When should I travel to get the best airfare?
Where do I go for answers to my travel questions?
What's the best and easiest way to plan and book my trip?

frommers.travelocity.com

Frommer's, the travel guide leader, has teamed up with **Travelocity.com**, the leader in online travel, to bring you an in-depth, easy-to-use resource designed to help you plan and book your trip online.

At **frommers.travelocity.com**, you'll find free online updates about your destination from the experts at Frommer's plus the outstanding travel planning and purchasing features of Travelocity.com. Travelocity.com provides reservations capabilities for 95 percent of all airline seats sold, more than 47,000 hotels, and over 50 car rental companies. In addition, Travelocity.com offers more than 2,000 exciting vacation and cruise packages. Travelocity.com puts you in complete control of your travel planning with these and other great features:

Expert travel guidance from Frommer's - over 150 writers reporting from around the world!

Best Fare Finder - an interactive calendar tells you when to travel to get the best airfare

Fare Watcher - we'll track airfare changes to your favorite destinations

Dream Maps - a mapping feature that suggests travel opportunities based on your budget

Shop Safe Guarantee - 24 hours a day / 7 days a week live customer service, and more!

Whether traveling on a tight budget, looking for a quick weekend getaway, or planning the trip of a lifetime, Frommer's guides and Travelocity.com will make your travel dreams a reality. You've bought the book, now book the trip!

Other Great Guides for Your Trip:

Frommer's Portable London from $85 a Day

Frommer's London

Frommer's Portable London

Frommer's England

Frommer's England from $60 a Day

Frommer's Europe

Frommer's Europe from $60 a Day

Frommer's Memorable Walks in London

Frommer's Irreverent Guide to London

Frommer's Born to Shop London

Europe For Dummies

London For Dummies

Here's what the critics say about Frommer's:

"Amazingly easy to use. Very portable, very complete."

—*Booklist*

♦

"The only mainstream guide to list specific prices. The Walter Cronkite of guidebooks—with all that implies."

—*Travel & Leisure*

♦

"Complete, concise, and filled with useful information."

—*New York Daily News*

♦

"Hotel information is close to encyclopedic."

—*Des Moines Sunday Register*

LONDON FROM $85 A DAY 2001

by Harriot Lane Fox

IDG Books Worldwide, Inc.
An International Data Group Company
Foster City, CA • Chicago, IL • Indianapolis, IN • New York, NY

About the Author

Harriot Lane Fox is a native Londoner and has lived in the city all her life. Her interest in travel began with an epic 3-month adventure in the United States after she left school. At university, she spent a year living and studying in France. Harriot's first job was as a public relations consultant, but 9 years ago she swapped sides to become a journalist. A former features editor of a business magazine, she is now a freelancer and writes on subjects as diverse as hotshot entrepreneurs and mouthwatering homes.

IDG Books Worldwide, Inc.

909 Third Ave.
21st Floor
New York, NY 10022

Find us online at **www.frommers.com**

ISBN 0-7645-6150-2
ISSN 1055-5331

Editor: Kelly Regan
Production Editor: Stephanie Lucas
Design by Michele Laseau
Staff Cartographers: John Decamillis, Elizabeth Puhl, Roberta Stockwell
Photo Editor: Richard Fox
Production by IDG Books Indianapolis Production Department

Special Sales

For general information on IDG Books Worldwide's books in the U.S., please call our Consumer Customer Service department at 1-800-762-2974. For reseller information, including discounts, bulk sales, customized editions, and premium sales, please call our Reseller Customer Service department at 1-800-434-3422.

Manufactured in the United States of America

5 4 3 2 1

Contents

4 Accommodations You Can Afford 72

5 Great Deals on Dining 129

6 Exploring London 187

List of Maps

An Invitation to the Reader

In researching this book, we discovered many wonderful places—hotels, restaurants, shops, and more. We're sure you'll find others. Please tell us about them, so we can share the information with your fellow travelers in upcoming editions. If you were disappointed with a recommendation, we want to hear about that, too. Please write to:

Frommer's London from $85 a Day, 2001
IDG Books Worldwide
909 Third Ave.
21st Floor
New York, NY 10019

An Additional Note

Please be advised that travel information is subject to change at any time—and this is especially true of prices. We therefore suggest that you write or call ahead for confirmation when making your travel plans. The authors, editors, and publisher cannot be held responsible for the experiences of readers while traveling. Your safety is important to us, however, so we encourage you to stay alert and be aware of your surroundings. Keep a close eye on cameras, purses, and wallets, all favorite targets of thieves and pickpockets.

What the Symbols Mean

✪ Frommer's Favorites

Our favorite places and experiences—outstanding for quality, value, or both.

The following abbreviations are used for credit cards:

AE	American Express	EC	Eurocard
CB	Carte Blanche	JCB	Japan Credit Bank
DC	Diners Club	MC	MasterCard
DISC	Discover	V	Visa

Find Frommer's Online

www.frommers.com offers up-to-the-minute listings on almost 200 cities around the globe—including the latest bargains and candid, personal articles updated daily by Arthur Frommer himself. No other Web site offers such comprehensive and timely coverage of the world of travel.

1

The Best of London from $85 a Day

Boy, do the millions of out-of-town Britons get cross when London hogs all the attention. I dread to think what their resting heart rate has been like for the past few years. Like the staccato rat-a-tat of an Uzi sub-machine gun, judging by the BBC's mailbag. Disgusteds of here, there, and everywhere always fire off a note to "Auntie" (the nation's nickname for the network) when something gets their goat. Like the £6 billion poured into sprucing up the capital of cool before the millennium. And then the months of media navel-gazing surrounding the mayoral election.

You can't really blame the public for reacting badly to the election. Opinionated locals may have forced Tony Blair to allow Ken Livingstone to run (though Blair did still expel him from the Labour party), but only a third of London's residents actually cared enough to vote. Poor Frank Dobson drew the short straw—yanked out of his ministerial job to fight off Ken for New Labour—only to be told by his spin doctors that beards are "dodgy" and he ought to shave his off. Amid snubs from his never-adoring public, the only enthusiastic reception he got was from a mob dressed up as furry blue rodents for an opportunistic marketing stunt.

It has been very trying for the blessed Tony Blair, whose halo slipped so far last year that it looked more like a hula hoop. Not even the arrival of another wee Blair—shortly after Tony's lawyer wife challenged government employment policy in court—could stem the tide of criticism. Baby Leo was a PR gift, the first baby born to a sitting (or pacing!) prime minister for centuries.

I can't say yet whether Mayor "Call me Ken" Livingstone will make the earth move. At press time, it's been all foreplay and no climax; he doesn't assume his responsibilities for another couple of weeks. He draws up his first budget in Spring 2001. And he and the assembly members can't even move into their new HQ, Norman Foster's giant glass display case by London Bridge, until 2002. In the meantime, they're paying £500 a pop to meet in an evangelical church.

That hasn't stopped London's tourism chief from submitting a wish-list, as though the mayor were his own personal good fairy. He wants 10,000 more hotel beds in the capital by 2005, to add to the thousands drummed up for the millennium; a 24-hour public transport system (Ken's big self-sell was keeping a lid on ticket-price increases); the paving over of hotspots like Trafalgar Square, an initiative that may kick off this spring; better use of the Thames, unlike last year's cock-up with the much-vaunted Central London Fast Ferry, which went virtually nowhere; and a mammoth city parking lot for buses, possibly at the Dome (RIP).

Oops, I knew I'd have to mention the D-word. As flopperoos go, London now can certainly claim a world-class one. When I heard that hair-loss clinics and alcoholism treatments were going to be allowed to advertise on British TV, I couldn't help thinking they'd have an eager audience in Dome-damaged civil servants, politicians, and supposed leisure experts. That Greenwich cow pat guzzled over £500 million and only got its last hand-out to stop going bust the very same day. As I write, the Dome's fate is still unknown, but it's due to be leased to a private operator.

That was pretty much the only millennial hiccup, except that the much-heralded river of fire was more of a trickle on the night. Even the much-criticized Royal Opera House relaunched on time to critical acclaim. London went BANG, using the calendar milestone as an excuse to pour £6 billion into celebrating modern achievements and redeveloping the institutions of the distant and not-so-distant past—museums, galleries, and theaters. The Tate Modern is a perfect example. This converted power station at Bankside was such an instant hit that the restaurant there simply stopped answering its phone (how's that for old-style customer service?).

And, boy, are Londoners proud of their city. That old empire-building arrogance was never dead, just dormant in the decades of Britain's declining power. But buttons are polished, chests puffed out, and they're standing by their beds ready to conquer the world. You can't blame them. Ever since Tony Blair wiped the Tories' eyes in 1997, people everywhere have been lauding Britain's capital as *the* happening place: with the hottest fashion designers; the rudest, most talented celebrity chefs, starring in a bubbling restaurant scene; fabulous theater, music, and dance; and artists breaking new boundaries, even Damien Hirst's post-pickled cow. There is an odd blast from the past, though. Hilton is giving the Playboy Bunny the kiss of life at a new chain of casinos—very 1970s and un-PC.

It would be interesting to know what one of the capital's newer residents thinks of that. Madonna had the press in knots trying to determine her London address—and, more importantly, what she paid for it! Laetitia Casta (the model who portrays Marianne, the national symbol of France) was also rumored to be buying a pied-à-terre here—though she was forced to deny her plans amid fierce protests on the other side of the Channel. As well as these two celebs, there are armies of imports whose names don't sell papers. And 6 million stopover visitors also answer London's siren call each year. A third of them are Americans, with the French and Germans close behind. So don't be surprised if you go several hours without hearing an English voice.

1 Frommer's Favorite Affordable London Experiences

- **Roam Along the River.** As a "favorite experience," I'm torn between two strolls. A newly spruced-up walk runs uninterrupted along the south bank of the Thames from the British Airways London Eye, opposite the Houses of Parliament, to Southwark, past a score of must-visit sights, including the Tate Modern and the wobbly but very beautiful Millennium Bridge. On the flip side, the toll-path heading west from Putney along the river could hardly be more different. The luminous tunnel of trees leads past the world's biggest urban wetland sanctuary to Hammersmith Bridge. Cross over there for a sunny summer's pint at one of the pubs between the string of north-bank boathouses.
- **Do That Continental Thing and Take to the Streets.** The city's social culture is changing, whether because of global warming or a general loosening of the

national corset. Now, it's not just Covent Garden where strollers and outdoor eaters can watch the street entertainment. The government chucked the Inland Revenue out of nearby Somerset House, which is between the river and the Strand. Millions have gone into refurbishing the big central courtyard, where there's nearly always something going on. The summer cafe on the river terrace is one of the most delightful cheap lunch spots in town. My other favorite thing is to pick up the Sunday paper and head to Soho for a late breakfast at one of the devilishly tempting patisseries. With the throngs of locals and visitors, it's like a Spanish *paseo.*

- **Get a Rooftop View.** The giant British Airways London Eye lifts you, at a crawling pace, 135 feet in the air for a staggering 25-mile view across the city. There are also stonking panoramas from the galleries in the dome of St. Paul's Cathedral, in the City, and from the tower of Westminster Cathedral. But you have to get out your wallet to enjoy all of these. Savvy travelers head for my favorite freebie, Tate Modern, to drink a toast to the superb skyline from the glass-walled cafe-bar on the roof of the old power station. See chapter 6.
- **Become an Art Critic.** Did you hear about the visitors to the Turner Prize exhibition at Tate Britain (another great freebie!) who played bouncy-bouncy on Tracey Emin's very creative unmade, and long-occupied, bed? Now, I'm not suggesting you become quite such a physical critic, but it is worth visiting White Cube^2 and Victoria Miro, both commercial galleries at the forefront of the Young British Artists phenomenon, to see what the fuss is all about. See chapter 6.
- **Stalk London's Ghostly Celebrities.** You can feel the aura of long-gone superbrains in the British Library Reading Room. Thomas Carlyle, Virginia Woolf, Mahatma Gandhi, Lenin, George Bernard Shaw, and Karl Marx all worked away in the blue, cream, and gold rotunda. Some of these famous names, Marx included, left their mortal remains at Highgate Cemetery, an eccentric showcase of Victorian funerary excess. It charges a small admission fee, while the library at the British Museum is free. See chapter 6.
- **Catch the Brits in the Act.** Apart from football, gardening is the hottest national passion. Even new London Mayor Ken Livingstone took half a day off after winning the election to tend to his neglected patch. And you can catch the locals at their most steamed-up when they open their private city spaces for only a pound or so to raise money for the National Gardens Scheme. They love to chat about their gardens, and why what went where, while you have a look around. Top that off with a visit to the Museum of Garden History or the Geffrye Museum, which replicates urban gardens through the ages; both are free. See chapter 6.
- **Time-Travel into Pageantry from the Past.** The Brits have had centuries to practice their pomp and circumstance, which is why they've got ceremonies like the Changing of the Guard at Buckingham Palace, Horse Guards Parade, and St. James's Palace, down to a fine art. The "new world" simply has nothing to match it. Prime Minister's Question Time, on Wednesday afternoons at 3pm, is another example. However hard young MPs, and women especially, lobby for reform, the old-guard schoolboys past their sell-by date resist change to their noisy traditions. See chapter 6.

Impressions

Anybody who enjoys being in the House of Commons probably needs psychiatric care.

—Ken Livingstone MP, in the *Evening Standard,* February 26, 1988

Central London

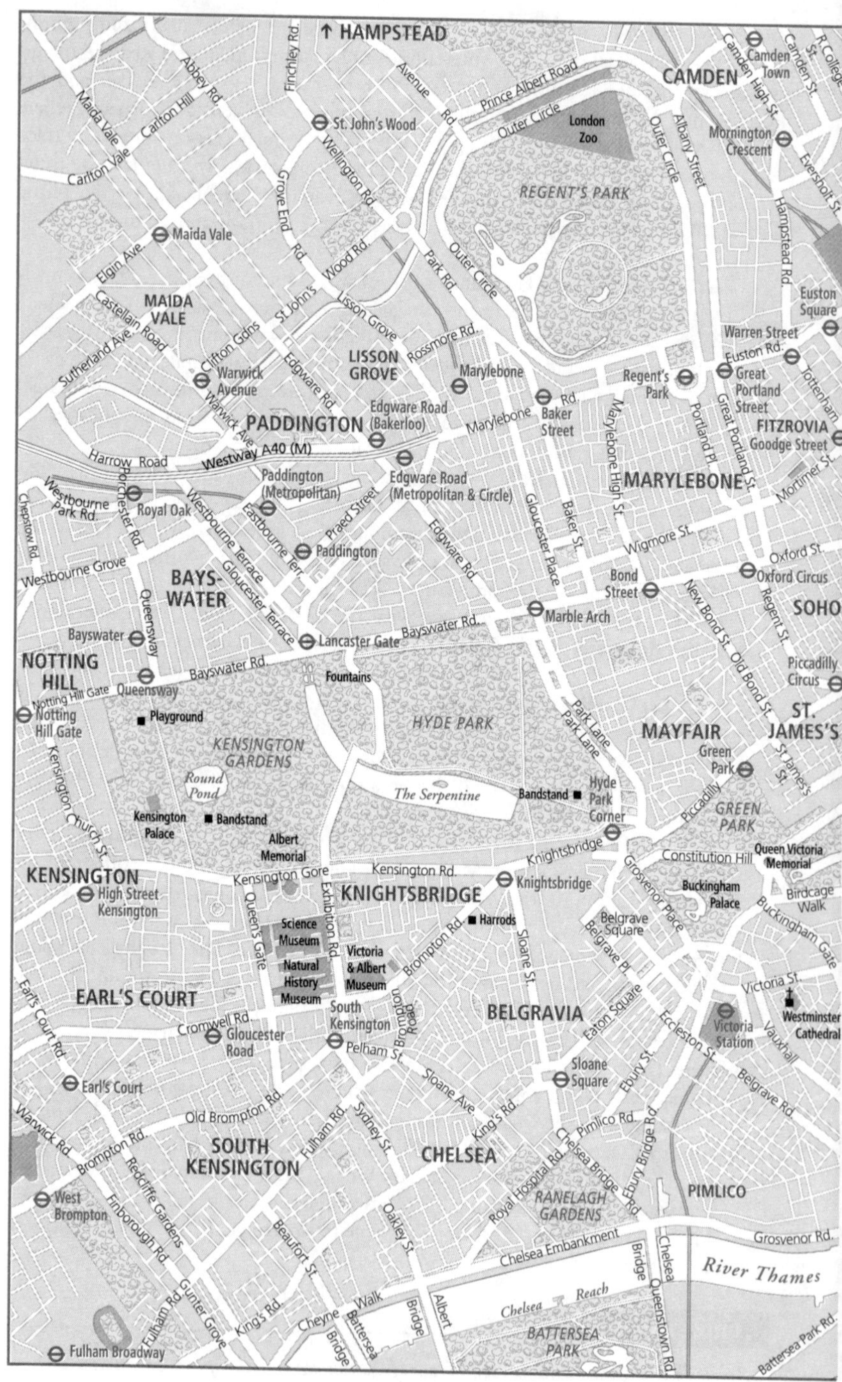

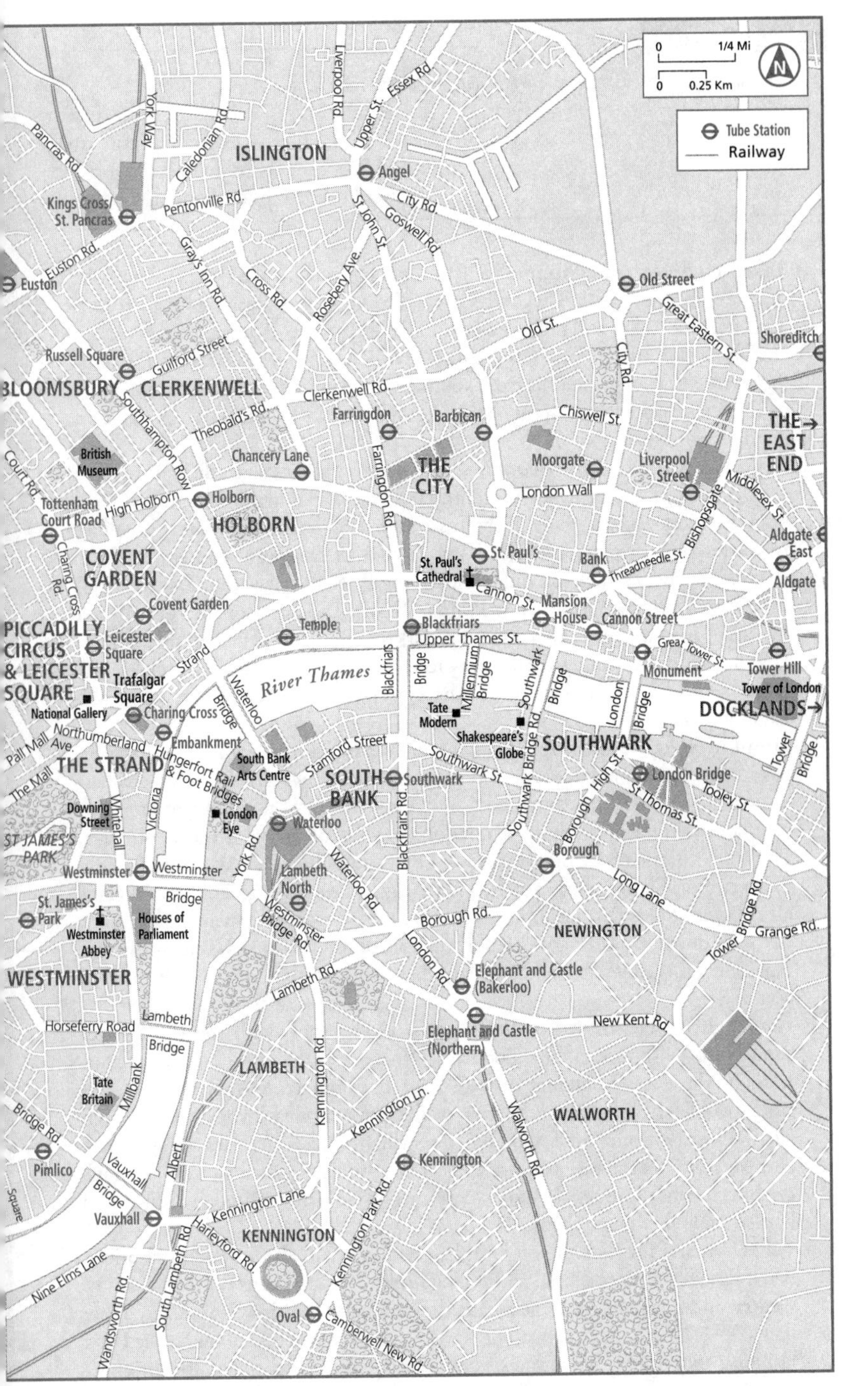
0 1/4 Mi
0 0.25 Km
Tube Station
Railway
ISLINGTON
Angel
Kings Cross/ St. Pancras
Euston
Old Street
Shoreditch
Russell Square
BLOOMSBURY
CLERKENWELL
Farringdon
Barbican
THE EAST END
British Museum
Chancery Lane
THE CITY
Moorgate
Liverpool Street
London Wall
Holborn
Tottenham Court Road
HOLBORN
COVENT GARDEN
St. Paul's
St. Paul's Cathedral
Bank
Aldgate East
Aldgate
Covent Garden
Temple
Blackfriars
Mansion House
Cannon Street
PICCADILLY CIRCUS & LEICESTER SQUARE
Leicester Square
Trafalgar Square
National Gallery
Charing Cross
Embankment
River Thames
Monument
Tower Hill
Tower of London
DOCKLANDS
Tate Modern
Shakespeare's Globe
SOUTHWARK
THE STRAND
South Bank Arts Centre
SOUTH BANK
Southwark
London Bridge
Downing Street
London Eye
Waterloo
ST JAMES'S PARK
Westminster
Lambeth North
Borough
St. James's Park
Westminster Abbey
Houses of Parliament
NEWINGTON
WESTMINSTER
Elephant and Castle (Bakerloo)
Elephant and Castle (Northern)
Horseferry Road
LAMBETH
Tate Britain
WALWORTH
Pimlico
Kennington
Vauxhall
KENNINGTON
Oval
Pancras Rd
York Way
Caledonian Rd
Liverpool Rd
Upper St.
Essex Rd
Pentonville Rd.
City Rd.
St John St.
Goswell Rd.
Euston Rd.
Gray's Inn Rd.
Cross Rd.
Rosebery Ave.
Great Eastern St.
Old St.
Guilford Street
Clerkenwell Rd.
Theobald's Rd.
Southhampton Row
Chiswell St.
Court Rd.
Farringdon Rd.
High Holborn
Middlesex St.
Bishopsgate
Charing Cross Rd.
Threadneedle St.
Cannon St.
Upper Thames St.
Great Tower St.
Strand
Waterloo Bridge
Blackfriars Bridge
Millennium Bridge
Southwark Bridge
Southwark Bridge Rd.
London Bridge
Tower Bridge
Northumberland Ave.
Pall Mall
Stamford Street
Southwark St.
Borough High St.
St Thomas St.
Tooley St.
Hungerford Rail & Foot Bridges
The Mall
Victoria
Whitehall
York Rd.
Blackfriars Rd.
Waterloo Rd.
Long Lane
Westminster Bridge
Westminster Bridge Rd.
Borough Rd.
London Rd.
Tower Bridge Rd.
Grange Rd.
Lambeth Rd.
New Kent Rd.
Lambeth Bridge
Kennington Rd.
Millbank
Kennington Ln.
Walworth Rd.
Bridge Rd.
Vauxhall Bridge
Albert
Square
Kennington Lane
Kennington Park Rd.
Harleyford Rd.
South Lambeth Rd.
Nine Elms Lane
Wandsworth Rd.
Camberwell New Rd.

Impressions

"As I was saying 14 years ago when I was so rudely interrupted . . ."

—Ken Livingstone, new Mayor of London, at his first press conference (May 5, 2000)—a cheeky allusion to Margaret Thatcher abolishing his old job as head of the Greater London Council

- **Take in a Show with "Auntie."** That's the nickname for the BBC among Brits of a certain generation. The Beeb, as it's also known, is always keen to recruit audiences for its TV and radio shows, and tickets are free. If you're a fan of quirky British humor, try and catch my Radio4 favorites, *The News Quiz* and *I'm Sorry I Haven't a Clue,* the latter hosted by famous jazzman Humphrey Littleton. Some of the references will be pretty obscure to out-of-towners, but I can guarantee a good giggle. See chapter 6.
- **Make like a Modern Mary Poppins.** Nannies have always taken their aristocratic charges to the park for a dose of healthy fresh air before heading home for afternoon tea. Today, you're more likely to see stay-at-home dads in charge, or young Aussie travelers saving up the cash to hop to another European country. They'll be heading for the scramble-on pirate ship at the Peter Pan playground in Kensington Gardens, a new memorial to Princess Diana. Look out for the rollercops, a dynamic duo in blue who patrol the park on inline skates. The other Mary Poppins treat is watching the keepers feed the Pelicans, descended from a pair given by the Russian ambassador in the 17th century, by the lake in St. James's Park. See chapter 6.
- **Drool over Aspirational Antiques.** London is like a man with two mistresses, passionate about contemporary culture but still in love with the past. So it's a fantastic place to browse for antiques. Go to a free pre-auction viewing of rare treasures and weird arcana at one of London's big salerooms—Christie's, Sotheby's, Phillips, or Bonhams. Serious treasure-hunters should set their alarm clocks for a dawn raid on Bermondsey market, where wily dealers come to sniff out bargains at 5:30am. There's Portobello market on Saturday—not quite such an early start, but scarf down your breakfast to beat the tourist hordes—and Camden Passage, especially on Wednesday and Saturday when stalls set up outdoors. See chapters 6 and 7.
- **Get High on Delicious Foodie Aromas.** Only people with steely willpower should risk a visit to London's food halls. Whether it's the tiled opulence of Harrods, or the empire-building poshitude of Fortnum & Mason, the delicious smells will have you reaching for your wallet and worrying if you'll have enough left over to pay your hotel bill. But it's such fun, and there are always a few cheaper treats that make great presents to take home. A new haunt of London's celebrity chefs, Borough Market is another must-visit for fresh produce and locally made foods. See chapter 7.
- **Label Yourself for Less.** If you love the brand but hate the astronomical prices, you'll do what I do and head for the handful of factory shops on the fringes of Central London. Did you know that the venerable Burberry is so funky these days it even does tartan bikinis! There are big discounts to be had on Nicole Fahri fashions, too, or chic homewares from Ocean, and the Villeroy & Boche china found only on the poshest tables. And nobody at home need know that you got a whopping discount instead of paying full price. For wannabe it-girls and -boys, there's one stop and that's Top Shop at Oxford Circus. It has persuaded a gang of

great designers to create exclusive collections that even show up in the pages of Vogue—in the cheap, cheap shopping section. See chapter 7.

- **Be a Good Sport.** Horseracing is much less snobby than you'd imagine from watching the Derby or Ascot on TV. One of my favorite ways to spend a summer Monday evening is to take the boat from the local station up the river to Windsor Racecourse, with a picnic and a bottle of fake champagne—you can buy a glass of the real stuff there. Greyhound racing at Wimbledon is a more raucous evening's entertainment, and dogs are an even dodgier bet. So stick to a pound each way. See chapter 7.
- **Steal a Musical Moment.** It's amazing how much more magical a concert can be when you're enjoying it for free! Lots of London's major arts venues do giveaways, perhaps to prove that they're worth all those millions of pounds from the public purse. Check out the FreeStage concerts at the Barbican Centre, Commuter Jazz in the foyer of the Royal Festival Hall, and the Monday lunchtime sessions at the Royal Opera House. And I've persuaded lots of friends to ditch their pay-up ethics and enjoy the summer opera at Holland Park Theater for free while sitting on the grass outside. See chapter 8.
- **Invest in the Theatrical Future.** The productions you'll see at the Royal Court Theatre could be on Broadway next year—it was the first to stage Conor McPherson's *The Weir.* Why wait and pay mortgageable ticket prices, when all seats here go for a fiver on Monday nights? If you're prepared to gamble, there's an even better deal as last-minute standbys at the downstairs stage cost a token 10p (16¢). The Soho Theatre also charges £5 ($8) a seat on Mondays and specializes in new writing. See chapter 8.
- **Go Early-Bird Clubbing.** Lots of London's nightspots start the evening as bars. Go before the DJ plugs in, and there's no cover charge. You could even find that it's happy hour. That's the deal at Bar Rumba, where drinks are two for the price of one between 5 and 9pm Monday to Thursday. A hot 'n' cool crowd comes for a different funky sound every night of the week. See chapter 8.
- **Cruise with the Cocktail Groupies.** These strange concoctions are so hip in London that superstar bar tenders—sorry, *mixologists*—have to fight off (or not!) their fans. At splurgy prices, cocktails are best kept as a happy-hour treat. Head for WKD, a club-bar in trendy Kentish Town, before 8pm for its house brew of Kahlua, Amaretto, Baileys, and milk. See chapter 8.

2 Best Hotel Bets on a Budget

Turn to chapter 4 for a full review of these hotels.

- **Best Overall Value: Arran House,** 77 Gower St., WC1 (☎ **020/7636-2186**), isn't a ritzy place. Indeed, the rooms are simple, and some are quite small. But look at what it offers at extremely competitive rates: roses rambling across a beautiful private garden; double-glazing masking traffic noise; a truly enormous full English breakfast (two types of bacon, sausages, fried bread, French toast, scrambled eggs, baked beans, tomatoes, grapefruit, toast and jam, orange juice, tea and coffee); use of the kitchen to make supper; self-service laundry facilities; and a very friendly welcome.
- **Best for Families:** It's the open-air swimming pool next door and video games in the basement that send **High Holborn Residence,** 178 High Holborn, WC1 (☎ **020/7379-5589**), to the top of the class. Since this student dorm is only a 10-minute walk to the heart of Covent Garden, there's always something to keep the little monsters happy and at a great price.

- **Best Cheap Break from the Kids:** Mrs. Wildridge doesn't allow little tykes under 10 to stay at **St. Charles Hotel,** 66 Queensborough Terrace, W2 (☎ **020/7221-0022**). I suspect she realizes that her miles of shiny bannisters—there are a lot of stairs—would be irresistible to daredevil young bottoms. This is a great place to stay if messy breakfasts and high-pitched excitement make your palms itch.
- **Best for Travelers with Disabilities:** Sadly, there aren't a lot of rivals for this recommendation. **Ibis Euston,** 3 Cardington St., NW1 (☎ **020/7388-7777**), has eight adapted units, and it is very close to useful train and tube lines, taxi ranks, and services for travelers at Euston. **Regent Palace Hotel,** Piccadilly Circus, W1 (☎ **020/7734-7000**) has only two units, but it is right in the thick of things.
- **Best for Nonsmokers:** The **Arosfa Hotel,** 83 Gower St., WC1 (☎ **020/7637-2115**), is certainly the worst for smokers. Mr. Dorta, the owner, has a nose like a truffle hound and chucks people out after just one sneaky puff.
- **Best for Gay Travelers:** Stay at the **New York Hotel,** 32 Philbeach Gardens, SW5 (☎ **020/7244-6884**), and you get the best of two very wonderful worlds. This B&B has a sauna, Jacuzzi, and fantastic garden. And you can pop next door to no. 30, the **Philbeach Hotel** (☎ **020/7373-1244**) for a spot of dinner or to cruise one of its famed Friday club nights.
- **Best View:** Last year, my vote went to **Travel Inn Capital, County Hall,** Belvedere Rd., SE1 (☎ **020/7902-1600**). Get someone to hold onto your ankles while you hang out of the window there and peer 'round the corner to enjoy *the* London view, across the river to the Houses of Parliament. But there's hot competition now from **Hotel Strand Continental,** 143 Strand, WC2 (☎ **020/7836-4880**), where rooms at the back look across the rooftops and through the middle of the restored courtyard at glorious Somerset House.
- **Best Jumbo Breakfast:** The Davies family not only cooks a huge fat-boy breakfast, they also give guests free run at a buffet of fruit, yogurt, croissants, and cereals, at **Harlingford Hotel,** 61–63 Cartwright Gardens, WC1 (☎ **020/7387-1551**). I'd take a doggy bag. For a very special local treat, check into **Vicarage Private Hotel,** 10 Vicarage Gate, W8 (☎ **020/7229-4030**). It's the only budget guesthouse I've seen with kippers (herring that is split open and smoked slowly over oak chips until it's golden brown) and porridge on the menu. As befits a Frommer's top tip, **Arran House** (see above) also sets out a bumper morning feast.
- **Best for Lazy Diners:** The French-Caribbean restaurant downstairs won a nomination in the best brasserie category at the London Carlton TV Restaurant Awards. Upstairs at **The Townhouse,** 24 Coptic St., WC1 (☎ **020/7636-2731**), you'll find very pretty and extremely cheap bathless sleeps. How they do it, I can't imagine, as this place is just the other side of New Oxford Street from Covent Garden.
- **Best for Serious Shoppers: The Ivanhoe Suite Hotel,** 1 St. Christopher's Place, W1 (☎ **020/7935-1047**), is in a little pedestrian enclave crammed with so many delicious boutiques that you might want to put a padlock on your wallet.
- **Best for Theater Buffs:** There are several contenders, but my vote goes to the **Regent Palace Hotel,** Piccadilly Circus, W1 (☎ **020/7734-7000**). The Piccadilly Theatre is just across the road. Shaftesbury Avenue and Drury Lane are just 'round the corner, and a double room costs less on the weekends than many B&Bs.
- **Best for Lighthouse-Keepers: The Windermere Hotel,** 142–144 Warwick Way, SW1 (☎ **020/7834-5163**), has a fantastic pair of wedge-shaped rooms

right at the top of the house with windows on two sides. If you flick the bedside light on and off, you can almost hear the sea.

- **Best for Interior Design Tips:** The **Rushmore Hotel,** 11 Trebovir Rd., SW5 (☎ **020/7370-0274**), is an extravaganza of muraled ceilings and stage-set bedrooms. Canopied beds and swagged drapes conjure up a Transylvanian castle. Because it's decorated with wit more than vast expense, you don't have to be extravagant to stay here. And the service is silky smooth.
- **Best for Animal Companionship:** Do you pine at every separation from your four-legged canine friend? Stay at **Jenkins Hotel,** 45 Cartwright Gardens, WC1 (☎ **020/7383-2067**), and Sam Bellingham will lend you one of his Labradors to walk for pet-replacement therapy.
- **Best Splurge Choice:** Ask for the Abba room, and the charming manager Graham Chapman will giggle and groan, probably at the same time. The owner of the **The Fielding Hotel,** 4 Broad Court, WC2 (☎ **020/7836-8305**) is awfully attached to his treasured gallery of kitsch 1970s pictures and keeps a firm hand on decor decisions. This isn't a luxe gold-tap joint, and breakfast is not included. But the location is superb, right by the Royal Opera House in Covent Garden, which is why so many of its guests are performers and their groupies.
- **Best for Party-Animals on a Shoestring:** As long as your shoestring is waterproof, go for **St. Christopher's Village,** 121 Borough High St., SE1 (☎ **020/7407-1856**). This £11-a-night ($17.60) hostel has a sauna and hot-tub on the roof, a nightclub in the basement, and subsidized pub grub. It's also just a few minutes' walk from the Globe, Tate Modern, and Borough Market.
- **Best for Net Addicts:** Guests pay a £5 ($8) set-up charge to have a computer in their room, then surf all they want for free at **InterneSt @ Portobello Gold,** 97 Portobello Rd., W11 (☎ **020/7460-4910**). Or they can just pop along to the cyber bar at this old converted pub, which is right in the middle of the antiques stalls during the Saturday market. Rooms are a very, very good value for Notting Hill.
- **Best for Easy Payment:** Brian and Arline Woutersz at **Kenwood House Hotel,** 114 Gloucester Place, W1 (☎ **020/7935-3473**), have got more air-miles under their belts than all the Miss Worlds put together. A British Airways pilot and former stewardess, they're super-attuned to travelers' needs and accept any major currency, as well as most credit cards.

3 Best Dining Bets on a Budget

See chapter 5 for a full review of these restaurants.

- **Best Overall Value:** Not only do you get two delicious dishes on the £7.50 ($12) early-bird menu, with tasting notes on the spices used, but it's happy hour at the same time in the downstairs bar when usually-pricey cocktails cost the same as chi-chi bottled beer elsewhere (£2.50/$4). So get on down to **Soho Spice,** 124–126 Wardour St., W1. (☎ **020/7434-0808**) to sample the stylish Indian cuisine.
- **Best Fixed-Price Bargain:** These fab dinner options set no early- or late-bird restrictions and are practically given away. Try a South Indian feast at **Diwana Bhel Poori House,** 121 Drummond St., NW1 (☎ **020/7387-5556**) for just £6.20 ($9.90), and you can bring your own wine with no charge. At **Le Mercury,** 140a Upper St., N1 (☎ **020/7354-4088**), the ex-French President Chirac's ex-chef Michel Hautin whips up a £5.95 ($9.50) set meal. Gobsmacking and certainly gob-filling!

- **Best Budget Blow-Out from a Celebrity Chef:** Marco Pierre White, Britain's baddest bad-boy of haute cuisine, does a cracking fixed-price lunch at **Mirabelle** for £14.95 to £17.95 ($23.90 to $28.70), 56 Curzon St., W1 (☎ **020/7499-4636**). For cuisine from the "school of" Stephen Bull, try the delicious Modern European food and wicked teas at **The Sculpture Garden at the Wallace Collection,** Hertford House, Manchester Sq., W1 (☎ **020/7563-9500;** Tube: Bond St). This lovely museum uses him as a consultant for its eaterie in the newly covered courtyard.
- **Best of the Brit Pack:** Veronica Shaw is passionate about food history and adapts discovered recipes that go back as far as 700 years. The £12.50 ($20) two-course menu is a great deal—generous enough to fuel Henry VIII, which it probably did, as well as high in entertainment value, with its charming explanatory notes. Make sure to book early to get a table at **Veronica's,** 3 Hereford Rd., W2 (☎ **020/7229-5079**).
- **Best Super-Healthy Super-Cheap Eat:** It has to be **Quiet Revolution,** 49 Old St., EC1. (☎ **020/7253-5556**). This soup manufacturer is approved by the Soil Association, which regulates "organic" producers, and it has twice won S.A. food awards. Soups come with every kind of information—grams of fat, carbohydrates, number of calories, and so on—and only cost from £2.75 to £5 ($4.40 to $8). It's in the middle of East London's artists ghetto. If you're not planning to head that way, head instead for one of the four branches of the almost-as-healthy **SOUP Works** in Soho and Covent Garden.
- **Best Barbecues:** Enjoy the sizzle and delicious smells of steaks, lamb, sausages, and corn-fed chicken cooked to order by the Hellbergs, who run **Arkansas Café,** Old Spitalfields Market, E1 (☎ **020/7377-6999**). Keir gets up at dawn to choose the best meat himself from Smithfield Market and posts up the life story of each cut.
- **Best for Vegetarians:** I don't like ignoring the veggie stalwarts, and you shouldn't either—particularly **Quiet Revolution** (see "Best Super Healthy Super Cheap Eat," above). But there's nothing to beat a meatless ethnic cuisine with a much longer tradition than any western Johnny-come-lately. South-Indian specialist **Woodlands,** 77 Marylebone Lane, W1. (☎ **020/7486-3862**), which has two other London branches, is the outpost of a family-run empire with over 20 restaurants across the sub-continent. Fixed-price dinners are a great value at £10.95 to £11.95 ($17.50 to $19.10).
- **Best for Nonsmokers:** You can't light up at **Wagamama,** 4a Streatham St. (off Coptic Street), WC1 (☎ **020/7323-9223**), and most smokers don't mind—the atmosphere is so frenetic, it probably won't even occur to them to do so. And no nicotine is allowed to yellow the shelves at top lunch spot, **Books for Cooks,** 4 Blenheim Crescent, W11 (☎ **020/7221-1992**). This mecca for gourmet bibliophiles tests recipes in a little kitchen at the back.
- **Best for a Romantic Dinner:** No restaurant can rival the cozy candlelit charm of **Andrew Edmunds,** 46 Lexington St., W1 (☎ **020/7437-5708**), where young locals whispering sweet nothings make up the bulk of the clientele. Afterward, wander the buzzy streets of Soho hand in hand. Aaaaaah.
- **Best for Bingeing with the Gang:** The £17.99 ($28.80) Grande Bouffe is a fabulously loony deal at one of the looniest restaurants in London: **Schnecke,** 58–59 Poland St., W1 (☎ **020/7287-6666**). Staff cram your table-top with 15 dishes from the Alsatian menu of flaming tarts, pizzas, and heart-stopping specials laden with cream, cheeses, onions, and wine. And you get a free beer, kitsch Europop, and cabbage-shaped door handles thrown in.

- **Best for Winos:** About 25 wines are sold by the glass to wash down your Kangaroo steak, at the **Cork & Bottle Wine Bar,** 44–46 Cranbourn St., WC2 (☎ **020/7734-7807**). All have chatty tasting notes written by the Australian owner and very unsnobby expert, Don Hewitson.
- **Best Booze-Less Bargain:** The meat for the kebabs at **Patogh,** 8 Crawford Place, W1 (☎ **020/7262-4015**) is left to marinate overnight, which is why they melt in your mouth. This Persian diner is unlicensed, so you can bring your own wine and don't even have to pay corkage.
- **Best View in Town:** The panorama across London's best-known landmarks from **Café Level 7 at Tate Modern,** Bankside, SE1 (☎ **020/7401-5020,** or 020/7887-8000 museum), is stupendous. The old power station has sprouted a glass-sided zit, high up on the roof, where lunchtime sarnies, soups, and substantial meals start at £2.50 ($4)—very democratic. It's also open for dinner on Friday and Saturday, but it's screamingly popular. So, if you can't get in, try Café Level 2, which also looks out at the river and serves the same menu, plus breakfast, too.
- **Best for a Grand Entrance:** The sweeping staircase down into the multileveled **Vong,** Berkeley Hotel, Wilton Place, SW1 (☎ **020/7235-1010**), could have been made for a royal entrance. And the £17.50 ($28) early- and late-bird menu is a fair deal for a "black plate" filled by Euro-celebrity chef Jean-Georges Vongerichten. Eat your heart out, Queenie.
- **Best for Spectators:** Raise yourself above hoi polloi in Covent Garden Piazza at **Chez Gerard at the Opera Terrace,** First Floor, Covent Garden Central Market, WC2 (☎ **020/7379-0666**). Even the stilt-walkers can't reach that high to interrupt your meal.
- **Best Distraction from a Dodgy Dinner Companion:** Sir Terence Conran's Soho eaterie, **Mezzo,** 100 Wardour St., W1 (☎ **020/7314-4000**), has turned itself into a mostly jazz-oriented live music venue and weekend quasi-club with a DJ. Diners never have to pay a cover charge, as long as they pick up their knives and forks before 10pm.
- **Best Comfort Food:** Cabbies know everything, and they're always right, as you'll find out if you travel by taxi. Their vote goes to **North Sea Fish Restaurant,** 7–8 Leigh St., WC1 (☎ **020/7387-5892**), for that national staple, fish and chips. For bangers and mash, the Brits' other favorite comfort food, check out **R.K. Stanleys,** 6 Little Portland St., W1 (☎ **020/7462-0099**), where the Magnificent Seven homemade sausages have a global twist.
- **Best for the Morning After: The Star Café,** 22 Great Chapel St., W1 (☎ **020/7437-8778**) does a fantastic all-day breakfast. And if the situation is grave enough, you can get a Bloody Mary from the pub downstairs. If it's near-fatal, steer clear of the weekend brunch at **Mash,** 19–21 Great Portland St., W1 (☎ **020/7637-5555**). The £10 ($16) set menus are a bumper reviver, but bad behavior tends to flash-back when people see the too-late advice proffered by the electronic Love Machine at the entrance.
- **Best Film-Set Decor: Momo,** 25 Heddon St., W1 (☎ **020/7434-4040**), is superbly and decadently Moorish as well as more-ish. This pasha's palace is full of the most luxurious fabrics and beturbanned staff—*Hideous Kinky* with cash to flash.
- **Best Gory Story:** The 17th-century it-girl Lady Elizabeth Hatton was murdered in Bleeding Heart Yard in the middle of her annual winter ball. Who can say she's not a see-through regular at **Bleeding Heart Tavern,** off Greville St., EC1 (☎ **020/7404-0333**), which you'll find in the yard today. This restored 1746 tavern serves earthy regional English cuisine and robust real ale.

2 Planning an Affordable Trip to London

London is one of the most expensive cities in the world, more so even than New York. But that doesn't mean you can't enjoy a marvelous, affordable vacation here; that's the raison d'être for this guidebook. Your trip will be much more fun—and certainly a lot smoother—if you plan it properly. This chapter is designed to help you do that, step by step.

1 The $85-a-Day Premise

Our premise is that two people traveling together can have a great time in London for only $85 a day per person. That will cover the price of a decent double room (often with an in-room shower, at least), a lunchtime refueling stop at a pub or cafe, and a fine feast at an ethnic restaurant in the evening. It's likely that you'll get a free, full breakfast at your hotel.

After searching the streets of London, we've come up with the best of the budget deals. And don't worry—this doesn't mean you'll have to stay at dingy dives or eat nasty food. You can do it for less than $85 if you want to, of course, and you can certainly do it for more. Included in the book are recommendations on how to do both.

We've found some gem hotels in hot locations. But keep in mind that most B&Bs and small hotels have to deal with the problem of being in ancient and odd-shaped buildings. Hotel managers try to compensate for this in various ways. For example, if there was one phrase I heard constantly on my tramp through the city, it was, "that's what people want"—usually referring to some new comfort introduced to keep their toughest customers, those choosy Americans, happy. That has its downsides: Putting in private bathrooms tends to jack the prices up. But so many small hotels have upgraded over the past couple of years that cheap rooms with shared facilities are generally comfortable, if simple. Bloomsbury, for example, is a real hot spot for typically English guesthouses catering to modest travelers. We've even found a couple of brilliant deals in hotels so central, just off Oxford Street in Marylebone, in Soho, and off the Strand, that you'll want to cut your credit cards up before venturing out the door. If you're on a very strict budget, check out both the YHA hostels and the funky commercial ones for the snowboarding generation. We've also reviewed the best student halls.

The biggest revolution for savvy travelers, though, has taken place on the eating scene. The Brits have discovered food, as the rest of the world knows it, in a big, big way. And it isn't just the high end that's changing. New cuisines and revamped old ones—Thai one year, sushi the next, North African in between—are storming through budget eateries. Now healthy food, from freshly squeezed this to organic that, is converting the meat-and-two-veggie crowd all across the city. Even pubs tend to offer much better fare, replacing congealed, prepacked sludge with hearty homemade dishes. Some have even turned into understated but achingly stylish restaurants, known rather unfortunately as "gastropubs." The selections in this book are designed to guide you to the best value options around and point out some of the locals' favorites. Take a break from sightseeing on at least 1 day, because it's at lunchtime that some of the celebrity chefs lower their prices enough to let in hoi polloi. If they aren't low enough, you can have a great value gourmet meal without even leaving Tate Modern, or the new wings at the National Gallery and National Portrait Gallery.

As for sightseeing, you can't get around the fact that some of the stock-in-trade sights are overpriced—Madame Tussaud's and Buckingham Palace, particularly. Don't be daunted though. You can enjoy a splendidly rich vacation at a host of free museums and galleries, the street and antiques markets, the rituals and ceremonies that make up London life, and just by strolling through the streets.

2 Fifty Money-Saving Tips

PRETRIP PLANNING AND TRANSPORTATION SAVINGS

1. Information pays; forewarned is forearmed. Old adages survive for a reason, and these are as important as ever when you're thinking of taking a trip. Read as much as you can about London before you go. Talk to people who've been there recently. Check in with the **British Tourist Authority** offices in New York or Chicago (see "Visitor Information," below) for a wealth of free information. The BTA pack has details about several discount deals: the **London GoSee card,** a 3- or 7-day saver pass to major museums and galleries (see tip 30, below); the **London for Less discount card and guidebook,** and **Great British Heritage Pass** (see tips 8 and 9, below). You'll also be able to get maps and helpful booklets like *Britain for Cyclists, Britain for Walkers,* and more.
2. Travel off-season. Airfares and B&B rates are cheaper and easier to get if you travel from late fall through early spring. Hotel/flight packages plummet by hundreds of dollars. And London is great in the winter. Cultural life is at full throttle, and sightseeing is more rewarding without the summer hordes. You don't have to go in darkest February—in March or October, you'll still reap financial benefits.
3. Reserve and pay in advance, especially if you plan to rent a car. If you book with an agency like **Europe by Car,** (☎ **800/223-1516** in the U.S., 800/252-9401 in Los Angeles, or 212/581-3040 in New York; www.europebycar.com), you'll pay half what a local British company will charge. Except the online-only **www.easyRentacar.com**. Its rates fluctuate according to demand: from £9 ($14.40) a day, even on a peak-season weekend if you book several weeks ahead, to £28 ($44.80), plus £5 ($8) car-prep fee. Great value for day-trips into the beautiful English countryside.

4. Fly during the week and early in the morning and save big money.
5. Shop around for your airfare. This will be the most expensive part of your trip, so it pays to do some legwork. Searching the Internet will turn up some great bargains. Alternatively, scour your newspaper for consolidators like **TFI Tours International** (☎ **800/745-8000** or 212/736-1140), which sells airline seats at a substantial—as much as 60%—discount. Certainly consult your travel agent, who will often be privy to special deals and package rates. Air carriers want to fill every seat on every flight, so they're constantly adjusting the pricing. Also investigate charter flights on scheduled airlines offered by reliable operators like the **Council on International Educational Exchange** (☎ **212/822-2600;** www.ciee.org). For information on all of these, see "Getting There" below, and "Planning Your Trip: An Online Directory," following this chapter.
6. Consider buying a **holiday package:** one low price that includes airfare, transfers, accommodations, and some sightseeing discounts. For example, in 2000, **Globus & Cosmos** (☎ **800/556-5454;** www.globusandcosmos.com) was offering a week in a smartish hotel in London for $1,239 (per person, peak season). The airlines have all become tour operators and put packages together, too. (See section 9 of this chapter for more information.)
7. Pack light. You won't need a porter, and you're less likely to succumb to the desire for a taxi. But pack small, too: no space just aching to be filled with shopping. *Note:* Luggage carts are free in London's airports.
8. Buy a **London for Less card and guidebook** for $19.95, valid for up to four people for 8 consecutive days. It gets you a 20% to 50% discount at many different attractions, on theater and concert tickets, in restaurants and shops, on tours, car rental, hotels, fees at Travelex foreign currency exchanges, and telephone calls. You may have neither the time nor the inclination to use all of the coupons. But with money off at the Royal Shakespeare Company, Royal Opera, Royal Ballet, and Royal Philharmonic, *plus* savings on admissions or tours at Buckingham Palace, the Tower of London, Westminster Abbey, Hampton Court Palace, Kensington Palace, and Kew Gardens, you're sure to cover the sign-on cost. Any extra shopping, at posh stores like Burberry, and dining discounts will be a bonus. The card and book are available in London at any tourist info center for £12.95 ($20.70). To buy them before you leave home and at a small discount, call ☎ **888/GO-FOR-LESS** in the U.S., or 937/846-1411 (www.for-less.com), or visit Britrail's **British Travel Shop,** 551 Fifth Ave., 7th floor, New York, NY, next to the BTA office.
9. The **Great British Heritage Pass** is great if you're planning any of the day-trips we suggest. You get free entry into almost 600 public and private historic properties owned by bodies including the National Trust, English Heritage, and Historic Royal Palaces. That means Hampton Court Palace, Kensington Palace State Apartments, and Royal Ceremonial Dress Collection (plus half-price at the Tower of London) in the city; Anne Hathaway's Cottage and Shakespeare's Birthplace in Stratford-upon-Avon; the Roman Baths and Pump Room in Bath; and Windsor Castle. Passes are valid for 7 days ($54), 15 days ($75), or a month ($102), no discounts for children. In the U.S. call **BritRail** (☎ **888/BRITRAIL;** www.raileurope.com) before you depart. In London, take your passport to the Britain Visitor Centre, 1 Regent St., SW1, or any

tourist information center, but you'll have to pay a bit more—£32, £45, and £60 ($51.20, $72, and $96) respectively.

10. Before you leave, also get a 3-, 4-, or 7-day **London Visitor Travelcard™,** which offers virtually unlimited travel on public transport and is not available in the United Kingdom. Contact your travel agent or BritRail (☎ **888/BRITRAIL;** www.raileurope.com). It has big advantages over buying a local pass when you get to London: You don't have to provide a passport photo and can travel at any time (in London, many passes are only after 9:30am). You can choose all zones or just Central London, which will cover most of what you need: Central zone (zone 1 and 2) adult passes cost $22 for 3 days, $27 for 4, and $32 for 7; child equivalents cost $9, $11, and $13. A one-way adult ticket inside zone 1 usually costs £1.70 ($2.70).
11. International phone calls are exorbitant. Though using a calling card overseas usually carries a surcharge, it's worth checking it out before leaving home: American Express cardholders should ask about the charges using the company's "Connections" plan. Also see what AT&T, MCI, and Sprint have to offer and whether it's worth switching your residential service to one of them.

    Much less hassle, though, and the traveler's very best friend, is **eKit** (www.ekit.com). Join for free on the Web, and you'll get free e-mail, cheap access to both voice-mail, and a "travel vault"—a secure place online to store passport and credit-card details, medical records, and so on—and super-cheap international calling rates. The lowest BT charges are only available on weekends, while eKit has one rate 24 hours a day. This is how they compare per minute: 26p (BT) and under 5p (eKit) to the U.S., 26p (BT) and under 10p (eKit) to Canada, 44p (BT) and 7p (eKit) to Australia and New Zealand. Hook up with eKit, and you can ignore all the bargain phone services plastering every newsagent window in London. These may look good but lines get jammed up, usually just when you want to call home.

    Note: Holders of International Student Identity Cards and Youth Travel Cards, and YHA members all get discounted phone calls.

ONCE YOU ARRIVE

12. Take public transport from the airport into the city. The Piccadilly Line on the Underground runs directly from Heathrow to Central London and costs only £3.50 ($5.60), instead of the £35 ($56) or more that a taxi would cost. That saves you over half a day's budget.
13. Don't use traveler's checks or moneychangers like American Express and other bureaux de change. Instead, go to an overseas ATM and withdraw money from your account at home (if you can). You'll get a much better deal because banks use a special wholesale rate. Do check with your bank first to make sure it isn't going to charge you a fee for this service. Above all, don't draw cash on a credit card; you'll pay exorbitant interest rates for that privilege.

ACCOMMODATIONS

14. When you're looking for a hotel, try a university area like Bloomsbury first. Other London neighborhoods worth investigating for a good supply of budget hotels are Paddington, Bayswater, Victoria, and Earl's Court.

15. Think about what you really want in a hotel room. If a private bathroom isn't crucial to you, you can save anywhere from £10 to £20 ($16 to $32) a night.
16. Negotiate the price. Check if the management will give you a discount for staying 3 nights or more. Suggest trade-offs—a lower price for a smaller room or a room minus TV, and so on. Ask for an old-style per-person (not room) rate: On a tight budget, a couple may be able to downgrade to a 4-foot-wide bed normally used as a single; with a bit more cash, you could get a good rate on a triple. If you're on a hotel-lined street like Sussex Gardens in Paddington, or Ebury Street near Victoria, keep checking out rooms until you find one you like for your price.
17. Think about alternatives to hotels and guesthouses. Many Londoners offer bed-and-breakfast in their homes, a cozy option that costs as little as £36 ($57.60) a night for two people in attractive West London through **Host and Guest Service** (☎ **020/7385-9922;** www.host-guest.co.uk).
18. Or be even braver and do a house swap, which costs nothing once you've paid the matchmaking service's fee: $30 a year through U.S.-based **HomeExchange.COM** (☎ **805/898-9660;** www.homeexchange.com); $60.80 with **Home Base Holidays** (☎ **020/8886-8752;** www.homebase-hols.com), established in London in 1986.
19. Depending on your threshold of pain, consider staying at a youth hostel, or at one of the dozens of university dorms. **High Holborn Residence** charges £57 to £67 ($91.20 to $107.20) for a twin, and provides two TV lounges, a bar with two pool tables, table tennis, 24-hour Laundromat, and a computer room.
20. Don't call home from a hotel phone unless you can access USA Direct or a similar company; and even then, check to see if there's a charge for the connection. Similarly, don't call direct from a pay phone, which may connect to carriers charging super-high prices.

DINING

21. Stay at a hotel providing a full breakfast, not the continental one that hotels are switching to now. We've noted which still serve the traditional cereals, bread, fruit, bacon, eggs, sausage, mushrooms, and tomatoes. That would cost you at least £6 ($9.60) a head outside the hotel.
22. Bring a knife, fork, plate, and corkscrew so that you can feast on delights from the splendid food halls at Harrods, Fortnum & Mason, Selfridges, on simpler fare from Tesco Metro and Marks & Spencer, or the super-fresh produce from the city's farmers' markets.
23. If spreading your own butter is not your style, then check out the ever-expanding range of budget eating options. A stop at one of the new soup kitchens will refuel pretty much anybody: There are four SOUP Works branches around Soho and Covent Garden, and prices start at £1.50 ($2.40) a cup.
24. At many a London restaurant, you'll find fixed-price and pre-theater menus. Depending on the neighborhood, a two-course meal could cost as little as £5.95 ($9.50), and many are £10 to £15 ($16 to $24). Even Marco Pierre White does lunch at Mirabelle in Mayfair for £14.95 ($23.92). Note, though, that most of these menus offer a very limited choice—that's why they're the price they are.
25. At many restaurants, service is included—don't make the mistake of tipping twice.

GETTING AROUND TOWN

26. Walk—it's the best way to explore the city and meet the locals. London is big, but it only takes a little forethought to schedule sights, shops, and fuel stops, neighborhood by neighborhood. That way, you can explore on foot and save on Tube costs, as well as on wasted downtime.
27. Take advantage of any discounts on public transport. Travelcards (see tip 10 above) allow you to ride the buses and Underground throughout the two zones of Central London for £3.90 ($6.25) a day and £18.20 ($29.10) a week. They make sightseeing so much more spontaneous, too.
28. For London's cheapest tour, ride the no. 11 bus from Liverpool Street to Fulham Broadway, or the no. 188 from Euston to Greenwich, or any of the other routes, for that matter. With a travelcard, you can go wherever you please inside the zones to which it applies.

SIGHTSEEING & ENTERTAINMENT

29. Buy a **London GoSee card** (www.london-gosee.com). This costs £16 ($25.60) for 3 days, £26 ($41.60) for 7 days, and £32 and £50 ($51.20 and $80) respectively for family cards. GoSee is always recruiting new partners and as this book went to press was good at 17 top museums and galleries last year. Anyone who did them all would have saved over £60, but you only have to visit six or seven make your money back. You can buy a GoSee card before you travel, at the British Travel Shop next to the BTA's Manhattan office (☎ **800/677-8585**); or through Global Tickets (☎ **800/223-6108;** www.globaltickets.com). Contact the BTA itself in Australia (☎ **2/9377-4400**) and New Zealand (☎ **9/303-1446**). In London, they're available from the participating museums, London Underground information centers, and at tourist information offices.
30. Surf the relatively new **www.britainsavings.com**, and download discount coupons for historic buildings, museums and galleries, attractions, bus tours, and river cruises: £1 ($1.60) off admission to a Barbican exhibition, for instance. It also lists all those with free admission. The promised dining, accommodation, and shopping discounts were few and far between when I looked.
31. London has lots of world-class free attractions and museums—the main galleries of the British Museum and the National Gallery, and the core collections at both Tate galleries, to name only four. Be organized, and decide exactly what you most want to see in a museum that does charge, and then check if they let people in for free in the last 45 minutes—many do.
32. Students who present their ID can usually get discounted admissions, as can seniors. From April last year, many of the really major museums and galleries stopped charging seniors completely.
33. Make creative sightseeing choices. Some of the best things in life are free. A walk down any street in London is bound to turn up several buildings

Seeing the Prime Minister in Action

The Prime Minister submits to a weekly grilling in the House of Commons, known as Question Time, on Wednesday from 3 to 3:30pm. British residents who want to see him not sweat should write for tickets to their local MP. Overseas visitors must contact their embassy. See chapter 6 for more information.

marked with blue plaques, showing someone famous once lived there or that it was the scene of a historic event. No one can charge you for looking, so enjoy the architecture, from the Tudor Staple Inn to the modern Lloyd's Building, to the brilliant interiors of Wren's or Hawksmoor's churches and the memorials that seem to line every one. Oh, and do make sure to walk across the marvelous Millennium Bridge (assuming they've sorted out the swinging hammock effect!). If you go to the park, opt for the classic iron bench, not a deck chair where bum-space costs money.

34. Stand and stare at the host of ceremonial events: the Changing of the Guard at Buckingham Palace, St. James's Palace and Whitehall, the Lord Mayor's Show, the Notting Hill Carnival, and a year-long list of many more (see "Calendar of Events" for details). You can enjoy the entertainment in the Piazza at Covent Garden any day—fire-eaters, mime artists, a jazz trio, who knows what—or visit the courtyard at Somerset House.
35. Take a seat in the galleries at the Old Bailey in the City, the Royal Courts of Justice in the Strand, and of course, the Houses of Parliament. They're all free and will give you a glimpse both into the past and into the institutions and social issues of contemporary London.
36. Visit a legion of long-dead celebrities at London's cemeteries. And not just High Gate—Brompton Cemetery on Old Brompton Road, Hampstead Cemetery on Fortune Green Road, and the Dissenters' Graveyard at Bunhill Fields in the City. The Pet Cemetery in Kensington Gardens was the fashionable last place to bury noble and not-so-noble cats and dogs, from Victorian times until 1867. Call ahead for permission to visit (☎ **020/7298-2117**).

NIGHTLIFE

37. Go to nightclubs early or very late to get a discount. For instance, **Bar Rumba** has a happy hour Monday to Thursday, 5 to 9pm, and there's no cover charge then. **The Clinic** in Chinatown is free before 10pm. Also clip out the Privilege Pass, printed weekly in listings magazine *Time Out*. And check Tower Records in Piccadilly Circus for cheap-deal flyers, which some of the clubs also post on their Web sites.
38. Queue at the kiosk in Leicester Square for half-price West End theater tickets. Or pop into an Internet cafe, and surf **www.lastminute.com** for right-now discounts. There are five handy branches of **easyEverything:** 358 Oxford St., W1 (☎ **020/7491-3936;** Tube: Bond St.); 9–16 Tottenham Court Rd., W1 (☎ **020/7436-1206;** Tube: Tottenham Court Rd.); 160–166 Kensington High St. (☎ **020/7938-1841;** Tube: Kensington High St.); 457–459 The Strand, WC2 (☎ **020/7930-4094;** Tube: Charing Cross); and 9–13 Wilton Rd., SW1 (☎ **020/7233-8456;** Tube: Victoria).
39. Go to matinees instead of evening performances. A top-price matinee will cost at least £5 ($8) less than a top-price evening ticket.

Cyber Deals for Net Surfers

It's possible to get some great deals on airfare, hotels, and car rentals via the Internet. So, before you take off, go grab your mouse and start surfing—you could save a bundle on your trip. Flip to "Planning Your Trip: An Online Directory" immediately following this chapter for information about the best travel Web sites.

40. On Monday nights, when all tickets are only £5 ($8), go to the Royal Court Theatre, which offers some of the city's most exhilarating and controversial contemporary drama in a totally revamped building.
41. Try out the London fringe like Soho Theatre, which fosters new writing and charges £11 ($17.60) at most for a seat—at least half what you'd pay at a blockbuster stage. Here, too, all tickets are £5 ($8) on Monday night.
42. Hunt down those free concerts. In churches at lunchtime, in the foyers of the Barbican Centre and the Royal Festival Hall, at the Royal Opera House, and at London's many drama and music schools. For example, students of Trinity College give free concerts in Hinde Street Church on most Thursday lunchtimes during term. Call all these places for information: **Central School of Speech and Drama**, 64 Eton Ave., NW3 (☎ **020/7722-8183**); the **Guildhall School of Music and Drama**; the **Barbican,** EC 1 (☎ **020/7628-2571**); the **Royal Academy of Dramatic Art**, 62–64 Gower St., WC1 (☎ **020/7436-1458**); **Royal Academy of Music**, Marylebone Rd., NW1 (☎ **020/7873-7373**); or **Trinity College of Music**, 11–13 Mandeville Place, W1 (☎ **020/7487-9647**).
43. At many a jazz or other music club, sitting at the bar instead of at a table can save you anywhere from £6 to £12 ($9.60 to $19.20) cover charge.
44. London has developed a happy-hour culture. Many bars offer discounted drinks—cocktails are the hip tipple these days—usually between 5:30 and 7:30pm, with prices slashed by 30% to 50%.

SHOPPING

45. Hang out at the outdoor markets: Camden Town on the weekends for a youth-oriented avant-garde experience akin to Canal Street in New York City; Bermondsey and Portobello for antiques; and Borough Market and the city's new farmers' markets for mouthwatering fresh produce.
46. Come to London in January, and shop in the sales. Virtually every store of every description knocks down its prices, and Londoners indulge in a frenzy of post-Christmas spending.
47. Check if there's a Designer Warehouse Sale during your stay. Mens- and womenswear are 40% to 80% off during these 3-day jamborees, usually at a photographic studio near King's Cross (see chapter 7).
48. Check out department stores Debenhams and Bhs (see chapter 7), as well as high street fashion chains like Top Shop: They've all invited big name designers to create small, exclusive collections for them, at unexclusive prices.
49. Trek a few extra Tube stops to find 25% to 80% discount on samples and ends of lines at London's handful of factory shops—Nicole Fahri and Burberry both have one.
50. Get your VAT refund—a whopping 17.5%. Fill out the appropriate forms in the shop; get the form and your receipt stamped at customs; and mail them back to the retailer.

3 Visitor Information

Information about London and traveling elsewhere in the country can be obtained from the **British Tourist Authority** (**BTA**). The BTA has two offices in the United States. The main one is at 7th Floor, 551 Fifth Ave., at 45th St., New York, NY 10176 (☎ **800/GO2BRITAIN** or 212/986-2200). It's open Monday to Friday from 9am to 6pm. A second office is located at 625 N. Michigan Ave., Suite 1001, Chicago, IL 60611 (no phone). Office hours are

9am to 5pm. The BTA Web site has sections tailored to each visitor nationality, so surf **www.visitbritain.com**.

You can also buy the following passes at the **British Travel Shop** store adjacent to the Manhattan BTA office: **London for Less** discount card to major London attractions (See tip 9, above) or order this by credit card from ☎ **888/GO-FOR-LESS** (www.for-less.com); the **British Heritage Pass** (See tip 9, above) gives you free entry into around 600 historic properties around the United Kingdom, or phone BritRail (☎ **888/BRITRAIL;** www.raileurope.com).

The BTA also maintains offices in **Australia,** at Level 16, Gateway, 1 Macquairie Place, Sydney, NSW 2000 (☎ **02/9377-4400**); in **Canada,** at 5915 Airport Rd., Suite 120, Mississauga, Ontario, LAV 1T1 (☎ **888/VISITUK** or 905/405-1840); in **Ireland,** at 18–19 College Green, Dublin 2 (☎ **01/670-8000**); and in **New Zealand,** at Suite 305, 3rd Floor, Dilworth Building, Auckland 1 (☎ **09/303-1446**).

In London, visit the main British Tourist Authority office in the **Britain Visitor Centre,** 1 Regent St., SW1 (no phone). It's open Monday 9:30am to 6pm, Tuesday to Friday 9am to 6:30pm, Saturday and Sunday 10am to 4pm (Saturday 9am to 5pm, June to September). There's a Globaltickets booking service for theater, sightseeing, and events; a bureau de change; and a Thomas Cook hotel and travel reservations office. And it's very busy.

For more information, check out our Online Directory immediately following this chapter.

4 Entry Requirements & Customs

DOCUMENTS

Citizens of the United States, Canada, Australia, and New Zealand need only a valid passport to enter Great Britain.

CUSTOMS

INTO THE U.K. Overseas visitors are allowed to import duty-free either 200 cigarettes, or 100 cigarillos, or 50 cigars, or 250 grams of tobacco; 2 liters of still table wine plus 1 liter of alcoholic drinks over 22% volume, or 2 liters of alcoholic drinks under 22%; 60cc of perfume and 250cc of eau de cologne. Other items can be imported free of tax, provided they're for personal use or, in the case of gifts, do not exceed £145 ($232) in value. Live animals, plants, and produce are forbidden. So are counterfeit and copied goods, and anything made from an endangered species: Leave your fake Rolex and your ivory jewelry at home.

Note: Duty-free sales ended for journeys within the European Community from April 1999. If you take a day-trip to France, for example, you'll pay local VAT and excise duty at the port or airport. However, passengers traveling to and from any non-EC country still benefit.

FOR U.S. CITIZENS Returning **U.S. citizens** who've been away for 48 hours or more are allowed to bring back, once every 30 days, $400 worth of merchandise duty free, plus 100 cigars, 200 cigarettes, and 1 liter of alcohol. You'll be charged a flat rate of 10% duty on the next $1,000 worth of purchases. Be sure to have your receipts handy. Pre-register on a form 4457 any valuable personal items you're taking with you, especially those not made in the U.S. (a Japanese laptop, for instance), to smooth the journey back through United States customs. On gifts mailed home, the duty-free limit is $100. You cannot bring fresh foodstuffs into the country; tinned foods, however, are allowed. The **U.S. Customs Service** publishes a useful free pamphlet *Know Before You Go*: call ☎ **202/354-1000,** or read it on the Web site (www.customs.ustreas.gov/travel/know.htm).

FOR CANADIANS For a summary of **Canadian** rules, read the booklet *I Declare* (publication no. RC4044), issued by **Revenue Canada** (☎ **613/993-0534;** www.ccra-adrc.gc.ca/publications). The personal exemption is CAN$750, and you can bring back duty free 200 cigarettes, 200 grams of tobacco, 50 cigars, and 1.5 liters of wine or 1.14 liters of liquor. In addition, you're allowed to mail gifts worth up to CAN$60 per package to Canada from abroad, provided they're unsolicited and don't contain alcohol or tobacco (write on the package "Unsolicited gift, under $60 value"). You should declare all valuables on the Y-38 form before leaving Canada, including serial numbers on things like expensive foreign cameras. *Note:* The CAN$750 exemption can be used only once a year and only after an absence of 7 days.

FOR AUSTRALIANS The duty-free allowance in **Australia** is A$400 or, for those under 18, A$200. Personal property mailed back from England should be marked "Australian goods returned" to avoid payment of duty. Upon returning to Australia, citizens can bring in 250 cigarettes or 250 grams of loose tobacco, and 1,125 milliliters of alcohol. If you're returning with valuable goods you already own, such as foreign-made cameras, you should file form B263. And you must declare all foodstuffs, even tins. A helpful brochure, *Know Before You Go,* is available from Australian consulates or **Australian Customs Services** (☎ **1/300-363-263;** www.customs.gov.au/travel/know.htm).

FOR NEW ZEALANDERS The duty-free allowance for **New Zealand** is NZ$700. Citizens over 16 can bring in 200 cigarettes, or 50 cigars, or 250 grams of tobacco (or a mixture of all three if their combined weight doesn't exceed 250 grams); plus 4.5 liters of wine or beer, and 1.125 liters of liquor. Any excess will be subject to duty and GST, where applicable, but Customs will only collect combined charges of over NZ$50. Most questions are answered in a free pamphlet, *Advice for Travellers,* available at consulates, and from New Zealand Customs: (☎ **0800/428-786** or 9/300-5399; www.customs.govt.nz/TRAVHOME/advice1.htm).

5 Money

CURRENCY

POUNDS & PENCE The British **pound** (£), a small, thick, pale-yellow coin, is divided into 100 pence (pennies). These come in 1p and 2p copper coins, and the silvery 5p, 10p, and 7-sided 20p and 50p coins. There are also large two-tone £2 coins. Notes are issued in £5, £10, £20, and £50 denominations.

CREDIT CARDS/ATMS

All major credit cards are widely accepted. However, be aware that budget hotels and restaurants often refuse American Express and Diners Club because of the merchant charges—the acceptability of Diners, particularly, fluctuates widely from year to year. In England, MasterCard is also called Access. Using

Currency Converter

Exchange rates are volatile. If you have access to the Web, you can get the right-now rate at **www.xe.net/currency**.

The British Pound & the U.S. Dollar

At this writing, $1 = approximately 62p (or $1.60 = £1), and this was the exchange rate used to calculate the dollar values in this book (rounded to the nearest nickel).

U.K.£	U.S.$	U.K.£	U.S.$
.05	.08	6.00	9.60
.10	.16	7.00	11.20
.25	.40	8.00	12.80
.50	.80	9.00	14.40
.75	1.20	10.00	16.00
1.00	1.60	15.00	24.00
2.00	3.20	20.00	32.00
3.00	4.80	25.00	40.00
4.00	6.40	30.00	48.00
5.00	8.00	35.00	56.00

plastic can be economical as well as convenient. Credit cards eliminate commissions for currency exchange. They also allow for delayed billing, which can work out to your advantage or disadvantage, depending on whether the dollar goes up or down with time.

Similarly, today you'll save money if you use an ATM rather than convert your home currency at a traditional bureau de change. The fees are generally lower and also the exchange rate is the "wholesale" rate, which is better. Obviously, you'll pay out less in fees if you minimize the number of transactions. Try to take out larger amounts on fewer occasions. Check with your bank before you leave about any charges, daily withdrawal limit, and whether you need a new pin number. It will also supply a list of overseas ATMs. To find out which overseas banks belong to the **CIRRUS** network, call ☎ **800/424-7787** (www.mastercard.com/atm). For **Visa Plus,** call ☎ **800/843-7587** (www.visa.com).

TRAVELER'S CHECKS

Although ATMs are an easier and cheaper way to get cash, some more safety-conscious travelers may prefer to stick traveler's checks in foreign currencies, which are still easily exchanged in London. Banks and companies like American Express and Thomas Cook offer the best rates. *Beware:* Private currency-exchange businesses that stay open late charge high commissions.

Sterling traveler's checks are accepted at most shops, restaurants, hotels, theaters, and attractions, except the smaller ones of all the above. But there are two drawbacks to carrying them. First, you'll have to exchange your money into pounds at home, where the transaction usually proves more expensive than it would in London. Second, you'll have to re-exchange unused pounds after the trip and pay again.

6 When to Go

Spring and fall are the best seasons for avoiding the hordes that descend on the major sights in summer. In winter, the weather in London can be very dreary—January and February are particularly grim—but the cultural calendar is rich, and the attractions much more peaceful.

What Things Cost in London	U.S.$
Taxi from Heathrow Airport to London	56.00
Underground from Heathrow to central London	5.60
Local telephone call	.16
Double room at Hallam Hotel (splurge)	164.00
Double room at More House (super-cheap)	64.00
Fish and chips for one, at The Rock & Sole Plaice	11.20
Lunch for one at most pubs	8.00
Celebrity-chef set menu for one, at Criterion Brasserie	28.70
Pint of beer	2.70
Coca-Cola in a restaurant	1.40
Coca-Cola in a can	.80
Roll of ASA 100 film, 24 exposures	4.15
Admission to Tate Modern	Free
Walking tour	8.00
Movie ticket	14.40
Cheapest ticket to see the Royal Shakespeare Company	9.60
Can of Heinz Baked Beans	.50

THE CLIMATE

London's infamous Jack the Ripper–friendly fog was never fog at all. It was the mucky exhaust from the coal fires that heated houses and blew forth from factory chimneys. Rigidly enforced air-pollution controls long ago made it an offense to use anything but smokeless fuel, so "fog" is no longer in the forecast. Rain, drizzle, and showers are, of course. A typical weather forecast any time of year predicts "scattered clouds with sunny periods and showers, possibly heavy at times." Temperatures are mild and rarely go below freezing in winter or above 75° Fahrenheit in summer—although there've been some major heat waves recently. El Niño and other natural phenomena have caused unusual weather patterns, including almost-summer warmth in March and hailstorms in May.

London's Average Daytime Temperature (°F) & Rainfall (inches)

	Jan	Feb	Mar	Apr	May	June	July	Aug	Sept	Oct	Nov	Dec
Temp.	39	39	42	46	52	57	60	60	57	51	44	41
Rainfall	3.5	2.5	2.8	2.4	2.5	2.5	2.4	3.0	3.1	3.3	3.5	3.7

HOLIDAYS

Businesses are closed on Christmas Day, for Boxing Day on December 26, and on New Year's Day, January 1: If any of these dates fall on a Saturday and/or Sunday, then the following Monday and/or Tuesday becomes a public holiday. A high proportion of offices, though not stores, actually close for the whole week between Christmas and New Year. In Britain, Good Friday is a public holiday as well as Easter Monday. There are also three bank holidays, on the first and last Mondays in May, and the last Monday in August. In London, shops, restaurants, museums, and other attractions tend to be much less quick to shut down, but there's no fixed policy. So call to check.

London Calendar of Events

January

- **Charles I Commemoration.** Banqueting House, Whitehall. Hundreds of men march through Central London dressed as cavaliers to mark the anniversary of the 1649 execution of King Charles I. Last Sunday in January.

February

- **Great Spitalfields Pancake Day Race.** Teams of four run in relays, doing that pancake-tossing thing. Noon on Shrove Tuesday (40 days before Easter) at Old Spitalfields Market, Brushfield St., E1 (☎ **020/7375-0441**). Why not join in? February 27.
- **Chinese New Year Parade.** Chinatown, at Gerrard and Lisle streets. Festive crowds line the decorated streets of Soho to watch the famous Lion Dancers and browse stalls crammed with crafts and delicacies (☎ **020/7734-5161**). Date varies each year.

March

- **The Oxford & Cambridge Boat Race.** The dark and light blues compete over a 4-mile course along the Thames from Putney to Mortlake. The race has been held since 1829, and crowds line the towpaths and fill the riverside pubs to cheer the teams on (**www.oubc.rowing.org.uk/**). March 24.

April

- **Flora London Marathon.** Almost 30,000 serious athletes and nutcases dressed up as giant chickens run 26 miles, from Greenwich to The Mall, SW1 (☎ **020/7620-4117;** www.london-marathon.co.uk). April 22.
- **National Gardens Scheme.** Enthusiastic amateurs and the not-so-amateur open up their private gardens to the public for a nominal entry fee on set days, organized by the charitable National Gardens Scheme. Pick up an NGS handbook from most bookstores for information, or contact the trust at Hatchlands Park, East Clandon, Guildford, Surrey, GU4 7RT (☎ **01483/211535;** www.ngs.org.uk). April to August.

May

- **Museums & Galleries Month.** Thousands of attractions all over Britain put on special exhibitions and events linked to common guiding themes (**www.24hourmuseum.org.uk**). May 1 to June 3.
- **May Fayre & Puppet Festival.** Procession at 10am; service at St. Paul's Covent Garden at 11:30am; then Punch & Judy until 6pm at this church where Samuel Pepys watched England's first show in 1662. Second Sunday in May.
- ✪ **Chelsea Flower Show.** This international spectacular features the best of British gardening, with displays of plants and flowers for all seasons. Set in the beautiful grounds of the Chelsea Royal Hospital, it is a world-class affair. For ticket information, write Shows Department, Royal Horticultural Society, Vincent Square, London SW1P 2PE (☎ **020/7649-1885;** www.rhs.org.uk). Tickets go on sale in December. May 22 to 25.
- **BOC Covent Garden Festival.** A celebration of the singing voice from cabaret to opera, in lovely old venues around the neighborhood (☎ **020/7413-1410;** www.cgf.co.uk). Last 2 weeks of May.

June

- **The Derby.** Pronounced "darby," this is one of the highlights of the flat racing season, at Epsom Racecourse in Surrey. Posh frocks, corporate suits, and much too much champagne, darling. (☎ **01732/470047;** www.epsomderby.co.uk). June 9.
- **Royal Ascot.** A 4-day midweek event held at Ascot Racecourse in Berkshire. The glamorous event of the racing season, as renowned for its fashion extravaganzas as for its high racing standards. The royal family attends. Remember the scene in *My Fair Lady?* (☎ **01344/876456;** www.ascot.co.uk). June 19 to 22.
- ✪ **Trooping the Colour.** Horse Guards Parade, Whitehall. On the Saturday closest to her official birthday, Elizabeth II inspects her regiments from an open carriage and receives the salute as they parade their colors before her. Quintessential English pageantry that still draws big crowds—many of them waiting to see a wretched young soldier faint in the heat under his ridiculous bearskin hat. Tickets are free and are allocated by ballot. Apply in writing between January and the end of February, enclosing an International Reply Coupon to: The Ticket Office, HQ Household Division, Chelsea Barracks, London SW1H 8RF. Canadians should apply to Royal Events Secretary, Canada House, Trafalgar Square, London SW1Y 5BJ.
- **Fleadh** (*Flah*). Exhausting all-day celebration of all things Irish, and more, in Finsbury Park, N4. Performers from Van Morrison, Elvis Costello, and Shane McGowan, to Ronan Keating from Boyzone and the Sawdoctors. Three stages, one for Irish stand-up comedy. Tickets £30 ($48) (☎ **020/7344-0044;** www.fleadhfestival.com). Usually the 2nd Saturday of the month.
- **The Covent Garden Flower Festival.** A free extravaganza of flowers, gardens, themed arts, and entertainments in the Covent Garden Piazza, celebrating the rich local cultural life. (**www.cgff.co.uk**). June 17 to 24.
- **Meltdown.** The Royal Festival Hall on the South Bank invites a celebrity artistic director (Nick Cave in 1999, Scott Walker last year) to host his or her dream festival, pulling together any art forms and performers they choose. (☎ **020/7960-4242;** www.meltdown.co.uk). Usually the last 2 weeks of June.
- **Royal Academy Summer Exhibition.** The world's largest open art exhibition and a great time to hear the critics at their catty best. Call ☎ **020/7300-8000** for info (www.royalacademy.org.uk). June to July.
- **London Mardi Gras.** The gay and lesbian event formerly known as Pride. A 2-week arts festival of club nights, plays, talks, and readings, culminating in the huge costumed march and parade from Hyde Park, through Piccadilly Circus and Trafalgar square, to Parliament Square, then a party at Finsbury Park, N4 (☎ **020/7494-2225;** www.londonmardigras.com). Usually last 2 weeks of June.
- **City of London Festival.** A 3-week extravaganza of over 100 events, covering every point on the musical spectrum, at venues from St. Paul's Cathedral to City livery company halls not normally open to the public (☎ **020/7368-8891;** www.city-of-london-festival.org.uk). Usually starting the 3rd week of June.
- ✪ **Wimbledon Lawn Tennis Championships.** This is a thrilling event where the posh and the people rub shoulders, and you can get right up close to the world's top tennis players. For full admission details, see "Spectator Sports," in chapter 6. June 25 to July 8.

July

- **Henley Royal Regatta.** A serious international rowing competition—the course covers more than a mile, against the current—with serious champagne socializing on the side. Held at Henley-on-Thames, Oxfordshire. Tickets are obtainable from the Secretary (☎ **01491/572153;** www.hrr.co.uk). July 4–8.
- **New Designers 2001.** Over 4,000 design graduates from all over Britain show their work at this giant degree show, held at the Business Design Centre in Islington. (☎ **020/7359-3535,** or 0870/735-2100 ticket hot line; www.newdesigners.com). July 5 to 8 and 12 to 15.
- **Greenwich & Docklands International Festival.** A week and a half packed with music, dance, and theater in historic buildings by the Thames—and street fun. (☎ **020/8305-1818;** www.festival.org). Usually early July.
- **Henry Wood Promenade Concerts.** World-famous summer musical season at Royal Albert Hall. Dating back to 1895, it runs the musical gamut from ancient to modern classics, and a bit of jazz, too, (see "Freebies," in section 1 of chapter 8). It's only £3 ($4.80) to rough it with the scrum of enthusiastic promenaders on the floor of the hall (☎ **020/7589-8212;** www.royalalberthall.com or www.bbc.co.uk/proms). Late July to mid-September.

August

- **Teddy Bears Picnic.** Around 1,000 kids and their furry friends enjoy free entertainment, from face-painting to workshops, at Battersea Park (☎ **020/8871-8107**). Usually 1st Friday afternoon in August.
- **Summer Rites.** Gay and lesbian fair with market stalls, bars, a funfair, concerts, and top DJs in Brockwell Park (☎ **020/7278-0995**). Usually early August.
- **Great British Beer Festival.** Organized by the Campaign for Real Ale. Olympia Exhibition Centre overflows with over 500 different ales, beers, ciders, and perries, brewed the traditional way. For information, contact CAMRA (☎ **01727/867201;** www.camra.org) or the Olympia box office (☎ **0870/904-0300**). Usually 1st week of August.

✪ **The Notting Hill Carnival,** Ladbroke Grove. One of the largest street festivals in the world, attracting more than half a million people to its 2-day celebration. Live reggae, steel bands, and soul music combine with great Caribbean food, camaraderie, and a charged atmosphere (**www.nottinghillcarnival.net**). August 26 to 27.

September

- **Thames Festival.** Fireworks, theatrical shows, sculpture, art exhibitions, bankside entertainment, a river pageant and torch-lit procession—all free and magical to behold (☎ **020/7928-0960;** www.thamesfestival.org). September 16.
- **London Open House Weekend.** A pat on the back for centuries of British architecture, as over 450 London buildings usually closed to visitors throw open their doors for the weekend, for free! Call ☎ **09001/600061** (www.londonopenhouse.co.uk). September 22 to 23.

October

- **Pearlies Harvest Festival.** London's famous Pearly Kings and Queens, with their fabulous coats encrusted with buttons, celebrate Harvest

Festival at St. Martin-in-the-Fields, in Trafalgar Sq., SW1 (☎ **020/7930-0089;** www.stmartin-in-the-field.org). Usually 1st Sunday in October.

- **Soho Jazz Festival.** Ten-day feast of jazz in local bars, cafes, and clubs—even impromptu sessions in Soho Square public garden, weather permitting (☎ **020/7437-6437**). Usually 10 days from the last Thursday in September.
- **Affordable Art Fair.** Held in Battersea Park, over 100 stands display work priced at under £2,000 ($3,200) (☎ **020/7371-8787;** www.wills-art.com). October 25 to 28.

November

- **State Opening of Parliament,** Whitehall and Parliament Square. Although the ceremony itself is not open to the public, crowds pack the parade route to see the royal procession (☎ **020/7291-4272;** www.parliament.uk). Late October or early November.
- ✪ **Fireworks Night.** Hyde Park, Battersea Park, and other public areas in London. Commemorates the "Gunpowder Plot," a Roman Catholic conspiracy to blow up King James I and his parliament in 1605. Huge bonfires are lit to burn effigies of the most famous conspirator, Guy Fawkes. Free. November 5 and closest Saturday.
- **London to Brighton Veteran Car Run.** More than 300 veteran cars from all over the world compete in this 57-mile run from London's Hyde Park to Brighton. Starts at 7:30am (☎ **01753/681736**). November 7.
- **London Film Festival.** Two-week fest of movies from all over the world, including big name premieres, at the National Film Theatre on South Bank and in West End cinemas (☎ **020/7928-3232;** www.lff.org.uk). From early November.
- **The Lord Mayor's Procession and Show.** Over 100 floats follow the new Lord Mayor in his gilded coach from Guildhall, in the City, to his inauguration at the Royal Courts of Justice in the Strand (☎ **020/7332-1456;** www.lord-mayors-show-org.uk). November 11, from 11am.

December

- **Spitalfields Festival.** Magical music by candlelight in Christ Church, Spitalfields, designed by Hawksmoor. Spin-off from 2-week festival in June (☎ **020/7377-1362** or 020/7377-0287). Usually week before Christmas.
- **Harrods' After-Christmas Sale,** Knightsbridge. Call ☎ **020/7730-1234** (www.harrods.com) for exact dates and hours. Late December.
- **New Year's Eve.** Drunken lemmings party at Trafalgar Square, where the fountains are switched off to prevent drowning and hypothermia. And lots more fun across the city, attempting to recapture the Millennium Eve spirit when fireworks lit up the Thames. To find the hottest hotspots, contact the London Tourist Board (☎ **020/7932-2000** or 020/7971-0026; www.londontown.com) or the BTA (see "Visitor Information," above).
- **Greenwich & Docklands First Night.** A fiesta of street theater, fireworks, music, and fun in the courtyard of the Royal Naval College, Greenwich. Tickets £3 ($4.80) (☎ **020/8305-1818;** www.festival.org/). December 31.

7 Health, Insurance & Other Concerns

MEDICAL REQUIREMENTS

Unless you're arriving from an area known to be suffering an epidemic, you don't need inoculations or vaccinations to enter Britain. If you're on medication, bring the doctor's prescription for any controlled substances you possess.

HEALTH INSURANCE

Citizens and residents of Australia and New Zealand are entitled to free medical treatment and subsidized dental care while in Britain. Americans and other nationals will usually have to pay up-front, except in accident and emergency departments (until referral). Doctors and hospitals are expensive: Even though it's not required of travelers, we recommend you take out health insurance. Most American travelers are covered by their hometown policies in the event of an accident or sudden illness on vacation. Also, some credit-card companies offer free, automatic travel-accident insurance, up to $100,000, when you buy tickets on their cards. Before spending money on additional protection, check to see that your health maintenance organization (HMO) or insurance carrier will cover you in foreign countries.

OTHER TRAVEL-RELATED INSURANCE

You can also protect your travel investment by insuring against lost or damaged baggage, and trip cancellation or interruption costs. These are often combined into a single comprehensive plan and sold through travel agents and credit-card companies. Contact the following for more information: **Access America** (☎ **800/284-8300;** www.accessamerica.com); **Travelex** (☎ **888/457-4602;** www.travelex-insurance.com); **Travel Guard International** (☎ **877/216-4885;** www.travel-guard.com); and **Wallach & Co** (☎ **800/237-6615;** www.wallach.com).

8 Tips for Travelers with Special Needs

FOR TRAVELERS WITH DISABILITIES

Before you plan a trip, consider joining **The Society for the Advancement of Travel for the Handicapped** (**SATH**), 347 Fifth Ave. Suite 610, New York, NY 10016 (☎ **212/447-7284;** www.sath.org). It costs $45 annually, $30 for seniors and students, to gain access to the society's vast network of connections in the travel industry. It provides information sheets on travel destinations and referrals to tour operators that specialize in traveling with disabilities. The quarterly magazine, *Open World for Disability and Mature Travel,* is full of good information and resources. A year's subscription is $18 ($35 outside the United States).

For information on traveling in Britain, contact **Holiday Care Services,** 2nd floor, Imperial Buildings, Victoria Road, Horley, RH6 7PZ (☎ **01293/774535;** www.holidaycare.org.uk), between 9am and 5pm on weekdays. The organization publishes 120 information sheets on different topics and regions. If you want more than two, the charge is 50p per sheet. Pay £15 ($24) to become a "friend," and receive a newsletter and holiday discounts. **Tripscope** (☎ **020/8580-7021**) provides a very helpful transport-information service for people with disabilities, Monday to Friday 9am to 4:45pm.

London's major museums and tourist attractions should all now be fitted with wheelchair ramps, but call **Artsline** (☎ **020/7388-2227**) for free advice on accessibility to theaters, galleries, and events around the city—including youth-oriented info. The phone line is open Monday to Friday from 9:30am to 5:30pm. It's common for theaters, nightclubs, and attractions to offer discounts, called "concessions," to people with disabilities. Ask for these before paying full price.

FOR GAY & LESBIAN TRAVELERS

The International Gay & Lesbian Travel Association (IGLTA), (☎ **800/448-8550** or 954/776-2626; www.iglta.org), links travelers up with the appropriate gay-friendly service organization or tour specialist. With around 1,200 members, it publishes quarterly newsletters, marketing mailings, and a membership directory updated quarterly. A lot of members are gay or lesbian businesses, but IGLTA is open to individuals, too, for $150 yearly, plus a $100 joining fee. Contact IGLTA for a list of agencies tied into its information resources. The purely online www.gaytoz.com or www.rainbownetwork.com are also both very comprehensive.

When you get to London, look out for the free *Pink Paper* (www.sonow.net) at gay bars, bookstores, and cafes—head straight for Old Compton Street in Soho. *Boyz* (www.boyznow.com) and *QX* (www.qxmag.co.uk) are excellent for city listings, gossip, and scenes, and glossy magazine pin-ups. *Time Out* (www.timeout.com) also has a good gay section. And lastly, for advice on pretty much anything, including accommodation, call the 24-hour **Lesbian & Gay Switchboard** (☎ **020/7837-7324;** www.llgs.org.uk).

We've also reviewed two gay hotels, the New York Hotel and the Philbeach (see "Earl's Court," in chapter 4), and you'll find information on "Gay & Lesbian London," in chapter 8, "London After Dark."

FOR SENIORS

In Britain, "senior citizen" usually means a woman at least 60 years old and a man at least 65. Seniors often receive the same discounts as students. Some are restricted to British citizens only, but check at all attractions, theaters, and other venues. From April last year, many of the major national museums and galleries abolished charges for seniors.

London's youth hostels welcome older guests. These are some of the cheapest accommodations in the city and are listed under "Super-Cheap Sleeps" in chapter 4.

Members of AARP have access to a purchase privilege discount program on hotels, car rentals, tours, and other travel facilities. For information, write or contact the **American Association of Retired Persons** (**AARP**), 601 E St. NW, Washington, DC 20049 (☎ **800/424-3410;** www.aarp.org). Anyone aged 60 and older, along with their spouses of any age (or a "significant other" 50 or older), can take advantage of an educational program sponsored by **Elderhostel,** 75 Federal St., Boston, MA 02110 (☎ **877/426-8056** or 617/426-7788; www.elderhostel.org). It sends almost 25,000 people, aged 55 plus, to school abroad every year. Courses last 2 to 4 weeks. Fees include airfare, meals, lodging, daily classroom instruction, and admission fees. Last year, a 10-night trip to London in peak season cost $2,689.

FOR STUDENTS

The **American Institute for Foreign Study,** River Plaza, 9 West Broad St., Stamford, CT 06902 (☎ **800/727-2437** or 203/399-5000; www.aifs.org) offers 3- to 12-week study/travel programs, costing from $3,700 to $7,000, including meals and housing. The **Institute for International Education,** 809 United Nations Plaza, New York, NY 10017 (☎ **212/883-8200;**

www.iie.org) also administers student applications for study-abroad programs in England and other European countries. Write or call ☎ **800/445-0443** for its free booklet, "Basic Facts on Study Abroad." It's also possible to enroll in summer courses at **Oxford University** (☎ **01865/270360;** www.ox.ac.uk), and **Cambridge** (☎ **01954/280398;** www.cam.ac.uk). For the latter, also contact Dr. Joann Painter, 714 Sassafras St., Erie, PA 16501 (☎ **814/456-0757**).

The best all-round resource for students, however, is the **Council on International Educational Exchange,** 205 E. 42nd St., New York, NY 10017 (☎ **212/822-2600;** www.ciee.org). The CIEE publishes a free magazine titled *Student Travels* and also runs a "Work in Britain" program for U.S. college and university students. It can also set you up with the $20 **International Student Identity Card** (**ISIC**). This is the only officially acceptable form of student identification, good for cut rates on rail passes, plane tickets, phone calls, and other discounts. It also provides you with basic health and life insurance and a 24-hour help line. A real best friend. If you're no longer a student but are still under 26, you can buy an **International Youth Travel Card** ($20), which will get you the insurance and some of the discounts (but not student admission prices in museums). CIEE has a London office at 28A Poland St., London W1V 3DB (☎ **020/7437-7767**).

ISIC cards are also available through CIEE's travel branch, **Council Travel** (☎ **800/226-8624;** www.counciltravel.com), the biggest specialist agency in the world. It offers discounts on plane tickets, rail passes, and the like. Ask for a list of offices in major cities so that you can keep the discounts flowing (and aid lines open) as you travel. The International Student Travel Confederation Web site (**www.istc.org**) is a useful source of advice and directions to member organizations all over the world. In London, your best bet is **USIT Campus,** 52 Grosvenor Gardens, London SW1W 0AG (☎ **0870/240-1010;** www.campustravel.co.uk), opposite Victoria Station.

For long-stays, students should check out the **Jenny Jones Agency,** 40 S. Molton St., W1 (☎ **020/7493-4801;** Tube: Bond St.), which rents out bedsits in Central London for £65 to £70 ($104 to $112) a week! Most of its private landlord clients only accept 6-month lets, though some will do 3 months. You can't book ahead, but just turn up at the agency's office, open Monday 2 to 5:30pm, Tuesday to Thursday 9.30am to 1.30pm and 2.30 to 5.30pm, and Friday 9.30am to 1.30pm. You must pay a month's rent in advance, plus the same again as a deposit, in cash or travelers checks (no credit cards), and should bring working references with you—sign up with a local temp agency—to prove you're not going to do them over.

The **University of London Student Union** (**ULU**), Malet Street, WC1 (☎ **020/7664-2000;** www.ulu.lon.ac.uk), caters to more than 70,000 students and may be the largest of its kind in the world. In addition to a gym and fitness center with squash and badminton courts, the Malet Street building houses several shops, bars, restaurants, a bank, a ticket-booking agency, and an STA travel office. And there's an action-packed schedule of gigs and club nights. Stop by or phone for information on university activities. The student union building is open Monday to Thursday from 8:30am to 11pm, Friday 8:30am to 1am, Saturday 9am to 1am, Sunday 9am to 10:30pm. Take the Tube to Goodge Street.

London's youth hostels are not only some of the cheapest sleeps, they're also great spots to meet other student travelers and pick up discounts to local attractions. You have to be a member of **Hostelling International** (**International Youth Hostel Federation**) and can sign up at all of them: $25 adults,

$15 for seniors, under-18s free. To apply in the United States and make advance international bookings, contact Hostelling International (AYH), 733 15th St. NW, Suite 840, Washington, DC 20005 (☎ **202/783-6161;** www.hiayh.org or www.iyhf.org). You can also book online—dorm-beds only—through the English Web site (www.yha.org.uk).

FOR WOMEN

Several Web sites offer advice for women on how to travel safely and happily. Run by Delta Airlines, the **Executive Woman's Travel Network** (www.delta-air.com/prog-serv/exec-womans-travel) offers tips on staying fit while traveling, eating well, finding special airfares, and dealing with many other women's travel issues. **Journeywoman Network** (www.journeywoman.com) is a very friendly gossip-net, advice shop, and portal, authored by women for women. Though dedicated to female travelers, **www.thepassport.co.uk** focuses largely on leaving the U.K. rather than inward-bound information. It does have hotel suggestions, but these are rather pricey. However, it merits inclusion because you can post questions to their on-site experts. It assumes women are independent travelers, too, and is hot on avoiding single-room supplements.

Lady Cabs (☎ **020/7254-3501**) is a great service to know about in London: It employs only women drivers.

FOR SINGLE TRAVELERS

One of the main drawbacks of traveling alone is the damnable single-room supplement. And while it's bliss to be totally independent, many people do miss having a partner in crime to giggle and gasp with. For all these reasons, it's worth contacting a traveler-matching service like **Vacation Partners** (☎ **800/810-8075;** www.vacationpartners.com). You pay $50 for "Coach Class" membership—$50 more to upgrade to "Business Class"—and receive four matches a year, based on a detailed questionnaire.

9 Holiday Packages

Package deals rarely undercut what you'll pay by hunting down the deepest discounts for each separate component of your holiday. However, writing one check after someone else has done all the planning work is a lot less of a hassle. And the discounts that tour operators and airlines can get with their buying power means you'll be staying in at least a 2- or 3-star hotel, rather than risking the vagaries of a guesthouse. So check the ads in your newspaper's travel section.

Fully shepherded tours—where a group travels together and shares the same preplanned activities—are not only unnecessary for a holiday based mainly in London, but you won't get the best out of this very vibrant city by "baa baaing" along en masse like sheep. Happily, packages don't have to be that regimented. Last year, top tour operator **Globus & Cosmos** (☎ **800/556-5454;** www.globusandcosmos.com) was offering a London at Leisure deal, including Saturday flights, 6 nights accommodation, a ½-day tour, discount vouchers, a London VisitorCard giving free travel on buses and Tubes, and a helpful "host service." It cost $1,536 for two people in January, rising to $2,478 in peak season.

We did the math to put that in context. Last July, two people would have spent around $1,700 to travel to London from JFK on cheap midweek flights from a consolidator, stay 6 nights in a modest bed-and-breakfast, and buy a bus tour, a London VisitorCard, and Tube tickets to and from Heathrow.

Airline packages are a comparative splurge, too. But they are flexible as to the day and time you can travel and what's included in the deal. You decide whether to buy from the menu of extras, such as tours, sightseeing, theater tickets, and so on. Then you go it alone—no having to dodge irritating new friends at breakfast. The packages below are representative prices quoted at press time for summer season—the two-person price drops by around $600 between October and March—with midweek flights, airport transfers, taxes, and 6 nights in a hotel: **American Airlines Vacations** (☎ **800/321-2121;** www.aavacations.com) was charging $1.934.40; **British Airways Holidays** (☎ **877/428-2228** or 800/359-8722; www.british-airways.com/vacations) threw in an open-top bus tour, too, on a Taste of London package for $2,341; **Continental Airlines Vacations** (☎ **800/772-4622;** www.flycontinental.com) threw in a few discount vouchers for attractions for $2,054.40; **United Airlines** (☎ **800/377-1816;** www.unitedvacations.com) sweetened its $1,828 deal with a London for Less discount card and guidebook; **Virgin Atlantic Vacations** (☎ **888/937-8474;** www.virgin-atlantic.com/vacations) was charging $2,464. **Qantas** (www.qantas.com) sells Jetabout Holidays only through travel agents.

British Travel International (☎ **800/327-6097;** www.britishtravel.com) can build you a package of discount deals and passes on planes, trains, automobiles, and buses, as well as accommodation. In Australia, contact **Explore Holidays** (☎ **2/9857-6200;** www.exploreholidays.co.au). The excellent U.K. travel agent **Trailfinders** (www.trailfinders.com.au) also has five Australian offices and claims to be able to offer up to 75% discount on standard prices when it tailor-makes a vacation: Sydney (☎ **02/9247-7666**); Melbourne (☎ **03/9600-3022**); Cairns (☎ **07/4041-1199**); Brisbane (☎ **07/3229-0887**); and Perth (☎ **08/9226-1222**). And try Qantas, too (☎ **1300/360-347;** www.qantas.com.au/holidays).

10 Getting There

BY PLANE

Around 90 scheduled airlines serve London, including these major American carriers: **American Airlines** (☎ **800/433-7300;** www.americanair.com), **Continental** (☎ **800/231-0856;** www.flycontinental.com), **Delta Airlines** (☎ **800/241-4141;** www.delta-air.com), **Northwest Airlines** (☎ **800/447-4747;** www.nwa.com), **TWA** (☎ **800/892-4141;** www.twa.com), and **United Airlines** (☎ **800/538-2929;** www.ual.com).

British Airways (☎ **800/247-9297;** www.british-airways.com) is the largest U.K. airline and goes everywhere, including Australia and New Zealand. **Virgin Atlantic Airways** (☎ **800/862-8621;** www.virgin-atlantic.com) flies from New York and Newark, New Jersey, as well as from Chicago, Boston, Las Vegas, Los Angeles, San Francisco, Orlando, Miami, and Washington, D.C. **Qantas** (☎ **1300/131313;** www.qantas.com) is the national Australian carrier, also serving New Zealand, and it code-shares with many foreign carriers. **Air New Zealand** (☎ **0800/737000;** www.airnz.com) flies daily to Heathrow.

FINDING THE BEST AIRFARE

London's popularity and the number of airlines flying there mean heavy competition for customers. So check local and national newspapers for special promotions and always shop around to find the cheapest fare.

The lowest-priced standard cattle-class fare usually carries some restrictions like advance-purchase, minimum stay, or a Saturday stopover, as well as penalties for altering dates and itineraries. Note, too, that weekday flights are slightly cheaper than weekend flights, and early mornings cheapest of all.

Make sure to check alternative ticket sources before buying direct from the airline. For instance, consolidators buy blocks of seats and sell them at a discount. Tickets are restrictive, valid only for a particular date or flight, nontransferable, and nonrefundable except directly from the consolidator, and they may also not earn frequent flier miles. There are rarely set advance-purchase requirements; if space is available, you can buy just before you fly. Always pay with a credit card, though, to protect yourself in case the consolidator goes belly up.

The lowest-priced bucket shops are usually local backroom operations with low profiles and overheads. Look for their tiny ads jam-packed with cities and prices in the travel or classified section of your local newspaper. Those that advertise nationally are rarely as competitive, but they often have toll-free telephone numbers and may be more reliable. In 2000, you could get a high-season round-trip ticket to London for $485. Here are some of the most reliable consolidators: **Arrow Travel** (☎ **212/889-2550**); **Cheap Tickets Inc.** (☎ **212/570-1179** or 800/377-1000; www.cheaptickets.com); **TFI Tours International** (☎ **212/736-1140** in New York State, or 800/745-8000); **Travel Land International Inc.** (☎ **212/268-6464**); and **Up & Away Travel** (☎ **212/889-2345**).

CHARTERS Another cheap way to cross the Atlantic is on a charter flight. Most operators advertise and sell their seats through travel agents, making them your best source of information on the deals available. Two well-known charter companies that do deal directly with passengers are **Travac,** (☎ **800/872-8800** or 212/563-3303, or 888/872-8327 for current fare quotes); and the CIEE-offshoot **Council Travel** (☎ **800/226-8624;** www.counciltravel.com).

FLYING INTO HEATHROW

Heathrow is a self-contained, self-sufficient micro-town about 13 miles from the middle of London, due west. As well as shops and restaurants, the airport has every kind of visitor service. You can save a lot of time by sorting things out here before going into the city. The vast majority of flights from North America, Australia, and New Zealand arrive at Terminals 3 and 4. Call **Heathrow** (☎ **0870/000-0123;** www.baa.co.uk) for any additional information.

VISITOR INFORMATION The **Airport Information** desks are at: **Terminal 3 Arrivals,** open daily from 5:30 to 10:30am; **Terminal 3 Departures,** open daily from 7am to 9:30pm; and **Terminal 4 Arrivals,** open daily from 5:30am to 10:30pm. The **London Tourist Board** has an information center in the Tube station concourse that connects with **Terminals 1, 2, and 3,** open daily from 8:30am to 6pm. And there is a Hotel & Traveller Centre in **Terminal 3 Arrivals,** open daily 6am to 11pm.

HOTEL RESERVATIONS **Expotel** has desks in the arrivals area of every terminal, open daily from 6am to 11pm. They will book you into any accommodation anywhere, even youth hostels, for a small fee.

CURRENCY EXCHANGE **American Express,** Terminal 4, Tube station concourse (☎ **020/8754-7057**) is open daily from 7am to 7pm. At all other

Make the Airline Pricing System Work for You

Increasingly sophisticated reservations software allows the airlines to practice yield management. They juggle twin priorities: filling the plane and making as much profit as possible from each flight. So, airlines constantly adjust the pricing of each seat on a particular flight according to the immediate demand. It sounds dodgy, but actually it's great for budget travelers who can play the hi-tech fare game, too. Save big money either by trawling the Internet, or by talking to a reliable travel agent or one of the companies that specialize in searching out low airfares.

Among the latter are: **A Better Airfare** (☎ 800/238-8371; www.better1.com); **AAAbsolute Savings** (☎ 800/359-4537); **Airline Bargain Finder & Ticket Sales** (☎ 800/727-1147); **1-800 Low Air Fare** (☎ 800/569-2473); **Fare Busters International** (☎ 800/618-0571); **Global Discount Travel Services** (☎ 800/497-6678); and **1-800 Fly Cheap** (☎ 800/359-2432; www.1800flycheap.com).

If you've got access to the Internet, surf **www.only-travel.com**. This lists several handy Web sites, including **Priceline** (www.priceline.com). Alternatively, **Intellitrip** (www.intellitrip.com) scans for the cheapest fares to your destination. For more information, consult "Planning Your Trip: An Online Directory," following this chapter.

bureaux de change, **British Airports Authority,** which runs Heathrow, guarantees that charges will match or beat at least one of Britain's big-four high street banks: for information on special deals, call ☎ **0800/844844.** The following companies have numerous branches, open daily at both terminals: **Thomas Cook** (☎ **020/8272-8073** T3 or 020/8272-8100 T4) is open in Arrivals from 5:30am to 10:15pm, and in Departures from 5:30am to 10pm; **Travelex** (☎ **020/8897-3501**) is permanently open in Arrivals, and from 5:30am to 10pm in Departures. There are ATMs throughout the airport.

CAR RENTALS Renting a car for holidays in London is unwise (see "Getting Around," in chapter 3). If you must, however, airport pick-ups are very convenient. The big rental agencies have branches at every Heathrow terminal: **Avis** (☎ **020/8899-1000**); **Budget Rent-a-Car** (☎ **0845/606-6669**); **Europcar** (☎ **020/8897-0811**); and **Hertz** (☎ **020/8897-2072**).

GETTING FROM THE AIRPORT TO TOWN There are lots of ways to get into London from Heathrow: It could hardly be simpler. Children under 5 travel free on most services.

The **Underground** is undoubtedly the best value. There are two airport Tube stations on the Piccadilly Line: one for Terminals 1, 2, and 3, and one for Terminal 4. The journey takes 50 to 60 minutes. Trains leave the airport from 5:08am to 11:49pm and arrive there from 6am to 1:07am (shorter hours on Sunday). Heathrow is in zone 6 and therefore not covered by most travelcards. One-way fares from zone 1, or Central London (see "Getting Around," in Chapter 3), are £3.50 ($5.60) for adults and £1.50 ($2.40) for children aged 5 to 15. If you miss the last Tube, the **N97 night bus** leaves every 30 minutes and costs £1.50 ($2.40) for adults and children. Call **London Transport Travel Information** (☎ **020/7222-1234;** www.londontransport.co.uk) for more information.

Heathrow Express (☎ **0845/600-1515;** www.heathrowexpress.com) is the new, super-luxxy, nonstop rail service to Paddington Station. It takes 15 minutes from Terminals 1, 2, and 3, and 20 minutes from Terminal 4. Trains leave Heathrow from 5:02am to 11:52pm and arrive there from 5:30am to midnight. All major airlines offer full luggage check-in at Paddington. Standard-class one-way tickets cost £12 ($19.20) for adults and £6 ($9.60) for children aged 5 to 15.

National Express (☎ **08705/747777** info or 08705/757747 credit-card bookings; www.gobycoach.com) runs two airport bus services and accepts online bookings. The **Airbus** leaves four times an hour from just outside every Heathrow terminal and goes to 23 stops in Central London. Ask your hotel or B&B if there's one close by, because this may be the most convenient option. The service runs from 5:15am to 10:15pm, and one-way tickets cost £7 ($11.20) for adults and £3 ($4.80) for children ages 5 to 15. The **Hotel Hoppa** runs between each terminal and the main Heathrow hotels from 5:30am to 11:30pm. One-way tickets cost £2 ($3.20). One child aged 5 to 15 travels free with each adult.

Hotelink (☎ **01293/532244;** www.hotelink.co.uk) is a door-to-door minibus service with desks at Terminals 3 and 4 Arrivals. It runs from 6am to 10pm daily, calls at its passengers' hotels only, and costs £12 ($19.20) for a one-way ticket.

Black taxis (see "Getting Around," in Chapter 3) are always available at Heathrow. The approximate fare to London is £35 ($56), which is a good value, door-to-door cost if you can fill the cab with the maximum five passengers and still have room for luggage. The taxi desk numbers are: **Terminal 3** (☎ **020/8745-4655**); **Terminal 4** (☎ **020/8745-7302**). To walk smugly past the tedious taxi line, book ahead with **Black Cab London** (☎ **877/405-7622** in the U.S., 020/8663-6400 from elsewhere overseas, or 0800/169-5296 in the U.K.; www.blackcablondon.co.uk). The driver will meet you in arrivals and help carry that jumbo Samsonite. Such convenience comes at luxury prices, of course. The ride from Heathrow into Central London will cost £52 ($83.20), instead of £35 ($56).

SPECIAL NEEDS There are **Help Points** throughout Heathrow. Use the green telephone to ask for a Help Bus (☎ **020/8745-5185**) to drive you around the airport, for a wheelchair, or just for general assistance. Travelers with disabilities can call the following numbers, in addition to those listed above, for advice or to make pre-arrangements: **Heathrow Travel-Care**

Smaller Airports

If you're flying to London on a no-frills flight, you may land at **Stansted** (☎ **01279/680500;** www.baa.co.uk). The National Express **Airbus** (see above) makes the journey to Victoria Station in about 1 hour and 40 minutes and costs £8 ($12.80) one-way. Charters and cheapie airlines also fly into **Luton Airport** (☎ **01582/405100**). The Greenline 757 bus leaves Luton Airport for London once an hour and takes 1 hour and 10 minutes. It costs £7 ($11.20) one-way. For information, call ☎ **08706/087261.** It's much faster, though, to take the Railair Coach to Luton Station, where you then catch the Luton Flyer train to London King's Cross. The total journey time is 38 to 43 minutes. The 24-hour service runs every 15 to 20 minutes at peak times, otherwise every hour. Tickets cost £9.50 ($15.20) one-way. Call National Rail Enquiries for further information (☎ **08457/484950**).

Onward! Short Hops Around Britain & Across the Channel

If you want to fly to Europe, or even up to Scotland, check out these no-frills airlines, which all fly from Stansted: **easyJet** (☎ **0870/600-0000;** www.easyjet.com), also from Gatwick; **Ryanair** (☎ **0541/569569;** www.ryanair.ie); **Virgin Express** (☎ **020/7744-0004;** www.virgin-express.com), Heathrow and Gatwick, too; and British Airways **GO** (☎ **0845/605-4321;** www.go-fly.com). Look for ads in local newspapers and on Tube stations as the fare war sees lower prices posted practically every day. Last June, Ryanair was offering summer round-trip specials, ranging from £9 ($14.40) to Glasgow up to £59 ($94.40) to Pisa, of leaning-tower fame.

(☎ **020/8745-7495**); and **London Transport's Unit for Disabled Passengers** (☎ **020/7222-5600**). One out of two London taxis can accommodate wheelchairs, or you can book **Vic Hughes** taxi service (☎ **020/8831-0770**).

FLYING INTO GATWICK

There are three ways of making the 25-mile trek into the city from Gatwick (☎ **01293/535353;** www.baa.co.uk). The most popular is the **Gatwick Express** train, which takes 30 to 45 minutes to reach Victoria. It costs a hefty £10.20 ($16.30) one-way. The station is just below the airport, and trains depart every 15 minutes from 6am to 10pm (hourly, on the hour, at other times). There is a second train option, post-privatization. **Connex South Central** charges £8.20 ($13.60) one-way, for a journey taking a ½ to ¾ hour, depending on how many stops it makes between Victoria station and the airport. For information on both, call National Rail Enquiries (☎ **08457/484950**), or pre-book through **www.thetrainline.com**.

You can also take the **Airbus** (☎ **08705/747777** info or 08705/757747 credit-card bookings; www.gobycoach.com). The 70-minute journey costs £8 ($12.80) one-way. Buses leave for Victoria Coach Station from Gatwick's North Terminal hourly.

BY TRAIN

Each of London's train stations is connected to a vast bus and Underground network, and there are phones, restaurants, pubs, luggage-storage areas, shops, and London Transport Information Centres, at all of them.

If you're **arriving from France,** the fastest way to get to London is by taking the HoverSpeed connection between Calais and Dover (see "By Ferry & Hovercraft," below), where you can pick up a train into the city. If you prefer the ease of one-stop travel, you can take the Eurostar train directly from Paris—or go there and back in a day for a very swanky excursion.

VIA THE CHUNNEL FROM THE CONTINENT Queen Elizabeth and President François Mitterrand officially opened the $15-billion Channel Tunnel in 1994. One of the great engineering feats of all time, this is the first link between Britain and the Continent since the Ice Age. (See "By Car," below, for details on Le Shuttle.)

Rail Europe (☎ **800/EUROSTAR;** www.raileurope.com) sells tickets on the **Eurostar** direct service between Paris Gare Du Nord and Brussels Central

Station and Waterloo in London. On the Continent, the train rips along at 186 m.p.h.; on the British side, it slows down to 100 m.p.h., at least until the track upgrade is completed. A standard round-trip between Paris and London costs $239, but you can cut that back to $199 with a 14-day advance purchase (nonrefundable) ticket—and special promotions go a lot lower, so check the newspapers. In London, make reservations for Eurostar at ☎ **08705/186186** (www.eurostar.com); in Paris, at ☎ **08/36353535** or 01/53607000; in Brussels, at ☎ **02/525-9292** (bookings only, no inquiries).

FROM ELSEWHERE IN THE U.K. If you're traveling to London from elsewhere in the United Kingdom, consider buying a **BritRail Classic Pass.** This allows unlimited rail travel anywhere during a set time period (Eurailpasses aren't accepted in Britain, although they are in Ireland). A second-class pass costs $265 for 8 days, $400 for 15 days, $505 for 22 days, and $600 for 1 month. Children under 5 travel free. One child aged 5 to 15 can travel free with each adult pass. All additional children pay half price. Seniors qualify for discounts. Travelers between 16 and 25 can purchase a **BritRail Classic Youth Pass,** which allows unlimited second-class travel: $215 for 8 days, $280 for 15 days, $355 for 22 days, or $420 for 1 month. There are also passes for three or four people traveling in a group, or for people who are only going to roam close to London, the **BritRail SouthEast** pass (see chapter 9).

You must purchase all special passes before you leave home: in the United States, at the **British Travel Shop** next to the Manhattan BTA office, or those in Australia and New Zealand (see "Visitor Information," above.). Or call ☎ **888/BRITRAIL** in the United States, 800/361RAIL in Canada (www.raileurope.com).

BY BUS

Whether you're coming from the Continent or from another part of the country, London-bound buses almost always go to (and leave from) **Victoria Coach Station,** Buckingham Palace Road, 1 block from the train station.

The **Tourist Trail Pass** is ideal for serious day-trippers and round-Britain tourers. This allows unlimited travel on a set number of days, not necessarily consecutive but falling within a fixed time period: either 2 days to be used within a 3-day period, for £49 ($78.40); 5 days travel, valid for 10, for £85 ($136); 7 days, valid for 21, for £120 ($192); or 14 days, valid for 30, for £187 ($299.20). The £9 ($14.40) discount cards available to under-25s and over-50s cut pass and individual ticket prices by 20% to 30%. You can buy all passes with a credit card, online or by phone, direct from **National Express** (☎ **08705/747777** info or 08705/757747 credit-card bookings; www.gobycoach.com); or, in person, at the Heathrow Central Bus Station and Victoria Coach Station, at National Express offices in St. Pancras station and Earl's Court Tube station, or at any travel agent displaying the National Express logo. The U.S. agent for National Express is **British Travel International** (☎ **800/327-6097;** www.britishtravel.com).

Bus connections to Britain from the Continent are not so much uncomfortable, as mind-blowingly tedious, especially when you think how quickly you could be traveling. But it is very cheap compared to the train, and plane except for specials on the no-frills carriers (see above). **Eurolines** is yet another part of National Express (☎ **08705/747777** info or 08705/757747 credit-card bookings; www.gobycoach.com). It goes to more than 450 destinations in Ireland and mainland Europe, with daily departures from Victoria to Belfast, Amsterdam, Brussels, Frankfurt, and others. For instance, there are three daytime buses to Paris each day: The journey takes 8½ hours and costs from £33 ($52.80) return. For a serious pilgrimage around Europe, check out the 30-day Eurolines Pass (£139/$224.40), which links you to 30 cities.

BY FERRY & HOVERCRAFT

For centuries, ships and ferries have crossed the English Channel carrying supplies, merchandise, and passengers. The shortest and closest routes from London are Dover to Calais, and Folkestone to Boulogne. Note that here, too, you pay less traveling out of season and during unsociable hours, and if you prebuy tickets rather than just turn up. To have any hope of squeezing on board in the summer and during public holidays, you must book anyway.

Check with the BTA (see "Visitor Information," above) for a full listing of ferries to the Channel Islands, Ireland, the Isle of Man, and around the host of Scottish islands. All the companies below put together stopover packages if you fancy a continental break from your London holiday. You can also get day-trip deals.

CAR & PASSENGER FERRIES **P&O Stena Line** (☎ **0870/600-0600,** or 561/563-2856 in the U.S.; www.posl.com) operates car and passenger ferries between Dover and Calais, 30 departures a day, with a journey time of 1 hour 25 minutes: Summer one-way tickets cost £120 to £165 ($192 to $264) for car and driver, or £24 ($38.40) for an adult foot passenger. **Sea France** (☎ **08705/711711;** www.seafrance.com) runs 15 departures a day, with a journey time of 1½ hours: One-way peak-season tickets cost £134 to £204 ($214.40 to $326.40) for car and driver, £15 ($24) for an adult foot passenger.

HOVERCRAFT & SEACATS Traveling by Hovercraft or SeaCat takes about half the time that a ferry does. **Hoverspeed** (☎ **0870/240-8070;** www.hoverspeed.co.uk) makes 6 to 12 hovercraft crossings to Calais from Dover, taking 35 minutes. Hoverspeed SeaCats take a little longer, 50 minutes, and there are five departures a day. One-way tickets on both cost £119 to £165 ($190.40 to $264) for car and driver, and adult foot passengers pay £24 ($38.40). The SeaCat also travels between Folkestone and Boulogne, up to four times a day, taking 55 minutes, and costing £109 to £149 ($174.40 to $238.40) for car one-way, and £24 ($38.40) for adult foot passengers. A hovercraft trip is great fun, even though you can't see out at all, as the vessel is technically "flying" over the water. **Stena Line** also runs SeaCats, from Stranraer, near Glasgow, to Belfast, and from Holyhead to Dublin. Call ☎ **08705/707070** (www.stenaline.com).

BY CAR

If you plan to take a rented car across or under the Channel, check with the rental company about license and insurance requirements before you leave. For car ferries, hovercraft, and SeaCats, check the details above.

LE SHUTTLE Le Shuttle (☎ **08705/353535;** www.eurotunnel.com) is the Channel Tunnel drive-on train service. Cars, charter buses, taxis, and motorcycles all do just that—drive on at Calais or Folkestone and off at the other end. It operates 24 hours a day, 365 days a year, running every 15 minutes during peak times and at least once an hour at night. No more weather-related delays or seasickness. Before boarding Le Shuttle, you'll stop at a toll booth to pay, then pass through Immigration for both countries at one time. The carriages are bright and air-conditioned, and you can get out of the car to stretch your legs. The total travel time between the French and English highway system is about 1 hour (35 minutes from platform to platform).

In summer especially, it's sensible to book rather than just turn up, because stand-by queues can be very long and slow. Prices vary according to the season, the day of the week, and the time of day. A late-night/crack-of-dawn round-trip fare would cost you £260 ($416) in the summer. If you make the return trip within 5 days, that plummets to £155 ($248). The single fare is half the price of a round trip.

There are restaurants, shops, and service stations on both sides of the Channel, and all the staff are bilingual. Hertz runs a scheme called **Le Swap** for passengers taking Le Shuttle, which allows you to switch cars at Calais to keep the local driving position—left- or right-hand.

Once you get to Folkestone, follow the signposts to the motorway to London. The capital has two ring roads, the inner A406 and the A205, and the M25 farther out. The M25 connects with the M40 to Oxford and Birmingham, the M1 to Leeds, the M4 to Bristol, and the M11 to Cambridge (and many others!). Once in London, I'd strongly suggest you get rid of the car: Parking is difficult and expensive, the streets are a maze, and the whole driving experience is a nightmare.

Planning Your Trip: An Online Directory

Frommer's Online Directory will help you take better advantage of the travel-planning information available online. Part 1 lists general Internet resources that can make any trip easier, such as sites for getting the best possible prices on airline tickets. In Part 2 you'll find some top online guides specifically for London.

This is not a comprehensive list, but a discriminating selection to get you started. Recognition is given to sites based on their content value and ease of use. Inclusion here is not paid for—unlike some Web-site rankings, which are based on payment. Finally, remember this is a press-time snapshot of leading Web sites; some undoubtedly will have evolved, changed, or moved by the time you read this.

1 Top Travel-Planning Web Sites

By Lynne Bairstow

Lynne Bairstow is the co-author of *Frommer's Mexico,* and the editorial director of *e-com* magazine.

WHY BOOK ONLINE?

Online agencies have come a long way over the past few years, now providing tips for finding the best fare and giving you suggested dates or times to travel that yield the lowest price if your plans are at all flexible. Other sites even allow you to establish the price you're willing to pay, and they check the airlines' willingness to accept it. However, in some cases, these sites may not always yield the best price. Unlike a travel agent, for example, they might not have access to charter flights offered by wholesalers.

Online booking sites aren't the only places to reserve airline tickets—all major airlines have their own Web sites and often offer incentives (bonus frequent flyer miles or Net-only discounts, for example) when you buy online or buy an e-ticket.

The new trend is toward conglomerated booking sites. By mid-2000, a consortium of U.S.- and European-based airlines is planning to launch an as-yet-unnamed Web site that will offer fares lower than those available through travel agents. United, Delta, Northwest, and Continental have initiated this effort, based on their success at selling airline seats on their own sites.

Check Out Frommer's Site

We highly recommend **Arthur Frommer's Budget Travel Online (www.frommers.com)** as an excellent travel-planning resource. Of course, we're a little biased, but you'll find indispensable travel tips, reviews, monthly vacation giveaways, and online booking. Among the most popular features of this site are the regular "Ask the Expert" bulletin boards, which feature Frommer's authors answering your questions via online postings.

Subscribe to Arthur Frommer's Daily Newsletter (**www.frommers.com/newsletters**) to receive the latest travel bargains and inside travel secrets in your e-mailbox every day. You'll read daily headlines and articles from the dean of travel himself, highlighting last-minute deals on airfares, accommodations, cruises, and package vacations.

Search our Destinations archive (**www.frommers.com/destinations**) of more than 200 domestic and international destinations for great places to stay and dine and tips on sightseeing. Once you've researched your trip, the online reservation system (**www.frommers.com/booktravelnow**) takes you to Frommer's favorite sites for booking your vacation at affordable prices.

The best of the travel-planning sites are now highly personalized; they store your seating preferences, meal preferences, tentative itineraries, and credit-card information, allowing you to quickly plan trips or check agendas.

In many cases, booking your trip online can be better than working with a travel agent. It gives you the widest variety of choices, control, and the 24-hour convenience of planning your trip when you choose. All you need is some time—and often a little patience—and you're likely to find the fun of online travel research will greatly enhance your trip.

WHO SHOULD BOOK ONLINE?

Online booking is best for travelers who want to know as much as possible about their travel options, for those who have flexibility in their travel dates, and for bargain hunters.

One of the biggest successes in online travel for both passengers and airlines is the offer of last-minute specials, such as American Airlines' weekend deals or other Internet-only fares that must be purchased online. Another advantage is that you can cash in on incentives for booking online, such as rebates or bonus frequent-flyer miles.

Business and other frequent travelers also have found numerous benefits in online booking, as the advances in mobile technology give them the ability to check flight status, change plans, or get specific directions from handheld computing devices, mobile phones, and pagers. Some sites will even e-mail or page passengers if their flight is delayed.

Online booking is increasingly able to accommodate complex itineraries, even for international travel. The pace of evolution on the Net is rapid, so you'll probably find additional features and advancements by the time you visit these sites. The future holds ever-increasing personalization and customization for online travelers.

TRAVEL-PLANNING & BOOKING SITES

Below are listings for sites for planning and booking travel. The following sites offer domestic and international flight, hotel, and rental-car bookings, plus news, destination information, and deals on cruises and vacation packages. Free (one-time) registration is required for booking.

Travelocity (incorporates Preview Travel). www.travelocity.com; www.previewtravel.com; www.frommers.travelocity.com

Travelocity is Frommer's online travel-planning and -booking partner. Travelocity uses the SABRE system to offer reservations and tickets for more than 400 airlines, plus reservations and purchase capabilities for more than 45,000 hotels and 50 car-rental companies. An exclusive feature of the SABRE system is its **Low Fare Search Engine,** which automatically searches for the three lowest-priced itineraries based on a traveler's criteria. Last-minute deals and consolidator fares are included in the search. If you book with Travelocity, you can select specific seats for your flights with online seat maps and also view diagrams of the most popular commercial aircraft. Its hotel finder provides street-level location maps and photos of selected hotels. With the **Fare Watcher** e-mail feature, you can select up to five routes and receive e-mail notices when the fare changes by $25 or more.

Travelocity's **Destination Guide** includes updated information on some 260 destinations worldwide—supplied by Frommer's.

Note to AOL Users: You can book flights, hotels, rental cars, and cruises on AOL at keyword: Travel. The booking software is provided by Travelocity/Preview Travel and is similar to the Internet site. Use the AOL "Travelers Advantage" program to earn a 5% rebate on flights, hotel rooms, and car rentals.

Expedia. expedia.com

Expedia is Travelocity's major competitor. It offers several ways of obtaining the best possible fares: **Flight Price Matcher** service allows your preferred airline to match an available fare with a competitor; a comprehensive **Fare Compare** area shows the differences in fare categories and airlines; and **Fare Calendar** helps you plan your trip around the best possible fares. Its main limitation is that like many online databases, Expedia focuses on the major airlines and hotel chains, so don't expect to find too many budget airlines or one-of-a-kind B&Bs here.

TRIP.com. www.trip.com

TRIP.com began as a site geared toward business travelers, but its innovative features and highly personalized approach have broadened its appeal to leisure travelers as well. It is the leading travel site for those using mobile devices to access Internet travel information.

TRIP.com includes a trip-planning function that provides the average and lowest fare for the route requested, in addition to the current available fare. An on-site "newsstand" features breaking news on airfare sales and other travel specials. Among its most popular features are Flight TRACKER and intelliTRIP. **Flight TRACKER** allows users to track any commercial flight en route to its destination anywhere in the United States., while accessing real-time FAA-based flight monitoring data. **intelliTRIP** is a travel search tool that allows users to identify the best airline, hotel, and rental-car rates in less than 90 seconds.

In addition, the site offers e-mail notification of flight delays, plus city resource guides, currency converters, and a weekly e-mail newsletter of fare updates, travel tips, and traveler forums.

Yahoo! Travel. www.travel.yahoo.com
Yahoo! is currently the most popular of the Internet information portals, and its travel site is a comprehensive mix of online booking, daily travel news, and destination information. The **Best Fares** area offers what it promises, plus provides feedback on refining your search if you have flexibility in travel dates or times. There is also an active section of Message Boards for discussions on travel in general and specific destinations.

LAST-MINUTE DEALS & OTHER ONLINE BARGAINS

There's nothing airlines hate more than flying with lots of empty seats. The Net has enabled airlines to offer last-minute bargains to entice travelers to fill those seats. Most of these are announced on Tuesday or Wednesday and are valid for travel the following weekend, but some can be booked weeks or months in advance. You can sign up for weekly e-mail alerts at the airlines' own sites (see "Getting There" in chapter 2) or check sites that compile lists of these bargains, such as **Smarter Living** or **WebFlyer** (see below). To make it easier, visit a site that will round up all the deals and send them in one convenient weekly e-mail.

Also popular are travel auction sites and services that let you name the price you're willing to pay for an air seat or a vacation package.

✪ **1travel.com. www.1travel.com**
Here you'll find deals on domestic and international flights and hotels. 1travel.com's **Saving Alert** compiles last-minute air deals so you don't have to scroll through multiple email alerts. A feature called "Drive a little using low-fare airlines" helps map out strategies for using alternative airports to find lower fares. And **Farebeater** searches a database that includes published fares, consolidator bargains, and special deals exclusive to 1travel.com. *Note:* The travel agencies listed by 1travel.com have paid for placement.

Bid for Travel. www.bidfortravel.com
Bid for Travel is another of the travel auction sites, similar to Priceline (see below), which are growing in popularity. In addition to airfares, Internet users can place a bid for vacation packages and hotels.

Cheap Tickets. www.cheaptickets.com
Cheap Tickets has exclusive deals that aren't available through more mainstream channels. One caveat about the Cheap Tickets site is that it will offer fare quotes for a route and later show this fare is not valid for your dates of travel—most other Web sites, such as Expedia, consider your dates of travel before showing what fares are available. Despite its problems, Cheap Tickets can be worth the effort because its fares can be lower than those offered by its competitors.

Staying Secure

More people still look online than book online, partly from fear of putting their credit-card numbers out on the Net. Secure encryption and increased experience with buying online have removed this fear for most travelers. In some cases, however, it's simply easier to buy from a local travel agent who can deliver your tickets to your door (especially if your travel is last-minute or if you have special requests). You can find a flight online and then book it by calling a toll-free number or contacting your travel agent, although this is somewhat less efficient. To be sure you're in secure mode when you book online, look for a little icon of a key or a padlock at the bottom of your Web browser.

LastMinuteTravel.com. www.lastminutetravel.com
Suppliers with excess inventory come to this online agency to distribute unsold airline seats, hotel rooms, cruises, and vacation packages. It's got great deals, but you have to put up with an excess of advertisements and slow-loading graphics.

Moment's Notice. www.moments-notice.com
As the name suggests, Moment's Notice specializes in last-minute vacation deals. You can browse for free, but if you want to purchase a trip you have to join Moment's Notice, which costs $25.

✪ Priceline.com. http://travel.priceline.com
Priceline lets you "name your price" for domestic and international airline tickets and hotel rooms. You select a route and dates, guarantee with a credit card, and make a bid for what you're willing to pay. If one of the airlines in Priceline's database has a fare lower than your bid, your credit card will automatically be charged for a ticket.

But you can't say when you want to fly—you have to accept any flight leaving between 6am and 10pm on the dates you selected, and you might have to make a stopover. No frequent-flyer miles are awarded, and tickets are nonrefundable and can't be exchanged for another flight. So if your plans change, you're out of luck. Priceline can be good for travelers who have to take off on short notice (and who are thus unable to qualify for advance purchase discounts). But be sure to shop around first, because if you overbid, you're required to purchase the ticket—and Priceline pockets the difference between what it paid for the ticket and what you bid.

Priceline says that over 35% of all reasonable offers for domestic flights are being filled on the first try, with much higher fill rates on popular routes (New York to San Francisco, for example). They define "reasonable" as not more than 30% below the lowest generally available advance-purchase fare for the same route.

SkyAuction.com. www.skyauction.com
An auction site with categories for airfare, travel deals, hotels, and much more.

Smarter Living. www.smarterliving.com
Best known for its e-mail dispatch of weekend deals on 20 airlines, Smarter Living also keeps you posted about last-minute bargains.

Travelzoo.com. www.travelzoo.com
At this Internet portal, more than 150 travel companies post special deals. It features a Top 20 list of the best deals on the site, selected by its editorial staff each Wednesday night. This list is also available via an e-mailing list, free to those who sign up.

Know When the Sales Start

While most people learn about last-minute weekend deals from e-mail dispatches, it can be best to find out precisely when these deals become available. Because these deals are limited, they can vanish within hours—sometimes even minutes—so it pays to log on as soon as they're available. Check the pages devoted to these deals on airlines' Web pages to get the information. An example: Southwest's specials are posted at 12:01am Tuesdays (Central time). So if you're looking for a cheap flight, stay up late and check Southwest's site to grab the best new deals.

Check Your E-mail While You're on the Road

You don't have to be out of touch just because you don't carry a laptop while you travel. Web browser–based free e-mail programs make it much easier to stay in e-touch.

Just open a freemail account at a browser-based provider, such as **MSN Hotmail (hotmail.com)** or **Yahoo! Mail (mail.yahoo.com).** AOL users should check out **AOL Netmail,** and **USA.NET (www.usa.net)** comes highly recommended for functionality and security. You can find hints, tips, and a mile-long list of freemail providers at **www.emailaddresses.com**.

Be sure to give your freemail address to the family members, friends, and colleagues with whom you'd like to stay in touch while you're in London. All you'll need to check your freemail account while you're away from home is a Web connection, easily available at Net cafes, copy shops, and cash- and credit-card Internet-access machines (often available in hotel lobbies or business centers) throughout the city. After logging on, just point the browser to **www.hotmail.com**, **www.yahoo.com**, or the address of any other service you're using. Enter your user name and password, and you'll have access to your mail, both for receiving and sending messages to friends and family back home, for just a few dollars an hour.

The excellent Net Café Guide (**www.netcafeguide.com**) suggests over 60 places to log on in London. Or check out easyEverything (**www.easyeverything.co.uk**). Entrepreneur Stelios Haji-Ioannou, of the cut-price airline Easyjet, is taking e-London by storm. By April 2000, he'd opened five cybercafes, with 2,300 screens available at bargain rates.

WebFlyer. www.webflyer.com

WebFlyer is a comprehensive online resource for frequent flyers and also has an excellent listing of last-minute air deals. Click on "Deal Watch" for a round-up of weekend deals on flights, hotels, and rental cars from domestic and international suppliers.

ONLINE TRAVELER'S TOOLBOX

Visa ATM Locator. www.visa.com/pd/atm/

MasterCard ATM Locator. www.mastercard.com/atm

Find ATMs in hundreds of cities in the U.S. and around the world. Both include maps for some locations and both list airport ATM locations, some with maps. *Tip:* You'll usually get a better exchange rate using ATMs than exchanging traveler's checks at banks, but check in advance to see what kind of fees your bank assesses for using an overseas ATM.

Intellicast. www.intellicast.com

CNN Interactive. www.cnn.com

The Weather Channel. www.weather.com

Weather forecasts for all 50 states and cities around the world. Note that temperatures are in Celsius for many international destinations, so don't think you'll need that winter coat for your next trip to Athens.

Universal Currency Converter. www.xe.net/currency

See what your dollar or pound is worth in more than a hundred other countries.

HM Customs & Excise Passenger Enquiries. **www.open.gov.uk**
U.S. Customs Service Traveler Information.
www.customs.ustreas.gov/travel/index.htm
Canada Customs and Revenue Agency. **www.ccra-adrc.gc.ca**
Australian Customs. **www.dfat.gov.au**
New Zealand Customs Service. **www.customs.govt.nz**
Wondering what you're allowed to bring in to the U.K. or bring back home? Check at these thorough sites, which include maximum allowances and duty fees.

2 The Top Web Sites for London

By Harriot Lane Fox

GETTING TO KNOW THE CITY

gaytoz guide/UK. **www.gaytoz.com**
Register with this cheeky site for a comprehensive London guide, e-mailed to you for free. Listings include hotels, bars, saunas, and general tourist information.

The Official Internet Site for London. **www.londontown.com**
The fab tourist board site will get you panting to start your trip. It lists events, accommodation, attractions, pubs and other places to live it up after dark, plus mini-area maps to download and daily specials including discount offers.

This is London. **www.thisislondon.com**
This comprehensive site from the *Evening Standard* includes a frank guide to dining, drinking, and clubbing. You can search for city attractions and events, and the Hot Tickets section offers independent advice on theater, music, and comedy.

✪ Time Out London. **www.timeout.com/london**
This excellent city guide has honest information on sightseeing, dining, lodging, shopping, entertainment, the gay scene, and fun for kids. It's a spin-off from the weekly magazine *Time Out,* the savvy travelers' bible.

GETTING AROUND

BAA: London Airports. **www.baa.co.uk**
Terminal maps for Heathrow, Gatwick, and smaller airports, and information about flight arrival times, duty-free shops, restaurants, and transport into London.

✪ London Transport. **www.londontransport.co.uk**
London Transport operates the Underground (subway), buses, and river ferries. This friendly site includes maps, schedules, fare information, and a new journey planner.

RailEurope. **www.raileurope.com**
This is where to find train fares and schedules and buy your tickets or discount passes for trips out of the city.

NEWSPAPERS

✪ Electronic Telegraph. **www.telegraph.co.uk**
From the conservative *Daily Telegraph* comes an unexpectedly exciting site, crammed with news, sports, entertainment reviews, and lifestyle features. And it's very, very fast.

Note to AOL Members

Digital City: London (Keyword: London) is a vibrant city guide that gives you the skinny on arts, dining, nightlife, and more. Culture buffs should try keyword: **Londonleisure.** You can also participate in AOL's active chat areas to see what others are saying, or pose a question of your own. Digital City: London is available on the Web at **london.digitalcity.com**.

Guardian Unlimited. **www.guardian.co.uk**
Imitating the paper's iconic design, the online *Guardian* serves up news, sports, entertainment reviews, and lifestyle features, and a link to its Sunday paper, *The Observer.*

Independent Online. **www.independent.co.uk**
The *Independent* has the usual local and world news, sports, and feisty columnists, but the site is visually bland and stores information several clicks deep.

The Times of London. **http://the-times.co.uk**
This venerable newspaper has an equally venerable-looking Web site, a good source for news, sports, and other London happenings. The *Sunday Times* is at **www.sunday-times.co.uk**.

WHERE TO STAY

For international Web sites that include hotel listings for London, see "Top Travel-Planning Web Sites," above.

✪ Automobile Association–UK. **www.theaa.co.uk**
This outstanding guide lists hundreds of places to stay, ranked by price and quality, and with apparently objective reviews. Many of the lodgings accept online bookings. You'll also find dining information with ratings based on food, service, atmosphere, and price.

British Hotel Reservation Centre. **www.bhrc.co.uk**
This consolidator deals with hotels and apartments for every budget, publishing the rack rate, its own price, and the resultant saving. You can search by hotel name, location, or proximity to attractions, and then book online.

Late Rooms. **www.laterooms.com**
Get big savings for bookings up to 3 weeks away at hundreds of London hotels. It gives official Star and Diamond ratings and a detailed description of each entry, but not reviews or photographs.

WHERE TO DINE

For further information on eating out, check the Automobile Association site and general city guides above.

Dine Online. **www.dine-online.co.uk**
Frank reviews sent in by diners, but restaurants are listed alphabetically and you can't search by price or postcode.

SIGHTSEEING, ACTIVITIES & ATTRACTIONS

The Big Bus Company. **www.bigbus.co.uk**
Routes and prices for tours of London in an open-top, double-decker bus. You can buy tickets online for a few attractions and theaters as well as for the Big Bus.

British Airways London Eye. www.british-airways.co.uk/londoneye
Get a Webcam preview of the most gobsmacking view in town—25 miles on a clear day from the 443-foot-high big wheel opposite the Houses of Parliament.

✪ **The British Museum. www.british-museum.ac.uk**
An essential guide to this peerless treasure trove. Use it or get lost in the museum for days. It lists temporary exhibits, gallery closures, and events. The photos are fabulous and download fast.

Harrods. www.harrods.co.uk
The labyrinthine store has posted a handy guide and printable maps of each floor. Learn about sales and see images of the Egyptian escalator, food hall, and much more.

Houses of Parliament. www.parliament.uk
A matter-of-fact guide to the Houses of Parliament, for interested citizens and visitors. It includes tour times and a schedule of when Parliament is in session.

✪ **The Insider's Guide to Shopping. www.inshop.co.uk**
Get the latest news on promotions, events, and sales across the capital, as well as advice on where to find the hottest items of the season, from womenswear to housewares.

✪ **London Transport Museum. www.ltmuseum.co.uk**
A fascinating virtual tour of this very child-friendly museum, which chronicles the development of London's public transport system from the early 1800s.

Madame Tussaud's. www.madame-tussauds.com
Take a virtual tour of the famous waxworks, including a behind-the-scenes glimpse of the real Pierce Brosnan posing for the James Bond model. The site also links to the London Planetarium and Rock Circus, Piccadilly.

The National Gallery. www.nationalgallery.org.uk
The National Gallery boasts some glorious masterworks. Browse through them here and check out new and visiting exhibitions.

Natural History Museum. www.nhm.ac.uk
A remarkably lively site, previewing the exhibitions and special programs. Click on the gallery guide to tour Dinosaurs, Creepy Crawlies, Wonders, and many more.

Official London Theatre Guide. www.officiallondontheatre.co.uk
Like the half-price ticket booth in Leicester Square, this site is run by the Society of London Theatres. Search by type of show, title, venue, or date, or view everything playing in London. Listings include summary, cast, times, prices, and each show's guaranteed run.

✪ **Original London Walks. www.walks.com**
London's longest-established guided walks company posts a day-by-day schedule of more than a dozen tours, from "Sherlock Holmes" to "Jack the Ripper Haunts."

Royal Palaces & Castles. www.royal.gov.uk/palaces
The monarchy's official site offers history, images, and descriptions of Buckingham Palace, Kensington Palace, and Windsor Castle. For more royal sights—the Tower of London, Hampton Court, Banqueting House, and Kew Palace—surf the excellent **www.hrp.org.uk**.

Shakespeare's Globe. www.shakespeares-globe.org
A rather earnest guide to productions, exhibitions, tours, and events at the magnificent reproduction of the 16th-century Globe theater. But more photos, please.

St. Paul's Cathedral. http://stpauls.london.anglican.org
Sightseeing details, a calendar of services and events, and the history of this remarkable landmark.

Tate Gallery. www.tate.org.uk
This is a visually arresting gateway to the original museum, now called Tate Britain, and the new Tate Modern at Bankside. You can also find details of the Liverpool and St. Ives galleries and touring exhibitions.

Victoria & Albert Museum. www.vam.ac.uk
Overambitious graphics and mysterious section headings make navigating this site a real chore. Best for basic details on the 146 glorious galleries of ceramics, fashion, high art, and so on. But practice deep breathing first.

✪ **Westminster Abbey. www.westminster-abbey.org**
A superb history and lots of photos of this magnificent Gothic church. Includes basic visitor information, tour schedules, and a section on royal coronations.

What's On Stage. www.whatsonstage.com
Theater listings and ticket information for the whole of the country by day, week, and month. The site carries recent reviews, news, and features on award-winners. A separate section covers classical music.

3

Getting to Know London

London is one of the most exciting cities in the world, and arriving here can be a bit of a shock for bleary-eyed and jet-lagged visitors. More than 8 million people live in the London area that sprawls across 600 square miles or more. Everything will probably seem too noisy, too dirty, too fast. But it will also feel marvelously familiar, as the red buses and black taxis you've seen in hundreds of movies are suddenly right there in front of you. Despite the bustle, the city is very visitor-friendly: It's laid out in distinct, manageable chunks and traveling between them is super easy on public transport.

This chapter will help you get your bearings. It provides a brief orientation and a preview of the city's most important neighborhoods. It also answers questions about how to use those lovely buses, as well as the Tube (less lovely on a sweaty summer's day!). The "Fast Facts" section covers all the essentials from navigating the phone system to where to get a cheap and chic haircut.

1 Orientation

VISITOR INFORMATION

The **Britain Visitor Centre,** 1 Regent St., SW1 (no phone) is open Monday 9:30am to 6pm, Tuesday to Friday 9am to 6:30pm, Saturday and Sunday 10am to 4pm (Saturday 9am to 5pm, June to September). It brings together the British Tourist Authority (www.visitbritain.com) and the English, Welsh, Scottish, and Irish Tourist Boards. There's a **Globaltickets** booking service for theater, sightseeing, and events; a bureau de change; and a **Thomas Cook** hotel and travel-reservations office. And it's very busy.

The **London Tourist Board** (☎ **020/7932-2000**) runs several **Tourist Information Centres,** too, offering similar services. The main one at **Victoria Station forecourt,** SW1, is open daily from 8am to 7pm from Easter to October. In winter, it closes 1 hour earlier Monday to Saturday, and opens from 8:30am to 4:30pm on Sundays. There are also centers at **Liverpool Street Tube station,** EC2, and the **Waterloo International arrivals hall,** SE1. The LTB recorded-information service (☎ **020/7971-0026**) offers premium-rate lines for different topics. The system is comprehensive but infuriating and, worse, costly. You're better off spending your time and money surfing the Web site, which is jam-packed with everything you need to know, and more (www.londontown.com).

Name That Street

The weird and wonderful street names in the City aren't really weird at all, but an intricate guide to centuries of history. The "bury" of Bucklersbury and Lothbury comes from *burh,* the word for the stone mansions built by Norman barons. Ludgate, Aldgate, and Cripplegate really were gates, the original ones to the city. The Barbican stands on the site of a watchtower. In the Middle Ages, *cheaps* were markets: hence modern street names like Eastcheap and Cheapside. As the city began to thrive as a commercial center, artisans and merchants gathered in particular streets. Today, you'll find Milk Street, Bread Street, and even Friday Street where fish was sold. South of the river in Southwark, where the city fathers banished all lowlife, is Clink Street. There used to be a prison there, hence the expression "in the clink."

More convenient than all of these is a **new information center** next to the Half-Price Ticket Booth in **Leicester Square.** It is run by Capital Link Partnership—a working group of local authorities, businesses, community representatives, and police—and opens from 10am to 6pm every day.

As you wander around the city, also look out for **i-plus** (www.cityspace.com) electronic booths, for touch-screen access to sightseeing information, online theater bookings, and so on. You can also send short e-mails for free—very handy, though the process is rather laborious. You'll find one opposite Kensington High Street Tube station, outside Pizza Express on King's Road (Chelsea), at Notting Hill Gate, and in the Bond Street Tube station shopping mall. The budget hotel chains Travel Inn and Ibis have them, as do the London Transport Museum, Madame Tussaud's, Natural History Museum, Theatre Museum, and the V&A.

CITY LAYOUT

Central London is like the jam in a doughnut, an amorphous rectangular blob rather than an official definition. Ask a local, and he'll probably tell you it means anything falling within the Circle Line on the Underground: the **City,** the **West End,** and a few bits west of that. Zone two of the Tube map loosely conforms to the broader definition of **Inner London. Greater London** includes the vast sprawling mass of suburbs.

The City is the oldest part of *Londinium,* as the Romans called it, and it covers a scant "Square Mile." That's still the nickname for what is now one of the world's leading financial centers. Villages then sprang up around the original settlement—**Bloomsbury, Holborn, Kensington,** and so on. Over time, these gradually melded together and became absorbed into the city proper. But each one still has its own heart and character, even today.

The West End is harder to pin down because it's so much more than a geographical term. Locals use it as shorthand meaning razzle-dazzle—the special streets where they shop by day and play by night. **Marble Arch** and **Hyde Park Corner,** with **Park Lane** running between them, mark the westernmost points. **Westminster** and **Victoria** stand by themselves, outside any catchall description. Then, west of the West End where the homes finally outnumber the offices, you come to **Bayswater** and **Notting Hill, Knightsbridge, Kensington,** and **Chelsea.**

This is the prime stamping ground for visitors. If you add on the best bits of Inner London—the cultural highlights close to the Thames at **South Bank, Bankside,** and

Southwark, stretching as far east as **Greenwich,** as well as the markets of **Islington** and **Camden,** and pretty **Hampstead** village, to the north—that makes an area of around 25 square miles.

FINDING YOUR WAY AROUND

Face it, you're going to get lost. Irrepressible organizers, the Victorians introduced the postcode system to show where a neighborhood is located in relation to the original post office in the City, itself EC1 for East Central. Moving west, the codes change from EC to WC (West Central) to W (West), and so on. Victoria is SW1 because it was the closest in that direction. Unfortunately, London expanded and boroughs began to be labeled alphabetically. Now all you can be sure of is the general direction: W4 is Chiswick, at least ¾ of an hour west of the West End.

Street names are completely random. And house numbers can work in several different ways: odd on one side of the street, even on the other; or in the right order, but up one side and back down the other. Murphy's law applies in spades: Wherever you start from, the target address is bound to be in the other direction.

STREET MAPS Check the detailed foldout street map included with this book; you may find it's all you need to get around.

Otherwise, the giveaways from hotels and tourist offices are a bit superficial. Serious explorers, wanting to venture farther afield, should go for the one and only ***London A to Z.*** Do a bag check on most locals, and you'll find one. They come in a bewildering range of different sizes, though the smallest isn't up to much. Unless you've got poor eyesight, when this may be too fine, I recommend the ***Mini A to Z,*** which costs £3.95 ($6.30) and still won't spoil your pocket-line. Even the smallest newsagent in Central London stocks them.

Neighborhoods in Brief

KNIGHTSBRIDGE Posh Knightsbridge is the first area you come to west of the West End and south of Hyde Park. It's very wealthy, and very fashionable in a way that is both solid establishment and gossip-column glitz. **Harrods** is the main attraction, of course. Green-liveried doormen will turn people away for having grubby clothing, ripped jeans, high-cut or cycling shorts, and bare midriffs or feet. The super-chic Harvey Nichols is 100 yards up the road toward Hyde Park Corner. Head for tea at the Lanesborough Hotel after that, because the covered central courtyard of what used to be St. George's Hospital is a delightful place to splash out on afternoon tea.

BELGRAVIA South of Knightsbridge, Belgravia reached the peak of its prestige in the reign of Queen Victoria, but for the new-moneyed and for those aristocrats whose forebears didn't blow all the family heirlooms, it's still a very chic address. The Duke of Westminster, who owns vast tracts of Belgravia and Chelsea, lives at Eaton Square. Architecture buffs will love the vanilla-ice-cream town houses, especially in the area's centerpiece, Belgrave Square. Budget travelers can hover on the verge of a smart address at the B&Bs in Ebury Street, though that is really Victoria.

CHELSEA This stylish district may start from the north bank of the Thames, west of Victoria, but the river is probably the least important thing about it. The action starts at Sloane Square, with Gilbert Ledward's Venus fountain at its center, and moves swiftly east down the dangerously captivating shopping heaven, the King's Road. The funkier high street names began to move in a few years ago, but it's still more chic than cheap, and retains a funky feel begun by Mary Quant's 1960s mini-skirt revolution

Where the Neighborhoods Are

Flip to the map, "Central London," on p. 4 for a clear picture of how all the neighborhoods described here actually fit together.

and built on by the doyenne of punk, Vivienne Westwood. Chelsea has always been a favorite of writers and artists, including Oscar Wilde, Henry James, and Thomas Carlyle, whose home you can visit. Residents today include aging rock stars (Mick Jagger), aging politicians (Margaret Thatcher), wealthy young Euromigrant families, and 30-something former "Sloane Rangers" of the 1980s. Temporary residents won't find many cheap places to stay, but there are a handful of good values and a mix of cheap pop-in eats and restaurants with excellent set meals.

KENSINGTON This is the heart of the Royal Borough of Kensington & Chelsea. The asthmatic William III started the royal thing in 1689 when he fled Whitehall in search of cleaner air (which is long gone). Queen Victoria was born in the house, by then renamed Kensington Palace and which the royals now call "KP." The late Princess Diana lived here, and it's still home to a gang of family members including Princess Margaret. You can visit (the palace, not the royals, though you may see the odd helicopter landing in the park). Kensington lies between Notting Hill, to the north, and South Kensington. There are a couple of great bathless budget sleeps just off Kensington Church Street, which is lined with by-appointment-only antiques shops and, at the bottom, several branches of the discount fashion store Amazon. Kensington High Street is a good mix of mainstream brands and bargains.

South Kensington is best known as home to London's major museums, in a row along Cromwell Road: the Natural History Museum, Victoria & Albert Museum, and the Science Museum. They're all built on land bought with the proceeds of Prince Albert's Great Exhibition of 1851. He gave his name to two spectacular landmarks here, too: the Royal Albert Hall, where the famous promenade concerts are held every year, and the Albert Memorial. His devastated wife Queen Victoria commissioned the latter from Sir George Gilbert Scott, and it was completed in 1872. It was recently restored to its full and super-excessive glory. South Ken, as it is often called, is stuffed to the gunwales with good value, self-catering accommodations—rather surprisingly. It's a prime holiday base for families.

EARL'S COURT This neighborhood has gone through many incarnations. It's west of South Kensington and was known between the wars as a staid residential district full of genteel ladies. It then became a haven for poor newcomers to Britain, both immigrants and backpackers, and young Brits buying an affordable first apartment. There are whole streets of budget hotels that really are dives. Things are changing, though. You can see it on the main street, Earl's Court Road, where the smarter cafe chains are starting to join the late-night fast-food joints with names that rip off KFC. The huge exhibition center brings in a lot of trade. Some hotels are upgrading to cater for it, providing good value budget sleeps. Earl's Court is the other big gay enclave, with gay hotels, bars, and pubs.

NOTTING HILL It wouldn't be surprising if Notting Hill became a victim of its own hype. The inexorable rise in house prices began in the mid-1990s. The press climbed on the bandwagon and hip media, music, and fashion luvvies rode in with it. Then there was the much-puffed film *Notting Hill,* with Hugh Grant and Julia Roberts—the nail in the neighborhood's coffin or the final rocket-blast to stratospheric status, depending on your view. Richard Curtis, who wrote the movie, sold his

Notting Hill house in 1999 for a rumored £1.4 million ($2.24 million). These days, achingly trendy restaurants and bars are opening one after the other at northern fringes, where true-blue Kensington (this is part of the Royal Borough, too) traditionally turned red in the council estates. Visitors flock here in hordes to visit the great Portobello Market, as you'll see if you stay at either of the good value sleeps we've found for you on this winding street. **Holland Park,** the next stop west, is a very chichi residential neighborhood, for fat wallets only. Richard Branson runs his Virgin empire from here. Budget travelers can get a fantastic cheap sleep at the youth hostel located in the middle of the park itself.

PADDINGTON & BAYSWATER Paddington has been the terminus for trains coming into London from the west and southwest since 1836. In recent decades, the station has had the usual effect, turning prosperous Georgian and Victorian terraces into scruffy sleeps for people passing through quickly. The area is about to enjoy a massive redevelopment around the canal basin, north of the station, and signs of a general smartening up are already apparent. There are good deals to be had here, only just west of the West End.

Bayswater is a generalization rather than a definable area, arising from the eponymous main road running across the top of Hyde Park. Walk 5 minutes from Paddington, and you'll come to it. The buzziest bit is **Queensway,** a street of cheap ethnic restaurants, cheap tacky shops, and an ice-skating rink, with the old Whiteley's department store, now a light and airy shopping mall, at the northern end. That is also where Westbourne Grove starts, an increasingly funky street that links up with Notting Hill.

MAYFAIR Bounded by Piccadilly, Hyde Park, Oxford Street, and Regent Street, Mayfair is filled with luxury hotels and grand shops. The Georgian town houses are beautiful, but many of them are offices now—real people don't live in Mayfair. Grosvenor Square (*Grov*-nor) is nicknamed "Little America" because it's home to the U.S. Embassy and a statue of Franklin D. Roosevelt. You must visit **Shepherd Market,** a tiny, rather raffish village of pubs and popular eateries: Sofra Bistro is a good and very reasonable Turkish restaurant. The old market was banned for "fornication and lewdness," among other things. Upmarket prostitutes still cater to loose-trousered politicians here.

MARYLEBONE Most visitors head to Marylebone to explore Madame Tussaud's waxworks or trudge up Baker Street in the virtual footsteps of Sherlock Holmes. Generally, this is an anonymous area, with most of the action in a strip running just north of Oxford Street. Robert Adam finished Portland Place, a very typical square, in 1780. Horatio Nelson's wife waited in Cavendish Square for the admiral to return from the arms of the sea and of Lady Hamilton. But the real must-visit is in Manchester Square: the mini–French chateau called Hertford House, which houses the Wallace Collection, one of London's loveliest free attractions. St. Christopher's Place is a pretty piazza with some reasonable restaurants and unreasonable boutiques close to Bond Street Tube. While budget hotels are as rare as hen's teeth here, you will find good value, big-roomed splurge hotels in Gloucester Place.

ST. JAMES'S Often called "Royal London," St. James's basks in its associations with everybody from the "merrie monarch" Charles II to Elizabeth II, who lives at its most famous address, Buckingham Palace. It starts at Piccadilly Circus and moves southwest, incorporating Pall Mall, The Mall, St. James's Park, and Green Park. Budget travelers must day-trip here to sample the lingering pomp. The English gentleman retreats here to his club, that traditional male-only bastion. Cheap eats may be hard to find, except close to Piccadilly Circus, but the parks are prime picnic territory. You can get the necessary, or stop for tea, at the world's most luxurious grocery store, **Fortnum & Mason.** It has kept explorers, empire-builders, and the warrior classes supplied with food parcels for over 200 years.

SOHO Cities are rarely sleaze-free, but few have their strip joints and red lights right next door to chi-chi restaurants, heavenly delis, thriving media companies, and a traditional fruit and veg market (Berwick Street). The council is enforcing ever more stringent controls on the sex trade by forcibly buying flats used as unlicensed brothels and selling them to charities that in turn develop social housing. Additionally, the infamous Moor Street triangle is to be demolished and replaced with a luxury hotel. Other projects to spruce up the gloriously cosmopolitan Soho haven't been so successful—the council reversed its disastrous traffic ban after only 6 months because among the pedestrians were too many winos, aggressive beggars, and pickpockets.

Soho is a wedge-shaped neighborhood. Its boundaries are Regent Street, Oxford Street (a mecca for mass-market shopping), Charing Cross Road, which is stuffed with antiquarian bookshops, and the theater-lined Shaftesbury Avenue. Urban streetwear stores are finally starting to push back the tide of tourist schlock on Carnaby Street, where the 1960s swung the hardest. In the middle of Soho, Old Compton Street is the heart of gay London. Cross Shaftesbury Avenue, and you come to Chinatown, which is small, yet authentic, and packed with excellent restaurants.

London's best-located youth hostel is in Soho, on Noel Street, and there are great deals at the Regent Palace near the point of the wedge at Piccadilly Circus. But that's it.

PICCADILLY CIRCUS & LEICESTER SQUARE Piccadilly Circus was named after the "picadil," a ruffled collar created by the 17th-century tailor, Robert Baker. It's packed with crowds morning, noon, and way past midnight, grazing on fast food. You don't need to do the same—Marco Pierre White's Criterion restaurant on Piccadilly Circus has great set menus. Then sample the delights of the Trocadero, if you dare. There's floor after floor filled with video games and noisy attractions, which the kids' will love. Its huge signs are part of a whole gallery of neon that illuminates the statue of Eros. **Leicester Square** is wall-to-wall neon, too, no longer the swish address it was when William Hogarth or the portrait painter to the nobility, Joshua Reynolds, lived here. It changed forever when the Victorians opened four towering entertainment halls, which today are cinemas. Crowds mill about until the early morning. It's tacky, but fun. Keep a tight hold on your wallet, as pickpockets cruise for careless tourists.

BLOOMSBURY Northeast of Piccadilly Circus, beyond Soho, Bloomsbury is the academic heart of London—much of the University of London, as well as several other colleges, are based here. All the same, it's quite a staid neighborhood. Writers such as Virginia Woolf, who lived here and put Bloomsbury into her book *Jacob's Room,* have fanned its reputation. She and her husband were unofficial leaders of a bohemian clique of artists and writers known as "the Bloomsbury Group." Russell Square is the main hub, and the streets around it are crammed with excellent value B&Bs. Most visitors come to see the treasure troves of the British Museum, and there are a few really good and good-value restaurants in the area.

Nearby is **Fitzrovia,** bounded by Great Portland Street, Oxford Street, and Gower Streets (lots of B&Bs there). Goodge Street is the main Tube and the village-like heart, with many shops and restaurants. It was the stamping ground of Ezra Pound, Wyndham Lewis, and George Orwell. The knobbly British Telecom Tower on Cleveland Street is one of London's best-recognized landmarks, but it's closed to the public. Visitors come to play "TV presenter" in the BBC Experience at the organization's head office in Portland Place. A great cheap sleep is the Carr-Saunder student dorm on Fitzroy Street.

HOLBORN This is the heart of legal London, where the ancient Inns of Court and Royal Courts of Justice lie. Dickens was a solicitor's clerk here when he was 14 and used the experience to good effect in *Little Dorrit.* Once you're off the traffic-laden High Holborn, time rolls back. The Viaduct Tavern, 126 Newgate St., was built over the notorious Newgate Prison. Holborn Viaduct was the world's first overpass. This is too business-like to be a hotel zone, stuck oddly between the West End and the City, and northeast of Covent Garden. But you'll get a great cheap sleep at the Holborn Residence student dorm.

COVENT GARDEN & THE STRAND The fruit and flower market moved to an unromantic modern shed south of the river in 1970, and Professor Higgins would find today's young women in Covent Garden far too fashionable for Eliza Doolittle–style experiments. This is a very fashion-oriented neighborhood, with more shopping and general razzle-dazzle than Soho, and certainly more tourists. It's quite pricey, too. The restored market hall is in the middle of a big pedestrian piazza and filled with little boutiques. The character of Covent Garden owes a lot to its long theatrical history, too, which is why there are so many great pre-theater deals at the restaurants. The Theatre Royal Drury Lane was where Charles II's mistress Nell Gwynne made her debut in 1665. And the actors' church designed by Inigo Jones, St. Paul's Covent Garden, holds memorials to many famous names from Ellen Terry to Boris Karloff to Vivien Leigh. The Royal Opera House is open again and is a glorious place to stop for coffee. Stay with visiting performers and fans at the eccentric Fielding hotel, just round the corner.

The **Strand** is a windy thoroughfare, lined with theaters and hotels (including the Savoy), which runs northeast out of Trafalgar Square toward the City, and marks the southern border of Covent Garden. In its heyday, it was a favorite haunt of Charles Lamb, Mark Twain, Henry Fielding, James Boswell, William Thackeray, and Sir Walter Raleigh. **Trafalgar Square** is a visitor must-see all by itself. Nelson's Column—the triumphal memorial to England's victory over Napoleon in 1805—is in the middle, and the National Gallery is on the northern side. Plans to pedestrianize the space between them could finally see ground broken this spring . . . allegedly.

WESTMINSTER Edward the Confessor launched Westminster's rise to political power when he moved out of London to build his royal palace there in the 11th century. Dominated by the Houses of Parliament and gothic Westminster Abbey, it runs along the Thames east of St. James's Park. Whitehall, which has long been synonymous with the armies of civil servants who really wield the power, is the main thoroughfare from Trafalgar Square to Parliament Square. Visit Churchill's Cabinet War Rooms, then peer through the gates shutting off Downing Street. *Chez* Blair is actually No. 11 because the Prime Minister's family wouldn't fit into No. 10, even before the surprise addition of baby Leo.

Westminster also takes in **Victoria,** a strange area that is both businessy and, because it's dominated by the station, full of cheap hotels. Go carefully because a lot of them are very nasty. The classiest ones are in Ebury Street on the fringes of Belgravia. Art lovers come here to visit Tate Britain.

THE CITY The City is where London began. Now it's one of the world's leading financial centers, and its institutions are recognized everywhere: the Bank of England (or the Old Lady of Threadneedle Street), the London Stock Exchange, and disaster-prone Lloyds of London. Much of the City was destroyed in the Great Fire of London, the Blitz, and later in the 1990s with some help from the IRA. Nowadays, it's a patchwork of the ancient and the very modern. You'll see some of the most outstanding or outlandish modern architecture here, depending on your viewpoint, jostling up against treasures like St. Paul's Cathedral. The Museum of London is home to 2000 years of history, including objects found during work on the Underground's Jubilee Line extension. If you go to the Barbican cultural center, take a ball of string with you—following the painted walk-this-way lines is hopeless in this concrete jungle. **Fleet Street** was home to Britain's newspapers before the "brave new world" of remote printing prompted a move out, mostly to Docklands.

There are two Ys and a youth hostel in the City, super-cheap and convenient, but it's not a very welcoming location. The City of London runs its own **Information Centre** at St. Paul's Churchyard, EC4 (☎ **020/7332-1456**).

CLERKENWELL London's first hospital was here, and then Clerkenwell evolved into a muck-filled 18th-century cattle yard, home to cheap gin distilleries. In the 1870s, it became the center of the new socialist movement: John Stuart Mill's London Patriotic Club was in Clerkenwell, as was William Morris's socialist press later in the 1890s. Lenin lived here while he edited *Iskra.* Neither West End nor City proper, its fortunes then dwindled, but they're on the up and up again today as old commercial buildings turn into chic lofts and new restaurants open. Art galleries and shops run by small designers line Clerkenwell Green. Gritty working life goes on as meat lorries rumble into Smithfield Market. London's oldest church is here, too, the Norman St. Bartholemew-the-Great.

DOCKLANDS Since 1981, when the London Docklands Development Corporation was set up, billions of pounds have gone into the most ambitious scheme of its kind in Europe. The nascent river-city runs east from Tower Bridge, encompassing the rundown areas of Wapping, the Isle of Dogs, the Royal Docks, and Surrey Docks. Though it is finally picking up speed, the redevelopment is still patchy, with little sense of community among the new minority residents of chic conversions and the underprivileged population. **Canary Wharf,** on the Isle of Dogs, is the jewel in Docklands' crown. Its 800-foot tower, designed by Cesar Pelli, is in the center of a covered piazza filled with shops. New skyscrapers are sprouting up around it now, like beans in a gargantuan allotment.

Londoners gripe about having to work in Docklands. It still feels very out on a limb. And the architects and planners have cleverly created wind tunnels that most certainly would be the envy of anyone who tests car aerodynamics for a living. But do take a trip on the Docklands Light Railway, which snakes above historic buildings and 21st-century shrines to big business. It's an amazing architectural theme park. Or take the Jubilee Line and catch a glimpse of Canary Wharf station, one of the most striking of all the hi-design stops on the new extension.

THE EAST END This collection of boroughs, east of the City, has long been one of the poorest areas of London. The Huguenots, fleeing religious persecution in France during the 16th century, were the first of successive waves of immigrants right up to the large Bengali population today. Yet, it's also home to the ultimate Londoner, the Cockney born within the sound of Bow Bells. This referred to the bells of St. Mary-le-Bow church, which rang the city curfew until the 19th century. The current ones are post-war replicas. Close to the docks, the East End was bombed to blazes during the Blitz. The most famous, or infamous, residents were the mad, bad, and very dangerous Kray twins. Nudging Clerkenwell on the western edge is **Hoxton,** the hottest hotbed of Young British artists and the entrepreneurs who know how to hype them. Otherwise, the few draws for visitors include the amazing Columbia Road flower market and the Whitechapel Bell Foundry, which cast Big Ben and both America's Liberty and Bicentennial bells, and is still in production today.

SOUTH BANK This is a loose definition, devised by Londoners on the north bank of the Thames, to define the only bit south of the river they're really interested in. As more and more redevelopment takes place, the definition widens. The core is the **South Bank Arts Centre,** now the largest cultural complex in Europe and still planning a big expansion. It houses the National Theatre, Royal Festival Hall, Hayward Gallery, National Film Theatre, and the Museum of the Moving Image, as well as several eateries. There's a great second-hand book market on the riverside walk there. The center lies between Waterloo Station and the Thames. Upriver, facing the Houses of Parliament, are the lofty observation wheel and city landmark, the British Airways London Eye, and County Hall. Once home to the Greater London Council, this is now part luxxy Marriott hotel and part budget-bargain Travel Inn, with the London Aquarium in the basement. Go downriver (west), and you come to **Bankside,** where Tate Modern opened last year in the old power station. The gallery's opening caused such huge excitement that the doors had to be policed to control visitor numbers, and the rooftop restaurant simply stopped answering the phone. The new Millennium Bridge, linking Bankside with the City, was just as big a hit—swaying dangerously under the hordes of people trying to walk across. With Shakespeare's Globe Theatre only a stone's throw away, this is a really exciting neighborhood. The London School of Economics student dorm, Bankside House, offers good quality, cheap accommodation close by, but you'll have to book in early (see review in chapter 4 for more information).

Farther west again, and you come to London Bridge and **Southwark.** Known as the outlaw borough, the city's medieval fathers banished the prisons, prostitutes, theaters, drinking dens, and so on to here—and Londoners through the ages crossed the river for R&R. Pilgrims rested here, too, on their way to Thomas à Becket's shrine, as recorded in Chaucer's *Canterbury Tales.* There's a feast of history to revisit in this rundown area that is starting to revive. To the east of the bridge, the glass-walled HQ for the London Mayor and the assembly, designed by Norman Foster, is due to be completed in 2002.

ISLINGTON Islington is just north of Clerkenwell and northwest of Bloomsbury. It's always had a hint of raffishness: Kenneth Halliwell killed his playwright lover Joe Orton here in 1967, and Islington is heaving with pub theaters, as well as the fringe Almeida, which has attracted such illustrious names as Ralph Fiennes and Kevin Spacey. Gentrification is fairly recent, though, and still patchy despite the much-publicized influx of the New Labour "chattering classes." Or the outflux of residents such as Tony and Cherie Blair (who went straight to 10 Downing St.). Visitors should head for the antiques market at Camden Passage, to look even if they can't afford to buy.

CAMDEN This is another North London must-visit. The Victorian slums that grew up around the canal have now transformed into a hip, if still patchily seedy, neighborhood, first attracting artists such as Lucien Freud and Frank Auerbach, and later the burgeoning Indie music industry. The biggest draw, and it is very big, is Camden Market. This isn't just a couple of stalls selling fruit and vegetables, but a whole village of off-beat streets, covered areas, and old buildings, specializing in everything from new-age crystals to cheap clothes, bootleg tapes, arty-crafty bits and bobs, and so on. The list is endless. Come early on a Sunday to beat the bumper summer crowds.

HAMPSTEAD & HIGHGATE People who live in Hampstead live in Hampstead, not in London. This is a delightful village-style almost-burb northwest of Regent's Park, with its own 800-acre patch of countryside, Hampstead Heath. Everybody from Sigmund Freud to D. H. Lawrence to Anna Pavlova to John Le Carré has lived here. The wealthy residents still number a host of A-list celebs, who joined the less famous locals a few years ago to try to fight off an invasion of a certain well-known U.S. burger chain. Hampstead makes a delightful day-trip and isn't that far by Tube.

Highgate is on the northeastern edge of the Heath, and almost as villagey. It's well worth a visit, if only to go to the famous Highgate Cemetery where Karl Marx and George Eliot are buried. There are marvelous mausolea, typically Victorian in their desire to show off.

PUTNEY & HAMMERSMITH It's a bit lazy to lump these boroughs together. But they're among the best bits of riverbank in London. There are boathouses all along this stretch of the Thames. The leafy path going westward along the south bank from **Putney** takes you past a network of reservoirs, now a bird sanctuary called WWT Wetland Centre, and it could be in the middle of the countryside. The famous Harrods Depository, a huge Victorian warehouse turned into chi-chi apartments, is just by Hammersmith Bridge. Cross over there, and continue along the north bank, with its succession of hugely popular pubs. The closest bar to the bridge is featured in the hit British movie *Sliding Doors* as home to the actor John Hannah's character's rowing club—remember his kiss with Gwyneth Paltrow in a boat in the pouring rain with the bridge as the backdrop?

GREENWICH This charming port village is just about as far as you can go east along the south bank of the river without leaving London. It's ground zero for the reckoning of terrestrial longitudes, and a UNESCO World Heritage site. Greenwich is used to fame, having enjoyed its first heyday in Tudor days. It enjoyed it much less last year, however, as its name was forever bracketed with doom, gloom, and wasted millions at the disastrous Dome. So don't say the "D" word when you visit the many historic delights of Greenwich—the 1869 tea clipper, *Cutty Sark;* the National Maritime Museum; and the markets.

2 Getting Around

BY PUBLIC TRANSPORTATION

The London Underground operates on a system of six fare zones. These radiate out in rings from the central zone 1, which is where visitors spend most of their time. It covers an area from the Tower in the east to Notting Hill in the west, and from Waterloo in the south to Baker Street, Euston, and King's Cross in the north. You will need a zone 2 ticket, though, for a trip to Camden or Hampstead. Note that all single tickets, round-trip, and one-day passes are valid only on the day you buy them. The city's buses used to share this system but **London Transport** (LT) simplified it last year: into zone 1 and the rest for single tickets, and four fare zones for passes.

Tube and bus maps should be available at all Underground stations, or you can download them from the excellent Web site (www.londontransport.co.uk). There are also **LT Information Centres** at several major Tube stations: Euston, King's Cross, Liverpool Street, Piccadilly Circus, Victoria, St. James's Park, and Oxford Circus. They're all open daily—except for the last two, which close on Sundays—from at least 9am to 5pm.

FARES Kids up to age 4 travel free on the Tube and buses. From 5 to 15, they qualify for children's fares, generally around 40% less than adults (children must pay full rates after 10pm on buses). Parents should bring recent pictures of their offspring, plus proof of their age, to the nearest Tube station (just in case, most have photo booths) and get a Child Photocard. It costs nothing, but kids must carry one. Adults will also need passport-size photographs if buying any travel pass valid for more than 1 day (see below).

Phoning Underground

London Transport runs a 24-hour travel hot line (☎ **020/7222-1234**), which provides up-to-the-minute recorded information at standard local phone rates on how each service is running, or not, as well as the option to speak to a live human being for any detailed queries. Call if you have **restricted mobility** of any kind. The escalators in London's Tube stations are in a hopeless state and need millions of pounds' worth of overdue upgrading. They are frequently either closed for repair or have one side turned off forcing passengers to walk down to the platform.

London Transport puts up its fares once a year in early January, usually adding 10p to every one-way fare, and filtering that increase through to other tickets and passes. The 2000 prices are as follows:

Single tickets within zone 1 on the Underground cost £1.50 ($2.40) for adults and 60p (96¢) for children. Simply double that for a return fare. The price of a book of 10 single tickets, a **Carnet,** is two-thirds that of the same number bought individually. This is available for travel only within zone 1 and costs £11 ($17.60) for an adult and £5 ($8) for children. Adult bus fares range from £1 ($1.60) for any journey including zone 1, otherwise 70p, £1.50, and £1 ($1.12, $2.40, and $1.60) respectively on night buses. The flat daytime rate for children is 40p (65¢); they pay adult fares on night buses. A **Saver 6** gives you six journeys for the price of five, zone 1 adult fares only.

TRANSPORTATION DISCOUNTS Anyone planning to use public transport a lot should check out the big range of passes that are valid across all public transport: the Underground, buses, and the Docklands Light Railway. These make travel even cheaper.

One-Day Travelcards can be used for unlimited trips after 9:30am Monday to Friday, and all day on Saturday, Sunday, and holidays, but not on night buses. Adults traveling within zones 1 and 2 pay £3.90 ($6.25). Children, however, have to buy an all-zone at £2 ($3.20). If you want to beat the tourist crowds and start before 9:30am, a **One-Day LT Card** is available for zones 1 and 2 for £5 ($8) per adult, and £2.50 ($4) per child.

Weekend Travelcards are valid for one weekend, plus the Monday if it's a national holiday, and on night buses. These cost £5.80 ($9.30) for adults in zone 1 and 2, and £3 ($4.80) for children (again, this is all-zone).

One-Week Travelcards really are unlimited: any amount of trips, any hour of the day, and night buses. It costs adults £15.30 ($24.50) for zone 1 and £6.50 ($10.40) for a child; the prices rise for a zone 1 and 2 pass to £18.20 and £7.50 ($29.10 and $12).

Family Travelcards are available to groups that include up to two adults, plus one to four children. These, too, can be used only after 9:30am during the week, but not on night buses. They cost £2.60 ($4.15) per adult in the group, and 80p ($1.30) per child.

Tube Time

Signal failures, conked-out trains, and general lunacy permitting, you can calculate how long a tube journey will take by allowing 3 minutes per stop. Don't forget to add in a bit extra if you have to change lines. Last year, a scout leader set a new record by visiting all 282 Tube stations in 19 hours, 59 minutes, and 37 seconds. Even more amazing, he only suffered a 30 minutes' delay. The things people do for fun!

Buy a Travelcard Before Leaving Home to Save Pounds

If you plan to use public transport a lot, you must buy a **London Visitor Travelcard** before you leave home. This is a special tourist deal, which includes discount vouchers for some of London's major attractions, and isn't available in the United Kingdom. Prices are set in your local currency—yippee! An answer to the strong pound. Passes can cover 1 to 4 (consecutive) days, or 1 week, either just for zone 1 or for the whole London Transport bus and Tube network, including the Docklands Light Railway and most British Rail suburban trains. You don't even need a passport picture, as you do for longer lasting travelcards bought in the United Kingdom. Central zone (zone 1 and 2) adult passes cost $22 for 3 days, $27 for 4, and $32 for 7; child equivalents cost $9, $11, and $13. An extra bonus: there are no time restrictions, and you can use it on night buses. Contact the nearest BTA or BritRail office (see "Visitor Information" and "Entry Requirements & Customs," in chapter 2 for addresses and phone numbers).

Bus passes, valid for travel only on London Transport buses, are available for all zones for 1 day at £3 ($4.80) per adult and £1 ($1.60) per child, and for 1 week at £11.50 and £4 ($18.40 and $6.40).

You can buy all these, as well as monthly and annual passes for longer stays, at Tube stations but not on buses. They are also available at tobacconists and newsagents with a **Pass Agent** sticker in their window.

THE UNDERGROUND

The Tube map is very easy to use. Every line has a different color: navy blue for the Piccadilly Line (the one that runs in from Heathrow), red for the Central Line, and so on. Station signs directing you to the different platforms refer to eastbound and westbound, or northbound and southbound, for each line as appropriate, and usually list a few well-known stops in that direction to help you. The front of the train and the electronic notice boards on the platforms, which say when the next train is due, will name the final destination, so get to know the names of stations at or near the ends of the lines you use most often. The **Docklands Light Railway** is an extension to the main system. Its driverless trains run on raised tracks east from Bank Tube station and Tower Gateway, close to Tower Hill. It operates daily at similar hours.

Except for Christmas Day, Tube trains run every few minutes from about 5:30am Monday to Saturday and 7am or so on Sunday. The times of the last trains vary from 11:30pm and 1am, as they head back to home base, generally out of Central London, with stations closing behind them. There are posters with times and frequencies in each station, and the time of the last train is usually scribbled on a board near the entrance.

There are two ways of buying tickets: at the station ticket window or using one of the push-button machines. Queuing at the window can be phenomenally time-consuming and irritating. That's virtually all the time at West End stations during the summer. Elsewhere, the rush hour clogs things up, especially on a Monday when lots of people renew weekly travel passes. You will have to go to the window, though, if you want to buy a pass valid for longer than a day. There are two kinds of machines: The first takes only coins, and the buttons are marked with little more than the price. There should be a poster listing fares to every other station close by. These machines make change until they run out of spare coins, again something that tends to happen at busy times. The other machine has a button for each station and type of ticket, and will tell you the price of your choice. It accepts coins and notes up to £10 until it runs out of change, usually just as you get to the front of the queue.

Hold onto your ticket throughout your ride because you'll need it to exit, and LT inspectors make random checks. Last year, transport bosses announced plans to axe the rigidly imposed penalty fare—£10 ($16) on Tubes and £5 ($8) on buses—but you should check and see if they followed through.

London Buses

London buses go places the Tube can only dream of. But such a comprehensive system makes for a very bewildering map. Most locals know only two routes: from home to work and to the West End, and often that's the same thing. If the map foxes you completely, call the LT Travel Line (see above), and they'll tell you how to get from A to B. Many bus stops have big street maps of the surrounding neighborhoods with bus numbers marked on major roads. It's a matter of tracing back from where you want to go, to where you are, and seeing where you have to change. And ask the driver or conductor to let you know when the bus has reached your destination, since you probably won't recognize it.

To stop a bus when you're on it, press the bell (or tug the wire running the length of the ceiling in an old bus). Without any signal, the driver won't stop unless passengers are waiting to get on the bus. If you're the one waiting, make sure to note whether it is a compulsory (white background on the sign) or a request stop (red background). At the latter, give a big wave or the bus won't stop.

Traveling by bus is a great way to see London, but it can be frustratingly slow, particularly in rush hour. Oxford Street is the worst for blockages, and often, you could walk the entire length of it on red double-deckers without ever having to touch the ground. Normal buses run until around midnight when night buses, with an N in front of the number, take over for the next 6 hours. On most routes, there's one an hour, and they all pass through Trafalgar Square, so if in doubt, head there. Many travel passes are *not* valid on night buses.

You buy single-trip bus tickets, not round-trip, only on the bus itself. On those routes that do still use the old Routemasters, you pay the conductor when he or she comes around. Many new buses are now driver-only, including the little one-deck Hoppers, and you pay as you get on. In either case, proffering a note bigger than £5, unless you're only expecting small change, is likely to produce some very fruity language, particularly from the notoriously eccentric conductors. If inspectors find you without a ticket, the on-the-spot fine is £5 ($8).

By Central London Fast Ferry

Tony Blair and his government have used the millennium as the spur to a broader initiative known as **Thames 2000.** Its goal is to regenerate the river and restore long-lost passenger transport services. A new all-day **Central London Fast Ferry** was meant to run from the Tate at Millbank to Docklands, stopping at eight of the most popular piers. But it immediately ran into problems and was only offering a limited commuter service last year. To find out if they've got their act together, call **Whitehorse Ferries** (☎ **0870/240-3240;** www.whitehorse.co.uk). Adults pay £1.90 ($3.05) and children £1 ($1.60) to travel between any two stops.

By Car

Please don't rent a car if you're planning a holiday in Central London. It really isn't worth it. Parking is an expensive nightmare. Gas (petrol in the U.K.) is very heavily taxed and stratospherically expensive—over 80p ($1.28) a liter, or $4.86 *a gallon.* It takes a while to get to know the city well enough to drive from A to B without going via Z, even with a navigator in the car. And London drivers are a combative, unforgiving lot. Why make things tough for yourself when the public transport is so good? The only reason to rent a car is for a day-trip into the countryside (not a city visit) or an extended tour round Britain. For travelers planning that kind of holiday, and for anyone determined to brave the city streets whatever anyone says, here's what you need to know.

RENTING A CAR

Most car-rental companies in Britain will accept U.S., Canadian, Australian, and New Zealand driver's licenses, provided you've held it for more than a year. You'll also need a passport. Many companies have a minimum age requirement, of either 23 or 25. Anyone with a record for drunk driving will have a problem renting a car.

You can save money by booking a car in your home country before you travel, usually at least 48 weekday hours ahead, and for periods of a week or more. But try and give more than 2 weeks' notice because some rental companies will then guarantee a home-currency rate. Obviously, you must call around to find the best quote. In each case, check if the price includes the 17½% value-added tax (VAT), personal accident insurance, and collision-damage waiver (CDW). Also remember to specify an automatic if that's what you're used to because most Brits drive stick-shifts.

Some of the big companies have North American toll-free numbers, and they're listed here, along with their main London branches: **Avis** (☎ **800/331-1084;** www.avis.com) is at 8 Balderton St., W1 (☎ **020/7917-6700**); **Budget Rent-a-Car** (☎ **0845/606-6669;** www.budgetrentacar.com) is at 89 Wigmore St., W1 (☎ **020/7723-8038**); **Hertz** (☎ **800/654-3001;** www.hertz.com) is at 35 Edgware Rd., W1 (☎ **020/7402-4242**). But make sure to check out **Europe by Car** (☎ **800/223-1516** nationwide, 800/252-9401 in Los Angeles, or 212/581-3040 in New York; www.europebycar.com), because it often undercuts the rest.

easyRentacar is a new venture from discount king Stelios Haji-Ioannou, which hires out Mercedes A-Class cars from a depot at London Bridge. You can only book online (www.easyrentacar.com). Rates fluctuate according to demand, so the deal is always better if you book ahead: 1 day costs from £9 to £28 ($14.40 to $44.80), plus a £5 ($8) car-cleaning fee. The only downside is that each car has easy's orange logo glowing along its side.

PARKING

The **Transport Committee for London** (☎ **020/7747-4760;** www.tcfl.gov.uk/avoid.html) is an invaluable source of information on how to avoid parking fines.

On-street parking is heavily regulated. Some areas are for residents with permits only. Some are for general use, either paid for at a meter next to the parking space or at an automatic Pay and Display ticket machine that covers a small length of street. Generalizations about where each is prevalent, the hours they operate, and how much they cost are very dangerous. Each local council makes different rules even for different areas within its own patch. Check the streetside notices and information on meters. Do not ever park on single or double yellow lines (or even stop for a second where there are red ones), zigzag white lines at the edge of the road, or in bus lanes.

Car-Rental Tip

British Airways (☎ **877/428-2228;** www.british-airways.com) gives Hertz so much business by booking cars for its passengers that it can offer discounted rates. If you're traveling with the airline, call at least a week ahead of departure from the United States or Canada, with your flight information ready.

Penalties are harsh, and any one of the following can apply whenever and wherever you break the rules. Council parking tickets/fines range from £40 to £80 ($64 to $128), with 50% off if you pay within 14 days. There is no discount on police fines, currently around £40 ($64). *Warning:* All unpaid tickets eventually end up back at the rental company. It has your details and will send a bill. If you still do not pay up, this will go on a central record and may prevent your re-entry into the United Kingdom at any time in the future.

To get rid of a Denver Boot, which normally takes an hour from the time you call the number on the clamping sticker, you'll have to pay £60 ($96). If your car is towed away, it will cost £125 ($200) to get it out of the pound, plus the cost of the parking ticket. If you do come back to an empty parking space, try the TCL 24-hour **Vehicle Trace Hotline** (☎ **020/7747-4747**): It will tell you which pound it's gone to.

Blue signs point the way to **National Car Parks (NCP)**, which are spread throughout the city. Prices vary, and most set a minimum stay of 2 hours. To give you an idea of how extortionate they are, that costs upwards of £7 ($11.20) in the West End, with 9 to 12 hours from £27 ($43.20). To find the closest, call NCP (☎ **08456/061061;** www.ncp.co.uk).

SPECIAL DRIVING RULES

Be sensible and buy a copy of the *British Highway Code,* available at most newsagents and bookstores. Otherwise, there are a few basic things to remember, apart from driving on the left side of the road. Except where indicated, the speed limit in Central London, as in any built-up area, is 50kmph (30 m.p.h.). In Britain, everyone in the car must wear a seatbelt, even passengers in the back. You may not turn right on a red light. Cars must stop as soon as a pedestrian steps onto a zebra crossing—the black-and-white-striped crosswalk. These are in the middle of the block, not at the corner, and are always well-lit.

BY TAXI

Black cabs carry up to five people and can make sound economic sense. All the drivers are licensed and have to pass a test called The Knowledge first, so they know London very well. Look for the yellow "For Hire" sign lit up on the roof and wave wildly. Before you get in, tell the driver where you want to go. Except in the West End, many drivers go home after midnight. You can order a cab but will have to pay an extra charge for the time it takes the taxi to get to you—up to £3.80 ($6.10). These two companies are both 24-hour: **Dial a Cab** (☎ **020/7253-5000**) and **Radio Taxis** (☎ **020/7272-0272**).

The minimum charge is £1.40 ($2.25), and the meter goes up in increments of 20p (30¢). You'll pay a flat-rate surcharge of 60p to 90p (95¢ to $1.45) depending on the time of day: generally after 8pm and between midnight and 6am on weekdays, and slightly different times at weekends, or public holidays. Other extras on the basic fare include 40p (65¢) for every passenger after the first one and 10p (16¢) for every piece of luggage over 2 feet long or that has to go in the driver's cab. If you have any complaints, call the **Public Carriage Office** (☎ **020/7230-1631**).

Minicabs are generally cheaper than black cabs. But drivers don't have to have a special license, and many won't know their way around any better than you do. Technically, they must operate from a sidewalk office or through phone bookings, and are not allowed to cruise for fares. They do, of course, particularly at main railway stations and late night in the West End—there are none of the guarantees you get with a black cab, and I would refuse the offer. Minicabs don't have meters. Always negotiate the fare with the office, and confirm it with the driver. Most firms are open round the clock, and you can pre-book for much later—or for the next morning if you've got an early start. Ask your hotel or B&B to recommend one. Or you can obtain a list of reputable companies from the **London Private Hire Association** (☎ **020/7258-1100**). Here are two names to start with: **Addison Lee** (☎ **020/7387-8888**) and **Lady Cabs** (☎ **020/7254-3501**).

BY BICYCLE

Serious cyclists should check out the **London Cycling Campaign,** Tress House, 3 Stamford St., SE1 9NT (☎ **020/7928-7220**), for information and advice on city two-wheeling. We have also suggested a place to rent bicycles in the section on "Organized Tours," in chapter 6.

Fast Facts: London

Airport See "Getting There," in chapter 2.

American Express American Express has almost a dozen city offices. The most central is at 30–31 Haymarket, SW1 (☎ **020/2484-9600;** www.americanexpress.com; Tube: Piccadilly Circus). This is open Monday to Friday 8:30am to 6:30pm, Saturday 9am to 6:30pm, and Sunday 10am to 5pm. Weekend afternoons are currency-exchange-only. Cardholders and anyone with American Express traveler's checks can receive mail there. The company has a 24-hour toll-free line to report lost or stolen cards (☎ **0800/521313**).

Baby-Sitters Many hotels and B&Bs can arrange baby-sitting for you (see the reviews in chapter 4). **Universal Aunts** (☎ **020/7386-5900**) has been up and running for 16 years. It charges £5.50 ($8.80) per daytime hour, and £4 ($6.40) after 6pm. The minimum booking is 4 hours, and the agency fee is £3.50 ($5.60) for up to 5 hours, and £6.50 ($10.40) thereafter. You will also pay the sitter's travel both ways. Call as far ahead as you can. **Pippa Pop-ins** 430 Fulham Rd., SW6 (☎ **020/7385-2458**) describes itself as a totally flexible 24-hour backup to parents. All of the staff are fully qualified. Kids are bound to find new friends at this urban funhouse. They can come for half a day for £40 ($64), or even a whole 10 hours for £55 ($88)—the same price as an overnight stay. Pippa Pop-ins can also do off-site baby-sitting or take kids around London.

Business Hours Minimum bank opening hours are Monday to Friday 9:30am to 3:30pm, but most close at 4:30pm. Some are also open Saturday 9:30am to noon. Offices are generally open Monday to Friday from 9am until 5 or 5:30pm. By law, pubs can open Monday to Saturday 11am to 11pm, and noon to 10:30pm on Sunday, and most London ones do keep these hours. Some right in the center have late licenses that let them close up to 4 hours later. Restaurants, other than cafes and other cheap eats, serve lunch from noon to 2:30pm, and dinner 6 to 10:30pm (see chapter 5). A few go on later. Stores are generally open Monday to Saturday from 9 or 10am to 6pm. Many stay open for at least 1 extra hour on a Wednesday or Thursday, depending on the neighborhood (see chapter 8). Some around touristy Covent Garden don't close until 7 or 8pm nightly. Supermarkets and many of the stores in busy shopping areas now also open for 6 hours, usually starting at 11am, on Sundays.

Camera Repair Whether your camera is digital, conventional, or video, **Sendean,** first floor, 105–109 Oxford St., W1 (☎ **020/7439-8418**) can help. It will give you a free estimate and do a fast repair. It is open Monday to Thursday 9:30am to 5:30pm, and Friday 9:30am to 6pm. Sendean accepts American Express, MasterCard, and Visa.

Car Rentals See "Getting Around," earlier in this chapter.

Climate See "When to Go" in chapter 2.

Currency See "Money" in chapter 2.

Dentists **Dr. Martin Rooms LDS RCS (ENG),** 13 Kensington High St., W8 (☎ **020/7937-3951**) runs a 24-hour service, including late-night emergencies and weekend cases. Or, you can try the **Dental Emergency Care Service,** Guy's Hospital, St. Thomas's St., SE1 (☎ **020/7955-2186**), a first-come, first-served clinic on the 23rd floor, Monday to Friday 8:45am to 3pm. On Saturday and Sunday, there is a service on the first floor from 9am to 3pm. These are both more suited to pain-killing than drastic action. Citizens of Australia and New Zealand are entitled to subsidized emergency dental care while in Britain.

Doctors The National Health Service now runs a telephone help line, **NHS Direct** (☎ **0845/4647**), which is a useful first port of call for noncritical illnesses. Otherwise, **Medcall,** 2 Harley St., W1 (☎ **0800/136106**) operates a late-night practice and 24-hour call-out. Citizens of Australia and New Zealand are entitled to free emergency medical treatment.

Documents See "Visitor Information," Entry Requirements & Customs," in chapter 2.

Driving Rules See "Getting Around," earlier in this chapter.

Drugstores The Brits call them chemists. **Zarfash Pharmacy,** 233–235 Old Brompton Rd., SW5 (☎ **020/7373-2798**) is open round the clock every day. **Bliss Chemist,** 5 Marble Arch, W1 (☎ **020/7723-6116**), is open daily 9am to midnight.

Electricity British appliances operate on the EU standard of 230 volts. If you're bringing a hair dryer, travel iron, shaver, and so on, you will need a transformer. If you plug an American appliance into any European electrical outlet without one, you will certainly ruin it and may even start a fire. British sockets take different three-pronged plugs than those in America and on the Continent. London department stores and most branches of **Boots the Chemist** sell adapters, in case you arrive without one. Some hotels and B&Bs may have one you can borrow.

Embassies & High Commissions This list will help you out if you lose your passport or have some other emergency:

- **Australia** The **High Commission** is at **Australia House,** Strand, WC2 (☎ **020/7379-4334;** www.australia.org.uk), and is open Monday to Friday from 9am to 5pm. Tube: Holborn, Temple.
- **Canada** The **High Commission** is at 38 Grosvenor St., W1 (☎ **020/7258-6600;** www.canada.org.uk), and is open Monday to Friday from 8am to 11am. Tube: Bond St.
- **New Zealand** The **High Commission** is at **New Zealand House,** Haymarket, SW1 (☎ **020/7930-8422;** www.newzealandhc.org.uk), and is open Monday to Friday from 10am to noon, and 2 to 4pm. Tube: Piccadilly Circus.
- **The United States** The embassy is at 24 Grosvenor Sq., W1 (☎ **020/7499-9000;** www.usembassy.org.uk), is open for walk-in enquiries 8:30am to 12:30pm, 2 to 5pm (to 5:30pm for phone calls). Tube: Marble Arch, Bond Street.

Emergencies Dial ☎ **999** free from any phone for police, fire, and ambulance.

Eyeglass Repair There are several chains of opticians with branches all along main shopping streets. **David Clulow** has 10 in Central London. The one in Soho is convenient, and it can handle most repairs: 70 Old Compton St., W1 (☎ **020/7287-1128**).

Holidays See "When to Go," in chapter 2.

Hospitals Around a dozen city hospitals offer 24-hour walk-in emergency care. The most central is **University College Hospital,** Grafton Way, WC1 (☎ **020/7387-9300**). The two best alternatives are **Chelsea & Westminster Hospital,** 369 Fulham Rd., SW10 (☎ **020/8746-8000**) on the Chelsea/Fulham border; and **St. Mary's Hospital,** Praed St., W2 (☎ **020/7886-6666**) in Paddington.

Hot Lines For police, fire, or ambulance, call ☎ **999** free of charge from any phone. Anyone who is distressed about anything can call the **Samaritans** (☎ **0345/909090;** www.samaritans.org.uk) at any time to hear a friendly voice. **Alcoholics Anonymous** runs a help line from 10am to 10pm every day (☎ **020/7352-3001;** www.alcoholics-anonymous.org.uk/), and **Narcotics Anonymous** does the same (☎ **020/7730-0009;** www.na.org).

Information See "Visitor Information," earlier in this chapter.

Internet Access Britain has got the surfing bug. There are **easyEverything** cyber cafes all over London, and we've listed their addresses in chapter 5. A few budget hotels will send and receive e-mails for you, and access is available in all hostels (see chapter 4). You can also send short e-mails for free from the many **i-plus** electronic information booths around the city (see "Visitor Information," above).

Legal Aid If you get arrested, call **Release** (☎ **020/7729-9904,** or 020/7603-8654 after hours) for free advice, counseling, and referrals.

Liquor Laws The government has promised to update the antiquated English and Welsh licensing laws, but probably not before the next election. There's no set date for Tony Blair to "go to the country," other than it must be within 5 years of his ousting the Tories—so before May 2002. In the meantime, no one under 18 can buy or consume alcohol, with one exception: 16- and 17-year-olds may purchase "beer, porter, or cider," with a table meal. Under-14s may enter some pubs, but only when accompanied by an adult and only if the pub has a family room, restaurant, or garden. Adults can buy beer, wine, and spirits in supermarkets, liquor stores (called "off-licences"), and many local grocery stores, during the same opening hours as pubs (see "Business Hours," above). Admission-charging nightclubs are allowed to serve alcohol to patrons until 3am or so. By law, hotel bars may serve drinks after 11pm to registered guests only. Do not drink and drive because the police are eagle-eyed and the penalties very stiff.

Lost Property If you lose something on the bus or Tube, wait 3 working days before contacting **London Transport Lost Property Office,** 200 Baker St., NW1 (☎ **020/7486-2496** recorded information), open Monday to Friday 9:30am to 2pm. **Taxi Lost Property,** 15 Penton St., N1 (☎ **020/7833-0996**), is open Monday to Friday 9am to 4pm, only for things left in black cabs. For buses, you need to call and find out which depots are at either end of that particular line (☎ **020/7222-1234**). There are also lost-property offices at all train stations and at Victoria Coach Station.

Mail Stamps cost 45p (72¢) for airmail letters weighing up to 10 grams and 40p (64¢) for postcards to anywhere outside Europe. Budget travelers can get more post for the pound by buying aerograms for 40p (64¢) each. The deal gets even sweeter at £2.20 ($3.50) for six plain aerograms and £2.70 ($4.30) for hard-to-find pictorial ones. For more information, call the **Post Office Counters Helpline** (☎ **0845/722-3344;** www.postoffice-counters.co.uk).

Maps See "City Layout," earlier in this chapter.

Newspapers/Magazines The *Guardian, Independent, The Times,* and *Daily Telegraph* are the so-called quality national daily newspapers, moving in stately broadsheet fashion from left to right across the political spectrum. The *Daily Mail* and *Express* are supposedly "middle-of-the road" tabloids. All have Sunday editions. (The *Guardian* has a sister paper, *The Observer.*) The *Evening Standard* is the only citywide local paper and publishes updated editions from 10am to around 5pm. Make sure to buy it on a Thursday for the excellent what's-on supplement, *Hot Tickets* (www.thisislondon.co.uk). Most Sunday broadsheets produce entertainment guides, too. But the bible is the weekly *Time Out* magazine (www.timeout.com). Many newsagents also sell the *International Herald Tribune, USA Today, Time,* and *Newsweek.*

Police Dial ☎ **999** in an emergency, free from any phone.

Post Office The main **Trafalgar Square Post Office,** 24–28 William IV St., Trafalgar Square, WC2, is open Monday to Saturday from 8am to 8pm. Travelers can receive mail, marked "Poste Restante," here and must bring identification to collect it. Most other post offices are open Monday to Friday from 9am to 5:30pm, and Saturday 9am to noon. Look for the red signs. To contact the Trafalgar Square Post office or find the nearest local one, call the **Post Office Counters Helpline** (☎ **0845/722-3344;** www.postoffice-counters.co.uk).

Rest Rooms The Brits have three main words for rest rooms: toilet, lavatory, and loo. You'll see the "Public Toilets" sign on streets, in parks, and in Tube stations. Some are free—St. Christopher's Place, near Bond Street, and the uninviting but well-maintained subway facilities at Tottenham Court Tube station. But keep a few 20p coins handy for the many paid-for ones. Big public buildings—museums, galleries, department stores, railway stations, and so on—have well-maintained facilities. There are top shop loos (no charge) at John Lewis, Oxford Street, Waterstone's in Piccadilly, and Peter Jones in Sloane Square, Chelsea. You'll get a glare and often a telling off if you use a pub rest room without buying a drink, so be discreet if you do it. The same goes for the really lavish ones in posh hotels.

Safety Violent crime is no more common in Central London than any other big city, and much less common than in many. Despite the slow urban regeneration of the desolate area around King's Cross, it is wise to leave York Way and Goods Way to the prostitutes and johns—a former director of public prosecutions was caught here in 1991—and avoid parks late at night. The usual rules apply: Don't take risks, keep wallets and purses hidden, bags held tightly to you, and never leave possessions unattended, even if only at your elbow or on the floor between your feet. And don't flash your cash, credit cards, or jewelry.

Salon A really great budget deal is the **Vidal Sassoon School,** 53 Davies Mews, W1 (☎ **020/7318-5205**), which trains recently qualified hairdressers. Men and women can get a classic or creative cut for £16.50 ($26.40), a third of the cost of one at Vidal Sassoon's world-famous salons. The academy is open

Monday to Friday between 10am and 3pm. Appointments may still be available that day if you call first thing in the morning, but it's better to book a couple of days ahead.

Smoking Most U.S. cigarette brands are available in London. Smoking restrictions are getting tougher all the time. You cannot light up anywhere on the Underground or on buses. Most restaurants have nonsmoking sections, and some even ban it completely. Things really are starting to change in budget hotels and B&Bs. A few don't allow smoking at all. More are now keeping some rooms as nonsmoking. In both cases, those that throw offenders out are few and far between. Ask for a change of room if telltale smells linger.

Taxes There are no separate county or city sales taxes in Britain. The national 17.5% value-added tax (VAT) is levied on most goods and services. The exceptions are books and unprepared food, which means groceries. Other useful ones to know are children's shoes and clothes, so check them out if you're a petite adult. The exemption also applies to takeaway food hence, the two price lists at those eateries that offer both. Hotels and restaurants usually include VAT in quoted prices, but check their policy, which should be written on tariffs and menus (all rates in this book include VAT). Foreign visitors can reclaim the VAT on any goods they're taking out of the United Kingdom. You need to ask for a form from the sales clerk at those stores participating in the scheme, which will usually have a notice up about it. Then show it and the goods at the VAT desk at the airport. Refunds cannot be processed after you arrive home. For more information, see chapter 7.

Taxis See "By Taxi," earlier in this chapter.

Telephones Several companies operate London phone boxes, each branded differently, but the largest is BT. There are also pay phones in most pubs and large public buildings, including railway and Tube stations, museums and galleries, and some department stores. Most accept any coin upward of 10p. Others take pre-paid BT phonecards, BT account cards, and credit cards. And many take both coins and cards. You can buy the phonecards in post offices and newsagents. Look for the green sign.

Pay-phone **call rates** are the same every day, all day. The minimum cost is 10p (16¢), for the first 67 seconds of a local call and 43 seconds of all other calls. The pro-rata cost works out, respectively, at 9p (14¢) and 15p (24¢) per minute. Pay phones accept up to four coins at a time. They don't make change so, unless you're calling long-distance, use small denominations.

Telephone Alert!

You may have noticed from the telephone numbers in this book that London has gone through yet another **change of area code**—to **020** for the whole city. You only need to use the code when calling from outside London. If you want to look up old friends, and haven't updated your address book yet, this is what you do: Take the "7" or "8" from the old inner London 0171 or outer London 0181 code, and tack it onto the front of the original phone number to make it 8 digits. For example, ☎ **0171/123-4567** becomes ☎ **020/7123-4567;** and ☎ **0181/123-4567** becomes ☎ **020/8123-4567.**

If that sounds like gobbledygook, call the free **BT Helpline** (☎ **0800/731-0202;** www.bt.com), which is open Monday to Saturday from 8am to 8pm.

Telephone Dialing Info at a Glance

- To call London from home, dial the international access code: ☎ **011** from the **United States** and **Canada,** ☎ **0011** from **Australia,** and ☎ **00** from **New Zealand.** Follow that with **44,** and then the area code minus its initial zero, and finally the number.
- To call home from London, the international codes are ☎ **001** for the **United States** and **Canada,** ☎ **0061** for **Australia,** and ☎ **0064** for **New Zealand.** Then add the area code minus any initial zero, and the number. Or, you can use these **long-distance access codes:** AT&T USA Direct (☎ **0800/890011**), MCI Call USA (☎ **0800/890222**), USA Sprint Global (☎ **0800/890877**), Canada Direct (☎ **0800/890016**), Telstra Direct for Australia (☎ **0800/890061**), and New Zealand Direct (☎ **0800/890064**).
- When you're in London, dial ☎ **100** for the U.K. national operator, ☎ **155** for the international operator, ☎ **192** for Directory Enquiries to find out a U.K. telephone number, and ☎ **153** for International Directory Enquiries.

In Britain, the main **toll-free** code is **0800,** but not all customer-service, information, or central-reservations lines use it. There are dozens of other special codes, which may be charged at the local rate (the 0845 numbers you'll see throughout the book), regional, or national rate (08705). Companies using the extortionate 50p-a-minute (80¢) premium rate should warn you about the cost at the start of a call. You can check any code with the operator (☎ **100**) to avoid nasty shocks.

Before using the **in-room phone** at your hotel or B&B, check the rates because these will often include massive surcharges.

Time Zone London's clocks are set on Greenwich Mean Time—5 hours ahead of U.S. Eastern Standard Time, 10 hours behind much of Australia, and 12 hours behind New Zealand. To find out the time, dial **Timeline,** (☎ **123**). Daylight saving time is used in Britain, too. The clocks move 1 hour back, to British Summer Time, on the last weekend of March and forward to GMT again on the last weekend of October.

Tipping The more expensive restaurants tend to add a service charge of 12½% to the bill. Cheaper ones sometimes do, more often if you're a big group. All should write their policy on the menu. If in doubt, ask. And make sure to check the bill before filling in the gap for a gratuity. In Britain, it is usual practice to tip cab drivers, staff in restaurants, hairdressers, some bars with table service, and hotels, but never pubs. Budget hotels and B&Bs will rarely add a percentage to the bill, so it is up to you. The usual amount on any occasion is 10%.

Transit Info **London Transport** runs a 24-hour help line (☎ **020/7222-1234**), providing schedule and fare information for buses, the Underground, and British Rail services within Greater London.

Useful Telephone Numbers **Talking Pages** (☎ **0800/192-192**) is a free dial-a-directory, which can give you the name, address, and phone number of any service you might need in London. The **Restaurant Switchboard** (☎ **020/8888-8080**) makes recommendations and reservations, also free of charge. It's open Monday to Friday from 9am to 7pm. The **Capital Radio Helpline**

(☎ **020/7484-4000**) will answer any legitimate question about London, the universe, or anything, from who wrote or starred in *High Fidelity,* to what are the first lines of your favorite pop song to where to hire a limo or what's hot for kids. It's open Monday to Friday from 10am to 10pm, Saturday from 8am to 8pm, and Sunday from 10am to 4pm.

Water London's water is safe to drink. Tap water is free in restaurants, so make sure to ask for it specifically if you don't want to pay for mineral water.

Weather For information on the weather up to 14 days ahead, call ☎ **0991/004400.** If you're allergic to rain and want a forecast for the weather several months' ahead of time, call **Weather Action** (☎ **020/7922-8844;** www.weatheraction.com).

4 Accommodations You Can Afford

Spend a night in the car. Hang a drape across half your bedroom. Climb a lot of ladders. Wash in a bucket. Whatever it is, do something to prepare yourself for the accommodations you'll find in London. The London Tourist Board (LTB) has done a great job with its campaign to create thousands more beds in the capital. For every newly built hotel room, another opens in an historic building. The picture-postcard architecture of the latter is certainly appealing, but the comforts inside won't win any awards for luxury. Authorities are strict about alterations. Bedrooms are small and often old-fashioned. Private bathrooms are mainly an afterthought and tiny. And there's rarely an elevator to bypass the precipitous stairs. Yet, the rates will take your breath away. It isn't that hotels and B&Bs are out to rip you off (at least not many of them!). Property prices in London have gone stratospheric—the government is even talking about subsidizing housing costs for low-paid "key workers" like nurses and teachers to stop them from deserting the city. I hate to be such a killjoy, but forewarned is forearmed.

There is some good news. London's B&Bs and small hotels have finally wised up to the Web. Many set up Internet sites for the first time in the past year. Now you can look before you buy, though the pictures you see might not always reflect the reality. The past year has also brought an end to the confusing, mysterious symbols stuck proudly on hotel and B&B doors. The three main rating organizations, the English Tourist Board, AA, and RAC, launched a new set of harmonized quality standards. Hotels must have a restaurant, liquor license, lounge, and private bathrooms in 75% of their rooms. They still get stars but must work harder to win them. Diamonds are now the symbol for all guest accommodations, a broad term that primarily refers to B&Bs. These new standards—and the magic word "millennium"—may be why many have tarted themselves up over the past couple of years.

Whatever you think of the quality of accommodation, demand is so strong and the average B&B so small that you really must book ahead. Most places guard against no-shows by charging 1-night's stay as a nonrefundable deposit. Some ask for full payment on arrival. A few still charge for accepting credit cards, though most have fallen into line on that one. And fewer still, the really sneaky ones, quote rates without VAT. Check all this out when you call.

A Tip for the Bedless

As much as I love the **London Tourist Board,** it sometimes makes life very difficult. Having changed the way its accommodation reservation service worked in 1999, last year the LTB decided to change it again—naturally everything was still up in the air when I called. Adrenaline junkies who arrive in London without a bed for the night should ring the main LTB number (☎ **020/7932-2000;** www.londontown.com), or go to the tourist information desks at the airport (see "Flying into Heathrow" in chapter 2) to find out what's what. One thing's for certain: You'll still have to pay a booking fee.

1 Tips for Saving on Accommodations

If you know where to look and what to ask for, you can find bargains in London. Just read on.

- **Book into a budget neighborhood.** You'll get better value where a lot of hotels compete. Try Bloomsbury first, then Paddington and Bayswater, and Victoria. Be careful in cut-price Earl's Court because there "budget" tends to mean "dive."
- **Consider your options.** If you can survive without a private bathroom, or with the WC outside the room, you can save £10 to £20 ($16 to $32) a night.
- **Ask for the breakfast menu.** A full English breakfast would cost at least £6 ($9.60) outside the hotel. It includes cereal, bread, fruit, bacon, eggs, sausage, and sometimes baked beans, tomatoes, and mushrooms. Many budget hotels have switched to continental breakfast (see the listings). That can mean anything from a bit of dry toast to a no-holds-barred buffet, so ask for the menu before booking.
- **Don't be afraid to bargain.** Most budget places now quote room rates, but ask for an old-style per-person price, particularly out of season. You may get a bigger room for only a few pounds more—a triple for two people, for example. With large hotels, the rack rate is the maximum charge for a room, and it includes 10% or 25% travel agent commission. You can often get that knocked off by making your own reservation.
- **Subcontract the legwork.** If you hate haggling, call a consolidator. These guys get a discount by buying or reserving in bulk, and pass the savings (or some of it, at least) on to you. Don't rely solely on consolidators, though; you can often do better dealing directly with hotels. The following are among the more reputable providers: **Hotel Reservations Network** (☎ **800/964-6835;** www.hoteldiscounts.com); and **British Hotel Reservation Centre** (☎ **020/7828-0601;** www.bhrc.co.uk). Online, try booking a hotel through **Arthur Frommer's Budget Travel** (www.frommers.com) and save up to 50%.
- **Hold Your Breath.** If you can bear the tension, wait until a few days before you fly and then scan **www.lastminute.com** for great discounts at posh hotels right in the heart of London. There are big savings to be had through **www.laterooms.com**, too, for bookings up to 3 weeks in advance. And the reservation site, **www.leisurehunt.com**, had some excellent August cheapies on offer in June.
- **Hunt down discounts.** Hotels won't often advertise ways to save money. But asking for special discounts never hurts. For example, hotels offer good rates for groups; they will also discount rates for individuals who are planning extended stays (this is more common in the off-season). Discounts vary from 5% to 10%;

Index of London Hotel Maps

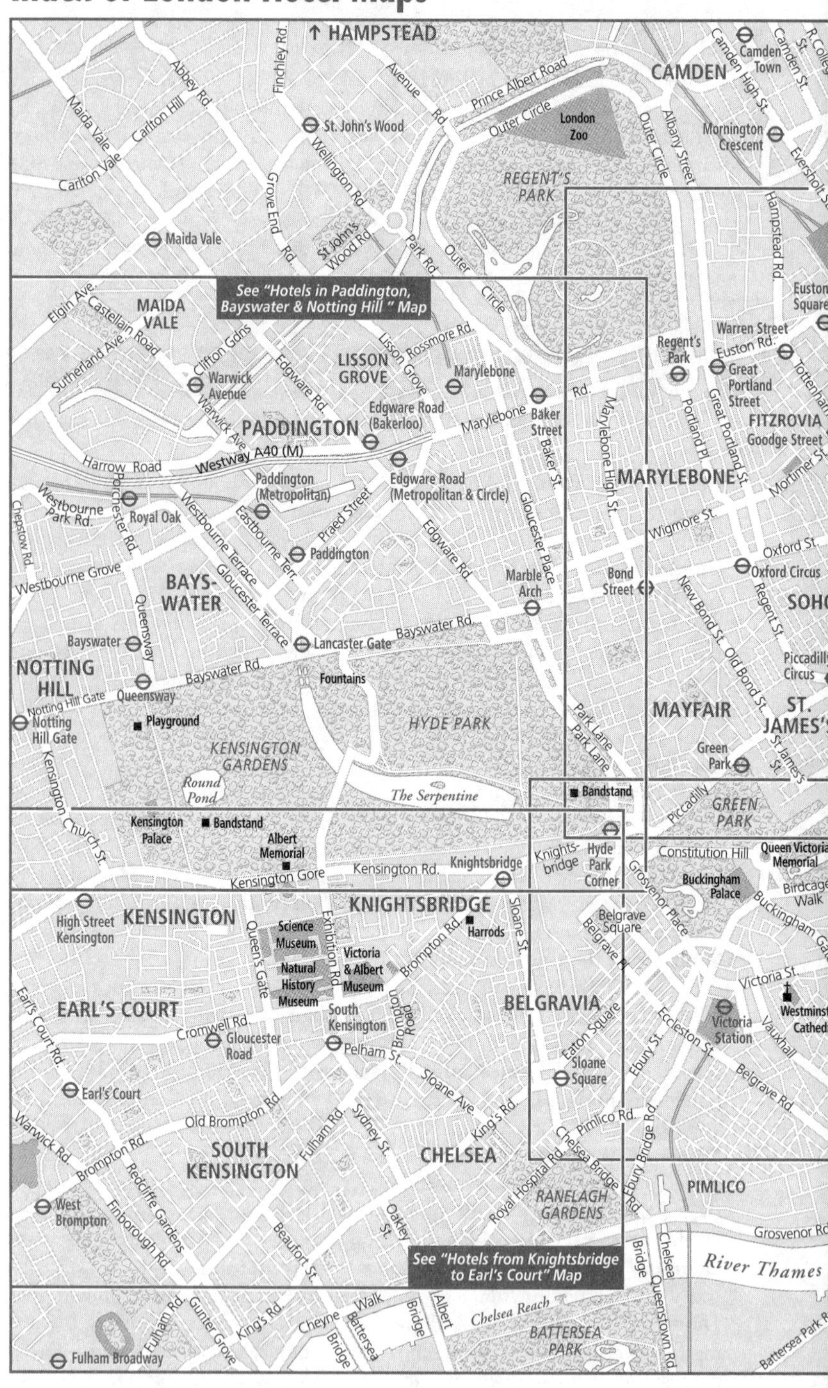

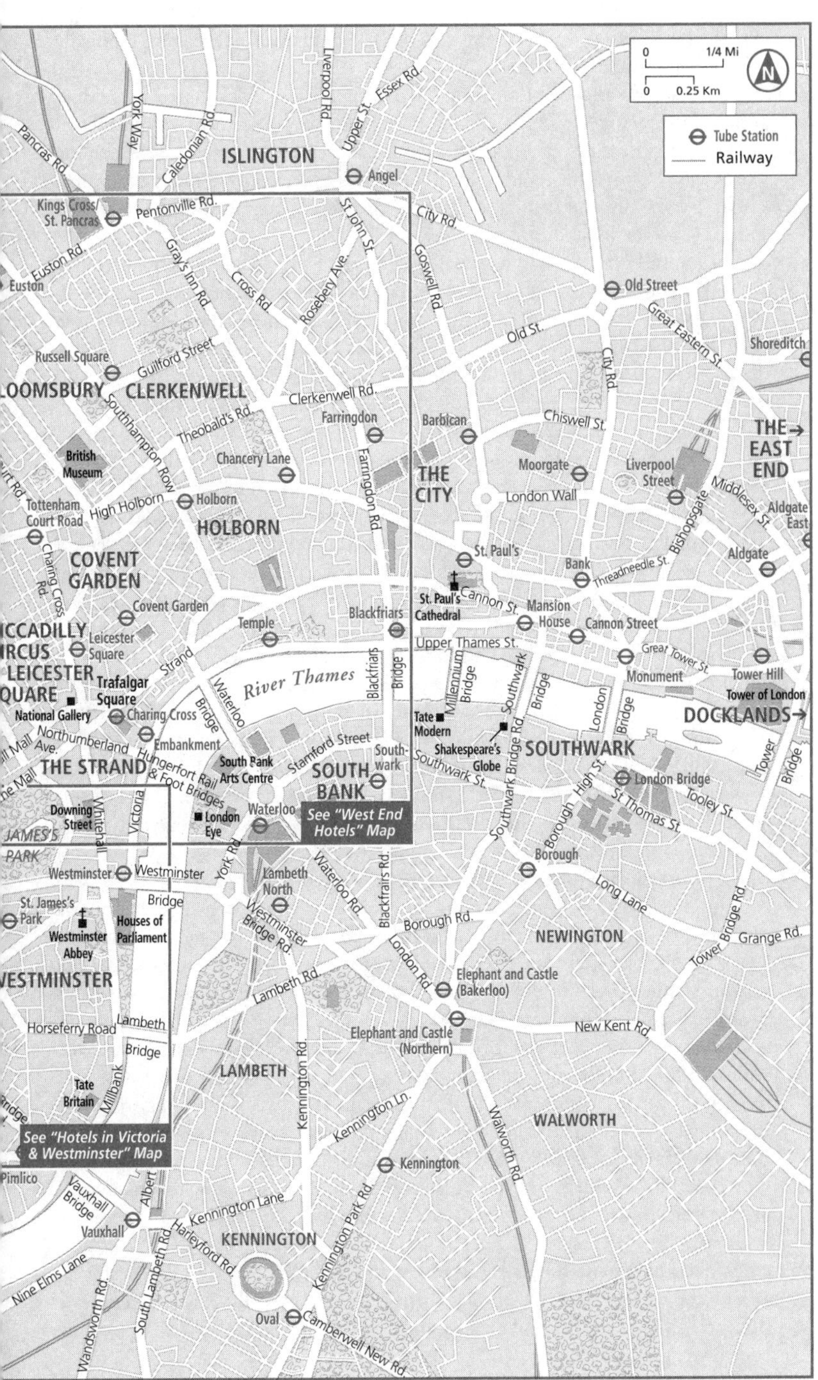

0
1/4 Mi
0
0.25 Km
N
Tube Station
Railway
ISLINGTON
Angel
CLERKENWELL
LOOMSBURY
HOLBORN
COVENT GARDEN
CCADILLY IRCUS
LEICESTER QUARE
THE STRAND
SOUTH BANK
THE CITY
THE EAST END
DOCKLANDS
SOUTHWARK
NEWINGTON
LAMBETH
WALWORTH
KENNINGTON
WESTMINSTER
JAMES'S PARK
Kings Cross/ St. Pancras
Euston
Russell Square
British Museum
Tottenham Court Road
Holborn
Chancery Lane
Farringdon
Barbican
Old Street
Shoreditch
Moorgate
London Wall
Liverpool Street
Aldgate East
Aldgate
St. Paul's
St. Paul's Cathedral
Bank
Mansion House
Cannon Street
Monument
Tower Hill
Tower of London
Covent Garden
Leicester Square
Trafalgar Square
National Gallery
Charing Cross
Embankment
Temple
Blackfriars
River Thames
Tate Modern
Shakespeare's Globe
South Bank Arts Centre
South-wark
London Bridge
Waterloo
London Eye
Downing Street
Westminster
St. James's Park
Westminster Abbey
Houses of Parliament
Lambeth North
Borough
Elephant and Castle (Bakerloo)
Elephant and Castle (Northern)
Tate Britain
Kennington
Vauxhall
Pimlico
Oval
Pancras Rd.
York Way
Caledonian Rd.
Liverpool Rd.
Upper St.
Essex Rd.
Pentonville Rd.
St John St.
City Rd.
Goswell Rd.
Euston Rd.
Gray's Inn Rd.
Cross Rd.
Rosebery Ave.
Guilford Street
Old St.
Great Eastern St.
Clerkenwell Rd.
Theobald's Rd.
Southampton Row
Chiswell St.
City Rd.
Farringdon Rd.
High Holborn
Middlesex St.
Bishopsgate
Threadneedle St.
Cannon St.
Charing Cross Rd.
Upper Thames St.
Great Tower St.
Strand
Waterloo Bridge
Blackfriars Bridge
Millennium Bridge
Southwark Bridge
London Bridge
Tower Bridge
Northumberland Ave.
Hungerford Rail & Foot Bridges
Stamford Street
Southwark St.
Southwark Bridge Rd.
Borough High St.
St Thomas St.
Tooley St.
Whitehall
Victoria
Mall
See "West End Hotels" Map
York Rd.
Westminster Bridge
Waterloo Rd.
Blackfriars Rd.
Westminster Bridge Rd.
Long Lane
Borough Rd.
London Rd.
Tower Bridge Rd.
Grange Rd.
Lambeth Rd.
Horseferry Road
Lambeth Bridge
Millbank
New Kent Rd.
Kennington Rd.
Kennington Ln.
Walworth Rd.
See "Hotels in Victoria & Westminster" Map
Vauxhall Bridge
Albert
Kennington Lane
Harleyford Rd.
Kennington Park Rd.
Nine Elms Lane
Wandsworth Rd.
South Lambeth Rd.
Camberwell New Rd.

extended stays range from 3 nights to a week. Ask about student rates, especially in Marylebone and Bloomsbury.

- **Play the supply-and-demand game.** Avoid high season. Most hotels make their annual rate increase in April and drop down again in October. Some budget places offer discounts of up to 20% from December to February, excluding Christmas. Business hotels need to fill beds at the weekend, so many offer great leisure breaks (see the box "The Bargain Business," later in this chapter), and some deals even apply during the week.
- **Think laterally.** This has to be the most unusual bed in London. One Saturday a month, February through November, families and small groups can zip back 400 years and stay on a replica of Sir Francis Drake's galleon, the **Golden Hinde** (☎ **08700/118700;** www.goldenhinde.co.uk; Tube: London Bridge, Monument). You'll help prepare for a pretend voyage, dressed in Tudor clothes, and sleep on the lower decks. And at £30 ($48) per person, it's about the same price as a bed-and-breakfast. (See page 232).
- **Go native.** Many Londoners offer bed-and-breakfasts in their homes. This is a cozy option, as long as you ensure the agency matches you up with a host with the right lifestyle—if you're anti-kids, not a family with an army of under-5s. The minimum stay is 2 nights, and breakfast is usually continental. You may have a private bathroom and lounge, or share with the owner, so rates vary. There are some very toney addresses, but staying in pretty West London (Chiswick, Putney, and Kew) is a better value. The LTB and some of the B&B agencies have launched the Bed & Breakfast and Hosts Association to set quality standards. The following three members are all well-established. Rates are per night and for two people sharing a room: **At Home in London** (☎ **020/8748-1943;** www.athomeinlondon.co.uk) from £67 ($107.20) Central London and from £52 ($83.20) West London; **Host and Guest Service** (☎ **020/7385-9922;** www.host-guest.co.uk) from £85 ($136) Central London and from £36 ($57.60) West London; **Uptown Reservations** (☎ **020/7351-3445;** www.uptownres.co.uk) from £90 ($144) Central London.
- **Make yourself at home.** All you need for a home exchange is a home that will accommodate visitors from London. The only charge is a small fee that allows you to list your property or to look at other people's; the rest is free. It sounds like a burglar's charter, but questionable hygiene standards are reported as the rare and only problem. Homeowners deal with each other directly. Successful swaps require meticulous groundwork: Ask a lot of questions, be honest about what you want and what you're offering. The U.S.-based **HomeExchange.COM** (☎ **805/898-9660;** www.homeexchange.com) has operated since 1966. You pay $30 to put your home on its site for a year, and anyone can e-mail you, via the company's Web site. It's up to you to respond and reveal your identity. **Home Base Holidays** (☎ **020/8886-8752;** www.homebase-hols.com) set up in London in 1986. Wannabe swappers pay £38 ($60.80) to view the password-protected listings and contact details online, or £55 ($88) for printed directories. It also has U.S. agents.
- **Consider apartment hotels or rooms with kitchens.** Staying in self-catering accommodations can cut down on expensive restaurant bills. And it often beats B&B prices for families and small groups, even accounting for having to buy your own eggs and bacon.

  If you can't live without smooth reception service, consider apartment hotels. I've recommended some under "Do-It-Yourself Deals" in each neighborhood.

Accommodations range from studios with kitchenettes to two-bedroom apartments, and hotel services. Minimum lengths of stay vary, and weekly rates are cheaper. Chi-chi South Kensington and Chelsea are chock-a-block with them. Robert and Polly Arnold own and run the very family-friendly **Emperors Gate Short Stay Apartments,** SW5 (☎ **020/7244-8409;** www.apartmenthotels.com). One-bedroom apartments, sleeping four, start at £99 ($158.40) per night for a minimum 2-night stay.

You can also rent an apartment. **Go Native** (☎ **020/7221-2028;** www.gonative.co.uk) manages private London homes for owners who are away for a while or rarely use their pied à terres. A short stay in a one-bedroom flat would cost from £500 ($800) a week—£650 ($1,040) for a fab pad, owned by an American architect, just a stone's throw from the Royal Opera House in Covent Garden. The rates drop the longer you stay, starting at 1 month. Mary and Simon Ette also provide a friendly and experienced service at **The Independent Traveller** (☎ **01392/860807;** www.gowithIT.co.uk): One-bedroom apartments in Central London start at £390 ($624) per week, minimum stay 3 nights. Other contacts for great deals include **Residence Apartments** (☎ **020/7727-0352;** e-mail: residence@btinternet.com) and the super-budget **Acorn Management Services** (☎ **020/7202-3311;** www.acorn-london.co.uk). The latter has links with Florida State University and lets out apartments year-round, with most offered May to August.

The **Jenny Jones Agency,** 40 South Molton St., W1 (☎ **020/7493-4801;** Tube: Bond St.) is a great source of super-cheap long stays: £65 to £70 ($104 to $112) a week for a bedsit in Central London! Most of its private landlord clients only accept 6-month lets, though some will do 3 months. You can't book ahead, but just turn up at the agency's office, open Monday 2 to 5:30pm, Tuesday to Thursday 9.30am to 1.30pm and 2.30 to 5.30pm, and Friday 9.30am to 1.30pm. You must pay a month's rent in advance, plus the same again as a deposit, in cash or traveler's checks (no credit cards). If you're a student, bring working references with you—sign up with a local temp agency—to prove you're not going to run off without paying. The agency gets very busy in September, which is just before the start of the university year.

- **Go back to school.** During the summer and sometimes at Easter, you can find budget lodging in university dorms. Accommodations at one of the six universities in Greater London (bed-and-breakfast) start at around £27 ($43.20) per person. The **British Universities Accommodation Consortium** (☎ **0115/950-4571;** www.buac.co.uk) publishes a directory and refers bookings for free. Or contact the three most central universities directly: **University of London**

A Note for Travelers with Disabilities

Travelers with disabilities will have a hard time maneuvering through a lot of budget accommodations—many B&Bs are in old buildings with steps up to the entrance, narrow doorways, and no elevator. The listings in this chapter include details of any special facilities. However, the best source of advice on where to stay is **Holiday Care Service** (☎ **01293/774-535;** www.holidaycare.org.uk). It publishes reams of information on every subject and will make hotel bookings for free, even for people who are not paid-up members ("friends"). For more information, see "Tips for Travelers with Special Needs" in chapter 2.

(☎ **020/7862-8880;** www.lon.ac.uk/accomm/); **University of Westminster** (☎ **020/7911-5807;** www.westminster.ac.uk/comserv/); **City University** (☎ **020/7477-8033;** www.city.ac.uk/ems/accomm1.htm).

- **Sleep super-cheap.** Professionally run, private hostels are multiplying like gremlins in London through companies like **Astor's** (see "Paddington & Bayswater" and "Bloomsbury," below) and Interpub, which owns **St. Christopher's** (see "Just South of the River," below). Beds cost from £12 to £20 ($17.60 to $32) per night. There are also seven **Youth Hostel Association** sites (☎ **020/7373-3400** centralized London reservations; www.yha.org.uk), the best of which are reviewed below. Remember, YHA members qualify for discounts at certain London attractions (the discounts vary by hostel), as well as cheap international phone calls and money-off meals. We have also reviewed the Barbican YMCA. For a full British address list and fact sheet, call the **National Council of YMCAs** (☎ **020/8520-5599;** www.ymca.org.uk).

2 Kensington & Chelsea

Citadines (☎ **020/7543-7878;** fax 020/7584-9166; www.citadines.com; e-mail: londonsouthkensington@citadines.com.) also has a cozy apartment hotel, with a fitness studio, here on Gloucester Road (Tube: Gloucester Road). Rates are lower than at Trafalgar Square, with studios for £93 to £103 ($148.80 to $164.80) a night if you stay 1 week. For more information, see "Covent Garden, The Strand & Holborn," below. Apartment-hotel seekers should also check out **Nell Gwynn House,** Sloane Ave., SW3 3AX (☎ **020/7589-1105;** fax 020/7589-9433; www.nghapartments.co.uk; reservations@nghapartments.co.uk). It's high quality but a bit impersonal, with rooms starting at £415 ($664) per week for a small two-person studio.

✪ **Abbey House.** 11 Vicarage Gate, London W8 4AG. ☎ **020/7727-2594.** www.abbeyhousekensington.com. 16 units, none with bathroom. TV. £45 ($72) single; £68 ($108.80) double/twin; £90 ($144) triple; £100 ($160) quad. Rates include full English breakfast. No credit cards. Tube: High St. Kensington, Notting Hill Gate.

Giving yourself the option to stay at Abbey House is one of the best reasons to go native and not have a private bathroom. There are none here, which is why it can charge these rates in such a posh part of town. It's only a short walk up to Notting Hill, or downhill to the more mainstream Kensington High Street. Abbey House, owned by Albert and Carol Nayach, is a gem set in a gracious Victorian square. The bright hallway has a checkerboard floor and wrought-iron staircase lined with lithographs of glum-faced royals. And the bedrooms are big for London. Simple but attractive in pastel colors, they all have new mahogany-style furniture and firm beds. The second-floor room at the front gets sole rights over the balcony above the front door, shaded by a stripy awning. The bathrooms are Laura Ashley style and impeccable; there's one for every three bedrooms. And there's a kitchenette, where you can make tea and coffee for free. The freezer is for ice but not storing cold drinks. The staff do treat you terribly well here, whether you need a hair dryer, baby-sitting, or restaurant

The Difference Between Singles, Twins & Doubles

In British English, a **single** is a room with one bed fitting one person. A **twin** has two beds, but each bed will accommodate only one person. A **double** has a bed big enough for two.

advice. They can even decipher the London bus map, which is no mean feat. By the time you read this, the hotel should also have a Web site.

Baden-Powell House. 65–67 Queen's Gate, London SW7 5JS. ☎ **020/7584-7031.** Fax 020/7590-6902. www.scoutbase.org.uk. E-mail: bph.hostel@scout.org.uk. 180 beds, all with bathroom (shower only). A/C TV. £65 ($104) single; £80 ($128) twin; £34 ($54.40) per adult triple; quad, £30 ($48) per adult, £20 ($32) per child under 16; dorm, £25 ($40) per adult, £17 ($27.20) per child. 6 units adapted for travelers with disabilities. Rates include full English breakfast. DC, MC, V. Tube: Gloucester Rd.

It pays to crunch the numbers before you stay at Scout HQ. The singles, triples, and quads work out to be more expensive than most B&Bs. But the twins are a good value, particularly for this fantastic location right next door to the Natural History Museum. And the dorms are virtually on par with youth hostels. Built in 1961, the Baden-Powell House is a big brick cube split into two parts. The Scout Association offices have a separate entrance around the corner on Cromwell Road. The commercial side consists of conference rooms, a restaurant, a new coffee shop, and the budget hotel. Hotel is a better word than hostel, after the recent £2-million ($3.2-million) refurb. The decor is institutional but comfortable, and spotlessly clean—white walls, bright-blue quilt-covers matching the carpet, and sturdy modern beds. The bunks in the dorms are unusual, interlocking at right angles like kids' building blocks, and the twin rooms are huge. All have new drop-in shower units, at a very high ratio in the dorms of one to every five beds. Tea- and coffeemakers are standard, and hair dryers are available at the reception desk. The hotel has also won three stars from the London Tourist Board for "Disabled Mobility." There's cheap Internet access, a tourist information point, launderette, and unwelcoming TV lounge. And if you can bear the traffic roar on the six-lane Cromwell Road, you can gaze out at the museum from the roof terrace. Baden-Powell House has an elevator and is totally nonsmoking.

Prince's Gardens Halls, Imperial College. Vacation Accommodation Office, Watts Way, Prince's Gardens, London SW7 1LU. ☎ **020/7594-9507.** Fax 020/7594-9504. www.ad.ic.ac.uk/conferences. E-mail: reservations@ic.ac.uk. 608 units. £35 ($56) single; £55 ($88) twin. Rates include full English breakfast. EC, MC, V. Open Easter and summer vacations. Tube: South Kensington. No children under 10.

British industry is forever complaining that not enough kids study science. Take them on a tour around here, and they'd switch subjects in a snap. Prince's Gardens is like a holiday camp. The maze of rooms is decorated in the usual student style, and most are singles, so book early if you want a twin. The long-heralded en-suite bathrooms won't be ready until Easter 2001. In the meantime, four rooms share a public facility. The best bit is that because Prince's Gardens is part of the campus at Imperial, you get to use all the on-site amenities. There are banking facilities as well as a bureau de change, a tourist information desk and travel agency, a medical center, launderette, TV lounge, and so on. You can even get a haircut. Guests also pay a discount rate at the sports center, as they would if they stayed at Imperial's Pembridge Gardens hall in Notting Hill. The Basics restaurant does pizza for half the price you'll pay anywhere else, and you can do a bar crawl without even leaving the complex. You will want to leave, though, because this is a fantastic location. Harrods, the Victoria & Albert Museum, the Natural History Museum, Kensington Gardens, Hyde Park, and the Royal Albert Hall are all within a short walk.

When you talk to the Vacation Accommodation Office, ask about the newly refurbished **Beit Hall,** next to Albert Hall. Due to open last September, its rates are only a little higher for a so-called superior room, many of which have private bathrooms: £42 ($67.20) single; £58 ($92.80) single with bathroom; £78 ($124.80) twin with bathroom; all include a full English breakfast.

Hotels from Knightsbridge to Earl's Court

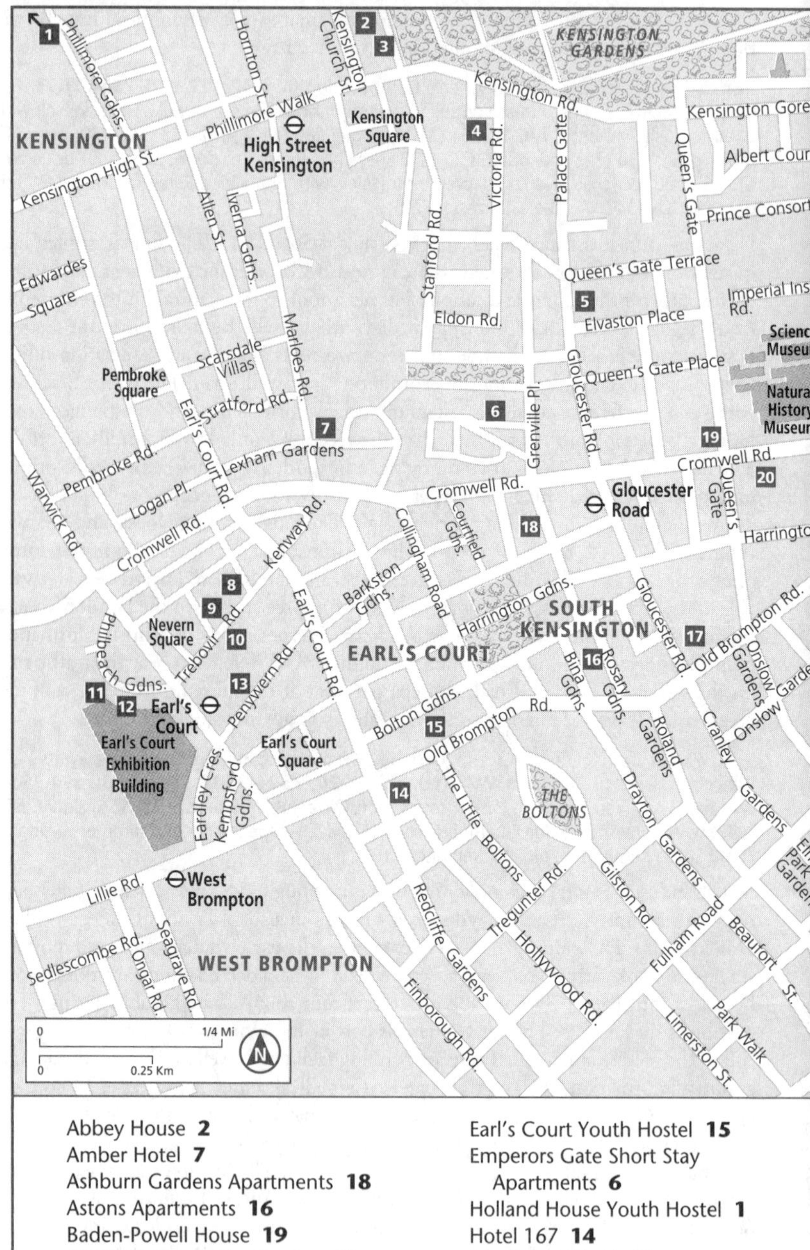

Abbey House **2**
Amber Hotel **7**
Ashburn Gardens Apartments **18**
Astons Apartments **16**
Baden-Powell House **19**
Citadines, South Kensington **5**
Clearlake Hotel **4**
Earl's Court Youth Hostel **15**
Emperors Gate Short Stay Apartments **6**
Holland House Youth Hostel **1**
Hotel 167 **14**
Mayflower Hotel **10**
More House **20**

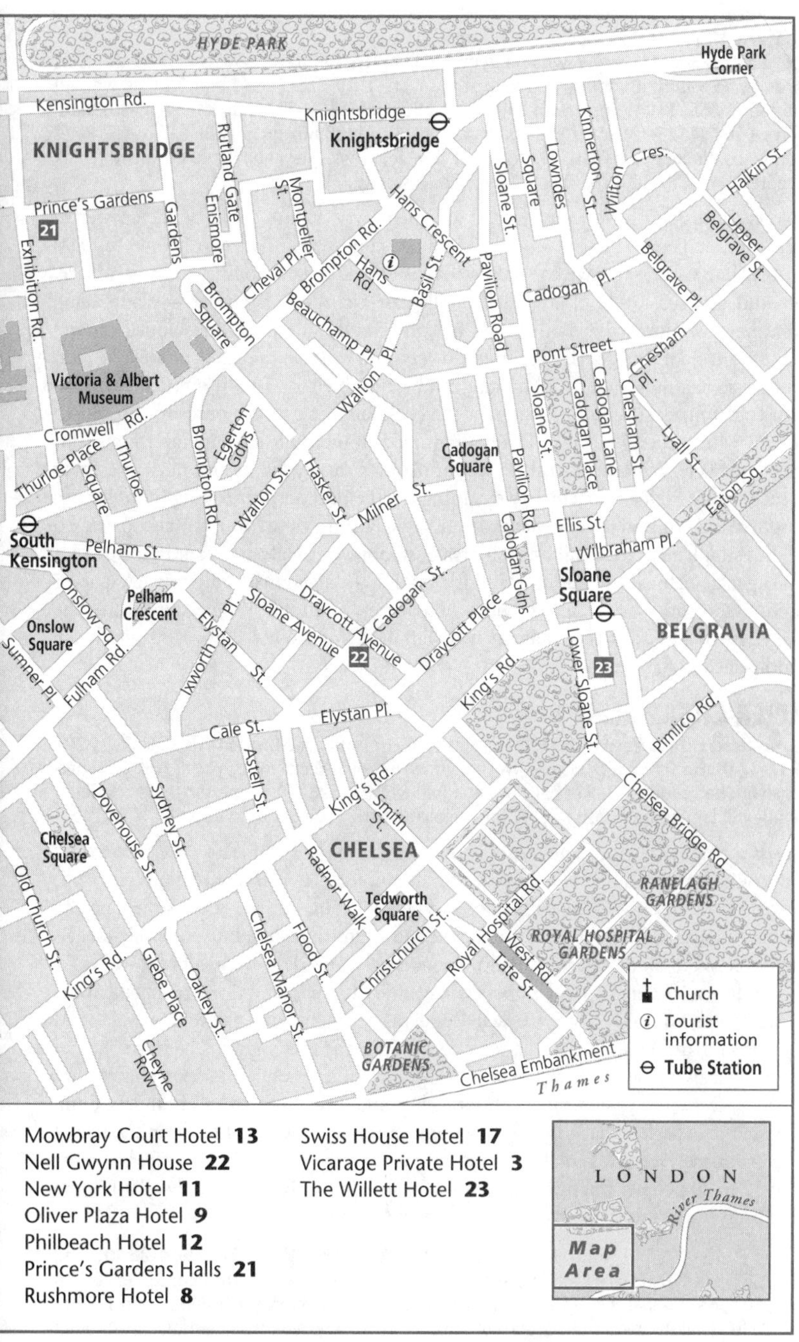
HYDE PARK
Hyde Park Corner
Kensington Rd.
Knightsbridge
Knightsbridge
KNIGHTSBRIDGE
Rutland Gate
Montpelier St.
Prince's Gardens
21
Gardens
Ennismore
Exhibition Rd.
Hans Crescent
Hans Rd.
Basil St.
Brompton Rd.
Cheval Pl.
Brompton Square
Beauchamp Pl.
Walton Pl.
Pavilion Road
Sloane St.
Lowndes Square
Kinnerton St.
Wilton Cres.
Halkin St.
Upper Belgrave St.
Belgrave Pl.
Cadogan Pl.
Pont Street
Chesham Pl.
Cadogan Place
Cadogan Lane
Chesham St.
Sloane St.
Lyall St.
Eaton Sq.
Victoria & Albert Museum
Cromwell Rd.
Thurloe Place
Thurloe Square
Thurloe
Brompton Rd.
Egerton Gdns.
Walton St.
Hasker St.
Milner St.
Cadogan Square
Pavilion Rd.
Ellis St.
Wilbraham Pl.
Cadogan Gdns
South Kensington
Pelham St.
Onslow Sq.
Pelham Crescent
Onslow Square
Sumner Pl.
Fulham Rd.
Elystan Pl.
Ixworth Pl.
Sloane Avenue
22
Draycott Avenue
Cadogan St.
Draycott Place
Sloane Square
BELGRAVIA
Lower Sloane St.
23
King's Rd.
Elystan Pl.
Cale St.
Pimlico Rd.
Astell St.
Sydney St.
Dovehouse St.
King's Rd.
Smith St.
Chelsea Square
CHELSEA
Chelsea Bridge Rd
Old Church St.
Radnor Walk
Tedworth Square
RANELAGH GARDENS
Royal Hospital Rd
Christchurch St.
Chelsea Manor St.
Flood St.
Oakley St.
Glebe Place
King's Rd.
West Rd.
Tate St.
ROYAL HOSPITAL GARDENS
Cheyne Row
BOTANIC GARDENS
Chelsea Embankment
Thames
Church
Tourist information
Tube Station
Mowbray Court Hotel 13
Nell Gwynn House 22
New York Hotel 11
Oliver Plaza Hotel 9
Philbeach Hotel 12
Prince's Gardens Halls 21
Rushmore Hotel 8
Swiss House Hotel 17
Vicarage Private Hotel 3
The Willett Hotel 23
LONDON
River Thames
Map Area

✪ **Swiss House Hotel.** 171 Old Brompton Rd., London SW5 OAN. ☎ **020/7373-2769.** Fax 020/7373-4983. www.swiss-hh.demon.co.uk. E-mail: recep@swiss-hh.demon.co.uk. 16 units, 15 with bathroom (most with shower only). TV TEL. £46 ($73.60) single without bathroom, £65 ($104) single with bathroom; £80–£90 ($128–$144) double/twin with bathroom; £104 ($166.40) triple with bathroom; £118 ($188.80) quad with bathroom. Rates include continental breakfast. Discount of 5% for 1-wk. stay and cash payment (U.S.$ accepted). AE, CB, DC, JCB, MC, V. Tube: Gloucester Rd.

If you've just gotta have your space, man, then Swiss House could be the answer to every prayer. Peter Vincenti lets out his huge family rooms to two people for £90 ($144). But you don't have to splurge because the standard doubles are a good size, too, and this is a lovely place. Guests walk past a curtain of greenery—plants hang from every window ledge, railing, and balcony—and under an old-fashioned canopy to the front door. Inside, chintz, dried flowers, and original fireplaces create a homey, country-style atmosphere. Traffic noise can be a problem on Old Brompton Road, so keep your fingers crossed for a room at the back looking over the peaceful communal garden, which guests can use. There are quite a number of nonsmoking rooms, but proprietor Peter Vincenti is realistic about people's sneaky habits and puts an ashtray in each room. He's an extremely welcoming and helpful host, providing room service of soups and "monster" sandwiches from midday until 9pm. You can also pay a £6 ($9.60) supplement for a full English breakfast. Someone will carry your bags up. Staff can organize baby-sitting, do the laundry, book tickets and taxis, buy the newspapers for you, and supply secretarial services. Hair dryers and cable TV are standard in the rooms. Swiss House is very popular with families, but around 80% of its guests are middle-aged U.S. tourists.

SUPER-CHEAP SLEEPS

✪ **Holland House Youth Hostel.** Holland Walk, Holland Park, London W8 7QU. ☎ **020/7937-0748.** Fax 020/7376-0667. www.yha.org.uk. E-mail: hollandhouse@yha.org.uk. 201 units, none with bathroom. £19.95 ($31.90) per adult; £17.95 ($28.70) per person under 18. Rates include full English breakfast. MC, V. Tube: Holland Park, High St. Kensington.

This is a magical setting. The hostel is right in the middle of a leafy public park, and you could be staying in a 400-year-old mansion. The accommodations are split between two buildings: One half is not-so-vintage 1950s, but the other is the amazing Holland House. Built in 1607, the redbrick and white-stone building has lovely crenellated decoration along the roof. Sadly, incendiary bombs destroyed half of it in World War II. In the summer, open-air opera is staged in the ruins, and if you're staying at the hostel, there's no need to buy a ticket. Residents, sitting around the ornamental pond in the courtyard, enjoy the music for free as it fills the evening air. The hostel has all the normal useful stuff like a kitchen, TV room, quiet room, laundry facilities, and Internet access. The cafeteria has a liquor license and serves cheap meals from 5 to 8pm. The only drawback is that a lot of school groups stay here, as you'll see from the crowd of kids outside Holland Park Tube every morning. Some dorms sleep 6 to 8, but most sleep 12 to 20 people, and there are no family bunkrooms. But you're only a 10-minute walk from two stations and a quick ride into the middle of town.

More House. 53 Cromwell Rd., London SW7 2EH. ☎ **020/7584-2040.** Fax 020/7581-5748. E-mail: more-house@surf3.net. 55 units, none with bathroom. £25 ($40) single; £40 ($64) double; £50 ($80) triple; £15 ($24) per person in a 4-to-6-bed dorm. Rates include full English breakfast. Discount of 10% for 1-wk. stay. No credit cards. Open summer vacation. Tube: South Kensington, Gloucester Rd.

The Sisters of St. Augustine run More House as an intercollegiate hall for students at the dozens of London colleges. It takes its name from Sir Thomas More, who was Henry VIII's Lord Chancellor until he quarreled with the king over the latter's divorce from Catherine of Aragon. Henry later beheaded More for refusing to acknowledge him as head of the Church of England. Sir Thomas lived in Chelsea and wrote his famous work, *Utopia,* here. More House is more of a good deal than ideal, and you don't have to give up your worldly wealth to enter. Its rates barely rise from year to year, which makes it an excellent value for London and almost half the price of non-student places in this overpriced area. The style is strictly institutional, unlike the luxxier student halls at Prince's Gardens or High Holborn. No more than six people share each toilet and shower or tub. There are tea- and coffeemakers, a microwave, a fridge, and a phone that accepts incoming calls on every floor. Pay phones are downstairs. And there's a launderette, as well as a couple of places where smokers can retreat. More House is in a great location, right across the road from South Kensington's museum row. It's a shame that, as at Baden-Powell House, that means staying on a six-lane arterial road.

DO-IT-YOURSELF DEALS

Ashburn Gardens Apartments. 3 Ashburn Gardens, London SW7 4DG. ☎ **020/7370-2663.** Fax 020/7370-6743. www.ashburngardens.co.uk. E-mail: info@ashburngardens.co.uk. 24 units, all with bathroom. TV TEL. £490–£665 ($784–$1,064) per wk. 1-bedroom apt.; £805–£1,155 ($1,288– $1,848) per wk. 2-bedroom apt. Higher rates apply Apr–Oct. Minimum stay 1 wk. No credit cards. Tube: Gloucester Rd.

Staying here off-season is one of the best deals in London. One-bedroom apartments undercut the B&Bs in toney South Kensington. And the bigger ones beat rates in budget neighborhoods, even accounting for guests having to fry their own bacon in the morning. In fact, it's little hardship to fill the generous rooms to capacity, including the lounge, unless you can't bear sofa beds. Ashburn Gardens is a small street that joins Cromwell Road midway between a big Sainsbury supermarket and London's museum row. Though it isn't busy itself, anyone sensitive to traffic noise should ask to be at the back and above the first floor to get more of a view. Mr. Aresti and his family have owned the business since 1974. Behind the Georgian facade and entrance hall, you'll find that everything has been refurbished and modernized. The decor is simple and comfortable, with hair dryers, satellite TV, and VCRs as standard. The beds were all new in 1998, as were the bathrooms and open-plan kitchens in 1999. Great maid service is part of the deal—more frequent than at a Citadines. They'll clean up every weekday, change the linen once a week and the towels on alternate days. These apartments are popular with families, so there's a whole cupboard of cribs, high chairs, and strollers at the reception desk. Using the sofa bed, you can fit four people in a one-bedroom and six people in a two-bedroom. Baby-sitting is available in the evening.

✪ **Astons Apartments.** 31 Rosary Gardens, London SW7 4NH. ☎ **800/525-2810** or 020/7590-6000. Fax 020/7590-6060. www.astons-apartments.com. E-mail: sales@astons-apartments.com. 53 units, all with bathroom (shower only). TV TEL. £60 ($96) single; £85 ($136) double, £120 ($192) designer double; £90 ($144) twin; £120 ($192) triple; £160 ($256) quad. Discount of 5% for 1-wk. stays. Children stay free in parents' room. AE, MC, V. Tube: Gloucester Rd.

Hosebay bought Aston's 4 years ago and has totally overhauled the three town houses. Behind that redbrick Victorian facade, you'll find the very model of a modern apartment hotel. Maids swoop through every day. The reception desk is manned around the clock. Laundry, dry cleaning, secretarial help, and a ticket-booking service are all on tap. And to celebrate finishing the job, Aston's has just jacked up its prices. Forget the singles and—a real shame—the great family room in the basement with its proper open-plan kitchen and a sofa bed for the kids. While the rest of the studios—"apartments" is a misnomer—do now verge on being a splurge, they're still a pretty good value and should impress even the most exacting guests. The bathrooms are new and all en-suite. The kitchenettes, behind foldaway doors, are fully equipped right down to cafetières, those mod glass coffeemakers. And satellite TV and ISDN lines are standard. What's really nice is that the refurb has actually enhanced Rosary Gardens' historic appeal—you can see your face in the lovely, polished, wood handrail on the stairs. The bedroom decor is comfortably English and pulled-together, with nice touches like cushions on the beds. Some studios do feel a bit small. My favorite is the second-floor twin with a balcony overlooking the quiet street. As this book went to press, Hosebay was in the process of tarting up another set of houses close by, so ask for an update when you call.

Clearlake Hotel. 18–19 Prince of Wales Terrace, London W8 5PQ. ☎ **020/7937-3274.** Fax 020/7376-0604. E-mail: clearlake@talk21.com. 25 units, all with bathroom (some with shower only). TV TEL. £55–£60 ($88–$96) double/twin studio; £75 ($120) triple studio; £93–£105 ($148.80–$168) 1-bedroom apt.; £110–£120 ($176–$192) 2-bedroom apt.; £192 ($307.20) three-bedroom apt. Weekly rates and long-stay discounts available. AE, DC, MC, V. Tube: High St. Kensington, Gloucester Rd.

Attention all honeymooners: Bring your crisp new marriage license, and the Clearlake will add to your bliss with a free bottle of bubbly. This is a splendidly ramshackle hotel that offers a range of fantastic-value, self-catering options. It would take a whole page to explain how many people each studio or apartment actually sleeps, and all the different deals. But it's helpful to know that Prince of Wales Terrace is a quiet street, opposite the park at the eastern end of Kensington High Street. Several of the big Victorian houses need repainting, but this is a solid-gold area. Turn a corner, and there's a charming, pastel-painted row of houses with plutocratic BMWs parked bumper-to-bumper outside. What really sells the Clearlake is the huge amount of space you get, except where modern partitions cut into the gracious proportions to make single rooms or toe-to-toe twins. Despite some recent redecoration (new carpets and furniture, and tidied-up bathrooms), many of the apartments resemble student digs—a junk-shop jumble of smart gilt mirrors, next to a host of 1970s horrors, and even theater props left over from plays the owner puts on. One of them has an old piano and a little patio. The studios are much tidier but still idiosyncratic. Stay 5 days, and you get maid service, although washing up and oven-cleaning cost extra. There are hair dryers and tea-/coffeemakers in every unit; videos to rent; laundry and dry-cleaning services; and cribs, strollers, and high chairs at the reception desk. And staff can arrange baby-sitting. Clearlake also has rooms without a kitchenette, and many rooms are nonsmoking.

WORTH A SPLURGE

Hotel 167. 167 Old Brompton Rd., London SW5 0AN. ☎ **020/7373-0672.** Fax 020/7373-3360. www.hotel167.com. E-mail: enquiries@hotel167.com. 19 units, all with bathroom. MINIBAR TV TEL. £72–£86 ($115.20–$137.60) single; £90–£99 ($144–$158.40) double/twin. Extra person £16 ($25.60). Rates include continental breakfast. AE, DC, MC, V. Tube: Gloucester Rd., South Kensington.

Hotel 167 does something rather unusual and does it rather well. London B&Bs tend to aspire to some variation on English style, whether out of a hotel pattern book or more individually put together. Not this one, though. It may live in a corner Victorian terrace house, but the decor is anything but old-fashioned. Frank Cheever has owned Hotel 167 for 20 years. He did the whole place over in 1988. You could travel round the world night by night, from a room that's a bit Scandinavian to one with a slightly Oriental feel, and through time from art-deco elegance to a more modern look. Sadly, because this is a small B&B, Mr. Cheever doesn't like to take special requests. The rooms all have hair dryers, access to in-house video, a fridge, tea-/coffeemakers, and the all-important double-glazing. Old Brompton Road is very busy, and the house is on a corner at the junction with the super-swanky Boltons. Hotel 167 mirrors the neighborhood, which has a large population of wealthy émigrés. Christie's has its auction rooms just down the road, and there are lots of chi-chi restaurants. The clientele score above average on the groove scale—after all, the band Manic Street Preachers did write a song about the place.

Vicarage Private Hotel. 10 Vicarage Gate, London W8 4AG. ☎ **020/7229-4030.** Fax 020/7792-5989. www.londonvicaragehotel.com. E-mail: reception@londonvicaragehotel.com. 18 units, 2 with bathroom (shower only). £45 ($72) single without bathroom; £74 ($118.40) double/twin without bathroom, £98 ($156.80) double/twin with bathroom; £90 ($144) triple without bathroom; £98 ($156.80) family room without bathroom. Rates include full English breakfast. No credit cards. Personal checks from U.S. banks accepted if received at least 2 mths. ahead of visit. Tube: High St. Kensington, Notting Hill Gate.

You see what happens when B&Bs start putting in en-suite bathrooms. Eileen Diviney, who runs Vicarage Private Hotel, did the first floor in 1999 and the second last year, following up by redecorating the rooms. An en-suite twin is a big splurge, at £24 ($38.40) more than a basic room. The ground-floor one at the back, number 3, is marvelous—peaceful, high-ceilinged, and furnished with a pretty painted tables and old-fashioned metal bedsteads. But you really don't have to splash out here. Most of the rooms are big—doubtless why 92% of the guests come from the United States, home of the ballpark bedroom. The ceilings are high up to the fourth floor. And every room may be different, but they're all in that Victorian country style to match the date of the house. Four bedrooms share each bathroom, and there are separate toilets to keep the traffic moving. If you're trying to weigh this B&B up against Abbey House right next door in this quiet Kensington Square, then there are other things to consider apart from the fancier decor here and marginally higher price. Vicarage Private Hotel has a TV lounge, instead of putting sets in the rooms. Hair dryers are standard, instead of at the reception desk. And you don't have to leave your room to make tea or coffee. Oh, and there are kippers (herring split open and smoked slowly over oak chips until it's golden brown) and porridge on a breakfast menu fit for warriors.

The Willett Hotel. 32 Sloane Gardens, London SW1 8DJ. ☎ **800/270-9206** in the U.S., or 020/7824-8415. Fax 020/7730-4830. www.eeh.co.uk. E-mail: willett@eeh.co.uk. 19 units, all with bathroom (shower only). TV TEL. £67–£87 ($107.20–$139.20) single; £90 ($144) small double/twin; £100 ($160) standard double/twin, from £145 ($232) deluxe double/twin; £155 ($248) triple. Rates include full English breakfast. AE, DC, MC, V. Tube: Sloane Sq.

You can imagine Miss Marple, Agatha Christie's elderly detective, coming up from the country to visit a friend here for tea. The Willett is in a quiet redbrick terrace, complete with mansard roof, bay windows, and a host of the other excesses beloved by the Victorians. This is the dream location for shopaholics, just off Sloane Square and a 5-minute walk to Chelsea's King's Road. Even Miss Marple, not a noted fashion plate, would appreciate being so close to the upper-crust holy of holies, the Peter Jones department store. Elegant English Hotels, which owns The Willett, has refurbished throughout in a ponderous traditional style to match the building. Deluxe means canopies over the beds, voluptuous swagged curtains, and matching armchairs. The bathrooms don't get much bigger though. The tiny standard twins are the ones to avoid, because you sleep head to head along one wall, but the small double is a fantastic value for this swanky area. Most of the rooms have fridges, tea-/coffeemakers, radios, hair dryers, and CNN as standard. Reception can supply laundry service, dry cleaning, secretarial help, complimentary newspapers, baby-sitting by arrangement, and limited room service. The porter will stagger upstairs with your bags. And best of all, guests can relax in the secluded communal garden. It's all just so civilized.

3 Earl's Court

Mayflower Hotel. 26–28 Trebovir Rd., London SW5 9NJ. ☎ **020/7370-0991.** Fax 020/7370-0994. members.aol.com/MAYFHOTEL/private/MAY.HTM. E-mail: mayfhotel@aol.com. 48 units, all with bathroom (some with tub only). TV TEL. £53–£65 ($84.80–$104) single; £69–£89 ($110.40–$142.40) double/twin; £89–£109 ($142.40–$174.40) triple; £99–£119 ($158.40–$190.40) family room. Rates include continental breakfast. Discount available for 3-day and weekday stays. AE, MC, V. Tube: Earl's Court.

The Mayflower looks like the woman next door, wearing her posh frock at the five 'n' dime so that nobody thinks she has to shop there. With its black pillars and showy window boxes, it's determined to look a cut above cut-price Earl's Court. Fortunately, the inside lives up to the promise. The owners have just overhauled the whole hotel, from restyling the breakfast room to look like a health-food cafe to repainting the hallways; a glazed greenhouse and private Internet cafe are next on the to-do list. The bedrooms, all refurbished, are very welcoming. The furniture matches the walls, which creates virtual space in smaller rooms, even those right under the roof with sloping ceilings (there is an elevator). Generally, they aren't a bad size for London, and if matching fabrics are your thing, the decor should press all the right buttons. There's a lovely second-floor family room that leads onto the front porch. Trebovir Road is used as a shortcut between the one-way main roads on either side of Earl's Court station. But every room is double-glazed, and the traffic dies down before midnight. Some are nonsmoking. Tea-/coffeemakers and CNN are standard. Irons, hair dryers, and adapter plugs are available at the reception desk. Staff can also organize room service (7 to 10pm), dry cleaning, newspapers, and secretarial help, and they can rent you a video. The Mayflower also has 35 attractive self-catering accommodations on busy Warwick Way, starting at £69 ($110.40) per night, or £420 ($672) per week, for a studio.

Mowbray Court Hotel. 28–32 Penywern Rd., London SW5 9SU. ☎ **020/7373-8285.** Fax 020/7370-5693. www.M-C-Hotel.mcmail.com. E-mail: mowbraycourthotel@hotmail.com. 82 units, 70 with bathroom (most with shower only). TV TEL. £48 ($76.80) single without bathroom, £55 ($88) single with bathroom; £60 ($94) double without bathroom, £70 ($112) double with bathroom; £75 ($120) triple without bathroom, £85 ($136) triple with bathroom; £84 ($134.40) quad without bathroom, £95 ($152) quad with bathroom; £100–£115 ($160–$184) family room without bathroom, £110–£125 ($176–$200) family room with bathroom; £154 ($246.40) 7-bed room. Rates include continental breakfast. AE, CB, DC, JCB, MC, V. Tube: Earl's Court.

Don't bother trying to guess which of the Dooley brothers you're speaking to on the phone. Tony and Peter will both call you "my dear" and sound exactly the same. The family opened the hotel 36 years ago, and it's one of the few cheap places in Earl's Court where it's safe to spend the night without a biohazard suit. It's the staff who need protection: When I visited, they were attacking the bathrooms with some hideously pungent substance, which is presumably why these are spotlessly clean. Mowbray Court is a friendly, old-fashioned, budget hotel, which even has a bar and lounge. The decor is a bit beige and dated, but that's a style choice because there's a regular renovation program. The Dooleys are devils with decorative plaster, and some of the new bathroom ceilings look like a frosted-icing moonscape. Four bedrooms share every public one. There's a von Trapp family room with seven beds in the basement of the main building and a handy triple with a little kitchen in the annex. Rooms at the back face the overground Tube line, but double-glazing keeps out the noise. Fifteen rooms are nonsmoking. Hair dryers, safes, trouser presses, satellite TV, and radios are standard. Staff can organize dry cleaning, laundry, baby-sitting, car rental, and tours. And—get this—there's even a Vidal Sassoon–trained visiting hairdresser.

New York Hotel. 32 Philbeach Gardens, London SW5 9EB. ☎ **020/7244-6884.** Fax 020/7370-4961. www.newyorkhotellondon.co.uk. 14 units, 12 with bathroom (most with shower only). TV TEL. £55 ($88) single without bathroom, £60 ($96) single with bathroom; £80–£100 ($128–$160) double/twin with bathroom; £100–£120 ($160–$192) triple with bathroom. Rates include continental breakfast. Tube: Earl's Court.

This is one of a pair of gay hotels next door to each other in a quiet crescent behind the exhibition center. The Philbeach is pure theatre, while this one is like a gents' club with extras. The New York is a fantastic value because guests get the use of a sauna and a big Jacuzzi. The hotel is a pretty, white, Victorian building with railings along the front and baskets of flowers hanging from the balconies. Swagged curtains, looping across the first-floor windows, are a hint of the poshness inside. These belong to the lounge, where cable TV is the only intrusion into a world of dark leather sofas and vases of lilies on polished furniture. The bedrooms are classic, too, with this matching that and coordinating with the other. All have tea-/coffeemakers, cable TV, fridge (on request), pants press and iron, and a hair dryer. Front bedrooms on the second floor lead onto the balcony, but I prefer number 3 at the back. It's a lovely bright double, with its own little terrace facing south across the garden. I'm not quite sure why, but there's a baby cannon out there, too. The garden is lovely with its fountain and gnarled wisteria. Guests can sit either in the sun at wrought-iron tables or under the shade of the awning. The hotel will organize dry cleaning and laundry, and offers limited room service.

Oliver Plaza Hotel. 33 Trebovir Rd., London SW5 9NF. ☎ **020/7373-7183.** Fax 020/7244-6021. www.capricornhotels.co.uk. E-mail: oliverplaza@capricornhotels.co.uk. 38 units, all with bathroom (some with shower only). TV TEL. £45 ($72) single; £65 ($104) double/twin; £78 ($124.80) triple; £80 ($128) quad; £100 ($160) family room. Rates include continental breakfast. AE, DC, EC, JCB, MC, V. Tube: Earl's Court.

The Oliver Plaza has one of the most bizarre bedrooms in London. It's right on top of the front porch in what looks like a dilapidated greenhouse. The double bed just—and I mean just—fits into the space, and you walk through a single to get to it. I'd love to recommend it, except you'd have to be a hothouse flower or an exhibitionist not to find it hugely uncomfortable. The Bhayani family also owns the Byron, one of our splurge choices in Bayswater, but here they've cut their cloth to match the budget area. With its slightly shabby pink and white paint, the outside is very pre-redevelopment Miami. Fortunately, the inside has all been refurbished, so don't worry that the dim hallway lighting disguises any nasties. While I still prefer Mowbray Court, Oliver Plaza is a good value, too. Many of the rooms have recently been done up in fleur-de-lys wallpaper, and they all have sparkling new bathrooms. In the basement, there's a double room that can link together with the one next door, which has two double beds and a single—a handy arrangement for big families. If the idea appeals, but you don't need so much space, ask about the other connecting options. Tea-/coffeemakers and hair dryers are standard, and staff can help with tour arrangements.

✪ **Philbeach Hotel.** 30–31 Philbeach Gardens, London SW5 9EB. ☎ **020/7373-1244.** Fax 020/7244-0149. www.philbeachhotel.freeserve.co.uk. E-mail: 10075.3112@compuserve.com. 40 units, 15 with bathroom (most with shower only). TV TEL. £35 ($56) budget single, £50 ($80) single without bathroom, £60 ($96) single with bathroom; £65 ($104) double without bathroom, £85 ($136) double with bathroom; £75 ($120) triple without bathroom, £95 ($152) triple with bathroom. Rates include continental breakfast. Discount available for 1-wk. stays. No 1-night stays on Sat. 20% discount in restaurant for guests. AE, DC, MC, V. Tube: Earl's Court.

The Philbeach is a one-stop entertainment bonanza for gay travelers and somehow manages to do it at budget rates. The conservatory restaurant, Wilde about Oscar, serves delicious French cuisine from about £15 ($24) for two courses, and residents get a 20% discount. The hotel has a chic, Soho-style basement bar, and the weekend club nights are a blast. There's a terrace, a dance floor, and a dressing service—wigs, clothes, shoes, and make-up—for transvestites (☎ **020/7373-4848**). The Philbeach is a really friendly place and attractive, too. As you go in, the gothic decor makes it look like an arts club, with chandeliers, navy walls printed with fleur de lys, and dark-painted dado rail. The rooms are more ordinary, though, and some are quite small. Go for one of the little mezzanine doubles. They share a terrace overlooking the lovely garden where vines snake across the trellis and flowers bloom in ornamental urns. One is en-suite, and the other shares a bathroom. It's about four bedrooms to every public facility. The Philbeach gets rowdier the higher you go up the house, so manager Ian Reynolds tries to put lesbians and straight couples on the second floor. Of course, if it all sounds a bit too over the top, you could always stay next door at the New York Hotel and come around here in the evening.

✪ **Rushmore Hotel.** 11 Trebovir Rd., London SW5 9LS. ☎ **020/7370-3839.** Fax 020/7370-0274. 22 units, all with bathroom (most with shower only). TV TEL. £65 ($104) single; £82 ($131.20) double; £94 ($150.40) triple; £99 ($158.40) family room. Rates include continental breakfast. Discount available for 1-wk. stays. 10% discount for seniors. Under-12s stay free in parents' room. MC, V. Tube: Earl's Court.

This gracious hotel makes art directors at interiors magazines go weak in the knees. The Rushmore experience begins with the Italianate paint effects in the hallway: classical scenes and cloudy ceilings. The breakfast room is stunning, too, paved in limestone, with wrought-iron furniture, lighting that flatters even after a heavy night, and architectural cacti in terra-cotta urns. Every bedroom is a different exuberant stage set, with the bathrooms just fabulously made-over, too. One has gothic looping curtains and a canopy over the bed, like Count Dracula's castle. In another, you'll find a chandelier and Louis XIV pale-blue walls, with panels sketched out in gold. There's a marvelous family room under the eaves, and a porter will carry up your bags. The Rushmore is rare in taking bookings for specific rooms (there are four for nonsmokers). Unfortunately, it still doesn't have a Web site where you can pick your favorite. Hair dryers, satellite TV, and tea-/coffeemakers are standard. Secretarial help, laundry and dry cleaning, and a booking service are on hand at the extremely welcoming reception desk. And you can sleep in on Sundays because breakfast goes on until 10am. Thank goodness this is in Earl's Court, or the Rushmore would certainly bust the budget.

SUPER-CHEAP SLEEPS

Earl's Court Youth Hostel. 38 Bolton Gardens, London SW5 0AQ. ☎ **020/7373-7083.** Fax 020/7835-2034. www.yha.org.uk. E-mail: earlscourt@yha.org.uk. 160 units, none with bathroom. £19.95 ($31.90) per adult; £17.95 ($28.70) per person under 18. Rates include bed linen and continental breakfast. MC, V. Tube: Earl's Court.

If you're going to stay somewhere cheap in Earl's Court, you're far better off going to the youth hostel than one of the dozens of super-budget hotels. At least you know what you're getting, and the location is great. This garden square is just north of Old Brompton Road. On the other side of the street, the millionaires' mansions in the Boltons mark the beginning of posh South Kensington. Earl's Court is backpacker central, and they flock to this hostel. The big, half-stuccoed Victorian building has a good mix of pretty basic dorms, from a few twins up to some with nine beds or more. You can surf the Internet, change money, and lock away your valuables. The hostel has both kitchen facilities and an on-site cafeteria, serving continental breakfast. It also makes packed lunches, if asked, but has stopped evening meals. That's not much of a loss since Earl's Court is jam-packed with cheap restaurants, as well as late-night shops—check the prices carefully because they can be exorbitant. And the more upmarket Gloucester Road is almost as close. The lounge has cable TV and video games (smokers get a space, too), and there's a launderette. But the really big plus is the little courtyard garden at the back.

WORTH A SPLURGE

✪ **The Amber Hotel.** 101 Lexham Gardens, London W8 6JN. ☎ **020/7373-8666.** Fax 020/7835-1194. 38 units, all with bathroom (some with shower only). TV TEL. £45–£90 ($72–$144) single; £90–£120 ($144–$192) twin; £80–£110 ($128–$176) double; £120–£130 ($192–$208) triple. Rates include continental breakfast. AE, CB, DC, MC, V. Tube: Earl's Court.

Staff at the Amber regret that Earl's Court is their nearest Tube stop and quickly add that the hotel is actually in Kensington. You can see why. This rather refined and professionally run establishment, on an elegant 1860s street north of Cromwell Road, bears very little relationship to the riff-raff closer to the station. But guests who get their timing right—certainly when there isn't a big exhibition at Earl's Court and probably in winter—still get an excellent deal. Check out the price range above. The private overseas owners recently funded the redecoration of the rooms and bathrooms on the mezzanine and fourth floors. Ask for a standard double on either, and you'll look out at the charming, private, terrace garden. There's even a top-whack, executive double, one of the few nonsmoking rooms, which has its own terrace. The decor is very pulled together and comfortable, with firm modern beds. The rooms are small to medium-size but have pants press, hair dryer, radio, tea-/coffeemakers, safe, complimentary toiletries, and satellite TV. The reception desk can organize dry cleaning. And the continental breakfast is a free-for-all banquet. You won't be able to read the list of the goodies without mentally running out of breath: boiled eggs, cheese, salami, cucumber, yogurt, croissants, muffins, olive bread . . . and on and on.

4 Notting Hill

✪ **The Gate Hotel.** 6 Portobello Rd., London W11 3DG. ☎ **020/7221-0707.** Fax 020/7221-9128. www.gatehotel.com. E-mail: gatehotel@thegate.globalnet.co.uk. 6 units, 5 with private bathroom (most with shower only). TV TEL. £55 ($88) single with bath and separate WC, £70 ($112) single with bathroom; £80–£90 ($128–$144) double with bathroom. Extra person £14 ($22.40). Rates include continental breakfast. MC, V. Tube: Notting Hill Gate.

Step out of The Gate Hotel on a Saturday morning, and you'll think you're on the set of *The Stepford Wives.* Portobello Road is the hottest tourist spot in London because of its market and antiques shops. It's a fun place to stay, if you don't mind crowds of people marching past as though an alien had control of their brains. The effect is less marked from inside, because double-glazing cuts out the chatter. The Gate's present owner—the rather gruff "just call me Debbie"—has run it for 21 years, but the hotel has been here since 1932. Look for a tiny, late-Georgian house, with a parrot living in the caged-in basement area in front. Sergeant Bilko used to entertain guests over breakfast, but now they eat in their bedrooms. Debbie has refurbished them all. The look is modern and attractive, with white-painted walls, paneled furniture, and blue carpet and linen. The bigger rooms are up narrow stairs lined with old photographs of the market, and each has a small sofa bed for an extra person. If you have a wild evening, remember the walls in the front rooms are supposed to curve as the Gate is on a bend in the road. All have a fridge, ceiling fan, and radio, with hair dryers at the reception desk. And if she likes you, Debbie will do your washing.

Manor Court Hotel. 7 Clanricarde Gardens, London W2 4JJ. ☎ **020/7792-3361.** Fax 020/7229-2875. 20 units, 16 with bathroom (shower only). TV TEL. £35 ($56) single without bathroom, £40–£50 ($64–$80) single with bathroom; £45–£60 ($72–$96) double/twin with bathroom; £55–£70 ($88–$112) triple with bathroom; £80 ($128) family room with bathroom. Rates include continental breakfast. Discount of 10% for 1-wk. stays. AE, DC, JCB, MC, V. Tube: Notting Hill Gate.

Manor Court is in a quiet cul-de-sac off Notting Hill Gate just where it turns into Bayswater Road. The gated enclave of swanky mansions at the edge of Kensington Gardens, known as Embassy Row, is just on the other side. The neighborhood gentrification is only just reaching Clanricarde Gardens and most of the Victorian stucco-fronted houses need repainting. By the time you get here, Manor Court will have put in new windows, which will do a lot to tidy up its front. It's a great deal on the fringes of an area where property prices are soaring—Portobello Road is only a 10-minute walk away. Manor Court is popular with families on holiday from the Continent. The decor is basic, with pale-yellow walls and blonde-wood furniture. And the bathrooms are clean, though some of the tiling shows signs of patching. Most of the rooms are a fair size for London, and there are mouth-watering original features. Check out the deep molding in the huge second-floor double room, which has access to the balcony through floor-to-ceiling windows. The smallest double has a strange reverse bathroom shape cut out of it, but there is a lovely, vaulted, window embrasure. My choice would be one of the triples, which would frankly be a squash at full capacity. They're a bargain for two people at the price, and you'll get a tub-shower, too. There are hair dryers at the reception desk.

Pembridge Gardens Halls, Imperial College. 28–32 Pembridge Gardens, London W2 4DX. ☎ **020/7594-9407.** Fax 020/7594-9504. www.ad.ic.ac.uk. E-mail: reservations@ic.ac.uk. 113 units, 58 with bathroom (shower only). £35 ($56) single without bathroom, £45 ($72) single with bathroom; £55 ($88) twin without bathroom, £65 ($104) twin with bathroom. Rates include continental breakfast. Open summer vacation. EC, MC, V. Tube: Notting Hill Gate. No children under 10.

The gracious houses on this quiet street look like sculpted ice cream and sell for multimillions. That may be why Imperial College charges the same rates here as at its main student hall, Prince's Gardens, even though this is much more Spartan. The location is fantastic, between Portobello Market and Kensington Gardens. And there are few local budget rivals—Manor Court Hotel is a bit cheaper, as is Portobello Gold, but only if you stay 7 nights. Pembridge Gardens has squeaky beds and big, functional, private bathrooms, which say "toilet" on the door in case you don't recognize them. There are signs everywhere, most more helpful since the three knocked-together houses are a real maze. The carpet in the hallways is new. And there are two kitchen-diners, equipped with microwaves, freezers, fridges, toasters, and kettles. Guests can brew up a cup of tea or coffee from the beverage pack in their room, or make a light snack as long as they bring their own utensils. The TV room is worth a visit, if only to see the moldings and pediment above the door. The hall also has a launderette, cold-drinks machines, video games, and a pool table. And guests here can use all the facilities at the main campus, the sports center and so on, which is three Tube stops away at South Kensington.

InterneSt @ Portobello Gold. 97 Portobello Rd., London W11 2QB. ☎ **020/7460-4910.** Fax 020/7460-4911. www.portobellogold.com. E-mail: chris@portobellogold.com. 5 units, 3 with bathroom (shower only). TV TEL. £45–£50 ($72–$80) single without bathroom, £60–£65 ($96–$104) single with bathroom; £52–£57 ($83.20–$91.20) double without bathroom, £70–£75 ($112–$120) double with bathroom. Rates include continental breakfast. Lower price Sun–Thurs. Discount for 1-wk. stays. MC V. Tube: Notting Hill Gate.

Whatever you do, do not try to make it to InterneSt until at least 6pm on a Saturday (in time for happy hour, in fact). The road closes during the day for Portobello Market, and there's zero chance of forcing intercontinental luggage—you know what I mean—through the solid crowds, let alone past the antique stalls that proliferate at the front of the building. In the old Princess Alexandra pub, Portobello Gold is a mini-life-support pod, catering to every need. The seafood and vegetarian restaurant is a local institution: Two courses could cost you as little as £13 ($20.80). The bar menu is almost as long, and dishes rarely top £7 ($11.20). And Web time is £1.50 ($2.40) per ½ hour, with free coffee, at the second-floor buzzbar. The e-revolution has staged a serious coup here, and that's what makes InterneSt special—apart from being cheap for London and very cheap for this popular area. Guests pay a minimal £5 ($8) set-up charge to have a computer in their room, then surf all they want for free. They're nice rooms, too: Small, simple, but freshly decorated. Portobello Road is quiet during the week, and the double-glazing should cut out the dawn chorus of stalls setting up on Saturday. If you like to wallow under the covers, ask for the 7-foot-long Captain's bed. For a very special treat (£20/$32 a head), make like a movie star, and tour London in Portobello Gold's 1952 Buick convertible—the chauffeur's uniform matches the green leather upholstery!

5 Paddington & Bayswater

Ashley Hotel. 15–17 Norfolk Sq., London W2 1RU. ☎ **020/7723-3375.** Fax 020/7723-0173. E-mail: ASHHOT@btinternet.com. 51 units, 40 with bathroom (shower only). TV TEL. £35.50 ($56.80) single without bathroom, £47 ($75.20) single with bathroom; £73 ($116.80) double/twin with bathroom; £94.50 ($151.20) triple with bathroom; £99 ($158.40) family room. Rates include full English breakfast. Discount available for children sharing parents' room. CB, DISC, MC, V. Tube: Paddington.

The Davies brothers started this place in 1967 when many British still didn't holiday abroad. They called it Tregaron to appeal to the Cornish and Welsh who arrived by train at Paddington. By 1975, they had bought two adjoining B&Bs and kept the names Oasis and Ashley so as not to scare off the regulars. The brothers only simplified matters in 1999, but this is an old-fashioned place and proud of it. There's an honesty box next to the Butler's Tea Shop, the hot-and-cold-drinks machine in the cozy lounge. Most guests still are British, and the young Matthew Davies, who has just taken over, is as choosy as his father and uncle about who he lets in—you won't find many construction workers here, despite all the local redevelopment. The bedrooms are neat, comfortable, and traditional, without trying for a cutesy English style, and Matthew is gradually redecorating them all. Tea-/coffeemakers and radios are standard, with hair dryers at the reception desk. The washbasins are in the rooms, because the bathrooms are tiny. You don't have to worry about the noise of staying in a room on the front, six of which have balconies. Norfolk Square, with its pretty public garden, is a rare oasis of calm in the Paddington bustle. At the back, ask to be above the second floor to avoid looking out on a wall. Kids will enjoy the unusual bunks in the basement family room, a single above a double.

Dolphin Hotel. 34 Norfolk Sq., London W2 1RP. ☎ **020/7402-4943.** Fax 020/7723-8184. www.dolphinhotel.co.uk. E-mail: info@dolphinhotel.co.uk. 32 units, 16 with bathroom (most with shower). TV TEL. £42 ($67.20) single without bathroom, £53 ($84.80) single with bathroom; £55 ($88) double/twin without bathroom, £70 ($112) double/twin with bathroom; £69 ($110.40) triple without bathroom, £80 ($128) triple with bathroom; £80 ($128) quad without bathroom, £94 ($150.40) quad with bathroom. Rates include continental breakfast (£2.50/$4 for full English). AE, DC, JCB, MC, V. Tube: Paddington.

Hotels in Marylebone, Paddington, Bayswater & Notting Hill

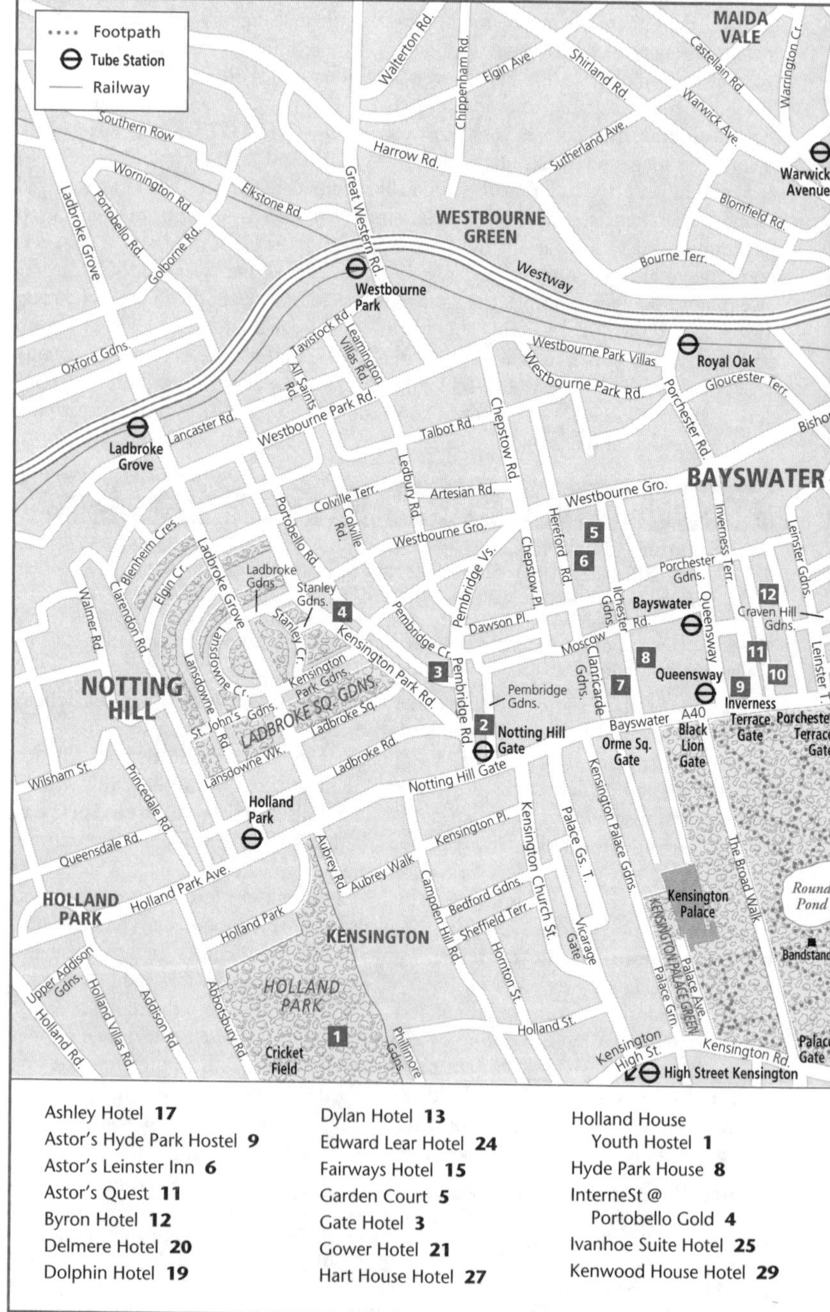

Ashley Hotel **17**
Astor's Hyde Park Hostel **9**
Astor's Leinster Inn **6**
Astor's Quest **11**
Byron Hotel **12**
Delmere Hotel **20**
Dolphin Hotel **19**
Dylan Hotel **13**
Edward Lear Hotel **24**
Fairways Hotel **15**
Garden Court **5**
Gate Hotel **3**
Gower Hotel **21**
Hart House Hotel **27**
Holland House Youth Hostel **1**
Hyde Park House **8**
InterneSt @ Portobello Gold **4**
Ivanhoe Suite Hotel **25**
Kenwood House Hotel **29**

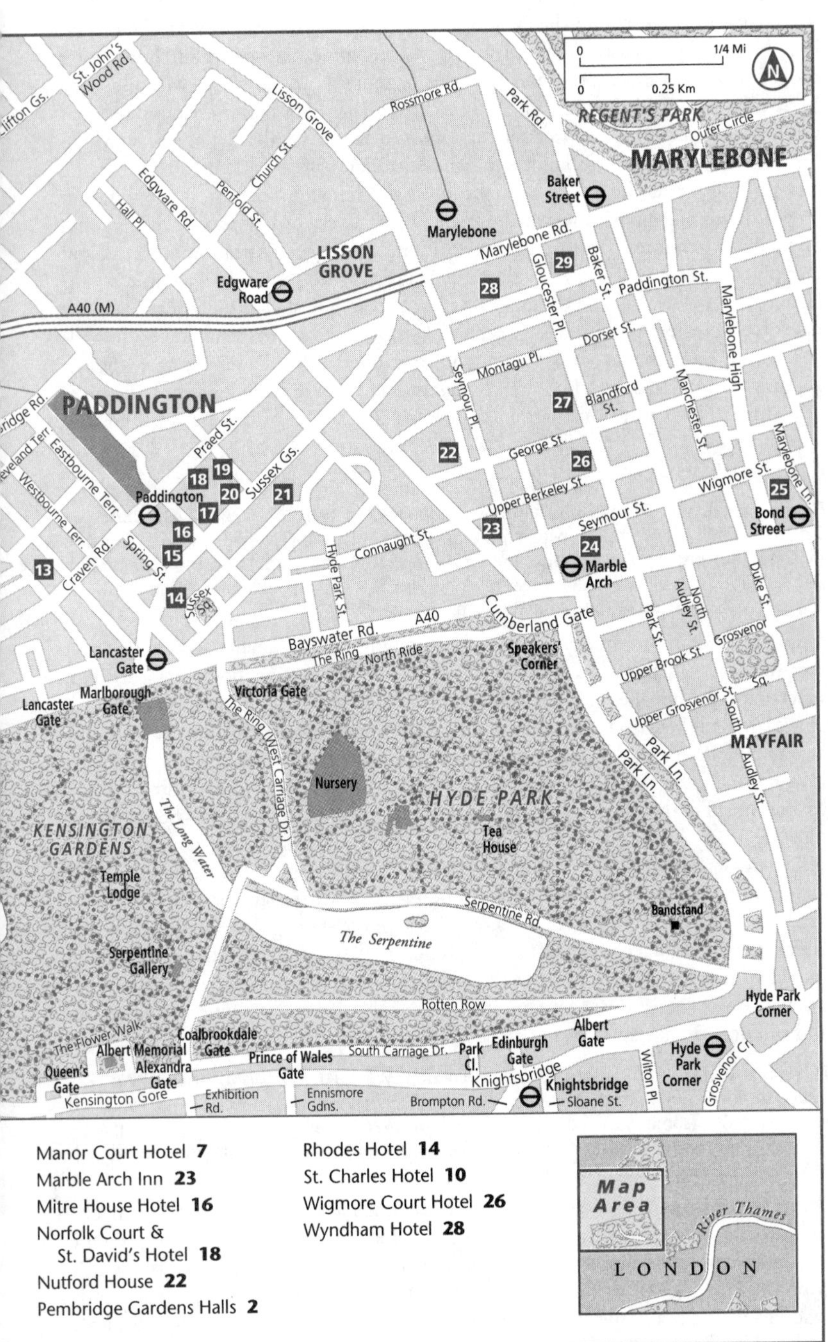

REGENT'S PARK
Outer Circle
MARYLEBONE
LISSON GROVE
PADDINGTON
MAYFAIR
HYDE PARK
KENSINGTON GARDENS
St. John's Wood Rd.
Lisson Grove
Rossmore Rd.
Park Rd.
Church St.
Penfold St.
Edgware Rd.
Hall Pl.
Marylebone Rd.
Gloucester Pl.
Baker St.
Paddington St.
Marylebone High
Dorset St.
Montagu Pl.
Seymour Pl.
Blandford St.
Manchester St.
George St.
Marylebone Ln.
Wigmore St.
Upper Berkeley St.
Seymour St.
Connaught St.
Hyde Park St.
Praed St.
Sussex Gs.
Eastbourne Terr.
Westbourne Terr.
Craven Rd.
Spring St.
Sussex Sq.
Bayswater Rd.
A40
A40 (M)
Cumberland Gate
Park St.
North Audley St.
Duke St.
Grosvenor Sq.
Upper Brook St.
Upper Grosvenor St.
South Audley St.
Park Ln.
The Ring
North Ride
The Ring (West Carriage Dr.)
The Long Water
Serpentine Rd.
The Serpentine
Rotten Row
South Carriage Dr.
The Flower Walk
Kensington Gore
Exhibition Rd.
Ennismore Gdns.
Brompton Rd.
Knightsbridge
Sloane St.
Wilton Pl.
Grosvenor Cr.
Baker Street
Marylebone
Edgware Road
Paddington
Lancaster Gate
Marble Arch
Bond Street
Knightsbridge
Hyde Park Corner
Speakers' Corner
Victoria Gate
Marlborough Gate
Lancaster Gate
Nursery
Tea House
Bandstand
Temple Lodge
Serpentine Gallery
Albert Memorial
Coalbrookdale Gate
Alexandra Gate
Queen's Gate
Prince of Wales Gate
Park Cl.
Edinburgh Gate
Albert Gate
0 1/4 Mi
0 0.25 Km
N
Map Area
River Thames
LONDON
Manor Court Hotel 7
Marble Arch Inn 23
Mitre House Hotel 16
Norfolk Court & St. David's Hotel 18
Nutford House 22
Pembridge Gardens Halls 2
Rhodes Hotel 14
St. Charles Hotel 10
Wigmore Court Hotel 26
Wyndham Hotel 28

Don't let the dread phrase "continental breakfast" turn you away from the Dolphin. It simply doesn't do justice to the extravaganza Mr. Moros lays on every morning. This is no bit of old dry toast, but a buffet with cheese, fairy cakes, yogurt and honey, eggs cooked any way, and more—and as many helpings as you can eat. Mr. and Mrs. Moros have run the Dolphin for 21 years. It's a charming place, certainly the best value in Norfolk Square and better than most in Sussex Gardens. The bedrooms do vary in size because every building on the Victorian square is designated as having architectural merit. You'll find wrought-iron balconies and some lovely moldings; in one of the second-floor rooms at the front, there's a very ornate panel, which would originally have framed a mirror. All the bedrooms are very comfortably decorated, and recently, too. The rooms have a table and chairs to write your postcards at, tea-/coffeemakers, satellite TV, and a fridge—the last two are unusual at the price. There are hair dryers at the reception desk. Secretarial services and baby-sitting are both available for an extra charge. And the Dolphin also offers limited room service, though Paddington is packed with pubs and restaurants and they're getting nicer all the time.

If there's no room at this particular inn, ask about their place next door: **Shakespeare Hotel,** 22–28 Norfolk Sq. (☎ **020/7402-4646;** fax 020/7723-7233; www.shakespearehotel.co.uk).

Dylan Hotel. 14 Devonshire Terrace, London W2 3DW. ☎ **020/7723-3280.** Fax 020/7402-2443. 18 units, 11 with bathroom (some with shower only). TV TEL. £35–£48 ($56–$76.80) single without bathroom; £55–£58 ($88–$92.80) double without bathroom, £58–£72 ($92.80–$115.20) double with bathroom. Rates include full English breakfast. AE, CB, MC, V. Tube: Paddington, Lancaster Gate.

Huge care and pots of money have clearly gone into this B&B, which makes this next remark rather uncharitable. The Dylan looks like a Victorian bordello. Dark red, mock-damask wallpaper lines the hallways below the dado rail, with red and gold flock above. And the stair-rods are painted gold. The style fits the date of the house but is so dramatic in one that is only medium size. And Mr. Felfeli, who has run the Dylan for 11 years, seems such a shy, retiring man. It took him 2 years to renovate from top to bottom. The bedrooms are bright and more restrained, but still carefully put together. Lampshades tone in with the printed wallpaper, and the carpet and pine furniture are new. Every room has an electric fan in summer and tea-/coffeemakers, and six of them also have a fridge. No bathroom worries here, either: They really do sparkle. Try to avoid the top of the house because the stairs go on forever, especially after eggs and bacon. The breakfast room is like a 1950s tea shop, with a collection of mugs and jugs hanging from the ceiling. All in all, the Dylan is a fantastic value. One of the cheaper B&Bs in Paddington, it's off the main drag facing a quiet public square and still only 5 minutes from the Tube station.

Fairways Hotel. 186 Sussex Gardens, London W2 1TU. ☎ **020/7723-4871.** Fax 020/7723-4871. www.fairways-hotel.co.uk. E-mail: info@fairways-hotel.co.uk. 17 units, 10 with bathroom (some with shower only). TV. £48 ($76.80) single without bathroom; £68 ($108.80) twin without bathroom; £75 ($120) double with bathroom. Rates include full English breakfast. MC, V. Tube: Paddington.

Fairways is a large, white, late-Georgian house, built in the style of John Nash. The inside is charming. Jenny Adams, who runs the B&B with her husband Steve, is quite a magpie, hence the collection of thimbles and Spode china in the breakfast room. The strong personal touch throughout Fairways—the halls and tiny lounge are recently redone—makes it a home away from home. There's a lovely first-floor double at the back, which has the biggest closet in London—great for style queens on tour. Two boudoir chairs flank a little lace-covered table, decorated with a vase of flowers. The fluffy pillows and quilt look like someone has been at them with a bicycle pump. And the bathroom has posh brass fittings. The basic twin is a good deal. The decor is a bit more mix 'n' match, but it's a nice-size room and only shares the bathroom with a single. Fairways may not throw as many extras as other local B&Bs, just a TV and hair dryer in each room, but there are compensations. As well as the friendly atmosphere, guests renting a car to travel out of London can park it for free at the front. The Mitre Hotel next door is the only other place to offer that. It's quite some compensation in a city where securing a private garage can cost six figures.

✪ **Garden Court.** 30–31 Kensington Gardens Sq., London W2 4BG. ☎ **020/7229-2553.** Fax 020/7727-2749. www.gardencourthotel.co.uk. E-mail: info@gardencourthotel.co.uk. 32 units, 16 with bathroom (some with shower only). TV TEL. £34 ($54.40) single without bathroom, £50 ($80) single with bathroom; £54 ($86.40) double/twin without bathroom, £65 ($104) twin with bathroom (no WC), £82 ($131.20) double/twin with bathroom; £72 ($115.20) triple without bathroom, £90 ($144) triple with bathroom; £80 ($128) family room without bathroom, £96 ($153.60) family room with bathroom. All rates include full English breakfast. MC, V. Tube: Bayswater, Queensway.

Edward Connolly's grandfather opened Garden Court almost 50 years ago. I fell for it from the moment I saw the jar of Everton mints at the reception desk. It's a good value for London, particularly the rooms without bathrooms (just over two share each public one), but other Bayswater B&Bs are cheaper. What you won't find elsewhere is such out-and-out appeal. The Victorian architect used Kensington Gardens Square to show off his full bag of tricks. The windows are a different shape on each floor, with different decorative moldings. Inside, Garden Court isn't luxxy—it's more like a much-loved home. The sitting room behind reception makes the grandest luggage store I've ever seen, with its ancestral portraits and silk orchids. The main lounge has some nice old furniture, more ancestors, fat novels to borrow, and free hot drinks. Sporting prints, a huge bowl of silk red roses, and a plaster bust wearing somebody's discarded tie decorate the hallway. There are only a few naff touches, like the modern paneling along the upper corridors. All the rooms are different: One has pretty yellow wallpaper and white painted furniture, another broad blue stripes that look hand-painted but aren't. Hair dryers are standard, and so is the friendly welcome. Second-floor, front bedrooms lead out onto balconies. Otherwise, the hotel has a terrace and access to the public gardens.

Gower Hotel. 129 Sussex Gardens, London W2 2RX. ☎ **020/7262-2262.** Fax 020/7626-2006. www.stavrouhotels.co.uk. E-mail: gower@stavrouhotels.co.uk. 21 units, 19 with bathroom (shower only). TV TEL. £34 ($54.40) single without bathroom, £44 ($70.40) single with bathroom; £48 ($76.80) double without bathroom, £66 ($105.60) double with bathroom. Rates include full English breakfast. MC, V. Tube: Paddington.

Make sure to tell Mario Stavrou that I sent you to his hotel because these fabulous rates—the best in Paddington—are only for Frommer's readers. Mario knows what discerning travelers want. Carpets, curtains, dressing tables, tea-/coffeemakers, pictures, quilts, and quilt covers—he's replaced them all over the past 3 years, as well as redoing the lounge and breakfast room. The new look is pulled-together and very comfortable. Elegant dark blue curtains match the big-check bedspreads and pale stripy wallpaper. The squishy leatherette headboards are a bit of an Abba-era throwback, but they seem to fit in and don't conceal any nasties, as fabric-covered ones might. Satellite TV is free. And there are new showers in all the bathrooms. The rooms are a good size, and in almost every one, you get more than you bargain for, or you can bargain with Mario for less. A twin or double room actually has a double bed and a single, and you can take it as a cut-price triple. Singles have a narrow double bed, but couples can take them at a discount, if they don't mind being a bit cramped. The only bedrooms without a bathroom are two doubles right under the eaves of the house. They're not a bad size either, despite the sloping ceilings, and a fantastic value if you can stand the climb. And you're above the heavy traffic noise, the big downside to balconied Sussex Gardens.

Hyde Park House. 48 St. Petersburgh Place, London W2 4LD. ☎ **020/7229-1687.** 15 units, 1 with bathroom (shower only). TV TEL. £28 ($44.80) single without bathroom; £42 ($67.20) twin without bathroom; £55 ($88) double with bathroom; £60 ($96) triple. Rates include continental breakfast. Discounts available off-season. No credit cards. Tube: Bayswater, Queensway.

This is a very simple B&B in a very toney part of town. Crown Prince Pavlos of Greece got married at the Greek Orthodox Cathedral of Saint Sophia on the opposite corner. Anyone staying at Hyde Park House in April 1999 would have seen a parade of European royals, including Prince William, arrive for the christening of the couple's first child. St. Petersburgh Place is a pretty row of terrace houses, with pocket-handkerchief gardens in front. Neon is a no-no, so look for the B&B's discreet black and gold sign. The bedroom decor is plain, the furniture mix 'n' match, and the sinks often hidden away in a cupboard. But John and Jeanette Toygar have just repainted and put in new carpets and curtains. They've also redecorated the shower units. And you do get good storage space, particularly in the second-floor twin, which has three jumbo floor-to-ceiling closets. Some of the rooms are small: The second-floor triple should really lose a bed. Hyde Park House doesn't have a breakfast room, so the Toygars deliver a small polystyrene tray with croissant, jams, and cheeses to your room—a nice thought, but that won't fuel a serious tourist for long. Luckily there's a fridge in each room to stock with top-up goodies (hair dryers are standard, too). Hyde Park House is more than reasonably priced, a short walk from Queensway and Portobello Road, and blissfully quiet.

Mitre House Hotel. 178–184 Sussex Gardens, London W2 1TU. ☎ **020/7723-8040.** Fax 020/7402-0990. www.mitrehousehotel.com. E-mail: reservations@mitrehousehotel.com. 70 rooms, all with bathroom (some with shower only). TV TEL. £65 ($104) single; £75 ($120) double/twin; £85 ($136) triple; £95 ($152) family room; £110 ($176) junior suite; £115 ($184) family suite. Rates include full English breakfast. AE, DC, EC, JCB, MC, V. Tube: Paddington.

The row of shiny 4×4s on the Mitre House forecourt should set off the budget-buster warning bell. Instead, it's a sign of how brilliantly the Chris brothers cater to families. There are rooms with a double bed and two singles. Family suites have a double with a private bathroom and a second room with two singles—fantastic if you're traveling with teenage mutants. Mitre House stretches across four late-Georgian houses on a corner, and superior family suites face quiet, leafy Talbot Square. These have a double and a single in one room, and a double bed in the other, with the toilet and tub-shower off a little private corridor. All the rooms are above average size for London and those at the back are quieter, too, though the view north across back alleys to Paddington isn't too inspiring. The wicker chairs and jagged-patterned fabrics are reminiscent of the geometric safari look so popular in the 1980s. Radios are standard. Hair dryers and tea-/coffeemakers are available at the reception desk. Junior suites make a good splurge choice, with lots of extra amenities and a Jacuzzi in the bathroom. Mitre House may not be the cheapest deal around, but it's a good value. As well as the big lounge and bar, you can get baby-sitting, dry cleaning and laundry service, safe-deposit boxes, and travel and tour advice. There is also an elevator.

Norfolk Court & St. David's Hotel. 14–20 Norfolk Sq., London W2 1RS. ☎ **020/7723-4963.** Fax 020/7402-9061. www.cityscan.co.uk/stdavidshotel. 69 units, 45 with bathroom (most with shower only). TV TEL. £44 ($70.40) single without bathroom, £55 ($88) single with bathroom; £64 ($102.40) double without bathroom, £74 ($118.40) double with bathroom; £95–£105 ($152–$168) family room. All rates include full English breakfast. AE, DC, MC, V. Tube: Paddington.

By January 2001, George and Foulla Neokleos will have finished the mammoth job of refurbishing all four of their buildings. The new look is unusual but appealing, with vanilla-painted walls and yellow picking out the moldings and original fireplaces. I'm not sure the latter is entirely a good idea. Norfolk Court & St. David's is a treasure trove of architectural details. One room even has a domed ceiling, and there's a lovely, stained-glass window on the stairs of no. 20. These Victorian houses have balconies across the front from which guests on the second floor can admire the pretty communal gardens. In the basement, there's a truly enormous and a very good value family room, that can fit five people and has a proper built-in shower. With the new units just put in at no. 14, two thirds of the rooms have private showers, all sparkling clean drop-in units that vary in size depending on what the bedroom can cope with. Satellite TV is standard, and hair dryers and tea-/coffeemakers are available at the reception desk. And Mr. Neokleos has been the breakfast king of Paddington for 26 years. Full English really does mean full, with mushrooms, tomatoes, and baked beans on top of all the rest.

✪ **Rhodes Hotel.** 195 Sussex Gardens, London W2 2RJ. ☎ **020/7262-0537.** Fax 020/7723-4054. www.rhodeshotel.co.uk. E-mail: chris@rhodeshotel.co.uk. 18 units, all with bathroom (most with shower only). A/C TV TEL. £55–£60 ($88–$96) single; £70–£80 ($112–$128) double/twin; £70–£95 ($112–$152) triple; £110–£125 ($176–$200) quad. Discount available for weekday and 3-day stays. Rates include continental breakfast. MC, V. Tube: Paddington.

When a tourist-board inspector said that the stairs and hallways here were a little "Spartan," Chris Crias was mortally offended. Suddenly, his plan to put in some new bathrooms, and spruce the place up in 1999, spiraled into an £80,000 ($128,000) decorating extravaganza. He and his wife have run the Rhodes for more than 20 years, and it always did have a touch of the theatrical—witness the velvet-curtained lounge with its huge murals of Greek amphora. But now the whole place is a gallery of paint effects. The walls are lacquered red below the dado rail on the stairs, and angels gaze down from the cloudy ceiling halfway up to the second floor. No other B&B can beat it for entertainment value. Mr. Crias is very proud of his firm new mattresses, too, as well as the recently installed air-conditioning and the new carpet in all the rooms. The bedroom decor is actually quite simple, and number 220 is my favorite. Halfway up the stairs, it has its own little private roof terrace, complete with table and chairs. The bunks in the family room are the poshest I've ever seen, dark wood and 3 feet wide. Mr. Crias quotes such a wide price range for each room to cater for people who want more space—two guests who take a triple, for example. Fridges, tea-/coffeemakers, and hair dryers are standard.

St. Charles Hotel. 66 Queensborough Terrace, London W2 3SH. ☎ **020/7221-0022.** Fax 020/7792-8978. www.stcharleshotel.fsbusiness.co.uk. E-mail: enquiries@stcharleshotel.fsbusiness.co.uk. 15 units, 11 with bathroom (most with shower only). £37–£45 ($59.20–$72) single without bathroom; £60–£69 ($96–$110.40) double/twin with bathroom. Rates include full English breakfast. Higher rates apply to 1-night stays. MC, V. Tube: Queensway, Bayswater. No children under 10.

The St. Charles is an excellent value. The bedrooms are big. The new shower rooms are big. And the prices are still pretty low, despite post-refurbishment rises. Queensborough Terrace must have been very grand when it was built in 1734. The half-stuccoed houses have porches over the front door and balconies along the second floor. You can spot the St. Charles by its old-fashioned hanging sign and green railings.

Sadly, most of the windows are not the Georgian originals, but that's because they're all double-glazed. But the inside will keep even demanding heritage-spotters happy. Ornate wrought-iron banisters curve away out of a huge entrance hall. There are marvelous moldings and fireplaces, too. And the lounge is paneled like a gentleman's club. Upstairs, the bedrooms are plain but bright, and Mrs. Wildridge, who has run the B&B for 18 years, recently put in a lot of really good-quality showers. Four rooms do still have their clean but shabby (except one just tidied up) units stuck bizarrely in a corner of the room. If you don't mind the lack of privacy, this knocks some pounds off the price. The amenities are minimal, of course, and there's no lift—it's a hard climb if you're on the top floor. But Hyde Park is at the end of the street, and you're only a 5-minute walk from good transport, cheap eats, and useful shops in Queensway.

SUPER-CHEAP SLEEPS

Astor's Hyde Park Hostel. 2–6 Inverness Terrace, London W2 3HY. ☎ **020/7229-5101.** Fax 020/7229-3170. www.scoot.co.uk/astorhostels/. E-mail: AstorHostels@msn.com. 200 units. £14–£16 ($22.40–$25.60) per person in a dorm. Rates include bed linen and continentall breakfast. Discount available for 1-wk. stays off-season. EC, MC, V. Tube: Queensway, Bayswater. 18–35 age restriction.

Astor's took over the former Methodist student hostel in 1998. It immediately called in an army of heavies to do over the three gracious Georgian buildings, chock-a-block with stunning original moldings. This isn't just another cheap sleep, but the company's London flagship. Taking advantage of the existing commercial kitchen, and a new late liquor license (until 2am), it has opened a funky bar and canteen-style eatery where the crazy murals, an Astor's hallmark, are now painted on back-lit removable boards. Enclosing the basement-level outdoor area with glass has created a games room, with a big space behind where the hostel shows movies every night. There's a laundry room, Internet facilities, and a guests' kitchen. The five- to eight-bunk dorms have had a lick of paint and new carpet. And in honor of the poshification, the upper age limit has risen to 35, instead of 30 as it is at Astor's four other hostels. Two of these are also in Queensway: **Leinster Inn,** 7–12 Leinster Sq., London, W2 4PR (☎ **020/7229-9641;** fax 020/7221-5255) famed for its weekend club nights, and the smaller, more laid-back **Quest,** 45 Queensborough Terrace, London, W2 8SY (☎ **020/7229-7782;** fax 020/7727-8106).

WORTH A SPLURGE

The Byron Hotel. 36–38 Queensborough Terrace, London W2 3SH. ☎ **020/7243-0987.** Fax 020/7792-1957. www.capricornhotels.co.uk. E-mail: byron@capricornhotels.co.uk. 45 units, all with bathroom (some with shower only). A/C TV TEL. £50–£75 ($80–$120) single; £96 ($153.60) double/twin; £120 ($192) triple; from £145 ($232) family room. Rates include full English breakfast. Discount of 10% for 4-night stays. AE, DC, JCB, MC, V. Tube: Bayswater, Queensway.

The blue plaque commemorating the Victorian composer, Sir William Sterndale Bennett, and the international flags above the entrance are a pretty good clue as to what you'll find inside The Byron Hotel. Like the Delmere in Paddington, it combines business-friendly service with an English theme, and at almost the same price. The decor is upper-crust country house, with a contemporary twist. There are sporting prints everywhere, and the bedrooms are all named after different stately homes. However, the inside of these old stucco-fronted houses has been reorganized, so don't expect palatial space. If that's a must, save a third off the bill and go up the road to St. Charles Hotel. The amenities at the Byron are excellent, though: air-conditioning, tea-/coffeemakers, hair dryers, radios, pants press, and modem access. The bathrooms are simple, but good-size and sparkling clean. The tub-showers have neither glass screens nor curtains. Instead, the Byron trusts its guests not to splash too much. Decorators get permanent jobs here, and everything is done up at least once every 3 years. They recently renovated the cozy lounge, with its well-stocked bar and supply of newspapers after breakfast. The Byron has a tour and car-rental desk, and offers dry cleaning and limited room service (5 to 11pm).

Delmere Hotel. 130 Sussex Gardens, London W2 1UB. ☎ **020/7706-3344.** Fax 020/7262-1863. www.delmerehotels.com. E-mail: Delmerehotel@compuserve.com. 38 units, all with bathroom (most with shower only). TV TEL. £78 ($124.80) single; £98 ($156.80) double/twin; £113 ($180.80) crown room; £115 ($184) triple. Rates include continental breakfast. Discount available. AE, DC, EC, JCB, MC, V. Tube: Paddington.

If there's one hotel Web site to keep an eye on, it's the Delmere's. When I looked, there was a fantastic promotion cutting high-summer rates by 15%, making it comparable to the local B&Bs. The Delmere calls itself a "boutique town-house hotel" (pretentious or what!), hence the gold nameplates and charming window boxes along the top of the late-Georgian porch, and the real-flame fire in the lounge. It caters to a mix of business and pleasure travelers. The rooms have modem outlets, as well as tea-/coffeemakers, hair dryers, radios, safes, and satellite TV. They are all recently refurbished and very comfortable, but the decor is a bit too safe for real elegance—except the crown room, of course, which is up under the eaves and has a Jacuzzi in the bathroom. The canopied bed, frilled tablecloth, and ruched blind make this one look like a rich widow's cabin on a cruise liner. Check out the bedrooms in the annex, which feel like having your own place. The windows look onto a small courtyard, though, so you may be able to hear the music from the hotel's jazz bar. And avoid the lower floor, which is a real hole in the ground. The La Perla restaurant does three-course meals for around £14 ($19.20) but bizarrely takes a break on Sundays, bank holidays, over Christmas, and for 3 weeks in the summer. Reception will provide limited room service (6 to 10pm), dry cleaning and laundry services, and newspaper delivery.

6 Marylebone

Like many student dorms, **Nutford House** on quiet Brown Street (☎ **020/7685-5000;** fax 020/7258-1781; www.lon.ac.uk/accomm/; e-mail: bursar.nutfurd@nutford.lon.ac.uk), opens to visitors during the summer and Easter vacations. The redbrick Edwardian building, just north of Marble Arch, used to be a home for distressed gentlewomen, and it has a beautiful garden. Yet it's half the price of anywhere else in the neighborhood: from £22 ($35.20) for a comfortable single room, to £43 ($68.80) for a twin, including full English breakfast (full-board also available). There's a 10% discount for 1-month stays; minimum 2 nights. No credit cards yet.

Edward Lear Hotel. 28–30 Seymour St., London W1H 5WD. ☎ **020/7402-5401.** Fax 020/7706-3766. www.edlear.com. E-mail: edwardlear@aol.com. 31 units, 4 with bathroom (1 with shower only). TV TEL. £48 ($76.80) single without bathroom, £58–£74.50 ($92.80–$119.20) single with bathroom; £67.50 ($108) double/twin without bathroom, £81–£92 ($129.60–$147.20) double/twin with bathroom; £81 ($129.60) triple without bathroom, £91–£102.50 ($145.60–$164) triple with bathroom. Rates include full English breakfast. Special rates for children. Children under 13 stay in parents' room at a discount during the week, and for free Sat–Sun; children under 2 stay free in parents' room. Discount of 10% for 1-wk. stays (not July–Aug) and for Internet bookings. MC, V. Tube: Marble Arch.

The Edward Lear has always been good value, and it will get even better—the only question is when. Previous reviews talked about the pretty Georgian houses with the most luxuriant window boxes in London; the excellent location, just behind Marble Arch; the warm professional welcome; and the charming lounge, hung with zoological drawings of parrots by artist and poet Edward Lear, who once lived here. Then came the "but . . . ," because the standards upstairs—up some very narrow-stepped stairs, in fact—just don't match up to the rest. The bedrooms aren't a bad size and have a faded charm, but the decor and bathrooms are scruffy and dated. But long-time owner Peter Evans has plans for a 2-year renovation program, as soon as the lease and hassles with changing old buildings are sorted out. In the meantime, this is still a great place to stay. Try for room 18, a double with its bathroom down a little flight of stairs. It looks over a mews at the back, instead of busy Seymour Street—there's no double-glazing at the Edward Lear. Basic rooms share a bathroom with only three other people. All have satellite TV, tea-/coffeemakers, hair dryers, and radios. And the Edward Lear has a price promise: If you find better value this close to Oxford Street, it'll refund you double the difference.

✪ **Ivanhoe Suite Hotel.** 1 St. Christopher's Place, Barrett St. Piazza, London W1M 5HB. ☎ **020/7935-1047.** Fax 020/7224-0563. www.hotels-centrallondon.co.uk. 7 suites, all with bathroom (some with shower only). TV TEL. £71 ($113.60) single; £85 ($136) double; £92 ($147.20) triple. Rates include continental breakfast. AE, DC, MC, V. Tube: Bond St.

The Ivanhoe Suite Hotel is a gem, but you don't have to be Daddy Warbucks to pay for it. St. Christopher's Place is a pretty piazza, just off Oxford Street, filled with designer boutiques and restaurants with tables outside. Its discreet entrance is next door to Sofra, the restaurant below the B&B—I was there at lunchtime and couldn't hear anything from downstairs, and diners have to move inside at 11pm. Each room has its own front-door bell, and guests can check on callers via the closed-circuit TV camera linked to their television. The Ivanhoe doesn't actually offer suites, but the rooms are big enough for a table and chairs, where you eat breakfast brought up to you in the morning. The fridge is stocked with mineral water and fruit when you arrive, and the rooms have a juice squeezer, tea-/coffeemakers, hair dryer, and pants press. CNN is standard. Movie channels cost a bit extra, or you can borrow a video from the reception desk. The rooms are attractive, and recently redecorated, with their bathrooms off a small lobby as you walk in. Mrs. Sofer, the proprietor for 29 years, aims to give people everything they want, before they know they want it. So there's limited room service, newspapers, laundry service, baby-sitting, and secretarial help. Some rooms face a narrow street, but she will try to arrange a view over the piazza fountain, if you ask.

Kenwood House Hotel. 114 Gloucester Place, London W1H 3DB. ☎ **020/7935-3473.** Fax 020/7224-0582. www.hotelconnectionsuk.com. E-mail: kenwoodhouse@yahoo.co.uk. 16 units, 11 with bathroom (most with shower only). TV. £38 ($60.80) single without bathroom, £48 ($76.80) single with bathroom; £50 ($80) twin without bathroom, £68 ($108.80) double/twin with bathroom; £80 ($128) triple with bathroom; £88 ($140.80) family room with bathroom. Rates include full English breakfast. Discounts for long stays and off-season. AE, CB, DC, MC, V. Tube: Baker St.

Gloucester Terrace has some of the biggest rooms in London. Madame Tussaud's is close to the northern end, while Oxford Street is due south. At over £10 ($16) a night cheaper than its neighbors, Kenwood House is a great value as long as these pluses (and the heartiest welcome in town) mean more to you than fancy decor. The hallway is old-fashioned mauve. Elsewhere, there are patches of crumbling plaster. And the bedrooms are comfortable but simple. Families of four do get masses of space in what used to be the master bedroom; its view to the back isn't up to much, but it's quiet. The traffic roar on Gloucester Place is relentless, and double-glazing still lets in a slight hum. The bathrooms are tiled and mostly large, and the showers clean despite some cracked grouting. They also have hair dryers. Ex-flight attendant Arline Woutersz and her airline pilot husband have been running the place for 24 years. These days, they'll even let you pay in any major currency. They'll also lend kettles, arrange baby-sitting, or help with tours.

Marble Arch Inn. 49–50 Upper Berkeley St., London W1H 7PN. ☎ **020/7723-7888.** Fax 020/7723-6060. www.rooms.demon.co.uk. E-mail: marble@rooms.demon.co.uk. 29 units, 23 with bathroom (shower only). TV TEL. £30–£45 ($48–$72) single without bathroom, £40–£60 ($64–$96) single with bathroom; £40–£50 ($64–$80) double without bathroom, £45–£70 ($72–£112) double/twin with bathroom; £60–£80 ($96–$128) triple with bathroom; £80–£110 ($128–$176) family room with bathroom. Rates include continental breakfast. Lower rates apply to bathrooms without WC and off-season. Discount of 5% for 4-night stays. AE, CB, DC, DISC, EC, JCB, MC, V. Tube: Marble Arch.

Mr. Kassam likes to tease his son, who's a fanatical soccer fan. If his club, Arsenal, is due to play a crunch match when you're staying, you'll find the place festooned with the other team's memorabilia. This is a friendly and extremely reasonable B&B, especially for somewhere just behind Marble Arch. Unlike Bloomsbury, this neighborhood has no halfway house between the dives and the deluxe. The rooms at the "inn" are tiny, and the showers are all drop-in units. Only parents with saintly children should even think about staying in a family room, particularly as they'll have to eat their continental breakfast there, too, since there's no dining room. The new furniture creates more space, but not much more. Parents who want separate rooms for older kids, or guests without any at all, get the best deal. Off-season, two people can take a triple and still pay less than in many other places. Anyone on a tight budget should consider foregoing a private shower because only two rooms share each public facility. Mr. Kassam knows he's got a space problem and works hard to compensate. Some rooms are nonsmoking. The decor is simple but fresh. There's a fridge and satellite TV in every room, as well as tea-/coffeemakers and a hair dryer, and the reception desk can help arrange tours. Oh, and Marble Arch Inn is not an inn at all, but there are several nearby.

✪ **Wyndham Hotel.** 30 Wyndham St., London W1H 1DD. ☎ **020/7723-7204.** Fax 020/7723-2893. www.wyndhamhotel.co.uk. E-mail: wyndhamhotel@talk21.com. 11 units, all with bathroom (most shower only). TV TEL. £40–£44 ($64–$70.40) single; £52–£55 ($83.20–$88) double/twin; £60–£65 ($120–$104) triple. Rates include continental breakfast. Discount of 10% for 1-wk. stays. EC, MC, V. Tube: Marylebone, Baker St.

Gordon Hamme used to be the world's biggest bullion dealer, based in London's Hatton Garden. He sold out, decided to run a B&B, and took over the Wyndham in spring 1999. He has turned what was a dated dump, on a pretty little terrace just off Marylebone Road, into a Georgian gem. A friend, who used to work at Sotheby's, has helped him find original period furniture. The major construction project involved putting fantastic £1,000 showers (the toilets are still shared) into all the bathrooms—except for room no. 22, the one I'd actually go for. It has lovely new tub-shower and private toilet, and looks out over the beautiful terraced garden. Terra-cotta-tiled last year, this is like an airy extension of the remodeled breakfast room, which leads directly outside. Guests can relax on a little roof terrace halfway up the stairs from the second floor. The rooms are small but attractive, and they all have a fridge, tea-/coffeemakers, and radios, as well as a basket of fruit to welcome arriving guests. And you can call down for sandwiches and salads and get your e-mail here. The Wyndham really is a charming retreat from the hard graft of sightseeing, and at absolutely giveaway rates.

Affordable Family-Friendly Accommodations

Ashburn Gardens Apartments *(see p. 83)* These one-bedroom and two-bedroom apartments score on every point. They're near London's best museums and its biggest city-center supermarket, and there are all sorts of baby equipment to borrow at the reception desk.

High Holborn Residence *(see p. 115)* Families on budgets should head straight for this place. Adults pay £65 ($88) for a twin with a bathroom, plus £5 ($8) for each child's foldaway bed. And you get reduced-price entry to the health club's open-air pool next door.

Mitre House Hotel *(see p. 96)* Whether you've got angelic under-10s or teenage monsters, this hotel has a solution to fit: from rooms with lots of beds to others that link together.

Mowbray Court Hotel *(see p. 86)* This is a really friendly budget hotel, from which you can book all sorts of tickets and tours. It has two enormous family rooms: One can sleep seven, and the other has a little kitchen where you can make the kids supper.

Swiss House Hotel *(see p. 82)* Big rooms, a quiet atmosphere, and a lovely communal garden at the back where the kids can burn off excess steam, all make this homey B&B a great family choice.

Travel Inn Capital, County Hall *(see p. 126)* It isn't just the price that makes this budget-chain hotel such a winner. The hotel restaurant has a kids' menu. The London Aquarium and McDonald's are in the same building. And it's London's number-one location—right on the river opposite the Houses of Parliament.

WORTH A SPLURGE

✪ **Hart House Hotel.** 51 Gloucester Place, London W1H 3PE. ☎ **020/7935-2288.** Fax 020/7935-8516. www.harthouse.co.uk. E-mail: reservations@harthouse.co.uk. 15 units, all with bathroom (some with shower only). TV TEL. £68 ($108.80) single; £98 ($156.80) double/twin; £118 ($188.80) triple; £135 ($216) quad. Rates include full English breakfast. AE, MC, V. Tube: Marble Arch, Baker St.

Andrew Bowden must have been the most pampered little boy in London. His parents used to run Hart House, and when he was 6 years old, maids brought him breakfast in bed to keep him out of guests' way. This is probably why this B&B is not only extremely welcoming, but one of the most professionally run in London. When I visited, staff in floral uniforms were even cleaning the walls. A Georgian town house, the entrance is like an august gentleman's club, until the polished paneling gives way to pretty floral wallpaper. The rooms are attractive and comfortable (and nonsmoking); all have been refurbished over the past few years. Double-glazing screens out the traffic roar on Gloucester Place. The top floor is the most recently redone, with one room gone to make way for an extra private bathroom. The double up here is the best deal: Mr. Bowden will probably give you a discount for the climb, and then carry your bags up himself. Room 6 is a huge twin at the back with a marvelous leaded, bay window, and its bathroom up a little flight of stairs. Every room has tea-/coffeemakers and a hair dryer. Hart House also offers a dry cleaning, laundry, and newspaper delivery service, and can arrange baby-sitting or an in-room massage.

Wigmore Court Hotel. 23 Gloucester Place, London W1H 3PB. ☎ **020/7935-0928.** Fax 020/7487-4254. www.wigmore-court-hotel.co.uk. E-mail: info@wigmore-court-hotel.co.uk. 18 units, 16 with bathroom (some with shower only). TV TEL. £51 ($81.60) single without bathroom, £60–£77 ($96–$123.20) single with bathroom; £78 ($124.80) double without bathroom, £90 ($144) double with bathroom; £115 ($184) triple with bathroom; £125 ($200) family room with bathroom. Rates include full English breakfast. Discount of 10% for 1-wk. stays. JCB, MC, V. Tube: Marble Arch.

Wigmore Court is a frustrating and contradictory place, which is what makes it so appealing. The owner, Najma Jinnah, knows the long climb to the fifth floor is a turn-off for a lot of guests, even though they get help with their bags, so she has introduced a reward system. Anyone who does make it to the top can sink into a four-poster bed to recover. There are two more, one each on the second and third floors. Sadly, because this is a small hotel, you'll have to soften Mrs. Jinnah's heart by saying it's your honeymoon or wedding anniversary to guarantee getting one. Budget travelers can get a very good deal here, too. There's a fourth-floor double, which is small for the hotel, but big for London since this is the gracious, Georgian Gloucester Place. It only shares a bathroom, one floor up, with a single and costs £17 ($27.20) less than the others. Though it faces the front, there is double-glazing throughout. The rooms at the back look over a mews. The decor is more relaxed than at Hart House, but six rooms are refurbished every year, and the hallway got a new look in 1999. The reception desk can supply secretarial help; hair dryers and tea-/coffeemakers are standard. Guests can also use the kitchen and laundry facilities, a big bonus normally restricted to budget B&Bs.

7 Soho & Oxford Circus

Regent Palace Hotel . Piccadilly Circus, London W1A 4BZ. ☎ **020/7734-7000.** Fax 020/7734-6435. www.forte-hotels.com. 918 units, 380 with bathroom (shower only). TV TEL. £59–£70 ($94.40–$112) single without bathroom; £59–£84 ($94.40–$136.90) double/twin without bathroom, £99–£109 ($158.40–$174.40) double/twin with bathroom; £85–£99 ($136–$158.40) triple without bathroom; £109–£128 ($174.40–$204.80) quad without bathroom. 2 units adapted for travelers with disabilities. Lower rates apply Sun–Thurs. Discount available for long stays. AE, DC, MC, V. Tube: Piccadilly Circus.

People who want their own bathroom have to splurge to stay at the Regent Palace, but that's rather missing the point. The hotel was purpose-built in 1915 before the phrase "en-suite" entered the dictionary. The bedrooms have basins, and only four share each block of three toilets and showers. The public bathrooms are kept locked to make sure they're always spotless, and the housekeeper will ride the elevator up at any time with the key and fresh towels. That's quite a deal at a weekday price that knocks spots off many B&Bs, even though breakfast is extra—around £5 ($8) for continental and £9 ($14.40) for full English. No problem: The giant wedge-shaped hotel is just off the southern end of Regent Street, with Soho and Piccadilly Circus right on the doorstep, both of which are chock-a-block with cheap eats. Granada took the Regent Palace over 3 years ago, when it took over Forte, and is slowly dragging it into the 21st century. It has installed private showers (no room for a toilet) in a third of the rooms. The decor is comfortable if a little heavy—lots of dark, wood veneer—and tea-/coffeemakers, radios, and pay-per-view movies are standard. The spruced-up lobby has a new Nescafé Coffee Shop, as well as a hotel/souvenir store, and looks like an air terminal now instead of a posh bus station—right down to the same dreadful weekend check-in queues. There's a laundry and dry-cleaning service, and a brasserie was due to open at the end of last year next to Callaghan's, the Irish-themed pub.

West End Hotels

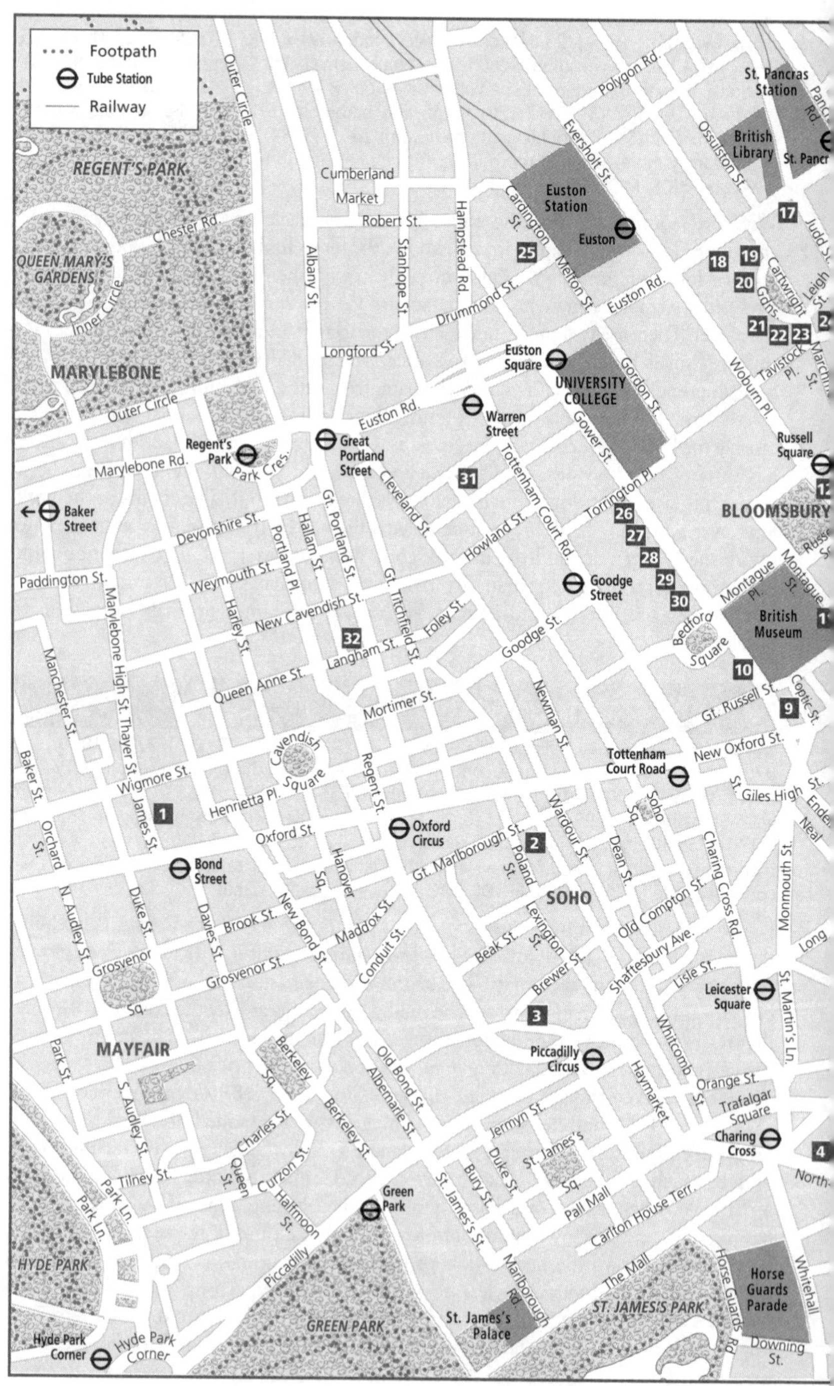

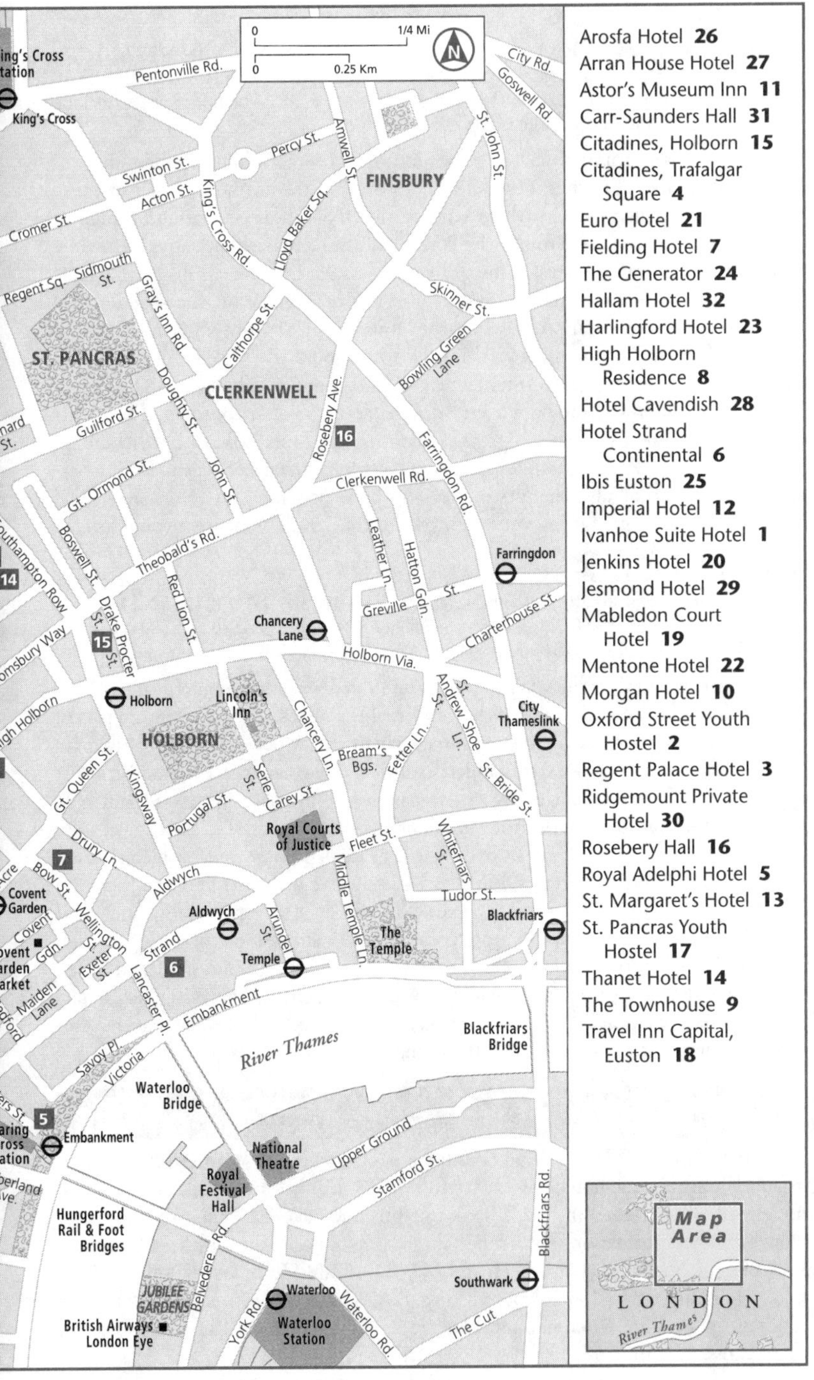
0
1/4 Mi
0
0.25 Km
N
King's Cross Station
King's Cross
Pentonville Rd.
City Rd.
Goswell Rd.
Percy St.
Amwell St.
St. John St.
FINSBURY
Swinton St.
Acton St.
King's Cross Rd.
Lloyd Baker Sq.
Cromer St.
Regent Sq.
Sidmouth St.
Gray's Inn Rd.
Calthorpe St.
Skinner St.
Bowling Green Lane
ST. PANCRAS
CLERKENWELL
Doughty St.
Rosebery Ave.
16
Farringdon Rd.
Guilford St.
John St.
Gt. Ormond St.
Clerkenwell Rd.
Leather Ln.
Hatton Gdn.
Farringdon
Boswell St.
Theobald's Rd.
Red Lion St.
Southampton Row
14
Greville St.
Charterhouse St.
Drake St.
Procter St.
15
Chancery Lane
Holborn Via.
Bloomsbury Way
Holborn
Lincoln's Inn
Chancery Ln.
St. Andrew St.
Shoe Ln.
City Thameslink
High Holborn
HOLBORN
Bream's Bgs.
Fetter Ln.
St. Bride St.
Gt. Queen St.
Kingsway
Serle St.
Carey St.
Portugal St.
Royal Courts of Justice
Fleet St.
Whitefriars St.
Drury Ln.
7
Middle Temple Ln.
Tudor St.
Aldwych
Bow St.
Covent Garden
Wellington St.
Aldwych
Arundel St.
Blackfriars
The Temple
Covent Gdn.
Exeter St.
Strand
6
Temple
Lancaster Pl.
Maiden Lane
Embankment
River Thames
Blackfriars Bridge
Savoy Pl.
Victoria
Waterloo Bridge
5
Embankment
National Theatre
Upper Ground
Royal Festival Hall
Stamford St.
Hungerford Rail & Foot Bridges
Belvedere Rd.
Blackfriars Rd.
Southwark
JUBILEE GARDENS
Waterloo
British Airways London Eye
York Rd.
Waterloo Station
Waterloo Rd.
The Cut
Arosfa Hotel 26
Arran House Hotel 27
Astor's Museum Inn 11
Carr-Saunders Hall 31
Citadines, Holborn 15
Citadines, Trafalgar Square 4
Euro Hotel 21
Fielding Hotel 7
The Generator 24
Hallam Hotel 32
Harlingford Hotel 23
High Holborn Residence 8
Hotel Cavendish 28
Hotel Strand Continental 6
Ibis Euston 25
Imperial Hotel 12
Ivanhoe Suite Hotel 1
Jenkins Hotel 20
Jesmond Hotel 29
Mabledon Court Hotel 19
Mentone Hotel 22
Morgan Hotel 10
Oxford Street Youth Hostel 2
Regent Palace Hotel 3
Ridgemount Private Hotel 30
Rosebery Hall 16
Royal Adelphi Hotel 5
St. Margaret's Hotel 13
St. Pancras Youth Hostel 17
Thanet Hotel 14
The Townhouse 9
Travel Inn Capital, Euston 18
Map Area
LONDON
River Thames

SUPER-CHEAP SLEEPS

Oxford Street Youth Hostel. 14–18 Noel St., London W1. ☎ **020/7734-1618.** www.yha.org.uk. E-mail: oxfordst@yha.org.uk. 75 units, none with bathroom. £21.80 ($34.90) per person in a twin; £20.55 ($32.90) per person in a 3-to-4-bed dorm. Rates include bed linen. MC, V. Tube: Oxford Circus. No children under 6.

This hostel is above some offices, in a location most people would kill for—and not just opposite Marks & Spencer's food hall. Noel Street is the northern border of Soho. The legendary Carnaby Street, where London first took off as cult fashion capital in the swinging 1960s, is just around the corner and hip new fashion shops are finally pushing back the trashy tourist traps. All the rooms are the same size—small. So, if you've got the cash, ask to share with one other person because the four-bedders feel like a cabin on a sleeper train. Unusually, the bunks are nice sturdy wooden ones, with crisp cotton sheets and the quilt turned back when you arrive. There are soft drinks and snack machines, as well as Internet access, in the lounge. The hostel is too small to have a restaurant and provides a very declinable £2.50 ($4) continental breakfast pack. The communal kitchen is a great excuse for a 5-minute walk to Berwick Street market. Go late on Friday afternoon, and you'll get huge scoops of vegetables at a bargain price. The hostel also changes money and posts new rates on Thursdays. So, if the pound gets stronger during your trip, good timing could win you a good deal.

WORTH A SPLURGE

Hallam Hotel. 12 Hallam St., Portland Place, London W1N 5LJ. ☎ **020/7580-1166.** Fax 020/7323-4537. 25 units, all with bathroom. MINIBAR TV TEL. £50–£86.50 ($80–$138.40) single; £95–£102.50 ($152–$164) double/twin. AE, DC, MC, V. Tube: Oxford Circus.

Mr. Universe had to turn sideways to fit through the door of his cabinette at the Hallam, and when he breathed out, his chest touched the opposite wall. There are two of these tiny singles, more like cryogenic storage chambers, which explains the big price range. A lot of celebs stay at this quiet, redbrick, Victorian hotel because it's just behind the BBC. You'll want to, as well, because it's only a 5-minute walk north of Oxford Circus. And the service from the fabulous Baker brothers is extremely eager: I had to wait and wait while guests had their bags carried up or tour problems sorted out. The rooms aren't sumptuous, but they are attractive with dark modern furniture and mock-Victorian bedside lights. They all have hair dryers, radios, and tea-/coffeemakers. And the space varies from compact in the smallest double to big enough in one of the twins to fit an extra foldaway bed. The bathrooms are spotless, though the lighting and sage green tiles create deep-sea gloom in the shower cubicles. The Hallam offers dry cleaning, a laundry service, baby-sitting, and free newspapers. And there is tea and coffee on tap in the little lounge/bar.

8 Bloomsbury

Travel Inn Capital (☎ **020/7554-3400;** fax 020/7554-3419; www.travelinn.co.uk) has another great value hotel at 1 Dukes Rd., WC1H 9PJ. It has similar rates, decor, and amenities as its hotel in South Bank (for this one, take the Tube to Euston); see below for more information. For a super-cheap sleep opposite the new British Library, check out the **St. Pancras Youth Hostel** (☎ **020/7388-9998;** fax 020/7388-6766; www.yha.org.uk; e-mail: stpancras@yha.org.uk) at 79–81 Euston Rd., NW1 2QS. Children under 3 are welcome, and cots are available. Take the Tube to Euston or King's Cross.

Arosfa Hotel. 83 Gower St., London WC1E 6HJ. ☎/fax **020/7636-2115.** 15 units, 2 with bathroom (shower only). TV. £37 ($59.20) single; £50 ($80) double/twin without bathroom,

£66 ($105.60) double/twin with bathroom; £68 ($108.80) triple without bathroom, £79 ($126.40) triple with bathroom; £92 ($147.20) quad with bathroom. Rates include full English breakfast. Surcharge of 2% to pay by credit card. JCB, MC, V. Tube: Goodge St., Russell Sq.

Gower Street has the best value B&Bs in Bloomsbury, beating Bedford Place and Cartwright Gardens hands-down. It's only a 15-minute walk at most from the West End. And you still get attractive accommodations, fine Georgian architecture, and oodles of local heritage. John Everett Millais, painter and founder of the Pre-Raphaelite Brotherhood, once lived in the house that is now the Arosfa. Mr. Dorta took over 7 years ago. He used to be the decorator at the Harlingford Hotel in Cartwright Gardens and is known for being unable to let a single paint chip go unrepaired. He has renovated throughout, and the sober decor has the pulled-together look you get in more expensive places. The bedrooms all have modern, dark-wood furniture, prints on the walls, and a little vase of silk flowers. Gower Street is less cozy than its rivals, but most B&Bs, including the Arosfa, have put in double-glazing against the heavy traffic noise, which is unusual for this price bracket. Three bedrooms share each spotless bathroom. There are free tea-/coffeemakers in the TV lounge, and hair dryers are available at the reception desk. The Arosfa is also completely nonsmoking. Mr. Dorta sends people into the garden, which all the guests can use. And he's a strong disciplinarian. One sneaky puff out of your bedroom window, and he'll ask you to go.

✪ **Arran House Hotel.** 77 Gower St., London WC1E 6HJ. ☎ **020/7636-2186** or 020/7637-1140. Fax 020/7436-5328. www.proteusweb.com/arran. E-mail: arran@dircon.co.uk. 28 units, 13 with bathroom (shower only). TV TEL. £45 ($72) single without bathroom, £55 ($88) single with bathroom; £55 ($88) double without bathroom, £60–£75 ($96–$120) double with bathroom; £73 ($116.80) triple without bathroom, £77–£93 ($123.20–$148.80) triple with bathroom; £79 ($126.40) quad without bathroom, £84–£97 ($134.40–$155.20) quad with bathroom; £88 ($140.80) 5-bed without bathroom, £110 ($176) 5-bed with bathroom. Rates include full English breakfast. MC, V. Tube: Goodge St., Russell Sq.

It's sad to get excited by something as ordinary as a kitchen, but that's the point. Most B&Bs don't let guests use theirs, and apart from Wigmore Court in Marylebone, none of the others that do are as nice as this. You can cook your own supper—great for budget travelers—and dine in style in the marvelous breakfast room. The family ought to sell tickets to see this mini-museum. Swords, coats of arms, and a mass of other memorabilia line the walls, all collected by the current proprietor's father, Major Richards. He also bought the classic film and theater posters that hang on the stairs. The bedrooms are simply decorated with white bedspreads and matching painted furniture. It seems that private bathrooms go together with original fireplaces. If you go for one with a shower, but no toilet, you'll get the best deal on Gower Street. The front rooms are double-glazed, and hair dryers and tea-/coffeemakers are standard. In the lounge, there's satellite and cable TV, as well as stacks of magazines and newspapers, and the Richards show videos three times a day on the bedroom TVs. The self-service laundry facilities are another big plus for any traveler. And you won't find a more beautiful garden than this. Roses ramble across a trellis, and each wrought-iron bench is hidden away in its own little gap in the greenery.

Euro Hotel. 53 Cartwright Gardens, London WC1H 9EL. ☎ **020/7387-4321.** Fax 020/7383-5044. www.eurohotel.co.uk. E-mail: reception@eurohotel.co.uk. 35 units, 9 with bathroom (some with shower only). TV TEL. £48 ($76.80) single without bathroom, £70 ($112) single with bathroom; £67 ($107.20) double/twin without bathroom, £87 ($139.20) double/twin with bathroom; £82 ($131.20) triple without bathroom, £102 ($163.20) triple with bathroom; £92 ($147.20) family room without bathroom, £112 ($179.20) family room with bathroom. Rates include full English breakfast. Special rates for children under 16. Discount of 10% for 1-wk. stays off-season. AE, MC, V. Tube: Euston, Russell Sq.

The kids' drawings that festoon the walls behind reception are a pretty heavy clue as to where the hotel's strength lies—as a favorite of families on holiday. Generally, prices are high for Cartwright Gardens, a pretty Georgian crescent in northern Bloomsbury that is already more expensive than Gower Street and farther away from the action. And unlike at the neighboring Harlingford, I couldn't see enough of a reason to pay the difference. However, the Euro does do a good value rate for children under 16 who share a room with their parents. You pay the normal single or double price, depending on the number of adults, plus £10 ($16) per child: For example, a basic family room for mom, pop, and two kids would cost £87 ($139.20) a night instead of £92 ($147.20). Toddlers under 2½ stay free, and you can borrow a high chair and cot at the reception desk. The Euro is an attractive place. The bedrooms have new pine furniture and carpet. Tea-/coffeemakers and radios are standard, and you get a free movie channel. Basic rooms only share a bathroom with one other—another good deal. Staff can provide hair dryers, e-mail, and fax services. And if the kids still need wearing out after a day on the tourist trail, you can hit the tennis court in the gardens opposite the hotel. The Euro will lend you rackets and balls.

Harlingford Hotel. 61–63 Cartwright Gardens, London WC1H 9EL. ☎ **020/7387-1551.** Fax 020/7387-4616. 44 units, all with bathroom (shower only). TV TEL. £70 ($112) single; £87 ($139.20) double/twin; £97 ($155.20) triple; £107 ($171.20) quad. Rates include full English breakfast. AE, DC, MC, V. Tube: Euston, Russell Sq.

Andrew Davies had big plans when I visited the Harlingford Hotel, a pretty, dove-gray, Georgian building on the corner of Cartwright Gardens and Marchmont Street. He was still being rather secretive, just muttering "Bloomsbury" and "theme." But by the end of 2000, there was a complete overhaul of the lounge and breakfast rooms. On either side of the front door, both are already very gracious with their arched windows and high ceilings. And if the way Mr. Davies has refurbished the rest of the hotel is anything to go by, the new literary look should be something really special. He's the young gun in the very welcoming family that owns the Harlingford and has put a huge amount of work into the place over the past couple of years. The results make its relatively high price for Cartwright Gardens much more justifiable. Wood paneling provides protection against poorly controlled suitcases as well as an attractive classic look. The bedrooms are not super-luxxy but have matching everything and are freshly decorated. There are new brass reading lamps and paneling around the beds. Tea-/coffeemakers are standard, hair dryers are available on request, and guests can use the ice dispenser. You can take your drink outside into the communal gardens opposite. All you have to do is ask for the key.

Hotel Cavendish. 75 Gower St., London WC1E 6HJ. ☎ **020/7636-9079.** Fax 020/7580-3609. www.hotelcavendish.com. E-mail: HOTEL.CAVENDISH@virginnet.co.uk. 20 units, none with bathroom. £34–£40 ($54.40–$64) single; £48–£66 ($76.80–$105.60) double; £69–£75 ($110.40–$120) triple; £88–£96 ($140.80–$153.60) quad. Rates include full English breakfast. Discount available for groups. AE, JCB, MC, V. Tube: Goodge St., Russell Sq.

Hotel Cavendish has a surprisingly raffish past. EMI used to book rooms for try-out bands; the Beatles also slept here when there were still five of them. Eluned Edwards' mother was running the B&B then. Guests today can spot their own stars in the making, as RADA, the famous drama school, is just across the road. When you compare rooms at similar hotels on Gower Street, you'll find that the clean, cozy, welcoming Hotel Cavendish battles with the Arosfa to be the cheapest. No two bedrooms are the same, but Mrs. Edwards is a big fan of William Morris wallpaper, so you'll find lots of that. All the rooms have candlewick bedspreads, cushions on the bed, and pretty furniture that might have come out of somebody's home. That's exactly what Hotel

Cavendish looks like—a home cleverly decorated on a budget. All the rooms have tea-/coffeemakers. Hair dryers are available at the reception desk. And the Edwardses recently put new power-showers into the shared bathrooms. Breakfast is served in a very pretty dining room complete with white-painted dresser and so many pictures you can barely see the space between them. Some rooms do have their own TV, or guests can watch the one in the lounge. Best of all, they can sit in the garden in the summer.

Ibis Euston. 3 Cardington St., London NW1 2LW. ☎ **020/7388-7777.** Fax 020/7388-0001. www.accor.com. E-mail: HO921@accor-hotels.com. 300 units, all with bathroom (shower only). TV TEL. £64 ($102.40) single; £69.95 ($111.90) double/twin. 8 units adapted for travelers with disabilities. Rates do not include breakfast. AE, DC, EC, MC, V. Tube: Euston.

Ibis is a chain of budget hotels, owned by the French group Accor, that has cloned itself all over the country (see "Near the Airport," below). It's a good deal for travelers who prefer up-to-date accommodations and are willing to forego the quirks of a B&B. Room rates compete with those on Gower Street, though breakfast is not included—buffet continental costs £5.25 ($8.40)—and it's twice as far to walk to the West End. You'd never choose the Ibis for the beauty of its location. The "wrong" side of Euston Road is a bit bleak and businessy; but around the corner on attractive Drummond Street, you'll find a cluster of Middle-Eastern delis. The Ibis has also made its modern redbrick building very welcoming with hanging baskets and striped awnings. The inside is appealing, too—the first floor has the open feel of a food court at a shopping mall. It encompasses the reception and lounge area, a railway-themed bar, and the restaurant, La Croisette, which is loosely styled as a South of France beach cafe. Supper is very reasonably priced both there and at Tracks. Upstairs, Ibis has refurbished its rooms, all of which are medium-size, and the look is simple, with curved built-in furniture. The next step was redoing the bathrooms in phases through to 2001. This hotel has an elevator, and you can send e-mail for free via the i-plus electronic information booth in the foyer.

✪ **Jenkins Hotel.** 45 Cartwright Gardens, London WC1H 9EH. ☎ **020/7387-2067.** Fax 020/7383-3139. www.jenkinshotel.demon.co.uk. E-mail: Reservations@jenkinshotel.demon.co.uk. 15 units, 7 with bathroom (most with shower only). MINIBAR TV TEL. £52 ($83.20) single without bathroom, £72 ($115.20) single with bathroom; £72 ($115.20) double without bathroom, £82 ($131.20) double with bathroom; £90 ($144) triple with bathroom. Rates include full English breakfast. MC, V. Tube: Euston, Russell Sq.

This is the only hotel I know that can lend guests a dog to walk. The charming Sam Bellingham, who has run it for 15 years, has two black Labradors and a chocolate-colored one, which lounge about cheerfully until required to act as surrogate family pets. Jenkins has been a hotel since the 1920s and once appeared in the PBS mystery series *Poirot.* It is the nicest, quietest, and best value on the crescent, though the smart porticoed entrance is actually in Burton Place. The rooms vary in size. Some are large by London standards and quite smartly decorated—the curtains and bedcover in one are a riot of leaves and ladybirds. Attractive brass bedside lamps and handsome antique reproductions grace the rooms, though there's the occasional scratched-up piece, too. Most of the twin beds can be zippered together if you want to sleep in a king-size. And there are a lot of goodies thrown in: fridges, safes, tea-/coffeemakers, hair dryers, and electric fans. Only two rooms share each public bathroom. An additional draw are the tennis courts in the lovely communal gardens opposite the hotel—you can borrow a racket and balls from the front desk. Cartwright Gardens is an attractive place to stay and has more of a neighborhood feel than much of Bloomsbury because of the local shops and little restaurants around the corner. Jenkins is completely nonsmoking.

Jesmond Hotel. 63 Gower St., London WC1 6HJ. ☎ **020/7636-3199.** Fax 020/7323-4373. 16 units, 5 with bathroom (shower only). TV. £33 ($52.80) single without bathroom, £43 ($68.80) single with bathroom; £49 ($78.40) double/twin without bathroom, £64 ($102.40) double/twin with bathroom; £76 ($121.60) quad without bathroom, £85 ($136) quad with bathroom. Rates include full English breakfast. MC, V. Tube: Goodge St., Russell Sq.

The Jesmond's proprietors, Mr. and Mrs. Beynon, travel to the United States a lot and worry about living up to the accommodation standards there. In many ways, they can't, like anyone running a small B&B in a listed building in Central London. A lot of the rooms are small, though the choice of blonde-wood furniture helps to counteract that and the cabinets around the in-room sinks provide extra storage. And only a few have private bathrooms. However, those that do are competitively priced, and those that don't are positively cheap. And the Beynons make sure the atmosphere and welcome are top-notch—they've been working at it for over 20 years. There are radios, as well as hair dryers and tea-/coffeemakers, in all the rooms. Those at the front also have double-glazing. Recently, the couple spruced up the lounge, and it really feels like home. It has a cold-drink machine and more free tea and coffee. If you're short of something to read, there are rows of books downstairs in the breakfast room. And this is one of the few places that still puts a fruit bowl out in the morning, instead of doling apples and bananas out from a guarded stash, even though guests pocket extra portions to take with them for lunch.

Mabledon Court Hotel. 10–11 Mabledon Place, London WC1H 9BA. ☎ **020/7388-3866.** Fax 020/7387-5686. 32 units, all with bathroom (shower only). TV TEL. £68 ($108.80) single; £78 ($124.80) double. Rates include full English breakfast. AE, DC, MC, V. Tube: Euston, Russell Sq.

Dating from the 1950s, Mabledon Court is a modern building by local standards, but it fits in well with the Georgian and Victorian neighbors. Originally, train drivers coming into Euston and King's Cross stayed here on London stopovers. Because it was originally built to be a hotel, there are no nasty surprises—tiny rooms squeezed out of larger ones. The Davies family, who also own the Harlingford around the corner in Cartwright Gardens, has been at the helm for 11 years, and they've recently completed a big refurbishment. The bedrooms have all had a fresh coat of paint, and new carpet, beds, and security chains on the doors. They have also replaced all the curtains and bedspreads. Hair dryers and tea-/coffeemakers are standard. Mabledon Court is one of the few places you'll find sheets and blankets, instead of quilts—when the Davies did a survey, people said they preferred them. This may be because the hotel has a lot of single rooms and 80% of guests are Brits on business. The bathrooms have sparkling white tiles and wooden floors, and paneling has lent the hallways a more upmarket air. And if you're a full English breakfast fiend, the pub next door has an all-day menu that includes black pudding. I'd say that was going native, but the natives are generally too namby-pamby to touch it. Mabledon Court has an elevator.

Mentone Hotel. 54 Cartwright Gardens, London WC1H 9EL. ☎ **020/7387-3927.** Fax 020/7388-4671. www.mentonehotel.com. E-mail: mentonehotel@compuserve.com. 42 units, 41 with bathroom (most with shower only). TV TEL. £42 ($67.20) single without bathroom, £60 ($96) single with bathroom; £79 ($126.40) double/twin with bathroom; £90 ($144) triple with bathroom; £99 ($158.40) family room with bathroom. Rates include full English breakfast. Discount available off-season and for long stays. AE, CB, DC, MC, V. Tube: Euston, Russell Sq.

The Mentone Hotel is the second one along from the south end of Cartwright Gardens. It's a bit cheaper than the neighboring Jenkins Hotel, and while the welcome is friendly and the decor new, it doesn't have quite the same charm. But you do get a big room here, which is not something you can say about many London B&Bs. The Mentone stretches across three houses and has been run by the same family for over 30 years. Simon Tyner took over from his mother in 1997, though she still looks after the hotel's hanging baskets and window boxes—she's won prizes for them in the past. Mr. Tyner has refurbished most of the bedrooms since then, and they've got nice matching quilt covers and curtains. What is unusual is that the family has resisted chopping up the original Georgian rooms, so the only funny shapes come from the private bathrooms, also recently redone. There's enough space in some for a small sofa, and though the ceilings are lower on the top floor, the rooms don't feel cramped. All have cable TV and tea-/coffeemakers, and you can borrow a hair dryer at the reception desk, as well as a key to get into the half-moon gardens opposite. Unlike the Euro and Jenkins hotels farther round the crescent, it doesn't lend out tennis equipment, so you'll have to bring your own to use the court.

✪ **The Morgan Hotel.** 24 Bloomsbury St., London WC1B 3QJ. ☎ **020/7636-3735.** Fax 020/7636-3045. 15 units, all with bathroom (most with shower only). A/C TV TEL. £57–£67 ($91.20–$107.20) single; £82 ($131.20) double/twin; £125 ($200) triple. Rates include full English breakfast. MC, V. Tube: Goodge St., Tottenham Court Rd.

It's a real treat to find a B&B with air-conditioning and double-glazing, particularly in an elegant, 18th-century terrace house. It makes staying at the Morgan Hotel completely painless, though Bloomsbury Street is at the busy southern end of Gower Street—a 10-minute walk to Covent Garden. It's more expensive than other local B&Bs (still cheaper than Cartwright Gardens), but then period-style decoration does tend to bump the price up. There are pretty floral bedspreads and decorative borders on the walls, and every room is different. If there are two of you, go for the first-floor room that opens onto the garden at the back, which no one else gets to use. The beds in one of the twins can be zippered together to make a king-size bed. But don't come here for a basic single room—the owner claims to get requests for the one on the first floor, but it's absolutely tiny, and there are much better deals elsewhere. The downside to the hotel is that it can only accommodate families of three in the same room. Otherwise, it's almost worth staying there just to see the breakfast room, an unusual and really appealing oak-paneled room where you all sit in wooden booths. Just up the road, Morgan has also got four fantastic one-bedroom apartments, which go for £100 ($160) a night including breakfast, or £140 ($224) to have a foldaway bed, and sleep three.

Ridgemount Private Hotel. 65–67 Gower St., London WC1E 6HJ. ☎ **020/7636-1141.** Fax 020/7636-2558. 34 units, 8 with bathroom (shower only). TV. £32 ($51.20) single without bathroom, £43 ($68.80) single with bathroom; £48 ($76.80) double/twin without bathroom, £62 ($99.20) double/twin with bathroom; £63 ($100.80) triple without bathroom, £75 ($120) triple with bathroom; £72 ($115.20) quad without bathroom, £86 ($137.60) quad with bathroom. Rates include full English breakfast. MC, V. Tube: Goodge St., Russell Sq.

The Ridgemount's Welsh proprietors, Royden and Gwen Rees, have a reputation for providing a warm-hearted welcome. They've run this B&B for 34 years, and some of their guests go back a long way, too. It's 13 years since one U.S. college started sending students to stay here every January during their exchange trips. Smiling group pictures are pinned up all over the breakfast room. If you want to stay at the Ridgemount, or any of the nicer Bloomsbury B&Bs, you will have to book ahead. A large part of the University of London is here, which guarantees an endless supply of customers. The Ridgemount stretches across two buildings, one of which still has all the original fireplaces and cornices. The decor is simple, with homey candlewick covers on the beds, and some of the rooms are quite small, particularly the basic twins. But if you're looking for a double room with a private bathroom, you'll have to stay a month in winter to find one cheaper on Gower Street. And by the beginning of this year, there were due to be several more en-suites, local council permitting. All the rooms on the front are double-glazed against the traffic noise. Free coffee and tea are available in the lounge, and you can borrow an electric fan at reception. Mr. and Mrs. Rees will even do laundry. And like most of the B&Bs on Gower Street, you can go out in the garden in the summer.

✪ **St. Margaret's Hotel.** 26 Bedford Place, London WC1B 5JL. ☎ **020/7636-4277.** Fax 020/7323-3066. 65 units, 10 with bathroom (most with shower only). TV TEL. £48.50 ($77.60) single without bathroom; from £60 ($96) double without bathroom, £75–£90 ($120–$144) double with bathroom. Rates include full English breakfast. MC, V. Tube: Russell Sq., Holborn.

The welcome at St. Margaret's inspires devoted loyalty. One lady guest stayed for 28 years. Mrs. Marazzi is the second generation of her family to run the B&B, which rambles over four houses. Take a ball of string if you want to find your room again. The rooms are simple, and no two are the same—short stays usually get the smaller ones. They are all nonsmoking. Access to CNN is standard. And you can borrow a fan from the reception desk and a hair dryer if you're staying in one of the rooms without one. Budget travelers should go for the cheap en-suite double, which has the toilet just outside. However, the Marazzis recently created some beautiful extra public bathrooms, so it's easy to survive the sharing experience. If you can afford it, room 53 is a marvelous, first-floor, family room, which two people can take for slightly more than an en-suite double. It has a king-size bed, a single bed, and a gray-tiled, private bathroom with a corner tub. And off it is a small private conservatory, looking onto the quiet communal garden, that all the guests can use. St. Margaret's has two lounges, one with a TV and the other for guests who prefer peace and quiet. Newspapers are delivered, and Mrs. Marazzi can arrange baby-sitting.

Thanet Hotel. 8 Bedford Place, London WC1B 5JA. ☎ **020/7636-2869** or 020/7580-3377. Fax 020/7323-6676. www.freepages.co.uk/thanethotel/. E-mail: thanetlon@aol.com. 16 units, all with bathroom (shower only). TV TEL. £65 ($104) single; £85 ($136) double/twin; £99 ($158.40) triple; £108 ($172.80) quad. Rates include full English breakfast. AE, MC, V. Tube: Russell Sq., Holborn.

Thanet is in a surprisingly quiet row of terraced Georgian houses linking Russell Square, which is like a London bus merry-go-round, and the more peaceful Bloomsbury Square. Bedford Place is also the closest of all the streets listed here to the heart of the West End—Covent Garden is little more than a ¼ mile away. It is easy to spot this guesthouse, with its blue awning and exuberant window boxes, and it still has the original tiles on the front step. It has won plaudits as a good budget bet for a long time, but prices have crept up. Thanet is a bit more expensive than St. Margaret's Hotel, which is across the way and more to my taste. These two illustrate how different London B&Bs can be. St. Margaret's offers simple decor and more public rooms than usual. The Orchard family, on the other hand, has gone for a rather solidly respectable style and no lounge. If you can, ask for the second-floor double, which has huge windows looking over the back garden, and is a bit bigger than some of the others. The slightly dated bathrooms are a bit of a squash and have disappointingly tiny washbasins, but at least, they're tidy. Tea-/coffeemakers, radios, and hair dryers are standard.

The Townhouse. 24 Coptic St., London WC1A 1NT. ☎ **020/7636-2731.** www.townhousebrasserie.co.uk. E-mail: townhousebrasserie@btinternet.com. 4 units, none with bathroom. MINIBAR TV. £25 ($40) single; £48 ($76.80) twin. Rates include continental breakfast. AE, DC, MC, V. Tube: Holborn, Tottenham Ct. Rd.

Get your fingers pushing phone buttons now; deals like this are as rare as an unchatty London taxi driver. Only a tiny handful of hotels so centrally located can match the twin-room price at The Townhouse—most are at least £10 ($16) a night more expensive. And none that do are as lovely as this. Think Zen-clotted cream. The furniture is all white and the decor vanilla, including the beautiful loopy curtains that ripple across the windows. And it's all sparkling new because The Townhouse, which is between the British Museum and Covent Garden, only started doing bed-and-breakfast in 1999. The singles are even more of a steal, at little more than what you'd pay to sleep with multiple snorers at a youth hostel. That's because they really are one-person big. There's one public bathroom for the six guests. Each bedroom has a tea-/coffeemaker and a fridge, and the twins get a little table and chairs to eat at. That's if you can resist the delicious food downstairs. Chef Lloyd Lewars has run this place with his wife Joanna for 4 years, winning a coveted nomination in the best brasserie category at the recent London Carlton T.V. Restaurant Awards (see chapter 5).

SUPER-CHEAP SLEEPS

Astor's Museum Inn. 27 Montague St., London WC1B 5BH. ☎ **020/7580-5360.** Fax 020/7636-7948. www.scoot.co.uk/astorhostels/. E-mail: AstorHostels@msn.com. 18 units, none with bathroom. £14–£17 ($22.40–$27.20) per person in a dorm. Rates include bed linen (not towels) and continental breakfast. Discount available for 1-wk. stays off-season. EC, MC, V. Tube: Russell Sq., Tottenham Court Rd., Holborn. 18–30 age restriction.

It's astonishing to find a bed this cheap within a 10-minute walk of Theaterland. The name is a bit misleading. Montague Street does run down the side of British Museum, but this isn't an inn, rather Astor's longest-established London hostel. Like those in Queensway and Victoria, it employs an age restriction. Unlike them, however, there are no in-your-face paint colors or murals, because of regulations protecting this Georgian terrace. Keeping the neighbors sweet means it's not a full-on party zone, either, but a cozier place where guests often go out in the evening together or have barbecues in the small internal courtyard. And there's even a ban on smoking in the kitchen by public demand. The hostel has just had a new paint job, as well as new carpeting; the lovely moldings are sky-blue and white, faux Regency style. Dorms sleep up to 11 and get very hot in summer. I visited on a fine spring day and practically had to strip. There are about eight people to a shared shower, all quite new. The lounge is nothing to shout about, but it does have Internet access. There is satellite TV and a shelf full of videos in the kitchen.

Carr-Saunders Hall, London School of Economics. 18–24 Fitzroy St., London W1P 5AE. ☎ **020/7323-9712.** Fax 020/7580-4718. www.lsevacations.com. E-mail: vacations@lse.ac.uk. 144 units, 2 with bathroom (tub only). TEL. £27 ($43.20) single without bathroom; £45 ($72) twin without bathroom, £50 ($80) twin with bathroom. Rates include full English breakfast. Open Easter and summer vacations. MC, V. Tube: Goodge St., Warren St. No children under 3.

There are dozens of student dorms in Bloomsbury because it's where so much of the University of London is based, as well as the University of Westminster. Carr-Saunders stands out by virtue of its location. This is really Fitzrovia and more like staying in the real world. Try for a room on one of the upper floors—Carr-Saunders is a modern-ish block with elevators—and you'll have a view to die for of one of London's best-known landmarks, the Telecom Tower, which is only two streets away. Children over 3 years old can stay in their parents' room, but there are no cots, so no babies. The decor is functional but tidy. London School of Economics has been upgrading the bathrooms, and it's about seven people to every shower. The hall has a lounge with TV, video games, a bar, and a launderette. There are kitchens on every floor, with just the basics for making light suppers, but you have to bring your own utensils. Or sample a £2

($3.20) supper in the canteen—what a bargain! This is definitely not as nice as LSE's High Holborn Residence, but the prices reflect that. And it is a fun area full of restaurants of every caliber and price. As you go south, Fitzroy Street turns into Charlotte Street, a long-time favorite among advertising agencies and graphic designers. Oxford Street is a 15-minute walk away at the bottom.

The Generator. Compton Place, off 37 Tavistock Place, London WC1H 9SD. ☎ **020/7388-7666.** Fax 020/7388-7644. www.the-generator.co.uk. E-mail: info@the-generator.co.uk. 217 units, none with bathroom. £38 ($60.80) single; £26 ($41.60) per person in a twin; £22 ($35.20) per person in a triple/quad; £15–£20 ($24–$32) per person in a dorm. Rates include bed linen, towels, and continental breakfast. Discount available for 5-night stays and for groups. MC, V. Tube: Russell Sq.

The Generator is hidden away through a scruffy hole in the wall in Tavistock Place. The hostel opened in 1995 in what used to be a police section house; inside, it's like a cross between the set of *Alien* and a hip Soho coffee bar. Aluminum pipes and blue neon lights snake across the ceiling in reception. The different floors are called Level 01, 02, and so on. And all the signage, including room numbers, is spray-stenciled, packing-crate-style. There's a nut on the door of the women's bathrooms and a bolt on the men's. The Spartan bedrooms, all nonsmoking and with bunks, are equipped with funky metal basins, and it's about eight people to every shower. The 800-bed Generator is more expensive than its rivals, except in the biggest dorms, and its rival Astor's Hyde Park Hostel can almost rival it for facilities but not quite. Here, the Turbine Lounge has satellite TV, pool tables, and video games; Internet access is in the Talking Heads room, a separate area with lots of tourist information. Breakfast is self-service in the Fuel Stop canteen, which also does a two-course supper for £5.25 ($8.40). There is no self-catering. The bar is very Soho, but prices are lower than even a local pub's, and it stays open until 2am. In fact, the only drawback to The Generator is that it caters for a lot of groups. Be prepared for hordes of kids on tour.

WORTH A SPLURGE

Imperial Hotel. Russell Sq., London WC1B 5BB. ☎ **020/7278-7871.** Fax 020/7837-4653. www.imperialhotels.co.uk. E-mail: info@imperialhotels.co.uk. 448 units, all with bathroom. TV TEL. £70 ($112) single; £94 ($150.40) double/twin. Rates include full English breakfast. AE, CB, DC, DISC, MC, V. Tube: Russell Sq.

A few pounds more expensive than Bloomsbury's toniest B&Bs, the Imperial is both a splurge and a very good deal. The decor isn't particularly plush. In fact, it's rather dated. What you do get, though, is an affordable, full-on, full-service hotel, just a stone's throw from Covent Garden and Soho. For a charge, guests can use the company's nearby health club. There are conference rooms, a car-rental desk, concierge, limited room service, dry cleaning, laundry service, newspaper delivery, and babysitting. It looks like a complete monstrosity from the outside—a huge, corrugated, concrete box taking up half the eastern side of Russell Square with a row of shops at street level. Some are useful, like the Hertz and American Express offices, but others sell cheesy souvenirs. The Imperial has 9 floors of bedrooms, and the third is nonsmoking. The hotel does a lot of tour-group business, but the rooms have stood up pretty well to the traffic. They're all a decent size and have excellent storage space, satellite TV, radios, and tea-/coffeemakers. Some also have pants presses, minibars, and hair dryers. Everything is sparkling clean. In most of the doubles and twins, the en-suite toilet and tub-shower are handily separate. If you'd rather forego the amenities and pay a few pounds less, check out its Web site because the company owns five other Bloomsbury hotels, including the no-frills **County Hotel** in Upper Woburn Place (☎ **020/7387-5544**).

Dining: The Atrium Lounge serves afternoon tea; the vast Elizabethan Restauran. does breakfast, lunch, and dinner; and the Day & Night Bar, an oasis of up-to-the-minute style, is open for light food and drinks until 2am. Imperial Hotels has a vineyard to make the Bordeaux house wine and a farm just outside London, which delivers produce every day.

9 Covent Garden, The Strand & Holborn

✪ **High Holborn Residence, London School of Economics.** 178 High Holborn, London WC1. ☎ **020/7379-5589.** Fax 020/7379-5640. www.lsevacations.com. high.holborn@lse.ac.uk. 428 units, 24 with bathroom (shower only). TEL. £34 ($54.40) single without bathroom; £57 ($91.20) twin without bathroom, £67 ($107.20) twin with bathroom; £77 ($123.20) triple without bathroom. 4 units adapted for travelers with disabilities. Rates include continental breakfast. Open summer vacation. MC, V. Tube: Holborn.

Rooms at the back of this hall look out over the topless sunbathers around the pool at the Oasis health club next door. But don't even think about requesting one, or the view you'll have is the one most people do, of the Shaftesbury Theatre and the traffic pouring down High Holborn—not roaring, though, because the whole place is double-glazed. This is a tip-top residence in a tip-top location. Turn a corner, and it's a 5-minute walk to Covent Garden, which is why it can charge B&B hotel rates. That, and the fact that the beds have the fattest, most civilized mattresses I've ever seen in a student hall. It's very popular with families, who pay £5 ($8) a night for a foldaway child's bed. An adult one costs £10 ($16), making this one of the cheapest triples in town. Blocks of six rooms lock together and share a toilet, shower, and kitchen—bring your own utensils. Every second floor has two extra shared tubs, and everything is in very good shape. Downstairs, there's a huge breakfast room-cum-lounge, where one of the vending machines sells Häagen-Dazs. There's a launderette, Internet access, several TV rooms, and a big bar with pool tables and video games. And, hey, check out that open-air pool: It's a great reviver, open from 7:30am to 9pm and only costs £2.90 ($4.65), or £1.10 ($1.75) for kids.

Hotel Strand Continental. 143 Strand, London WC2R 1JR. ☎ **020/7836-4880.** Fax 020/7379-6105. 22 units, none with bathroom. TV. £32 ($51.20) single; £45 ($72) twin; £40 ($64) double; £50 ($80) family room. Rates include continental breakfast. Discount of 10% for 1-wk. stays. MC, V. Tube: Temple.

The Strand Continental is like the set of an art-house movie about the dying days of the British Empire. The hotel is part of the India Club, which Krishna Mennon, the first Indian High Commissioner to Britain, set up after independence. The members may be third generation, but little else has changed—the cash register in the bar looks like a manual typewriter. It certainly isn't posh, but this little hotel has become an exceptional deal since a charming Indian couple, Mr. and Mrs. Marker, took over what was then a backpackers' last resort in 1998. They've repainted and recarpeted everywhere, except the utilitarian linoleum-covered stairs. There are new bedcovers, curtains, furniture, and TVs. At the moment, up to six rooms share a tub and a shower. But the Markers promise that work will start early this year on putting in private bathrooms. I'm not quite sure where! The bedrooms with their simple new decor and 4½-foot-wide double beds are tiny. But if you've a taste for the quirky, pay the extra to get a little more space in a triple, still virtually given away. Choose one at the back for an amazing view, through the middle of the just-restored Somerset House (see "London's Top Attractions," in chapter 6). The club's canteen-style restaurant is one of those food critics' "secrets"—two courses cost £11 ($17.60). Don't worry, the delicious smells are pretty well-contained.

The Bargain Business

Business hotel chains do offer great value splurges, if you ignore the very luxxiest budget-busters. Special rates, designed to lure in leisure travelers, mean many city-center 3-star (or more) sleeps cost little more than a pricey B&B. The rates below are per night, for two people sharing a room, bed-and-breakfast. Ask about half board, too, and their special interest packages, especially if you're planning a trip out of town (see chapter 9). Savvy bargain hounds know it's always worth surfing hotel chain Web sites for excellent e-deals, too.

- **Best Western** (☎ **0845/774-7474;** www.bestwestern.co.uk): Eight hotels; 2-night Getaway Breaks any day; from £80 ($128). The best value Best Western hotel is Raglan Hall in Highgate. Only 15 minutes by Tube from the West End, it's in a quiet residential area and has a delightful garden and terrace.
- **Choice Hotels Europe** (☎ **0800/444444;** www.choicehotelseurope.com): 14 hotels; weekend leisure breaks Friday to Sunday; from £65.50 ($104.80). The Choice 2- and 3-star hotel brands are Comfort Inn and Quality Hotels. There are two very conveniently located in Victorian terraced houses in Bayswater and Kensington. Don't expect fantastic luxury—just enjoy the fantastic prices.
- **Forte Posthouse** (☎ **0845/740-4040;** www.forte-hotels.com): four hotels; Leisure Savers, 1-night stays Friday to Sunday only, 2-night-plus stays must include Saturday; from £90 ($144). If you can afford to fork out a bit more (£126/$201.60), go for the Kensington Posthouse. Not only does it have a health club and swimming pool, but this hotel is just off buzzy Kensington High Street and very handy for visits to Kensington Palace and the major museums.
- **Hilton** (☎ **0800/856-8000;** www.hilton.com): 10 hotels; EscapeAways; from £99 ($158.40). Many of these hotels are out of our price range but not

DO-IT-YOURSELF DEALS

Citadines, Trafalgar Square. 18–21 Northumberland Ave., London WC2N 5BJ. ☎ **020/7766-3700.** Fax 020/7766-3766. www.citadines.com. E-mail: trafalgar@citadines.com. 187 units, all with bathroom. 16 studios and a 1-bedroom apt. suitable for travelers with disabilities. A/C TV TEL. £111–£117 ($177.60–$187.20) studio; £164–£174 ($262.40–$278.40) 1-bedroom apt.; £199–£209 ($318.49–$334.40) 2-bedroom apt. Lower rates apply to 1-wk. stays. AE, CB, DC, JCB, MC, V. Tube: Charing Cross, Embankment.

"Aparthotel" chains are new to London, at least on a large scale, and it was this French company that pioneered the concept. Trafalgar Square opened in 1998 and is the Citadines London flagship. The *Ghost Busters*–style 1930s building, which the company totally gutted, used to be the members' hotel for the Commonwealth Club next door. Inside, it's all marble-tiled and corporate now, with an impeccable 24-hour welcome. The studios sleep two on a seriously deluxe and easy-to-use sofa bed—double or twin. You get an armchair, a table, chairs, and a built-in desk, and there's enough room to move around if you can't be bothered to put away the bed. The sparkling white kitchenettes are fully equipped, down to a dishwasher and the essential extractor fan. The apartments have the same arrangement, with the tub-shower and toilet separate to cut down on awkward traffic jams. Four people sharing a one-bedroom make the rate very competitive for the area. Fill a bigger one, with two bedrooms up a flight of stairs, and you'll get a real bargain. Every unit controls its own heating and air-conditioning. The phones have voice-mail. Safes, satellite TV, vacuum cleaners, the fab 4-star Hilton Hyde Park, which has Nintendo consoles in every room if the notorious British weather turns against you.

- **Holiday Inn (☎ 0800/897121;** www.basshotels.com/holiday-inn): seven hotels; Weekender Plus, check restrictions; maximum two adults and two children sharing, free dinner for children under 12; from £107 ($171.20). Darling, I wouldn't stay anywhere but the Garden Court in Welbeck Street, W1, just north of Oxford Circus—such a nice class of clientele.
- **Jarvis Hotels (☎ 0845/730-3040;** www.jarvis.co.uk): four hotels; Jarvis-breaks any day; from £99 ($158.40). The Jarvis Hotel, next to Marylebone Tube and train station, is only a stone's throw from Madame Tussaud's and the Planetarium.
- **Radisson Edwardian (☎ 0800/374411;** www.radissonedwardian.com): nine hotels; Breakaways any day but cheaper at weekends; from £105 ($168). From its name and curlicued logo, you know this hotel group is about classic English style. Go for the good value Vanderbilt in South Kensington: The smart decor is more than compensation for staying on busy Cromwell Road.
- **Thistle Hotels (☎ 0800/181716;** www.thistlehotels.com): 21 hotels; leisure breaks any day; minimum 2 nights; from £100 ($120). For the best deals but scant aesthetic stimulation, go for one of the two ugly modern Thistles in King's Cross—the Royal Scot and London Ryan Hotels. For a few pounds more, though, you can buy a more traditional sleep at the brilliantly located Bloomsbury Park (between Russell Square and Holborn), or the Kensington Palace, at the eastern end of the high street opposite Kensington Gardens.

and irons are standard. There's a launderette, and the reception desk can organize dry cleaning and extra maid services—otherwise, it's one towel change a week. And one whole floor is nonsmoking. Citadines has a deal with the Commonwealth Club, so you can have breakfast there. It's expensive, £6.50 ($10.40) for continental and £8.50 ($13.60) for full English, but it's worth doing once just to see the stunning modern restaurant. For a cheaper sleep, try the clone: **Citadines Holborn,** 94–99 High Holborn, London, WC1V 6LF (☎ **020/7395-8800;** fax 020/7395-8789; e-mail: holborn@citadines.com; Tube: Holborn). Studios cost £91 ($145.60) a night if you stay 1 week.

WORTH A SPLURGE

✪ **The Fielding Hotel.** 4 Broad Court, Bow St., London WC2B 5QZ. ☎ **020/7836-8305.** Fax 020/7497-0064. www.the-fielding-hotel.co.uk. E-mail: reservations@the-fielding-hotel.co.uk. 24 units, all with bathroom (shower only). TV TEL. £76 ($121.60) single; £100 ($160) double/twin, £115 ($184) superior double/twin; £130 ($208) double suite with sitting room. Rates do not include breakfast. No 1-night bookings on Sat. AE, DC, MC, V. Tube: Covent Garden. No children under 13.

The Fielding is another hotel that should exist only on film. It almost did, as a gangster's bedroom in *Mona Lisa,* the British hit starring Bob Hoskins about a prostitute and her protector. The crew couldn't use the room because the hapless former manager rushed out and redecorated. The Fielding did keep a hilariously kitsch painting from the set, and it fits right in. The whole hotel is a clean, tidy, and regularly renovated 1970s time warp—clearly a very good decade for the owner, who keeps an iron grip on decor decisions. Despite the best efforts of his charming manager, Graham Chapman, the narrow hallways and stairs are brown and orange, and metallic glam-rock pictures and chocolate-box alpine scenes cover the walls. Other than that, the bedrooms are attractive with comfortable new beds and faded coverlets and curtains. And the Fielding has finally upgraded its famously antiquated electrics and plumbing—there are lovely new bathrooms throughout. Tea-/coffeemakers are standard, but breakfast is not included. As Mr. Chapman says, the hotel doesn't score marks for extra bits-and-bobs. But it is in a pretty pedestrian street just around the corner from the Royal Opera House—the source of many of its guests, both performers and Placido Domingo's female fans. And it really is one of a kind. I defy anyone staying here not to have a huge happy grin on his face.

Royal Adelphi Hotel. 21 Villiers St., London WC2N 6ND. ☎ **020/7930-8764.** Fax 020/7930-8735. www.royaladelpji.co.uk. E-mail: info@royaladelphi.co.uk. 47 units, 34 with bathroom (some with shower only). TV TEL. £50 ($80) single without bathroom, £68 ($108.80) single with bathroom; £68 ($108.80) double/twin without bathroom, £90 ($144) double/twin with bathroom; £120 ($192) triple with bathroom. Rates include continental breakfast. AE, DC, MC, V. Tube: Embankment, Charing Cross.

The Royal Adelphi is a favorite with London Marathon runners, so you'll have to book very early to stay here in April. Forget slipping on the Lycra or funky chicken suit: The first thing the athletes do when they arrive is book their lucky room for the year ahead. The hotel may be a "splurge," but it's a cheap one and a fantastic value for where it is. The street was named after the 17th-century courtier, George Villiers, Duke of Buckingham. It's a little pedestrian enclave, packed with sandwich shops and restaurants, which links the river to the Strand just by Trafalgar Square. Office workers flood here to buy their lunch before going to sunbathe in Victoria Embankment Gardens. In the evening, it gets the overflow crowd from Covent Garden. The only downside is the noise—Buckingham Street, on the other side of the hotel, is much quieter. There's double-glazing throughout, and some windows look onto a lightwell in the center of the building, a dubious plus. The rooms are modest, too, and there's no air-conditioning, so they do get hot in summer. The decor is respectable rather than plush, with heavy wood-veneer furniture built in, but manager, Ian Gillan, recently renovated them all. Tea-/coffeemakers, hair dryers, and new radio alarm clocks are standard. The lounge and hotel bar (open 24 hours for guests) show distinct signs of wear and tear, but who's going to notice that when there's so much going on outside?

10 Victoria & Westminster

Astor's also has a small hostel here, the **Victoria Hotel** on Belgrave Road, SW1 (☎ **020/7834-3077;** fax 020/7932-0693). It's one of the cheaper ones, at £12.50 to £14 ($20 to $22.40) per person in a dorm. For more information, see "Paddington & Bayswater," above.

✪ **Collin House.** 104 Ebury St., London SW1W 9QD. ☎/fax **020/7730-8031.** 13 units, 8 with bathroom (shower only). £52 ($83.20) single with bathroom; £65 ($104) double/twin without bathroom, £78 ($124.80) double/twin with bathroom; £90 ($144) triple without bathroom. Rates include full English breakfast. No credit cards. Tube: Victoria.

You could easily walk straight past the discreet slate nameplate announcing Collin House. That would be a real shame because it's one of the best B&Bs on Ebury Street. For a start, it's well worth foregoing a private bathroom, even though all the showers

Hotels in Victoria & Westminster

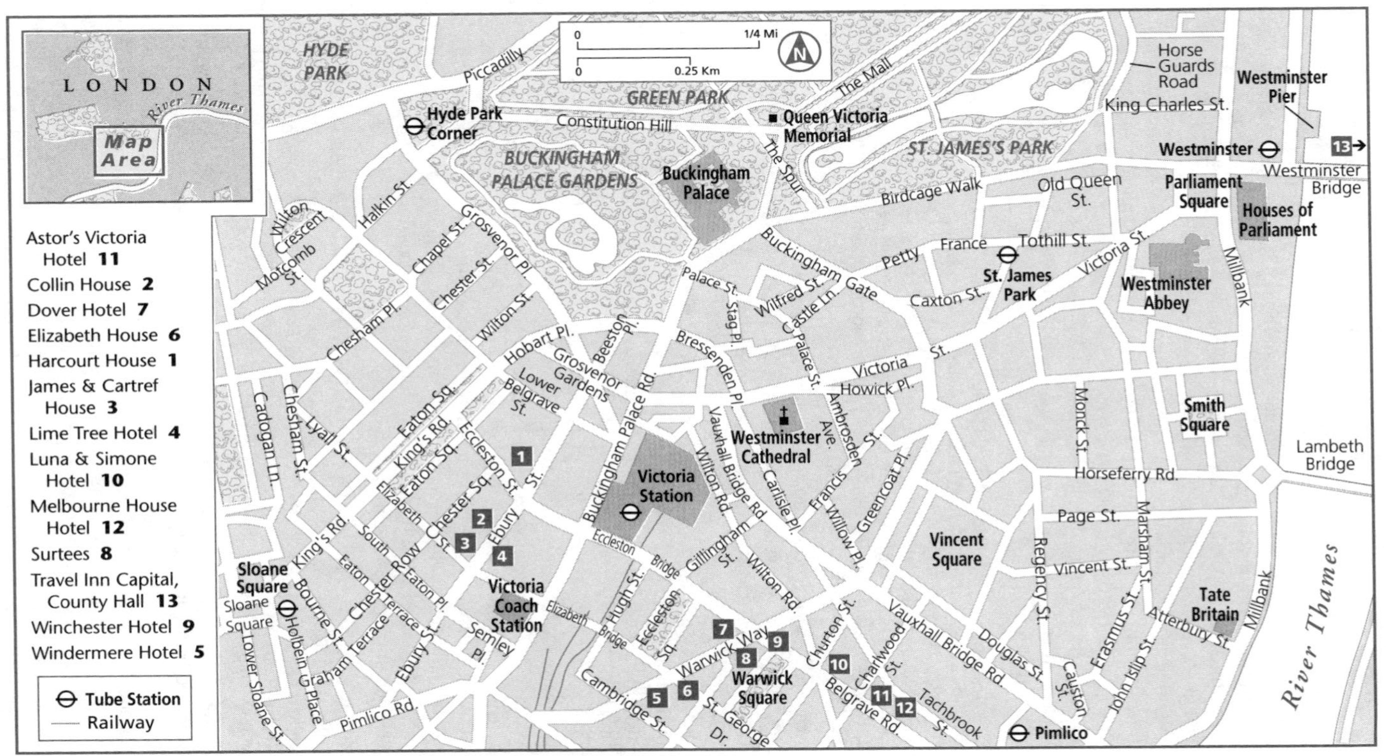

are all new, because there are never more than two bedrooms sharing each public facility. As well as having more money to go out on the town with, you'll get a room at the back, which is blissfully quiet. All the en-suites look out onto Ebury Street, and there is no soundproofing. However, if you don't mind traffic noise, go for the twin on the second floor. An untypically big room, it is also one of the five with new decoration. The armchair, carpet, and new printed wallpaper all tone together in pinky apricot, making it very cozy. Other recent renovations include new carpet on the stairs, where the original Victorian banisters curve outward like ribs on a skeleton. Mr. Thomas is now planning to convert the first-floor bedroom into a lounge. None of the other Ebury Street B&Bs listed here have got one, as the buildings are quite small. Let's hope he's as clever about it as he has been with the basement breakfast room. The look there is half-canteen, half-chapel, which disguises the cramped space. Collin House is nonsmoking throughout.

Dover Hotel. 42–44 Belgrave Rd., London SW1V 1RG. ☎ **020/7821-9085.** Fax 020/7834-6425. www.rooms.demon.co.uk. E-mail: dover@rooms.demon.co.uk. 33 units, 27 with bathroom (shower only). TV TEL. £40–£55 ($64–$88) single without bathroom; £50–£70 ($80–$112) double/twin with bathroom; £60–£75 ($96–$120) triple with bathroom; £70–£110 ($112–$176) family room with bathroom. Rates include continental breakfast. Lower rates apply Dec–Feb (excluding Christmas holiday). Discount of 5% for 4-night stays. AE, CB, DC, DISC, EC, JCB, MC, V. Tube: Victoria.

Belgrave Road is a good choice for art lovers, because the higher the house numbers get, the shorter the walk to Tate Britain at Millbank. It would take about 15 minutes from the Dover Hotel, and Victoria is under 10 minutes in the other direction. These two houses are part of a short terrace of smaller, brick-fronted houses on the eastern side of the street. Mr. Kassam took over in 1990. Since then, he has redecorated throughout, upgraded the showers, and recently put in new bedroom furniture, including some really ugly modern headboards. The bigger rooms—none are really that big—have decent-size closets, while the smaller ones have a hanging rail with a shelf above. Mr. Kassam's theory is that travelers don't care how much storage space they have. He obviously hasn't seen the jumbo suitcases that stream through Heathrow every day. Tea-/coffeemakers and hair dryers are standard, as well as clock radios and satellite TV, which is quite unusual at this price range, and some rooms are nonsmoking. There's a cold-drinks machine in the reception area. Breakfast is continental, but at least, it's self-service, so guests can go back as often as they want. The Dover may lack some of the quirky charm of Ebury Street rivals, but it is also a few pounds cheaper and very good value out of season.

Elizabeth House. 118 Warwick Way, London SW1V ISD. ☎ **020/7630-0741.** Fax 020/7630-0740. E-mail: elizabethhouse@compuserve.com. 30 units, 9 with bathroom (most with shower only). £30 ($48) single without bathroom, £40 ($64) single with bathroom; £50 ($80) twin without bathroom, £60 ($96) twin with bathroom; £18–£21 ($28.80–$33.60) per person in multi-share room. Rates include continental breakfast. MC, V. Tube: Victoria.

Warwick Avenue is a rather pretty street of small Victorian terrace houses with half-stuccoed fronts and iron railings. So it's a bit of a shame that traffic thunders down it from early morning until nearly midnight. That's partly why the B&Bs here are around £10 ($16) a night cheaper than those in posher Ebury Street. Elizabeth House is neat, clean, and a good value, particularly in comparison to some of its grotty neighbors. A lot of them are the sort of places that don't even try to entice you in by making the outside cheerful. The bedroom decor is plain, occasionally tired—never let it be said that any pictures darkened the walls—but comfortable, and there is ample storage space. The owner, Mr. Amin, has still got the bathrooms on his nonshrinking to-do list, both putting in new ones and sprucing up the old. One of his three buildings still has no en-suites. Elizabeth House does have a TV lounge with an excellent collection of guidebooks and holiday trash reading. In the summer, guests can sit out at tables and chairs in a large courtyard at the back, that fortunately is quiet and a real treat. And Elizabeth House also offers laundry facilities.

Harcourt House. 50 Ebury St., London SW1W 0LU. ☎ **020/7730-2722.** Fax 020/7730-3998. www.harcourthousehotel.co.uk. E-mail: harcourthouse@talk21.com. 10 units, all with bathroom (shower only). TV. £60 ($96) single; £75 ($120) double/twin; £90 ($144) triple. Rates include full English breakfast. Discounts for 3-night stays in winter. AE, MC, V. Tube: Victoria. No children under 18 except by prior arrangement.

Step through the door of Harcourt House, and you'll think the clock has spun back to the last century. For the past 3 years, the Woods have lovingly redecorated the whole of this early Victorian town house to recapture the original style and atmosphere. It's fantastically theatrical. Heritage junkies will love it, so long as they're not too pedantic about details, but other guests may find it rather dark. And it is a fraction cheaper than the other Ebury Street B&Bs listed. The hall and stairs are painted crushed blackberry below the dado rail, with sea-green above and over the ceiling. The rooms themselves, which have reproduction brass bedsteads (plus hair dryer and tea-/coffeemaker), are two-tone maroon and rich yellow. The only place where modern decoration is allowed to intrude—and it's a wise choice—is in the bright-tiled bathrooms. The Woods are clearly avid antiques hunters. The hall and stairs are lit with crystal chandeliers and decorated with junk-shop finds like the framed montage of Titanic memorabilia. The breakfast room, which is surprisingly light and bright, used to be the old kitchen. It has a real-flame fire and a restored wood-and-slate floor. Don't worry, no nasty Victorian cold cuts have made it onto the full English breakfast menu.

James & Cartref House. 108–129 Ebury St., London SW1W 9DU. ☎ **020/7730-7338** or 020/7730-6176. Fax 020/7730-7338. www.jamesandcartref.co.uk. E-mail: jandchouse@cs.com. 20 units, 11 with bathroom (shower only). TV. £50 ($80) single without bathroom; £65 ($104) double without bathroom, £78 ($124.80) double with bathroom; £85 ($136) triple without bathroom, £98 ($156.80) triple with bathroom. Rates include full English breakfast. AE, MC, V. Tube: Victoria.

Ebury Street calls itself Belgravia, but this is no hushed tycoon's enclave. Instead, it's a bustling road, with traffic zooming toward Victoria, a 10-minute walk away. There are dozens of places to stay either side of the junction with Elizabeth Street, where office workers join wealthy residents in the deli queues. Confusingly, James House and Cartref House are separate B&Bs on opposite sides of the road, both run by the very welcoming Derek and Sharon James. The main difference between them is in the number of private bathrooms. Most of them are in James House, but they're very small, so you might be better off without one—especially since only three rooms share public facilities. One thing: Kids have to be over 12 to stay in the top bunk in the James House family room. All the bedrooms are very nicely decorated: Mrs. James makes the curtains and bedcovers herself. Tea-/coffeemakers and hair dryers are standard. And both houses are nonsmoking. But the best news of all is that the Jameses have just put in proper permanent fans, giving you the coolest night's sleep on the whole of Ebury Street. Ask for a room with a wall-mounted one, as they've got more puff than those blowing down from the ceiling. Derek James is very proud of them, but his real pride and joy are still the zapper-controlled fans in both of the delightful conservatory dining rooms. Late-sleepers ought to be warned—breakfast stops at 8:30am, horribly early, at least by my slug-a-bed standards, whereas most B&Bs go on until around 9am.

Luna & Simone Hotel. 47–49 Belgrave Rd., London SW1V 2BB. ☎ **020/7834-5897.** Fax 020/7828-2474. E-mail: lunasimone@talk21.com. 36 units, 22 with bathroom (shower only). TV TEL. £35–£45 ($56–$72) single with bathroom; from £50 ($80) double without bathroom, £60–£70 ($96–$112) double with bathroom; £66–£90 ($105.60–$144) triple with bathroom. Rates include full English breakfast. JCB, MC, V. Tube: Victoria, Pimlico.

The family-run Luna & Simone stands out by a mile on this scruffy street. With the outside freshly painted, it gleams bright white like the icing on a wedding cake. New glass panels, etched with the hotel name, now partly shield the sides of the entrance porch. Usually, this sort of gentrification is the early warning sign of a bid for a posher class of guest. So it's reassuring to find the Luna & Simone prices pegged at B&B levels, especially as the owners have splashed out on the inside, too. The renovation has also taken in all the bedrooms, which vary widely in size, hence the price ranges. Most have desks, though, and all are equipped with hair dryers and tea-/coffeemakers. Ask about the bathrooms because some are extremely small—as long as you haven't got banana fingers, you might just fit both hands in the washbasin. The reception area is all new, as is the breakfast room, now totally nonsmoking. The look of both is light and simple, with modern curves, a refreshing change in Victorian building. The owners have put a luggage storage area into the old cellar under the pavement, so reception should never get to look like a charity appeal.

Melbourne House Hotel. 79 Belgrave Rd., London SW1V 2BG. ☎ **020/7828-3516.** Fax 020/7828-7120. 15 units, 13 with bathroom (most with shower only). TV TEL. £30 ($48) single without bathroom, £55 ($88) single with bathroom; £75 ($120) double/twin with bathroom; £95 ($152) triple with bathroom; £110 ($176) family room. Rates include full English breakfast. MC, V. Tube: Pimlico, Victoria.

Bathrooms are real crunch zones. They're expensive and hard work to maintain, and small budget hotels can really let guests down. Not so at Melbourne House. In one of the bathrooms, the gleaming gray tiles that I thought were brand-spanking-new turned out to be 6 years old. John Desira and his wife have run this B&B for 25 years. Everything is spotless, and there is no smoking allowed. Don't come here if you're looking for frills and fancy fabrics, though. The rooms are quite a good size for central London, but the decor is very simple for the price—plain walls and candlewick bedspreads. The Desiras have just replaced the carpets, beds, and furniture (a desk and ample storage space). All the shower units were new in 1999. Each room has tea-/coffeemakers and a hair dryer. There's a good family room for parents traveling with two teenage children, which combines a double, a twin, and a private bathroom. The lounge has had a face-lift, too. Gone at last are the squishy black armchairs that could have come straight out of a 1970s bachelor pad. In fact, the only disappointment at Melbourne House is that the full English breakfast isn't all-you-can-eat, as it is in many B&Bs. Mrs. Desira looked appalled at the thought, so don't try asking for more.

Surtees. 94 Warwick Way, London SW1V 1SB. ☎ **020/7834-7163** or 020/7834-7394. Fax 020/7460-8747. www.surtees-hotel.co.uk. E-mail: booking@surtees-hotel.co.uk. 10 units, 8 with bathroom (shower only). TV. £45 ($72) single without bathroom, £40 ($64) single with bathroom; £50 ($80) twin without bathroom, £55 ($88) twin with bathroom; £50 ($80) double without bathroom, £65 ($104) double with bathroom; £65 ($104) triple without bathroom, £75 ($120) triple with bathroom; £80 ($128) family room without bathroom, £90 ($144) family room with bathroom. Rates include full English breakfast. AE, CB, DC, DISC, EC, JCB, MC, V. Tube: Victoria, Pimlico.

Ahmed Akoudad has owned Surtees Hotel for 15 years and now runs it with his wife. You can't miss it. Festooned with hanging baskets, this is one of only a few buildings on its block with the bricks painted white above the first floor. Inside, it's very clean and well cared for. Mr. Akoudad does much of the work on the B&B himself and has spruced up most of the rooms, each one in a different style. He has also sorted out the bizarre, open-topped shower and toilet cubicles that some of them used to have, so no need now for diplomacy. Number 7, a basic twin on the top floor, is a good choice because it doesn't have to share the public facilities with any other room. There are also good deals to be had in the basement family rooms, as long as you don't mind looking out onto an internal courtyard. There's one that combines a single room with a triple, which three people can take for £20 ($32) per person. You get quite a lot of bang for your buck in terms of other amenities. Tea-/coffeemakers, satellite and cable TV, radios, and irons are standard, and you can borrow cots and VCRs at the reception desk.

Winchester Hotel. 17 Belgrave Rd., London SW1 1RB. ☎ **020/7828-2972.** Fax 020/7828-5191. 19 units, all with bathroom (shower only). TV. £75 ($120) double; £100 ($160) triple; £120 ($192) quad. Rates include full English breakfast. No credit cards. Tube: Victoria.

The Winchester is another big, white, Victorian house. To find it, look for greenery trailing over a porch where the hotel name is picked out in gold over black. There are lots of treats here for architecture buffs. The first-floor double room at the back has incredibly elaborate cornices. The proprietor, Jimmy McGoldrick, hasn't hacked the building about so you'll find the original moldings on the upper floors, too. The curtains complement them nicely, looping across the windows into tiebacks. The decor isn't super-grand, but it is fresh, clean, and attractive. On the second floor, you can walk out through floor-to-ceiling windows onto both the porch and the balcony that runs across the front. An unusual boon for four unattached friends traveling together is the all-single-bed family room in the basement, which has its own big bathroom. All the rooms have better-than-average storage space, and new carpet went down in 1999. The only catch is they're a bit short of amenities for the price. There's only a TV and radio. But the private bathrooms are the real thing, not drop-in units, and have glass-doored showers. And Mr. McGoldrick will cook you up a jumbo-size English breakfast, which he claims is the best in London. "Put it this way," one of his staff said, "If you don't like eggs, you'll get a pig on your plate. If you don't like bacon, you'll get a hen."

WORTH A SPLURGE

✪ **The Lime Tree Hotel.** 135–137 Ebury St., London SW1W 9RA. ☎ **020/7730-8191.** Fax 020/7730-7856. www.limetreehotel.co.uk. E-mail: info@limetreehotel.freeserve.co.uk. 26 units, all with bathroom (shower only). TV TEL. £75 ($120) single; £100–£110 ($160–$176) double/twin; £140 ($224) triple; £160 ($256) quad. Rates include full English breakfast. AE, CB, DC, MC, V. Tube: Victoria. No children under 5.

David and Marilyn Davies ran Ebury House, across the road, until 1994 when they moved to The Lime Tree Hotel. Mr. Davies is hugely competitive when it comes to winning prizes for his window boxes, and there are twice as many here as on any other house in the street. Flowers run rampant not only across the first floor, but in the basement, too, and boxes hang from the front railings and second-floor balcony. The Lime Tree is just as attractive inside. There are deep cornices in the hall, and statues and flowers sit in the alcoves up the stairs. The more expensive rooms are quite luxurious—swagged curtains, canopies, cushions on the beds, and pretty furniture. There is one on the first floor that leads out to a table and chairs on its own little terrace. The lower price applies to doubles and twins on the upper floors, which are more restrained but still very attractive. Don't expect a lift as part of your splurge, though. The authorities are very stringent about what they'll let people do to listed Victorian houses. All bedrooms have a tea-/coffeemaker, hair dryer, and safe. And the bathrooms are squeaky clean with glass-doored showers. The dining room is on the first floor, and in the summer, many guests take their breakfast out into the rose garden.

Windermere Hotel. 142–144 Warwick Way, London SW1V 4JE. ☎ **020/7834-5163.** Fax 020/7630-8831. www.windermere-hotel.co.uk. E-mail: windermere@compuserve.com. 22 units, 20 with bathroom (some with shower only). TV TEL. £67 ($107.20) single without bathroom, £80–£88 ($128–$140.80) single with bathroom; £75–£84 ($120–$134.40) double without bathroom, £84–£136 ($134.40–$217.60) double with bathroom; £132 ($211.20) triple with bathroom. Rates include full English breakfast. AE, CB, MC, V. Tube: Victoria.

People have been holidaying on this site, at the top end of Warwick Way, ever since the Middle Ages. The abbots and monks of Westminster Abbey and English kings and princes used to come to the Abbott's Grange for a bit of time-out. The Windermere itself dates from 1857, and it became one of the first-ever B&Bs in the area 24 years later. You can spot it today by the pale blue-painted stucco porch and pillars, a much grander architecture than the cluster of B&Bs down the street. Owner Nicholas Hambi and his wife have completely refurbished over the past 5 years. The big top-price double on the second floor was an experiment to see if people will splurge in a B&B. It's more like a minisuite, with canopied bed, sofa, and armchairs, and really expensive-looking curtains. It worked, and the Hambis are extending a toned-down version of the look into the others. My favorites are the pair of wedge-shaped rooms right at the top of the house—with windows on two sides, it feels like sleeping in a lighthouse. Budget travelers get fair deal at the Windermere, too: The basic double comes with a key to a hallway bathroom that no one else can use. Every room is double-glazed and has a hair dryer, safe, tea-/coffeemaker, modem outlet, and satellite TV. Eight of the rooms are nonsmoking, as are all the public areas.

Dining: The Hambis run a much-praised evening restaurant, called the Pimlico Rooms after the original B&B's name. It serves modern British and European food; two courses cost from £11 ($17.60). The bar is extraordinarily well-stocked, and the Hambis offer room service from 10am to 11pm.

11 The City & Clerkenwell

The **City of London Youth Hostel,** 36 Carter Lane, London, EC4V 5AB, (☎ **020/7236-4965;** fax 020/7236-7681; www.yha.org.uk; e-mail: city@yha.org.uk) is in a Victorian building that used to be the St. Paul's Cathedral choir school. Singles cost £26.80 ($42.90) and twins £50 ($80) per room; it's £19.70 to £23.30 ($31.50 to $37.30) per person in a dorm. There are family bunkrooms, but the hostel can't take groups because of parking restrictions on its quiet back street. Take the Tube to Blackfriars or St. Paul's.

SUPER-CHEAP SLEEPS

Barbican YMCA. 2 Fann St., London EC2Y 8BR. ☎ **020/7628-0697.** Fax 020/7638-2420. E-mail: admin@barbican.ymca.org.uk. 196 units, none with bathroom. £25 ($40) single; £21 ($33.60) per person in a twin. Rates include bed linen and full English breakfast. Weekly half-board rates are £150 ($240) single and £126 ($201.60) per person in a twin. CB, DC, DISC, MC, V. Tube: Barbican.

This 16-floor monster Y is one of the newer ones in London. It may not look very convenient, but the Tube station serving the Barbican arts complex is only two stops from the Piccadilly Line to Heathrow. And it takes 10 minutes to walk to St. Paul's. The Y sleeps around 250 people, and there are a lot of long-stay guests. So book as far in advance as possible. The decor is Spartan with shared bathrooms and a TV in the lounge. But the facilities are fantastic and pull in desk-bound city types during the week to work off their business lunches. The health club (£5/$8) has a gym and offers enough different kinds of exercise class to make your head spin. There's a sauna, tanning beds (just lie about the weather when you get home), massage rooms, and a sundeck. Reception is manned 24 hours a day and can lend you a hair dryer or lock up your valuables. You obviously get the best value by buying a week's half board. Even if you want more freedom, it's handy to have a cheap restaurant on-site. Barbican is not as deserted as some of the city out of working hours, but don't expect it to be like staying in the West End. The smaller sister hostel, **London City YMCA,** is a 5-minute walk away on Errol Street (☎ **020/7628-8832**).

Rosebery Hall, London School of Economics. 90 Rosebery Ave., London EC1R 4TY. ☎ **020/7278-3251.** Fax 020/7278-2068. www.lsevacations.com. E-mail: rosebery@lse.ac. uk. 449 units, 18 with bathroom (shower only). TEL. £26–£31 ($41.60–$49.60) single without bathroom; £36–£46 ($57.60–$73.60) twin without bathroom, £57 ($91.20) twin with bathroom; £55 ($88) triple without bathroom. 2 units adapted for travelers with disabilities. Rates include linen and full English breakfast. Open Easter and summer vacations. MC, V. Tube: Angel.

If you like browsing through market stalls, you'll love Rosebery Hall. Walk the 10 minutes to Angel, and there's one of the best markets in London for fruit and vegetables, cheap clothes, and household goods. Chapel Market dates from the 1860s and stretches for 200 yards at the weekend. Antiques buffs and lovers of memorabilia have to go a little farther to find Camden Passage where Islington's New Labour middle classes flock for bargains but have to haggle very hard to get them. South down Rosebery Avenue toward Clerkenwell is scruffy Exmouth Market. The hall may look out-of-the-way, and the tree-lined avenue is a bit of a highway. But you can see Sadler's Wells Theatre from some of the rooms, and there are lots of local restaurants. If you can, come at Easter because the rates are lower. You'll also pay less if you take a smaller twin. Some of the rooms are en-suite, otherwise there are shower blocks, as well as kitchenettes, on every floor. This is a well-maintained, if functional, modern building. Full English breakfast is included, and you can take it outside to the garden patio in the summer. The new bar looks like an airplane hangar, and the hall also has a launderette.

12 Just South of the River

Bankside House, London School of Economics. 24 Sumner St., London SE1 9JA. ☎ **020/7633-9877.** Fax 020/7574-6730. www.lsevacations.com. E-mail: bankside-reservation@ lse.ac.uk. 564 units, 306 with bathroom (shower only). TEL. £28 ($44.80) single without bathroom, £41 ($65.60) single with bathroom; £56 ($89.60) twin with bathroom; £73 ($116.80) triple with bathroom; £84 ($134.40) family room with bathroom. 32 units adapted for travelers with disabilities. Rates include full English breakfast. JCB, MC, V. Open summer vacation only. Tube: Southwark.

Culture buffs are falling over themselves to book in to this student hall, so make sure to call as far ahead as you can. Imagine finding somewhere to stay right behind the new Tate Modern at Bankside and Shakespeare's Globe Theatre. It's also 5 minutes' walk to the new Southwark Tube station on the Jubilee line, which links the maritime village of Greenwich (a UNESCO World Heritage site) to Bond Street and shopping heaven. Like High Holborn Residence, this isn't a super-cheap sleep, but then you do get rather more than a souped-up camp bed and a pin-board. Bankside House is a new building and more like a hotel—for a start, the mattresses are that lovely fat sort. When it began welcoming tourists in 1996, it mostly catered to youth groups, but the guest list is much more varied now that this historic, but once very run-down, neighborhood has become one of the most vibrant in London. Bankside House even has four rooms especially designed for families, with travel cots and high chairs available at the reception desk. Tea-/coffeemakers are standard, as there are no kitchenettes here, and there's a launderette, ironing room, games room, bar, and television lounge. The hall also has a cheap and cheerful restaurant where three courses cost around £7.50 ($12).

✪ **Travel Inn Capital, County Hall.** Belvedere Rd., London SE1 7PB. ☎ **020/7902-1600.** Fax 020/7902-1619. www.travelinn.co.uk. 313 units, all with bathrooms. TV. £64.95 ($102.40) single, double/twin, and family room (max. 4 people). Units adapted for travelers with disabilities. Rates do not include breakfast. AE, DC, MC, V. Tube: Waterloo, Westminster.

No budget hotel ever had a more astonishing location. County Hall is a mammoth 1920s monument to civic pride, across the Thames from the Houses of Parliament. It used to be home to the Greater London Council until Margaret Thatcher finally managed to abolish that left-wing thorn in her side in 1986. Now millionaires at the Marriott, which occupies the plum parts of County Hall, enjoy *the* London view. Guests at the Travel Inn, sadly, do not. Some rooms look downriver—though you can't see much water these days, since the British Airways London Eye, the 135-foot-high observation wheel, is parked right next door. Most face into a big central courtyard or out at luxury apartments behind. And once you're inside, you might be anywhere. There are 6 floors (5 nonsmoking) of bland identical corridors, but that's what budget chains do. The rooms are quite big, the decor good quality, and radios, hair dryers, and tea-/coffeemakers are standard. The price is an absolute steal, though the kids get a sofa bed in the family room and breakfast is not included. Continental costs £4.50 ($7.20), full English is £6.50 ($10.40), and under-10s can eat what they want for £3 ($4.80). The restaurant also serves a children's dinner menu, which is useful since there are few places to eat close by. If you walk round to the riverbank promenade, there's a McDonald's at the bottom of County Hall, next to the London Aquarium. There are also restaurants at the South Bank Centre, a 15-minute walk along the river. You can buy tickets for events there, as well as send e-mail for free, via the i-plus electronic information booth, in the foyer.

SUPER-CHEAP SLEEPS

✪ **St. Christopher's Village.** 165 Borough High St., London SE1 1NP. ☎ **020/7407-1856.** Fax 020/7403-7715. www.st-christophers.co.uk. 246 units, none with bathroom. £20 ($32) per person in a twin; from £12 ($19.20) per person in a 4-to-12-bed dorm. Full facilities for travelers with disabilities. Rates include continental breakfast. Discount available for 1-wk. stays. MC, V. Tube: London Bridge, Borough.

There is no cheaper place to stay in London. Or at least nowhere that would pass a rodent check. And definitely not with a hot tub as part of the deal. The hostel is in three buildings on busy Borough High Street. The first opened above the historic St. Christopher's Inn (no. 121 Borough High St.), where the floors are wonky, but the rooms are clean, and the showers are all new. (Don't stay here at the weekend if you're an early-bedder, because the pub goes ballistic and the floors are paper-thin.) Then, it expanded up above the stylish Orient Espresso coffee shop just up the road (no. 59), with much quieter dorms above where post–Generation X-ers and families with children under drinking age tend to stay. The really big bang happened in summer 1999, when the company gutted some marvelous old buildings and turned them into what it calls a backpacker's dream—PR puff, but I'd have to agree with it. There's an American diner-style bar called Belushi's, a roof-top deck with a sauna and hot tub, a nightclub in the basement, and so on and so on. There's none of the usual self-catering arrangements: Instead, St. Christophers subsidizes the food (£3.50/$5.60 for a hot meal) and drink. The area is a bit grotty, but on the rise like an Exocet missile, with the mouthwatering Borough Market round the corner, and Tate Modern only a few minutes away. And you're treading in the footsteps of Chaucer, Dickens, and Shakespeare.

St. Christopher's has 50 beds at similar prices at a hostel at 48–50 Camden High St. NW1 (Tube: Camden Town, Mornington Crescent), which you book through the Village telephone number above.

13 Farther Afield

HAMPSTEAD

The lovely **Hampstead Heath Youth Hostel,** 4 Wellgarth Rd., London NW11 7HR (☎ **020/8458-9054;** fax 020/8209-0546; www.yha.org.uk; e-mail: hampstead@yha.org.uk) used to be a college for nursery nurses and has its own garden. It charges £19.70 ($31.50) per person in a dorm, £17.30 ($27.70) for under-18s. Under-3s are welcome (cots available). Take the Tube to Golders Green.

WORTH A SPLURGE

La Gaffe. 107–111 Heath St., London NW3 6SS. ☎ **020/7435-8965.** Fax 020/7794-7592. www.lagaffe.co.uk. E-mail: La-Gaffe@msn.com. 18 units, all with bathroom (some with shower only). TV TEL. £65–£80 ($104–$128) single; £90–£125 ($144–$200) double. Rates include continental breakfast. AE, MC, V. Tube: Hampstead.

David Soul once stayed at La Gaffe. So did Oliver Reed. But they went for one of the honeymoon suites, of course, which have a four-poster bed, Jacuzzi, and a steam shower—sadly, these are super-splurges. Even the standard rooms are quite pricey, but this is a fantastic location and a really lovely hotel. Staying 30 minutes from Central London isn't too big a hardship, and Hampstead is certainly the place to do it. If you don't bump into a 1970s celeb at the hotel, then you might easily in the village, as it's home to many of them. This is where the rich and famous banded together with the not-so-famous to fight a vociferous battle against unsightly intrusion by a certain well-known burger chain. Hampstead is beautifully preserved and full of hip fashion stores and restaurants with their tables outside. La Gaffe is only a few minutes away from the Tube station toward the Heath. It opened in the 1970s—a great decade—above the restaurant of the same name, and Lorenzo Stella has now taken over the running of it from his parents. He has just built a conservatory on top of the roof terrace, a great vantage point. Other than the stars' favorite, the rabbit warren of rooms is small, which is typical of early Georgian houses, but they are comfortable and attractive with coordinating fabrics. All are nonsmoking and have tea-/coffeemakers and hair dryers. Breakfast is a bumper buffet.

NEAR THE AIRPORT

Hotel Ibis Heathrow (☎ **020/8759-4888**) is next to the Posthouse on Bath Road. Just refurbished, the rates, amenities, and decor replicate the Ibis Euston (see "Bloomsbury," above), without the railway theme. An en-suite double/twin is £69.95 ($111.90). To get here from the airport, take the Hotel Hoppa bus: H3 from Terminals 1 to 3, H13 from Terminal 4.

✪ **Harmondsworth Hall.** Summerhouse Lane, Harmondsworth, Middlesex, UB7 OBG. ☎ **020/8759-1824.** Fax 020/8897-6385. www.harmondsworthhall.com. 10 units, 7 with bathroom (shower only). TV TEL. £40 ($64) single without bathroom, £45 ($72) single with bathroom; £50–£60 ($80–$96) double/twin with bathroom; £70 ($112) family room with bathroom. Rates include full English breakfast. Discount available for longer stays. V. Bus: U3 from Heathrow Terminals 1–3 or West Drayton train station.

Harmondsworth is the perfect place to get over jet lag or catch a last glimpse of picture-book England to take home with you. This pretty little village has two pubs, an old-fashioned post office, and an 800-year-old church mentioned in the Domesday Book. It takes only 15 minutes to get to one of the world's busiest airports, yet the village isn't even under the flight path. Harmondsworth Hall is a rambling, 17th-century, redbrick house, with wrought-iron gates leading into a lovely country garden where there's even a Tudor cannon. The inside is beautiful, with a checkerboard floor in the hall, coffered ceiling in the wood-paneled breakfast room, an elegant drawing room, and Turkish carpets everywhere. But it's not like a museum, rather a cherished home. The rooms have lovely old furniture, too, and each one is decorated differently. Number 6 is my favorite—a huge double with a polished wood floor. Try and avoid the rooms in what was originally a separate cottage, because they're relatively modern. Hair dryers and tea-/coffeemakers are standard. Elaine Burke, who has run Harmondsworth Hall for 4 years, recommends the local taxi company (☎ **01865/ 444333**), which charges £6 ($9.60) for the trip to or from the airport. Book very very early as there are lots of regulars.

Heathrow Posthouse. 118 Bath Rd., Hayes, Middlesex, UB3 5AJ. ☎ **0870/400-9040.** Fax 020/8564-9265. www.posthouse-hotels.com. 186 units, all with bathroom. A/C MINIBAR TV TEL. £59–£119 ($94.40–$190.40) single, double, or twin. Lower rates apply Fri–Sat. AE, DC, MC, V. Hotel Hoppa bus: H2 from Terminals 1–3.

Bath Road runs along the Heathrow perimeter fence and all the big international names are here—Hilton, Sheraton, Marriott, and so on. The two budget hotels are right at the London end. Go for the business-friendly Posthouse for a weekend stay because you'll get more for the same money than at the Ibis next door. But stay away during the week when rates soar by nearly 30%. Granada has spent £1.3 million ($2.1 million) on giving the first floor at the Posthouse a smart new look. That includes the restaurant, where breakfast costs £11.95 ($19.10) during the week and £7.50 ($12) at weekends. It has also overhauled the second and fourth floors. Guests have to pay £20 ($32) extra for a redecorated room. Unless you're a big fan of contrasting wood veneers; you need to talk on the phone in the bath; or want a modem point, it isn't worth it for an airport stopover. All the rooms are classically masculine and luxxier than the Ibis. They're not a bad size either, with spotless bathrooms off the mini-lobby on the way in. Tea-/coffeemakers, hair dryers, and pants presses are standard, and half the rooms are nonsmoking. Built in the 1960s, the Posthouse looks like a roll of toilet paper. Many of the rooms face into a wide central courtyard, but the sound-proofing is so effective that guests often ask to face the airport—allegedly.

Great Deals on Dining

5

The locals get really bored by the constant slurs cast on British cooking. It can even cause them to forget their manners. And rightly so. That sad old cliché is about as accurate as the one that says the city is permanently enveloped in a pea-soup fog. The last 2 decades have seen an explosion of new eateries, new tastes, and new stars emerging from the kitchen. Today, London is one of the great food capitals of the world.

The Brits have dusted down their traditional dishes, robust comfort food like mother used to make before she started rushing down to the supermarket for a prepacked meal. Bangers and mash is a gourmet treat. Other chefs have aimed higher and taken the sort of upper-crust recipes the legendary Mrs. Beeton described in her Victorian cooking bible and given them a modern global twist.

A favorite for late-night lager-fuelled binges (at least *that* cliché still stands), Indian restaurants are rising to the top of the food chain again as purveyors of fine cuisine. And they're not the only ones. Great institutions all over the city are ditching institutional grub long past its sell-by date. First came the transformation of nicotine-stained "boozers" into innovative bare-boards restaurants, rather unfortunately called "gastropubs"—though locals will look at you very strangely if you ask for directions to the nearest one. Now London's major museums and galleries are giving the gourmet West End a run for its money. The new Tate Modern, and the revamped National Gallery, National Portrait Gallery, and Wallace Collection all serve up consummate contemporary cuisine in surroundings even Sir Terence Conran would kill for.

At the last count, Conran had 17 restaurants in the capital, typifying a particularly London phenomenon. The restaurant pioneers and celebrity chefs of a decade ago have become big businesses and cloned their ideas so successfully that flashy new eateries no longer generate the same buzz. Don't expect to find your heroes sweating into the soup when you dine at one of their places. We need a new term, something like the "school of . . ." phrase collectors use for artworks that came out of the Old Masters' studios.

The good news for budget travelers is that once a revolutionary concept turns into a fat-cat formula, that leaves space again at the bottom for a new generation of exciting cheap eats. If there's one common theme, or mission almost, it's the pursuit of "real" food, both richly wicked and virtuously fat-free, made from hand-reared ingredients with a mile-long pedigree that's often explained on the menu. The

Index of London Restaurant Maps

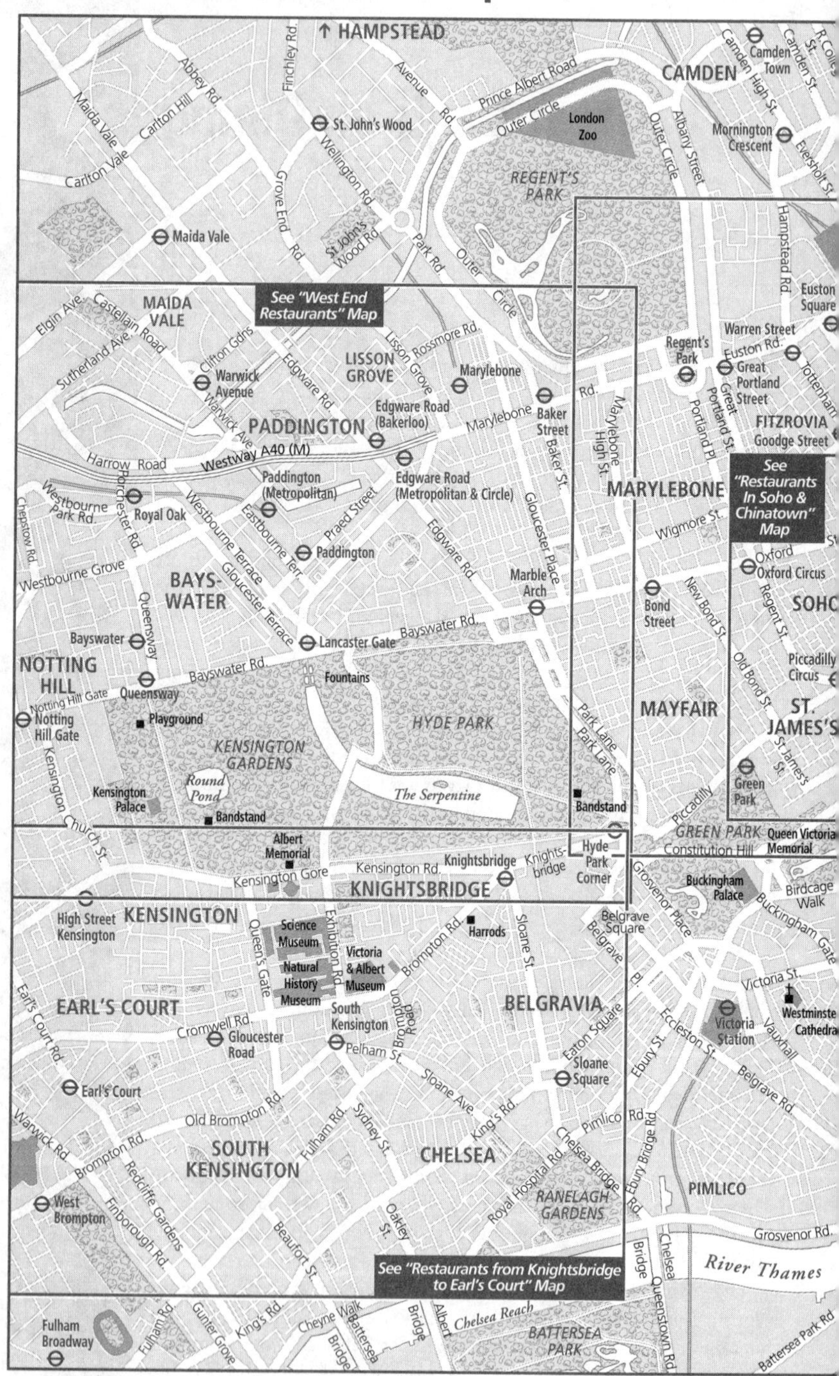

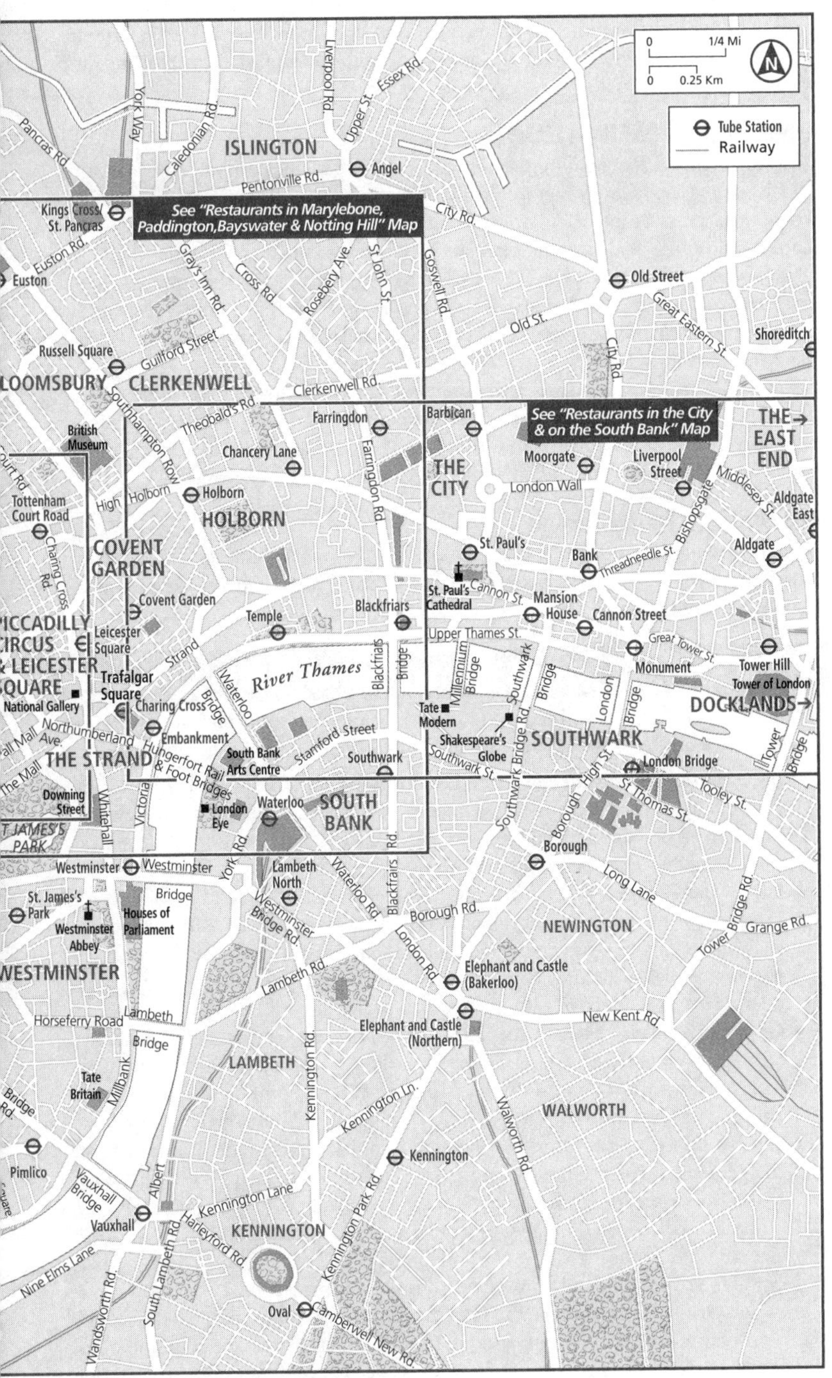

1/4 Mi
0.25 Km
N
Tube Station
Railway
ISLINGTON
Angel
Pentonville Rd.
York Way
Caledonian Rd.
Liverpool Rd.
Upper St.
Essex Rd.
Pancras Rd.
Kings Cross/St. Pancras
See "Restaurants in Marylebone, Paddington,Bayswater & Notting Hill" Map
City Rd.
Euston Rd.
Euston
Gray's Inn Rd.
Cross Rd.
Rosebery Ave.
St John St.
Goswell Rd.
Old Street
Great Eastern St.
Old St.
City Rd.
Shoreditch
Russell Square
Guilford Street
BLOOMSBURY
CLERKENWELL
Clerkenwell Rd.
Southampton Row
Theobald's Rd.
Farringdon
Barbican
See "Restaurants in the City & on the South Bank" Map
THE EAST END
British Museum
Chancery Lane
Farringdon Rd.
THE CITY
Moorgate
Liverpool Street
London Wall
Middlesex St.
Aldgate East
Tottenham Court Road
High Holborn
Holborn
HOLBORN
Charing Cross Rd.
COVENT GARDEN
St. Paul's
Bank
Threadneedle St.
Bishopsgate
Aldgate
St. Paul's Cathedral
Cannon St.
Mansion House
Covent Garden
Temple
Blackfriars
Cannon Street
PICCADILLY CIRCUS & LEICESTER SQUARE
Leicester Square
Upper Thames St.
Great Tower St.
Tower Hill
Monument
Tower of London
Strand
Trafalgar Square
Waterloo Bridge
River Thames
Blackfriars Bridge
Millennium Bridge
Southwark Bridge
London Bridge
National Gallery
Charing Cross
Tate Modern
DOCKLANDS
Northumberland Ave.
Embankment
Stamford Street
Shakespeare's Globe
SOUTHWARK
Tower Bridge
The Mall
THE STRAND
Hungerfort Rail & Foot Bridges
South Bank Arts Centre
Southwark
Southwark St.
Southwark Bridge Rd.
High St.
London Bridge
Tooley St.
Downing Street
Whitehall
Victoria
London Eye
Waterloo
SOUTH BANK
Borough High St.
St Thomas St.
ST JAMES'S PARK
York Rd.
Blackfriars Rd.
Borough
Westminster
Westminster Bridge
Lambeth North
Waterloo Rd.
Long Lane
St. James's Park
Westminster Abbey
Houses of Parliament
Westminster Bridge Rd.
Borough Rd.
NEWINGTON
Tower Bridge Rd.
Grange Rd.
WESTMINSTER
London Rd.
Lambeth Rd.
Elephant and Castle (Bakerloo)
Horseferry Road
Lambeth Bridge
New Kent Rd.
Elephant and Castle (Northern)
LAMBETH
Kennington Rd.
Tate Britain
Millbank
Bridge Rd.
Kennington Ln.
WALWORTH
Walworth Rd.
Kennington
Pimlico
Vauxhall Bridge
Albert
Kennington Lane
Kennington Park Rd.
Vauxhall
Harleyford Rd.
KENNINGTON
Nine Elms Lane
South Lambeth Rd.
Oval
Camberwell New Rd.
Wandsworth Rd.

concern about healthy eating, prompted by a wave of food scares, is a big cultural change. And a legal one: Restaurants have to 'fess up to enquiring diners if they use genetically modified foods.

A NOTE ON RESERVATIONS

Most restaurants accept bookings, except the super-cheap ones, and it's always wise to call ahead to save having to wait for a table. Regretfully, very few have wised up to the Web yet, at least as a tool for two-way communication, as you'll see from the rare e-mail addresses in listings. So do scan the reservations sites on the Internet. Celebrity chef Gary Rhodes is one of the backers behind what I think is the best one, **www.toptable.co.uk**. It is chatty and user-friendly, covers over 1,000 London restaurants, carries independent reviews, reveals celebrity-dining gossip, and offers regularly changing special deals. And there's no reservation fee.

For straight information, surf **www.thenosebag.net**. It groups over 5,000 restaurants, bars, diners, and cafes by clickable Tube stations on a London Underground map. It's very quick, very handy, and, though it was very new when I looked, plans to include reviews from critics and any diners who would like to contribute.

RESTAURANT HOURS

Restaurant hours vary, but lunch is usually noon to 2:30pm and dinner 6 to 10:30pm. Some shut down on Sundays or, if not, for one weekday meal. You'll never go hungry, though, because the city is stuffed with all-day cafes and diners.

1 Eat Without Losing Pounds: Money-Saving Tips

Seasoned bargain-hunters will recognize many of these dining tips, but it never hurts to have a checklist. And some of the weird local customs do need translating.

- **Sign Up for Discount Deals.** The **London for Less** card gets you 25% off the final bill, for food and drink, at 90 restaurants. YHA members also get a few dining bribes—perhaps a free dessert with a Hard Rock Cafe meal—which you can find out about when you book into a hostel.
- **Check the Charges.** Left to their own devices, Brits tip 10%, and so should you. However, some restaurants automatically add an "optional" 12% to 15% service charge. Check when you book, and knock it off if you're at all dissatisfied. A few restaurants also include a cover charge—normally £1 ($1.60). If your choice does, make sure to get your money's worth in free aperitif nibbles.
- **Go for Fixed-Price Menus.** You'll notice from the reviews that many restaurants offer great-value fixed-price meals, either at lunch, dinner, or for pre- and post-theater, which usually means 5:30 to 7pm, and after 10pm.
- **Bring Your Own Booze.** There are still a few unlicensed eateries left in London. You can take your own drink, saving pounds on inflated restaurant prices. Some charge a small fee per bottle, known as "corkage." Here's a BYOB directory: Mandola (see section 5), Books for Cooks (see section 5), Patogh (see section 6), Centrale (see section 7), Diwana Bhel Poori House (see section 9), October Gallery Café (see section 9), Food for Thought (see section 10), Quiet Revolution (see section 12), and Upper Street Fish Shop (see section 16).
- **. . . or Drink Theirs When It's Half-Price.** These restaurant-bars all have happy hours, but not always every day and not on all drinks. Check ahead to find out if your favorite tipple is on the list: Browns (see section 8), Cactus Blue (see section 4), Soho Spice (see section 7), and Speakeasy at Christophers (see section 10).

- **Net Savings.** Web sites like www.toptable.co.uk and www.lastminute.com post dining deals, usually sweetening standard menu prices with money off booze.
- **Get Your Timing Right.** There are big gastronomic compensations for braving a trip to London in January and February, because that's when several cheap-meal deals run. The *Financial Times* (www.ft.com) lists around 100 restaurants that offer a two-course lunch for £5 to £10. The *Times* (www.the-times.co.uk) does a similar thing, but you have to collect vouchers. Neither had confirmed details when we called, but you'll spot the promotion on their front pages.

2 Restaurants by Cuisine

Afternoon Tea

Brown's Hotel (Mayfair)
Dorchester (Mayfair)
Fountain Restaurant at Fortnum & Mason (St. James's)
The Lanesborough (Knightsbridge)
Waldorf Meridien (Covent Garden)

American

Arkansas Café (The City)
Blues Bistro and Bar (Soho & Chinatown, *P-T*)
Christopher's (Covent Garden, *P-T*)
Hard Rock Cafe (Mayfair)
Joe Allen (Covent Garden, *P-T*)
Planet Hollywood (Soho & Chinatown)

American Southwest

Cactus Blue (Chelsea & S. Kensington, *S*)

Belgian

Belgo Centraal (Covent Garden, *F-P*)

British Diner

Café in the Crypt (Covent Garden, *S-C*)
Café Grove (Notting Hill, *S-C*)
Chelsea Kitchen (Chelsea & S. Kensington, *S-C*)
The Star Café (Soho & Chinatown, *S-C*)

British/Modern

Andrew Edmunds (Soho & Chinatown)
The French House Dining Room (Soho, *S*)
The House (Chelsea & S. Kensington, *S*)
Shampers (Soho)

British/Traditional

Browns (Mayfair)
George (The City)
R.K. Stanleys (Bloomsbury & Fitzrovia)
Rules (Covent Garden, *S*)
Simpson's-in-the-Strand (Covent Garden, *S*)
Veronica's (Bayswater, *F-P*)

Chinese

China City (Soho & Chinatown)
Jenny Lo's Teahouse (Victoria)
Royal China (Bayswater)

Chinese/Cantonese

Golden Dragon (Soho & Chinatown)
Mr Kong (Soho & Chinatown)

Chinese/Northern

Yming (Soho & Chinatown, *P-T*)

Eclectic

Books for Cooks (Notting Hill, *F-P*)
Capital Radio Cafe (Soho & Chinatown)
Rainforest Café (Soho & Chinatown)

European

Vingt-Quatre (Chelsea & S. Kensington)

Key to Abbreviations: *F-P* = Fixed-Price *P-T* = Pre-Theater *S* = Splurge *S-C* = Super-Cheap

European/Modern

Aurora (Soho & Chinatown, *S*)
Bank (Covent Garden, *P-T*)
Corney & Barrow (Covent Garden)
Granita (Islington, *F-P*)
Mezzo (Soho & Chinatown, *F-P*)
Mirabelle (Mayfair, *F-P*)
Odette's (Camden, *F-P*)
Le Pont de la Tour (Just South of the River, *F-P*)
Teatro (Soho & Chinatown, *P-T*)
Villandry (Bloomsbury & Fitzrovia, *S*)

Fish & Chips

North Sea Fish Restaurant (Bloomsbury & Fitzrovia)
The Rock & Sole Plaice (Covent Garden)
Seashell (Marylebone, *F-P*)

French

Le Mercury (Islington, *S-C*)

French Brasserie

Brasserie St. Quentin (Knightsbridge, *F-P*)
Café Bohème (Soho & Chinatown)
Oriel (Chelsea & S. Kensington)

French/Modern

Criterion Brasserie (Soho & Chinatown, *S*)

French/Traditional

Chez Gerard (Covent Garden, *S*)
L'Escargot (Soho & Chinatown, *P-T*)
Mon Plaisir (Covent Garden, *P-T*)
Schnecke (Soho, *F-P*)

French-Caribbean

Townhouse Brasserie (Bloomsbury & Fitzrovia, *F-P*)

Gastropubs

Bleeding Heart Tavern (The City)
The Chapel (Marylebone)
The Eagle (Clerkenwell)
The Engineer (Camden)

Global

Cork & Bottle Wine Bar (Soho, *F-P*)
Giraffe (Marylebone)
Lola's (Islington, *F-P*)
October Gallery Café (Bloomsbury & Fitzrovia, *S-C*)

Greek

Daphne (Camden, *F-P*)
Lemonia (Camden, *F-P*)

Indian

Cafe Lazeez (Chelsea & S. Kensington, *F-P*)
Café Spice Namaste (The City, *S*)
Soho Spice (Soho & Chinatown, *F-P*)
Veeraswamy (Mayfair, *F-P*)

Indian/South

Diwana Bhel Poori House (Bloomsbury & Fitzrovia, *S-C*)
Malabar Junction (Bloomsbury & Fitzrovia, *F-P*)
Woodlands (Marylebone, *F-P*)

Indonesian

Nusa Dua (Soho & Chinatown, *F-P*)

Italian

Bertorelli's (Covent Garden)
Carluccio's (Bloomsbury & Fitzrovia, *S-C*)
Centrale (Soho & Chinatown, *S-C*)
Vasco & Pierro's Pavilion (Soho & Chinatown, *F-P*)

Japanese

Tokyo Diner (Soho & Chinatown, *F-P*)

Japanese/Noodles

Wagamama (Bloomsbury & Fitzrovia)

Japanese/Sushi

YO! Sushi (Soho & Chinatown)

Mediterranean

Mash (Bloomsbury & Fitzrovia, *S*)
Zoe (Marylebone)

MIDDLE EASTERN

Café Diana (Notting Hill, *S-C*)
Patogh (Marylebone, *S-C*)

NORTH AFRICAN

Momo (Mayfair, *F-P*)

PAN-ASIAN

Itsu (Chelsea & S. Kensington)
Wok Wok (Chelsea & S. Kensington)

PIZZA

Ask (Chain)
Oliveto (Victoria)
Pizza Express (Chain)
Pizza on the Park (Knightsbridge)

POLISH

Wódka (Chelsea & S. Kensington, *F-P*)

RUSSIAN

Trojka (Camden)

SANDWICHES

Pret a Manger (Chain)

SCOTTISH

Boisdale (Victoria, *F-P*)

SEAFOOD

Café Fish (Soho & Chinatown, *F-P*)
Fish! (Just South of the River, *S*)
Livebait (Covent Garden, *P-T*)
Lou Pescadou (Earl's Court, *F-P*)

SOUP

Quiet Revolution (Clerkenwell, *S-C*)
Soup Opera (Chain)
SOUP Works (Chain)

SPANISH

Cambio de Tercio (Chelsea & S. Kensington, *S*)

SPANISH/NORTH AFRICAN

Moro (Clerkenwell, *S*)

SUDANESE

Mandola (Notting Hill)

TEX-MEX

Café Pacifico (Covent Garden)

THAI

Sri Siam (Soho & Chinatown)

THAI-FRENCH

Vong (Knightsbridge, *S*)

TURKISH

Sofra (Covent Garden, *P-T*)

VEGETARIAN

Cranks Vitality & Health Care (Chain)
Food for Thought (Covent Garden, *S-C*)
Mildred's (Soho & Chinatown)
The Place Below (The City)
Woodlands (Marylebone, *F-P*)

WINE BAR

Cork & Bottle Wine Bar (Soho, *F-P*)
Corney & Barrow (Covent Garden)
Ebury Wine Bar (Victoria)
Shampers (Soho)

3 Knightsbridge

Pizza on the Park. 11 Knightsbridge SW1. ☎ **020/7235-5273.** Reservations required for music room. Main courses £6–£10 ($9.60–$16); breakfast menu £4–£4.95 ($6.40–$7.90). AE, DC, MC, V. Mon–Fri 8:15am–midnight, Sat–Sun 9:15am–midnight. Tube: Hyde Park Corner. PIZZA.

Pizza on the Park is one of the most popular jazz venues in London and pulls all the big names. Sadly, you do have to pay extra for the basement gigs: Monday to Saturday £18 ($28.80); Sundays £12 ($19.20). But come here Sunday lunchtime, and there's live background music—not jazz, usually—upstairs as well. This is a very superior pizza joint, with high ceilings, dramatic pillars, and tables set with fresh flowers.

Restaurants from Knightsbridge to Earl's Court

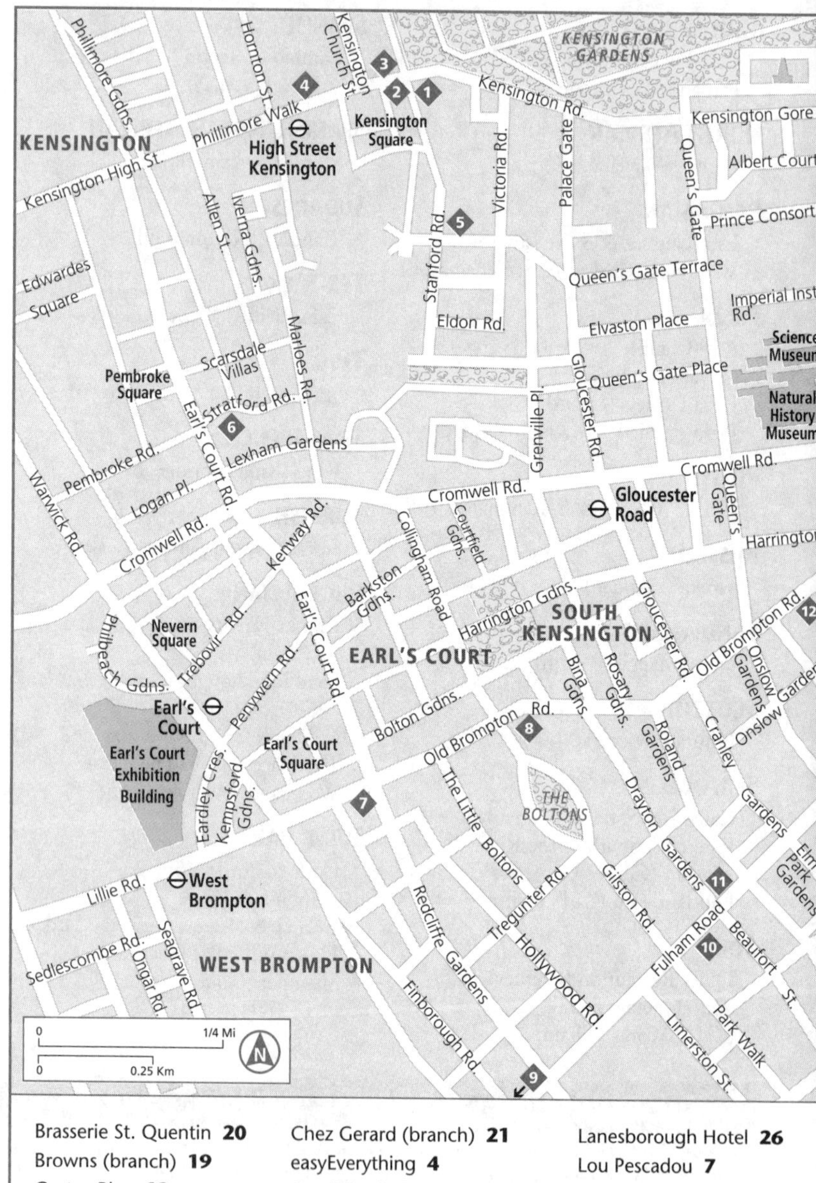

Brasserie St. Quentin **20**
Browns (branch) **19**
Cactus Blue **13**
Café Lazeez **12**
Cambio de Tercio **8**
Chelsea Kitchen **15**
Chez Gerard (branch) **21**
easyEverything **4**
Good Cook **1**
The House **17**
Itsu **18**
King's Head & Eight Bells **14**
Lanesborough Hotel **26**
Lou Pescadou **7**
Nag's Head **23**
Oriel **16**
Pizza on the Park **25**
Stratfords **6**

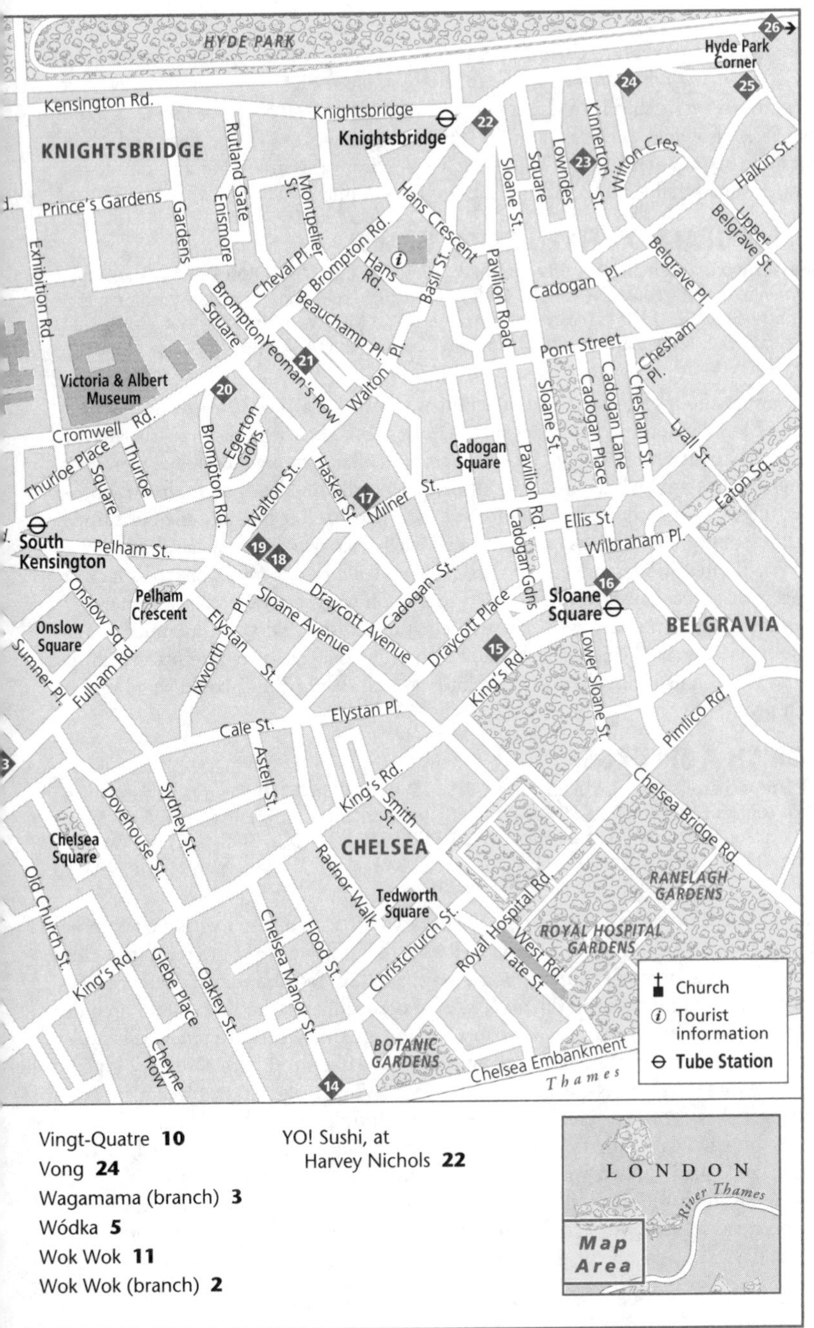

HYDE PARK
Hyde Park Corner
Kensington Rd.
Knightsbridge
Knightsbridge
KNIGHTSBRIDGE
Rutland Gate
Prince's Gardens
Gardens
Ennismore
Montpelier St.
Hans Crescent
Sloane St.
Lowndes Square
Kinnerton St.
Wilton Cres.
Halkin St.
Upper Belgrave St.
Exhibition Rd.
Cheval Pl.
Brompton Rd.
Hans Rd.
Basil St.
Pavilion Road
Cadogan Pl.
Belgrave Pl.
Brompton Square
Beauchamp Pl.
Victoria & Albert Museum
Yeoman's Row
Walton Pl.
Pont Street
Chesham Pl.
Sloane St.
Cadogan Place
Cadogan Lane
Chesham St.
Cromwell Rd.
Thurloe Place
Thurloe Square
Egerton Gdns.
Brompton Rd.
Walton St.
Hasker St.
Cadogan Square
Pavilion Rd.
Lyall St.
Eaton Sq.
Milner St.
Ellis St.
Cadogan Gdns
Wilbraham Pl.
South Kensington
Pelham St.
Onslow Sq.
Pelham Crescent
Onslow Square
Sumner Pl.
Fulham Rd.
Ixworth Pl.
Elystan St.
Sloane Avenue
Draycott Avenue
Cadogan St.
Draycott Place
Sloane Square
BELGRAVIA
King's Rd.
Lower Sloane St.
Pimlico Rd.
Elystan Pl.
Cale St.
Astell St.
Sydney St.
Dovehouse St.
King's Rd.
Smith St.
Chelsea Bridge Rd.
Chelsea Square
CHELSEA
Radnor Walk
Tedworth Square
RANELAGH GARDENS
Old Church St.
Chelsea Manor St.
Flood St.
Christchurch St.
Royal Hospital Rd.
West Rd.
Tate St.
ROYAL HOSPITAL GARDENS
King's Rd.
Glebe Place
Oakley St.
Cheyne Row
BOTANIC GARDENS
Chelsea Embankment
Thames
Church
Tourist information
Tube Station
Vingt-Quatre **10**
Vong **24**
Wagamama (branch) **3**
Wódka **5**
Wok Wok **11**
Wok Wok (branch) **2**
YO! Sushi, at Harvey Nichols **22**
LONDON
River Thames
Map Area

It used to be part of the Pizza Express chain, and the food still harks back to those days: lots of tomato on the base and interesting toppings. My long-time favorite is the *Quattro Formaggi,* but anyone prone to cheese-induced nightmares ought to avoid it because it is very rich. The restaurant loses form a bit when it comes to pasta. Pizza on the Park also does breakfast until 11:30am—great after a dawn start and all-in wrestling session at Harrods. The nicest view is from the inside looking out at the park. Pavement tables are a bit too close to heavy traffic.

GREAT DEALS ON FIXED-PRICE MEALS

Brasserie St. Quentin. 243 Brompton Rd., SW3. ☎ **020/7589-8005.** Reservations recommended. Main courses £12–£18 ($19.20–$28.80). Fixed-price lunch/pre-theater menu £11.50 ($18.40), £10 ($16) vegetarian. AE, DC, MC, V. Mon–Sat noon–3pm, Sun noon–3:30pm; Mon–Sat 6–11pm, Sun 6:30–10:30pm. Tube: Knightsbridge, South Kensington. FRENCH.

I've always thought Brasserie St. Quentin was a bit of a rip-off, with the prices it charges for the admittedly stylish main courses. But then it is right on the border between Knightsbridge and South Kensington. Local wallets are gold-lined, or at least designer label, as you'll see from the affluent, generally middle-aged or almost, clientele (there's a reassuringly high number of French, too). But the brasserie has earned itself big plus points with its excellent value fixed-price two-course meals, both lunch and pre-theater. It offers a blend of classic and updated French fare, from roast rack of lamb with parsley crust, to moist pan-fried salmon with sorrel sauce. Vegetarians get a run at most of the starters but are oddly left out in the cold when it comes to à la carte main courses—which is a shame, because this is a very attractive place with its chandeliers, etched mirrors, and tablecloths so well starched they could stand up on their own.

WORTH A SPLURGE

✪ **Vong.** Berkeley Hotel, Wilton Place, SW1. ☎ **020/7235-1010.** Reservations essential. Main courses £12.75–£29.75 ($20.40–$47.60); fixed-price lunch £16.50–£20 ($26.40–$32); black plate menu pre-/post-theater £17.50 ($28). AE, CB, DC, DISC, MC, V. Mon–Fri noon–2:30pm, Sat–Sun brunch 11:30am–2pm; Mon–Sat 6–11:30pm, Sun 6–10pm. Tube: Hyde Park Corner, Knightsbridge. THAI-FRENCH.

Vong is the London outpost of Jean-Georges Vongerichten. You'll either curl up in embarrassment or feel like a million dollars walking down from the reception area into this chic, basement, dining room—so make sure to dress up for the occasion. Vong is a visual feast, with brilliant flashes of orange-mandarin, single-stem orchids on the tables, and plates you want to take home. And the Thai-French cuisine is innovative and lightly hot: The delicious lobster daikon roll with rosemary ginger dip is an example. This is one of the five appetizers that make up the black plate pre- and post-theater menu. You'll also get a crab spring roll with tamarind dipping sauce, prawn satay with fresh oyster sauce, tuna and vegetables wrapped in rice paper, and quail rubbed with Thai spices and served with a cress salad. Seafood lovers can ditch the quail and take salmon slices in a scallion pancake with green peppercorns instead. Vegetarians can swap selections, too. If you can, fast for a couple of days and add on the divine warm Valrhona chocolate cake with lemongrass ice cream. It's extraordinary.

4 Chelsea, South Kensington, Kensington & Earl's Court

Itsu. 118 Draycott Ave., SW3. ☎ **020/7584-5522.** Sushi £2.50–£3.50 ($4–$5.60) per dish. AE, MC, V. Mon–Sun noon–11pm. No smoking in the restaurant. Tube: South Kensington. SUSHI/PAN-ASIAN.

Itsu is the brainchild of Julian Metcalfe who created Pret a Manger, the first chain of hip and healthy sandwich shops, which revolutionized the British lunch market. It does have the super-fashionable conveyor belt, the circling food on white, red, black, and gold plates to show the different prices. But simple sushi is the rogue element on a menu that subverts tradition with pan-Asian and Western influences. On the cheapest white plates, for instance, you'll find salmon sushi, a sweet omelet roll with chives, and the vegetarian Californian roll. Salmon has a big part on the menu, from the smoked variety with avocado and flying fish eggs, to some marinated with chives, or turned into sashimi. I tried not to look at the £3.50 gold plates, to avoid temptation. Grilled chicken with green soba noodles looked too good to resist, though, and was. Itsu is evangelically healthy, except for the oddball crème brulée on the black-plate list. So have a last cigarette in the bar upstairs as the restaurant is nonsmoking.

Oriel. 50–51 Sloane Sq., SW1. ☎ **020/7730-2804.** Main courses £4.95–£11.75 ($7.90–$18.80). AE, DC, MC, V. Mon–Sat 8am–10:45pm, Sun 9am–10:30pm. Tube: Sloane Sq. FRENCH BRASSERIE.

Oriel is *the* Chelsea rendezvous. It's such a fantastic location, right on the corner of Sloane Square, and everyone knows it. Posh 17 year olds, back from boarding school, meet their dates here or gangs of their mates. Green-clad country folk, who rarely come to London, flocked to Oriel before and after their famous 1998 protest march. And then there's your average Joe Blow. It's always hopping, so if you're planning to eat rather than grab a coffee-stop or a quick drink (wine by the glass is very reasonably priced), try to arrive a little ahead of normal mealtimes. The upstairs is classic brasserie, with big mirrors, square-topped tables, and high ceilings. There are a few pavement tables for people-watching. Downstairs, marshmallow sofas make you never want to leave. The food is a good value, from *moules marinières* (mussels) to salads or sausage and mash. Oriel has vegetarian dishes and will provide reduced-price portions for the kids.

Vingt-Quatre. 325 Fulham Rd., SW10. ☎ **020/7376-7224.** Main courses £7–£10 ($11.20–$16). AE, MC, V. Open 24 hours. Tube: Gloucester Rd., Fulham Broadway. EUROPEAN.

This is a proper diner, which serves proper food 24 hours a day. It's a West London institution and pretty unique across the whole city. Bedraggled partygoers, all untucked and blurring at the edges, roll in here hour by hour, whether to finish off the night with steak and fries or to officially mark the achievement of a *nuit blanche* with a rip-roaring English breakfast. Of course, you don't have to stay up all night to eat here. It's a great spot for a standard supper that isn't standard at all. The menu changes regularly, but diners can enjoy a delicious Caesar salad with quail eggs, or black tagliatelle with chili oil and grilled baby squid. If you do come for a session in the wee small hours, don't worry too much about getting back to your bed because Fulham Road is one of the more reliable places for finding a taxi.

Wok Wok. 140 Fulham Rd., SW10. ☎ **020/7370-5355.** Main courses £6–£10 ($9.60–$16). AE, DC, MC, V. Mon noon–10:45pm, Tues–Thurs noon–midnight, Fri–Sat noon–11:45pm, Sun noon–10:30pm. Tube: South Kensington. PACIFIC RIM.

Where to Go for a 24-Hour Munchie Fix

However cosmopolitan London gets, it still can't grasp the round-the-clock thing. There are a few places to assuage the munchies if they strike at an inconvenient hour but only a few, and some are only open 24 hours during the weekend. On Friday and Saturday, dirty stop-outs head for **Café Bohème** (see section 7). The legendary Soho diner, **Bar Italia,** 22 Frith St., W1 (☎ 020/7437-4520; Tube: Tottenham Court Rd.) is round-the-clock on Saturday and Sunday. The never-closers are the mainly gay **Old Compton Café,** 34 Old Compton St., W1 (☎ **020/7439-3309;** Tube: Leicester Sq.); the omelet and shake place, Clerkenwell's **Tinseltown,** 44–46 St. John St., EC1 (☎ **020/7689-2424;** Tube: Barbican, Farringdon); the nearby multi-ethnic snack shop, **The Knosherie,** 12–14 Greville St., EC1 (☎ **020/7242-5190**); the **Brick Lane Beigel Bake,** 159 Brick Lane, E1 (☎ **020/7729-0616;** Tube: Shoreditch); and **Vingt-Quatre** (see section 4).

Minimalist noodle bar Wok Wok is a fast food concept that does a good job of slowing down. You can make a quick stop for a quick bite, but the focus is on more leisurely dining at pedestal Formica tables. Combining culinary influences from all over Southeast Asia, the focus is on fresh ingredients and healthy-ish eating. Nothing is threateningly authentic, and the menu is brief and to the point. The Thai dishes pack the most satisfying punch. There's a very zippy rare beef salad and super-moist fish cakes. The *udon* noodles in broth with prawns, fish, chicken, squid, egg, and shiitake mushrooms, kept me quiet for a long time, except for a few appreciative "mmm's." Don't come here if you're a dead-set dessert person, because they're not up to much. Otherwise, Wok Wok is a good value, particularly for South Kensington. Other branches, useful to know about, are 67 Upper St., N1 (☎ **020/7288-0333;** Tube: Angel); 7 Kensington High St., W8 (☎ **020/7938-1221;** Tube: High St. Kensington); and 10 Frith St., W1 (☎ **020/7437-7080;** Tube: Tottenham Court Rd.).

SUPER-CHEAP EATS

Chelsea Kitchen. 98 King's Rd., SW3. ☎ **020/7589-1330.** Main courses £2.25–£4 ($3.60–$6.40); fixed-price meals from £5 ($8). No credit cards. Mon–Sun 8am–11:30pm. Tube: Sloane Sq. DINER/COFFEE SHOP.

This is a sister to the Stockpot chain, which also has a diner on King's Road. The Chelsea Kitchen is a lot more convenient, though, as you don't have to trek so far from Sloane Square, and the food is marginally less reminiscent of the dreadful school dinners the Brits grow up on. The cuisine is still not haute by any stretch of the imagination, but it is a fantastically good deal. The menu never ever changes. It runs from omelets and burgers to salads and more substantial hot dishes, such as goulash, spaghetti bolognese, and braised lamb chops. Of course, you can have fat fries with everything. Chelsea Kitchen is no-frills on the decor side, too, with polished wooden tables and bottom-numbing booths. The service sometimes sorely lacks a smile. But the prices are so "Old World" that it gets screamingly busy, particularly in the evening.

GREAT DEALS ON FIXED-PRICE MEALS

✪ **Cafe Lazeez.** 93–95 Old Brompton Rd., SW7. ☎ **020/7581-9993.** E-mail: cafelazeez@compuserve.com. Reservations recommended. Main courses £6.95–£14.50 ($11.10–$23.20); fixed-price meals £11.95–£15 ($19.10–$24). AE, DC, MC, V. Mon–Sat 11am–1am, Sun 11am–10:30pm. Tube: South Kensington. INDIAN.

Cafe Lazeez has twice won Carlton TV's Best Indian Restaurant award. It's another place that has ditched flock wallpaper and canned ethnic music for a cool modern approach, evolving new dishes but losing nothing of its authenticity in the kitchen. There's a bar/brasserie on the ground floor with the dining room upstairs. In summer, diners hang out on a terrace framed with flower boxes. There's so much good stuff to choose from and at such a range of prices, that you'd have to go back several times to work out which is the best deal. The £30 fixed-price menu for two is a great value. It starts with delicious barbecued meat: kebabs and chicken tikka with naan bread. The main course includes spicy sautéed chicken, lamb, aubergines, cumin potatoes, dhal, rice, more naan, and coffee. Alternatively, the £15.50 ($24.80) House Feast—a host of different meats cooked in the tandoor oven—could easily feed two people. Just ask for extra cutlery. There are two other branches: at 88 St. John St., EC1 (☎ **020/7253-2224;** Tube: Barbican, Farringdon) and at the Soho Theatre, 21 Dean St., W1 (☎ **020/7434-9393;** Tube: Tottenham Court Rd.).

Lou Pescadou. 241 Old Brompton Rd., SW5. ☎ **020/7370-1057.** Reservations essential. Main courses £7.80–£13.40 ($12.50–$21.45); weekday fixed-price lunch £9.90 ($15.85); weekend fixed-price meal £13.50 ($21.60). AE, DC, MC, V. Daily noon–3pm; Mon–Fri 7pm–midnight, Sat–Sun 6:30pm–midnight. Tube: Earl's Court. SEAFOOD.

You can't miss Lou Pescadou's porthole front window. The fishy theme carries on inside, with scallop ashtrays, marine-blue oilcloths on the tables, and boat pictures hanging on the walls. An evening at this old-fashioned restaurant can be a bit of a pantomime, too. Service is enthusiastic but often chaotic. Food standards can be patchy. Yet the restaurant has a loyal local clientele, mostly slightly older. It is very well-placed for anyone staying in Earl's Court. And you can sit out on the pavement during the summer. I definitely wouldn't go à la carte, but the weekend fixed-price menu is a pretty good value for three courses. If you get a shellfish option, make sure it comes with Lou Pescadou's deliciously velvety mayonnaise. Main courses are sturdy and old-fashioned, from whole seabass grilled with fennel to smoked haddock with juniper butter. I'd actually go for one of the meat dishes, also classically French—the chef really knows how to cook a steak, with shallot sauce, *saignant.*

A Frommer's reader kindly wrote to tell us about her "marvelous culinary experience" at the sister restaurant, **Stratfords,** 7 Stratford Rd., W8 (☎ **020/7938-3435**). Service was attentive: The waiter deboned her companion's Dover sole at the table, "to perfection." Her salmon was moist and delicious. The vegetables were "crisp and flavorful." And the wine was delightful. So we are delighted to pass on her recommendation.

Wódka. 12 St. Alban's Grove, W8. ☎ **020/7937-6513.** Reservations recommended. Main courses £10.90–£13.50 ($17.45–$21.60); fixed-price lunch £10.90–£13.90 ($17.45–$22.25). AE, DC, MC, V. Tube: High St. Kensington, Gloucester Rd. POLISH.

This Polish restaurant in South Kensington takes a new eclectic look at old classic dishes, served amid the simple modern decor. The two- and three-course fixed-price lunches are a great value. You might start with a meal-in-itself, such as *zur* (sausage and sour rye soup), or light fluffy blinis with aubergine mousse. The main courses are likely to include at least one Western European dish, the delicious fishcakes probably, so don't worry if Eastern has never been your bag. If you've got a bit of spare cash, then come in the evening instead. It's a much better time to enjoy Wódka's real specialty: the mile-long menu of vodkas, served by the shot or carafe. There's every flavor under the sun, from bison grass to rose petal, or a honey one that's served hot. You'll find some real hen's teeth, too, like the Genghis Khan from Mongolia. You can see why this is a firm favorite with locals and not-so-locals who want to kick their heels up.

WORTH A SPLURGE

Cactus Blue. 86 Fulham Rd., SW3. ☎ **020/7823-7858.** Reservations required for dinner. Main courses £10–£14 ($16–$22.40). AE, CB, DC, DISC, MC, V. Mon–Fri 5:30–11:45pm, Sat noon–11:45pm, Sun noon–11pm. Tube: South Kensington. AMERICAN SOUTHWEST.

Cactus Blue has all the icons of the American Southwest—dhurrie-upholstered banquettes; copper tables, chairs, and bar; portraits of Native-American leaders imported from Santa Fe; and an impressive collection of cacti. The happy buzz comes from people who are dressed nicely and have traveled far to enjoy food that is a great deal more upmarket than most American Southwest/Mexican ventures in London. It's not difficult to dine reasonably by mixing and matching appetizers and side orders: guacamole with crunchy root vegetable crisps, and South Fork skewered chicken fillets with pecans. But the main courses read so deliciously on the menu, and turn out to be even more so, that it would be a real shame not to splurge. Could you bear to watch a plate of marlin steak with roast mushrooms and garlic mash settle down in front of somebody else? I couldn't, and it was a great combination. Cactus Blue serves brunch from noon on Sundays, adding five kinds of eggs, plus sandwiches, to the regular menu. Happy hour goes from 5:30 to 7:30pm (all evening on Monday), when cocktails are £3.50 ($5.60) and bottled beer still a pricey £2.20 ($3.50). Enjoy your pick from 40-plus tequilas. And there's live jazz every Tuesday and Wednesday.

✪ **Cambio de Tercio.** 163 Old Brompton Rd., SW5. ☎ **020/7244-8970.** Reservations required for dinner. Main courses £9–£15 ($14.40–$24). AE, MC, V. Daily 12:30–2:30pm; Mon–Sat 7–11:30pm, Sun 7–11pm. Tube: South Kensington. SPANISH.

Several changes of chef have done nothing to dent the standards or the popularity of the stylish Cambio de Tercio. It's what they call a destination restaurant. Behind the small storefront, that opens up in summer, lies a dramatic interior, decorated in a rich yellow with damask-spread tables and chairs swathed in burgundy cloth. It might be too in-your-face for people with a strong interest in animal rights, because the walls are hung with pictures of bullfights and a matador's cloak and swords. The charming Spanish staff guides you through a menu of regional delights. The disembodied haunch and trotter in the window are a big clue to the house specialty—from the expensive plate of ham Jabugo, made from acorn-fed black pig, to the suckling pig Segovia style. Contrarily I went for the brilliantly conceived poached eggs with grilled asparagus, Basque wine mousseline, and sautéed foie gras. Not only should you dress up a bit for this place, but starve yourself beforehand.

The House. 3 Milner St., SW3. ☎ **020/7584-3002.** Reservations recommended. Fixed-price lunch £14.50 ($23.20), fixed-price dinner £23 ($36.80). AE, DC, MC, V. Mon–Fri noon–2:30pm; Mon–Sat 6–11pm. Closed 2 wks. in Aug, Christmas–New Year. Tube: South Kensington, Sloane Sq. MODERN BRITISH.

A lot's changed here since restaurant group Searcy-Corrigan took over last year and installed the highly regarded chef Graham Garrett. The one regret is that this has meant an end to the £10 ($16) three-course lunch: Now it's £14.50 ($23.20), which I think is too much of a splurge at midday. However, if you do fancy splashing out, then book in for dinner. There's no à la carte, but the fixed-price menu offers lots of choices—except for vegetarians, as is too often the case with robust modern British cuisine. I couldn't finish my ham hock with foie gras and artichoke terrine, but only because it was so rich. And I had to leave room for two more hearty courses: asparagus risotto, then rhubarb, mango, and custard tart. On a residential street in Chelsea, the House is the epitome of an elegantly traditional restaurant. Itd dining rooms, each are furnished with antiques and fresh flowers, and a fire roars in the hearth on cold days.

Dial-A-Dinner

Stuck in a rented apartment with the kids? Plotting a romantic evening in your hotel room? Then call **Room Service Deliveries** (☎ **020/7644-6666;** www.roomservice.co.uk). You can order from a book of menus from over 150 London restaurants, including **Café Lazeez** (see "Great Deals on Fixed-Price Meals" in section 4) and **Yming** (see "Pre-Theater Bargains" in section 7). The company has a mobile alcohol license and will bring anything from champagne to Jack Daniels. The minimum order is £10 ($16) and delivery is £4 ($6.40). You'll be in stellar company. Many of the clients are celebs hiding out from their adoring public. Jay Kay of Jamiroquai is a regular, as are the Oasis crew—Liam and Noel Gallagher. And the delivery guys' chins hit the deck daily as supermodels come to the door when they were expecting Miss Smith.

5 Notting Hill & Bayswater

NOTTING HILL

✪ **Mandola.** 139–143 Westbourne Grove, W11. ☎ **020/7229-4734.** Reservations recommended for dinner. Main courses £6–£9.50 ($9.60–$15.20). AE, MC, V. Mon–Sun noon–midnight. Tube: Notting Hill Gate. SUDANESE.

The secret of this little local restaurant is out. Mandola started out as the half-hearted annex to the take-out joint next door. Now it has grown into an attractive, laid-back, and mildly eccentric restaurant, and into yet another storefront. And the food is superb. The best deal in the home of good deals is the £10.50 ($16.80) starter, which gives two diners free run at everything the salad bar has to offer. "Salad bar" sounds like a motorway service station and doesn't do this justice. Options include white cabbage in peanut sauce, aubergine *salata aswad,* Sudanese falafel, and so on. Each would cost over £2 ($3.20) on its own, and you get pita bread to accompany them. Main courses are just as simple and just as irresistible, from super-tender meats in pungent sauces to the vegetarian stews. And the friendly staff will bring a flask and coffee set to the table. Mandola is unlicensed, so you can bring your own wine for £1 corkage per bottle.

SUPER-CHEAP EATS

Café Diana. 5 Wellington Terrace, Bayswater Rd., W2. ☎ **020/7792-9606.** Main courses £5–£8.50 ($8–$13.6), sandwiches £1.60–£4.20 ($2.55–$6.70). AE, DC, MC, V. Daily 8am–11pm. Tube: Notting Hill Gate. MIDDLE EASTERN.

It started out simply as a catchy name for a cafe so close to the park and Kensington Palace. Then Princess Diana heard about it and popped in for a cappuccino. She brought the first photograph, too, a smiling black-and-white shot with her signature scrawled across the bottom. Now the cafe is like a shrine, with barely an inch of space uncovered. There are shots of the princess in diamonds, playing with her children, visiting land-mine victims. One still has a black ribbon across the corner. Framed letters from her office thank the staff for their birthday wishes. History doesn't relate whether she preferred chicken tikka or lamb kofta kebabs. You can get a proper meal, but there are better value options. The pita breads filled with falafel, hummus, and kebabs are big and delicious, as are western versions like crispy bacon, chicken, and mayonnaise. And Until 4pm Café Diana does endless combinations of a greasy-spoon breakfast, which is why the clientele ranges from construction workers to tourists on a pit stop.

Surf 'n' Slurp @ the Best Internet Cafes

The first cyber cafe opened in London in 1994 to plaudits from the style press and puzzled bemusement from the masses. In e-volutionary history, that's like talking about the invention of the wheel—even local newsagents have sprouted scruffy surferias. The handy **www.netcafeguide.com** can give you a full London listing.

Now we're entering the Henry Ford phase, only this time the color is **easyEverything** orange. By mid-2000, there were already five of these giant Internet cafes in the capital (2,300 screens). The radical charging system is nothing like the usual £3 ($4.80) for half an hour. Surfers buy credit, not minutes. The minimum spend is £1 ($1.60), and the amount of time you get for that is in inverse proportion to how busy the branch is. The rate is adjusted every 5 minutes and posted on video screens, a bit like a money market. Your ticket has a user-ID, which notes the current rate when you first log on. That becomes your rate. You'll never pay more, but if things quiet down and the time-value of a pound improves, then you get more minutes, too—£1 could buy anything from 15 minutes to 6 hours. Avoid afternoons and early evenings. easyEverything never closes, and creatures of the night could even get to surf for free. A caffeine boost is also only a £1. Check www.easyeverything.com for new branches to add to this list: 358 Oxford St., W1 (☎ **020/7491-3936;** Tube: Bond St.); 9–16 Tottenham Court Rd., W1 (☎ **020/7436-1206;** Tube: Tottenham Court Rd.); 160–166 Kensington High St. (☎ **020/7938-1841;** Tube: Kensington High St.); 457–459 The Strand, WC2 (☎ **020/7930-4094;** Tube: Charing Cross); and 9–13 Wilton Rd., SW1 (☎ **020/7233-8456;** Tube: Victoria).

Note: You can send short e-mails for **free** from any of the dozens of **i-plus** electronic information kiosks around the city. You don't need to have an e-mail address. The downsides are: This is one-way communication; the maximum is 500 characters (about 90 words); and the touch-screen is irritating if you're used to typing arpeggios on a keyboard. To find out where the nearest kiosk is, see "Visitor Information," in chapter 3.

✪ **Café Grove.** 253a Portobello Rd., W11. ☎ **020/7243-1094.** Sandwiches and light meals £2–£7 ($3.20–$11.20). No credit cards (but soon). Winter 9am–5pm; summer Mon–Sat 8:30am–11pm. Tube: Ladbroke Grove. BRITISH DINER.

This is the perfect refueling spot after a morning of hunting down bargains at Portobello Market. In the summer, diners sit out on the roof terrace, enjoying the bustle below. It naturally gets a lot quieter during the week and in winter. Café Grove looks like a scruffy campus hangout from the 1970s, despite the freshly painted walls, and the menu is a mixture of the worthy and the wicked. You can breakfast your way around the world here—on porridge, hot muesli and maple syrup, huevos rancheros, pancakes, or croque monsieur. The very ungreasy All-Day Breakfast could stop a truck with its huge plate of bacon, sausages (vegetarian or "carnivorous"), tomato, fried eggs, mushrooms, baked beans, potatoes, and toast. For those who like their lunch to look like lunch, there are salads, build-your-own sandwiches, and homemade cakes. Café Grove serves wine and beer, but not Coke or Pepsi. And prepare for a dirty look if you smoke. You can also buy organic olive oil.

Great Deals on Fixed-Price Meals

✪ **Books for Cooks.** 4 Blenheim Crescent, W11. ☎ **020/7221-1992.** Reservations essential. Main courses £8 ($12.80); fixed-price meal £12 ($19.20). AE, DC, MC, V. Mon–Fri sittings at noon, 12:30, 1, and 1:30pm; Sat at noon, 1, and 1:45pm. Tube: Ladbroke Grove, Notting Hill Gate. ECLECTIC.

To eat at this amazing little store, you'll have to book well ahead: at least 1 week for weekdays, and 6 for a table at the weekend. Just off Portobello Road, this mecca for gastronomes stocks over 8,000 cookbooks. Staff can give really authoritative advice on which books to trust, where the measurement of ingredients should be taken with a pinch of salt, and which chefs clearly haven't tried out their dishes in a home environment. Because Books for Cooks constantly tests recipes in its open-plan kitchen. Each day a different freelance chef comes to cook lunch, and neither staff nor diners at the five tables squeezed in at the back of the store know what they're going to make until they arrive with the ingredients. Whatever it is, this is an astonishing value at £12 ($19.20) for three courses. The only downside is the envious stares at your plate from browsing shoppers. Books for Cooks is also unlicensed, but you can bring your own wine for no extra charge.

BAYSWATER

✪ **Royal China.** 13 Queensway, W2. ☎ **020/7221-2535.** Reservations recommended. Main courses £6–£40 ($9.60–$64); fixed-price dinner £23–£29 ($36.80–$46.40). AE, DC, MC, V. Mon–Thurs noon–11pm, Fri–Sat noon–11:30pm, Sun 11am–5pm; dim sum to 5pm daily. Tube: Bayswater, Queensway. CHINESE.

This restaurant has really put noses out of joint in Chinatown because the plaudits keep rolling in for its dim sum, which is reckoned to be the best in London. Royal China is marvelously over-ornate, with Hong Kong casino-style, black-and-gold paneling and female staff dressed in glittering sequins. But you don't have to be a high roller to dine here: Even pushing it, a dim sum extravaganza is unlikely to set you back much more than £10 ($16). The most popular dish, and deservedly so, is the roast pork puff—crisp pastry holding a wonderfully sumptuous filling. The touch is always light as air, whether on the standard menu dumplings or daily specials, such as a delicate mangetout combination. No wonder Sundays here are as big a scrum as the Harrods sale. Come during the week when it's a lot more peaceful, and the staff are more likely to have their happy faces on—but not that much more likely!

Great Deals on Fixed-Price Meals

✪ **Veronica's.** 3 Hereford Rd., W2. ☎ **020/7229-5079.** Reservations essential. Main courses £10.50–£18.50 ($16.80–$29.60); fixed-price menu £12.50–£16.50 ($20–$26.40). AE, CB, DC, MC, V. Mon–Fri noon–2:30pm, 6:30–11:30pm. Tube: Bayswater, Notting Hill Gate. TRADITIONAL BRITISH.

Veronica Shaw has won a cartload of awards for her unique style of cuisine. At her cozy restaurant, she adapts discovered recipes that go back as far as 700 years and puts charming explanatory notes in the menus. She spent 2 years painstakingly training Edmund Yoro before he took over as head chef. All the dishes list whether they're low fat, high fiber, vegan, or suitable for vegetarians. The house specialty is Fillet oak—richly-flavored, char-grilled beef, finished and served between smoking planks of wood. Otherwise, the menu changes with the seasons. The £12.50 ($20) two-course meal is a fantastic value. There's a choice of around three starters and puddings, and four main courses. To give you an idea, last year a special menu celebrated 2000 years of cooking in the British Isles. The simple sallet ("salad" to you and me) was anything

Restaurants in Marylebone, Paddington, Bayswater & Notting Hill

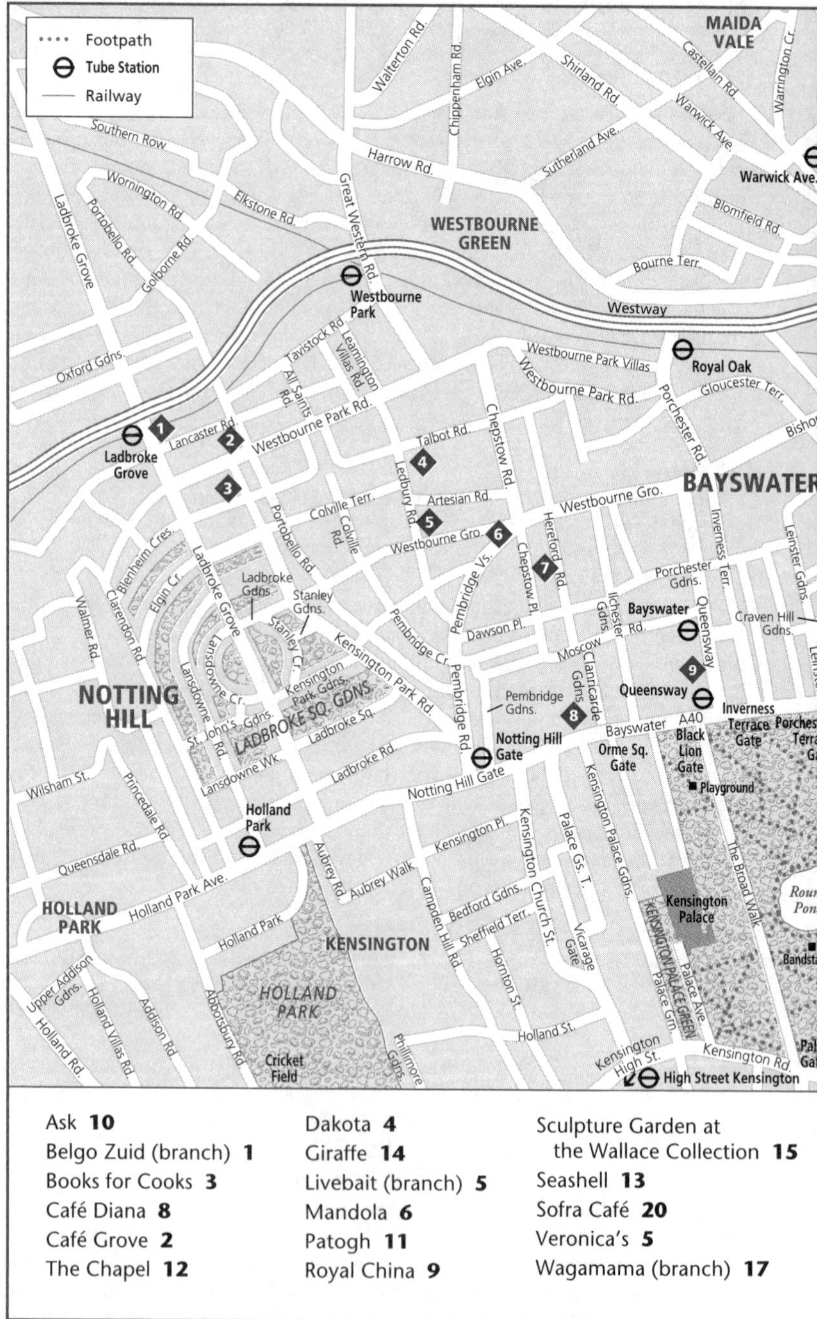

Ask **10**
Belgo Zuid (branch) **1**
Books for Cooks **3**
Café Diana **8**
Café Grove **2**
The Chapel **12**
Dakota **4**
Giraffe **14**
Livebait (branch) **5**
Mandola **6**
Patogh **11**
Royal China **9**
Sculpture Garden at the Wallace Collection **15**
Seashell **13**
Sofra Café **20**
Veronica's **5**
Wagamama (branch) **17**

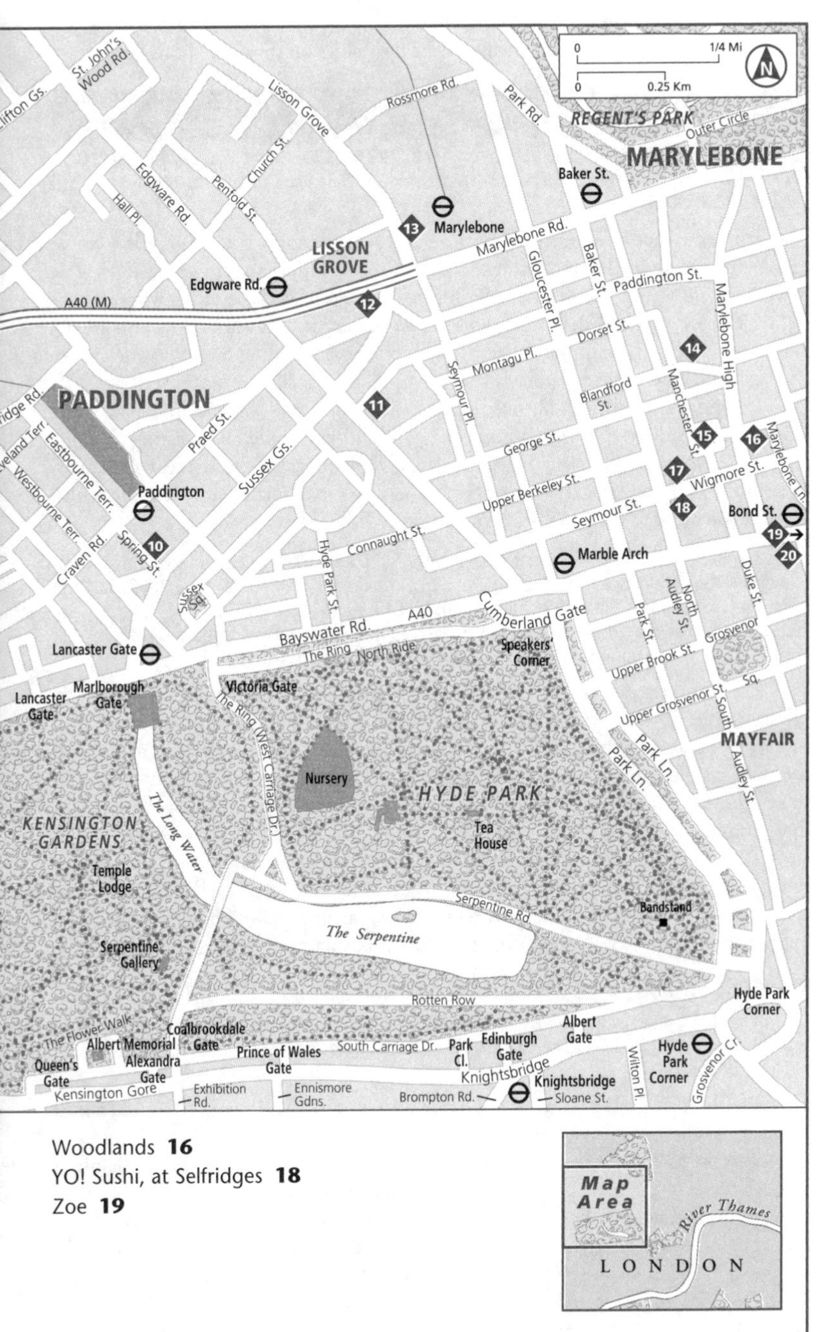

Woodlands **16**
YO! Sushi, at Selfridges **18**
Zoe **19**

but simple: asparagus, raw broccoli, carrot, orange, toasted almonds, marinated raisins, and salad cream from a 19th-century recipe, which a cheeky note suggested Heinz may have pinched. Ask for one of the few tables on the softly lit terrace.

6 Marylebone

✪ **Giraffe.** 6–8 Blandford St., W1. ☎ **020/7935-2333.** Main courses £6.95–£10.95 ($11.10–$17.50). MC, V. Mon–Fri 8am–midnight, Sat–Sun 9am–midnight. Tube: Baker St., Regent's Park. GLOBAL.

The first thing staff see when they turn up at this hard-working restaurant is a queue of eager eaters, and that's at 8 o'clock in the morning! It doesn't take reservations after 8pm, so be sneaky and book for 7 or 7:30pm, so you can stay all evening without having to wait for a table. I defy anyone not to leave Giraffe in a warm glow of contentment, not only because of the delicious food, but because of the friendly atmosphere. This is a café-cum-diner as well as a restaurant. Filling lunchtime snacks start at £3.50 ($5.60), and though there's no fixed-price menu, you needn't spend more than £15 ($24) in the evening. Go with a bunch of pals, and you could all be eating in a different country, from English herby sausages, to Moroccan-spiced meat dishes, to something with enough garlic to win you honorary French nationality. Giraffe is also at 46 Rosslyn Hill, NW3 (☎ **020/7435-0343;** Tube: Hampstead).

Zoe. 3–5 Barrett St., St. Christopher's Place, W1. ☎ **020/7224-1122.** Reservations recommended. Main courses £5.75–£10 ($9.20–$16) in cafe, £7.95–£14.75 ($12.70–$23.60) in restaurant; restaurant fixed-price menu £10.75–£13.50 ($17.20–$21.60). AE, DC, MC, V. Restaurant Mon–Fri noon–3pm, Mon–Sun 6–11:30pm; cafe daily 11:30am–11:30pm; bar noon–11pm, happy hour 5:30–7pm. Tube: Bond St. MEDITERRANEAN.

Zoe is in an piazza just off Oxford Street, surrounded by chic boutiques. Do keep an eye on the nearby sculpture fountain if it's a windy day: I was caught off guard by a sudden wet blast. Zoe has seating for 80 diners outside, with funky heaters to ward off the chill. People circle like drivers in a car park, ever ready to grab an empty table. The smarter restaurant is downstairs and offers some great fixed-price menus, either two or three courses, and at lunch as well as dinner. The cafe prices are so reasonable that it's a toss-up which is a better value. Though defining itself as modern European, the cuisine makes more than a nod to the Far East: upstairs with smoked chicken, Thai vegetable and rice vermicelli salad; downstairs with Cuan oysters with ginger granita. The menu changes regularly, but the friendly staff will explain everything.

SUPER-CHEAP EATS

✪ **Patogh.** 8 Crawford Place, W1. ☎ **020/7262-4015.** Reservations recommended. Main courses £4–£7.50 ($6.40–$12). No credit cards. Daily noon–11:30pm. Tube: Edgware Rd. MIDDLE EASTERN.

The no-frills, but very friendly, Patogh is a haven for a raffish crowd by day and a host of diners in the know by night. If you like simple but great quality Persian cooking, you'll love it, too. The kebabs are legendary. Left to marinate overnight, the lamb or chicken melts in the mouth. The skewers come on a huge circle of seeded bread, with yogurt dips and Middle-Eastern salad. The meat is all organic, and the spices create a riot of color. You'll never want to have a kebab made by anyone else again. If they're not you're thing, there are plenty of other choices, from chicken pieces to a whole host of ready-prepared salads and starters under the glass counter. There's hummus, marinated tomato, and other *meze* (small entrees). You could stack a plate high without coming close to busting the budget. Patogh is unlicensed, too, so you can bring your own cheap bottle of wine or beer, and you won't even be charged any corkage.

GREAT DEALS ON FIXED-PRICE MEALS

Woodlands. 77 Marylebone Lane, W1. ☎ **020/7486-3862.** Reservations essential on weekends. Main courses £3.50–£10.95 ($5.60–$17.50); fixed-price lunch £5.99–£11.95 ($9.60–$19.10), fixed-price dinner £10.95–£11.95 ($17.50–£19.10). AE, DC, MC, V. Daily noon–3pm, 6–11pm. Tube: Bond St. SOUTH INDIAN/VEGETARIAN.

This is one of three London outposts of a family-run empire, which has over 20 restaurants across India. It's a great place to try really authentic South Indian cooking. *Dosais*—funnel-shaped pancakes made from semolina and filled with spicy vegetables—are one of the specialties. Another must-try are the *Uthappam,* a crisp pancake made from spiced lentil and rice flower, topped with tomato and onion. The fixed-price menus are a great value. A *thali* will include some different vegetable curries, dahl (spiced, pureed lentils), rice, and bread. And the size of the meal seems to grow disproportionately to each small rise in price. Carnivorous diners must not let themselves be put off by the fact that Woodlands is vegetarian. This is a very attractive place, with several small dining rooms, each furnished with well-set tables and wooden chairs. The other city center branch is at 37 Panton St., SW1 (☎ **020/7839-7258**). Take the Tube to Leicester Square or Piccadilly Circus.

7 Soho & Chinatown

✪ **Andrew Edmunds.** 46 Lexington St., W1. ☎ **020/7437-5708.** Reservations recommended. Main courses £8.50–£11.50 ($13.60–$18.40). AE, MC, V. Mon–Sat 12:30–3pm and 6–10:45pm, Sun 1–3pm and 6–10:30pm. Tube: Oxford Circus, Piccadilly Circus. MODERN BRITISH.

Andrew Edmunds hates to think of itself as a stop on the tourist trail. In fact, it asked to be taken out of the guide. But this is such a good deal that we pretended we hadn't heard. The restaurant has grown organically, from an early start as a wine bar, and is attached to the print gallery next door. Popular for formal, and not so formal, business lunches by day, it becomes the haunt of young couples on romantic candlelit dinners in the evening. They have to whisper their sweet nothings because the tables are pretty close together. The handwritten menu changes frequently but always offers modern European cuisine in healthy portions: like wild mushroom risotto cake with salad and parmesan at the cheaper end, or splurgier duck breast with pumpkin and potato cakes in a juniper berry *jus* (that's a posh word for gravy). The desserts are delicious classics, from tiramisu to plum-and-almond tart. Finish up with a portion of Stilton.

Café Bohème. 13–17 Old Compton St., W1. ☎ **020/7734-0623.** Reservations recommended for dinner. Main courses £6–£12.50 ($9.60–$20). AE, DC, MC, V. Mon–Thurs 7am–3am, Fri–Sat 24hrs., Sun 9am–midnight. Tube: Leicester Sq. FRENCH BRASSERIE.

This is a favorite Soho hangout, despite the smokey atmosphere and *faux* French feel. It isn't just because Café Bohème is one of the few places in London that you can stagger into at any time of the day or night, at least on Friday and Saturday. There is a real buzz to the place, with a mix of young things and not-so young ones all looking for a good time at a reasonable price. The food is classic French bistro—from big sandwiches, omelets, and salads, to mussels, duck confit, and fillet of beef with onion marmalade. You can dine very well on two starters for under £10 ($16). Only two desserts appear on the menu, but if you feel let down by the time you get that far, I'd be very surprised. There is an enormous wine list and some eyebrow-raising cocktails, including one made of Sambuca, vodka, and Tabasco, called a Dead Line. An earlier-closing **Bohème Kitchen & Bar** (☎ **020/7734-5656**) has opened next door at nos. 19 to 21 Old Compton Street, with an open kitchen in the middle.

Capital Radio Cafe. Leicester Sq., WC2. ☎ **020/7484-8888.** Main courses £8–£12 ($12.80–$19.20); children's menu for under-8s £3.99 ($6.40). AE, DC, MC (accepts U.S.$). Mon–Sat 11:45am–midnight, Sun noon–11pm. Tube: Leicester Sq. ECLECTIC.

Young kids and teens love to visit this loud, glitzy emporium created by London's popular Capital Radio 95.8FM. And parents will enjoy taking their under-8s because there's a cut-price children's menu that includes a free drink and ice cream. It's very much in the Hard Rock Cafe style. The cavernous restaurant is wall-to-wall video screens. There are regular celebrity appearances. And you can listen to the DJs spin disks live on air all day. If you can eat in this frenzied atmosphere, the menu covers most teenage and youth favorites: burgers, sandwiches, salads, potato skins, chicken wings, and something a little more homegrown: bangers and mash. Like nearby Covent Garden, Leicester Square is jam-packed with people enjoying themselves at night, so do keep an eye out for pickpockets. Keep an eye out for stretch limos and skinny movie stars, too, because most London premières happen at the Empire cinema here.

✪ **China City.** White Bear Yard, 25a Lisle St., WC2. ☎ **020/7734-3388.** £4.50–£8.50 ($7.20–$13.60); fixed-price menu £15 ($24). AE, MC, V. Mon–Sat noon–11:45pm, Sun 11:30am–11:15pm. Tube: Leicester Sq. CHINESE.

This gigantic restaurant can seat up to 500 people, yet it's one of Chinatown's most relaxing locations. Walk through a gated archway, off busy Lisle Street, and you'll find a real slice of the Orient—a quiet courtyard with a fountain. The dining rooms, on 2 glass-fronted floors, are furnished with broadly set tables and bamboo chairs. Service varies from the usual off-hand style of Chinatown to surprisingly friendly, but you won't know which you'll get until you arrive. The cuisine is a mixture of old dim sum favorites and clever new ones with lacy fungi—the menu is à la carte rather than the traditional choice from the trolley. There's also a big range of casseroles, seafood, chicken, and so on to choose from for the main course. There is a minimum charge of £10 ($16), but diners can stuff themselves for that, which is why this restaurant is not listed under "Fixed-Price." China City also has a take-out service.

Golden Dragon. 28–29 Gerrard St., W1. ☎ **020/7734-2763.** Reservations recommended. Main courses £6–£18 ($9.60–$28.80); fixed-price menus £10.50–£20 ($16.80–$32). AE, DC, MC, V. Mon–Sat noon–11:45pm, Sun 11am–11:45pm. Tube: Leicester Sq. CANTONESE.

The crowds of local Chinese diners who come here back up the claim that the Golden Dragon serves up some of the best dim sum in town. There can be nothing but praise for the honey-glazed spare ribs, steamed eel with black-bean sauce, and sliced marinated duck with garlic dipping sauce. If you like, you can wash it down with po li or jasmine tea. Again, the service is variable but often because the staff is so busy rather than any deliberate rudeness. And the Golden Dragon is an appealing place, decked out in Chinese-holiday style. If you decide on dim sum, make sure to try the steamed scallop dumplings and prawn cheung fen. A real blowout shouldn't cost you more than £15 ($24), but you'll have to get here before 5pm. And do book, especially on Sundays when the place is packed.

Mildred's. 58 Greek St., W1. ☎ **020/7494-1634.** Reservations not accepted. Main courses £5.10–£6.90 ($8.15–$11.05). Mon–Sat noon–11pm, Sun 12:30–6:30pm. No credit cards. No smoking. Tube: Tottenham Court Rd. VEGETARIAN.

Mildred's is a smashing lunch spot that's open in the evenings, too, though not the best one for a long linger. This is a small cafe, and you may have to share a table. But with the very continental-style *passeo* that takes over Soho's streets at night, who'd want

AT&T Access Numbers

Aruba	800-8000	**Czech Rep. ▲**	**00-42-000-101**
Australia	**1-800-551-155**	Egypt●(Cairo)‡	510-0200
Austria●	**0800-200-288**	France	0-800-99-0011
Bahamas	1-800-872-2881	**Germany**	**0800-2255-288**
Barbados✚	1-800-872-2881	**Greece●**	**00-800-1311**
Belgium●	**0-800-100-10**	Guam	1-800-2255-288
Bermuda✚	1-800-872-2881	**Hong Kong**	**800-96-1111**
Cayman Isl.✚	1-800-872-2881	**Hungary**	**06-800-01111**
China, PRC▲	10811	**India ✖,➤**	**000-117**
Costa Rica	0-800-0-114-114	**Ireland ✓**	**I-800-550-000**

AT&T Direct® Service

AT&T Access Numbers

Aruba	800-8000	**Czech Rep. ▲**	**00-42-000-101**
Australia	**1-800-551-155**	Egypt●(Cairo)‡	510-0200
Austria●	**0800-200-288**	France	0-800-99-0011
Bahamas	1-800-872-2881	**Germany**	**0800-2255-288**
Barbados✚	1-800-872-2881	**Greece●**	**00-800-1311**
Belgium●	**0-800-100-10**	Guam	1-800-2255-288
Bermuda✚	1-800-872-2881	**Hong Kong**	**800-96-1111**
Cayman Isl.✚	1-800-872-2881	**Hungary**	**06-800-01111**
China, PRC▲	10811	**India ✖,➤**	**000-117**
Costa Rica	0-800-0-114-114	**Ireland ✓**	**I-800-550-000**

Israel	**1-800-94-94-949**	**Philippines** ●	**105-11**
Italy ●	**172-1011**	**Portugal** ▲	**0800-800-128**
Jamaica ●	1-800-872-2881	Singapore	800-0111-111
Japan ● ▲	**005-39-111**	**Spain**	**900-99-00-11**
Malaysia ●	**1800-80-0011**	**Switzerland** ●	**0-800-89-0011**
Mexico ● ▽	**01-800-288-2872**	Thailand ❮	001-999-111-11
Neth. Ant. ✪	001-800-872-2881	**Turkey** ●	**00-800-12277**
Netherlands ●	**0800-022-9111**	**U.K.**	**0800-89-0011**
New Zealand ●	**000-911**	**U.K.**	**0800-013-0011**
Panama	800-001-0109	**Venezuela**	**800-11-120**

FOR EASY CALLING WORLDWIDE

1. Just dial the AT&T Access Number for the country you are calling from. *2.* Dial the phone number you're calling. *3.* Dial your card number.

For access numbers not listed ask any operator for **AT&T Direct®** Service. In the U.S. call 1-800-331-1140 for a wallet guide listing all worldwide AT&T Access Numbers.

Visit our Web site at: www.att.com/traveler
Bold-faced countries permit country-to-country calling outside the U.S.

- ● Public phones may require coin or card deposit to place call.
- † Outside of Cairo, dial "02" first.
- ▲ May not be available from every phone/payphone.
- ✚ Public phones and select hotels.
- ✓ Use U.K. access number in N. Ireland.
- ❮ When calling from public phones, use phones marked "Lenso."
- ▽ When calling from public phones, use phones marked "Ladatel."
- ✖ Not available from public phones.
- ➤ Available from phones with international calling capabilities or from most Public Calling Centers.
- ✪ From St. Maarten or phones at Bobby's Marina, use 1-800-872-2881.

When placing an international call ***from*** the U.S., dial 1 800 CALL ATT.

Israel	**1-800-94-94-949**	**Philippines** ●	**105-11**
Italy ●	**172-1011**	**Portugal** ▲	**0800-800-128**
Jamaica ●	1-800-872-2881	Singapore	800-0111-111
Japan ● ▲	**005-39-111**	**Spain**	**900-99-00-11**
Malaysia ●	**1800-80-0011**	**Switzerland** ●	**0-800-89-0011**
Mexico ● ▽	**01-800-288-2872**	Thailand ❮	001-999-111-11
Neth. Ant. ✪	001-800-872-2881	**Turkey** ●	**00-800-12277**
Netherlands ●	**0800-022-9111**	**U.K.**	**0800-89-0011**
New Zealand ●	**000-911**	**U.K.**	**0800-013-0011**
Panama	800-001-0109	**Venezuela**	**800-11-120**

FOR EASY CALLING WORLDWIDE

1. Just dial the AT&T Access Number for the country you are calling from. *2.* Dial the phone number you're calling. *3.* Dial your card number.

For access numbers not listed ask any operator for **AT&T Direct®** Service. In the U.S. call 1-800-331-1140 for a wallet guide listing all worldwide AT&T Access Numbers.

Visit our Web site at: www.att.com/traveler
Bold-faced countries permit country-to-country calling outside the U.S.

- ● Public phones may require coin or card deposit to place call.
- † Outside of Cairo, dial "02" first.
- ▲ May not be available from every phone/payphone.
- ✚ Public phones and select hotels.
- ✓ Use U.K. access number in N. Ireland.
- ❮ When calling from public phones, use phones marked "Lenso."
- ▽ When calling from public phones, use phones marked "Ladatel."
- ✖ Not available from public phones.
- ➤ Available from phones with international calling capabilities or from most Public Calling Centers.
- ✪ From St. Maarten or phones at Bobby's Marina, use 1-800-872-2881.

When placing an international call ***from*** the U.S., dial 1 800 CALL ATT.

© 1/2000

Restaurants in Soho & Chinatown

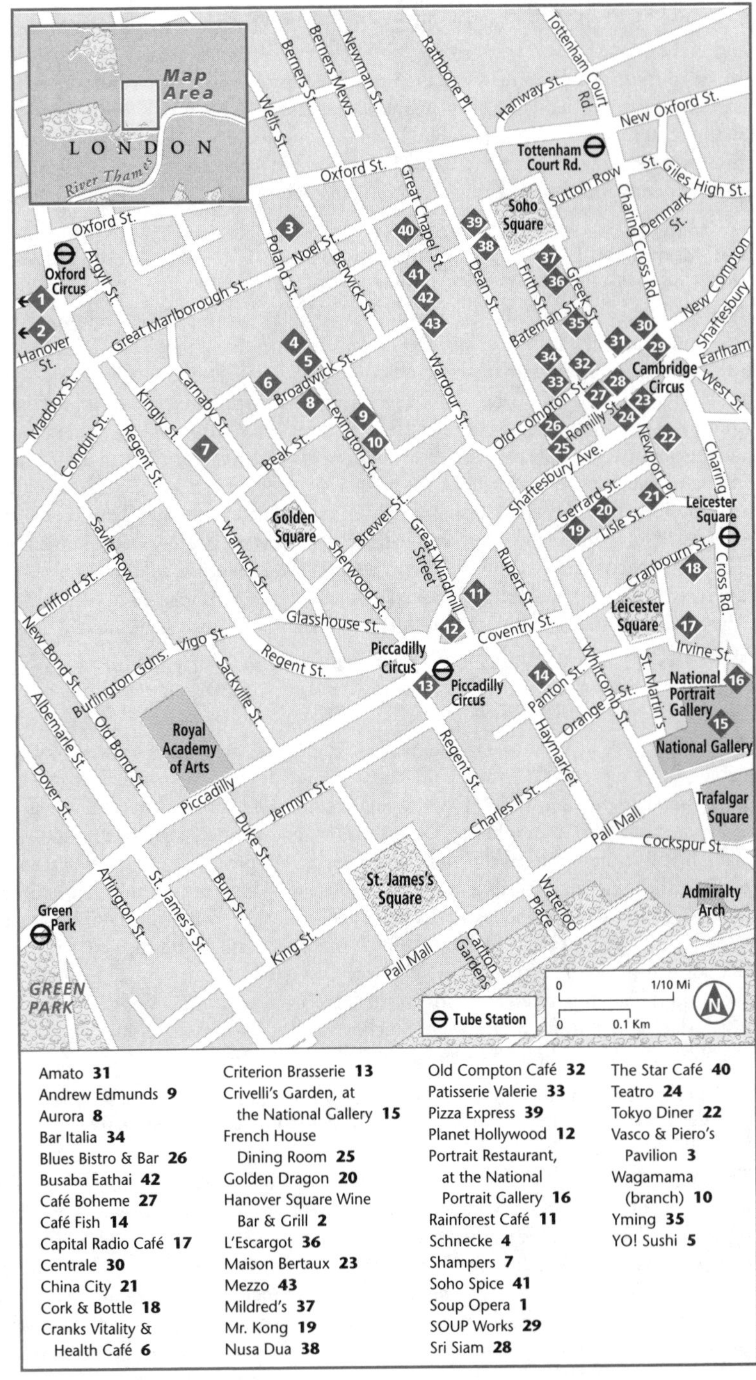

to stay inside? Mildred's may look like a product of the current trend for healthy eating in London, but it's been around since the days when vegetarian meant lunatic fringe to most people and few restaurants offered meatless options. All the vegetarian ingredients are naturally grown—or laid, in the case of the free-range eggs—and used in the right season wherever possible. Legumes cooked every which way are a firm fixture, as are stir-fries. The menu changes every day and becomes very wicked when you get to dessert. And Mildred's also stocks organic wines.

Mr Kong. 21 Lisle St., WC2. ☎ **020/7437-7341.** Reservations required for weekend dinners. Main courses £6–£18; fixed-price dinner £9.30–£22 ($14.90–$35.20). AE, DC, MC, V. Daily noon–3am. Tube: Leicester Sq., Piccadilly Circus. CANTONESE.

Nobody comes to Mr Kong for interior-decorating advice, but they would to get the low-down on truly authentic but innovative Cantonese cooking. This rather shabby restaurant is so popular that, while others in London shorten their hours, it's busy until 3am every night of the week. The cheaper fixed-price menu includes soup, a choice of three main courses—beef with black bean sauce, for instance—and rice. The more expensive one covers four courses and is a lot better value. Go with either, however, and you may get a visit from the green-eyed monster when you see what others have ordered from over 150 dishes listed on three different menus. The Chef's Specials could be Mandarin chicken with jellyfish, or frog's legs in ginger wine, or fish lips. The daily specials are generally a bit cheaper and less exotic. Or you can choose from the regular selection: Sliced pork, salted egg, and vegetable soup is a house specialty. The service is extremely friendly, and the menu translated into English.

Shampers. 4 Kingly St., W1. ☎ **020/7439-9910.** Main courses £8–£12 ($12.80–$19.20). AE, DC, MC, V. Mon–Sat noon–11pm. Closed Sat in Aug. Tube: Oxford Circus, Piccadilly Circus. WINE BAR/MODERN BRITISH.

The atmosphere at Shampers is laid-back and fairly stylish, despite its incredibly naff name. That's more to do with the off-Soho clientele it attracts than the decor, which is the standard wooden tables, posters, and candles. Right behind Regent Street, this is a great place to pop into for a good value bite and reasonably priced drinks—especially if you've just splurged the budget on a shopping spree. The food is robust modern British, sometimes with a Euro twist, sometimes with a hint of the east. Chicken and ginger and pak choi soup is a £3.50 ($5.60) filler, or go for the good value plate of delicious cured meats at £5.50 ($8.80). If that isn't going to fill the gap, try one of the hot dishes like pan-fried calves' liver with bacon, mashed potato and spinach, or the famous ham and cheese pie with salad. There are always fish and vegetarian dishes of the day, as well as fresh salads and quiche. Most of the wines are only available by the bottle, but there should be enough by the glass to satisfy.

Sri Siam. 16 Old Compton St., W1. ☎ **020/7434-3544.** Reservations recommended. Main courses £7–£10.50 ($11.20–$16.80). AE, DC, V. Mon–Sat noon–3pm and 6–11:15pm, Sun 6–10:30pm. Tube: Leicester Sq. THAI.

The long, narrow dining room at Sri Siam is divided into intimate dining areas softly lit with sconces, where black lacquer chairs are set at tables decked with fine white tablecloths. Banana leaves painted on the walls try to lend a tropical air. Sri Siam was one of the early pioneers in the Thai food boom, and with its consistently good service, it's still a favorite, despite being more expensive than hole-in-the-wall rivals. The attractively presented dishes here are usually well-spiced, though some will disappoint and others ought to carry a perspiration warning—hot-and-sour papaya salad is one such. Try the marinated fish grilled in banana leaf and served with two sauces (chili or tamarind plum); the spicy stir-fried pork with basil, chili, and garlic; or diced chicken

Sinful Soho: Dens of Delicious Iniquity

Whoever said the Brits are so-serious in public and only sin behind closed doors had obviously never been to Soho. I'm not talking about sleazy strip joints, but the wicked delights of the neighborhood's famous patisseries. The French had to show them how to do it, but supposedly stodgy Londoners have taken to sweet flaky pastries, tarts, and cakes with a vengeance. Just watch the shameless hordes that flock here on a Sunday. The most venerable patisserie is **Maison Bertaux,** 28 Greek St., W1 (☎ **020/7437-6007**), and I defy you to pass by its delectable window without wanting to dunk a brioche in a cup of coffee. Not unless it's to visit **Patisserie Valerie,** 44 Old Compton St., W1 (☎ **020/7437-3466**), *the* place to gawk at greedy film and theater types who've fallen for its chocolate truffle cake. The crowds are smaller at **Amato,** 14 Old Compton St., W1 (☎ **020/7734-5733**) but its alcoholic chocolate-and-coffee mousse cake is to die for.

with lemongrass and red chili. So many delicious alternatives, and that's before even mentioning Thai noodle dishes like *pad thai.* If you find yourself traveling east, visit the sister restaurant **Sri Siam City,** 85 London Wall, EC2 (☎ **020/7628-5772**).

✪ **YO! Sushi.** 52 Poland St., W1. ☎ **020/7287-0443.** Sushi selections from £1.50–£3.50 ($2.40–$5.60) per plate; children's dishes £1–£1.50 ($1.60–$2.40). AE, DC, MC, V. Daily noon–midnight. Tube: Oxford Circus. No smoking. SUSHI.

From the razzmatazz surrounding the 1997 launch of YO! Sushi, you'd have thought no one in London had ever tasted Japanese food before. They had, of course, but never in quite such a deliberately funky setting. YO! Sushi rivals NASA for hi-tech gadgets. Talking drink trolleys circle the restaurant like R2D2, and diners pick out what they want. Sushi-making robots turn out 1,200 pieces an hour, which circle around on the longest conveyor belt of its kind in the world. The different colored plates indicate the price. Diners tuck into tuna, sashimi, and so on, until full enough to ask for a plate count. Do keep a running tally, or this could turn out to be a budget-buster. Kids love it, too, and there are toned-down dishes for them, from chicken nuggets to cigar-shaped fish fingers. Founder Simon Woodroffe used to design rock-'n'-roll stages, and he's won countless awards for this venture, which he is launching in New York. **YO! Below** (☎ **020/7439-3660**) is a Japanese beer and sake hall, open downstairs at Poland Street until 1am, with metered, self-service, booze piped to every table. YO! Sushi is also at the Harvey Nichols store in Knightsbridge, SW1 (☎ **020/7235-6114**) and Selfridges on Oxford Street, W1 (☎ **020/7318-3944**).

SUPER-CHEAP EATS

Centrale. 16 Moor St., W1. ☎ **020/7437-5513.** Main courses £3.50–£5.50 ($5.60–$8.80). No credit cards. Daily noon–9:45pm. Tube: Leicester Sq., Tottenham Ct. Rd. ITALIAN.

This ought to be the ideal choice for diners who've splurged on theater tickets and want a cheap eat. But beware: The portions at Centrale are so huge that a tired traveler might fall asleep halfway through the first act. This isn't a spot for a romantic assignation, or for people who don't like people, but the old-fashioned no-frills restaurant has a great deal of charm and a very loyal clientele. People in their night-out finery mix with students on a shoestring and business people snatching a bite, all crammed together on black vinyl banquettes at narrow, red Formica-topped tables. The starters are traditional budget menu items like minestrone soup. You can eat meat for the main course. But forget all that, and do what everyone else does and plump for pasta. Often, you'll get more pasta than whatever's supposed to go with it, so go for a sauce with cheap ingredientsmd]mushroom is a good choice. And don't forget to bring a bottle of wine with you (corkage is 50p/80¢).

The Star Café. 22 Great Chapel St., W1. ☎ **020/7437-8778.** Reservations recommended. Main courses £4.25–£5.95 ($6.80–$9.50). No credit cards. Mon–Fri 7am–4:30pm. Tube: Tottenham Court Rd. BRITISH DINER.

This ex-pub has been run by the same family for 65 years and is proud to boast of being the oldest cafe in Soho. A favorite cheap eat for media luvvies on a lunch break, it's more caff than cafe. The walls of the main floor are hung with old, enamel, shop signs and, would you believe it, radio sets. The no-frills menu does include a salad bar in the summer. Otherwise, the staples include things like jacket potatoes, toasted sandwiches, and pasta, with daily luncheon specials such as roast chicken with crispy bacon stuffing, steak and onion pie, or salmon fillet with broccoli. Most people come for the all-day, full English breakfast, though, and that includes vegetarians who get a very superior spread with peppers and diced roast potatoes. The service is so smooth that you'll probably fall off your chair if your last meal was in Chinatown. Sadly, The Star Café is closed in the evenings, as well as at weekends.

GREAT DEALS ON FIXED-PRICE MEALS

Café Fish. 36–40 Rupert St., W1. ☎ **020/7287-8989.** Reservations recommended. Canteen fixed-price lunch £7.50–£15.50 ($12–$24.80); main courses £8.50–£18 ($13.60–$28.80);. AE, DC, MC, V. Mon–Fri noon–3pm; Mon–Sat 5:30–11:30pm, Sun 5:30–10:30pm. Tube: Leicester Sq. SEAFOOD.

Café Fish has the stark modern look of a modern livebait restaurant. The first-floor tables in the first-floor canteen are elbow-knockingly close together in a pretty decent-size space, but you still must book to get into this very popular restaurant. The fixed-price lunches start at one main course, saving around £2 ($3.20) off the price of most à la carte dishes. For £11.50 ($18.40), diners can add on a starter—Mediterranean seafood soup or four rock oysters, for instance. Before you gasp with horror, this is lunchtime, remember, and the simpler option goes a long way—definitely no need to reach for the sky and have three courses. There are only three dishes on the set menu, but then the choice is limited in the canteen anyway: You have to bust the budget and book the more welcoming upstairs restaurant for a broader selection. All the fish is super-fresh, and the service is attentive and friendly.

✪ **Cork & Bottle Wine Bar.** 44–46 Cranbourn St., WC2. ☎ **020/7734-7807.** Main courses £6.95–£11.95 ($11.10–$19.10); bistro lunches £10–£12 ($16–$19.20). Tube: Leicester Sq. WINE BAR/GLOBAL.

The leafleting has stopped. Aki, the Nigerian head chef at the Cork & Bottle, has convinced the wildlife lobby that he hasn't got a team of big-game hunters doing the dodgy for him. The kangaroo, crocodile, emu, and other exotic meats are all from farmed animals. The menu spans Pacific Rim, Afro-Caribbean, with some good British and European staples, too. And it's a good value in the evening, as well as with the fixed-price lunch. This very unusual wine bar is in a cozy basement bar in the heart of London's theater district—don't go until after 8pm if you want a seat. There are about 25 wine selections available by the glass, with chatty tasting notes written by the Australian owner Don Hewitson. Last summer, after we went to press, Don opened a new bar for "Cork & Bottle graduates" with fatter pay packets: **Shiraz,** 12 Upper St. Martin's Lane, WC2 (☎ **020/7379-7811**). Aki spent a few weeks in Australia training with Don's famous TV chef brother, Iain Hewitson, before taking over here, too.

The third West End wine bar is closed on the weekends: **The Hanover Square Wine Bar & Grill,** 25 Hanover Sq., W1 (☎ **020/7408-0935;** Tube: Oxford Circus).

Mezzo. 100 Wardour St., W1. ☎ **020/7314-4000.** Reservations recommended. Mezzonine: main courses £4.50–£10.95 ($7.20–$17.50); fixed-price lunch and pre-theater menu £8.90–£11.90 ($14.25–$19.05). Mezzo: main courses £11.25–£21.50 ($18–$34.40); fixed-price lunch and pre-theater menu £12.50–£15.50 ($24.80). AE, JCB, MC, V. Mezzonine: Mon–Fri noon–3pm, Sat noon–4pm; Mon–Thurs 5:30pm–1am, Fri–Sat 5:30pm–3am. Mezzo: Mon–Fri, Sun noon–3pm; Mon–Thurs 6pm–midnight, Fri–Sat 5:30pm–1am (Crustacea bar to 3am), Sun 6–11pm. Tube: Piccadilly Circus, Tottenham Court Rd. MODERN EUROPEAN (Mezzo)/CONTEMPORARY ASIAN (Mezzonine).

Terence Conran opened the 700-seater Mezzo in 1995. The gargantuan restaurant had a lot of doubters then, and there are some today who dismiss it as a naff hangout for attention-seekers. But it's a fun naff hangout. The first-floor Mezzonine, if that isn't a contradiction, has just had a huge overhaul. It now has a large lounge bar and serves what it calls contemporary Asian cuisine. The modern European restaurant downstairs was also due for a makeover last autumn. Let's hope it sorts out the noise problem, an unfortunate by-product of being this big. As is haphazard, though super-willing, service: I once waited half an hour for a friend, and he was 10 feet away behind a pillar all the time. Both floors offer two- or three-course fixed-price meals, which are always changing. Mezzonine is clearly cheaper, and I prefer it, as long as I can sit far away from the entrance. As part of its revamp, Mezzo is also turning itself into a live music venue—respected cabaret singers, bluesy jazz trios, and bands playing covers of vinyl hits. It's free entry Sunday to Tuesday and free for diners before 10pm Wednesday to Saturday, £5 ($8) after 10pm and for nondiners before midnight. On Friday and Saturday, a D.J. takes over after the band and goes on until 2:45am.

Nusa Dua. 11 Dean St., W1. ☎ **020/7437-3559.** Reservations recommended. Main courses £4–£7.80 ($6.40–$10.85); fixed-price menu £15.50 ($24.80). AE, MC, V. Mon–Fri noon–2:30pm; Mon–Thurs 6:30–11:30pm, Fri–Sat 6:30pm–midnight, Sun 6:30–10:30pm. Tube: Leicester Sq. INDONESIAN.

Nusa Dua is popular with people from the Indonesian Embassy, or so the restaurant says. You could dismiss that as PR puff, except that the food here generally is excellent and the *rijsttafel* is certainly an excellent deal. That's the fixed-price meal: It means "rice table" in Dutch. What you get is a huge selection of the kitchen's best dishes, all from the Malay Peninsula: beef cooked in coconut milk, or marinated in soy sauce, and so on This is not a place for tender taste buds since the menu is hot and spicy throughout (Nusa Dua also has copies printed in braille). The fish is extra special: fried with pineapple in hot green chili sauce or steamed with spring onion in ginger and oyster sauce. My favorit, is pomfret with shallots in a sweet soy sauce. The ambience is casual, the service over both floors relaxed, and the furnishings basic bamboo. In the summer, you can request one of the four tables outside on the pavement.

✪ **Schnecke.** 58–59 Poland St., W1. ☎ **020/7287-6666.** Reservations recommended. Main courses £5.99–£15.99 ($9.60–$25.60); fixed-price menu £11–£21 ($17.55–$33.60); Grand Bouffe £17.99 ($28.80). AE, DC, MC, V. Mon–Fri noon–3:30pm and 6–11:30pm, Sat noon–11:30pm, Sun noon–11pm. Tube: Oxford Circus. FRENCH/ALSATIAN.

Schnecke is even barmier than the monkish Belgo chain, which the same restaurant entrepreneurs sold for £10 million a couple of years ago. It celebrates the heart-stopping cuisine of Alsace, a border region that France and Germany played pass-the-parcel with for centuries. The menu boasts flaming tarts (sounds politer as *tartes flambées!*), pizzas, spicy sausages, and specialties—24 dishes in all, laced variously with cream, cheeses, onions, wine, and *choucroute* (a.k.a. sauerkraut). The DIY fixed-price menu selector lets you pick a starter (£3.99/$6.40) and main course (£6.99 or £10.99/$11.20 or $17.60), and add on a dessert, too (£3.49, £3.99, or £5.99/$5.60, $6.40, or $9.60). But the outrageous Grande Bouffe is the best deal: Staff cram your tabletop with 15 of the most popular dishes, and you can finish yourself off with a £2 ($3.20) shot of fruit-flavored schnapps. Both options include a free beer. Don't come if you hate kitsch Europop—like the cabbage-shaped door handles and prices quoted in Euros, it's all part of the joke. There's a second branch in Islington: 80–82 Upper St., N1 (☎ **020/7226-6630;** Tube: Angel).

✪ **Soho Spice.** 124–6 Wardour St., W1. ☎ **020/7434-0808.** E-mail: info@sohospice.co.uk. Main courses £8–£14 ($12.80–$22.40); fixed-price lunch and pre-theater menu £7.50 ($12); 3-course seasonal menu £15.95 ($25.50). AE, DC, MC, V. Mon–Thurs 11:30am–12:30am; Thurs–Sat 11:30am–3am, Sun 12:30–10:30pm. Tube: Leicester Sq., Tottenham Court Rd. INDIAN.

The food at this successful modern 100-seater restaurant is as stylish as the decor. Antique spice jars and brilliantly colored powders line the window, and there's a storytelling spice card attached to each menu. Waiters wearing brightly colored kurtas serve diners seated at wood tables. The list of familiar favorites—chicken *tikka,* tandoori lamb, and spicy prawn curry—is supplemented by a seasonal three-course menu focusing on a particular Indian regional cuisine. Punjabi, for example, means such dishes as *rara gosht,* lamb cooked in the tandoor and then stir-fried with cardamon and dried ground ginger *masala.* The two-course lunch or pre-theater deal offers a choice of appetizers like *aloo palak Bhaji* (potatoes and spinach blended with spicy graham flour) or crisp fried chicken drumsticks, followed by a choice of three main dishes. One is always vegetarian. Happy hour at the basement bar runs Monday to Saturday from 5 to 7pm, when cocktails are all £2.50 ($4) instead of £4.95 ($7.90). Try a Bollywood Buzz, a combination of apricot brandy and sweet vermouth spiced with a ginger-stuffed apricot and topped with ginger ale. There's a D.J. on Friday and Saturday nights. Reservations are only taken for groups of six people or more.

Amin Ali is also a partner in a great new cheap eat, **Busaba Eathai,** 106–110 Wardour St., W1 (☎ **020/7255-8650;** Tube: Piccadilly Circus, Tottenham Court Rd.), where tasty bowls of Thai noodle soup cost around £5 ($8).

Tokyo Diner. 2 Newport Pl., WC2. ☎ **020/7434-1414.** Reservations not accepted. Fixed-price lunch £5.95–£12.90 ($9.50–$20.70); main courses £6–£13 ($9.60–$20.80). MC, V. Daily noon–midnight. Tube: Leicester Sq. JAPANESE.

This 3-story restaurant on the edge of Chinatown is the diametric opposite of somewhere like YO! Sushi. There's no talk of brand values here, simply great value fast food in traditional, Japanese-diner style. And it has lots of Japanese customers. The wooden tables are small and cramped, but nobody seems to mind (you can only book if there are six of you or more). The fixed-price menu changes daily but is a guaranteed blowout, particularly at the higher price. The bento boxes are a great value, too, at around £10 ($16), given that they include rice, noodle salad, salmon sashimi salad, and a main dish, which might be pork or chicken *tonkatsu,* or chicken, salmon, or mackerel teriyaki. If you really want to save money, make a meal from the *donburi*—boxes filled with rice topped with seasoned egg and chicken, perhaps, or chicken flambéed in teriyaki sauce. You can get sushi and sashimi, too. Tea to wash it all down is free or go for a Japanese beer, slightly cheaper here than at pubs.

✪ **Vasco & Piero's Pavilion.** 15 Poland St., W1. ☎ **020/7437-8774.** Reservations recommended. Main courses £8.50–£14.50 ($13.60–$23.20) at lunch; fixed-price dinners £16.50–£19.50 ($26.40–$31.20). AE, JCB, MC, V. Mon–Fri noon–3pm and 6pm–1am, Sat 7–11pm. Tube: Oxford Circus. ITALIAN.

This small, comfortable, Italian restaurant attracts a business and sophisticated older crowd who consider it their secret favorite hideaway—folks like "Call me Ken" Livingstone, the London mayor. Unfortunately, too many of them have written glowingly about it in newspaper columns and you must book ahead. The Matteucci family has run the restaurant for 30 years, and the welcome is one of the warmest around—and Vasco still does much of the cooking. The unpretentious cuisine is light and fresh, with flavors clear as a bell, whether in marinated anchovies or asparagus that has been perfectly cooked al dente. Many of its ingredients come from local producers in Umbria. The fixed-price menus change daily, and you can choose either two or three courses from a fantastic selection of seven or eight of each. Ask what's best that day, and order it. Calves' liver and homemade pasta are house specialties.

Vasco's son Paul is managing a new northern outpost in swanky Hampstead, where you can easily eat for under £20 ($32): **Caffe Umbria,** 108 Heath St., NW3 (☎ **020/7431-4696;** Tube: Hampstead).

PRE-THEATER BARGAINS

✪ **Blues Bistro and Bar.** 42–43 Dean St. W1. ☎ **020/7494-1966.** E-mail: reservations@bluesbistro.com. Reservations recommended. Bistro main courses £6.95–£15.70 ($11.10–$25.10), pre-theater menu Mon–Tues, Sat–Sun £10 ($16); bar food £1–£6.50 ($1.60–$10.40). AE, MC, V. Mon–Thurs noon–midnight, Fri noon–1am, Sat 5pm–1am, Sun 5pm–midnight. Tube: Leicester Sq., Tottenham Court Rd. AMERICAN.

This sleek Soho joint is frequented by media types and a very friendly party crowd. The slim-line art-deco-ish dining room is like the Orient Express, but the cuisine is up-to-the-minute American. It also has possibly the best deal in town for early-birds. If you come on the right day—and you'll be p*@@ed if you don't—you can have three courses for £10 ($16). And not just any old nosh chucked together for no-account paupers, but fragrant onion soup with a gruyere crouton (a bit breath-testing), followed by a succulent salmon fillet, and a wicked chocolate marquise to finish. But that ain't the end of the temptations. If you do go à la carte, have a starter at around £5 ($8), plus a pudding for £4.25 ($6.80), or £6.95 ($11.10) with a glass of sweet muscat wine. The serpentine front bar is a great place to meet for an aperitif, though you might not want to leave once you see the menu there: crostini (posh baby open sandwiches) for £1 ($1.60), hot canapes up to £3 ($4.80), or a plate of hot tartlets only £6.50 ($10.40). Think of all this as an excuse to come back and back.

L'Escargot. 48 Greek St., W1. ☎ **020/7437-2679.** Reservations recommended. Main courses £12.95 ($20.70); fixed-price lunch and pre-theater menu £14.95–£17.95 ($23.90–$28.70). AE, DC, MC, V. Mon–Fri 12:15–2:15pm; Mon–Sat 6–11:30pm. Tube: Leicester Sq., Tottenham Court Rd. TRADITIONAL FRENCH.

Dining in a Michelin 1-star restaurant for £14.95 ($23.90) is a fantastic value. We've put L'Escargot in the pre-theater section because this is serious food, in seriously elegant surroundings, and you ought to make a real occasion of it. Cut the gallery tour because you'll still get your art fix here: The walls are hung with works by Marc Chagall, Joan Miró, and David Hockney. Andrew Thompson has taken over as executive head chef and changes the first-floor restaurant's *Du Jour* fixed-price menu every week. Diners get to choose from three starters, main courses, and desserts, all classic French dishes perfectly executed. Just to whet your appetite, this is what you could be eating: paupiette of smoked salmon with pickled cucumber, followed by stuffed rabbit leg; or swap one of those for chocolate tart with praline ice cream. Pure bliss. Vegetarians must check the menu before they book because choices are limited. Prices are higher in the upstairs Picasso Room, but the service is uniformly impeccable.

✪ **Teatro.** 93–107 Shaftesbury Ave., W1. ☎ **020/7494-3040.** Reservations essential. Main courses £14.50–£18.50 ($23.20–$29.60); fixed-price lunch and pre-theater menu £15.50–£18 ($24.80–$28.80). AE, DC, MC, V. Mon–Fri noon–3pm; Mon–Sat 6–11:45pm. Tube: Piccadilly Circus. MODERN EUROPEAN.

You'll have to work hard to find Teatro: It lives up on the second floor of an old multistory car park where Greek Street meets Shaftesbury Avenue. Actress Lesley Ash and her footballer husband Lee Chapman opened the minimalist Teatro to enormous hype in 1998, and it has been collecting plaudits ever since. The bar is members-only, so watch for celebs on the stairs. But when you look at the main course prices and then taste the delicious modern European cuisine, you'll realize why the pre-theater menu is such a good deal. The menu has enough choices to baffle the indecisive. You get two courses and might start with a sumptuous garlic and leek soup, or finish with a really wicked treacle tart and double cream, with cider-braised pork belly and puy lentils as the main course. Everything is executed with flair and the best ingredients. The only downside is that the wine list is expensive.

YMing. 35–36 Greek St., W1. ☎ **020/7734-2721.** Main courses £6–£12 ($9.60–$19.20); fixed-price menu (served noon–6pm) £10 ($16). AE, CB, DC, DISC, MC, JCB, V. Mon–Sat noon–11:45pm. Tube: Leicester Sq. NORTHERN CHINESE.

Light and airy like a hotel dining room, YMing is a tranquil antidote to more in-your-face local rivals. The large tables are prettily set, the service is smooth and unobtrusive, and the food is superb northern Chinese cuisine. Even though à la carte prices aren't outrageous, we recommend the pre-theater menu, which includes three courses. The dishes change regularly but will include a choice of appetizer (crispy won ton, spring roll, tofu, or aubergine in spiced salt, for example), followed by a main course like fish slices in Chinese wine sauce or braised tofu. If duck, prawn, or lamb are on the list, go for it. The sizzling dishes are among the most popular—prawns with fresh mango, or lamb with fresh leek or with ginger and spring onion. You can finish up with coffee or sip YMing's excellent tea all the way through.

WORTH A SPLURGE

✪ **Aurora.** 49 Lexington St., W1. ☎ **020/7494-0514.** Reservations recommended. Main courses £10.75–£12 ($17.20–$19.20). MC, V. Daily for coffee 8am–midnight; lunch 12:30–3pm, dinner 6:30pm–midnight. Tube: Piccadilly Circus, Oxford Circus. MODERN EUROPEAN.

This is a delightful place for basking in the summer sunshine. Instead of filling your lungs with carbon monoxide at some pavement table in one of Soho's narrow streets, go to Aurora's idyllic courtyard in the back. There are only six outside tables, so book ahead. Inside, the restaurant has cozy modern-rustic walls and wooden tables, lit by candles set in a treasured mass of old drips. The menu follows the seasons—globe artichokes, spring lamb, and lemongrass and coriander vichyssoise—and is put together by someone with a very open mind, its influences eclectically European. Aurora is even better value on booze. It only got a liquor license a year ago and is keen not to alienate diners used to bringing their own bottle. So while £12 ($19.20) for the cheapest bottle isn't exactly cheap, it's a fair bit cheaper than you'll find in rival splurge restaurants. If you think Aurora is out of reach even with that bonus, come just for coffee any time after 8am and out of mealtimes.

✪ **Criterion Brasserie.** 224 Piccadilly, W1. ☎ **020/7930-0488.** Reservations essential. Main courses £12–£15 ($19.20–$24); fixed-price lunch £14.95–£17.95 ($23.90–$28.70); fixed-price dinner £17.95 ($28.70), order before 6:30pm. AE, DC, MC, V. Mon–Sat noon–2:30pm, 5:30–11:30pm; Sun 5:30–10:30pm. Tube: Piccadilly Circus. MODERN FRENCH.

This used to be the only place where diners could sample the cooking of Michelin 3-star bad boy Marco Pierre White without remortgaging their home (the fixed-price dinner at his Oak Room in the Meridien Hotel runs to $88 per person). Now his superlative restaurant, Mirabelle in Curzon Street (see section 8, "Mayfair," below), offers a fixed-price lunch for the same price. But it is still well worth coming to the Criterion. Right on Piccadilly Circus, the inside is like a Byzantine palace with its fantastic gold vaulted ceiling, and you can just picture the scene at the dinner dances hosted here in the 1920s. The staff is often pressed for time but the modern French cuisine is superb. Don't try the three-course early dinner, unless you eat at the speed of lightning. Save the Criterion for a lunchtime blowout on your last day. The hot favorite when I went was the ballottine of salmon with herbs and *fromage blanc,* and risottos are always a real star performer.

✪ **The French House Dining Room.** 49 Dean St., W1. ☎ **020/7437-2477.** Reservations recommended. Main courses £8.50–£14.50 ($13.60–$23.20). AE, DC, MC, V. Mon–Sat noon–3pm, 6–11:15pm. Tube: Leicester Sq., Piccadilly Circus. MODERN BRITISH.

If you believe in ghosts, then this is the place to come. The pub downstairs was the unofficial Free French headquarters during World War II, then a legendary hangout of artists like bohemian Soho stalwart Francis Bacon. The informal dining room is tiny and simply decorated, with wooden floors and paneling. Like its sister restaurant, St. John in Clerkenwell, the French House is a firm believer in not wasting a morsel of any beast. They call it nose-to-tail eating and have published a cookbook with the same name. Calves' liver, sweetbreads, ox tongue, and bone marrow move on and off the seasonal menu, which changes twice a day. Don't worry if you think offal is awful, though. More restrained carnivores can choose from the mouthwatering list of familiar animal parts and chicken cooked every which way. There are always a couple of fish options and something for vegetarians. And the desserts would break the diet resolve of a supermodel, from lemon tart to homemade ice cream.

8 Mayfair

Browns. 47 Maddox St., W1. ☎ **020/7491-4565.** Reservations recommended. Hot sandwiches and main courses £6.95–£13.95 ($11.10–$22.30). AE, CB, DC, DISC, MC, V. Mon–Sat noon–10pm. Tube: Oxford Circus. TRADITIONAL BRITISH.

Browns takes the brasserie idea and makes it terribly English. The most famous one is in Oxford, where mummies and daddies take their student children for tea. The food is a little predictable, but it's robust, generally well put together, and a pretty good value for money. That's a rare treat in Mayfair, where restaurants tend to cater to the super-affluent and child-free. Browns is divided into two sections, filled with wood paneling, old glass, and mirrors. The restaurant is at the back beyond the bar, which is a popular after-work meeting point—during happy hour, between 5 and 7pm, cocktails start at £3.95 ($6.30). The food ranges from pastas, salads, and sandwiches, to honest-to-goodness main courses such as steak, mushroom, and Guinness pie. There are lighter, more modern dishes, too. I went for char-grilled chicken breast with tarragon butter. It could have had more tarragon, but then I'm an herb fiend. For dessert, bread-and-butter pudding is a firm favorite. There are two other branches, at 82 St. Martins Lane, WC2 (☎ **020/7497-5050**), and 114 Draycott Ave., SW3 (☎ **020/7584-5359**).

West End Restaurants

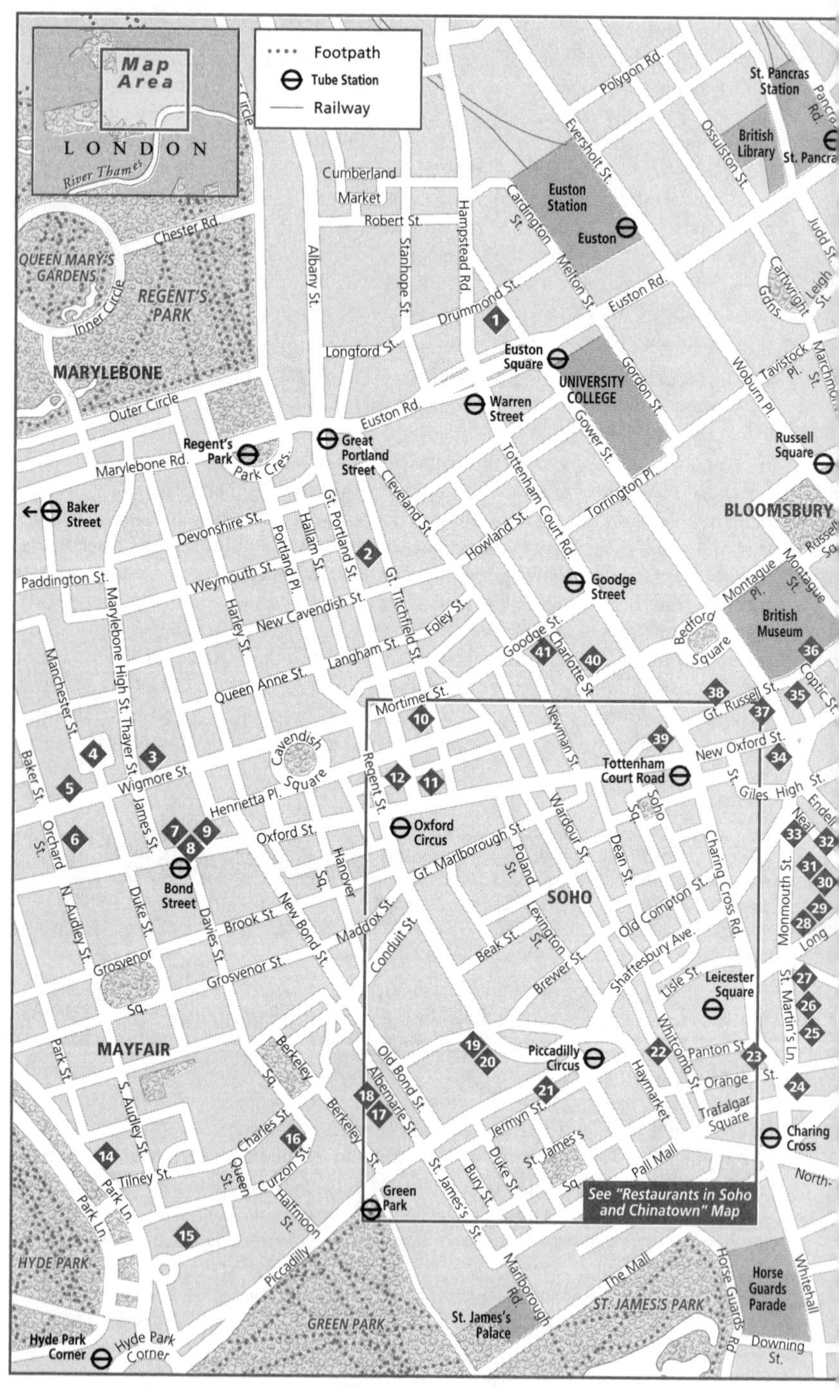

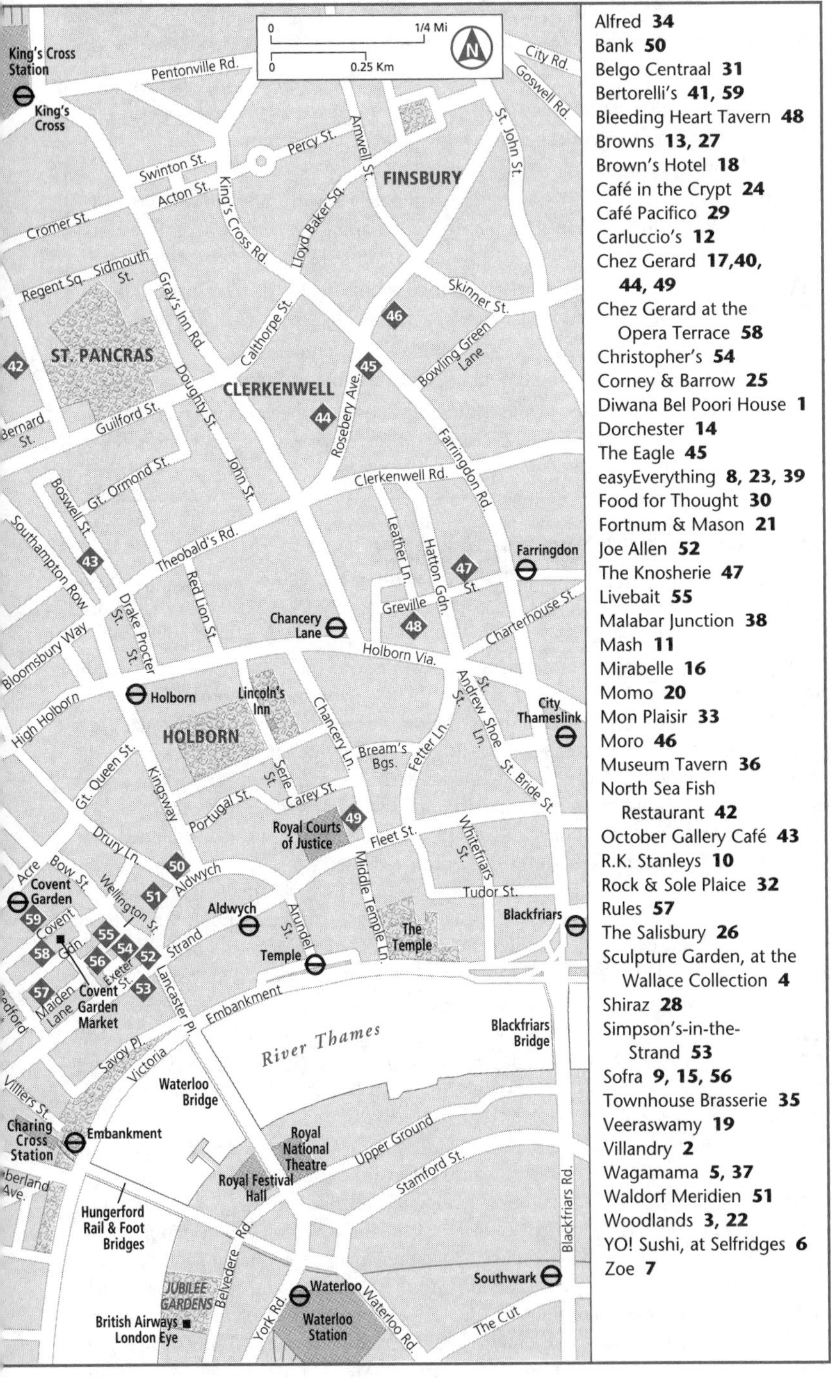
0
1/4 Mi
0
0.25 Km
N
King's Cross Station
King's Cross
Pentonville Rd.
City Rd.
Goswell Rd.
Swinton St.
Acton St.
Percy St.
Amwell St.
St. John St.
FINSBURY
Cromer St.
King's Cross Rd.
Lloyd Baker Sq.
Regent Sq.
Sidmouth St.
Gray's Inn Rd.
Calthorpe St.
Skinner St.
Bowling Green Lane
ST. PANCRAS
CLERKENWELL
Doughty St.
Rosebery Ave.
Bernard St.
Guilford St.
Farringdon Rd.
Gt. Ormond St.
John St.
Clerkenwell Rd.
Boswell St.
Southampton Row
Theobald's Rd.
Leather Ln.
Hatton Gdn.
Farringdon
Red Lion St.
Greville St.
Charterhouse St.
Chancery Lane
Drake St.
Procter St.
Bloomsbury Way
Holborn Via.
Holborn
Lincoln's Inn
St. Andrew St.
Shoe Ln.
City Thameslink
High Holborn
HOLBORN
Chancery Ln.
Bream's Bgs.
Fetter Ln.
St. Bride St.
Gt. Queen St.
Kingsway
Serle St.
Carey St.
Portugal St.
Royal Courts of Justice
Fleet St.
Whitefriars St.
Drury Ln.
Aldwych
Acre
Bow St.
Covent Garden
Wellington St.
Middle Temple Ln.
Tudor St.
Aldwych
Arundel St.
The Temple
Blackfriars
Covent Gdn.
Strand
Temple
Exeter St.
Lancaster Pl.
Covent Garden Market
Maiden Lane
Embankment
River Thames
Blackfriars Bridge
Savoy Pl.
Victoria
Villiers St.
Waterloo Bridge
Charing Cross Station
Embankment
Royal National Theatre
Upper Ground
Royal Festival Hall
Stamford St.
Hungerford Rail & Foot Bridges
Belvedere Rd.
Blackfriars Rd.
JUBILEE GARDENS
Waterloo
Southwark
British Airways London Eye
York Rd.
Waterloo Station
Waterloo Rd.
The Cut
Alfred 34
Bank 50
Belgo Centraal 31
Bertorelli's 41, 59
Bleeding Heart Tavern 48
Browns 13, 27
Brown's Hotel 18
Café in the Crypt 24
Café Pacifico 29
Carluccio's 12
Chez Gerard 17,40, 44, 49
Chez Gerard at the Opera Terrace 58
Christopher's 54
Corney & Barrow 25
Diwana Bel Poori House 1
Dorchester 14
The Eagle 45
easyEverything 8, 23, 39
Food for Thought 30
Fortnum & Mason 21
Joe Allen 52
The Knosherie 47
Livebait 55
Malabar Junction 38
Mash 11
Mirabelle 16
Momo 20
Mon Plaisir 33
Moro 46
Museum Tavern 36
North Sea Fish Restaurant 42
October Gallery Café 43
R.K. Stanleys 10
Rock & Sole Plaice 32
Rules 57
The Salisbury 26
Sculpture Garden, at the Wallace Collection 4
Shiraz 28
Simpson's-in-the-Strand 53
Sofra 9, 15, 56
Townhouse Brasserie 35
Veeraswamy 19
Villandry 2
Wagamama 5, 37
Waldorf Meridien 51
Woodlands 3, 22
YO! Sushi, at Selfridges 6
Zoe 7

Affordable Family-Friendly Restaurants

Capital Radio Cafe (*see p. 150*) Your kids won't recognize the DJs' names, but they'll love the clatter and noise of all-day live broadcasts at this restaurant from London's leading independent music radio station. If they're lucky, one of their pop idols will pop in, too, for a star appearance.

Rainforest Café (*see p. 182*) This place will pacify any grumpy kid who wanted to go to Disneyland. Animatronic animals roar, and birds screech from the riot of jungly vegetation. And there are even fake storms. Take a pair of earplugs.

YO! Sushi (*see p. 153*) Smart-aleck, talking robots deliver drinks to your table. Plus, there's unyucky food for kids, who haven't graduated to sushi yet.

Carluccio's (*see p. 165*) In typical Italian style, so unlike the chilly Brits, this cafe welcomes *i piccoli* (small children) with open arms and tasty baby pizzas.

Café Pacifico (*see p. 167*) While Mom and Pop chug the delicious margaritas, the kids can draw a lovely family picture with the crayons provided by this Tex-Mex restaurant.

GREAT DEALS ON FIXED-PRICE MEALS

✪ **Mirabelle.** 56 Curzon St., W1. ☎ **020/7499-4636.** Reservations essential. Main courses £12.50–£25 ($20–$40); fixed-price lunch £14.95–£17.95 ($23.90–$28.70). AE, CB, DC, MC, V. Daily noon–2:30pm and 6–11:30pm. Tube: Green Park. MODERN EUROPEAN.

As long as you don't get a primeval urge to wash your meal down with a £30,000 ($48,000) bottle of 1847 Chateau d'Yquem, this is the best value mouthful of Marco Pierre White you will ever eat. The lower priced, two-course, fixed-price lunch costs less than most of his main courses. And the food is sensational: really tricky ingredients timed perfectly, and very clearly defined tastes. The entrance to Mirabelle is pretty nondescript but behind it lies a lounge decorated with tongue-in-cheek murals, then the long bar, and finally the brasserie-style restaurant. Diners are a little cramped, but who cares. And on sunny days, you can sit out on the terrace. The menu changes seasonally but includes MPW classics. The two courses could be terrine of duck with foie gras and potatoes, in a beetroot dressing, and then hot smoked salmon with horseradish cream. A few extra pounds will get you a dessert or a selection of oozing French cheeses. This offer is good only at lunchtime, so take a break between shopping in Oxford Street, say, and a visit to the Royal Academy on Piccadilly.

Momo. 25 Heddon St., W1. ☎ **020/7434-4040.** Reservations essential. Main courses £9.75–£16.50 ($15.60–$26.40); fixed-price lunch £13–£16 ($20.80–$25.60); weekend brunch £15 ($24). AE, CB, DC, DISC, MC, V. Mon–Fri 12:30–3pm, Sat–Sun noon–4:30pm; Mon–Sat 7–11pm. Tube: Piccadilly Circus. NORTH AFRICAN.

Momo launched with such fanfare that it was bound to be hip for a while, and then Madonna threw a bash here. I had to wait 6 weeks for a supper booking, having navigated through the incredibly irritating automated telephone system. The furor has died down a bit, but it's still worth calling before you leave home. The exotic ambience is 60% of the appeal. Beaded curtains add a casbah mystique; glowing lanterns cast patterns on the stucco walls; and the swathes of fabrics are pure sensuality. If you're tall, ask for a banquette, or you'll be crippled by the end of the evening. The best deal is weekend brunch: Oriental, English, Mediterranean, or American. Each menu includes five dishes that are liberal interpretations of their respective nationalities—cumin in the American sauté potatoes, for instance. I recommend the Oriental, which includes a delicious sweet-and-spicy pigeon pie with almonds and cream. Don't expect a heavy hand with the spices, though. In fact, for bolder taste buds, there may not be enough. Last year, Momo opened a Moroccan tearoom, **Cheb Momo,** next door at no. 23 Heddon Street (☎ **020/7734-3999**).

Veeraswamy. 99–101 Regent St., W1. ☎ **020/7734-1401.** Reservations recommended. E-mail: action@realindianfood.com. Main courses £9.75–£13.50 ($15.60–$21.60); lunch and pre-/post-theater menu £11–£14 ($17.60–$22.40); Sun menu £15 ($24). AE, DC, MC, V. Mon–Sat noon–2:30pm and 5:30–11:30pm; Sun 12:30–3pm and 5:30–10:30pm. Tube: Piccadilly Circus. INDIAN.

Veeraswamy will surely prove the most extraordinary Indian restaurant you've ever encountered. It's hip, painted in vibrant colors, with frosted-glass panels dividing up the sections, and ultra-modern furniture. Only a few pictures remain from the old days. Established in 1926 by a general and an Indian princess, Veeraswamy claims to be the oldest Indian restaurant in London. Over the years, it has been the haunt of princes and potentates, from the Prince of Wales to King Hussein and Indira Gandhi. The clientele are still pretty prosperous if less august today, and they're certainly well-fed by the time they leave. For starters, the stir-fried oysters with coconut and Kerala spices are sublime. For an exotic, and only mildly sweaty, choice, try the shanks of lamb curried in bone stock and spices. Unless you're in the mood to splurge, this isn't the place to sample lots of different dishes. Go for a great-value fixed-price menu instead.

There is also a sister restaurant in Fulham: **Chutney Mary,** 535 King's Rd., SW10 (☎ 020/7351-3113; Tube: Fulham Broadway). The decor is pure colonial club and seven ex-pat masterchefs dish up delicious regional cuisines. Main courses range from £9.25 to £15.75 ($7.65–$25.20); lunch and post-theater menu £12.50 ($20); Sunday brunch £15 ($25.60).

9 Bloomsbury & Fitzrovia

R.K. Stanleys. 6 Little Portland St., W1. ☎ **020/7462-0099.** Reservations recommended. Main courses £7–£10.50 ($11.20–$16.80). AE, MC, V. Mon–Fri noon–11:30pm, Sat 5:30–11:30pm. Tube: Oxford Circus. TRADITIONAL BRITISH.

R.K. Stanleys may look like an American diner, with its red leatherette banquettes and metal-edged chairs, but the cuisine is determinedly British. Bangers and mash are the specialty but with a very modern twist. R.K. Stanleys Magnificent Seven homemade sausages range from Caribbean, bratwurst, and jerk to game sausages with crispy pancetta, glazed parsnips and cabbage, or the vegetarian cheese-based Glamorgan. Thai sausages come with noodles and chicken with couscous. For nonsausage fans, there are other main courses, such as braised lamb shanks and Thai fishcakes. Wise diners pace themselves because portions are large; start with wood pigeon salad, or finish with treacle tart or the homemade ice cream. Choose from a huge range of British cask ales, keg ales, lager stout, and porter. And you can buy wine by the glass. The service is charming, and the atmosphere laid back. Fred Taylor's first restaurant was the successful **Alfred,** 245 Shaftesbury Ave. (☎ **020/7240-2566;** Tube: Tottenham Court Rd.), which offers a wider range of inventive and robust British cooking in Formica-topped canteen style (main courses £9 to £15.90/$14.40 to $24.80).

Wagamama. 4a Streatham St. (off Coptic St.), WC1. ☎ **020/7323-9223.** Main courses £4.70–£7.20 ($7.50–$11.50). AE, MC, V. Mon–Sat noon–11pm, Sun 12:30–10pm. Tube: Tottenham Court Rd. No smoking. JAPANESE NOODLES.

This is an enduring London hot spot even though the novelty has worn off. Stone stairs lead down to a dining room set up with ranks of long shared tables like a traditional Japanese noodle bar. Staff punch the orders into handheld electronic keypads

Moveable Feasts

There's nothing more blissful on a sunny summer's day than raiding a deli and carrying off the scrumptious spoils to dine alfresco. London is full of green spaces that are great for picnics. Get there early at lunchtime and mark out your patch, because the locals grab any chance to leave their desks.

That's particularly true of Soho Square, a grassy oasis right in the heart of the West End (Tube: Tottenham Court Rd.). There are lots of nearby places to pick up the necessary stuff. The **Marks & Spencer Food Hall,** 458 Oxford St., W1 (☎ **020/7935-7954**), has deli fare and pre-chopped veggies and salad for busy yuppies. It sells sandwiches to huge queues of people, too. I'd also recommend **I Camisa & Son,** 61 Old Compton St., W1 (☎ **020/7437-7610**), which is a scented heaven of Italian sausages, cheeses, and olives. Then pop around the corner to **Berwick Street market** for salad ingredients and great bread.

Kids will love Coram's Fields, on the eastern edge of Bloomsbury (Tube: Russell Sq.). Adults need to be accompanied by a young one for admittance. It's a wonderful inner-city farm with hens, horses, sheep, and pigs on the site of the old Foundling Hospital. **Bloomsbury Cheeses,** 61b Judd St., WC1 (☎ **020/7387-7645**), will sort you out with a mammoth range of cheeses, obviously, and wine, olives, and delicious bread. **Alara Wholefoods,** 58–60 Marchmont St., WC1 (☎ **020/7837-1172**), is great for salads and sandwiches.

Fortnum & Mason, 181 Piccadilly, W1 (☎ **020/7734-8040**), is the only place to go before setting off to Green Park (Tube: Green Park or Hyde Park Corner). Its food halls will demand iron self-control. The obvious supply store for a picnic by the Serpentine in Hyde Park or, if you don't mind the walk, the Round Pond in Kensington Gardens, is another famous food hall: **Harrods,** 87–135 Brompton Rd., SW1 (☎ **020/7730-1234**).

My last hot tip for a picnic spot is Holland Park (Tube: Holland Park). If you can, go on summer's evening with candles and sit on the grass outside the temporary tented opera stage in the ruins of Holland House. The music is magical. You can stock up at two upmarket local stores: **Harts the Grocers,** 82 Holland Park Ave., W11 (☎ **020/7727-7332**); and **Cullens,** 112–114 Holland Park Ave., W11 (☎ **020/7221-7511**).

Note: Do take a picnic if you go to the **Royal Botanic Garden Kew** or **Hampton Court Palace** to enjoy on the banks of the Thames (see "London's Top Attractions," in chapter 6).

that send a radio signal to the kitchen. The thread noodles come in soups, pan-fried, or else served with various toppings. This place is kid heaven: The menu actually tells you to slurp as the extra oxygen adds to the taste. For a hearty dish, try the chili beef ramen—char-grilled sirloin, chilies, red onion, parsley, and spring onions served in a chili-soup base. It's served with parsley, pickled pepper, bean sprouts, and lime, which you add to the dish. Each dish is cooked and served immediately, so if you're dining with a group, be prepared for individual meals to arrive at different times. And don't expect to linger too long in the bus-station bustle. Wine, sake, beer, and raw healthful juices are available. Wagamama is also at 10a Lexington St., W1 (☎ **020/7292-0990**); 101a Wigmore St., W1 (☎ **020/7409-0111**); 26a Kensington High St., W8 (☎ **020/7376-1717**); and 11 Jamestown Rd., Camden Town, NW1 (☎ **020/7428-0800**).

SUPER-CHEAP EATS

Carluccio's. 8 Market Place, W1. ☎ **020/7636-2228.** Main courses £4.50–£7.50 ($7.20–$12). AE, MC, V. Mon–Fri 8am–11pm, Sat 11am–11pm, Sun 11am–10pm. Tube: Oxford Circus. ITALIAN.

Antonio Carluccio was one of the first celebrity chefs in Britain. That the locals no longer think of Italian cuisine simply as pizza and soggy lasagne, but instead a rich patchwork of regional specialties, is largely due to him. The cafe uses many imported ingredients and still manages to be a mega-cheap eat. Make a quick lunch stop for soup and antipasti starting at £3.60 ($5.75), or come for an evening reviver. Even if you choose the most expensive items for each course—a huge plate of antipasti, followed by moist grilled swordfish, then a cheesy tour of regional Italy—and have the most expensive aperitif, glass of wine with the meal, and coffee, you'd still spend under £30 ($48). Choose the cheapest, and it'd be £16.50 (£26.4), including drinks. It's the sort of place that adapts to fit any purse: There are cheaper dishes for infants; the deli can provide top picnic pickings; and Carluccio's will even sell you a Vespa!

✪ **Diwana Bhel Poori House.** 121 Drummond St., NW1. ☎ **020/7387-5556.** Main courses £4–£6.20 ($6.40–$9.90); buffet lunch £4.50 ($7.20); fixed-price menu £6.20 ($9.90). AE, DC, MC, V. Daily noon–11:30pm. Tube: Euston, Warren St. SOUTH INDIAN.

It's hardly worth pulling out your credit card to pay for a meal as cheap as this. Diwana Bhel Poori House absolutely disproves the cliché that cheap has got to mean nasty, except in the 1970s decor. The buffet lunch is still under a fiver and tummy-tinglingly good if you avoid the oilier dishes. At other times, you'll be hard pressed to spend more than £10 ($16) a head and can set up your own buffet of South Indian vegetarian dishes for everyone to share. The dosais—semolina pancakes filled with spicy potato and vegetables—are a delight; there are several different ones to choose from. If you go for the fixed-price *thali,* hold back from ordering anything else, because it's a bonanza of breads, bhajees, dahl, rice, vegetables, and pickles. Diwana Bhel Poori House has a sister restaurant across the road, Chutney's, but it's more expensive. And this one is unlicensed: you can bring wine and there's no corkage fee.

October Gallery Café. 24 Old Gloucester St., WC1. ☎ **020/7242-7367.** Main courses £4.40–£5.60 ($7.05–$8.95). AE, MC, V. Tues–Sat 12:30–2:30pm. Closed Easter wk., Aug, and Christmas wk. Tube: Holborn. GLOBAL.

The October Gallery is a charitable trust that works to promote multi-ethnic contemporary art. A short walk from the British Museum, the old Victorian school building has a theater, a gallery, and a club room, as well as the cafe, with its pinewood floor and polished tables, and walls hung with bright artworks. This is only a lunch place, but it is so popular that you really must get here early, or there'll be nothing left but a few crumbs, and certainly no tables in the delightful central courtyard (the only place you can smoke). The short menu is transglobal, naturally, and ever-changing, from hummus and pita bread to chicken cacciatore, always with a vegetarian dish, fish on Friday, a salad or two, plus a wicked dessert. The cafe isn't licensed, so if you fancy a boozy lunch, you'll have to bring a bottle with you. Corkage is £1 ($1.60).

GREAT DEALS ON FIXED-PRICE MEALS

Malabar Junction. 107 Great Russell St., WC1. ☎ **020/7580-5230.** Fixed-price bar meal (served noon–5pm) £3.50 ($5.60); main courses £6–£8 ($9.60–$12.80). AE, MC, V. Daily noon–3pm, 6–11:30pm. Tube: Tottenham Court Rd. SOUTH INDIAN.

Okay, so the choice is minimal—chicken, lamb, or vegetarian—but how could anyone resist the offer of a bumper plate of curry for just £3.50 ($5.60)? This attractive restaurant serves excellent South Indian cuisine, specifically dishes from Kerala.

Behind an unprepossessing entrance, the domed atrium dining room is furnished with elegant potted palms and tables decorated with fresh orchids, and a languid tropical air hangs over the whole place. House specialties include *masala dosai,* a traditional Kerala pancake, filled with potato *masala* and served with *sambar* and chutney; and *utthappam,* a cross between a pizza and an open pancake, topped with chopped onions, green chilies, and tomatoes, and spiced with curry and ginger. The unusually rich lamb *kurma* is prepared with cashew nuts, sultanas, and tomatoes in a creamy sauce. Every dish is a taste sensation: Do try the green bananas flavored with spices and onions, or *Kalan,* which is sweet mango and yam cooked with coconut, yogurt, cumin, and green chilies. After their bar meal, I defy anyone not to come back for more.

✪ **Townhouse Brasserie.** 24 Coptic St., WC1. ☎ **020/7636-2731.** E-mail: townhousebrasserie@btinternet.com. Reservations recommended. Main courses £9–£16 ($14.40–$25.60); fixed-price menus £9.95–£13.45 ($15.90–$21.50). AE, DC, JCB, MC, V. Mon–Fri noon–11pm, Sat 4–11:30pm, Sun 10am–6pm. Tube: Holborn, Tottenham Court Rd. FRENCH-CARIBBEAN.

Chef Lloyd Lewars runs this brasserie with his wife Joanna, and his Chinese-Jamaican background is evident in his work. The fixed-price meals are excellent value for either two courses or three. You get a limited choice of three dishes at each stage, always including one vegetarian, so you might want to ask for a run-down before you book. Disappointment is very unlikely, though. The menu changes quarterly, but fish is a specialty and game makes a big appearance in winter. If you're on a tighter budget or counting the calories, the Townhouse Brasserie offers the perfect solution with the "light meal" list between the starters and main courses. Light is a relative term and I was more than satisfied with my seafood crêpe—and with the atmosphere, too. This little converted town house is full of good and not-so-good artworks, bright colors, and cozy wooden banquettes. The Townhouse also has a fantastic value B&B: £25 ($40) single, £48 (76.80) twin. See chapter 4.

WORTH A SPLURGE

Mash. 19–21 Great Portland St., W1. ☎ **020/7637-5555.** Main courses £9.50–£15.50 ($15.20–$24.80); brunch £10 ($16). AE, DC, MC, V. Restaurant Mon–Fri noon–3:30pm, Sat–Sun noon–4pm; Mon–Sat 6–11pm. Bar Mon–Sat 11am–1am, Sun noon–4pm. Tube: Oxford Circus. MEDITERRANEAN.

The Love Machine at the entrance flashes romantic epigrams as people open the doors. One of the more flip is "The best way to a man's heart is to leave him." That and the video screens in the women's toilets giving glimpses into the men's are why people either love or hate Mash. Oliver Peyton opened the sleek and gargantuan resto-deli in 1998. It has one of London's first microbreweries, the huge tanks visible at the back of the first-floor cafe. Couches invite customers to linger. The cuisine is Mediterranean-Italian, of sorts: Paper-thin pizzas, with bizarre toppings such as crispy duck, cucumber, Asian greens, and hoisin sauce appear from a wood-fired grill. Main courses are either baked (like whole sea bass with gherkin and caper mayonnaise) or roasted (like the pork cutlet with wilted radicchio, new potatoes, French beans, and anchovy butter). This is a great place to come for a full-works brunch on the weekend: The Mash menu, American, and vegetarian all cost £10 ($16).

✪ **Villandry.** 170 Great Portland St., W1. ☎ **020/7631-3131.** Reservations recommended. Main courses £7.50–£15 ($12–$24). AE, CB, DISC, MC, V. Mon–Sat 8–11:30am, 12:30–3pm, 7–10pm; Sun noon–3pm. Tube: Great Portland St. No smoking in restaurant. MODERN EUROPEAN.

Eating here is like joining the exuberant village feast after the summer fair. Villandry used to be a byword in Marylebone, and it has surely conquered hearts in its bigger and better site on Great Portland Street. It combines a bustling deli with the airy restaurant, which is decked out refectory-style with plain walls, white covers over the tables, arts-and-crafts chairs, and wooden floors. A lot of the food here is organic, and the menu changes twice a day. The lines blur between starters and main courses, so while you could stagger out wondering how to pay for the rest of your vacation, it's quite possible just to graze through the lower end. Tuna carpaccio is marvelous. Villandry focuses on seasonal cuisine, so the ingredients will be super-fresh. Villandry was planning to open a bar last year for wine, juice, and coffee. It also does breakfast and brunch.

10 Covent Garden & The Strand

Bertorelli's. 44A Floral St., WC2. ☎ **020/7836-3969.** Cafe main courses £7.50–£12.25 ($12–$19.60); restaurant main courses £10.90–£14.50 ($17.45–$23.20). AE, DC, MC, V. Mon–Sat noon–3pm, 5:30–11:30pm. Tube: Covent Garden. ITALIAN.

Bertorelli's is right across the street from the revamped Royal Opera House and has just revamped itself. The cuisine hasn't changed though: Why muck about with a formula that delivers robust modern Italian dishes with such a stylish hand? Head straight for the cheaper cafe downstairs, where you'll find heart- and stomach-warming dishes such as the delicious salad of roasted peppers, aubergines, and artichokes dressed in a fine, warm vinaigrette, followed by chicken on rosemary potatoes with wild mushrooms, spinach, and anchovy butter. Eat slowly because the starters are so good they can overwhelm the main courses. If you want to go freestyle, there are lots of pizzas and pastas to choose from—the gnocchi baked with mushrooms and artichokes in a walnut pesto is to die for. Otherwise, the *secundi piatti* are rather pricey. Groupe Chez Gerard owns Bertorelli's now, but the cheerful, bustling atmosphere make this feel like your neighborhood favorite. There's a second, more expensive branch in Fitzrovia: **Bertorelli's,** 19–23 Charlotte St., W1 (☎ **020/7636-4174;** Tube: Goodge St.).

Café Pacifico. 5 Langley St., WC2. ☎ **020/7379-7728.** Main courses £6.75–£13 ($10.80–$20.80). AE, JCB, MC, V. Mon–Thurs noon–11:45pm, Fri–Sat noon–12:45am, Sun noon–10:45pm. Tube: Covent Garden. TEX-MEX.

Café Pacifico opened in 1978 and claims to be London's oldest Mexican restaurant. The evening menu spans Tex-Mex favorites and modern Mexican dishes like roast pork fillet with chili and apple stuffing, and new potatoes in a rosemary chili sauce. Most people come this party joint for the classics, though, and it is good at most of them, unlike the over-packaged chains that dominate this small niche in the market. The menu arrives with a complimentary bowl of nachos and salsa, and runs from Taquitos to smoked chicken quesadillas and giant prawn fajitas. The *Degustacion del Pacifico* (£9.50/$15.20) is a meal in itself, with a little bit of everything, and the best value. And you can wash it all down with any one of 60 tequilas, nine Mexican beers, and a huge list of cocktails. It's a great place for families. Café Pacifico has a children's menu and crayons to lend. Evening reservations are accepted Sunday through Tuesday.

SUPER-CHEAP EATS

Café in the Crypt. St. Martin-in-the-Fields, Duncannon St., WC2. ☎ **020/7839-4342.** Rolls and sandwiches £2.50–£3.10 ($4–$4.95); main courses £5.50–£6.10 ($8.80–$9.75). No credit cards. Mon–Sat 10am–8pm, Sun noon–8pm. Tube: Charing Cross. BRITISH DINER.

Right on Trafalgar Square, this is a great place to grab a bite to eat between a visit to the National Gallery and marching off down The Mall to Buckingham Palace. Or pop in with the kids after a session at the church's brass rubbing center. Head for the door on the side of the building, down the steps to the brick-vaulted crypt. Simple healthy food costs a lot less here than at more commercial places. It's a self-service cafeteria, where diners pick from a big salad bar and a choice of two traditional main courses—you really might find shepherd's pie here. The other light-lunch options include filled rolls and delicious cups of soup. The menu changes daily, but one fixture is that most traditional of British desserts, bread-and-butter pudding (bread soaked in eggs and milk with currants or sultanas and then oven-baked). Super-light for something super-wicked.

Food for Thought. 31 Neal St., WC2. ☎ **020/7836-9072** or 020/7836-0239. Main courses £2.30–£5.70 ($3.70–$9.10). No credit cards. Mon–Sat 9:30am–8:30pm, Sun noon–5pm. Tube: Covent Garden. No smoking. VEGETARIAN.

Food for Thought is an enduring stalwart of the vegetarian movement, which manages to lure in a broad clientele because of its unpreachy wholesome food and very cheap prices. It's a pop-in kind of a place, and you're best off popping in for brunch or maybe a strawberry scone for tea, because it's tiny and mobbed both at lunchtime and for the recently introduced £5 ($8) evening special dish. The decor is simple with pine tables, fresh flowers, and original art on the fresh whitewashed walls. There are a handful of outdoor tables, but you'll probably have to sit downstairs, which in summer is about the only reason to go elsewhere. The menu always features a quiche and a vegetable stir-fry. Otherwise it will have a few salads, stews, and hot dishes along these lines, always with vegan and gluten-free options. The puddings look irresistible, sitting up on the bar, and in the eating, most do manage to disguise their virtuousness. The cafe is unlicensed, so bring your own bottle: There's no corkage fee.

GREAT DEALS ON FIXED-PRICE MEALS

✪ **Belgo Centraal.** 50 Earlham St., WC2. ☎ **020/7813-2233.** Reservations recommended. Lunch £5 ($8); main courses £7.95–£17.50 ($12.70–$28); Belgo Complet fixed-price menu £12.95 ($20.70). AE, DC, MC, V. Mon–Thurs noon–11:30pm, Fri–Sat noon–midnight, Sun noon–10:30pm. Tube: Covent Garden. BELGIAN.

Hip young trendies usually turn their nose up at blatant concept restaurants, but the Belgian national dish of *moules, frites,* and *bière,* served at long refectory tables by staff dressed as monks, has become an entertainment icon. A kilo pot of mussels, prepared any one of three ways, will set you back between £10.95 and £12.95 ($17.50 and $20.10). The only quibble is that sometimes there's too much broth. There are non-seafood dishes, and you'll find them on the fixed-price lunch: either wild boar sausages served with Belgian mash and a beer, or two lighter dishes with mineral water. The pricier Belgo Complet starts with a *salade liègeoise,* then *moules,* plus either a beer or ice cream. But for sheer gluttony, nothing can outdo the Beat the Clock menu. It runs from 5 to 6:30pm on weekdays. Whatever time you order at, that's what the meal will cost—£5.45, for instance. There are three huge dishes to choose from and wash down with a free drink. This is a fun place, if you can hack the noise and pace, and it's got a Belgian beer hall, too. Other branches are **Belgo Noord,** 71 Chalk Farm Rd., NW1 (☎ **020/7672-0718;** Tube: Chalk Farm); **Belgo Zuid,** 124 Ladbroke Grove, W10 (☎ **020/8982-8400;** Tube: Ladbroke Grove); and the **Bierdrome,** 173 Upper St., NW1 (☎ **020/7226-5835;** Tube: Highbury, Islington, Angel).

PRE- & POST-THEATER BARGAINS

Bank. 1 Kingsway, WC2. ☎ **020/7234-3344.** Reservations recommended. Main courses £10–£24; fixed-price lunch and pre-theater dinner £13.90–£17.50 ($22.25–$28). AE, CB, DC, JCB, MC, V. Mon–Fri 7:30–10:30am and noon–3pm, Sat–Sun 11:30am–3:30pm (brunch); daily 5:30–11:30pm. Tube: Covent Garden, Holborn, Temple. MODERN EUROPEAN.

The chefs are part of the frenetic exciting performance here, rushing around in the kitchen behind a big glass window like fish at feeding time. Bank was a bank until an extremely hip conversion stripped bare the structural girder, put in a suspended, armour-plated ceiling, and turned it into London's most stylish brasserie. You could come here for the weekend brunch (there is a children's menu then, too), but it'll cost you. Better to feast on the pre-theater menu, then head to the bar where you can spy on the 100 or so other diners. Great value for either two or three courses, the seasonal cuisine brings together Continental and Southeast Asian influences in the sort of harmony the supra-national organizations can only dream of: from seared rare spiced tuna with mango salad, to roast rabbit with couscous and spiced crab. The only quibbles are that the service can be a bit too quick—this is another place with a handheld electronic ordering system—and the tables are close together.

✪ **Christopher's.** 18 Wellington St., WC2. ☎ **020/7240-4222.** Reservations recommended. Brunch £5–£13; main courses £11–£28 ($17.60–$44.80); pre- and post-theater menu £14.50–£17.50 ($23.20–$28). AE, DC, JCB, MC, V. Mon–Fri noon–3pm, Sun noon–4pm; daily 5–midnight. Tube: Covent Garden. AMERICAN.

It's worth coming to Christopher's to gawk at the dramatic decor. A grand stone staircase links the 3 floors of this former bank building. The long main dining room has a soaring ceiling and ornate stucco carvings. The suitably luxxy cuisine gives classic American dishes a punchy modern and international twist. So, as well as huge steaks and grills, or Maryland crab cakes and Maine lobster, you'll find dishes like baked cod with Roquefort and watercress mash. The wine list is loyal to the United States, too. The pre- and post-theater menu is a great value, particularly if you're not a dessert fiend—I am and thought I'd died and gone to heaven after Pennsylvania red-berry strudel with lemon sherbet. There's a brunch menu, too, spiced up with dishes like huevos rancheros and lobster club sandwich. On Saturdays, it's served in the laid-back **Speakeasy** bar, where you'll find light eats and lower prices at any time—and happy hour 8:30 to 9:30pm Monday to Saturday.

✪ **Corney & Barrow Wine Bar.** 116 St. Martin's Lane, WC2. ☎ **020/7655-9800.** Bar food around £5 ($8); brunch £6.50 ($10.40); main courses £9.50–£14.95 ($15.20–$23.90); late-night platters for 2 people £9.95–£30 ($15.90–$48), fixed-price lunch and pre-theater menu £10.95–£12.95 ($17.50–$20.70). Cover £5–£7.50 ($8–$12) after 11pm. Mon–Tues noon–midnight, Wed–Sat noon–2am. AE, DC, MC, V. Tube: Leicester Sq. WINE BAR/MODERN EUROPEAN.

Corney & Barrow's first West End wine bar (it has around 11 branches in the City) swaps the classic cellar-style decor for limestone, granite, marble, and mohair. But the 50-strong wine list is still very reasonable with bottles starting at around £11 ($17.60)—30 are sold by the glass from £2.80 ($4.50). The food is good value, too. Bar snacks are all under £5 ($8) and include deep-fried cod cakes with tartar sauce and griddled foie gras on toast. And this is a great place to satisfy late-night stomach rumblings: between 11pm and 2am, Corney & Barrow serves jumbo platters for two people that make very fair-priced meals, as long as you're not sharing one with a monster muncher. There's Middle-Eastern meze, Oriental bits and bobs to dip in this and that, seafood, fruit, or veggie. But do get here before 11pm, or there's a £5 to £7.50 ($8 to

$12) cover charge. Otherwise, the upstairs brasserie has a very economical fixed-price menu, both at lunch and in the early evening, with either two courses or three, both including coffee.

Joe Allen. 13 Exeter St., WC2. ☎ **020/7836-0651.** Reservations essential. Main courses £7.50–£14.50 ($12–$23.20); fixed-price lunch £12–£14 ($19.20–$22.40); pre-theater menu £13–£15 ($20.80–$24); weekend brunch menu £14.50–£16.50 ($23.20–$26.40). AE, MC, V. Mon–Fri noon–1am, Sat 11:30am–1am, Sun 11:30am–midnight. Tube: Covent Garden. AMERICAN.

This dark wood-paneled basement, with its ridiculously discreet entrance, is a thespian institution where Londoners dining late rub shoulders with the cream of West End talent. It's a great game matching the flesh-and-blood faces to those staring down from from the dozens of theater posters. You'll have to splurge to join them or stick to starters and salads where the portions are pretty generous. Joe Allen does have good value pre-theater deals, though, for two or three courses. The menu changes daily, except for the perennial bowl of chili, and the cuisine is a mix of classic down-home dishes and others that look suspiciously like modern British cooking—roast guinea fowl with new potatoes roasted in balsamic vinegar, and blueberry and ginger relish. But brownie lovers really can close their eyes and feel like they've never left home. The service is sometimes perfunctory, and the tables are too close together, but the lively atmosphere and live jazz on Sunday nights are enough of a compensation.

Livebait. 21 Wellington St., WC2. ☎ **020/7836-7161.** Reservations recommended. Main courses £14–£20.75 ($22.40–$33.20); fixed-price lunch and pre-/post-theater menu £12.50–£15.50 ($20–$24.80). AC, DC, MC, V. Mon–Sat noon–3pm, 5:30–11:30pm (10:30pm in the bar). Tube: Covent Garden. SEAFOOD.

Livebait is one of the friendliest and most exciting restaurants in London. If you like fish so fresh that it still looks surprised, then you'll love this retro white-tiled caff. There's a cheap way to enjoy it, too: Settle down in the bar for a bowl of cockles and a mixed-green salad, and it'll only cost you £6.20 ($9.90). In the restaurant, you have to have a main course. The fixed-price menus are all a steal, and early booking is essential. You get two or three courses, and two dishes to choose from in each. I started with fish soup with aiöli. The garlic-laden mayonnaise was dynamite. Vacation logistics probably make a pre- or post-theater visit more achievable, and it's great to find somewhere you can eat late as well as on top of your English tea. Livebait makes no concessions to seafood haters. It has also been spawning new branches: 43 The Cut, SE1 (☎ **020/7928-7211;** Tube: Waterloo, Southwark), and 175 Westbourne Grove, W11 (☎ **020/7727-4321;** Tube: Bayswater, Queensway).

Mon Plaisir. 21 Monmouth St., WC2. ☎ **020/7836-7243.** Main courses £8.60–£13.95 ($13.75–$22.30); pre-theater menu plus glass of wine £11.95–£14.95 ($19.10–$22.30); fixed-price lunch £14.95 ($23.90); fixed-price dinner plus glass of wine £23.50 ($37.60). AE, DC, MC, V. Mon–Fri noon–2:15pm; Mon–Sat 6–11:15pm. Tube: Covent Garden/Leicester Sq. FRENCH.

Mon Plaisir is the *grande dame* of French restaurants. It has only changed hands, from one family to another, once since it opened in the 1940s. Behind the narrow glass front lies a warren of charming rooms, hung with pans and posters, where diners are packed in like sardines. Things have changed just a fraction in the past few years since chef Patrick Smith, a veteran of several well-known London restaurants, came in. He hasn't ditched the classics—*quelle idée!* You'll still find good old-fashioned coq au vin, snails, and so on. But new dishes have crept onto the menu, such as roast duck breast with Szechwan pepper and beetroot and onion marmalade. The pre-theater menus are either two courses or three if you fancy finishing with something like profiteroles and chocolate sauce. Sadly, service is sometimes nose-in-the-air and it can get a little touristy because Mon Plaisir is such an institution.

Sofra. 36 Tavistock St., WC2. ☎ **020/7240-3773.** Mixed meze £5.45 ($8.70); main courses £6.95–£14.95 ($11.10–$23.90) with most under £10 ($16); fixed-price lunch £8.95 ($14.30); pre- and post-theater menu £9.95 ($15.90). AE, DC, MC, V. Daily 12pm–12am. Tube: Covent Garden. TURKISH.

Sofra is a very modern Turkish eating house. The cuisine is completely authentic, although the food is not as spicy as some chili fans would like. And the portions aren't as generous as they are at more basic ethnic restaurants. But the ingredients are super-fresh and so is the way they're treated. The chef goes light on the oil, chargrilling instead, which is part of what owner Huseyin Ozer promises—clean healthy food. The fixed-price meals are a fantastic value, comprising 11 mezes and meat dishes—super-tender diced lamb, velvety hummus, the classic Middle Eastern eggplant dish, *Imam Bayildi,* and on and on. It's a great way of avoiding the perennial problem, first of zero self-control at the sight of a delicious menu, and then catatonic shock at the bill. There are eight little sisters to this place: The best is **Sofra Cafe,** 1 St. Christopher's Place, W1 (☎ **020/7224-4080;** Tube: Bond St.). Or go for Sunday lunch at **Sofra Bistro,** 18 Shepherd St., W1 (☎ **020/7493-3320;** Tube: Green Park, Hyde Park Corner).

WORTH A SPLURGE

✪ **Chez Gerard at the Opera Terrace.** First Floor, Covent Garden Central Market, WC2. ☎ **020/7379-0666.** Reservations essential. Main courses £9.90–£16.40 ($15.85–$26.25); fixed-price weekend lunch and daily dinner £15.95–£20 ($25.50–$32). Cover charge £1 ($1.60). AE, DC, MC, V. Mon–Sat 11am–11:30pm, Sun 11am–10:30pm. Tube: Covent Garden. FRENCH.

Until the Royal Opera House reopened, with its new Amphitheatre restaurant and terrace, Chez Gerard had no competition as the finest site in Covent Garden. For budget eaters, it still is the best most of the time as is the general public can only have lunch at the ROH. Chez Gerard is right on top of the old market, and you can look down on the throngs in the piazza. The clientele has a definite air of affluence, especially in the evening when companies aren't picking up the tab, yet the fixed-price menu is a remarkable value because Chez Gerard heads straight in with three courses and the higher price is for four. If it weren't for the £1 ($1.60) cover charge, which brings freshly baked bread, anchovy butter, and olives at the start of the meal, and toasted almonds at the end, it wouldn't have to be a splurge at all. The cuisine is traditional French, delivered in a very attractive modern way. The gravadlax will melt in your mouth, and the corn-fed chicken from Périgord in France, where it is the local specialty, will put you off the supermarket variety forever. There are six other branches: 31 Dover St., W1(☎ **020/7499-8171;** Tube: Green Park); 3 Yeomans Row, SW3 (☎ **020/7581-8377;** Tube: Knightsbridge); 119 Chancery Lane, WC2(☎ **020/7405-0290;** Tube: Chancery Lane); 8 Charlotte St., W1 (☎ **020/7636-4975;** Tube: Tottenham Court Rd., Goodge St.); 64 Bishopsgate (☎ **020/7588-1200;** Tube: Liverpool St.); 84–86 Rosebery Ave., EC1 (☎ **020/7833-1515;** Tube: Farringdon).

Rules. 35 Maiden Lane, WC2. ☎ **020/7836-5314.** E-mail: info@rules.co.uk. Reservations essential. Main courses £15.95–£19.95 ($25.50–$31.90); weekday fixed-price menu (served 3–5pm) £19.95 ($31.90). AE, DC, MC, V. Mon–Sat noon–11:15pm, Sun noon–10:15pm. Tube: Charing Cross, Covent Garden. TRADITIONAL BRITISH.

This wonderful, ultra-British restaurant has been around for 200 years and seems likely to survive another 200. Lily Langtry and Edward VII used to tryst here, and it's about the only place in London where you'll see a bowler hat these days. But despite the hammy quaintness, Rules is a very modern restaurant operation. It supports the current "Keep Britain Farming" campaign and markets the house specialty, "feathered and furred game," as healthy, free range, additive-free and low in fat. The fixed-price menu is a splurge, but it's still a great deal because you can select two courses from anything on the very broad menu. Head straight for the biggest budget busters—lobster and asparagus salad with mango dressing, followed by fallow deer with spiced red cabbage, blueberries, and bitter chocolate sauce—and you'll save around £10 ($16). The food is delicious: traditional yet innovative, until you get to the puddings, which are a mix of nursery and dinner-dance classics. The wine list is definitely dinner-dance, but Rules does have three brown ales, so try one of them instead.

Simpson's-in-the-Strand. 100 Strand, WC2. ☎ **020/7836-9112.** E-mail: simpsons@savoy-group.co.uk. The Grand Divan main courses £11.95–£22.95 ($19.10–$36.70); fixed-price breakfast £13.50–£15.95 ($21.60–$25.50); fixed-price lunch and pre-theater menu £14.50–£17.75 ($23.20–$28.40); Sunday lunch £21.95 ($35.10), ½-price for under-12s. AE, DC, MC, V. Mon–Fri 7–11am; daily noon–2:30pm; Mon–Sat 5:30–11pm, Sun 6–9pm. Tube: Charing Cross. TRADITIONAL BRITISH.

If you want to experience grand British dining, as few British remember it, then you can't do better than Simpson's. Tailcoated waiters still wheel trolleys of joints around the ornate paneled Grand Divan restaurant—23 saddles of lamb and 25 roast sirloins of Scottish beef each day. Simpson's is the sort of place where even Bart Simpson would talk in a whisper. But don't be nervous, because the main menu has a very funky modern twist, with white peaches sweetening the roast mallard duck, or butternut gratin nestling up to the seared monkfish. The fixed-price menus are the best value. But for a real treat, splash out on a Simpson's Great British Breakfast: a bowl of porridge, cereal, or stewed fruit, followed by a plate piled with sausage, scrambled eggs, American and Canadian bacon, black pudding, grilled mushrooms, and tomato. And there's fresh juice, coffee, toast, and pastries to go with it. Pay another £3 ($4.80), and you'll get lamb kidneys, deadly but delicious fried bread, bubble and squeak (mashed fried potatoes with greens), baked beans, and lamb's liver. Just make sure your health coverage is up to date. The Adam-style upstairs restaurant, Simply Simpsons, is lighter, brighter, and more European, and main courses cost £8.95 to £16 ($14.30 to $25.60). (It has the same telephone number.)

11 Victoria

Ebury Wine Bar & Restaurant. 139 Ebury St., SW1. ☎ **020/7730-5447.** Reservations recommended. Main courses £9.50–£16 ($15.20–$25.60). AE, DC, MC, V. Mon–Sat noon–3pm, Sun noon–2:30pm; daily 6–10pm. Tube: Victoria. WINE BAR.

The main courses should make this place a splurge, but you can have an equally good meal for the price of a single dish if you stick to the 20 or so choices on the entrée and salad menus. For instance, my best friend's chicken-and-bacon terrine with red onion marmalade, followed by a Caesar salad—all rousing an "mmm" of appreciation—cost £10 ($16). I did go for a main course, because I'm a sucker for sausages—in this case, rich mushroomy ones with mash and onion gravy, which also cost £10 ($16). The menu changes faster than a socialite with a full diary, except for such improbably but scrumptious regulars as Mars Bar spring roll. Oooh, count those extra pounds. Count them too if you decide to lubricate your meal with one of a host of very fine wines. Is it any wonder that the tarted-up bar and old-fashioned restaurant draw such an eclectic clientele of local workers and smart Belgravia residents?

✪ **Jenny Lo's Teahouse.** 14 Eccleston St., SW1. ☎ **020/7259-0399.** Reservations not accepted. Main courses £5–£6.50 ($8–$10.40). No credit cards. Mon–Sat 11:30am–3pm, 6–10pm. Tube: Victoria. CHINESE.

Jenny Lo's father was Britain's best-known Chinese cookery writer. His restaurant, Ken Lo's Memories of China, is still going strong in nearby Ebury Street but falls on the expensive side. This teahouse, however, is more than affordable. The simple but stylish decor—long shared tables, wooden chairs, and bright splashes of color—accurately mirrors the fresh cuisine. Jenny Lo doesn't use the old Chinese standard, monosodium glutemate. There's a short menu, mainly rice, soup noodles, and wok noodles, ranging from the standard to ones with a southeast Asian twist (hot coconut), and from the light to quite substantial. Try the luxurious black-bean seafood noodles. Side dishes, rather than starters, include such street-food classics as onion cakes. You can't make reservations, but the staff is extremely friendly and helpful, which soothes any irritation if you have to wait for a space. Jenny Lo has also commissioned her own tonic teas from Chinese herbalist Dr. Xu. Long life and happiness are both on the menu here.

Oliveto. 49 Elizabeth St., SW1. ☎ **020/7730-0074.** Main courses £7–£10 ($11.20–$16). AE, CB, MC, V. Mon–Fri noon–3pm, Sat–Sun noon–4pm; daily 7–11:30pm. Tube: Victoria. PIZZA.

This is yet another example of a cheaper offshoots spawned by a successful restaurant, which offers the same quality but faster food—Oliveto is the baby of Olivo, just 'round the corner. The focus is on pizza, and there are 15 different and deliciously crisp alternatives to choose from. Our favorites are the *quattro stagioni* made with mozzarella, tomato, sausages, prosciutto, mushroom, and squash; and one made with Gorgonzola, arugula, tomato, and mozzarella. There are always a few pasta dishes—a delicious linguine al granchio made with fresh crabmeat, garlic, and chili, for example. Oliveto has a very mixed clientele, from platinum credit-carded families who live in Belgravia and young Pimlico singles out for a relaxed supper. If you are feeling a little more flush, try **Olivo,** 21 Eccleston St., SW1 (☎ **020/7730-2505**). Main courses cost £9.50 to £15 ($15.20 to $24), and the cuisine is robust, modern Italian.

GREAT DEALS ON FIXED-PRICE MEALS

✪ **Boisdale.** 15 Eccleston St., SW1. ☎ **020/7730-6922.** E-mail: info@boisdale.co.uk. Reservations recommended. Main courses £6.90–£19.80 ($11.05–$31.70); fixed-price menus £14–£17.45 ($22.40–$27.90). AE, DC, MC, V. Bistro Mon–Fri noon–2:30pm; Mon–Sat 7–11pm, Sun noon–10:30pm. Bar Mon–Sat to 1am. Tube: Victoria. SCOTTISH.

Boisdale is clan territory. Owned by Ranald Macdonald, the very model of a modern chieftain-in-waiting, its bar boasts London's biggest range of hard-to-find single malt whiskies and a tartan menu to match. The cheaper fixed-price meal is a cultural treat you'll want to boast about at home: a hearty fish soup, then haggis made by the world famous McSween in Edinburgh, neeps (mashed swede), and tatties (mashed potato). This is the dinner that Robert Burns wrote his famous ode in praise of and which guests salute as it's brought to the table at the annual celebration of his birthday on January 25th. If centuries of tradition can't persuade you to try oatmeal and sheep's innards, then there is a more expensive fixed-price meal, with a wide choice of starters and main courses, which are bound to include venison, salmon, and Scottish beef, perhaps with a hint of the Continental in the styling. The only thing that might stop you from coming here is a strong aversion to smoke: What else would a fat cat want to go with the single malt other than a big fat Cuban cigar?

12 The City & Clerkenwell

THE CITY

George. Great Eastern Hotel, Liverpool St., EC2. ☎ **020/7618-7300.** E-mail: restaurantres@great-eastern-hotel.co.uk. Main courses £7.50–£9.25 ($12–$14.80). AE, DC, MC, V. Mon–Sun 11am–11pm. Tube: Liverpool St. TRADITIONAL BRITISH.

Turn right out of Liverpool Street Station, and Terence Conran's biggest venture to date is at the next corner. The Great Eastern dates back to the era of slow train travel, when every major terminus had a major hotel. With his business partners, Conran spent over 2 years refurbishing this place, opening five new restaurants in 2000.

George is my favorite. It serves those hearty dishes everyone tells you to expect in England but that are relatively hard to find. The manager calls it "comfort food." Try *toad in the hole*—sausages baked in gloriously fluffy batter, a bit like a waffle with a secret. Or fish and chips with mushy peas—the gloopy green stuff the Prime Minister's pal Peter Mandelson thought was guacamole on an ill-fated outing to meet the people. And it's very reasonably priced.

If that isn't your bag, then pop into **Miyabi** (☎ **020/7618-7100**): rice and noodle soups, salads, sashimi, sushi, tempura, and main courses are very good and very, very good value £4 to £8 ($6.40 to $12.80); open Monday to Friday noon to 3pm and 6 to 11pm (noon to 7pm for take-out). **Terminus** (☎ **020/7618-7400**) is the original hotel diner and keeps to the railway timetable—in opening from 6:30am to midnight, not because it never opens on time. Forget the oddly expensive main courses, which start at £11.50 ($18.40), and come for the tapas, which costs £10 ($16) for three dishes. Or even just for coffee. **Aurora** is out of our price range, and there are several fish restaurants in this listing that are a better value than **Fishmarket.**

Arkansas Café. Unit 12, Old Spitalfields Market, E1. ☎ **020/7377-6999.** Main courses £4.90–£13 ($7.85–$20.80). MC, V. Mon–Fri noon–2:30pm, Sun noon–4pm. Tube: Liverpool Street. AMERICAN.

The U.S. Embassy swears by the high-class barbecuing skills of Keir and Sarah Hellberg. If you're swish enough to get onto the Independence Day guest list there, you'll probably find them catering the party. Arkansas Café is at the retired Spitalfields Market, and diners sit out in the covered central space and enjoy the sizzle and delicious smells while the Hellbergs cook steaks, lamb, sausages, and corn-fed chicken to order!—my burger was so perfectly rare that I thought I heard it moo. If you call ahead, to allow for the 10-hour cooking time, they'll even do you a whole pig! Mr. Hellberg chooses the best cuts of meat himself from Smithfield market, and posts its provenance up at the cafe. Plump for a jumbo sandwich as a cheaper option or take the meat on its own. That's not really on its own, of course, because there are down-home potato and vegetable salads to have on the side and Mr. Hellberg's secret barbecue sauce on every table. The beef brisket and ribs are home-smoked, the puddings so baaad they're good enough to cue an impromptu Meg Ryan moment.

✪ **The Place Below.** St. Mary-le-Bow, Cheapside, EC2. ☎ **020/7329-0789.** www.theplacebelow.co.uk. Main courses £6–£7 ($9.60–$11.20). MC, V. Mon–Fri 7:30am–2:30pm. Tube: St. Paul's, Bank. No smoking. VEGETARIAN.

St. Mary-le-Bow is a beautiful Christopher Wren church built on the site of a much earlier one. Today, the arched Norman vaults are home to one of the most atmospheric and delicious cheap eateries in The City—a blissful escape from The City's brash commercialism. The menu changes daily, with a bit of curry added to this, Caribbean fruits to that, and Italian influences showing in the other. You'll always find a hot dish

Restaurants in the City & on the South Bank

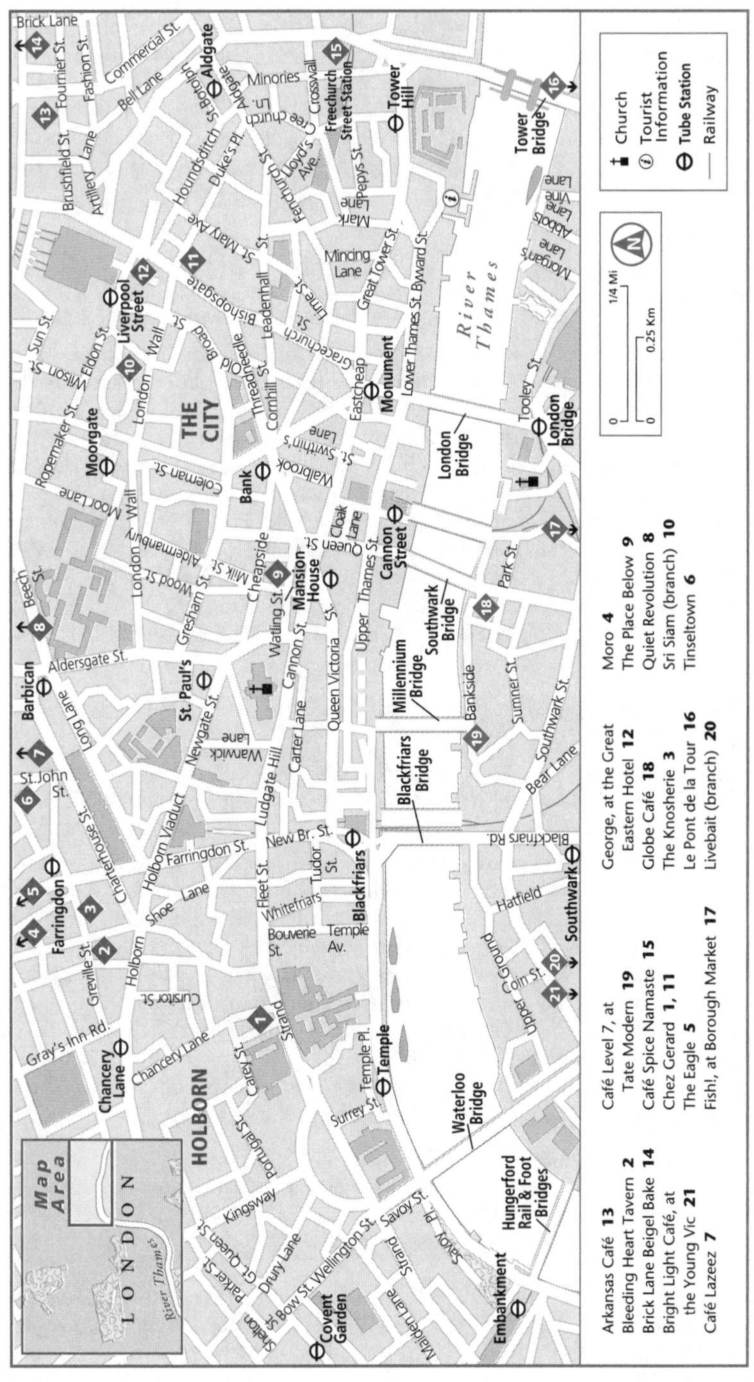

of the day, soup, quiche, and two salads (one dairy-free): My cashew-and-lentil pâté was deliciously moist. Then misbehave with a brownie or pat yourself on the back with fruit salad. The Place Below has embraced the U.S. habit of unlimited refills of coffee or tea, and that's rarer than hen's teeth in London. There's seating for 50 outside—good for outcast smokers. Or you can take the food away with you and save on the VAT. The Place Below is hoping to refurbish and begin opening in the evening, too, perhaps by July this year.

WORTH A SPLURGE

Café Spice Namaste. 16 Prescot St., E1. ☎ **020/7488-9242.** Reservations recommended. Main courses £7.75–£14.50 ($12.40–$23.20). AE, DC, MC, V. Mon–Fri noon–3pm and 6:15–10:30pm, Sat 6:30–10:30pm. Tube: Aldgate, Tower Hill, Tower Gateway. INDIAN.

The modern Indian cuisine at this wonderful restaurant is some of the finest you will find in London. Cyrus Todiwala must be running out of wall space at home for all the congratulatory letters. His menu travels through Goa, Hyderabad, Madras, and North India, plus some Parsee specialties. You could be careful—pick an appetizer or a starter size portion of a main course, and add a couple of side orders—and come away only £10 ($16) poorer, but that'd be a real shame. I chose one of the weekly specials, a most unusual and delicious Kangeroo Tikka Masaledar. The meat, which can be very chewy in the wrong hands, was meltingly tender. If you've got space, finish with the Parsee toffee ice cream made with intensely sweet, sun-dried Indian apricots. The menu has a little history of each dish and explanation of how it's made. The old Victorian magistrate's court is always full to bursting, so go on a Saturday night because it'll be much more relaxed then.

CLERKENWELL

SUPER-CHEAP EATS

Quiet Revolution. 49 Old St., EC1. ☎ **020/7253-5556.** Soups from £2.75–£5 ($4.40–$8). No credit cards. Mon–Fri 8am–5pm, Sat–Sun 10am–2pm. Tube: Old St. SOUP.

Quiet Revolution really is revolutionary. This soup manufacturer is not only approved by the Soil Association, which regulates "organic" producers. It has also twice-won S.A. food awards, among a host of other impressive trophies. With this new cafe-diner, Quiet Revolution can finally serve its delicious and super-healthy nosh direct to the public. Nosh like the Polska Tomato soup—suitable for vegans, 35 calories per 100g, 5g of carbohydrate, 1.3g of fat. Every variety, from Luscious Leek to Carrot & Coriander, carries this wealth of detail. Quiet Revolution even filters the water "seconds before adding it to the stock." All very reassuring, but I'm fairly relaxed about such things and just relished the fabulous flavors. This is a great place to refuel between visits to the hot local art scene (see "Young, British, and Hung in East London," in chapter 6). Quiet Revolution is unlicensed, so bring your own wine.

WORTH A SPLURGE

Moro. 34–36 Exmouth Market, EC1. ☎ **020/7833-8336.** Mororestaurant@hotmail.com. Reservations recommended. Main courses £9.50–£14 ($15.20–$22.40); tapas £2.50–£4.50 ($4–$7.20). Mon–Fri 12:30–10:30pm, Sat 6:30pm–midnight. AE, DC, MC, V. Tube: Angel, Farringdon. SPANISH/NORTH AFRICAN.

On the run-down City fringes, Clerkenwell has become a very hip neighborhood in recent years. If you didn't know that, then an evening at Moro will quickly put you in the picture. It opened 4 years ago, has amassed a pot full of awards, and gets better every day. The decor is clattery, modern minimalist—bare walls and stripped wood—with a new quieter conservatory corner. The Spanish and North African cuisine is earthy and powerful. You can dine extremely reasonably on delicious tapas, but splurge, if you can, because the kitchen uses only the best ingredients, organic where possible. The charming staff will explain any of the exotic mysteries on the menu. Highly recommended are the perfectly cooked, wood-roasted bream with fennel, garlic, and paprika, and the stewed long-horn beef, like no cowboy ever had it, with prunes, chard, and potatoes. Two courses will probably set you back around £20 ($32). Giving up dessert isn't too much of a sacrifice, as the choice is limited.

13 Just South of the River

GREAT DEALS ON FIXED-PRICE MEALS

Le Pont de la Tour. Butler's Wharf, 36d Shad Thames, SE1. ☎ **020/7403-8403.** Reservations essential. Restaurant main courses £17.50–£25 ($28–$40); pre-/post-theater menu £19.50 ($31.20); fixed-price lunch £28.50 ($45.60). Bar and grill main courses £13–£18.50 ($21.60–$29.60); fixed-price lunch £14.95–£17.50 ($23.90–$28). AE, JCB, MC, V. Mon–Fri and Sun noon–3pm; Mon–Sat 6–11:30pm, Sun 6–11pm. Tube: Tower Hill, London Bridge. MODERN EUROPEAN.

Until Sir Terence Conran opened his five new restaurants at The Great Eastern Hotel in Liverpool Street last year, this was the diamond in his dining empire. Tony Blair brought Bill and Hillary here in 1998. It has a restaurant, bar and grill, plus a food and wine store and a bakery, and can get very hectic. The best deal is the fixed-price menu in the grill, where the food is delicious but simpler than in the restaurant. My calf's liver and bacon made me wonder just what the school cook had been doing to produce such muck out of similar ingredients all those years ago. Sadly, the offer only applies to lunch. But you can do the cheap-skate's two-step: Around £12 ($19.20) would get you, for instance, pork rillettes with toast and cornichons, and passion fruit bavarois. Pay a very little more to swap one of those for six slippery Irish rock oysters. Seafood is a big thing down here. The only way to eat upstairs is on a still pricey pre- or post-theater menu. Wherever you dine, bring a sweater if it's fine, and ask to sit out on the terrace and enjoy the magical nighttime lights shining on Tower Bridge.

WORTH A SPLURGE

✪ **Fish!.** Cathedral St., Borough Market, SE1. ☎ **020/7234-3333** central reservations, or 020/7836-3236. Reservations recommended. Main courses £7.80–£16 ($12.50–$25.60). JCB, MC, V. Mon–Sat 11am–2:45pm and 5:30–10:30pm, Sun noon–3:30pm and 5:30–9:30pm. Tube: London Bridge, Borough. SEAFOOD.

Southwark is one of the oldest parts of London. Now that Tate Modern has opened on Bankside and scruffy old warehouses are turning into swanky flats, it is also one of the hippest. Another neighborhood draw is the foodie mecca, Borough Market, which is where you'll find Fish! The design is futuristic diner, all glass and steel—a bit noisy at busy times—and the style is evangelical. Notes on place mats detail why fish is good for you and how it should be caught. Ticks against a list of 20 fish on the choose-your-own menu show you which are available that day, to be grilled or steamed as you like, with a choice of five accompanying sauces. Chips cost extra but are perfectly cooked and well worth it. There are lots of other options: fish pies, swordfish club sandwiches, and so on. And if you go for a starter, make it the fish soup, which is superbly executed. You might even be able to sucker anti-fish kids with the tuna bolognese and fishy toys. There are new branches at Canary Wharf and Battersea, plus five more opening at "can't tell you yet" locations by the end of last year. You can book at any of them through the central reservations number above.

Gourmet Cultural Eats

If you've had time to glance at chapter 6, you'll know that many of London's major national museums and galleries have sprouted stupendous new extensions. In honor of their steel, stone, glass, and glistening white paint, the chaps behind the scenes have turned their attention to the art of fine dining, too. The best gourmet cultural eats are listed below—and all but the Wallace Collection serve dinner at least 1 night a week.

And here are a few more places to nourish body and soul: **The Royal Court Theatre** (see p. 271) in Sloane Square, **The Royal Opera House** (see p. 280) in Covent Garden, **Somerset House** (see p. 203) in the Strand, the **British Museum's** new Great Court (see p. 195), Bankside's **Vinopolis** (see p. 229), and **Shakespeare's Globe Theatre** (see p. 272). If you are "doing" the South Bank and Bankside, stop in at **Bright Light Café,** run by delicious deli Konditor & Cook, at the Young Vic, 66 The Cut, SE1 (☎ **020/7620-2200** for reservations; Tube: Waterloo, Southwark). Open noon to 8pm, Monday to Saturday, it has that fake-sunshine lighting designed to combat Seasonal Affective Disorder!

- **Café Level 7 at Tate Modern,** Bankside, SE1 (☎ **020/7401-5020** or 020/7887-8000 museum; Tube: Mansion House or St. Paul's and cross over Millennium Bridge, Southwark). Right under the glass roof extension on top of the old power station, this cafe has the best dining views in London. It is also an excellent value. Lunchtime sandwiches, soups, and substantial meals cost £2.50 to £7.50 ($4 to $12). Evening main courses are £7.50 to £12.45 ($12 to $19.90). It's screamingly popular, so if you can't get in, try Café Level 2 instead, which still looks out on the river and serves the same menu, plus breakfast, too. Level 7 is open Monday to Friday 11:45am to 3pm, Saturday to Sunday 11:45am to 4pm; Friday to Saturday 7 to 11pm. Level 2 Sunday to Thursday 10am to 6pm, Friday to Saturday 10am to 10pm. MODERN BRITISH.

14 Farther Afield

ISLINGTON

SUPER-CHEAP EATS

Le Mercury. 140a Upper St., N1. ☎ **020/7354-4088.** Main courses £5.85 ($9.35); fixed-price meal £5.95 ($9.50). MC, V. Mon–Sat 11am–1am, Sun noon–11:30pm. Tube: Islington/Highbury. FRENCH.

Hold the front page! Le Mercury has lured top chef Michel Hautin, who used to cook for French President Chirac, to Islington and ratcheted up its fixed-price menu price by an extortionate 45p. In an area that's seen an influx of new moneyed residents and restaurants to cater for them, Le Mercury is an unnatural phenomenon: down-home French cooking, delivered in one-price main courses and dynamite three-course deals. That's why this upbeat storefront restaurant gets so crowded. You can order the fixed-price menu right through the day until 6pm. Choose from smoked mackerel and avocado salad with port sauce or a soup of the day. Of the four main courses, I went for salmon fishcakes and was mildly irked that vegetables cost an extra £1.95 ($3.10)—an unjustly Scrooge-like reaction at this price. Desserts are a bit dull, to be honest, unless you're a fan of chocolate butter pudding. The à la carte dinner is a lot more exciting and not a dirty word at these prices: £2.85 ($4.55) for starters, £3.85 ($6.15) for main courses, the same as above for veggies, £2.75 ($4.40) for dessert, and £2.45

- **Crivelli's Garden at the National Gallery,** Trafalgar Square, WC2 (☎ **020/7747-2869;** Tube: Charing Cross, Leicester Sq.). Gaze down at London's most famous landmark, Nelson's Column, from this cafe-bar-restaurant on the third floor of the new Sainsbury wing. Two tips: Stick to the cafe during the day, for light meals costing £4.50 to £8.50 ($7.20 to $13.60); or book ahead for dinner on late-opening Wednesday night for a £14.50 ($23.20) early-bird treat. Open daily, cafe-bar 10am to 5:30pm, restaurant 11:30am to 5pm, both to 9pm on Wednesday. MEDITERRANEAN.
- **The Portrait Restaurant & Bar at the National Portrait Gallery,** St. Martin's Place, WC2 (☎ **020/7312-2490;** Tube: Charing Cross). Another spectacular view, across West End chimney pots from the new glass-roofed Ondaatje Wing. Try the lounge-bar for light lunchtime treats, £6.50 to £7.95 ($11.10 to $12.70). Restaurant main courses are pricey at £10.75 to £14.95 ($17.20 to $23.90), but come for dinner anyway and have two starters for the same price. Restaurant open daily 11:45am to 2:45pm, Thursday to Friday 5:30 to 8:30pm; lounge-bar 11:30am to 5:30pm. MODERN BRITISH.
- **The Sculpture Garden at the Wallace Collection,** Hertford House, Manchester Sq., W1 (☎ **020/7563-9500;** Tube: Bond St). The eaterie in the new covered courtyard is best for cheap light lunches and wicked gooey teas, or great value, proper meals inspired by celebrity chef Stephen Bull, who is "food director" here. Posh main courses cost £7.50 to £11.50 ($12 to $18.40), or snaffle a bunch of starters at £3.50 to £4.75 ($5.60 to $7.60). Pastries, cakes, and savory bites cost £1.50 to £4.95 ($2.40 to $7.90). Restaurant lunch noon to 3pm, cafe snacks and tea 10am to 5pm. MODERN EUROPEAN.

($3.90) for rocket-fuel coffee laced with rum, brandy, vodka, or Amaretto, to make you forget how close together the tables are and how hard the gateback chairs.

Great Deals on Fixed-Price Meals

Granita. 127 Upper St., N1. ☎ **020/7226-3222.** Reservations recommended. Main courses £9–£14 ($14.40–$22.40); fixed-price lunch £11.95–£13.95 ($19.10–$22.30); fixed-price Sun dinner £12.50–£14.95 ($20–$23.90). MC, V. Wed–Sun 12:30–2:30pm; Tues–Sun 6:30–10:30pm. Tube: Islington/Highbury. MODERN EUROPEAN.

This used to be one of Tony and Cherie Blair's favorite dining places before they quit Islington and moved onto greater things. Superb cuisine and blonde-on-blonde, minimalist decor have ensured Granita an enduring spot at the top of the hip restaurant tree. Diners who go à la carte will appreciate the meal-on-a-plate approach, which avoids the need to bump the bill up by adding side orders. But the short fixed-price menus, either two or three courses, are excellent value. There are about three choices at each stage, modern European dishes with nods to the Middle East and Southeast Asia. And these change weekly to keep Granita's many regulars entertained. You might find sautéed calves' liver with artichokes, broad beans, sage, and lemon. Or a hearty pea and sorrel soup. Char-grilling is a favorite cooking method, particularly delicious when it comes to rump of beef with Middle Eastern spices. And the desserts would make Martha Stewart green with envy.

✪ **Lola's.** The Mall Building, 359 Upper St., N1. ☎ **020/7359-1932.** Reservations essential. Main courses £9.75–£15.50 ($15.60–$24.80); fixed-price lunch £10–£15 ($16–$24). AE, DC, MC, V. Mon–Fri noon–2:30pm, Sat–Sun noon–3pm; Mon–Sat 6–11pm, Sun 7–10pm. Tube: Angel. GLOBAL.

Upstairs from the antiques market in an old tram shed, the light floods in through acres of glass to create a delightful conservatory dining room. At night, Lola's is a perfect place for star-gazing. Or it would be, if diners weren't concentrating so hard on more earthly things—the highly rated, simple but inventive, cooking. The hand-written menu changes daily, and includes peasant and modern European dishes, with detours through the Middle East, Pacific Rim, and North America. There are some fine bistro dishes, like steak and frites, grilled tuna salad niçoise, and poached chicken breast with aiöli and vegetable salads. But I'd recommend skipping past those to more ambitious roast halibut with panzanella-style couscous. The weekday fixed-price lunches are excellent value, especially to top off a visit to the market. But you can dine reasonably in the evening, too, on a couple of starters. The wine list is just as global and includes some very fair-priced bottles. On weekends, Lola's offers an eclectic brunch.

CAMDEN

Street food and hole-in-the-wall cafes are the cheapest option and super-abundant in Camden. Cruise any section of the market to find a bewildering array of kebabs, hot dogs, falafel, and pizza starting at around £2 ($3.20) a pop. For healthier fare, head for Camden Green Market in the railway arches behind the Stables Great Hall.

Trojka. 101 Regent's Park Rd., NW1. ☎ **020/7483-3765.** Reservations essential for weekend dinner. Main courses £5.50–£8 ($8.80–$12.80); fixed-price lunch £6.95 ($11.10). AE, DC, MC, V. Mon–Fri 8:30am–10:30pm, Sat–Sun 9am–10:30pm. Tube: Chalk Farm. RUSSIAN.

A raffish literary crowd, lollyed-up locals, and folks from the home country, all flock here for delicate borscht or blinis filled with smoked salmon and trout, aubergine caviar, and a host of other delights. It's most fun on Friday and Saturday nights (£1/$1.60 cover charge), when the Russian musician serenading the room creates a really festive atmosphere—there's soft canned music the rest of the time. Blinis are all under £4 ($6.40). As well as the fixed-price lunch, check both the specials on the blackboard and the main dishes on the regular menu, because the portions are huge enough to fuel a winter trek across the steppes, and the prices so reasonable that you won't bust the bank. I was shocked to hear that Trojka had completely redecorated in 1999, but thankfully nothing hs changed. The big room, with its clattery floors, is still full of post-war furniture, still painted bright yellow and pea green, still hung with gilt mirrors and a few kitsch pictures—and still reassuringly charming.

GREAT DEALS ON FIXED-PRICE MEALS

Daphne. 83 Bayham St., NW1. ☎ **020/7267-7322.** Reservations essential on weekends. Fixed-price lunch £5.75 ($9.20); main courses £6.50–£13 ($10.40–$20.80). MC, V. Mon–Sat noon–2:30pm and 6–11:30pm. Tube: Camden Town. GREEK.

I've spent many a lunchtime at this veteran Camden eatery because attached to the small dining room is an even tinier terrace festooned with vines and a spacious roof terrace, where tables are hotly fought over. Daphne is a simple place, the tables covered with green gingham and walls decorated with scenes of Greece. The food is freshly and lovingly prepared by the family-owners, and mostly pretty reliable as well as a very good value at the price. You'll find all the traditional Greek specialties such as moussaka, *kleftiko* (joint of lamb baked with lemon and spices), and *afelia* (cubes of pork marinated in wine and cooked with coriander). But it's the grilled seasonal fish—sea bass, mullet, and swordfish, with a squeeze of lemon and freshly chopped parsley, for example—where Daphne comes into its own. The wine list favors Greek and Cypriot wines, but there is a short selection of French bottles.

Lemonia. 89 Regent's Park Rd., NW1. ☎ **020/7586-7454.** Reservations essential. Fixed-price lunch £6.75–£7.95 ($10.80–$12.70); main courses £7.25–£13.50 ($11.60–$21.60); meze £13.50 ($21.60). MC, V. Sun–Fri noon–3pm; Mon–Sat 6–11:30pm. Tube: Chalk Farm. GREEK.

This long-established restaurant offers a classic Greek menu prepared better than practically any other you'll find in London. It's a charming place, which more than lives up to its name: Lemons are absolutely everywhere. The mix of polished wood and marble-topped tables cluster near the fully open front window, up on a dais, and in the conservatory. There are even a few out on the pavement. If you don't want to come this way for lunch, then the meze, which gets you a mixed bag of starters and main courses, is a fantastic deal. Otherwise, top recommendations include the moussaka, which is a triumph of eggplant, zucchini, potatoes, tomatoes, and ground beef in a creamy sauce, and the subtly flavored *afelia* (cubes of pork marinated in wine, coriander seeds, and spices). Lemonia is deservedly very popular. Expect crowds of happy locals, especially on the weekend when the ritual is to walk off the feast on Primrose Hill, and revel in one of the best views across London.

✪ **Odette's.** 130 Regent's Park Rd., NW1. ☎ **020/7586-5486.** Reservations essential. Main courses £11–£16.50 ($17.60–$26.40); fixed-price lunch £12.50 ($20). AE, DC, MC, V. Mon–Fri 12:30–2:30pm; Mon–Sat 7–11pm. Tube: Chalk Farm. MODERN EUROPEAN.

Get out your travel pass, posh frock, and autograph book for celeb-nabbing, and hurry to Odette's for the three-course weekday fixed-price lunch. To be able to set such a great price, this posh restaurant cuts out all choice. The seasons dictate the marginally modern European menu, but it might be something like ox-cheek soup, fillets of John Dory, then glazed banana and fresh berries with pistachio ice cream. If you ask really nicely, the charming staff may swap one option for you. If they don't, two courses of such fine cuisine and at such an elegant restaurant are still a fantastic deal. Odette's is a converted town house, with a conservatory and opulent dining room, hung with gilt mirrors of all shapes and sizes, on the first floor and a bar in the basement. The wine list is formidably long, but it includes half-bottles or wine by the glass. Odette's will also supply children's portions at a reduced price.

15 Best of the Budget Chains

The past 2 decades have brought a massive explosion in restaurant chains to Britain—low-concept, pseudo-ethnic, cafe this and cafe that. They aren't my cup of tea, so I've left them out. The best funky newcomers and familiar favorites are cloning themselves just as prolifically, but each branch has a personality of its own.

Pizza Express introduced the Italian staple to Britain when even metropolitan Londoners talked about filthy foreign muck. It's still the quality benchmark, and a pizza will cost you £4.45 to £7.45 ($7.10 to $11.90). There are over 60 branches across London. One of the liveliest is in Soho: 10 Dean St., W1 (☎ **020/7437-9595;** Tube: Tottenham Court Rd., Leicester Sq). Surf the Web site for a full list (www.pizzaexpress.co.uk). Newcomer **ASK** is putting up a very worthy challenge. It uses chi-chi ingredients familiar in posher cuisine—goat cheese, sun-dried tomatoes, and so on. It's a restaurant, not a joint, with cool modern decor and smooth service. Yet pizza prices are very reasonable at £4 to £6.70 ($6.40 to $10.70). There are about 20 ASKs—

look for the blue neon signs. Two are extra handy for budget hotels: in Paddington, at 41 to 43 Spring St., W2 (☎ **020/7706-0707**); and Victoria, at 160 to 162 Victoria St., SW1 (☎ **020/7630-8228**).

There are three friendly faces for U.S. travelers who want a taste of home. Choose between mega-queues, but great burgers (from £7.25/$11.60), at **Hard Rock Cafe,** 150 Old Park Lane, W1 (☎ **020/7629-0382;** Tube: Hyde Park Corner); or more local diners, and even better but pricier burgers (from £8.95/$14.30), at **Planet Hollywood,** Trocadero, 13 Coventry St., W1 (☎ **020/7287-1000;** Tube: Piccadilly Circus). The third, and nuttiest, U.S. chain to arrive in London is the **Rainforest Café,** 20 Shaftesbury Ave., W1 (☎ **020/7434-3111**). This is themed dining on steroids: jungly vegetation, rocks and waterfalls, tropical birds and wailing animatronic animals, thunderclaps and sudden storms—as if London needed pretend ones. There's a kids' menu, and grown-ups can choose between standard fast food and more exotic Asian concoctions for £6.75 to £14.95 ($10.80 to $23.90).

Healthy meals-in-a-cup are definitely big in London, even if they haven't reached the super-iconic status that Al's Soup Kitchen International in New York acquired when *Seinfeld* immortalized Al as the Soup Nazi. These two are my pick of the bunch, and both are a great value. Also check out the excellent **Quiet Revolution,** in Clerkenwell.

SOUP Works is a funky U.S.-style operation, with rows of huge metal saucepans along the counter. The flavors change regularly, but prices start at £1.50 ($2.40) for 8oz. of something like lentil, carrot, and cumin. There are also 12, 16, or jumbo 32oz. pots—the biggest makes a delicious, if messy, shared meal. Breakfast in a cup is a cheap way to start the day: coffee and porridge with two toppings (white chocolate and raisins . . . mmm) for £2.25 ($3.60). There are four branches clustered around Soho and Covent Garden. The one near Leicester Square, at 15 Moor St., W1 (☎ **020/7734-7687;** www.soupworks.co.uk) is great for late-night slurps, open until 11pm Monday to Thursday and midnight on Friday and Saturday. **Soup Opera** promises you'll be able to "squelch" the plum tomatoes in its soups. Prices include a piece of bread and fruit, and start at £2.50 ($4) for a 12oz. carton—this place doesn't bother with 8oz. There are six branches, and I'd try one near Oxford Circus at 2 Hanover Sq., W1 (☎ **020/7629-0179;** www.soupopera.co.uk).

Cranks has been churning out meat-free hot meals, snacks, cakes, and drinks, eat-in and take-out, since the days when vegetarianism was viewed as deeply subversive. It's had a face-lift and now calls itself **Cranks Vitality & Health Cafe.** The new star dish is a 95% fat-free, 200-calorie, stir-fry at £2.95 ($4.70). My favorites of the five West End branches are: 23 Barrett St., W1 (☎ **020/7495-1340**), and 8 Marshall St. (☎ **020/7437-9431**).

Eat in or take out, **Pret a Manger** is *the* quick snack stop. Sandwiches are its specialty, with such luxurious fillings that you must grab a stack of napkins to catch the lateral ooze. Or you can grab a cappuccino, sushi box, or wicked cake. There are 65 branches. The helpline will tell you the nearest (☎ **020/7827-8887**). To refuel after a visit to the Tower of London, go to: 1 Great Tower St., EC3 (☎ **020/7283-4722**).

16 Only in London

AFTERNOON TEA

If you're over in August, book in to a Friday **Celebritea** at the Royal National Theatre (☎ **020/7452-3000;** www.nt-online.org; Tube: Waterloo, Southwark, Embankment). Theatrical giants talk about their work while you scoff your cream tea. The event starts at 2:30pm and costs £7 ($11.20).

MAYFAIR

✪ **Brown's Hotel.** Albemarle and Dover sts., W1. ☎ **020/7493-6020.** Reservations required for 3 and 4:45pm sittings on weekdays. No denim, shorts, or sneakers, but no jacket required. £19 ($30.40). AE, DC, MC, V. Daily 3–6pm. Tube: Green Park.

This quintessentially understated, oh-so English hotel (the oldest 5-star in London) is justifiably famous for its country-house afternoon tea. Tailcoated waiters tend to guests reclining in armchairs in the paneled drawing room. It's a lot of money, but you certainly won't need dinner after a session here. Tea starts with a fine array of ham and mustard, smoked salmon, egg, and many other sandwiches. Scones with clotted cream and jam follow that. And then you'll have your pick of scrumptious cream cakes and pastries. Brown's serves its own blended tea, among a long list of others. You don't have to dress up, although there is a no-denim dress code, but that is part of the occasion.

Dorchester. 54 Park Lane, W1. ☎ **020/7629-8888.** Reservations recommended. Dress smart casual. Fixed-price tea £19.50–£29.50 ($31.20–$47.20). Daily 3–6pm. AE, DC, JCB, MC, V. Tube: Hyde Park Corner.

The Promenade may not have quite the limitless luxury of the Ritz's Palm Court, but it's a pretty close-run thing. Gold decoration and marble floors and pillars make this a very posh corridor in which to take afternoon tea. The Dorchester is famed for its pastries: The fluffy scones that follow the sandwich first course, and the strawberry tart, white chocolate parcel, coffee éclair, and the host of other cakes will send you out into the Mayfair early evening, happy but crawling on your hands and knees.

ST. JAMES'S

Fountain Restaurant at Fortnum & Mason. 181 Piccadilly, W1. ☎ **020/7734-8040.** Ice-cream afternoon tea £12.95 ($20.70). AE, DC, MC, V. Mon–Sat 8:30am–8pm. Tube: Green Park, Piccadilly.

Fortnum & Mason is such a world-famous name that it's mobbed with tourists. The ice-cream tea at the downstairs Fountain restaurant includes a pot of own-blend tea, chocolate shells filled with scoops of vanilla ice cream, freshly baked scones with clotted cream and strawberry jam, and then a slice of one of a selection of cakes. It's great for the kids, not just because it's their kind of meal, but because there's so much noise that no one will notice if they goof around.

KNIGHTSBRIDGE

The Lanesborough. Hyde Park Corner, SW1. ☎ **020/7259-5599.** Reservations recommended. Dress smart casual. Fixed-price teas, Lanesborough £20.50 ($32.80), Belgravia £26.50 ($42.40); minimum £7.50 ($12). AE, DC, JCB, MC, V. Mon–Sat 3:30–6pm, Sun 4–6pm. Tube: Hyde Park Corner.

The Lanesborough occupies prime position right on Hyde Park Corner in what used to be the St. George's Hospital. The glass-covered central courtyard, where you take afternoon tea, is flamboyantly elegant and modeled on the Brighton Pavilion. The hotel has its own smokey blend of tea, among several others, to wash down the three-course Lanesborough menu. This starts with sandwiches, moves through hot buttered crumpets, as well as scones with lemon curd, jam, and clotted cream, to climax with sinful cakes: Chocolate mousse in a white chocolate case is a must. The dearer Belgravia adds strawberries and champagne on top. The staff is extremely charming and welcoming.

COVENT GARDEN

Waldorf Meridien. Aldwych, WC2. ☎ **020/7836-2400.** Reservations recommended, essential on weekends. Fixed-price tea £21–£28 ($33.60–$44.80); tea dance £25–£28 ($40–$44.80). AE, DC, MC, V. Mon–Fri 3–5pm; tea dance Sat 2:30–5pm, Sun 4–6:30pm. Tube: Covent Garden, Aldwych.

The teas are delicious in the airy elegant Palm Court every day of the week, but the weekend tea dances are a special treat. Two-left-feet shufflers and two-step champions, young and old, happily circle together while the silver cutlery and Wedgwood china tinkles in the background. It's a marvelously old-fashioned way to work off a dozen mini-sandwiches, pastries, and squelchy cakes.

FISH & CHIPS

MARYLEBONE

Seashell. 49–51 Lisson Grove, NW1. ☎ **020/7224-9000.** Main courses £7.95–£15 ($12.70–$24); 3-course fixed-price menu served until 7pm £9.50 ($15.20). AE, MC, V. Mon– Fri noon–2:30pm, Sun noon–2:45pm; Mon–Fri 5:00–10:30pm. Tube: Marylebone.

Seashell epitomizes the changing place of fish and chips in British food culture. That sounds pompous, I know, but you'll have to visit to understand the gulf between this and what used to be the workers' cheap and cheerful staple. The clientele is varied, from a host of tourists doing the London thing, to cabbies. The latter are generally a good sign that you're not going to be ripped off. And Seashell is very good value for a place that is so well known, even if it is not the very best fish and chips in town. Diners walk through the take-out area at the front and sit at wooden booths. As well as the usual cod, Seashell sells hugely popular fish cakes and hot pots filled with seafood. Dover sole tops the price list. If you take the early three-course supper, there's absolutely no chance of going hungry by the time you've polished off one of the traditional puddings.

BLOOMSBURY

✪ **North Sea Fish Restaurant.** 7–8 Leigh St., WC1. ☎ **020/7387-5892.** Main courses £6.95–£15.95 ($11.10–$25.50). AE, DC, MC, V. Mon–Sat noon–2:30pm, 5:30–10:30pm. Tube: Russell Sq., King's Cross.

Locals love North Sea's version of what is, of course, the national dish. It has a different marketing approach to the old-fashioned Seashell in Marylebone. Here the look is deliberately upmarket country-cozy, even down to the stuffed fish. Diners at the rear of the chippie sit on velvet-covered chairs at wooden tables. You'll find a good mix of cabbies on a tea break, local academics, and tourists here. Dining in, you could do two starters—smoked mackerel and scampi, perhaps—or one and a portion of deliciously crispy fat chips, for under £6 ($9.60). The best deal, though, is the enormous seafood platter, which comes with bite-size, battered pieces of lots of different sorts of fish and seafood. You can go for straight cod, of course, or skate, haddock, plaice, all brought in fresh from Billingsgate every morning. And I'll salute any diner who's got room for one of the traditional puddings after that.

COVENT GARDEN

The Rock & Sole Plaice. 47 Endell St., WC2. ☎ **020/7836-3785.** Reservations recommended (dinner). Eat in £7 ($11.20); take-out £5 ($8). DC, MC, V. Mon–Sat 11:30am–10:30pm (11:45pm for take-out), Sun noon–10pm. Tube: Covent Garden.

Endell Street is a peaceful oasis only 1 block away from Covent Garden's unrelenting crowd scene. But it's still best to avoid The Rock & Sole Plaice in the early evenings: Theater-goers queue up here to refuel before the curtain goes up. It opened in 1871 and claims to be London's oldest surviving fish-and-chip shop. The decor is very Covent Garden, with theatrical posters and pavement tables. Fortunately, the prices are anything but. The Dover sole certainly has to be the cheapest in town at £11 ($17.60), and the other fish are half that price. Choose from halibut, mackerel, tuna, haddock, plaice, or cod. If you've never tried skate, then do because it's a moist, flaky fish with a wonderful flavor. The chips are thick and wedge-shaped, and you can add on mushy peas, pickled onions, and . . . mmm, smell that breath. For non-fish-eaters, there's steak-and-kidney and several other pies, plus sausage in batter.

PUBS & GASTROPUBS

No tradition is sacrosanct as restaurateurs bid to turn London into a world food capital. The days when pub grub just meant soggy pie and chips were long over anyway, but now even the places serving honest no-frills fare, made on the premises, are facing a powerful challenge. All hail the conquering gastropub. It's an unfortunate name, hinting at some dodgy stomach complaint from a dodgier than usual old-style meal. But one thing these new foodie haunts don't cause is many complaints, unless it's about the prices. Swapping nicotine-stained wallpaper for chi-chi minimalist restaurant walls, and beer bellies for a sleeker-figured clientele, costs roughly double what you'd have paid for a meal before. But the food is usually innovative, global, and delicious—and if you choose the right place, excellent value.

Traditionalists needn't despair. There are still lots of good old boys who serve good food all day. For a really hearty homemade pie, for about £6.50 ($10.40), try the **Salisbury,** 90 St. Martin's Lane, WC2 (☎ **020/7836-5863**). It's in the heart of theaterland and mingles traditional decor with chi-chi modern art. You can get hot food from 11am until 11pm (Sunday noon–10:30pm). Farther north, in Bloomsbury, there's a great place to stop after a visit to the British Museum. The **Museum Tavern,** 49 Great Russell St., WC1 (☎ **020/7242-8987**), can fix you up with a very decent beef-and-ale pie, or a ploughman's lunch for £5 to £6 ($8 to $9.60) at any time of the day. Built as a jail in 1780, the **Nag's Head,** 53 Kinnerton St., SW1 (☎ **020/7235-1135**), is supposed to be the smallest pub in London. Wash down the shepherd's pie or gourmet sausages with one of the big range of on-tap real ales. The food will cost you £4.50 to £5.25 ($7.20 to $8.40), a bargain in Belgravia. The **King's Head & Eight Bells,** 50 Cheyne Walk, SW3 (☎ **020/7352-1820**), is in Chelsea, close to where Carlyle, Swinburne, and George Eliot used to live. The patrons are still pretty glitzy. Daily specials include sausage or fish 'n' chips, and cost £5 to £6 ($8 to $9.60).

MARYLEBONE

The Chapel. 48 Chapel St., NW1. ☎ **020/7402-9220.** Main courses £8–£12.50 ($12.80–$20). AE, DC, MC, V. Daily noon–2:30pm and 7–10pm. Tube: Edgware Rd.

The Chapel more than earns the epithet, gastropub. The food is ambitious, beautifully executed, and primarily modern European. The blackboard scrawl lists a handful of daily starters, from brie en route to parma ham and Tuscan bean salad in a filo basket. Main courses may sound traditional (many don't) but have a very modern twist, like the pork with caramelized apples. The desserts are extremely wicked. Twenty-five wines are available by the glass. And the bare-boards interior is bright and spacious.

THE CITY & CLERKENWELL

✪ **Bleeding Heart Tavern.** Bleeding Heart Yard, off Greville St., EC1. ☎ **020/7404-0333.** Reservations essential in restaurant. Main courses, tavern £6.95–£10.95 ($11.10–$17.50), bistro £6.95–£12.50 ($11.10–$20), restaurant £9.95–£16.95 ($15.90–$27.10); bar menu £3.50–£6.95 ($5.60–$11.10). AE, DC, JCB, MC, V. Tavern Mon–Fri 11am–11pm; bistro noon–3pm); restaurant noon–2:30pm; 6–10:30pm (both). Tube: Chancery Lane, Farringdon. MODERN BRITISH.

The story of Bleeding Heart Yard is every bit as gory as you hope it will be. The beautiful 17th-century it-girl Lady Elizabeth Hatton was murdered here, after walking outside with the European ambassador during her annual winter ball. Today, this is a very remarkable gastropub. The restored 1746 tavern is the London flagship of regional brewery and wine merchant, Southwold Adnams. It is *the* place to quaff real ale (from £2.20/$3.50 a pint) with the sort of earthy cooking you can imagine Thomas Hardy describing, were he writing today. My luscious deep-fried Somerset brie with gooseberry compote, ale-fed Suffolk pork sausages with mash and cider onion gravy, and sticky apple pie came to £15.70 ($25.12).

There are two other parts to this trencherman's heaven, with successively higher prices. Though you can drink wine in the tavern, the choice represents a mere fraction of the miraculous wine list in the bistro, from £10 ($16) a bottle or £2.50 ($4) a glass. Three courses, of a similar style cuisine, costs a couple of pounds more here. For a real splurge (£15.45/$24.70 minimum for two courses), head for the ever-so French restaurant downstairs, where the name of every dish is like a two-line love letter.

The Eagle. 159 Farringdon Rd., EC1. ☎ **020/7837-1353.** Main courses £8–£12 ($12.80–$19.20). No credit cards. Mon–Sat 12:30–3:30pm and 6:30–10:30pm; Sun 12:30–3:30pm. Tube: Farringdon. MEDITERRANEAN.

Justly celebrated for its food, The Eagle is more like a cafe-restaurant than a traditional pub, and it's packed for lunch. The fresh ingredients are displayed in baskets at the bar. The short menu—a jumble of starters and main courses—always has hearty soup and a variety of Mediterranean delights. The grilled marinated leg of lamb with Catalan ratatouille, humming with garlic and rosemary, was yummy. And at £1 ($1.60) a pop, who could resist several of the melting Portuguese custard tarts. Not me! There are about 15 wines available by the glass from £2.20 ($3.50).

CAMDEN

The Engineer. 65 Gloucester Ave., NW1. ☎ **020/7722-0950.** Reservations recommended. Main courses £9–£15.50 ($14.40–$24.80). MC, V. Mon 7am–10pm, Tues–Sun 7am–10:30pm. Tube: Camden Town, Chalk Farm.

The Engineer was one of the gastropub pioneers. It has huge glass windows and scrubbed tables in the bar, restaurant, and garden. The modern European cuisine is elaborate, with a few global influences. It's pricey, but skinny wallets can fill their stomachs with simple but delicious meals in a bowl, while the less restricted have something like the dreamy lemon-scented risotto of yellow-pepper puree, gorgonzola, and walnuts. And splurgers gorge on whole roasted sea bass. The menu changes every 2 weeks, and the meat is all organic. This is a delightful place and screamingly busy, with locals popping in for its very good coffee as well as to eat. Do book ahead.

6

Exploring London

The Queen's scissor hand must have been ready to drop off last year after cutting so many miles of official ribbon. London is like a gold-rush town. Spurred on by the millennium, the public and commercial sector invested £6 billion in sprucing up the city's tourist facilities. Not since the era of the great Victorian philanthropists has there been such a museum and gallery boom. But the old patriarchal elitism has no place at the dozens of new attractions and stunning modern extensions. The collections are no less awesome, but the displays now sizzle with interactivity to bring the past alive, make history relevant to today, and flash a foretaste of the future. Last year also saw the opening of the Millennium Bridge, linking the City to Bankside. The second of the twin Hungerford footbridges, between Westminster and the South Bank, will be completed early this year. Even the extremely ambitious plan to make London's busiest roundabout, Trafalgar Square, fit for humans again may start this spring. At last, the "urban renaissance" is more than just civic hot air.

One big fat blot did mar this lovely landscape—the flop to end all flops, the Dumb . . . oops, Dome. As this book went to press the government was talking about handing over control to Nomura, the Japanese bank that bought the site in August 2000. One month later Nomura dropped its plans to create a theme park and pulled out of the deal, citing a litany of problems that made the Dome management look even more hopeless than people had thought they were. So we'll just have to wait and see if anyone can rescue this white elephant!

A NOTE ON PRICES

Many of the city's major national museums and galleries stopped charging for children in 1999, and from April last year, that extended to seniors. The government has now put forward a proposal to cut admission for adults. Tax issues associated with their charitable status mean the institutions would lose heavily if they stopped charging altogether. So, the Culture Secretary has offered to help fund a new standard £1 ($1.60) ticket beginning in September 2001. Check with his department's Web site (www.culture.gov.uk) or with the London Tourist Board (see below).

A family ticket usually covers two adults and two children, but sometimes you can take an extra offspring. The age limit to qualify as a child varies widely, from 15 to 18, while under-5s get free admission to most attractions.

WHERE TO GET YOUR SIGHTSEEING INFO

The **London Tourist Board** (☎ **020/7932-2000** or 020/7971-0026; www.londontown.com) will fall over itself to help you. So will **London Transport** (www.londontransport.co.uk), which has put together a brilliant set of fold-out miniguides on themes from showbiz to royal London, as well as on specific neighborhoods. Also look for the space-age **i-plus** kiosks, at bus stops, on high streets, and at several of London's major attractions. Touch the screen for information on attractions and public transport, and to buy theater tickets online. For details on where to find all of the above, see "Visitor Information," at the start of chapter 3.

As ever, the weekly *Time Out* magazine (www.timeout.com) has great up-to-the-minute ideas. Also surf the one-stop **www.24hourmuseum.org.uk**, a gateway to virtually every museum in the country.

1 Cheap Thrills: How to Save on Sightseeing

Many big London attractions have pegged their prices over the past couple of years, knowing that visitors from overseas will faint from shock when they do the reverse exchange calculation. But many still put a big dent in the wallet. The prime way to save money is to take advantage of all the free museums, galleries, and historic buildings—as long as you hard-heartedly resist all invitations to make a donation. Here's a handy directory, in the same order as the listings: British Museum, National Gallery, Somerset House, Tate Britain, Tate Modern, the churches and Westminster Cathedral in section 3 of this chapter, Bank of England Museum, Guildhall, Middle Temple Hall, Ben Uri Art Society, British Library, Geffrye Museum, Kenwood House & Iveagh Bequest, Museum of Garden History, National Army Museum, National Portrait Gallery, Percival David Foundation of Chinese Art, Royal Hospital Chelsea, Serpentine Gallery, Sir John Soane Museum, Wallace Collection, Whitechapel Art Gallery, Leighton House, William Morris Gallery, and Bethnal Green Museum of Childhood. Phew! Now tell me that isn't enough to keep even a performance-enhanced tourist happy for several trips to London.

There are lots more ways to have fun for free, or at least very cheaply, so take a look at the suggestions below.

FREEBIES

- Squeeze in a lightning-late visit to the big museums that don't charge for entry from about ¾ of an hour before they close: **Natural History Museum** (see p. 200), **Science Museum** (see p. 202), **Victoria & Albert Museum** (see p. 207), and **Museum of London** (see p. 224).
- Most museums and galleries put on dozens of tours, talks, and workshops, and many do it for free. As well as the ones listed above, the **British Library** (see p. 218), **British Museum** (see p. 195), **Tate Britain** (see p. 203), and **Tate Modern** (see p. 204) get top scores for this.
- Many of the city's beautiful churches put on free lunchtime concerts. For a full list, contact the **City Information Centre** (☎ **020/7332-1456**). The newly people-friendly **Royal Opera House** (see p. 280) does the same thing every Monday at 1pm during the season. So does the **Royal Festival Hall** (see p. 281), informally in front of the Festival Buffet Café, noon to 2pm daily. Jazz buffs should head to **The 100 Club** (see p. 284) for a cover-free Friday lunch.
- Visit the **Houses of Parliament** (see p. 197) to watch a debate, from the **Strangers' Galleries,** in the rowdy Commons or the eccentric Lords. The PM

Hot Tip: Where to Find Free E-mail

You can send short e-messages for free from any **i-plus** electronic information kiosk, even if you don't have your own e-mail address. Keep an eye out for the slim, silvery kiosks at the London Transport Museum, Madame Tussaud's, Natural History Museum, Theatre Museum, and the V&A.

---

answers questions on Wednesday at 2:30pm. Sessions run from mid-October to the end of July, with recesses at Christmas and Easter.

- Go to the **Old Bailey** or the **Royal Courts of Justice** to marvel at the barristers weaving their Machiavellian arguments (see section 5, "Institutions as English as Shepherd's Pie," below).
- Catch the **Changing of the Guard** (see the box later in this chapter) at Buckingham Palace, Horse Guards, or St. James's Palace, or the **Ceremony of the Keys** (see the box later in this chapter) at the Tower of London. Lots of luvverly toy soldiers!
- Got something to say? Then sound off at **Speaker's Corner,** in the northeast corner of Hyde Park. Every Sunday, anarchists, stand-up comics, religious fanatics, would-be politicians, and the deeply eccentric come here to spout their opinions and grievances.
- There's lots more outdoor fun to be had in **Covent Garden Piazza** and **Somerset House** (see p. 203), where Londoners come to hang out and watch the street entertainment.
- Go to a free **pre-auction viewing** at one of London's big salerooms (see p. 251). It's a rare chance to see bizarre and fabulous treasures normally held in private collections.
- Pick up a bite to eat at one of the city's **food halls** (see p. 261). Harrods gives good sensory overload amid lavish decor. Fortnum & Mason has a tradition that dates back 3 centuries. The stylish Fifth Floor at Harvey Nichols was once Princess Di's favorite.
- **Go to market** for a full day of fun. Say it's antiques you're after—head to **Portobello Road.** If your taste runs more to funk and new-age knick-knacks, head off early on Saturday to **Camden.** See "Markets," in chapter 7.

DISCOUNT STRATEGIES

For full details of the discount cards below, see "Fifty Money-Saving Tips," in chapter 2.

- **London GoSee card.** Buy this great 3- or 7-day open-sesame, and the more attractions you go to, the more money you'll save. Last year, 17 top museums and galleries took part in the program: Anyone who did them all would have saved over £60. Even if the proposed £1 ($1.60) adult ticket does go ahead from September (see "A Note on Prices," above), GoSee will still be a great deal, especially as it recruits yet more attractions.
- The **London for Less card and guidebook** costs $19.95 and gets you a 20% to 30% discount at many different attractions, including the pricey Madame Tussaud's, and 30% to 50% off organized tours.
- Equally useful, particularly if you're planning day-trips out of London, is the **Great British Heritage Pass.** There are 7- or 15-day, and 1-month options, and you only need to visit around 5 of the 600 historic castles and houses covered to make your money back.

Central London Sights

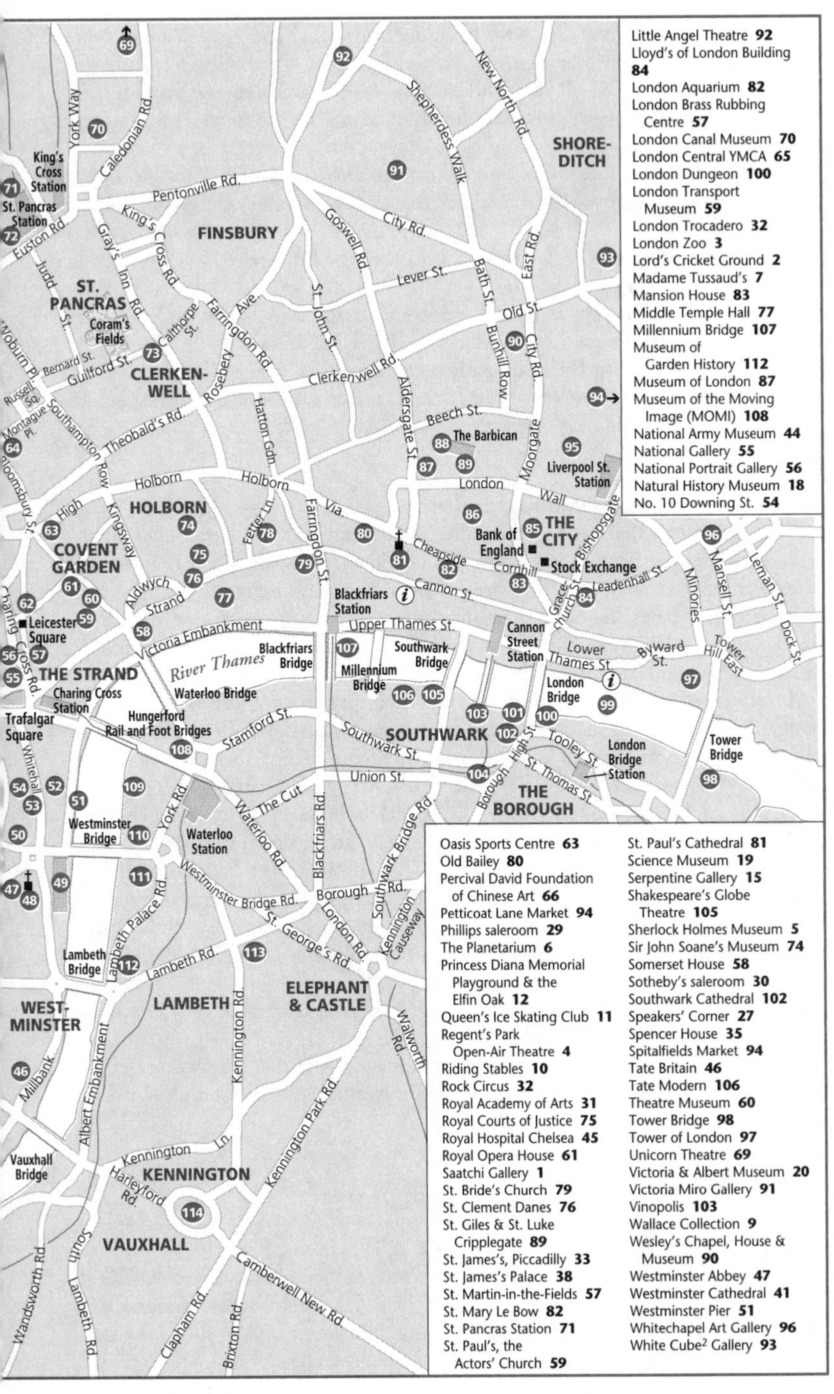

Little Angel Theatre 92
Lloyd's of London Building 84
London Aquarium 82
London Brass Rubbing Centre 57
London Canal Museum 70
London Central YMCA 65
London Dungeon 100
London Transport Museum 59
London Trocadero 32
London Zoo 3
Lord's Cricket Ground 2
Madame Tussaud's 7
Mansion House 83
Middle Temple Hall 77
Millennium Bridge 107
Museum of Garden History 112
Museum of London 87
Museum of the Moving Image (MOMI) 108
National Army Museum 44
National Gallery 55
National Portrait Gallery 56
Natural History Museum 18
No. 10 Downing St. 54
Oasis Sports Centre 63
Old Bailey 80
Percival David Foundation of Chinese Art 66
Petticoat Lane Market 94
Phillips saleroom 29
The Planetarium 6
Princess Diana Memorial Playground & the Elfin Oak 12
Queen's Ice Skating Club 11
Regent's Park Open-Air Theatre 4
Riding Stables 10
Rock Circus 32
Royal Academy of Arts 31
Royal Courts of Justice 75
Royal Hospital Chelsea 45
Royal Opera House 61
Saatchi Gallery 1
St. Bride's Church 79
St. Clement Danes 76
St. Giles & St. Luke Cripplegate 89
St. James's, Piccadilly 33
St. James's Palace 38
St. Martin-in-the-Fields 57
St. Mary Le Bow 82
St. Pancras Station 71
St. Paul's, the Actors' Church 59
St. Paul's Cathedral 81
Science Museum 19
Serpentine Gallery 15
Shakespeare's Globe Theatre 105
Sherlock Holmes Museum 5
Sir John Soane's Museum 74
Somerset House 58
Sotheby's saleroom 30
Southwark Cathedral 102
Speakers' Corner 27
Spencer House 35
Spitalfields Market 94
Tate Britain 46
Tate Modern 106
Theatre Museum 60
Tower Bridge 98
Tower of London 97
Unicorn Theatre 69
Victoria & Albert Museum 20
Victoria Miro Gallery 91
Vinopolis 103
Wallace Collection 9
Wesley's Chapel, House & Museum 90
Westminster Abbey 47
Westminster Cathedral 41
Westminster Pier 51
Whitechapel Art Gallery 96
White Cube² Gallery 93
SHORE-DITCH
FINSBURY
ST. PANCRAS
CLERKEN-WELL
HOLBORN
COVENT GARDEN
THE STRAND
THE CITY
SOUTHWARK
THE BOROUGH
LAMBETH
ELEPHANT & CASTLE
WEST-MINSTER
KENNINGTON
VAUXHALL
River Thames
King's Cross Station
St. Pancras Station
The Barbican
Liverpool St. Station
Bank of England
Stock Exchange
Blackfriars Station
Cannon Street Station
London Bridge Station
Waterloo Station
Charing Cross Station
Trafalgar Square
Leicester Square
Coram's Fields
Blackfriars Bridge
Southwark Bridge
Millennium Bridge
Waterloo Bridge
Hungerford Rail and Foot Bridges
London Bridge
Tower Bridge
Westminster Bridge
Lambeth Bridge
Vauxhall Bridge

- Search the relatively new **www.britainsavings.com**, and download discount coupons for historic buildings, museums and galleries, attractions, bus tours, and river cruises: £1 ($1.60) off admission to an exhibition at the Barbican, for instance. It also lists all those with free admission. The promised dining, accommodation, and shopping discounts were few and far between when I looked.
- Be sure to buy either a **London Transport Travelcard** or a **London Visitor Travelcard,** so that you can catch the bus and Tube as often as you want for one cheap flat fee.
- Join the **Youth Hostel Association,** either the local England & Wales branch, or the international one, and you'll get discounts on lots of London attractions, from the London Aquarium and Madame Tussaud's, to Tower Bridge and St. Paul's Cathedral (see our "Fifty Money-Saving Tips," in chapter 2).
- Check out **The Big Bus Company** (see "Organized Tours," below): It often packages cut-price, fast-entry tickets to hot London attractions, as well as guided walks and river cruises, along with its famous 24-hour tickets.

FESTIVALS

The millennium **String of Pearls Festival** was so successful it may become an annual, or biannual, event—that was still under discussion when we went to press. During the yearlong celebration, more than 50 great London institutions, along the Thames from Greenwich to Kew, let visitors in to see places normally off-limits. The schedule was bursting with parades, concerts, street theater, special performances, fireworks, exhibitions, and special tours. Surf the festival Web site for info (www.stringofpearls.org.uk), or call the **London Tourist Board** (see above).

Museums & Galleries Month (www.24hourmuseum.org.uk) is a certainty, though. From May 1 to June 3, thousands of attractions all over the country put on special exhibitions and events linked to three common guiding themes. On the first night, many stay open until midnight—a great reason to come in May. Unless you'd rather wait for **London Open House** (☎ **09001/600061;** www.londonopenhouse.co.uk), on September 22 to 23, when more than 450 architectural treasures, normally off limits to you and me, open to the public for a whole weekend . . . for free! Tour the governors' and directors' rooms at the **Bank of England** (for its museum, see section 5 later in this chapter); or **Lloyd's of London,** the Lime Street home of the British insurance market, where the traditional ship's bell tolls once for bad news and twice for good behind the ultra-modern facade; or the glorious Gothic giant, **St. Pancras Station** and Sir George Gilbert Scott's pinnacled Midland Grand Hotel (now offices), on Euston Road.

What a dilemma. But don't tie yourself in knots because there's always something going on—anniversaries, historic pageants, festivals, and carnivals. Consult our "London Calendar of Events" in chapter 2.

Suggested Itineraries

Europeans often poke fun at the hectic pace of Americans, Australians, and New Zealanders trying to squeeze in as many of the "hits" as their brief vacations will allow. Pay no attention. Familiarity tends to make the locals blasé towards their national treasures. The itineraries below are designed for long-distance visitors, so skip a few stops if you'd prefer a more leisurely pace. If you're here for 2 days or more, I'd highly recommend joining a walking tour for a very cheap, efficient, and fun way to see the city.

If You Have 1 Day

Take the Tube to Charing Cross or Embankment (there's only 1 block between them) and cross into Trafalgar Square, the most famous square in London and the city's unofficial hub. Here, the commercial West End meets The Mall, the regal avenue that leads to Buckingham Palace, and governmental Whitehall. Nelson's Column is in the middle of the square, with the National Gallery facing it to the north and the church of St. Martin-in-the-Fields, east at about 2 o'clock.

Turn down Whitehall and visit Banqueting House to see the nine magnificent, allegoric ceiling paintings by Rubens. If you're quick, you'll be out again in time to watch the Changing of the Guard across the road at Horse Guards (at 11am Monday to Saturday, 10am on Sunday). Walking on down Whitehall, you'll come to the Cenotaph, the moving memorial to all those who fell in the two world wars. No. 10 Downing Street, usually the Prime Minister's official residence, is right opposite. It was too small for the Blair family, so you'll have to keep your eyes peeled on no. 11 to catch a glimpse of baby Leo. Whitehall ends in Parliament Square, which is flanked by Big Ben, the spectacular Houses of Parliament, and Westminster Abbey.

After a late lunch and a quick breather, walk across Westminster Bridge and take a flight on the British Airways London Eye. The giant 443-foot-high observation wheel on the south bank will give you a 25-mile bird's-eye view of the London landmarks you haven't got time to visit.

If You Have 2 Days

Follow the 1-day itinerary but at a more leisurely pace and in reverse. So start your Whitehall stroll from Parliament Square, cross the beautiful St. James's Park to arrive at Buckingham Palace for the 11am Changing of the Guard. Then pop into the National Gallery in Trafalgar Square. Pop out again and continue north along Charing Cross Road, turn right on Long Acre, and visit Covent Garden. You're spoilt for choice there: shopping, street entertainment, or a visit to the gobsmacking Royal Opera House.

Make your second day the one for hitting some of "London's Top Attractions," below. The British Museum, with its new Great Court, is a must, especially as you can now visit the celebrated British Library Reading Room. At lunchtime, head east to St. Bride's Church, on Fleet Street for the free recital (Tuesday, Wednesday, and Friday at 1:15pm, or Sunday at 11am and 6pm). Then carry on to St. Paul's Cathedral. From there, you won't be able to resist a visit to Tate Modern. Housed in the old power station, it looms across the Thames at the end of the lit-up Millennium Bridge.

If You Have 3 Days

Spend days one and two as described above, but leave out Tate Modern, and make day three a Bankside and South Bank special. You can start at either end of the Millennium Mile riverside walk, but I'd recommend a ride in the British Airways London Eye first, before queues build up. Then stroll along the Thames to the South Bank Centre for a fascinating backstage tour of the Royal National Theater, and a bite to eat during a lunchtime concert at the Royal Festival Hall. Next stop Tate Modern. End the day, if you can, with a show at Shakespeare's Globe Theatre.

If You Have 4 Days or More

With the big stuff done on your first 3 days, use your last one to explore other historic neighborhoods, enjoy more of the city's cultural scene, or shop. For option one,

Sights from Knightsbridge to Earl's Court

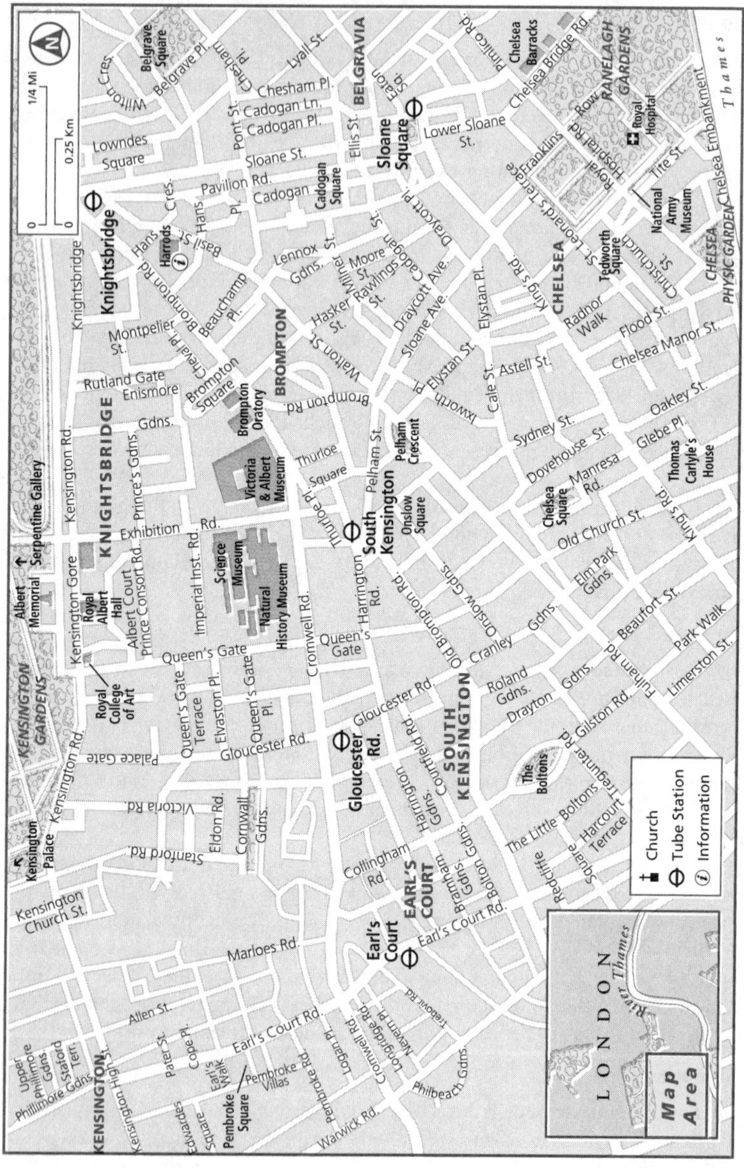

take a boat down river to Greenwich, perhaps, or the other way to Hampton Court. Alternatively, head for South Kensington to see the spectacularly overhauled British Galleries at the V&A and the new Welcome Wing at the Science Museum. Diana fans might want to stop at Kensington Palace, nearby in Kensington Gardens. Turn east, instead, and walk along the edge of the park to Knightsbridge if you yearn for the Harrods experience.

2 London's Top Attractions

British Museum. Great Russell St., WC1. ☎ **020/7323-8000,** or 020/7580-1788 for recorded info. www.thebritishmuseum.ac.uk. Main galleries free; £2 ($3.20) donation requested. Special exhibitions £4.50 ($7.20) adults, £2 ($3.20) students, free seniors and under-16s. Mon–Sat 10am–5pm, Sun noon–6pm. Tube: Russell Sq., Tottenham Court Rd.

The British Museum spent £97 million redeveloping the space left vacant—almost 40% of the Bloomsbury complex—when the British Library decamped to its new home. A comic hiccup briefly threatened to turn the project into an inglorious fiasco: The company reconstructing the south portico used the wrong stone and English Heritage, the funding body, almost made them take it down again. It relented and the Queen cut the ribbon in December. Sir Norman Foster has created a stunning glass-and-steel roof to cover the 2-acre **Great Court** at the center of the museum, previously filled with book stacks. The ethnographic collections are returning bit by bit from the Museum of Mankind to fill several exhibits, including **The Sainsbury African Galleries.** There's also a new education center, restaurants, and coffee shops in this huge public space. After closing time, the Great Court becomes a self-contained cultural center. Call for details of free and almost-free talks, tours, concerts, and children's workshops that run day and night.

The real excitement, though, is that for the first time the public can visit the extraordinarily beautiful copper-domed **British Library Reading Room,** in the middle of the Great Court. Designed by Robert Smirke and completed in 1857, it inspired Thomas Carlyle, Virginia Woolf, Mahatma Gandhi, Lenin, George Bernard Shaw, Karl Marx (who wrote *Das Kapital* here), and a host of other great names. Restored to its original blue, cream, and gold glory, it now houses the museum's books on the upper floors and **The Walter and Leonore Annenberg Center** below. The **Paul Hamlyn Library** is an open-access treasure trove of around 25,000 titles on civilizations and societies. Visitors can go online (as can Internet users) at the multimedia center and tour a super-sophisticated virtual British Museum. That's quite a technological feat.

From a collection purchased from Sir Hans Sloane in 1753, the museum has grown through acquisition and gifts into one of the richest storehouses of antiquities, prints, drawings, manuscripts, and *objets d'art* in the world. Only a small percentage is on display at one time, though the museum is slowly bringing more of its treasures out of mothballs. Its most celebrated possessions include: the **Rosetta Stone,** acquired from Napoléon after his defeat at Alexandria; the much fought-over **Elgin Marbles; George III's library** (almost 13,000 volumes); **James Cook's South Sea Islands collection;** the **Mausoleum of Halicarnassus,** from Constantinople; and the ever-popular **Egyptian mummies.**

Buckingham Palace. The Mall, SW1. ☎ **020/7839-1377,** 020/7799-2331 for recorded info, 020/7321-2233 for credit-card bookings, or 020/7839-1377 for visitors with disabilities to reserve tickets for palace tours. www.royal.gov.uk. Tours of the State Rooms £10.50 ($16.80) adults, £8 ($12.80) seniors, £5 ($8) under-18s, £22.50 ($36) family ticket. 2nd week in Aug to early Oct daily 9:30am–4:15pm. Queen's Gallery closed until 2002. Royal Mews £4.30 ($6.90) adults, £3.30 ($5.30) seniors, £2.10 ($3.40) under-18s, £10.70 ($17.10) family ticket. Oct–July Mon–Thurs noon–4pm; Aug–Sept Mon–Thurs 10:30am–4:30pm; times are very tentative so call ahead. Tube: Victoria, St. James's Park, Green Park.

Buckingham Palace is Her Maj's official London residence, and supposedly the one she likes least of all her homes. You know she's there when the royal standard is flying. The palace has 600 rooms, of which the Queen and the Duke of Edinburgh only occupy a suite of 12. The rest are used by the royal household or for posh functions, banquets, and investitures, like last year's promotion of great screen dames Elizabeth Taylor and Julie Andrews to Dame Commanders of the Order of the British Empire.

King George III and Queen Charlotte bought the house from the Duke of Buckingham in 1762, but it was George IV who converted it into a palace. He commissioned John Nash to add some grandeur, which he did by adding wings at the front and extending those at the back, all for £700,000. Neither George nor his brother William IV actually lived here, and by the time Queen Victoria came to the throne, doors wouldn't close, windows wouldn't open, bells wouldn't ring, and the drains were clogged. Victoria sent Nash packing and Edward Blore completed the repairs. But it quickly became too small for an official residence. So, in 1847, the queen had the East Front built, facing The Mall, and moved Marble Arch from the palace forecourt to the top of Park Lane. Sir Aston Webb designed the existing facade in 1913.

The Queen first opened the 18 **State Rooms,** including the **Throne Room,** in 1993 to help raise money to repair Windsor Castle after the fire. Overlooking the 45-acre gardens, where the Queen gives her famous summer parties, the State Rooms contain pictures, tapestries, and furniture from the superb royal collections. Queen Victoria's vast ballroom—the ceilings are 45 feet high and there's room to park 35 double-decker buses—was added to the tour for the first time last year. You can only visit during August and September when the royal family is on holiday. Tickets can be purchased in person, from 9am on the day you want to take the palace tour: Eager tourists start queuing at sunrise, and an hour-long wait is the rule. Booking a fixed-time ticket by phone, or asking the Visitor Office for an application form, is less hassle, but only the £10.50 ($16.80) rate is available in advance.

Much better value is the **Royal Mews** (entrance in Buckingham Palace Road). These superb working stables house the royal carriages, including the gold state coach used at every coronation since 1831, and the horses that draw them. The **Queen's Gallery** is closed for refurbishment until 2002.

✪ **Hampton Court Palace.** East Molesey, Surrey. ☎ **020/8781-9500** for recorded info, or 020/8781-9666. www.hrp.org.uk. Admission £10.50 ($16.80) adults, £8 ($12.80) students and seniors, £7 ($11.20) under-16s, £31.40 ($50.25) family ticket. Mid-Mar to mid-Oct Mon 10:15am–6pm, Tues–Sun 9:30am–6pm; mid-Oct to mid-Mar Mon 10:15am–4:30pm, Tues–Sun 9:30am–4:30pm. Park dawn–dusk. Closed Dec 24–26. Train: Waterloo to Hampton Court. 30-min. journey time. Travel after 9:30am on cheap day-return ticket, £4.70 ($7.50) adults, £2.35 ($3.75) children. River launch: From Westminster pier, calling at Richmond and Kew (☎ **020/7930-2062**). 3–4-hr. journey time. Leaving Westminster 10:30, 11:15am, and noon (add 1hr. for Richmond departures, 1½hr. for Kew); returning from Hampton Court at 3, 4, and 5pm; all dependent on the tide. Tickets cost £10 ($16) one-way or £14 ($22.40) return from Westminster, £5 or £8 ($8 or $12.80) from Richmond, £7 or £11 ($11.20 or $17.60) from Kew; under-16s half-price.

This magnificent palace sits on the banks of the Thames, about 15 miles southwest of London. Henry VIII's pleasure-loving lord chancellor, Cardinal Wolsey, took the then-country house in 1515 as a retreat from the city's poisonous air and water. His grandiose remodeling plan called for 280 rooms, new courtyards and gardens, and a staff of 500. When the cardinal fell into disfavor in 1528, the ever-grasping king confiscated his property. Henry spent a whopping £18 million in today's money and turned Hampton Court into a very sophisticated palace—with bowling alleys, "real tennis" courts, a chapel, pleasure gardens and a hunting park, **The Great Hall** for dining, and a 36,000 square-foot kitchen.

Queen Elizabeth I came to live at Hampton Court in 1559. She planted the gardens with new discoveries, such as tobacco and potatoes, brought back by Sir Francis Drake and Sir Walter Raleigh from South America. Under the Stuarts, the palace

Changing of the Guard

Looking more like toy soldiers than honed fighting machines, these poor men somehow do their duty, apparently oblivious to kids pulling silly faces and the clicking of holiday snaps. **Changing of the Guard** takes place at **Buckingham Palace** daily from April through July at 11:30am, and on alternate days August through March; at **St. James's Palace,** St. James's St., W1 (Tube: Green Park) at 11:15pm, same dates; and at **Horse Guards** (Tube: Charing Cross) Monday through Saturday at 11am, and 10am on Sunday. Bad weather and state events disrupt the ceremony, so call ahead to check (☎ **0839/123411**).

collections grew and grew with hundreds of new paintings and other lavish objets d'art. Charles II banished the gloom of Cromwell's brief stay here, with his very lively court and many mistresses.

William and Mary found the palace apartments old-fashioned and uncomfortable, so they commissioned Sir Christopher Wren to make improvements and asked such artists as Grinling Gibbons, Jean Tijou, and Antonio Verrio to decorate the rooms. Later, Anne redid the chapel, and Verrio and Thornhill painted murals in her drawing rooms. George III ended royal occupation—his grandfather used to box his ears in the State Apartments, so he hated the place.

The highlights for visitors to Hampton Court are the **Tudor Kitchens** and the **King's Apartments,** as well as the **Wolsey Rooms** and **Renaissance Picture Gallery.** One of Henry VIII's wives, the headless Catherine Howard, has been sighted several times in the **Haunted Gallery.** The grounds are splendid, especially the famous **maze** and the **Privy Garden.** Capability Brown, who designed the gardens, planted the Great Vine in 1769, and it still bears fruit—come during the late-August harvest and you can sample them.

Hampton Court is a fantastic day out. There are restaurants, cafes, and shops, too, but I recommend taking a picnic. There are special events and festivals throughout the year, all designed, like the costumed guides, to bring centuries of history to life.

✪ **Houses of Parliament.** Bridge St. and Parliament Sq., SW1. ☎ **020/7219-4272** House of Commons or ☎ **020/7219-3107** House of Lords. www.parliament.uk. Free admission, subject to recess and sitting times. Guided tours available during 6-wk. summer recess. House of Commons: Wed 9:30am–1:30pm, Mon–Wed 2:30–10:30pm; Thurs 11:30am–7:30pm; and Fri 9:30am–3pm. House of Lords: Mon–Thurs 9:30am–1pm (last entry noon); occasionally Fri. Queue at St. Stephen's entrance, near the statue of Oliver Cromwell. Debates usually run until 10pm and often into the night; lines shrink after 6pm. For tickets to Prime Minister's Question Time, Wed 3–3:30pm, write to your MP (overseas residents, to your embassy). Tube: Westminster.

The Houses of Parliament, with their trademark clock tower, are the ultimate symbol of London. Edward the Confessor built the first palace here, and the site was home to the monarchy and court until Henry VIII's time. But, in 1834, a fire lit to burn the Exchequor's tally sticks got out of control, sparing only Westminster Hall (1097), which is not open to the public, and the Jewel Tower (see section 6 later in this chapter). Charles Barry designed the neo-Gothic extravaganza (1840) you see today. Augustus Welby Pugin created the paneled ceilings, tiled floors, stained glass, clocks, fireplaces, umbrella stands, and even inkwells. There are more than 1,000 rooms, 100 staircases, and 2 miles of corridors. **Big Ben** is not the clock tower, as people think, but the largest bell in the chime. It weighs close to 14 tons and was named after the first commissioner of works.

The parliamentary session runs from mid-October to the end of July, with breaks at Christmas and Easter. Visitors can watch debates from the Strangers' Galleries in both houses. Many MPs have called for sittings to begin in the morning, and for an end to the ridiculously late nights. The Commons Modernization Committee was due to report on this and other issues last summer. So call to check, as the hours may have changed. Last year, MPs also finally agreed to allow **guided tours** during the summer recess: For info, call ☎ **020/7945-5504** (www.tourguides.co.uk).

Most visitors are struck by how small the **Commons chamber** is. It was rebuilt in precise detail in 1950 after being destroyed during the Blitz of 1941. Only 437 of the 651 MPs can sit at any one time; on the rare occasions when most of them turn up, the rest crowd noisily around the door and the **Speaker's chair.** The ruling party and opposition sit facing one another, two sword lengths apart, though from the volume of the argy-bargy you'd think it was more like 2 miles. The **Mace,** on the table in the middle, is the symbol of Parliament's authority. The queue for the **House of Lords** is usually shorter, as debates here are less crucial and a lot more polite. The chamber is fantastically opulent, decorated with mosaics and frescoes. The Lord Chancellor presides over proceedings from his seat on the **Woolsack,** a reminder of the days when wool was the source of Britain's wealth. You'd think such tradition made the place sacrosanct. Yet, last year, New Labour made all the hereditary peers pitch to keep their privileges and ousted 600 of them.

Kensington Palace State Apartments and Royal Ceremonial Dress Collection. Kensington Gardens. ☎ **020/7937-9561.** www.hrp.org.uk. Admission £10 ($16) adults, £8 ($12.80) seniors and students, £7 ($11.20) under-16s, £29.10 ($46.55) family ticket. Additional charge for temporary exhibitions. Mar–Oct daily 10am–5pm; Oct–Mar daily 10am–4pm. Tube: Queensway, High St. Kensington.

Kensington Palace has been a pilgrimage site ever since Princess Diana's death in August 1997. People flocked to the gates after the news was announced and carpeted the ground with hundreds of flower tributes. Plans for a Diana memorial garden roused such vehement local opposition, because of fears it would draw unmanageable crowds, that the money has instead gone into a Peter Pan children's playground with a huge pirate galleon, nearby in the park.

The asthmatic William and his wife Mary bought this house, owned by the Earl of Nottingham, in 1689 to escape from the putrid air enveloping Whitehall. The royal couple then commissioned Sir Christopher Wren to remodel the modest Jacobean mansion. Queen Anne, who came to the throne in 1702, laid out the gardens in English style, had the Orangery built after designs by Nicholas Hawksmoor, and died here in 1714 from apoplexy brought on by overeating. The first two Georges lived at Kensington Palace. George III abandoned it in favor of Buckingham House (now Palace, too). But his fourth son, Edward Duke of Kent, did have apartments here, and his daughter, the future Queen Victoria, was born and baptized at Kensington Palace. The Archbishop of Canterbury and the Lord Chamberlain roused her from sleep here on June 27, 1837, with news of the death of her uncle, William IV and her succession to the throne. That night was the first she had ever slept outside her mother's room. Three weeks later, she moved into Buckingham Palace.

Today, Princess Margaret, the Duke and Duchess of Gloucester, and Princess Michael of Kent all have apartments here. Only the **State Apartments,** filled with art treasures from the Royal Collection, and **Royal Ceremonial Dress Collection** are open to the public. See the **Cupola Room,** where Queen Victoria was baptized, and marvel at William Kent's magnificent trompe l'oeils and paintings in the **King's Drawing Room, Presence Chamber,** and on the **King's Staircase.** The dress collection displays court fashions and uniforms from 1760, including dresses worn by the

Queen. This year is the centenary of Victoria's death, so look out for commemorative events. And you can have lunch or tea in the Orangery.

Madame Tussaud's & the Planetarium. Marylebone Rd., NW1. ☎ **020/7935-6861.** www.madame-tussauds.com. Madame Tussaud's £11 ($17.60) adults, £8.50 ($13.60) seniors, £7.50 ($12) under-16s. Planetarium £6.30 ($10.10) adults, £4.85 ($7.75) seniors, £4.20 ($6.70) under-16s. Combined ticket £13.45 ($21.50) adults, £10.30 ($16.50) seniors, £8 ($14.40) under-16s. Madame Tussaud's: opening time varies by season (9, 9:30, and 10am), closing at 5:30pm. Planetarium daily 10am–5:30pm. Shows run every 40min., 12:20–5pm, weekends/holidays from 10:20am. Closed Dec 25. Tube: Baker St.

Madame Tussaud had an extraordinary life. Born Marie Grosholtz, she learnt the craft from her mother's doctor employer, who had a talent for wax modeling. Such was her renown that Louis XIV and Marie Antoinette appointed her as their children's art tutor. Gruesomely, Marie later had to make death masks of the king and queen, after their execution in 1793, to prove her loyalty to the revolution and get out of Laforce Prison. You can see several casts from her original molds—a spooky 3-D Voltaire, for instance—at this "museum." But most of its space is devoted to modern superstars, from Sadam Hussein to Mel Gibson, in whose pockets staff once found a pair of ladies knickers. Craftsmen take more than 200 measurements from each star sitter. And stars know they're on the wane when Tussaud's boils their figure down and uses the wax to make someone else—there's enough in the 400 figures for 16,000 candles. Actor Robert Carlyle has just joined the **Garden Party,** wearing rather more clothes than he did in either *The Full Monty* or *The Beach*—he donated a pair of Levi's, a denim jacket, and trainers to dress his model. The dungeon-level **Chamber of Horrors** is the stuff tourist traps are made of. It "honors" Charles Manson, Jack the Ripper, and Dracula, as well as burning Joan of Arc at the stake and doing grisly unmentionables to Gunpowder Plotter Guy Fawkes. Madame Tussaud's is expensive and rather overrated, but it attracts more than 2.5 million visitors a year. So get there early to get a jump on the crowds.

Next door, the **London Planetarium** is a much more specialist attraction, and not my cup of tea, as it happens. But if you're going to Madame Tussaud's anyway, it's worth spending the extra couple of pounds for a combined ticket. This copper-domed London landmark is not only the largest planetarium in Europe, it was the first (1995) to install the state-of-the-art Digistar II projection system. As well as re-creating an earth-based view of 9,000 stars and planets scattered across the night sky, computer graphics take you on a *Starship Enterprise* journey past exploding nebulae right to the edge of the universe. There are also interactive exhibits to play on before the show.

National Gallery. Trafalgar Square, WC2. ☎ **020/7747-2885.** www.nationalgallery.org.uk. Main galleries free; Sainsbury wing, £3–£7 ($4.80–$11.20) during some special exhibitions. Wed 10am–9pm, Thurs–Tues 10am–6pm. Closed Jan 1, Good Friday, and Dec 24–26. Tube: Charing Cross, Leicester Sq.

This gallery houses Britain's collection of more than 2,300 paintings dating from 1260 to 1900, as well as masterpieces on loan from private collectors. It's arranged in four time bands. The **Sainsbury Wing** shows work from 1260 to 1510 by such artists as Giotto, Botticelli, Leonardo da Vinci, Piero della Francesca, and Raphael. The **West Wing** takes on the next 90 years, and El Greco, Holbein, Bruegel, Michelangelo, Titian, and Veronese. The **North Wing** holds the 17th-century masters, Rubens, Poussin, Velázquez, Rembrandt, and Vermeer. Van Dyck's *The Abbé Scaglia* entered the collection in 1999, given by a private owner in lieu of inheritance tax. Works by Stubbs, Gainsborough, Constable, Turner, Canaletto, van Gogh, Corot, Monet, Manet, Renoir, and Cézanne are all in the **East Wing.** For the past two summers, from May to September, the National Gallery has let natural daylight illuminate many of the paintings, particularly in the Sainsbury Wing, to magical effect—the colors are truer, and it cuts down on flare and shadow from the frames. You'll need to choose a sunny day for your visit, though, because artificial help steps in if it gets too gloomy.

There's a free (donation invited) audio guide to every painting on the main floor, and free guided tours start at 11:30am and 2:30pm every day, plus at 6:30pm on Wednesday evenings. In the Sainsbury Wing, stop in the Micro Gallery and use one of the 12 workstations to view the visual encyclopedia on every painting in the collection. If paintings are your passion, then check out the talks at the gallery—most are free. There are also two excellent eateries: the **Crivelli's Garden** restaurant (☎ **020/7747-2869;** see chapter 5) in the Sainsbury Wing and the **Pret à Manger** sandwich cafe in the basement of the Main Building. (To gallery-hop at no charge, see "Hot Tip: Traveling Inter-Tate for Free," later in this chapter.)

Natural History Museum. Cromwell Rd., SW7. ☎ **020/7942-5000** or 020/7942-5011. www.nhm.ac.uk. Admission £7 ($11.20) adults; £4.50 ($7.20) concessions; free seniors and under-17s; free Mon–Fri after 4:30pm, Sat–Sun after 5pm. Mon–Sat 10am–5:50pm, Sun 11am–5:50pm. Clore Education Centre Tues–Fri 2:30–5pm (term-time); Mon–Fri 10:30am–5pm, Sat 10:30am–5pm, Sun 11:30am–5pm. Closed Dec 23–26. Tube: South Kensington.

Sir Hans Sloane was such a prolific collector that his treasures overflowed the British Museum. Hence the decision to build this vast terra-cotta building (1881), with its towers, spires, and nave-like hall, fit "for housing the works of the Creator." The huge **dinosaur** skeletons are awe-inspiring, and the earthquake and volcano simulations in the **Earth Galleries** hint at the terror of the real thing. However, this museum, too, can display only a fraction of its treasures—animal, vegetable, and mineral. An exciting project is set to revolutionize all that, opening not only the collection stores, but also the science labs, to public view. Phase I of the Darwin Centre will be ready in 2002. The museum already has the new Clore Education Centre, where kids can look at real specimens with video microscopes and bug-hunting magnifying glasses, build their own Web site, and take part in regular events.

✪ **Royal Botanic Gardens Kew.** Richmond, Surrey. ☎ **020/8332-5622,** 020/8332-5655 for events, or 020/8332-5633 for tours. www.kew.org. Admission £5 ($8) adults, £3.50 ($5.60) late entry 45 min. before buildings (glasshouses/galleries) close, £3.50 ($5.60) concessions, £2.50 ($4) under-17s, £13 ($20.80) family ticket. Feb–Mar daily 9:30am–5:30pm, buildings close 5pm; Apr–Sept Mon–Fri 9:30am–6:30pm, Sat–Sun 9:30am–7:30pm, buildings close 5:30pm; Sept–Oct daily 9:30am–6pm, buildings close 5:30pm; Nov–Feb daily 9:30–4:15pm, buildings close 3:45pm; last admissions ½ hr. before closing. Queen Charlotte's Cottage open bank holidays only. Kew Palace is closed for renovations until 2002. Tube: Kew Gardens. Train: From Waterloo to Kew Gardens or Kew Bridge; cheap day-return after 9:30am £3.10 ($4.95) adults, £1.55 ($2.50) concessions and children. River Launch: from Westminster Pier (☎ **020/7930-2062**) to Kew Pier (☎ **020/8940-3891**); £11 ($17.60) return adults, £5 ($8) children. Leaving Westminster 10:30, 11:15am, and noon; returning from Kew every hr. 3:30–6:30pm.

More than 240 years of plant collecting, cultivation, and scientific research have won Kew such international renown that it ranks alongside the Taj Mahal and the Grand Canyon as a UNESCO World Heritage Site. Augusta, widow of Frederick Prince of Wales, started the first small botanical garden here in 1759. But it was Sir Joseph Banks, made director by George III in 1772, who laid the foundations of its fame. He had voyaged to Australia with Captain Cook on HMS *Endeavour* and urged other collectors to scour the world for specimens. Today, there are more than 35,000 different plants in this magnificent park, which covers 300 acres amassed from the royal Kew and Richmond estates. Its borders, arboretum, lakes, glasshouses, follies, museums, galleries, and working buildings are a lasting testament to countless famous names from Capability Brown to architects John Nash, Sir William Chambers, and Decimus Burton.

The glasshouses are huge, from the 4-acre Victorian **Palm House** (1844–48), to the 1987 addition, the **Princess of Wales Conservatory.** This exuberant Eden is split into 10 climactic zones growing sci-fi cacti, spooky orchids, mangrove swamps, and more. The **Evolution House** is a wild walk through 3.5 billion years of plant development, past a fuming volcano and a set of dinosaur footprints. The **Marianne North Gallery** houses more than 800 paintings by this botanical artist and intrepid 19th-century traveler. The **Museum,** across the lake from the Palm House, is well worth a visit for its wonderful oddities: a Pacific Islands newspaper printed on beaten bark, rubber dentures, and a shirt made from pineapple fiber. The working buildings are not open to the public, but you can watch researchers in the **Jodrell Laboratory** from the colonnade. As for the garden, its wonders are to numerous to list, but spring is magical, as a million and a half crocuses bloom into a sea of color.

Kew has four entrances: nearest to Kew Gardens tube station is Victoria Gate, with its **visitor center** and shop; Main Gate is closest to Kew Pier and Kew Bridge station, and the **Orangery café-shop;** a mile from there and nearest to the **Pagoda** folly and the **Pavilion Restaurant,** is Lion Gate; Brentford Gate is next to the car park.

Sadly, **Kew Palace** is closed for restoration at least until 2002. The enchanting **Queen Charlotte's Cottage** is only open on bank holiday weekends. For information on both, call ☎ **020/8940-3321** (www.hrp.org.uk).

✪ **St. Paul's Cathedral.** St. Paul's Churchyard, EC4. ☎ **020/7246-8348** or 020/7246-8319. stpauls.co.uk. Admission £5 ($8) adults, £4 ($6.40) students and seniors, £2.50 ($4) under-17s. Mon–Sat 8:30am–4pm; Sun for worship only. Tube: St. Paul's, Mansion House.

No one who saw the wedding of Prince Charles and Lady Diana in 1981 will ever forget the image of the royal carriages approaching St. Paul's. This magnificent cathedral is 515 feet long and 36 feet high to the cross on the dome, which dominated the contemporary skyline. Christopher Wren laid out the whole base first to thwart interference from his paymasters, who harassed him constantly over the 35 years it took to complete the building (1675–1710). Buried in **the crypt,** Wren's epitaph says it all: *"Lector, si monumentum requiris, circumspice"* ("Reader, if you seek his monument, look around you"). The **outer dome** was so huge and heavy he had to put a smaller one inside it, with a brick cone sandwiched in between, to support it. Frescoes depicting the life of St. Paul line the **inner dome.** You can see them best from the **Whispering Gallery,** famous for its amazing acoustics, which can project a murmur to the other side of the dome. A second steep climb leads to the **Stone Gallery,** and a third to the highest **Inner Golden Gallery,** with the views ever more awe-inspiring.

Many artists worked on the decoration. Grinling Gibbons carved the choir screens and stalls, and the organ case. Francis Bird sculpted the statues on the west front. Tijou was responsible for the chancel gates. Caius Gabriel Cibber carved the phoenix above the motto "Resurgam" on the south pediment. And master mason William Kempster designed the geometric staircase in the southwest tower. This tower holds **Great Tom,** the bell rung when a member of the royal family, the Bishop of London, the Dean of St. Paul's, or the lord mayor dies. In the ambulatory, the **American Memorial Chapel** pays tribute to soldiers killed in World War II.

Guided tours of the cathedral and crypt take place at 11, 11:30am, 1:30, and 2pm, and cost £3.50 ($5.60) for adults, £3 ($4.80) concessions, £1 ($1.60) children, plus admission. **Audio guides** are available in five languages until 3pm: £3 ($4.80) for adults, £2.50 ($4) for children, £7 ($11.20) for a family, plus admission. **Triforium** tours take in the library, geometric staircase, the West End gallery, and Trophy Room where Wren's Great Model is on display. Tickets are £10 ($16), including admission. Call Monday to Friday, 9am to 4pm, to book. Also check the cathedral diary for

St. Paul's Cathedral

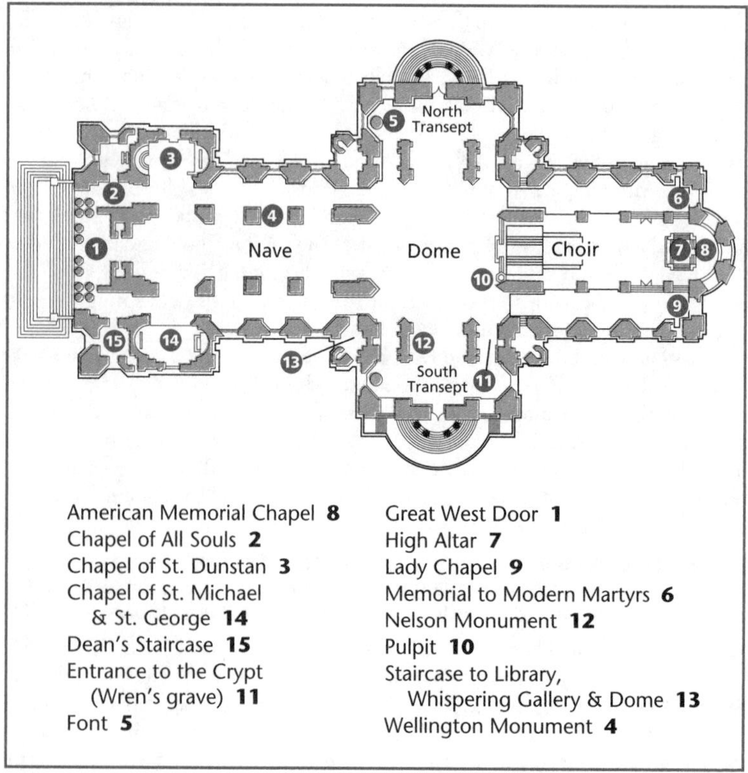

frequent closures, special services, free (and cheap) talks, and concerts. There are often organ recitals at 5pm on Sunday, at no charge. Fuel up at the Crypt Café first.

✪ **Science Museum.** Exhibition Rd., SW7. ☎ **020/7942-4000** or 020/7942-4455. www.sciencemuseum.org.uk. Admission £6.95 ($11.10) adults, £3.50 ($5.60) students, free seniors and under-17s; free after 4:30pm. Daily 10am–6pm. Closed Dec 24–26. Tube: South Kensington.

The massive £45 million **Wellcome Wing** opened last June and has revolutionized the museum. The striking cantilevered building houses six new exhibitions presenting the latest developments in science, medicine, and technology. The blue glass of the West Wall and blue interior lighting magnify the funky sci-fi feel. Find out what the kids might look like in 30 years using spacey IT in the ***Who am I?*** gallery, which explores the biomedical sciences and the human identity. For a more intimate portrait, check out the gory digital cross-sections in ***The Visible Human Project. Antennae*** is a rolling display of the latest scientific breakthroughs. This is fantasyland for gadget geeks and kids, who'll love the mad interactivity. Art installations by Marc Quinn, Yinka Shonibare, Darrell Viner, and other big names on the ultra-modern scene, should pacify science-hating culture buffs. And there's a 450-seat IMAX cinema on the first floor.

Another huge new gallery, **Making the Modern World,** links the Wellcome Wing to the old museum. Using some of the most iconic treasures of the permanent collection—Apollo 10, Stephenson's Rocket, and the fleece from famous Scottish clone, Dolly the Sheep—it charts 250 years of technological advances and their effects on our culture.

The new galleries are stunning, but don't let them dazzle you into forgetting the rest of this marvelous museum. It is home to many pioneering machines: Arkwright's spinning machine, for instance, and the Vickers "Vimy" aircraft, which made the first Atlantic crossing in 1919. The basement is dedicated to children, with water, construction, sound and light shows, and games for 3 to 6 year olds in the **garden,** and the **Launch Pad** for 7 to 15 year olds. Of course, the Wellcome Wing is even more ambitious: its first-floor **Pattern Pod** aims to convert kids to science from the age of 3 months.

✪ **Somerset House, the Courtauld Gallery, and Gilbert Collection.** Somerset House, Strand, WC2. ☎ **020/7845-4600** Somerset House, 020/7848-2526 the Courtauld, or 020/7420-9400 Gilbert Collection. www.somerset-house.org.uk. Courtyard, river terrace, Seamen's Waiting Hall free. Joint admission to Courtauld Gallery and Gilbert Collection £7 ($11.20) adults, £5 ($8) seniors, free under-18s. Courtyard 7:30am–9pm (7pm in winter). Galleries and exhibitions Mon–Sat 10am–6pm, Sun noon–6pm. Closed Jan 1, Dec 24–26. Tube: Temple, Covent Garden, Charing Cross.

The Queen Mother once remarked what a pity it was that the courtyard at Somerset House was being used as a workers' car park. It was just the spur needed by the long-running campaign to open up the 1,000-room civil service palace, designed in 1776 by Sir William Chambers, to the public. The government moved the Inland Revenue and the Lord Chancellor's Department elsewhere. The Heritage Lottery Fund coughed up millions to restore the buildings, the courtyard with its new fountain, and the stunning river terrace, where there's now a summer cafe, cheaper than the new restaurant indoors. And last May, the QM duly returned to open the "new" people's playground. It's a cross between Covent Garden Piazza and the Barbican or South Bank Centre—high culture and "street" entertainment. There will be open-air performances, tours, talks, and workshops. It costs nothing to visit the courtyard and river terrace, which link the Strand to the Embankment, or **The Seamen's Waiting Hall,** where naval officers waited to collect their commissions. The restoration is proceeding in phases, as will the opening of parts of the buildings. Last Autumn, the State Hermitage Museum in St. Petersburg was due to unveil an offshoot here. **The Hermitage Rooms** will display pieces from the Russian Imperial collections. Very, very exciting, so call for details.

In Somerset House since 1989, the **Courtauld Gallery** (www.courtauld.ac.uk) is now expanding into the tarted-up South Building. The gallery's chief benefactor, textile mogul Samuel Courtauld, collected impressionist and post-impressionist paintings, which are still its real strength—Manet's *Bar at the Folies Bergères;* Monet's *Banks of the Seine at Argenteuil; Lady with Parasol* by Degas; *La Loge* by Renoir; Van Gogh's *Self-Portrait with Bandaged Ear;* and several Cézannes, including *The Card Players.* But you'll find work by most great names (lots of Rubens), right up to modern greats Ben Nicholson, Graham Sutherland, and Larry Rivers.

The **Gilbert Collection** (www.gilbert-collection.org.uk) is also in the South Building, plus two new galleries in the vaults beneath the river terrace, originally stables and workshops, then a store for birth and death certificates. The glittering gold, silver, and mosaics were valued at £75 million when Arthur Gilbert donated the collection to the nation in 1996. Visitors can drool over 800 pieces, amassed by Gilbert and his late wife, Rosalinde, starting in the 1960s when British museums had trouble raising money to stop the export of national treasures—there are objects here from Princess Diana's old home, Althorp.

✪ **Tate Britain.** Millbank, SW1. ☎ **020/7887-8000.** www.tate.org.uk. Free admission to permanent collection; temporary exhibits £6–£7.50 ($9.60–$12) adults, £4–£5 ($6.40–$8) concessions, £16–£18 ($25.60–$28.80) family ticket. Daily 10am–5:50pm. Closed Dec 24–26. Tube: Pimlico. Central London Fast Ferry: Millbank Pier.

The new Tate Modern at Bankside may have been making all the noise, but the shifting around of collections has also seen a huge overhaul at the original gallery, founded in 1897 and endowed by sugar magnate Sir Henry Tate. The exciting Centenary Development reaches fruition this year. It boosts exhibition space by 34% with a suite of airy new galleries on the lower floor of the northwest wing, refurbished ones above, and stripped-bare space at the heart of the building. That's the new home for **Art Now,** with its strong focus on new media and experimental work by foreign artists living in London and Brits based here and abroad. All in all, artists are going to muck in much more at the gallery, curating shows or exhibiting their work within the collection. Having handed International Modernism over to Bankside, Tate Britain can now concentrate on British work dating back to 1500. It has ditched the chronological displays and gone, like the new gallery, for a thematic approach: **Private and Public** includes portraits and scenes of daily life; **Artists and Models** explores nudes and self-portraiture; **Literature and Fantasy** is for visionary artists such as Blake and Spencer; and **Home and Abroad** looks at the landscape artist at home and abroad. Juxtaposing very different kinds of work isn't always successful, but the vibrancy of the place can't help but give you a rush. And with more space and less artistic ground to cover, you won't have to stalk your favorite painting for months, waiting for its brief foray out of storage. Also, really important people, like Gainsborough, Constable, Hogarth, and Hockney, get a room to themselves, which should pacify the traditionalists.

Like all Britain's major arts institutions, open access is the mantra. The imposing wrought-iron gates have gone. The surrounding gardens have been transformed. And the guided tours, gallery talks (Monday to Friday 11:30am, 2:30, and 3:30pm, and Sunday 3pm), auditorium lectures, and films, are mostly free—as it is to use the Art Trolley, designed to entertain kids aged 3 to 11, and available Sunday 2 to 5pm in term-time, all week during the holidays. Tate Britain also has shops, a good cafe and espresso bar, and a restaurant. At the latter, a three-course lunch is available at the not-very-accessible price of £18.50 ($29.60)—check out Tate Modern, instead.

✪ **Tate Modern.** Bankside, SE1. ☎ **020/7887-8000,** or 020/7887-8888 for events. www.tate.org.uk. Free admission to permanent collection; temporary exhibitions £8.50 ($13.60). Sun–Thurs 10am–6pm, Fri–Sat 10am–10pm, galleries open at 10:15am. Closed Dec 24–26. Tube: Mansion House and St. Paul's (cross over Millennium Bridge), Southwark. Central London Fast Ferry: Bankside Pier.

The BBC nearly didn't televise any of the Queen Mother's 100th birthday celebrations, yet it eagerly devoted much of its main news programs to the party launching Tate Modern. The media attention was phenomenal. Then, so is this gallery—the first new standalone space on this scale for hundreds of years. Swiss architects Herzog and de Meuron have transformed the defunct Bankside Power Station, designed by Sir Giles Gilbert Scott (of red telephone box fame), into a cathedral of modern art. Except for a 2-story glass addition on the roof that beams light down inside, the vast bunker-like facade looks pretty much as it ever did, right down to the London grime. Then you enter the building, down a ramp into the old turbine hall. Left empty, its huge

Hot Tip: Traveling Inter-Tate for Free

As one of the whizz-bang deals supporting the launch of Tate Modern, a ½-hourly **Art Bus** shuttled between it and Tate Britain, via the National Gallery, with those nice folks at www.msdwcard.co.uk paying the fare. The service may run again this year (mid-May to September), if a fat corporate sponsor coughs up the necessary funding. So ask at the galleries if you can still travel around for free.

dimensions (500 feet long by 100 feet high) make you feel like Gulliver in *Brobdingnag.* Stainless steel lifts and escalators carry visitors up to three floors of ultra-plain white galleries. The display space is so big that 60% of the collection will be on view—almost as much as used to be in storage. The work is arranged into four themes: **Landscape/Matter/Environment, Still Life/Object/Real Life, History/Memory/Society,** and **Nude/Action/Body.** In some rooms, paintings are next to sculptures next to installations. Others are devoted to a single artist—like the marvelous Joseph Beuys sculptures. The first big temporary exhibition, **Century City: Art and Culture in the Twentieth-Century Metropolis,** takes place February through April. This looks at nine cities, across the world, that at some time reached a definable creative flashpoint—Paris in the 1910s, for example, or New York in the 1970s.

There's no such thing as a flash visit to Tate Modern. Set aside half a day if you can. Free guided tours start at 10:30, 11:30am, 2:30, and 3:30pm every day. There's also a busy talks program (free or £7 to £10/$11.20 to $16), family fun, and a workshop project for budding creatives aged 15 to 23 years old (Raw Canvas). But if you only do one thing at Tate Modern, make that a visit to the Café on Level 7 (☎ **020/7401-5020;** see chapter 5): inside the glass roof, it has spectacular views across the Thames and the Millennium Bridge to St. Paul's Cathedral. It is also open on Friday and Saturday for dinner until 11pm. Mobbed from the moment it opened, the Café had quickly had to stop taking bookings.

Tower Bridge Experience. SE1. ☎ **020/7378-1928** or 020/7403-3761. www.towerbridge.org.uk. Admission £6.25 ($10) adults, £4.25 ($6.80) seniors and children. Apr–Oct daily 10am–6:30pm; Nov–Mar daily 9:30am–6pm. Last entry is 1¼ hr. before closing. Closed Jan 17, Dec 25–26. Tube: Tower Hill, London Bridge.

Here's a London landmark you must not miss—possibly the most celebrated and photographed bridge in the world, and a reminder never to underestimate the English in a business deal. A certain American tried to buy it, but asked for London Bridge by mistake, as he discovered when he unpacked his enormous parcel to find nary a tower in sight. Despite its Gothic appearance, Tower Bridge dates from 1894, and the twin towers are made of steel clad in stone. Inside them, interactive exhibits trace the history and construction of the bridge, whose architect Horace Jones died before it was completed. In the south tower, you can see the old (pre-1976) hydraulics used to raise and lower the bridge—not that big a thrill unless you're an engineer. It uses electrical power now, and about five ships a day pass through in the summer months. Even if you don't catch one in the act, the views from the pedestrian walkways are glorious, to St. Paul's, the Tower, and the distant Houses of Parliament. Opening times change daily and are only announced 1 day in advance, so call to check.

Tower of London. EC3. ☎ **020/7709-0765.** www.hrp.org.uk. Admission £11 ($17.60) adults, £8.30 ($13.30) students and seniors, £7.30 ($11.70) under-16s, £33 ($52.80) family ticket. Mar–Oct Mon–Sat 9am–5pm, Sun 10am–5pm; Nov–Feb Tues–Sat 9am–4pm, Sun–Mon 10am–4pm. Last tickets sold 1hr. before closing. Last entry to buildings 30min. before closing. Closed Jan 1, Dec 24–26. Tube: Tower Hill. Docklands Light Railway: Tower Gateway. Central London Fast Ferry: Tower Pier.

The Tower of London is the most perfectly preserved medieval fortress in Britain. Over the centuries, it has served as a palace and royal refuge in times of trouble, a prison, a military base, and supplies depot; home to the Royal Mint and the Royal Observatory; and finally a national monument. It has only twice come into practical use since the late 19th century: in World War I, 11 spies were held and executed here; then, in World War II, Rudolph Hess was a prisoner here for 4 days, and another spy got his just desserts.

The Ceremony of the Keys

Every night for 700 years, the guards have secured the Tower of London defenses with the **Ceremony of the Keys.** The chief yeoman warder marches out across the causeway at 10 o'clock precisely to lock the entrance gate, then returns with the guard to do the same at the Byward Tower. As the pair approaches the Bloody Tower, the sentry cries, "Halt, who goes there?" and the chief yeoman warder replies "The Keys." "Whose keys?" comes the demand. "Queen Elizabeth's keys." The sentry presents arms, and the chief warder raises his Tudor bonnet, yelling, "God preserve Queen Elizabeth." The ritual ends with a rousing "amen" from the whole guard. Tickets to see it are free. Write at least 1 month in advance, enclosing an International Reply Coupon, to: Ceremony of the Keys, 2nd floor, Waterloo Block, HM Tower of London, London EC3N 4AB.

The oldest part, and focal point, is the massive White Tower, built in 1078 by the Norman king, William the Conqueror, to protect London and discourage rebellion among his new Saxon subjects. Every king after him added to the main structure, so that when Edward I completed the outer walls in the late 13th century, they enclosed an 18-acre square. Walk round the top of them for a bird's-eye view of how the Tower of London would have looked in its heyday.

The ✪ **Crown Jewels**, glittering in the **Jewel House** in Waterloo Barracks, are the real must-see. No words can do justice to the Imperial State Crown, encrusted with 3,200 precious stones, including a 317-carat diamond. A moving walkway is meant to keep visitors flowing through, but it can still be a long wait. The **Martin Tower** exhibition, *Crowns & Diamonds: The Making of the Crown Jewels,* tells the stories of two of the world's most famous diamonds, the Koh-i-Noor and Cullinan II, as well as of a botched attempt to steal the State regalia in the late 17th century.

Visitors with a more ghoulish bent should start at The Chapel Royal of St. Peter ad Vincula, which contains the graves of all the unfortunates executed at the Tower. The Scaffold Site, where the axeman dispatched seven of the highest-ranking victims, including Henry VIII's wives, Anne Boleyn and Catherine Howard, is just outside. Everyone else met their end on Tower Green. Imagine their terror as they arrived by boat at the dread **Traitors' Gate.**

The **Bloody Tower** was where Richard of Gloucester locked up his young nephews while he usurped his crusading brother Edward IV. The princes' bodies were later found by the White Tower. How they died remains a mystery, despite the obvious suspect. Today, an exhibit recreates how Sir Walter Raleigh might have lived during his 13-year imprisonment after the Gunpowder Plot against James I.

The royal menagerie moved out in 1834 to form the new London Zoo—all except the **ravens.** Legend has it Charles II was told that if they ever left the Tower the monarchy would fall. Ever since, a few birds have been kept in a lodging next to Wakefield Tower, looked after by a yeoman warder. The **yeoman warders,** or Beefeaters, have guarded the Tower for centuries. Now usually retired soldiers, they lead tours every half hour from 9:30am to 3:30pm and give vivid talks at 9:30 (not Sunday), 11:30am, 2:15, and 4:30pm.

As well as the daily **Ceremony of the Keys** (see box above), there's a diary of State events: Call for info. **Beating of the Bounds** takes place every third year (next in 2002) on Ascension Day, the Thursday 40 days after Easter. A painter marks out the boundaries on the ground to signal the Tower's independence from the jurisdiction of the city.

Tower of London

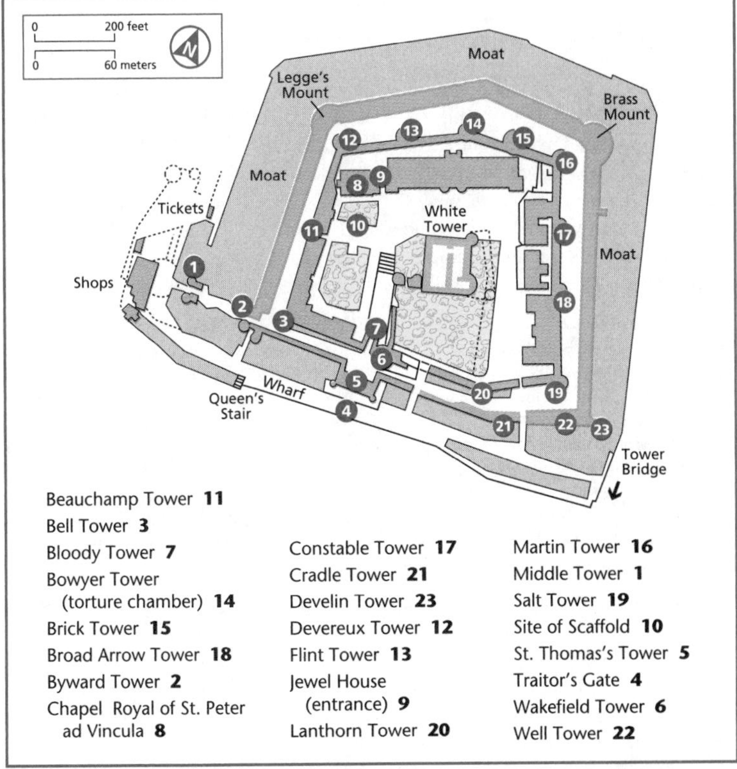

✪ **Victoria & Albert Museum.** Cromwell Rd., SW7. ☎ **020/7942-2000.** www.vam.ac.uk. Admission £5 ($8) adults; additional fee for some special exhibitions; free seniors, under-18s, and students; free late entry after 4:30pm. Daily 10am–5:45pm. Closed Dec 24–26. Tube: South Kensington.

The V&A is a treasure house devoted to the decorative and fine arts. It has more than 4 million objects, 7 miles of galleries, and plans for an ultra-modern, and ultra-controversial, extension. Designed by Daniel Libeskind, The Spiral won't open until 2005—there's not even a hole in the ground yet. Right now, work is focusing on a £31-million overhaul of the British Galleries. As at so many museums, the patriarchal approach is history: no more dazzling the hoi-polloi with treasures protected in glass cases. Instead, there'll be pieces to handle, video re-creations of how they were used, and commentaries on taste by historical figures and today's top designers. Iconic objects, such as the **Great Bed of Ware,** which Shakespeare mentions in *Twelfth Night,* will tell the story of Britain's 400-year rise (1500–1900) to world power and cultural authority. This vivid right-in-there experience launches in November.

The V&A collections are fabulous: sculpture, furniture, fashion, textiles, prints, paintings, photographs, silver, glass, ceramics, and jewelry—from Britain and all over the world. The Art and Design Galleries are arranged by place or date, showing visual relationships and cultural influences. The Materials and Techniques Galleries trace the development of a particular material, in form, function, or technique. Temporary exhibitions in the diary for 2001 include: **Contemporary Fashion** (photography) in the Canon Gallery, which runs until February or March; and The Victorians, on from April through July.

Not only is the museum worth a good long visit, but there are so many regular activities you'll want to keep coming back. Free guided tours take place daily on the hour, 10:30am to 3:30pm, and family tours 1:30 to 5pm on Saturdays and other times during school holidays (for full details of child-friendly fun, call ☎ **020/7942-2197**). Specialist gallery talks start at 1pm. There are demonstrations every Saturday from 2 to 5pm. And Wednesday is **Late View** (admission £3/$4.80), an after-hours jamboree of themed lectures (plus £5/$8), exhibitions, entry into certain galleries, and live music. You can have a very English supper at the New Restaurant (main courses £10.50/$16.80), or stick to an aperitif glass of wine (£2.10/$3.35) and eat somewhere cheaper later.

✪ **Westminster Abbey.** Dean's Yard, SW1. ☎ **020/7222-5152,** 020/7222-5897 Chapter House, or 020/7233-0019 Pyx Chamber and Abbey Museum. www.westminster-abbey.org. Admission £5 ($8) adults, £3 ($4.80) seniors and students, £2 ($3.20) under-16s, £10 ($16) family ticket. Chamber House, Pyx Chamber, and Abbey Museum £2.50 ($3.20) adults, £1.90 ($3.05) seniors and students, £1.30 ($2.10) under-16s; reduced with Abbey admission, free with guided and audio tour. Cloisters, College Garden, St. Margaret's Church free. Abbey Mon–Fri 9:30am–4:45pm, Sat 9:30am–2:45pm, last admission 1hr. before closing, Sun for worship. Chapter House Apr–Oct 10am–5:30pm; Nov–Mar 10am–4pm. Pyx Chamber and Abbey Museum daily 10:30am–4pm. Cloisters 8am–6pm. College Garden Apr–Sept 10am–6pm; Oct–Mar 10am–4pm. St. Margaret's Church Mon–Fri 9:30am–3:45pm, Sat 9:30am–1:45pm, Sun 2–5pm. Tube: Westminster.

St. Peter ordered Sebert, king of the East Saxons, to build the first church here in the 7th century and then materialized at the consecration. No wonder the devout Edward the Confessor chose the site to found his new abbey. The king didn't make it to the consecration in 1065, dying 4 days beforehand. Westminster Abbey is neither a cathedral nor a parish church, but a "royal peculiar," under the jurisdiction of the dean and chapter, and subject only to the sovereign.

Largely dating from the 13th to 16th centuries, it has played a prominent part in British history—most recently, with the funeral of Princess Diana. Every coronation since 1066 has taken place here. The oak **Coronation Chair** was made in 1308 for Edward I. It held the ancient **Stone of Scone,** on which the kings of Scotland were crowned. The English seized the stone in 1296 and refused to return it until a couple of years ago. Visit the **Norman Undercroft,** to see the replica coronation regalia, as well as ancient funeral effigies. The abbey is guardian of the nation's memories. Five kings and four queens are buried near the **Shrine of Edward the Confessor,** which is behind the high altar. Geoffrey Chaucer sowed the seeds for **Poets' Corner,** when he was buried here in 1400—in his case, because he worked for the abbey. Ben Jonson is there, standing upright, as well as Dryden, Samuel Johnson, Sheridan, Browning, and Tennyson. The practice of putting up literary memorials began in earnest in the 18th century with a full-length figure of Shakespeare. But the sinner Oscar Wilde didn't get a memorial window until 1995. There are historical figures from every field, but only one painter, Godfrey Kneller. The **Tomb of the Unknown Soldier** honors all those who fell in World War I. The nameless man lies under Belgian stone in soil brought back from the battlefields of France.

Guided tours of the abbey, lead by the vergers, cost £3 ($4.80). These start at 10, 10:30, 11am, 2, 2:30, and 3pm (not Friday) during the week April through October; at 10, 11am, 2, and 3pm (2:30pm on Friday) on winter weekdays; and at 10, 11am, and 12:30pm on Saturday year-round. Call ☎ **020/7222-2072** to book. Audio guides are only £2 ($3.20). With both, you get discounted entry to the **Chapter House** (1245–55) in the east cloister, the nearby **Pyx Chamber,** and the **Abbey Museum,** all under the care of English Heritage. Call the abbey for a diary of concerts and talks.

Westminster Abbey

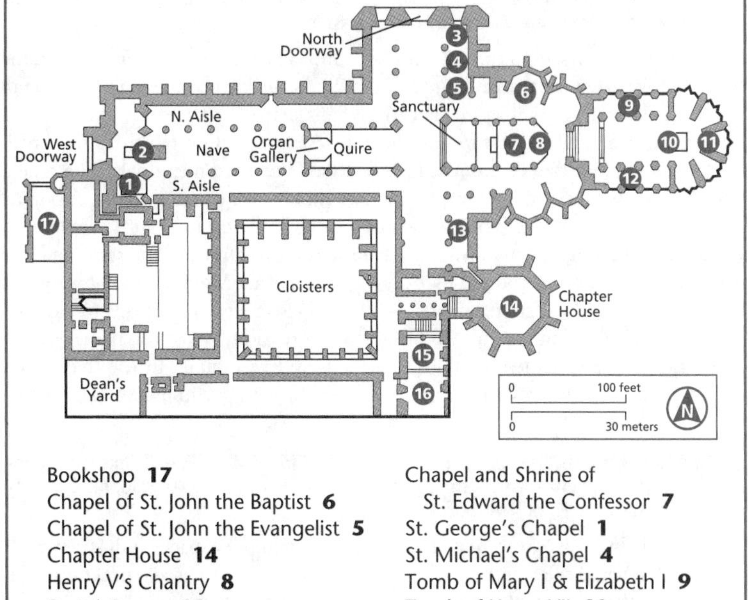

Bookshop **17**
Chapel of St. John the Baptist **6**
Chapel of St. John the Evangelist **5**
Chapter House **14**
Henry V's Chantry **8**
Poets' Corner **13**
Pyx Chamber **15**
Royal Air Force Chapel & Battle of Britain Memorial Window **11**
St. Andrew's Chapel **3**
Chapel and Shrine of St. Edward the Confessor **7**
St. George's Chapel **1**
St. Michael's Chapel **4**
Tomb of Mary I & Elizabeth I **9**
Tomb of Henry VII **10**
Tomb of Mary, Queen of Scots **12**
Tomb of the Unknown Soldier & Memorial to Churchill **2**
Undercroft Museum **16**

3 Churches, Cathedrals & a Cemetery

Many of the churches listed below put on **lunchtime concerts.** Tickets are usually free, although it's customary to leave a small donation. The **City Information Centre,** St. Paul's Churchyard, EC4 (☎ **020/7332-1456**) can give you a full list. It's open from 9:30am to 5pm, daily April through September and weekdays October through March, and 9:30am to 12:30pm on winter Saturdays.

✪ **Brompton Oratory.** Thurloe Place, Brompton Rd., SW7. ☎ **020/7808-0900.** Free admission. Daily 6:30am–8pm. Tube: South Kensington.

The priests of the Institute of the Oratory, founded by St. Philip Neri, serve this amazing church. Architect Herbert Gribble modeled it after the Chiesa Nova in Rome. Completed in 1884, its baroque extravagance marked the revival of the long disenfranchised English Catholicism. Brompton Oratory has the third widest nave in Britain after Westminster Cathedral and York Minster. The marble statues of the apostles are by Mazzuoli and were originally in Siena Cathedral. The Oratory is famous for its beautiful **musical services**—the organ has nearly 4,000 pipes—and for the Latin mass, sung at 11am on Sunday.

Highgate Cemetery. Swain's Lane, N6. ☎ **020/8340-1834.** East Cemetery £2 ($3.20); West Cemetery £4 ($6.40); £1 ($1.60) to bring a small camera. East Cemetery Apr–Oct Mon–Fri 10am–5pm, Sat–Sun 11am–5pm; Nov–Mar closes at 4pm. West Cemetery tours

Apr–Oct Mon–Fri at noon, 2, and 4pm, Sat–Sun also at 11am and 3pm; Nov–Mar Sat–Sun at noon, 1, 2, and 3pm. Tube: Archway. No under-8s in the West Cemetery.

Serpentine pathways wind through this beautiful cemetery, which is laid out around a huge, 300-year-old cedar tree. Opened in 1829, it quickly became so fashionable that 3 decades later a new graveyard had to be consecrated on the other side of Swain's Lane. You have to take a tour to visit the old western cemetery, but that's no hardship as the guides are extremely knowledgeable about Victorian memorials. The funerary rituals, like so much of the culture at that time, were extraordinarily elaborate—witness the tomb-lined **Egyptian Avenue,** which leads up to the catacombs in the **Circle of Lebanon.** Scientist **Michael Faraday,** poet **Christina Rossetti,** and many other famous figures are buried here. The grave of **Karl Marx,** marked by a gargantuan bust, lies in the eastern cemetery—the Chinese government helps to pay for its upkeep. You'll also find the grave of novelist **George Eliot,** whose real name was Mary Anne Evans. Please remember the cemetery is still very much in use. No children under 8 can enter the western side, and you will have to pay to use a small camera—no video allowed.

St. Bride's Church. Fleet St., EC4. ☎ **020/7353-1301.** Free admission. Mon–Fri 8:30–4:30pm, Sat 9:30am–4:30pm, Sun 9:30am–12:30pm and 5:30–7:30pm. Concerts at 1:15pm on Tues, Wed, and Fri. Tube: Blackfriars.

St. Bride's is in Fleet Street, once the heart of Britain's newspaper industry, which is why it is known as the "journalists' and printers' church." Archaeological excavations, carried out after the bombing of 1940, discovered a Roman house preserved in the crypt—there's a museum there now. St. Brigit of Ireland founded the first Christian church here, and the present one is the eighth on the site. After the Great Fire, Sir Christopher Wren supervised the rebuilding, which cost £11,430. The spire was added later. This "madrigal in stone"—four octagonal tiers capped by an obelisk, itself topped off with a ball and vane—is 234 feet tall and supposedly inspired the wedding cakes of a 17th-century Fleet Street pastry cook. St. Bride's has had many famous parishioners, including writers John Dryden, John Milton, Richard Lovelace, and John Evelyn. The diarist Samuel Pepys and his eight siblings were all baptized at St. Bride's. There are concerts every Tuesday and Friday, and an organ recital on Wednesday.

St. Clement Danes. Strand, WC2. ☎ **020/7242-8282.** Free admission. Mon–Fri 9am–4pm, Sat–Sun 9am–3pm. Tube: Temple (closed Sun), Charing Cross, Blackfriars.

No one knows for certain where the "Danes" comes from, but there was a wooden Saxon church on this site. Rebuilt in stone in the late 10th century, it survived the Great Fire but was declared unsafe. Sir Christopher Wren (him again!) was commissioned to rebuild it, though James Gibbs designed the spire. Samuel Johnson attended services regularly at St. Clement Danes. And Bishop George Berkeley and the wife of poet John Donne are buried here. Gutted in the Blitz, it was rebuilt in the late 1950s and underwent another big renovation in 1999. This is the RAF's church and contains memorials to the British, Commonwealth, and American airmen who flew in World War II. It is also thought by some people to be the church immortalized in the nursery rhyme, "Oranges and lemons say the bells of St. Clement's." Each child at the attached primary school receives an orange and lemon after the special annual service. (In fact, the rhyme probably refers to St. Clement Eastcheap, which is on the riverfront where citrus fruits were unloaded.)

St. Giles & St. Luke Cripplegate. Fore St., EC2. ☎ **020/7638-1997.** www.users.globalnet.co.uk/~stgiles. Free admission. Mon–Fri 9am–5pm, Sat 9am–noon, Sun for services. Tube: Moorgate, Barbican.

St. Giles was founded in the 11th century and named after the patron saint of cripples. The church survived the Great Fire, but the Blitz left only the tower and walls standing. Oliver Cromwell became betrothed to Elizabeth Bourchier at St. Giles in 1620. John Milton, author of *Paradise Lost,* was buried here in 1674. More than a century later, someone opened his grave, knocked out his teeth, stole a rib bone, and tore some hair out of his skull. So much for nutty celebrity-souvenir hunters being a modern phenomenon.

St. James's Church. 197 Piccadilly, W1. ☎ **020/7734-4511.** Free admission. Daily 8am–7pm. Recitals Mon, Wed, and Fri at 1:10pm. Courtyard market: antiques Tues, crafts and souvenirs Wed–Sat. Tube: Piccadilly Circus, Green Park.

In the late 17th century, the thriving city expanded its western borders into a new aristocratic enclave known as St. James's. Its patrons naturally commissioned Sir Christopher Wren to build their parish church, while Grinling Gibbons carved the reredos, organ case, and font. Diarist John Evelyn wrote, "There is no altar anywhere in England, nor has there been any abroad, more handsomely adorned." As might be expected, this church has rich historical associations. William Blake, the poet and artist, and William Pitt, who became England's youngest prime minister at age 24, were both baptized here. Caricaturist James Gillray, auctioneer James Christie, and coffeehouse founder Francis White are all buried at St. James's. The church has seen some pretty colorful weddings, too—none more so than that of explorer Sir Samuel Baker to a woman he had bought at a slave auction in a Turkish bazaar. St. James's holds lunchtime recitals on Monday, Wednesday, and Friday, with an irregular program of inexpensive evening concerts and talks as well. The market is a bit of a scrum, but worth a look for odd little gifts amid the crafty kitsch.

✪ **St. Martin-in-the-Fields.** Trafalgar Sq., WC2. ☎ **020/7930-0089** for church info, 020/7839-8362 for box office, or 020/7930-9306 London Brass Rubbing Centre. www.stmartin-in-the-field.org. Free admission to church and lunchtime recitals; evening concerts £6–£16 ($9.60–$25.60). Brass rubbings from £4 ($6.40). Church daily 9am–6pm (except during services); London Brass Rubbing Centre Mon–Sat 10am–6pm, Sun noon–6pm. Tube: Charing Cross, Leicester Sq.

This church is one of the most beautiful and best-loved in London. Though there's been a place of worship here since 1220, the current building dates from 1726. Designed by James Gibbs, the intricate plasterwork ceiling enhances the simple nave. Curiously, the parish boundary passes through the middle of Buckingham Palace, and the names of many royal children appear on the baptismal registry. The Queen Mother, who lives at Clarence House, is a parishioner. St. Martin's is famous for its music: Handel played the organ here (not the current 3,637-pipe instrument, which was installed in 1990), and Mozart is on the list of past performers. There are free lunchtime concerts (Monday, Tuesday, and Friday), as well as evening recitals from Thursday to Saturday. Many are by candlelight, and the program leans heavily towards the baroque, with performances by the Academy of St. Martin-in-the-Fields and other chamber orchestras. The choral music during the three Sunday services is sublime. Evensong is the most quintessentially Anglican, usually at 5pm, but call ahead for specific times.

In the crypt of St. Martin's is the **London Brass Rubbing Centre,** which has about 100 medieval and Tudor church brasses—knights, ladies, kings, merchants, and heraldic animals—as well as unusual Celtic patterns and early woodcuts of the zodiac. There are lots of new designs this year to celebrate the center's 25th anniversary. Materials and instruction are provided, and it's great fun. The gift shop stocks Celtic jewelry as well as courtly mementos, and many of the artworks in the crypt gallery are also for sale. If you have time, take a break for a luvverly cuppa or a delicious homemade meal at **The Café-in-the-Crypt** (see chapter 5).

St. Mary Le Bow. Cheapside, EC2. ☎ **020/7248-5139.** Free admission. Mon–Thurs 6:30am–6pm, Fri 6:30am–4pm. Lunchtime concerts Thurs 1:05pm. Dialogues Tues 1:05pm during school terms. Closed major holidays and the week after Christmas and Easter. Tube: St. Paul's, Bank, Mansion House.

Traditionally, to be a true Cockney, you must be born within the sound of Bow bells—the ones that ring at this church. St. Mary's colorful history has been marked by a series of bizarre incidents. The first happened in 1091, when a storm ripped off the roof. Then, in 1271, the church tower collapsed, killing 20 people. In 1331, Queen Philippa and her ladies-in-waiting plummeted to the ground when a wooden balcony collapsed during a joust to celebrate the birth of the Black Prince. The Great Fire destroyed the church, and it was rebuilt by the great architect Wren—not a disaster, of course. St. Mary's was rededicated in 1964 after a big restoration. As well as the Thursday lunchtime concerts, the rector holds discussions with an intriguing range of guests, from museum curators to movie directors, and representatives of other faiths every Tuesday during school terms.

St. Paul's, The Actors' Church. Bedford St., WC2. ☎ **020/7836-5221.** Free admission. Mon–Fri 8:30am–4:30pm. Tube: Covent Garden.

The Drury Lane Theatre, the Theatre Royal, and the Royal Opera House are all within the parish of St. Paul's, so it's little wonder that it has become known as the actors' church. Inside, you'll find dozens of memorial plaques dedicated to such thespian luminaries as Vivien Leigh, Laurence Harvey, Boris Karloff, Margaret Rutherford, and Noël Coward, to name but a few. It is also the last resting place of wood-carver Grinling Gibbons, writer Samuel Butler, and the doctor's daughter Margaret Ponteous, who was the first victim of the Great Plague in 1665. Famous baptisms here have included that of landscape painter J. M. W. Turner and librettist W. S. Gilbert. Despite substantial and repeated restoration work over the years, particularly after a fire in 1795, the church is still largely how Inigo Jones designed it for the Earl of Bedford in the 17th century, with its quiet garden piazza in the rear. St. Paul's celebrates the Eucharist at 11am on Sunday. Every second Sunday of the month, there is choral evensong at 4pm.

Southwark Cathedral. Montague Close, London Bridge, SE1. ☎ **020/7367-6700.** www.dswark.org. Cathedral admission by donation, suggested £2.50 ($4); visitor center exhibition, prices to be announced. Daily 8:30am–6pm. Tube: London Bridge.

This is another of London's truly ancient places of worship, going back more than 1,000 years. The present church dates from the 15th century, though it was partially rebuilt in 1890. An exciting new visitor center is designed to teach people about the history of Southwark, the outlaw borough "of players and poets, prostitutes, paupers and prisons, pilgrims and patients," which made up the medieval parish. Chaucer and Shakespeare both worshipped here, and to this day, there is a birthday service held annually for the Bard—don't miss his carved memorial. Another rare treasure is the wooden effigy of a knight dating to 1275. Southwark Cathedral has seen many important historical events, from the marriage of James I of Scotland and Mary Beaufort in 1424, to the Tudor Bishop of Winchester's consistory court, which condemned seven of the Marian martyrs to death. Later, the bishop's retro choir was rented to a baker and even used as a pigsty. Southwark Cathedral has a notable choir, so it's worth attending a service here just for the music. Otherwise, there are free concerts every Thursday at 1pm and a program of other events.

Wesley's Chapel, House & Museum. 49 City Rd., EC1. ☎ **020/7253-2262.** Chapel is free; house and museum £4 ($6.20) adults, £2 ($3.10) under-18s. House (audio-guide) and museum Mon–Sat 10am–4pm (closed Thurs 12:45–1:30pm, worshippers welcome), Sun noon–2pm. Music recital every Tues at 1:05pm. Tube: Old St., Moorgate.

John Wesley, the founder of Methodism, established this chapel in 1778 as his London base. There's a day-long service every year on November 1 to celebrate the occasion, and another on May 24 to mark his full conversion. This simple man, who traveled the length and breadth of England on horseback and preached in the open air, is buried in a grave behind the chapel. The building somehow survived the Blitz but later fell into serious disrepair, until a major restoration in the 1970s. The museum in the crypt traces the history of Methodism up to the present day. Across the road in **Bunhill Fields** is the Dissenters Graveyard where Daniel Defoe, William Blake, and John Bunyan are buried. Come here for one of the Tuesday lunchtime music recitals.

Westminster Cathedral. Ashley Place, SW1. ☎ **020/7798-9055.** www.westminstercathedral.org.uk. Cathedral and Sun organ recitals free; tower £2 ($3.20) adults, £1 ($1.60) under-16s. Cathedral, daily 7am–7pm; Campanile lift Apr–Nov daily 9am–5pm, Dec–Mar Thurs–Sun 9am–5pm. Tube: Victoria.

The land this cathedral stands on once belonged to the monks of Westminster Abbey, who used it for a market and feast-day fairs. After the dissolution of the monasteries under Henry VIII, it changed hands several times, until finally chosen as the site for the Middlesex County Prison of Tothill Fields. When the prison fell into disuse in 1882, Cardinal Henry Edward Manning bought the land for what was to become the premier Roman Catholic church in Britain—the new Archbishop of Westminster, the Most Reverend Cormac Murphy-O'Connor was installed here last year. John Francis Bentley designed the massive brick-and-stone edifice (1903)—360 feet long and 156 feet wide—in spectacular Byzantine style. The richly decorated interior uses 100 different kinds of marble: dark green for the eight marble columns supporting the nave, yellow for those holding up the huge **baldachino** over the high altar. Mosaics emblazon the chapels and the vaulting of the sanctuary. The controversial Stations of the Cross are the work of famous sculptor Eric Gill. One of the biggest thrills is taking the lift to the gallery at the top of the 273-foot-tall campanile for a fantastic panoramic view over London. Another is attending a free Sunday organ recital or sung mass. Music is an extremely important part of cathedral life and has been since composer Sir Edward Elgar premiered his celebrated choral work, the oratorio setting of Cardinal Newman's *The Dream of Gerontius* (a piece initially regarded as a failure but later acclaimed), at its opening. Call for information on the concert program.

4 Memorials & Monuments

Gone but not forgotten. Since ancient times, nations have honored the supreme sacrifices and great successes of their famous dead with imposing public memorials. Last year finally saw the unveiling of a very fitting celebration of the life of Princess Diana. The £1.3-million **Peter Pan playground,** in Kensington Gardens (also see Albert Memorial, below), is a wonderland with a huge pirate galleon for children to scramble about on. This replaced the idea for a memorial garden, which roused huge opposition from local residents, who feared they'd be besieged by crowds of pilgrims.

But the torturous debate about how to commemorate Diana was nothing compared to the great Trafalgar Square question. One of the plinths near the base of Nelson's Column has been empty for 160 years while city grandees have debated who deserves immortalization. The latest special committee finally decided last year. And they fudged it! The plinth will remain empty, a home for temporary exhibits, as it has been in recent years. Memorials are a tricky issue. There are so many different constituencies to satisfy these days. It's harder to be a hero. Not to mention ra-ra patriotism is largely left to the great modern sporting battles.

In fact, modern Britain could hardly be more different than the nation that built **Nelson's Column.** The admiral's victory at the Battle of Trafalgar in 1805 staved off the French invasion. It also cost him his life. "Men started at the intelligence, and turned pale, as if they had heard of the loss of a dear friend," wrote poet Robert Southey. It took until 1843 to complete the 185-foot Corinthian column, a copy of one in the temple of Mars Ultor (the Avenger) in Rome. Bronze reliefs on the sides of the pedestal commemorate Nelson's most famous battles. The lions, by Landseer, were added in 1843. If plans to pedestrianize the north side of Trafalgar Square get the go-ahead (work could start in Spring 2001), you'll be able to marvel once more at the glory of Nelson's Column, from the steps of the National Gallery, without bumper-to-bumper buses spoiling the view.

This is only the first phase of a much bigger urban renaissance project (www.worldsquares.com) that will eventually extend down Whitehall and spruce up Parliament Square. That's where you'll find the **Cenotaph,** a very simple, but emotionally eloquent, memorial to the fallen of World Wars I and II. Designed by Sir Edwin Lutyens, it is the center of Remembrance Day ceremonies on November 11.

Last on our list of notable London monuments is the extraordinary **Albert Memorial,** put up by Victoria in Kensington Gardens to commemorate her beloved husband. The queen was so devastated by Albert's premature death from typhoid fever in 1861 that she withdrew from public life for more than a decade and wore her trademark black until she died in 1901. Unveiled again in 1998 after a 10-year restoration, this Gothic icon is in better condition than when it was built to designs by Sir George Gilbert Scott. Gilding removed in World War I glows opulently once more, and craftsmen have carefully replaced missing statuary and mosaics. Railings protect the memorial, but you can take a guided tour behind them on Sundays at 2 and 3pm. To book, call ☎ **020/7495-0916** (www.tourguides.co.uk): Tickets cost £3 ($4.80) for adults, and £2.50 ($4) for concessions.

Note: **Westminster Abbey** and **St. Paul's Cathedral** both contain memorials to many famous people and events, as do the holy places listed in the section above.

5 Institutions as English as Shepherd's Pie

It may seem a bit odd to single anything out as being quintessentially English when all the attractions in this chapter are a product of, and often celebrate, the very powerful national culture. But some experiences are so unrepeatable, in the best possible sense, that they merit special attention. As well as those listed below, don't miss the rowdy **debates in the House of Commons** (see "Houses of Parliament," section 2 of this chapter), and the equally passionate crowds at London's great sporting venues. **Lord's** cricket ground, the home of rugby union at **Twickenham,** and the world-famous **All England Lawn Tennis Club** at Wimbledon all have museums, too, and put on guided tours (see "Spectator Sports," below).

Bank of England Museum. Threadneedle St., EC2. ☎ **020/7601-5545.** www.bankofengland.co.uk. Free admission. Mon–Fri 10am–5pm, and 2nd Sat in Nov for Lord Mayor's Show. Closed bank holidays. Tube: Bank.

The museum is actually within the Bank of England. It traces the fascinating history of the "Old Lady of Threadneedle Street" from its foundation by Royal Charter in 1694 to its modern role as the nation's central bank. Gold glitters temptingly in ancient ingots and the modern market bar, and a new display lets you feel how heavy they are. There are also displays of bank notes, coins, and the pikes and muskets used to defend the bank. Forget the Data Protection Act—the private financial papers of such famous clients as the Duchess of Marlborough, George Washington, and Horatio

Sights North of Hyde Park

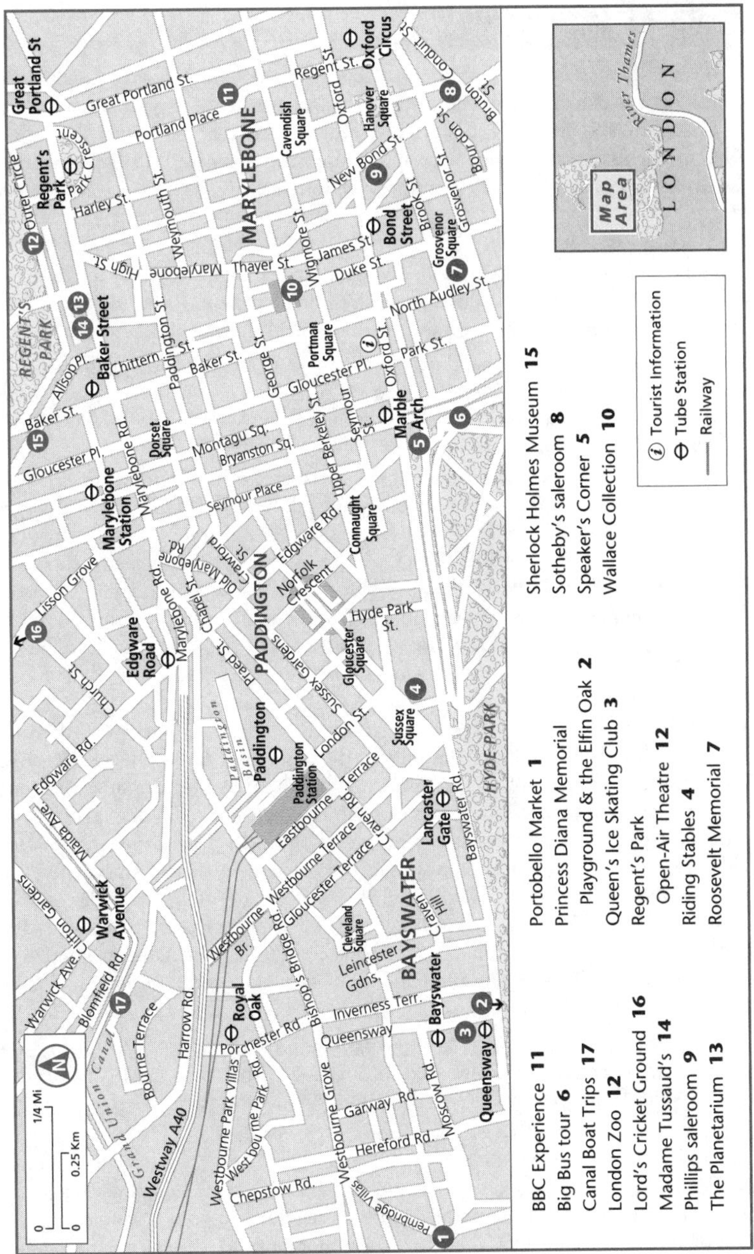

Nelson are there for everyone to nosey through. There is even an interactive presentation that gives an intriguing insight into the intricacies of bank note design and production. The Bank of England is an extremely tough monitor of how notes are pictured in printed matter. You can only show a very small proportion of the surface area in an illustration, in case someone uses it as counterfeit money. Call ☎ **020/7601-5491** to

Visiting Mansion House

To tour Mansion House, the official residence of the Lord Mayor of London, you must send a request for tickets to the Principal Assistant-Diary, Mansion House, London EC4N 8BH (☎ **020/7626-2500**). If you can't be bothered or didn't request tickets in time, come anyway because this impressive Palladian building is well worth a gawk. Simply hop on the Tube to Bank.

---

find out about the host of events at the museum, including special entry to the "inner sanctum"—the governors' and directors' posh entertaining rooms—during September's Open House Weekend (see "Festivals," in section 1 of this chapter).

BBC Experience. Broadcasting House, Portland Place, W1. ☎ **0870/603-0304** for bookings. www.bbc.co.uk/experience. Admission £7.50 ($12) adults, £6.50 ($10.40) seniors, £5.95 ($9.50) students, £4.95 ($9.90) under-16s, £19.95 ($31.90) family ticket. Tours take 1½hr., starting Mon 11am, Tues–Sun 10am, last tour 4:30pm. Tube: Oxford Circus.

The fab BBC Experience takes you behind the scenes of this quintessential British institution, which the locals, for some reason, call "Auntie." There's something to entertain everyone. History buffs will enjoy the treasures from the radio archives, dramatically presented in **BBC: The Early Years 1922–1952.** A new exhibition, **BBC: Sight and Sound 1950–2000,** combines rare TV news footage and much loved shows with newer big productions. You can watch the Coronation, the fall of the Berlin Wall, *Monty Python*, *Black Adder*, *Pride and Prejudice*, even the *Teletubbies* (is that really a landmark?). Another new display reveals the secrets of one of the BBC's most ambitious adaptations ever, *Gormenghast,* from the trilogy by Mervyn Peake. It got mixed reviews, but the special effects used to create the fantasy kingdom are phenomenal, and you can flick a button to turn the set from day into night. The BBC Experience is even more of a must-visit now that the rival Museum of the Moving Image is closed for refurbishment. Visitors can take part in a radio drama, commentate on sports, edit a scene from Britain's top soap opera, *EastEnders*, present a weather bulletin, and much more. The shop is a great source of gifts, such as tapes and videos of classic and modern drama. The BBC grew out of Broadcasting House, designed by G. Val Myers in 1932, long ago, shifting many of its operations to **BBC Television Centre,** Wood Lane, W12. You must pre-book to tour the West London complex—call the number above. (See the "Freebies," at the start of chapter 8 for information on tickets to TV and radio shows.)

Guildhall. Off Gresham St., EC2. ☎ **020/7606-3030.** www.corpoflondon.gov.uk. Free admission. May–Sept daily; Oct–Apr Mon–Sat 10am–4:30pm. Closed Jan 1, Good Friday, Easter Monday, Dec 24–26, and for ceremonial occasions. Tube: Bank.

This has been the seat of government (for the city of London only, and not to be confused with the new Mayor Ken's mob) for more than 800 years. The Guildhall itself dates from 1411 and has the largest medieval crypt in a capital crawling with crypts. The building has been restored, with great care, on several occasions, notably after the Great Fire and again after the Blitz. Among the decorations are the banners of the 100 livery companies and inscriptions in the windows recording the names of all the lord mayors since 1189. Some of them also merit a monument, as do Churchill, Wellington, and Nelson. Statues of the legendary giants Gog and Magog guard the institution. The Court of Common Council meets here, in public, at 1pm on the third Thursday of each month.

Middle Temple Hall. Middle Temple Lane, EC4. ☎ **020/7427-4800.** Free admission. Mon–Fri 10–11:30am and 3–4pm. Call to check if closed for special ceremonies. Tube: Temple.

This is like a very posh canteen for the barristers who keep their chambers nearby, so visiting hours are tailored not to disturb their prosperous lunching. Built in 1573, the hall has an imposing double hammer-beam roof. Elizabeth I donated an oak from Windsor Park to make the 29½-foot bench table. Well worth a visit if you're wandering through this arcane legal village anyway.

✪ **Old Bailey.** Newgate St., EC4. ☎ **020/7248-3277.** Free admission. Public viewing galleries Mon–Fri 10:30am–1pm and 2–4pm. Tube: St. Paul's. No under-14s.

This is the nation's Central Criminal Court, affectionately known as the Old Bailey after a street that runs nearby. It has been the scene of many famous trials, including those of Oscar Wilde, Lord Haw Haw, and the Yorkshire Ripper. Take a seat in one of the public viewing galleries to watch the bewigged barristers presenting their cases to the high court judges, who include the Lord Chancellor and the Lord Chief Justice. It's a fascinating experience. The Old Bailey opened in 1907 on what used to be the site of the infamous Newgate Prison. An addition was built in the 1970s and now has 19 courtrooms and holding cells for 70 prisoners. Justice crowns its dome, and a Recording Angel, supported by Fortitude and Truth, stands above the entrance. If you go down into the basement, you can see a patchwork remnant of the original city walls.

Note: All visitors and their property will be searched, and admittance denied to anyone with cameras, electronic equipment (mobile phone, pager, radio, and so on), large bags, food, or drink. The court cannot look after anything for you, so leave all of the above at your hotel.

Royal Courts of Justice. Strand, WC2. ☎ **020/7947-6000.** www.open.gov.uk. Free admission. Sessions Mon–Fri 10:30am–1pm and 2–4pm. Court in recess Aug–Sept. Tube: Temple.

At these 88 courts, mainly civil cases are heard. Visitors can take a seat at the back of a courtroom to watch justice, allegedly, in action. Designed by G. E. Street, the neo-Gothic court buildings (1874–82) contain more than 1,000 rooms and 3½ miles of corridors. Sculptures of Christ, King Solomon, and King Alfred grace the front door, glowing importantly under the marvelous new floodlighting. On the second Saturday in November, the annually elected Lord Chief Justice swears in the new Lord Mayor of London. The millennium video about the history of the Royal Courts may still be in the hall—plans weren't finalized as we went to press. The same goes for tours to parts of the building not normally open to the public. So call to check.

6 More Museums, Galleries & Historic Buildings

Apsley House, The Wellington Museum. 149 Piccadilly, Hyde Park Corner, W1. ☎ **020/7499-5676.** Admission (includes audio guide) £4.50 ($7.20) adults, £3 ($4.80) concessions, free seniors and under-18s. Tues–Sun 11am–5pm. Closed Jan 1, Good Friday, May 1, and Dec 24–26. Tube: Hyde Park Corner (exit 3).

Once known as "No. 1 London" because it was the first house outside the tollgate, Apsley House has been the magnificent city residence of the dukes of Wellington since 1817. The name comes from its first owner, the Earl of Bathurst, Baron Apsley. Wellington moved in on his return from a triumphant military career in India, Spain, and Portugal, culminating in the victory over Napoléon at Waterloo. He entertained very extravagantly, dining off the gorgeous Sèvres Egyptian Service that Napoléon had commissioned for Josephine, and a vast silver Portuguese service with a 26-foot-long centerpiece. Wellington's heroic military success earned him lavish gifts as well as royal respect. No wonder the original Robert Adam design (1771–78) had to be enlarged to house the duke's treasures. Today, the house is crammed with silver, porcelain, sculpture (note the nude statue of Napoléon by Canova on the main staircase), furniture, medals, and 200 or more paintings by Velázquez, Goya, Rubens, Brueghel, Steen, de Hooch, and other masters. It's one of the few great London town houses where such collections remain intact and the family is still in residence: The eighth Duke of Wellington and his son have private apartments.

Banqueting House. Opposite Horse Guards Parade, Whitehall, SW1. ☎ **020/7839-8918.** www.hrp.org.uk. Admission £3.80 ($6.10) adults, £3 ($4.80) seniors and students, £2.30 ($3.70) under-16s. Mon–Sat 10am–5pm. Last admission 4pm. Closed Dec 24–Jan 1, Good Friday, and for government functions. Tube: Charing Cross, Embankment, Westminster.

This is all that remains of the great Palace of Whitehall after the fire of 1698. A masterpiece of English Renaissance (1619–22) architecture, it was designed by Inigo Jones for James I. The main hall was obviously for posh banqueting (as it still is today), hence the nine magnificent ceiling paintings by Rubens, depicting the Divine Right of Kings. You can also visit the undercroft (crypt), somewhere the king could get drunk with his mates. On a somber note, the bust of Charles I above the entrance reminds visitors that he was beheaded in front of the building. Combine a visit with watching the Changing of the Guard, at Horse Guards opposite (see the box below).

Barbican Art Gallery. Level 3, Barbican Centre, Silk St., EC2. ☎ **020/7382-7105.** www.barbican.org.uk. Admission £6–£10 ($9.60–$16) adults; £4–£7.50 ($6.40–$12) students, seniors, and under-15s. Mon–Tues and Thurs–Sat 10am–6pm, Wed 10am–8pm, Sun noon–6pm. Tube: Barbican, Moorgate.

This space is the Barbican Centre's main gallery, and it regularly exhibits exciting shows of historic and contemporary work, including photography and some low culture surprises. The highlight of last year was **The Art of Star Wars,** 250 original models, costumes, paintings, and drawings, on loan from the Lucasfilm archives in California. The Concourse Gallery on level "0" has been sexily rechristened **The Curve.** The exhibitions tend to have a multicultural bent and are open from 10am to 7:30pm on Monday, Wednesday, Friday, and Saturday, until 6pm on Tuesday and Thursday, and from noon to 7:30pm on Sunday. Another great free reason to come to the Barbican.

Ben Uri Art Society. The Manor House, 80 East End Rd., N3. ☎ **020/8349-5724.** www.ort.org/benuri. Free admission. Sun–Thurs 11am–4pm. Closed for Jewish festivals and bank holidays. Tube: Finchley Central.

Named after Bezalel Ben Uri, who crafted the tabernacle in the Old Testament, the society has played a central role in the cultural life of Anglo-Jewry. Last year, it finally moved into its new home at the Jewish Arts & Cultural Centre in Finchley, where it holds both temporary art exhibitions and displays its own collection. This is one of the most prominent in Europe, with more than 700 works by artists such as David Bomberg, Mark Gertler, Jacob Epstein, Leon Kossoff, Jacob Kramer, Frank Auerbach, and R. B. Kitaj.

Also at the center is **The Jewish Museum** (☎ **020/8349-1143;** www.jmus.org.uk), a sister to the one in Camden (see below), as well as a shop, cafe, and a lovely garden that grows one of every plant mentioned in the bible.

The British Library. 96 Euston Rd., NW1. ☎ **020/7412-7332.** www.bl.uk. Free admission. Galleries and public areas Mon and Wed–Fri 9:30am–6pm, Tues 9:30am–8pm, Sat 9:30am–5pm, Sun 11am–5pm. Tours of public areas: Mon, Wed, Fri 3pm, Sat 10am and 3pm;

tickets £4 ($6.40) adults, £3 ($4.80) concessions. Tours including a reading room: Tues 6:30pm, Sun 11:30am and 3pm; tickets £5 ($8), £4 ($6.40) concessions. Tube: St. Pancras.

This is a national research library and is responsible for Britain's printed archive. Legally, publishers must send in one copy of everything they produce. This new building in St. Pancras was one of the longest-running and problematic projects that London had ever seen, taking decades to come to completion. Designed by Colin St. John Wilson, critics first condemned it as an eyesore, and then changed their minds when it finally opened in 1998. There was a noisy blip last year when the library, which went £400 million over the construction budget, launched its *Adopt a Book* appeal to raise yet more funds for conservation. If you find a spare £1,000 in your holiday budget, you too could have your name attached to a rescued book in grateful thanks. The three exhibition spaces are well worth a visit. The **John Ritblat Gallery** displays the permanent collection of treasures brought from the library's old home, the British Museum: the *Magna Carta*, Tyndale's *New Testament*, Shakespeare's first folio, and more. Throughout, there are audio stations where visitors can listen to poets and writers reading from their works (James Joyce from *Finnegan's Wake,* for example) and other recordings. Truly amazing, though, are the interactive exhibits that allow you to flip through an illuminated manuscript, such as Leonardo's *Notebooks.* A second gallery is used for temporary exhibitions, and the third, **The Workshop of Words, Sounds & Images,** traces the history of book production from the earliest written documents to the current digital revolution—and there are regular free book-craft demonstrations. Also in the busy events diary are free Monday lunchtime talks, based on the collections, and Friday lunchtime author visits and discussions held in the excellent British Library shop.

✪ **Cabinet War Rooms.** Clive Steps, King Charles St., SW1. ☎ **020/7930-6961.** www.iwm.org.uk. Admission £5 ($8) adults, £3.60 ($5.80) students and seniors, free under-16s. Apr–Sept daily 9:30am–6pm (last admission 5:15pm); Oct–Mar daily 10–6pm (last admission 5:15pm). Closed Dec 24–26. Tube: Westminster, St. James's Park.

This warren of underground rooms served as Churchill's nerve center and the secret HQ of the British government during World War II. It is preserved exactly as it was back then: the Cabinet Room, where the PM, his ministers, and military men made their crucial decisions; the Map Room, where they plotted out the progress of the war and the status of the military campaigns; the Telephone Room, where so many calls were placed and received from FDR; even the PM's Emergency Bedroom. In 1995, the Heritage Lottery Fund bought what are known as the Churchill Papers for the nation. The core of the collection is held at the Churchill Archives Centre in Cambridge, but there are always pieces on display here—the exhibit changes every 3 months. It is eerie and oddly exciting imagining the great man and his staff living their secret subterranean life.

Design Museum. 28 Shad Thames, at Butler's Wharf, London, SE1. ☎ **020/7403-6933.** www.designmuseum.org. Admission £5.50 ($8.80) adults, £4.50 ($7.20) students and under-16s, £4 ($6.40) concessions, £15 ($24) family ticket. Daily 11:30am–6pm. Tube: Tower Hill (then walk over the bridge) or London Bridge (then walk along the Silver Jubilee Walk Way).

This beautiful riverside space is a temple to international design and how it affects our lives. The Permanent Collection explores the development of mass production through thematic displays. Find out why icons such as the Volkswagen Beetle or the anglepoise lamp look the way they do. The ever-changing Review Gallery showcases hot innovations, prototypes, and concepts that are shaping the future of architecture, fashion, technology, furniture, and engineering. The Temporary Gallery is just that, a space for visiting exhibitions—there's one on Brunel at the beginning of the year. The museum shop is great browsing territory, selling everything from designer socks to sleek alarm clocks. The museum's **Blue Print Café** is an unflashy Conran eaterie, delicious but sadly rather expensive, with a breathtaking view to Tower Bridge from its terrace. The Design Museum really is a feast for all the senses.

Dulwich Picture Gallery. Gallery Rd., SE21. ☎ **020/8693-5254.** www.dulwichpicturegallery.org.uk. Admission £4 ($6.40) adults; £3 ($4.80) seniors; free concessions, students, and under-16s; free on Fri. Tues–Fri 10am–5pm, Sat–Sun (bank holiday Mon) 11am–5pm. Closed Jan 1, Good Friday, and Dec 24–26. Tube: Brixton, then P4 bus. Train: North Dulwich, West Dulwich.

This is the oldest public picture gallery in Britain, dating back to 1817. Last year, the Queen cut the ribbon on a marvelous new wing, comprised of extra exhibition space, a lecture hall, cafe, and working studio. Designed by Rick Mather Architects, an airy glass cloister very successfully closes the union with Sir John Soane's beautiful original building. The Dulwich Picture Gallery was set up to house a superb collection of 16th- and 17th-century European Old Masters, put together at the behest of the King of Poland for his national museum. Forced to abdicate before paying his English art dealer for works by Canaletto, Gainsborough, Poussin, Rembrandt, Rubens, and Van Dyck, he never took possession. Temporary exhibitions three times a year bolster the Dulwich collection with important works on loan from all over the world—until April, *Murillo: Scenes of Childhood.* Free introductory tours take place every Saturday and Sunday at 3pm. And there is a whole new program of talks, concerts, evening events, and art-based children's workshops.

Fenton House. Hampstead Grove, NW3. ☎ **020/7435-3471.** Admission £4.20 ($6.70) adults, £2.10 ($3.35) children, £10.50 ($16.80) family ticket. Mar Sat–Sun 2–5pm; Apr–Oct Sat–Sun 11am–5pm, Wed–Fri 2–5pm. Closed Nov–Feb. Tube: Hampstead.

This lovely house, built in 1693, belonged to a (somewhat self-aggrandizing?) merchant named Fenton in the 18th century. In the 1950s, then-owner Lady Binning handed it over to the National Trust with her fine collection of Oriental and European porcelain, needlework, and furniture. Now it is also home to the famous Benton Fletcher collection of early keyboard instruments, all in working order, including a 1612 harpsichord that Handel probably played. You'll feel as if you've stepped back into a much more gracious time. You can imagine elegant ladies walking in the beautiful rose-scented gardens, while the gardener slaved away in the kitchen garden.

Florence Nightingale Museum. St. Thomas' Hospital, 2 Lambeth Palace Rd., SE1. ☎ **020/7620-0374.** www.florence-nightingale.co.uk. Admission £4.80 ($7.70) adults, £3.60 ($5.75) children and concessions. Mon–Fri 10am–5pm, Sat–Sun 11:30am–4:30pm, last admission 1hr. before closing. Closed Good Friday, Easter Sunday, Dec 25–Jan 2. Tube: Westminster, Waterloo.

Florence Nightingale founded her School of Nursing here in 1860. She dedicated her life to improving hospital standards, the quality of nursing, and public health, and the exhibits in this museum illustrate how she achieved her goals. The reconstruction of a ward in Scutari Hospital located in war-torn Crimea shows exactly the ghastly scene that fired her reforming zeal. Nightingale's copious notebooks are here, too, as well as a bracelet she wore woven from her mother's and sister's hair (there is more of her jewelry at the National Army Museum; see below). There are free guided tours every day, and entrance tickets are valid for a month.

Geffrye Museum. Kingsland Rd., E2. ☎ **020/7739-9893.** www.geffrye-museum.org.uk. Free admission. Tues–Sat 10am–5pm, Sun and holidays noon–5pm. Closed Jan 1, Good Friday, and Dec 24–26. Herb garden and period garden rooms open Apr–Oct. Tube: Liverpool St., then no. 149 or 242 bus.

This gem of a museum is devoted to the history of English domestic interiors of the urban middle classes from 1600 to 2000. Based in the old Ironmongers' almshouses

(1715), it's worth a visit for the architecture alone. Each era is recreated with a fusion of outside landscaping and interior design. Time-travel past Elizabethan oak, fine Georgian aesthetics, and ornate Victoriana, to the era of art deco, post-war utility, and the 1960s plastic explosion—all with gardens to match. Special exhibitions explore a wide variety of themes. In December, the rooms sparkle with festive decorations, as 400 years of Christmas tradition come to life. There's also a shop, restaurant, and design center, which is usually one of the venues for **Hidden Art,** an East London design fair and festival of open-studio days at the end of November (see "Crafts," in the shopping chapter).

Hayward Gallery. South Bank Centre, Belvedere Rd., SE1. ☎ **020/7960-4242.** www.hayward-gallery.org.uk. Admission varies but is usually around £6 ($9.60) adults, £4 ($6.40) concessions, free under-12s, £14 ($22.40) family ticket. Tues–Wed 10am–8pm, Thurs–Mon 10am–6pm. Tube: Waterloo, Embankment.

This highly regarded modern art gallery is wedged between the Royal National Theatre and the Royal Festival Hall, at the South Bank Centre. Built in 1968 (the era of "brutalist" architecture!), it has one of the largest and most versatile spaces in Britain. It puts on a very eclectic range of shows, which conform to one of four different formats and aims: single artists, historical themes and artistic movements, other cultures, and contemporary. The highlights of this year include *Know Thyself: Art & Science of the Human Body from Leonardo to Now,* and exhibitions of Goya and Brassai. There is always a wide program of events, scheduled around an exhibition: concerts, talks, children's workshops, video-recorded interviews with the artist, and so on. There are also free hour-long gallery talks from 6:30pm on Tuesdays, and artists are around for an informal chat about an exhibition on Wednesday from 4:30 to 7:30pm and Sunday from 1 to 4pm. Get here early on weekends, because the queues for big-name shows are staggering.

Imperial War Museum. Lambeth Rd., SE1. ☎ **020/7416-5000.** www.iwm.org.uk. Admission £5.50 ($8.80) adults, £4.50 ($7.20) concessions, free seniors and children; free daily after 4:30pm. Daily 10am–6pm. Closed Dec 24–26. Tube: Lambeth North, Waterloo.

The Imperial War Museum excels in commemorating and re-creating 20th-century conflicts, not only to honor the sacrifice of those who fought in them but also to make sure they never happen again. A clock in the basement grimly records the running total of the human cost of war—over 100 million people now. The new Holocaust Exhibition, opened last June, continues that tradition. Four years in the making, it uses heartrending historical material—a funeral cart from the Warsaw Ghetto, victims' diaries and photograph albums, part of a deportation railcar—to tell the story of the Nazi persecution of the Jews and other groups during World War II. Eighteen survivors have given their testimony, showing the effect of the Holocaust on families, while other exhibits explain the grand political context and the spread of anti-Semitism across Europe after the First World War. Life in the trenches during that earlier conflict is the subject of another exhibit, as is the Blitz of WWII, which dramatically re-creates an air raid with sound, scents, and other special effects. Other permanent collections include the dirty tricks and tales of espionage in **Secret War** and **Conflicts Since 1945,** which explores all modern wars from Korea to Bosnia.

It seems fitting that this building should be the home of such a museum. Built in 1815, it was part of the Royal Bethlehem Hospital (Bedlam), where "distracted" patients were kept chained to the walls, plunged into water, or whipped when they became violent. In the 17th and 18th centuries, the Bedlam insane asylum was one of the major London "sights," and visitors paid a hefty entrance fee.

Institute of Contemporary Arts (ICA). The Mall, SW1. ☎ **020/7930-3647,** or 020/7930-6393 for recorded info. www.ica.org.uk. Galleries Mon–Fri £1.50 ($2.40) adults, £1 ($1.60) seniors; Sat–Sun £2.50 ($4) adults, £2 ($3.20) seniors; free with cinema or show ticket. Daily noon–7:30pm. Tube: Piccadilly Circus, Charing Cross.

The publicly assisted ICA is a major forum for the avant-garde arts. It runs two galleries, as well as a theater, cinema, media center, cafe, bar, bookshop, and lecture program. Since it opened in 1948, many artists have held their first solo shows at the ICA. Among the more recent are Damien Hirst, Helen Chadwick, Gary Hume, and Steve McQueen. The admission price is to cover the institute's day membership. If you are attending a movie or performance here, you can take in the galleries at no extra cost.

Jewel Tower. Abingdon St., Westminster, SW1. ☎ **020/7222-2219.** www.english-heritage.org.uk. Admission £1.50 ($2.40) adults, £1.10 ($1.75) seniors, 80p ($1.30) under-16s. Apr–Sept daily 10am–6pm; Oct daily 10am–5pm; Nov–Mar daily 10am–4pm. Closed Dec 24–26. Tube: Westminster.

Opposite the Houses of Parliament, this is one of only two surviving buildings from the medieval Palace of Westminster. It was built around 1365 so that Edward III had somewhere to stash his treasures. The exhibition explains how Parliament works, and a touch-screen computer runs a virtual-reality tour of both houses.

Jewish Museum. 129 Albert St., Camden Town, NW1. ☎ **020/7284-1997.** www.jewmusm.ort.org. Admission £3 ($4.80) adults, £1.50 ($2.40) children, £7.50 ($12) family ticket. Sun–Thurs 10am–4pm. Closed Jewish and public holidays. Tube: Camden Town.

This museum opens a window into the history and religious life of the Jewish community. The History Gallery has medieval notched, wooden tax receipts and loving cups presented to the lord mayors of London by the Spanish and Portuguese Synagogue. The exceptional Ceremonial Art Gallery houses ritual objects of great beauty like a 16th-century Italian synagogue ark, Nathan Meyer Rothschild's *Book of Esther,* and silver Torah bells crafted in London. This year, from February to May, the museum is showcasing the work of artist Simeon Solomon. From June to November, *By the Rivers of Babylon* will explore the culture of the Jews of Iraq.

The sister **Jewish Museum,** The Manor House, 80 East End Rd., N3 (☎ **020/8349-1143**) traces the history of immigration and settlement in London, with displays like the reconstructions of East End tailoring and furniture workshops. Mirroring its work on Holocaust education, a moving exhibition traces the life of one London-born survivor, Leon Greenman. It is open 10:30am to 5pm Monday to Thursday and closes at 4:30pm on Sunday. Admission is £2 ($3.20) for adults, £1 ($1.60) concessions, and free for children.

Kenwood House & Iveagh Bequest. Hampstead Lane, NW3. ☎ **020/8348-1286.** www.english-heritage.org.uk. Free admission. Apr–Sept daily 10am–6pm; Oct–Mar daily 10am–4pm. Tube: Archway, Golders Green, Hampstead, and Highgate, then no. 210 bus from outside all stations.

English Heritage, which looks after Kenwood for the nation, has just given the palatial house a makeover—and what a makeover. Gone are the chilly, rather institutional, blues and grays, replaced by deep, harem-like colors that flout the core conservators' code—thou shalt remain true to the original design of a historic building at all times—which English Heritage usually polices relentlessly. But then few historic buildings can boast such an astounding art collection, left to the nation, with the house, by Lord Iveagh in 1927. It includes the **Rembrandt** self-portrait, voted Britain's favorite picture, and **Vermeer's** *The Guitar Player,* and many others, for which the bold new interiors are a perfect foil. This wedding-white house, remodeled by

Robert Adam in the late 18th century, is high on Hampstead Heath, overlooking the lake, and famous for its summer open-air concerts (see chapter 8).

London Canal Museum. 12–13 New Wharf Rd., King's Cross, N1. ☎ **020/7713-0836.** www.canalmuseum.org.uk. Admission £2.50 ($4) adults, £1.25 ($2) seniors and students. Tues–Sun 10am–4:30pm. Closed Dec 24–26. Tube: King's Cross.

The museum is in a warehouse on the Regent Canal, where famous ice-cream maker Carlo Gatti used to store the ice blocks shipped in from Norway in the mid-19th century. You can peer down into one of the two huge ice wells, partly excavated underneath the building. The museum tells the story of Gatti and others like him who made their living along and on these man-made waterways. Until April, there will be an exhibition on architect John Nash and his patron the Prince Regent, who gave his name to this canal. Another, running from July to October, will trace the history of the Grand Junction Canal. Tickets to the monthly lecture cost the same as admission to the museum, and there are sometimes theater performances as well.

London Transport Museum. The Piazza, Covent Garden, WC2. ☎ **020/7565-7299** for recorded info, or 020/7879-6344. www.ltmuseum.co.uk. Admission £5.50 ($8.80) adults, £2.95 ($4.70) concessions and under-16s, £13.95 ($22.30) family ticket. Sat–Thurs 10am–6pm, Fri 11am–6pm (last admission 45 min. before closing). Closed Dec 24–26. Tube: Covent Garden, Charing Cross.

This fantastic museum, in the old Covent Garden flower market, traces the 200-year history of public transport in London, from the days when cabs were horse-drawn and the pollution squelchy. Like a Noah's Ark for machinery, it has examples of just about everything, from omnibuses to trams to Tube trains, as well as paintings, posters, working models and interactive exhibits. Kids love it. Actors bring the past to life, playing characters like a 1906 tunnel miner and a World War II clippie (bus conductor to you). There's a busy program of workshops, usually free with admission, during half-terms and school holidays, as well as gallery talks at 6:30pm on a Wednesday (£6/$9.60). The museum even organizes guided London tours, with a transport bent of course, on the river, Tube, or bus (£8/$12.80). The shop here is terrific and known for models, posters, and other original gifts.

The London Transport Museum can only display about 400 of the 370,000 items in its massive collection, so it has taken over a defunct Tube shed in West London for storage and as a locale to work on conservation. Twice a month, it opens to the public. Some Fridays there are guided tours, which include access to parts of **The Depot** not normally open to visitors. Tickets cost £9.50 ($15.20), and you must book ahead. On an open day, from 11am to 5pm one Sunday, you can explore the main shed and its vehicles, machinery, signs, and shelters, as well as enjoy the program of talks, stalls, and themed displays. Same-day tickets can be purchased at a cost of £6.95 ($11.10). Call for dates (then take the Tube to Acton Town).

Museum of Garden History. St. Mary-at-Lambeth, Lambeth Palace Rd., SE1. ☎ **020/7401-8865.** www.museumgardenhistory.org.uk. Free admission. Sun–Fri 10:30am–5pm. Closed mid-Dec to late Feb. Tube: Lambeth North.

This museum is devoted to *the* quintessential British passion and the gardeners, botanists, and collectors who've nurtured it. It holds a marvelous collection of historic tools and artifacts, too. Follow the lives of great plant gatherers like the royal gardeners to Charles I and II, John Tradescant and his son (also John), who are buried here, and Captain Bligh of mutiny fame, as well as stories about such beloved English gardeners as Gertrude Jekyll. The museum's own patch is planted in a 17th-century Knot Garden design and contains many rare plants introduced into the country by the Tradescants.

Those Must Be *Some* Petunias . . .

One in four British women prefer spending time in the garden to having sex, or so said a survey in the very hip *New Eden* magazine, which took the nation's pulse for its 1999 launch.

Another space inspired by historical Persian design, the Garden of the Ark, is open on Wednesdays from April to October. The museum is south of the Thames, in a historic church and churchyard, and serves morning coffee and lunchtime snacks.

✪ **Museum of London.** 150 London Wall, EC2. ☎ **020/7600-3699.** www.museumoflondon.org.uk. Admission £5 ($8) adults, £3 ($4.80) seniors, free children; free from 4:30pm. Tickets valid 1yr. Mon–Sat 10am–5:50pm, Sun noon–5:50pm. Tube: St. Paul's, Moorgate, Barbican.

For anyone interested in London's history, this is the place to begin. In fact, you may not have to go anywhere else: Not only is this the biggest and most comprehensive city museum anywhere in the world, but it is genuinely engaging and creative. Two floors of exhibits trace London's development from Roman times to the 1990s, using models, artifacts, reconstructions, and audio-visual presentations. Among the highlights are a reconstruction of a Roman interior and a Roman complex; a bedroom in a merchant's house from the Stuart period; the lord mayor's coach; a brilliant, audio-visual, dioramic presentation on the Great Fire with a voiceover reading diarist Samuel Pepys' account; a Victorian barber's shop; and the original elevators from Selfridges department store. The museum's archaeologists get called in at the start of most big building projects in London. The skeletons of 160 medieval paupers and prostitutes, uncovered in Southwark during work on the Jubilee Line, all ended up at the museum. In 1999, the team discovered the body of a wealthy young Roman woman in a sarcophagus at Spitalfields. Finds like these generally go on display once the study and conservation process is completed. Every year, there are three big temporary exhibitions often looking at the social culture of modern city life. Many of the resident experts take part in the talks, museum tours, and workshops program (free to £4/$6.40), as well as leading London walks and outside visits (£3 to £10/$4.80 to $16).

National Army Museum. Royal Hospital Rd., Chelsea, SW3. ☎ **020/7730-0717.** www.national-army-museum.ac.uk. Free admission. Daily 10am–5:30pm. Closed Jan 1, Good Friday, early May, Dec 24–26, public holiday. Tube: Sloane Sq.

This is the British Army's own museum and tells the soldier's story, starting from 1415. It is crammed with life-size models, medals (including 30 original Victoria Crosses), paintings of battle scenes by Gainsborough and Reynolds, weapons, and uniforms. Among the highlights are a 420-square-foot model of the Battle of Waterloo, with its 70,000 model soldiers; the skeleton of Napoleon's horse, Marengo; and the saw that was used to amputate the leg of Lieutenant-General, the Earl of Uxbridge during the battle. Even more offbeat is the now-stuffed cat brought back from Sebastopol by a sentimental officer during the Crimean War. Each exhibit aims to let you inside the soldiers' everyday lives—Henry V's archers shivering at Agincourt, Wellington's troops standing shoulder to shoulder at Waterloo, and British Tommies scrambling over the top at the Somme. Visitors can actually experience what it was like to live and work in a World War I trench, as well as try on an excruciatingly uncomfortable civil war helmet, or test the frightening weight of a cannonball. One gallery focuses on the contribution women have made to the army and armed conflict. A new Modern Army Gallery opens this year, focusing on today's high-tech military force.

Lunchtime talks take place most Thursdays at 1pm, and the theme changes every month.

National Portrait Gallery. St. Martin's Place, WC2. ☎ **020/7306-0055.** www.npg.org.uk. Free admission. Mon–Fri 10am–9pm, Sat–Sun 10am–6pm. Closed Jan 1, Good Friday, May 1, Dec 24–26. Tube: Leicester Sq., Charing Cross.

The National Portrait Gallery has a rather curious claim to fame: The escalator rising out of the entrance hall to the refurbished Tudor galleries is one of the largest in London. The Queen opened the marvelous new Ondaatje Wing, now the heart of the NPG, last May. It is built in a courtyard pinched from the neighboring National Gallery in exchange for a less convenient wing. The reshuffle and bright white new build has created a much more logical flow through the collection. What Madame Tussaud's does with wax models, this gallery does with 10,000 paintings and 250,000 photographs—chart the history of the nation through its famous faces—and it's an equally strong barometer of who's in and who's out. Last year, the curators consigned Helmut Newton's portrait of Margaret Thatcher, among others, to the historical section, to make room for such right-now icons as David Beckham (Posh Spice's footballer husband), *Harry Potter* author J. K. Rowling, and Ralph Fiennes. The permanent collection is displayed chronologically, and you'll find Henry VII, Henry VIII, and Sir Thomas More, all painted by Holbein, the only extant portrait of Shakespeare, and T.S. Eliot by Sir Jacob Epstein. There are endearing amateur daubs, too, including one of Jane Austen by her sister. Touch-screen terminals in the IT Gallery allow visitors to surf the entire collection.

Temporary exhibitions take on big themes and single artists. There are three on display from February to May: *Return to Life, A New Look at the Portrait Bust*; the first museum retrospective for American photographer Rollie McKenna; and the first retrospective in a British museum for another photographer, Horst. *The Beautiful and the Damned,* June to October, looks at the development of portrait photography in the 19th century. *Painted Ladies,* starting in October, focuses on the court of Charles II.

The National Portrait Gallery puts on lots of lunchtime and weekend events, many of which will now take place in the new lecture theater. In addition to the cafe, there is the stunning **Portrait Restaurant & Bar** (☎ **020/7312-2490;** see chapter 5), looking out across the rooftops from under the Ondaatje Wing's glass roof.

Percival David Foundation of Chinese Art. 53 Gordon Sq., WC1. ☎ **020/7387-3909.** Free admission. Mon–Fri 10:30am–5pm. Closed bank holidays. Tube: Russell Sq., Euston, Euston Sq., Goodge St.

Sir Percival David presented this collection of Chinese ceramics, the finest outside China itself, and a library of books on art and culture to the University of London in 1950. There are over 1,700 objects, dating mainly from the 10th to 18th centuries. Not only are they exquisitely beautiful, but some bear inscriptions ordered by emperors such as Qianlong (1736–95). The stoneware from the Song (960–1279) and Yuan (1279–1368) dynasties are exceptional and include examples of very rare Ru and Guan wares. You'll certainly recognize the blue-and-white porcelains.

The Planetarium. See Madame Tussauds & The Planetarium in "London's Top Attractions," above.

Notice of Attractions Closings

Sadly, the **Museum of the Moving Image,** at the South Bank Centre, is closed for redevelopment, as is the **Wembley** national sports stadium.

Rose Theatre Exhibition. 56 Park St., SE1. ☎ **020/7593-0026.** Admission £3 ($4.80) adults, £2.50 ($4) seniors and students, £2 ($3.20) children, £8 ($12.80) family ticket. Daily 10am–5pm. Tube: London Bridge.

In 1989, this theater saw the light of day for the first time in centuries during excavations for the building of an office block. The heritage and performing arts crowd lobbied hard and, in the end successfully, for its preservation (under a pool of water) and opening to the public. Built in 1587, it was the first-ever theater on Bankside, the medieval equivalent of the West End. While a video, narrated by actor Sir Ian McKellen, tells the dramatic story of the Rose, amazing lights come on under the water to illuminate the remains.

Royal Academy of Arts. Burlington House, Piccadilly, W1. ☎ **020/7300-8000.** www.royalacademy.org.uk. Admission varies, depending on the exhibition. Sat–Thurs 10am–6pm, Fri 10am–8:30pm. Closed Dec 25, Good Friday. Tube: Piccadilly Circus, Green Park.

The illustrious Sir Joshua Reynolds and Thomas Gainsborough were founding members of The Royal Academy. When it opened in 1768, this was the nation's first art school and the first institution to hold an annual art exhibition. In June to July, it's one of the world's biggest open shows of contemporary painting, sculpture, and drawing, and most of the pieces are for sale. The hanging panel's choices always excite frenzied media debate—as the main exhibition program does sometimes. Until April, the galleries are full of Caravaggio, Anibale Carracci, and Rubens in *The Birth of Baroque in Rome.* In the Sackler Wing, from March through June, is a visiting show of drawings for *The Divine Comedy* by Botticelli and Dante. The year-round stalwart is the Friends Room, which displays the recent work (also often for sale) of Royal Academicians. Or, you can come in January to see, and maybe invest in, pieces by hot young artists at the end of 3 postgraduate years at the Royal Academy schools.

Royal Hospital Chelsea. Royal Hospital Rd., SW3. ☎ **020/7730-5282.** Free admission. Mon–Sat 10am–noon, 2–4pm, Sun 2–4pm (not Oct–Mar). Tube: Sloane Sq.

Charles II founded this dignified institution in 1682, inspired by the Hôtel des Invalides in Paris, as a home for veteran soldiers. Hence the statue of the king, by Grinling Gibbons, in the courtyard. Sir Christopher Wren completed the series of buildings in 1692, and there's been little change to his design, except for minor work done by Robert Adam in the 18th century and the addition of Sir John Soane's stables in 1814. In the main block, you can look around the museum, chapel, and hall, where the Duke of Wellington lay in state for a week in 1852. So many people thronged to see him that two were crushed to death. The east and west wings are dormitories for around 400 ex-servicemen pensioners, dressed in blue uniforms for everyday, red ones on ceremonial occasions. The lovely grounds play host to the annual Chelsea Flower Show (see page 24).

Saatchi Gallery. 98a Boundary Rd., NW8. ☎ **020/7624-8299.** Admission £4 ($6.40), £2 ($3.20) seniors, under-12s free. Thurs–Sun noon–6pm. Tube: St. John's Wood, Swiss Cottage.

Charles Saatchi has amassed one of the largest independent collections of contemporary British and international art in the world. In December 1998, he sold off a small fraction to fund bursaries for new artists. Around 130 works, including some of Damien Hirst's pickled cow, were up for grabs amid a violent art-world protest that he would completely distort the market. Saatchi is famous for launching new homegrown artists and for creating brand names, as befits an ex-adman—first the Young British Artists, then Neurotic Realism. The Young Americans shows do the same for American artists. The gallery has rotating displays from Saatchi's vast holdings. Enter through the unmarked metal gateway of what was once, appropriately, a paint warehouse.

Serpentine Gallery. Kensington Gardens (near Albert Memorial), W2. ☎ **020/7402-6075.** www.serpentinegallery.org. Free admission. Daily 10am–6pm. Tube: Lancaster Gate, South Kensington.

This delightful gallery opened 30 years ago in a 1934 tea pavilion in Kensington Gardens—I recommend combining a visit here with a lazy picnic in the park. Now more than 400,000 people a year come to see the stimulating exhibitions of modern and contemporary art, arranged by theme or single artist. On Saturday at 3pm, artists and critics usually provide visitors with an informal introduction to the work on display.

Sherlock Holmes Museum. 221b Baker St., NW1. ☎ **020/7935-8866.** www.sherlock-holmes.co.uk. Admission £6 ($9.60) adults, £3.50 ($5.60) under-17s. Daily 9:30am–6pm. Tube: Baker St.

Our hero, the quintessential English detective "resided" at this literary address from 1881 to 1904. It's not really a museum—nothing about Sir Arthur Conan Doyle, for instance—but a re-creation of the Victorian chambers as they might have been if they had ever been. In the living room, you can pick up Sherlock Holmes's pipe, don a deerstalker, and take a photograph of yourself horsing around. Other "exhibits" include Dr. Mortimer's stick from *The Hound of the Baskervilles* and numerous letters written to Holmes asking him to solve individual mysteries and his "replies." There's now an exhibition area on the top floor, too, with more scenes from the tales of you know who. But it's not worth the ticket unless you're a real Holmes fan.

✪ **Sir John Soane's Museum.** 13 Lincoln's Inn Fields, WC2. ☎ **020/7405-2107.** www.soane.org. Free admission (£1 donation requested). Tues–Sat 10am–5pm; first Tues of each month also 6–9pm. Tube: Holborn.

Collector and architect Sir John Soane (1753–1837) was the son of a bricklayer who apprenticed himself to George Dance the Younger and Henry Holland before opening an architectural practice of his own. He married into great wealth and began collecting the objects displayed in this wonderful house, which he both designed and lived in. It is enchanting, stuffed full of every kind of amazing this and that—architectural fragments, casts, bronzes, sculpture, and cork models. Get some tips from Soane's use of colored glass and mirrors to create reflections of architectural details and other dramatic effects. The collection of paintings includes works by Turner, three Canalettos, and two series of paintings by Hogarth, *An Election* and *The Rake's Progress.* Other works, including a wonderful group of Piranesi drawings, are ingeniously hung behind special movable panels in the Picture Room. Of special note is the sarcophagus of Seti I (Pharaoh 1303–1290 B.C.). Soane bought it for £2,000, a price so steep that it stopped the British Museum in its tracks. A gallery opened in April 1995 displays changing exhibitions of architectural drawings from Soane's collection of over 30,000, which includes works by Dance, Sir Christopher Wren, Sir William Chambers, and Robert and James Adam. It's particularly entrancing when it's candlelit during the evening opening time.

Spencer House. 27 St. James's Place, SW1. ☎ **020/7499-8620.** www.spencerhouse.co.uk. Admission only on timed tour ticket: £6 ($9.60) adults, £5 ($8) seniors and children 10–16. Sun 10:30am–5:30pm (closed Jan and Aug). Tube: Green Park. No under-10s.

John, the first Earl Spencer, who was an ancestor of Princess Diana, married his sweetheart Georgiana Poyntz secretly at Althorp and soon set about building the splendid

Looking for the Globe?

For info on tours and the exhibition at **Shakespeare's Globe Theatre,** see chapter 8.

Backstage Tours

London is a wonderland for lovers of the performing arts, budding thespians, and stalwarts of the local am-dram. There are several stages where you can step behind the footlights to hear tall theatrical tales and see exactly what goes into creating the spectacular performances. Backstage tours cost from £3.50 to £6 ($5.60 to $9.60), whether at the publicly funded **Royal National Theatre** (see chapter 8), **Barbican** (see section 6 of this chapter), and **Royal Opera House** (see chapter 8), or at commercial West End theaters. These three all put on blockbuster productions: the **London Palladium,** Argyll St., W1 (☎ **020/7494-5091;** Tube: Oxford Circus), the **Theatre Royal Drury Lane,** Catherine St., WC2 (☎ **020/7494-5456;** Tube: Covent Garden), the **New London Theatre,** Drury Lane, WC2 (☎ **020/7405-1568;** Tube: Holborn). This is fabulous low-budget fun, so book as far ahead as possible.

Other must-visits include the **Rose Theatre** (see section 6 of this chapter) and the exhibition and tour at **Shakespeare's Globe Theatre,** both of which whiz you back to the 17th century. The **BBC Experience** (see section 5 of this chapter) reveals the hi-tech secrets of making radio and TV shows.

Spencer House (1756–66) in St. James. Today, it is the only 18th-century private palace in London still intact. Quite an achievement since it stopped being a home in 1927 and was then rented out to the Ladies' Army and Navy Club, Christie's, and British Oxygen Gases Ltd. The painstaking restoration began in 1987, and Spencer House now glows opulently, returned to its original splendor. The Spencers were a very wealthy couple; the diamond buckles on his honeymoon shoes alone were valued at £3,000. The eight staterooms were some of the first neoclassical interiors created in London by John Vardy and James Stuart. The Palm Room is so called because of the series of gilded palm trees. The Painted Room contains superb gold furniture set against an elegant mural celebrating the Triumph of Love. There is no unsupervised wandering; you have to take the tour. There's no pre-booking so come early to avoid a long wait.

✪ **Theatre Museum.** Russell St., WC2. ☎ **020/7943-4777.** www.vam.ac.uk. Admission £4.50 ($7.20) adults; £2.50 ($4) concessions, seniors, and under-16s. Tues–Sun 11am–6pm. Daily guided tours at 11am, 2, and 4pm; makeup demonstrations at 11:30am, 1, 2:30, 3:30, and 4:30pm; costume workshops at 12:30 and 3pm. Closed all bank holidays. Tube: Covent Garden, Charing Cross.

This offshoot of the Victoria & Albert Museum holds the national collections of everything relating to the performing arts—theater, ballet, opera, music hall, pantomime, puppetry, circus, and rock 'n' pop. The costume cupboard is fabulously darling and so are the paintings, photographs, and memorabilia. Great theater transports the audience into a parallel world, and so does a great museum, which this is. You can smell the greasepaint, hear the roar of the crowd, as it tells the story of the development of the British stage, from Shakespeare to the present day, with stage models, posters, props, audio-visual displays, and souvenirs of such legendary British thespians as Garrick, Kean, and Irving. See how makeup artists create special effects at daily demonstrations, and try on costumes from the Royal Shakespeare Company and the Royal National Theatre. The museum also has a big Diaghilev archive, which is the basis of a display about the Ballet Russe and its revolutionary influence on dance in the West, thanks to choreographer Michael Fokine and costume and set designer Leon Bakst.

Vinopolis, City of Wine. 1 Bank End, SE1. ☎ **020/7940-8300.** www.vinopolis.co.uk. Admission £11.50 ($18.40) adults, £4.50–£10.50 ($7.20–$16.80) concessions. £1 ($1.60) discount for advance booking. Daily 10am–5pm. Tube: London Bridge.

This newish attraction is even more expensive than Madame Tussaud's and, for my money, isn't really worth it. The basic premise is flawed—wine and wine-making is hard enough to illustrate without trying to hold visitors' interest throughout such an enormous space. The soaring vaulted rooms are beautiful, but the museum relies too much on wine-bottle pyramids and serried ranks of fuzzy over-blown-up photos of vineyards. And the personal audio guides are infuriating. Each exhibit has a three-digit code to punch in to hear the information, which is the only reason why you'll find yourself spending hours here. To be fair, there is some light relief. You get three wine tastings at tables set up in the relevant regional rooms, with your admission ticket. Even so, I'd counsel you not to bother. Instead, come and refuel at the **Cantina Vinopolis** between visits to the other, seriously excellent attractions at Bankside (see below).

Wallace Collection. Hertford House, Manchester Sq., W1. ☎ **020/7563-9500.** www.the-wallace-collection.org.uk. Free admission. Mon–Sat 10am–5pm, Sun noon–5pm. Tube: Bond St.

According to the terms of Lady Wallace's bequest, this collection must remain "unmixed with other objects of art." Sir Richard Wallace was the illegitimate heir of the Marquis of Hertford, and the fifth generation to add to the acquisitions of exquisite furniture, armour, paintings, and decorative arts in the family's London home. Nothing can be loaned or added to the perfect time capsule of 19th-century Anglo-French taste. There's so much to delight the eye here—Sèvres porcelain, Limoges enamels, 17th-century Dutch paintings, 18th-century French (Watteau, Fragonard, and Boucher) and British art, and Italian majolica. To celebrate its centenary as a national museum, architect Rick Mather (who also created the new wing at the Dulwich Picture Gallery) has redesigned the neglected basement into a study center for lectures, workshops, and object-handling sessions. Four new galleries hold temporary shows, explain the craft of conservation and house pieces previously in store. But the really flashy bit is the sculpture garden and restaurant (see chapter 5) under a glass roof covering the internal courtyard. For free tours of the restored spaces and the new, come at 1pm any weekday, or 11:30am on Wednesday and Saturday, 3pm on Sunday.

Young, British & Hung in East London

The neighborhood around Hoxton Square has become a vibrant creative community, hotching with young British artists and hot new galleries. Entrepreneur Jay Jopling, who has a fine line in creating bankable stars, from Damien Hirst to Gary Hume and the Chapman brothers, has turned an old warehouse into a new gallery, **White Cube^2,** 48 Hoxton Sq., N1 (☎ **020/7930-5373;** www.whitecube.com). It is open Tuesday to Saturday 10am to 6pm. My other recommendation is also new, on two enormous floors of an industrial building: **Victoria Miro,** 16–18 Wharf Rd., N1 (☎ **020/7734-5082**), is also open Tuesday to Saturday 10am to 6pm. Turner prizewinner Chris Ofili, of elephant dung fame, is one of her artists. To visit both of these, take the Tube to Old Street.

Whitechapel Art Gallery. Whitechapel High St., E1. ☎ **020/7522-7888.** www.whitechapel.org. Free admission. Tues and Thurs–Sun 11am–5pm, Wed 11am–8pm. Closed holidays. Tube: Aldgate East.

This is one of London's leading galleries and *the* place to see up-and-coming British contemporary artists. It exhibited Picasso's haunting *Guernica* in 1939 and has been on the cutting edge ever since, having introduced such high-profile names as Tony Bevan, Lucian Freud, and Cathy de Monchaux to the public. This is its centenary year, so expect a series of special events and exhibitions. You'll have to come back in 2001 for the biannual Whitechapel Open, a huge show of jury-selected works by artists working in the East London creative colony.

7 Maritime & Waterfront Sights

The Thames is once more becoming the hub of London life, as you'll see from the listings below, which travel from east to west through the city. For a handy tourist guide, surf **www.riverthames.co.uk**.

WOOLWICH

Thames Barrier. Unity Way, Woolwich, SE18. ☎ **020/8305-4188.** Admission £3.40 ($5.45) adults, £2 ($3.20) seniors or children 5–17. Call for opening times. Tube: North Greenwich. River launches: Westminster, Charing Cross, Tower, and Greenwich piers.

This giant feat of engineering, which looks like a row of mini–Sydney Opera Houses, opened in 1984 to protect London from flooding. It consists of four giant gates, each weighing 3,000 tons and as high as a 5-story building, and six smaller ones. When closed, they seal the upper river off from the sea. It's reckoned that the three paint jobs it will need over the next century will cost £75 million. The Visitor Centre on the south bank shows how the thing works.

GREENWICH

Note that the **Greenwich Passport Ticket** gets you reduced price combined entry to the Cutty Sark, National Maritime Museum, and the Royal Observatory Greenwich. Available at all three, it costs £12 ($19.20) for adults and £9.60 ($15.35) for concessions.

Cutty Sark. King William Walk, Greenwich, SE10. ☎ **020/8858-3445.** www.cuttysark.org.uk. Admission £3.50 ($5.60) adults, £2.50 ($4) children. Daily 10am–5pm. Closed Dec 24–26. Docklands Light Railway: Cutty Sark for Maritime Greenwich. Central London Fast Ferry: Greenwich Pier.

This 19th-century sailing clipper is one of the most famous to have survived its era. Built in Dumbarton, it launched in 1869, too late to succeed in the tea trade, which had been taken over by steamers after the opening of the Suez Canal. Instead it carried Australian wool, circling the globe round the Cape of Good Hope on the outward journey and Cape Horn on its return. Designed for speed, the Cutty Sark could cover almost 400 sea miles a day. It was restored in 1922 and has been in dry dock since 1954. On board, you'll see how tough life was for the Victorian crew and officers. The Long John Silver Collection of merchant ship figureheads is the biggest in the country, and there are some fine maritime paintings and prints. Go below deck for hands-on activities.

✪ **National Maritime Museum, The Royal Observatory Greenwich, and The Queen's House.** Romney Rd., Greenwich, SE10. ☎ **020/8858-4422** or 020/8312-6608. www.nmm.ac.uk. Admission: Museum £7.50 ($12) adults, £6 ($9.60) concessions; Royal Observatory £6 ($9.60) adults, £4.80 ($7.70) seniors; combined entry £10.50 ($16.80) adults, £8.40 ($13.45) concessions; free under-16s. Daily 10am–5pm. Closed Dec 24–26. Rail:

Charing Cross to Maze Hill. Docklands Light Railway: Cutty Sark, Greenwich. Central London Fast Ferry: Greenwich Pier.

Even before the refurbishment and the building of 12 new galleries (£21 million spent in all), this Greenwich landmark was one of the largest maritime museums in the world. The ceremonial opening in 1937 was the first duty of the new King George VI after the abdication crisis. The collection contains 2,500 ship models, 4,000 paintings, 50,000 charts, and 750,000 ship plans, plus hundreds of scientific and navigational instruments. It even has the bullet-pierced coat Nelson was wearing when he died. Until September, there is a heroic exhibition called *South: The Race to the Pole*. The expansion has allowed the museum to use very modern interactive technology to look at very modern maritime issues and the effect of the past on today: how pollution threatens the sea, new ways of exploring its ultimate depths, pleasure-cruising, and much, much more. On Saturdays, a workshop in the All Hands gallery explores seafarers' lives through the ages. It runs from 2 to 4pm, except on the first Saturday of the month when there's a guest presenter and a longer session, 12:30 to 4:30pm. Also look out for the family activity trails.

The Royal Observatory Greenwich hit the super-dizzy heights of stardom on millennium eve, as all time is measured from the Prime Meridian Line here. High on a hill with magnificent views across the Thames, the Observatory was founded in 1675 by Charles II as part of his quest to determine longitude at sea. Clockmaker John Harrison eventually solved the problem in 1763, and received £20,000 for his pains. You too can stand astride the meridian (with a foot in each hemisphere) and set your watch precisely by the falling time-ball, which is how shipmasters set their chronometers from 1833 on. The observatory has a collection of historic timekeepers and astronomical instruments, and Britain's largest refracting telescope. The telescope dome is open on Monday mornings, with actual stargazing allowed 1 evening a month. Planetarium shows happen every weekday afternoon and on Saturdays from Easter to the end of August: £2 ($3.20) for adults, £1.50 ($2.40) for kids.

The innovative Inigo Jones designed **The Queen's House** (1616) for Anne of Denmark, wife of James I. She died before it was completed, so Charles I in turn gave it to his queen, Henrietta Maria. The house's cantilevered tulip staircase was the first of its kind. The royal apartments give a wry insight into the niceties of court etiquette: Only visitors of the highest rank made it through the full sequence of seven rooms to the royal bedchamber. The millennium exhibition here worked so well that the house is likely to remain a display space. But that, and the charging policy, had yet to be decided as we went to press.

Royal Naval College. King William Walk, off Romney Rd., Greenwich, SE10. ☎ **0800/389-3341** or 020/8269-4747. www.greenwichfoundation.org.uk. Admission £3 ($4.80) adults, £2 ($3.20) concessions, free under-16s; free after 3:30pm and Sun. Daily 10am–4:30pm. Closed Good Friday and Dec 24–26. Rail: Charing Cross to Maze Hill. Docklands Light Railway: Cutty Sark, Greenwich. Central London Fast Ferry: Greenwich Pier.

Sir Christopher Wren designed this complex as a naval hospital in 1696. Its four blocks, named after King Charles, Queen Anne, King William, and Queen Mary, are split into two sections so as not to block the view of the river from The Queen's House. Greenwich Palace stood on the site before that, from 1422 to 1640. If you're in the neighborhood, do stop in here to see Thornhill's magnificent Painted Hall where Nelson lay in state in 1805. You can also visit the Georgian chapel of St. Peter and St. Paul, or come at 11am on Sunday for the choral Eucharist. The Navy moved out of the college in 1998, and it is now home to departments of the University of Greenwich and other public organizations.

TOWER BRIDGE

The iconic **Tower Bridge** is a must-visit, of course, as is the **Tower of London** (see section 2 in this chapter for a review of both) on the north bank. Facing it across the river is the new HQ for the new Greater London Authority, designed by Norman Foster. Wander down and see how work is progressing on the giant glass display case, which is due to complete in 2002.

HMS Belfast. Morgan's Lane, Tooley St., SE1. ☎ **020/7940-6300.** Admission £5 ($8) adults, £3.80 ($6.10) seniors, free under-16s. Mar–Oct daily 10am–6pm; Nov–Feb daily 10am–5pm. Closed Dec 24–26. Tube: London Bridge, Tower Hill. Central London Fast Ferry: London Bridge City.

This 11,500-ton, 32-gun battle cruiser played a vital role in World War II—during the Normandy landings, the sinking of the *Scharnhorst* in the Battle of the North Cape, and on the terrible Arctic convoy route to North Russia. HMS *Belfast* has nine decks to explore, from the Bridge to the boiler and engine rooms. Along the way visitors can operate anti-aircraft guns and imagine what life was like for the sailors in the Mess decks. Cramped but pretty boozy is the answer, by all accounts: from 1950 to 1952, when the ship served in the Far East, the crew consumed 56,000 pints of Navy rum, along with 134 tons of meat and 625 tons of potatoes. HMS *Belfast* is a much-loved landmark. When it left the Thames in 1999 for a checkup at Portsmouth (the first time in 20 years), thousands of Londoners came to watch. There are special kids' events during school holidays.

BANKSIDE

Greenwich may have been the millennial hotspot, but nothing can beat Bankside for high-octane buzz. This once-scruffy neighborhood has got it all, from the very ancient to the super-modern, and enough of it to keep you buzzing for days. Check out **Tate Modern** (see section 2 of this chapter), **Shakespeare's Globe Theatre** (see chapter 8), **Southwark Cathedral** (see section 3 of this chapter), **Vinopolis** (see above), and, nearby, **Borough Market** (see "Markets," in chapter 7) and the ancient **The George** (see "Pubs," in chapter 8).

Opened last May, the **Millennium Bridge** is the first new foot-crossing on the Thames since the 19th century and a photo opportunity to rival the best in the capital. Sir Norman Foster designed the £14-million streak of steel and light. From Bankside, it looks like a space-age causeway leading straight to St. Paul's Cathedral.

Golden Hinde. St. Marie Overie Dock, Cathedral St., SE1. ☎ **08700/118700.** www.goldenhinde.co.uk. Admission £2.50 ($4) adults, £2.10 ($3.35) concessions, £1.75 ($2.80) children, £6.50 ($10.40) family ticket; pre-booked guided tour £3 ($4.80) adults, £2.60 ($4.15) concessions, £2.25 ($3.60) children. Daily, call for opening times. Tube: London Bridge, Monument.

The *Golden Hinde* is a meticulous replica of the galleon in which Sir Francis Drake circumnavigated the globe (1577–80). Purists may mutter "theme park," but this is no cardboard sham, having sailed over 140,000 miles itself since the 1973 launch, even repeating Drake's historic feat. It's very hot on the educational stuff. During half-terms and holidays, you can drop the kids off for a 4-hour workshop where they'll learn to load cannons, sing Tudor sailing songs, and discover the horrors of barber surgery. Prices vary, and you need to book ahead. Families and small groups can even stay overnight. Actors play the officers and crew preparing for a voyage, while visitors join the work dressed in Tudor clothes, eat rather better food than the sailors would have done, and sleep on the lower decks. If you've got the bottle for it, this is fantastic fun, and at £30 ($48) per person, about the same price as a budget bed-and-breakfast.

Tales from the Riverbank

The **Millennium Mile** is part of a big initiative to improve pedestrian access to the Thames. This marvelous river walk runs uninterrupted along the south bank from the British Airways London Eye, opposite Westminster, to Southwark, past a score of must-visit sights and attractions. For great info on this stretch of the river, surf **www.southbanklondon.com**. A new **Thames cycle route** also opened last summer, linking the two Tate galleries. See "Organized Tours," below for information on where to rent your two wheels.

SOUTH BANK

The twin foot-crossings next to **Hungerford Bridge** (for trains only until now) are another millennium project. Suspended from steel pylons, they link the West End to the South Bank, with its mammoth arts center (see chapter 8). The new view of the **Houses of Parliament** is stupendous. The £26-million project completes in April.

British Airways London Eye. Jubilee Gardens, SE1. ☎ **0870/500-0600.** www.britishairways.com/londoneye. Admission £7.45 ($11.90) adults, £5.95 ($9.50) concessions. Apr–Oct daily 9am–dusk; Nov–Mar daily 10am–6pm. Tube: Waterloo, Westminster.

At 443 feet high, this is the world's tallest observation wheel (don't say "Ferris;" it's a dirty word to these guys). On the south bank, next to County Hall and facing across to the Houses of Parliament, the ½-hour slow-mo "flight" gives "passengers" a stunning 25-mile view over the capital—including into the Buckingham Palace garden, much to the Queen's annoyance. Ironically, it's better when the sun isn't shining, as the glare makes it difficult to see out. I was twiddling my thumbs after 10 minutes or so. There is a human guide with you to help identify landmarks, but I'd have preferred the sort of map you often find in mountain cable cars. Also, the movement is so slow as to be imperceptible—no adrenaline rush here. Despite those quibbles, it is worth the trip, but book your "boarding ticket" (the hand of BA lies very heavily) to avoid too much hanging about.

HAMMERSMITH

The path along the south bank of the Thames, between Putney and Hammersmith bridges, is one of the loveliest walks in London. The urban clatter seems miles away in the green-lit tunnel of trees. It's so quiet—even the rowers glide by almost noiselessly on the river below. The only downside is the stream of arrogant cyclists who assume, quite rightly, that you'll chicken out first and jump out of their way.

WWT The Wetland Centre. Queen Elizabeth's Walk, SW13. ☎ **020/8409-4400.** www.wetlandcentre.org.uk. Admission £6.50 ($10.40) adults, £5.25 ($8.40) seniors, £4 ($6.40) children, £17 ($27.20) family ticket. Summer daily 9:30am–6pm; winter 9:30am–5pm. Tube: Hammersmith, then bus nos. 33, 72, 209, or 283.

This 105-acre wetland habitat, just by the river, is the first to be created on such a scale in any capital city anywhere. The Wildfowl & Wetland Trust shifted thousands of tons of concrete and recycled 500,000 cubic meters of soil to turn the old Barn Elms reservoirs and waterworks into this Site of Special Scientific Interest. The views across it from the observatory in the visitor center are astonishing. There are multimedia displays, a restaurant, and shop there, too. The three outside exhibitions focus on World Wetlands (the Hawaiian lava flow to the African floodplains), Waterlife, and British pondlife living on the Wildside. A great place to take a break from pounding the capital's pavement.

8 At Home with Famous Artists & Writers

When you walk the streets of London, you're walking through hundreds of famous past lives. The city has nurtured so many artists and writers that there's somebody's former home on every other street, around every other corner. English Heritage (☎ **020/7973-3000;** www.english-heritage.org.uk) commemorates each significant spot with a blue-and-white plaque and has done so for 120 years. There are more than 700 on walls all over London (at Jimi Hendrix's Mayfair lair and Mahatma Gandhi's student digs in Fulham, as well as the homes of artists and writers). Geoffrey Chaucer lived above Aldgate, in the city, until 1386. Playwright Joe Orton lived on Noel Road in Islington until his murder in 1967. Oscar Wilde, Dylan Thomas, Agatha Christie, George Orwell, D. H. Lawrence, George Bernard Shaw, Rudyard Kipling, William Blake—the list goes on and on. Usually, the blue plaque is all that's left to mark the past, but there are some exceptions. (For a re-created fictional life, see the "Sherlock Holmes Museum," in section 6 above.)

Carlyle's House. 24 Cheyne Row, SW3. ☎ **020/7352-7087.** Admission £3.50 ($5.60) adults, £1.75 ($2.80) under-17s. Apr–Oct only, Wed–Sun 11am–5pm. Tube: Sloane Sq.

Writer and historian Thomas Carlyle lived in this Queen Anne terrace house from 1834 until his death in 1881. Many a famous figure visited the "Sage of Chelsea" here, including Chopin, Dickens, Tennyson, and George Eliot, who lived just around the corner on Cheyne Walk. Virtually unaltered, the house contains the original furniture and many books, portraits, and mementos from his day. The walled Victorian garden has also been restored and is a delight.

The Dickens House Museum. 48 Doughty St., WC1. ☎ **020/7405-2127.** www.dickensmuseum.com. Admission £4 ($6.40) adults, £3 ($4.80) students and seniors, £2 ($3.20) children, £9 ($14.40) families. Mon–Sat 10am–5pm. Open Christmas Day. Tube: Russell Sq., Chancery Lane.

This terraced house on the edge of Bloomsbury was home to Victorian London's quintessential chronicler for only 2 years (1837–39). In that time, though, Dickens produced some of his best-loved works, including a portion of *The Pickwick Papers, Nicholas Nickleby,* and *Oliver Twist.* His letters, furniture, and first editions are on display in glass cases in rooms restored to their original appearance.

Dr. Johnson's House. 17 Gough Sq., Fleet St., EC4. ☎ **020/7353-3745.** www.drjh.dircon.co.uk. Admission £4 ($6.40) adults, £3 ($4.80) students and seniors, £1 ($1.60) under-16s, free under-10s, £9 ($14.40) family ticket. May–Sept Mon–Sat 11am–5:30pm; Oct–Apr Mon–Sat 11am–5pm. Tube: Blackfriars, Chancery Lane.

The house is one of the last of its age surviving in the city. It's tucked away behind Fleet Street, on a little square at the end of an ancient labyrinth of alleys and passages. Samuel Johnson lived here from 1748 to 1759, while he compiled the first comprehensive English dictionary. In the top garret, six copyists stood transcribing the entries. Johnson sat elsewhere reading and making lists of words from the best literature of the time. You can actually see the original dictionary, published in 1755, as well as letters, prints, portraits, and other memorabilia. But there are very few furnishings to help paint a picture of Johnson entertaining his illustrious friends, Joshua Reynolds, David Garrick, Edmund Burke, Oliver Goldsmith, and James Boswell.

Freud Museum. 20 Maresfield Gardens, Hampstead, NW3. ☎ **020/7435-2002.** www.freud.org.uk. Admission £4 ($6.40) adults, £2 ($3.20) students, free under-12s. Wed–Sun noon–5pm. Tube: Finchley Rd.

Sigmund Freud lived in Maresfield Gardens for a year after he and his family fled Vienna and the Nazis in 1938. A brief stay, but time enough for him to complete

Moses and Monotheism here and entertain friends like H.G. Wells. The rooms are full of memorabilia including furniture, paintings, photographs, and letters. Freudians will enjoy seeing the replica of his Viennese consulting room, complete with couch, and some of his collection of Egyptian, Roman, and Asian antiquities. The museum also shows archive films.

Keats House. Keats Grove, NW3. ☎ **020/7435-2062.** www.cityoflondon.gov.uk. Admission £3 ($4.80) adults, £1.50 ($2.40) concessions, free under-16s. Free admission to garden. Daily Easter to mid-Dec only, call for opening times. Tube: Hampstead, Belsize Park.

John Keats, the romantic poet, lived in this charming Regency cottage in Hampstead from 1818 to 1820. He fell in love with Fanny Brawne, his neighbor's daughter, but had to leave her to winter in Italy, where he died the following year, because of his tuberculosis. While at the cottage, Keats penned "Ode to a Nightingale"—a first edition is on display with books, diaries, letters, memorabilia, and some original furnishings. For the next few years, the museum will close every winter for conservation and restoration. It reopens at Easter with a free festival of special events. During the summer, there is general opening on some days, guided tours, lectures, concerts, and visits by appointment on others. Call to find out the schedule.

Leighton House. 12 Holland Park Rd., W14, off Melbury Rd. ☎ **020/7602-3316.** Free admission. Wed–Mon 11am–5:30pm. Guided tours £2 ($3.20) Wed and Thurs at noon. Tube: High St. Kensington.

This fine example of high Victoriana was the home of Frederic, Lord Leighton (1830–96), a classical painter and president of the Royal Academy. Built between 1867 and 1879 to designs by George Aitchison, it expresses Leighton's vision of a private palace devoted to art. The most stunning element is the exotic Arab Hall with its central fountain and remarkably beautiful gilt mosaic frieze of birds and animals. The authentic Iznik tiles add their own brilliance to the space. Similar fantasy infuses the studio's gilded dome and apse. The house has a fine collection of Victorian art, including works by Leighton, Edward Burne-Jones, Millais, and their contemporaries. There are temporary exhibitions throughout the year.

Linley Sambourne House. 18 Stafford Terrace, W8. ☎ **020/8994-1019.** www.victorian-society.org.uk. Admission £3.50 ($5.60) adults, £2.50 ($4) seniors, £2 ($3.20) under-16s. Mar–Oct only, Wed 10am–4pm; guided tours Sun 2:15, 3:15, and 4:15pm. Tube: High St. Kensington.

This was the home of Edward Linley Sambourne (1844–1910), a leading cartoonist for *Punch* magazine in the late Victorian and Edwardian era. The house is deliciously cluttered and retains most of the original decor, including wall decorations, fixtures, furniture, and paintings by Linley and his friends. There's even wallpaper by William Morris himself.

William Morris Gallery. Lloyd Park, Forest Rd., E17. ☎ **020/8527-3782.** www.lbwf.gov.uk/wmg. Free admission. Tues–Sat and 1st Sun of each month, 10am–1pm and 2–5pm. Closed all bank holidays. Tube: Walthamstow.

Designer, socialist, poet, publisher, and manufacturer of furniture and wallpaper, William Morris was an extraordinarily talented man. Fascinated by the medieval period and the richness of craftsmanship that prevailed then, he became a prime leader in the Arts and Crafts movement. Fans of Morris will not want to miss the permanent collection here, which traces his career through his vast output and writings. There are cozy bits of memorabilia, too—the coffee cup he always used on weekly visits to the Edward Burne-Jones. In turn, the latter's work often forms part of the upstairs temporary exhibits on the artists in Morris's circle, known as the Pre-Raphaelites.

9 Especially for Kids

The London Tourist Board has a **What's On for Children** recorded information line (☎ **0839/123404**). There are also pages in the listings magazine, ***Time Out,*** dedicated to special events and ways of entertaining the kids. You'll have spotted some winners, already, in our listings: touring the **Tower of London,** seeing the **Changing of the Guard** at Buckingham Palace, climbing to the top of **Tower Bridge,** taking a "flight" in the **British Airways London Eye,** or shivering the timbers of the pirate galleon in **Princess Diana memorial playground,** at Kensington Gardens. All the major museums are shaking off their dusty image, not only with interactive exhibits, but fun workshops, too. Topping the hit list are the **Science Museum,** the **London Transport Museum,** the **Museum of London,** the **Theatre Museum,** the **British Museum, Tate Modern,** and the **V&A.** Two more places offering sneakily educational role-playing are **Shakespeare's Globe Theater** (see chapter 8) and the **Golden Hinde. Madame Tussaud's** is always a hit, as is the **BBC Experience.** You should also try the **London Brass Rubbing Centre** in the crypt at St. Martin-in-the-Fields.

Bethnal Green Museum of Childhood. Cambridge Heath Rd., E2. ☎ **020/8980-2415.** www.vam.ac.uk. Free admission. Mon–Thurs and Sat–Sun 10am–5:50pm. Closed Jan 1, Dec 25–26. Tube: Bethnal Green.

A great collection of toys, dolls, dollhouses, games, puppets, children's costumes, and other kids' stuff.

✪ **Little Angel Theatre.** 14 Dagmar Passage, Islington, N1. ☎ **020/7226-1787.** Tickets £5–£7.50 ($8–$12). Box office Mon–Fri 10am–5pm, Sat–Sun 9am–5pm. Tube: Angel, Highbury, Islington.

This magical theater is the only one like it in London. It puts on a huge variety of puppet shows from fairy tales to adaptations of children's books, by its own company and visiting masters of the art. Performances take place on weekends at 11am and 3pm, from September to July, and during half-terms and the Christmas holidays. It's not for children under 3, and some shows are designated for certain age groups.

London Aquarium. County Hall Riverside Building, Westminster Bridge Rd., SE1. ☎ **020/7967-8000.** www.londonaquarium.co.uk. Admission £8.50 ($13.60) adults, £6.50 ($10.40) seniors, £5 ($8) under-15s, £24 ($38.40) family ticket. Daily 10am–6pm. Closed at Christmas. Tube: Westminster, Waterloo.

After Margaret Thatcher abolished the Greater London Council, its huge offices on opposite Westminster lay empty for years. Part of County Hall is now a luxxy Marriott Hotel, part is a budget Travel Inn, and there's a fun palace down in the basement, which includes the London Aquarium. It is one of the largest in Europe, with 650,000 gallons of water for the fish to slosh about in. The two main tanks contain hundreds of varieties of marine life from the Atlantic and Pacific—come and see the sharks (quite young and rather small) being fed at 2:30pm on Tuesday, Thursday, and Saturday. Kids enjoy the shallow Beach Pier where they can touch stingrays and other fish, and there are less alarming but equally yucky things to stroke in the Touchpool. Other zones whiz you through a rainforest, mangrove swamp, coral reef, and an

Fishy Fun Fact

The Thames must be getting cleaner. Last year, a 5-foot porpoise was spotted playing tag with cruise boats right by County Hall. Perhaps it had come to try and liberate its fishy friends from the London Aquarium!

English stream on a summer's day. In total, there are 67 viewing panels, countless sound effects, and even pumped-out smells. Call for details on feeding times—perhaps you'd rather watch the messy-eating piranhas—and talks.

London Dungeon. 28–34 Tooley St., SE1. ☎ **09001/600-0666.** www.thedungeons.com. Admission £9.95 ($15.90) adults, £8.50 ($13.60) students, £6.50 ($10.40) under-15s (must be accompanied by an adult). Apr–Sept daily 10am–6:30pm; Oct–Mar daily 10am–5:30pm (last admission 1hr. before); late openings July–Aug. Closed Dec 25. Tube: London Bridge.

This state-of-the-art horror chamber has huge appeal for kids with a taste for the gruesome and ghoulish. But it will frighten and upset the sensitive and the very young, so be careful. It re-enacts the goriest events from British history in the most vivid way possible, in the dark: one night in the bloody life of Jack the Ripper, the passing of a death sentence that sends you by barge through Traitors' Gate, a medieval city ransacked by invaders, and more. A new roaring red tableau on the Great Fire of London opened last year.

The London Trocadero. Piccadilly Circus, W1. ☎ **09068/881100.** Sun–Thurs 10am–midnight, Fri–Sat 10am–1am. Closed Dec 25. Tube: Piccadilly Circus.

This giant entertainment mall is a kid's idea of heaven, but parental hell. **SegaWorld** (☎ **020/7734-2777**) has 6 floors of arcade games and electronic wizardry, available to anyone with enough 20p and £1 coins, over 43 inches tall, and accompanied by an adult if they're under 16. **Funland** (☎ **020/7287-8913**) has virtual-reality bowling, bumper cars, flight simulators, and more. **007 Licence to Thrill** (☎ **020/7434-1007**) is a test-run for wannabe spooks. Walk down the MI6 corridor to Q's gadget lab and a mission briefing: £5.95 ($9.50) adults, £3.95 ($6.30) children. The **Pepsi Max drop ride** (☎ **020/7434-0300**) does just that—rockets you up 9 floors to the roof, dangles you for a millisecond, then plummets 135 feet to the basement—for a mere £3 ($4.80), as long as you're over 47 inches tall. There's also the **Pepsi London IMAX Theatre** (☎ **020/7494-4153**). That's even before you start talking about the trashy souvenir shops, junk eateries, and general million-decibel din. (Also see **"Rock Circus,"** below).

London Zoo. Regent's Park, NW1. ☎ **020/7722-3333.** www.londonzoo.co.uk. Admission £9 ($14.40) adults, £8 ($12.80) students and seniors, £7 ($11.20) children 4–14. Mar–Oct daily 10am–5:30pm; Nov–Feb daily 10am–4pm. Closed Dec 25. Tube: Camden Town. London Waterbus: From Camden Lock or Little Venice; for joint boat trip–zoo entry tickets, see "Boat Tours," below.

Zoos have had a rough ride in recent years, amid mounting concerns over the humane treatment of animals and waning public interest. London Zoo is no exception, and it was under threat of closure for some time. Rescued by a lottery grant, the zoo has opened a state-of-the-art education center, which puts it back at the forefront of science, as well as making it a great attraction again. **Web of Life** promotes conservation and biodiversity. It brings visitors right up close and personal with the animals and uses interactive displays, too. There's still all the old stuff, of course: the children's zoo, elephants, lions, tigers, penguins, and chimps, plus a small aquarium, and reptile and insect houses. Pick up a copy of the daily-events guide to find out the feeding times of your favorite animals, and so on.

Rock Circus. London Pavilion, Piccadilly Circus, W1. ☎ **020/7734-7203.** www.madame-tussauds.com. Admission £8.25 ($13.20) adults, £7.25 ($11.60) seniors and students, £6.25 ($10) under-16s. Sun–Mon and Wed–Thurs 10am–8pm, Tues 11am–8pm, Fri–Sat 10am–9pm. Closed Dec 25. Tube: Piccadilly Circus.

Rock Circus always used to earn more brickbats than riotous applause, with its not-very-like them waxworks of dubious icons. But it has recently had a face-lift, with a totally new audio-visual kit, animatronics, and an attempt, at least, to keep up to date with fickle music trends—Jay Kay of Jamiroquai is in there. Concert designer Mark Fisher has created an exclusive Rock Circus after-show party, with an ultimate Best of British soundtrack. There are reproductions of a VIP green-room and a Madonna video shoot, and memorabilia from the obvious (Roy Orbison's Fender Telecaster guitar) to the eccentric (a giant telephone-box-shades of *Dr. Who*—that Oasis emerged through onto the set on the Be Here Now tour). So give Rock Circus another chance. *Note:* All the hair used on the models is real!

The Unicorn at the Pleasance. The Pleasance Theatre, Carpenter Mews, North Rd., N7. ☎ **020/7609-1800.** www.unicorntheatre.com. £5–£9.50 ($8–$15.20). Tube: Caledonian Rd.

This is London's oldest professional children's theater company. Founded in 1948, it puts on plays and entertainment for 4-to-12-year olds, either adaptations of old favorites like *Sleeping Beauty* or commissioned works. Performances usually take place at 10:15am and 1:30pm Tuesday to Friday during school terms, 11am (Saturday only), and 2:30pm at weekends. Call to check and to get the holiday schedule.

10 Parks & Gardens

PRIVATE

From April through August, enthusiastic amateurs and the not-so-amateur open their private gardens to the public, organized by the **National Gardens Scheme,** to raise money for charity. This is a chance to see the British at their most passionate, allegedly, for a nominal entry fee—a pound or two at the most. You can pick up an NGS handbook, listing which garden is open on what day, from most bookstores. Or contact the NGS at Hatchlands Park, East Clandon, Guildford, Surrey, GU4 7RT (☎ **01483/211535;** www.ngs.org.uk).

The **Chelsea Physic Garden,** at 66 Royal Hospital Rd. (enter from Swan Walk), SW3 (☎ **020/7352-5646;** www.cpgarden.demon.co.uk), is the second-oldest botanical garden in England. Behind its high walls is a rare collection of exotic plants, shrubs, and trees, many more than 100 years old. Founded in 1673 by the Society of Apothecaries to teach apprentices how to identify medicinal plants, its main function is still research and education. Among labeled plants you'll find those that gave us aspirin, steroids, and other common medicines. Admission is £4 ($6.40) for adults, £2 ($3.20) for students and children. The garden is open April through October, on Wednesday noon to 5pm, and 2 to 6pm on Sunday; the resident English Gardening School holds lectures throughout the summer. Take the Tube to Sloane Square.

PUBLIC

Behind Kensington High Street, **Holland Park** is one of the city's most entrancing parks—an oasis of woods and gardens set around the ruins of Holland House. That's where the open-air theater and opera (☎ **020/7602-7856**) take place in the summer, ousting the noisy peacocks. There's an adventure playground for kids and lots of sports facilities (squash, tennis, cricket, golf nets, and football): Call ☎ **020/7602-2226** for reservations. Also worth seeking out is the Japanese Kyoto Garden. A summer ballroom is now an upscale restaurant, and there's a cafe, too. Take the Tube to High Street Kensington.

Regent's Park, Hyde Park, Kensington Gardens, Green Park, and St. James's Park all come under the aegis of the **Royal Parks Agency** (☎ **020/7298-2000;** www.royalparks.co.uk). Most organize guided walks around the monuments and hidden historical byways, as well as taking part in a Summer Festival of music, theater, and children's events. Wood-and-cloth deck chairs are ubiquitous, and fee collectors seem to appear from nowhere to startle visitors who didn't realize they had to pay a couple of quid to sit down. So stick to the benches and grass.

✪ **Hyde Park** (☎ **020/7298-2100**) is the largest, the most popular, and the most symbolic of all London's parks. The aptly named Serpentine Lake, created in the 1730s, is the most notable feature in all 350 acres. Take a boat out, lounge by its side, or swim from the Lido—make sure you've had your shots if you do, though, as the guano quota is pretty high. Or go horseback riding (see "Staying Active," below) along Rotten Row, a corruption of route du roi, laid out by King William III from the West End to Kensington Palace.

On Sunday the park really comes alive. People flock to the contemporary Serpentine Gallery (☎ **020/7402-6075;** see section 6 above for details), while artists of dubious talent hang their works along the Bayswater Road railings. The northeast corner, near Marble Arch, becomes ✪ **Speaker's Corner.** Anyone can stand on a soapbox here and speak on any subject—expect a few good nutcases. This tradition is often touted as an example of Britain's tolerance of free speech. In fact, the ritual began several hundred years ago when condemned prisoners were allowed a few final words before they were hanged on Tyburn gallows, which stood on the very same spot. Take the Tube to Marble Arch.

Kensington Gardens (☎ **020/7298-2117**) abuts the western perimeter of Hyde Park, and it's hard to spot the join. Laid out in the early 18th century, the trees, lawns, and criss-crossed paths stretch out to Kensington Palace (see section 2 above) on the opposite side. There, you can wander around the edges of the sunken gardens, enjoy a bite at the Orangery, and while away some time on one of the many benches. Perhaps near the Round Pond, where enthusiasts make their model boats buzz between the ducks. Close to the northwestern entrance to the park is the Peter Pan playground, a memorial to Princess Diana, where kids can clamber about on a mock pirate galleon. And do show them the Elfin Oak. In the 1930s, Ivor Innes carved hundreds of little gnomes, goblins, and fairies peering out of the nooks and crevices in a 10-foot-high tree stump. Repainted in glowing colors, it really is enchanting. Near the Long Water, you'll find the famous bronze statue of Peter Pan with his rabbits. And, on the south side of the park, near Queen's Gate, is the overpoweringly gothic Albert Memorial. The Pet Cemetery in Kensington Gardens was the fashionable last resting place for cats and dogs, noble and not-so-noble, from Victorian times until 1867. Call ahead for permission to visit. Take the Tube to Queensway or Bayswater.

Regent's Park (☎ **020/7486-7905**) was once Henry VIII's private hunting ground—as were most of the royal parks—but it is the people's playground now. In summer, you'll see people walking their dogs; playing cricket, soccer, and baseball; doing gymnastics; and throwing Frisbees. Besides the zoo, it's famous for the boating lake, summer open-air theater (☎ **020/7486-2431;** see chapter 8), and brass band concerts on Holme Green. There are 30,000 blossoms and 400 different varieties in Queen Mary's rose garden. And don't miss the Italianate decorations in the Avenue Gardens, the Japanese Gardens, and the wildflowers that grow along the banks of Regent's Canal. In the northwestern corner of the park stands Winfield House, the home of the American Ambassador, while a short distance south of it is the London Mosque. The park was conceived in 1811 by the Prince Regent and John Nash as part of an elaborate remodeling of London. Get there by Tube to Regent's Park, Baker Street, or Camden Town.

Opposite Buckingham Palace, **St. James's Park,** The Mall (☎ **020/7930-1793**), is perhaps the most beautiful of all of London's parks. It was landscaped by Le Notre and John Nash. The famous lake and Duck Island are a waterfowl sanctuary for lots of species, including coots and white and Australian black swans, which give the park a romantic atmosphere. Come at 3pm to see the keepers feeding the pelicans, descendants of a feathered present given by a 17th-century Russian ambassador. You can get a great view of Buckingham Palace from the bridge. Lots of benches and plenty of grass and shade make this an ideal picnicking place. Take the Tube to St. James's Park.

Named for its absence of flowers (except for a short time in spring), **Green Park** (☎ **020/7930-1793**) provides ample shade from tall trees that make it a picnic bower. For other places to *déjeuner sur l'herbe,* and where to buy supplies, see chapter 5. Don't forget to check out the marvelous gardens at Hampton Court Palace, or the Royal Botanic Gardens Kew: see "London's Top Attractions," earlier in this chapter for both.

Also, check out the **WWT The Wetland Centre,** in section 7 above.

11 Organized Tours

Joining an organized tour might sound like grim death to some independent travelers, but this is a useful way both to orient yourself when you arrive and to make the most of limited time. And the guides are a mine of quirky tales, as well as historical facts. For seriously quirky sightseeing, nothing beats **London Frog Tours** (see "Boat Tours," below).

If you're thinking multimodal, man, check out **The Big Bus Company** (see "Bus Tours," below), which has a great value 1-day package that includes walks and cruises. Otherwise, **Tour Guides,** 57 Duke St., London W1M 5DH (☎ **020/7495-5504;** www.tourguides.co.uk) is a fab one-stop shop for tours by car, coach, or on foot, in and out of London.

WALKING TOURS

London's most interesting streets are best explored on foot, and several inexpensive walking-tour companies will lead you along some fascinating routes. Most hotels have information about where to meet up with the guides.

The Original London Walks, P.O. Box 1708, London NW6 4LW (☎ **020/7624-3978;** www.walks.com) has for over 40 years offered an amazing array of themes, from spies, to royalty, to rock-'n'-roll legends. Try a historic Thames-side pub crawl, or trace the footsteps of Princess Diana, led by well-known actors, top Blue Badge guides, and experts in every field. The famous "Jack the Ripper" walk leaves daily at 7:30pm from Tower Hill Tube station. Try and go when Donald Rumbelow, a retired city policeman and authority on the subject, is leading the tour—Sunday and Monday, plus alternate Fridays. Tours cover up to 1½ miles and take around 2 hours: £5 ($8) adults, £3.50 ($5.60) seniors and students. It's an even better bargain if you buy a **Discount Walkabout Card** (£1.50/$2.40), which gets you student rate for every walk after the first one. This company also does out-of-London **Explorer Day** tours every Saturday (see chapter 9).

Every night is fright night on walking tours with historian and ghost researcher **Richard Jones,** 67 Chancery Lane, London WC2A 1AF (☎ **020/8530-8443;** www.london-ghost-walk.co.uk). He sets off at 7:30pm from Bank Tube station. Tickets cost £5 ($8) adults, £3.50 ($5.60) concessions, and you must book ahead.

Two of the capital's best museums (listed above) show their expertise on excellent tours. A **Museum of London** guide (☎ **020/7600-3699;** www.museumoflondon.org.uk) tells tales of archaeological digging along the Thames foreshore, on a walk from St. Paul's Cathedral to the Tower of London. Tickets are a steal at £3 ($4.80). The **London Transport Museum** (☎ **020/7565-7299;** www.ltmuseum.co.uk) charges £8 ($12.80) for trips with a transport bent. Call both for up-to-date details.

Seeing London by Bus

Buy a **Travelcard** (see "Getting Around" in chapter 3), and you can tour all over London on the top of a red double-decker anytime you want. The no. 11 bus has one of the best routes—Liverpool Street Station to Fulham Broadway, via King's Road, Westminster Abbey, Whitehall, Horse Guards, Trafalgar Square, the National Gallery, the Strand, Law Courts, Fleet Street, and St. Paul's Cathedral; the no. 188 runs from Euston to Greenwich; and a great new service was due to launch this April, traveling from Covent Garden past the British Airways London Eye, Tate Modern, and the Globe, to the Tower of London. Nicknamed the **Ecobus** because of its especially low emissions, nobody knew what number it would carry as we went to press, so call the London Transport hot line (☎ **020/7222-1234**) or surf www.southbanklondon.co.uk for info.

BICYCLE TOURS

For a slightly faster pace (been to the gym lately?), try the **London Bicycle Tour Company,** 1a Gabriel's Wharf, 56 Upper Ground, London SE1 9PP (☎ **020/7928-6838;** www.londonbicycle.com; Tube: Waterloo, Blackfriars). You'll cover 7 to 8 miles in 3½ hours or so, with a well-earned refreshment break. Tickets cost £12 ($19.20), including bike rental. If you want to go solo, the company rents out bikes for £2.50 ($4) an hour, or £12 ($19.20) for the first day and then £6 ($9.60) a day, or £36 ($57.60) a week, with discounts for kids.

BUS TOURS

If your time is more limited than your budget, a comprehensive bus tour may be your best bet. **The Big Bus Company** (☎ **020/7233-9533;** www.bigbus.co.uk) leaves from Green Park, Victoria, and Marble Arch daily, from 8:30am to 7pm (4:30pm in winter) on three different routes that take anywhere from 1½ to 2½ hours. Tickets include a river cruise and walking tours, and cost £14 ($22.40) for adults and £6 ($9.60) children. They are valid for 24 hours and allow you to hop on and off at 60 different locations. Big Bus often puts on special offers, too, throwing in cheap theater tickets, fast-entry to popular attractions, and so on, which can be a fantastic deal: Call to get the low-down. The **Original London Sightseeing Tour** (☎ **020/8877-1722;** www.theoriginaltour.com) has been going since the Festival of Britain in 1951. The 2-hour tour leaves from Piccadilly Circus, Victoria, Baker Street, or Marble Arch, every 6 minutes, from 8:30am to 7pm. This one has 90 stops to hop on and off at during the day. It costs £12.50 ($20) for adults, £7.50 ($12) for under-17s, and you can buy tickets on board or at any London Transport or London Tourist Board office.

BOAT TOURS

The latest addition to the city's tour scene is a fabulously loopy idea. **London Frog Tours** (☎ **020/7928-3132;** www.frogtours.com) has adapted several World War II amphibious troop carriers, known as DUKWs, to civilian comfort levels, painted them screaming yellow, and now runs 80-minute road and river trips. Tours start behind County Hall, rumble through Westminster and up to Piccadilly, gathering bemused stares all the way. But that's nothing to the reaction when the DUKW sploshes into the river at Vauxhall for the 30-minute river cruise. The high ticket price of £13 ($20.80) for adults, £10 ($16) concessions, £7 ($11.20) children, and £34 ($54.40) for families is worth it in holiday-snap value alone.

The Thames has always served as the city's highway, and there are 23 piers along its London stretch, from Hampton Court to Gravesend in the estuary. At the last count, more than 10 companies were running river cruises and ferry trips. You'll find a full schedule on the London Transport Web site (www.londontransport.co.uk), or pick up its excellent **Thames River Services** booklet, at most Tube stations and tourist information offices. *Note:* All river activity is much reduced in winter.

The best value, both pound-per-minute and for flexibility, is the **Crown River Cruises** service from Westminster to St. Katherine's Dock, stopping by the South Bank Centre and London Bridge, from 11am to 7:30pm in peak season. A return ticket costs £5.80 ($9.30) for adults, £4.80 ($7.70) concessions, and £3 ($4.80) under-16s. It's valid for a day, and you can hop on and off to sightsee. Don't forget: You can go to Hampton Court and the Royal Botanic Gardens Kew by boat. Those trips are dearer, and there are fewer headline sights on the way, but it does make a great day out (see "London's Top Attractions," above).

The government's Thames2000 initiative was supposed to include a new all-day **Central London Fast Ferry** running between eight of the most popular piers. But it immediately ran into problems and was only offering a limited commuter service last year. To find out if they've got their act together, call Whitehorse Ferries (☎ **0870/240-3240;** www.whitehorse.co.uk). Adults pay £1.90 ($3.05) and children £1 ($1.60) to travel between any two stops.

You can also take a boat along the Regent's Canal. **Jason's Trip** (☎ **020/7286-3428;** www.jasons.co.uk; Tube: Warwick Ave.) operates a 90-minute tour from the wharf opposite no. 60 Blomfield Rd. in Little Venice. The narrow boat leaves at 10:30am, 12:30, and 2:30pm and takes you past Brownings Island (so called because Robert Browning lived there), through the Maida Hill Tunnel and Regent's Park, to Camden Lock. The round-trip price is £5.95 ($9.50) for adults and £4.50 ($7.20) for children; £4.95 ($7.90) and £3.75 ($6), respectively, one-way. **London Waterbus Company** (☎ **020/7482-2660;** Tube: Warwick Ave., Camden Town) travels the same stretch of canal, leaving every hour from 10am to 5pm. The fares are as follows: one-way £4 ($6.40) adult, £2.60 ($4.15) seniors and children; round-trip £5.50 and £3.50 ($8.80 and $5.60). An all-in-one ticket including admission to London Zoo costs £9.90 ($15.84) adults, £8.90 ($14.25) seniors, £7.10 ($11.35) children, from Little Venice; and £9.20, £8.20, and £7.10 ($14.70, $13.10, and $11.35), respectively, from Camden Lock. A stupendous bargain, if you look at the zoo's ticket prices (see above).

12 Staying Active

GOLF

You'll have to travel into the burbs if you want to tee off while you're here. Contact the **English Golf Union** (☎ **01526/354500;** www.uk-golf.com) to find out where.

HORSEBACK RIDING

Both these stables take groups out riding in Hyde Park every day except Monday and charge £30 ($48) an hour for adults, £25 ($40) for children: **Hyde Park Stables,** 63 Bathurst Mews, W2 (☎ **020/7723-2813**); and **Ross Nye Stables,** 8 Bathurst Mews, W2 (☎ **020/7262-3791**). You can't gallop or jump, only amble rather sedately around the sandy track. Both get booked up early for weekends. Take the Tube to Lancaster Gate or Paddington.

ICE-SKATING

Broadgate Ice Rink. Broadgate Circus, Eldon St., EC2. ☎ **020/7505-4068.** Admission £5 ($8) adults, £3 ($4.80) seniors and students; skate rental £2 ($3.20) adults, £1 ($1.60) students

Where to Go for Sports Info

The English are passionate about sports, and there's no better way to get to know and understand them than to watch them watching the play. **Sportsline** (☎ **020/7222-8000**) will answer any questions, on where to work out as well as where to spectate, Monday through Friday from 10am to 6pm.

---

and seniors. Nov–Mar only, Mon–Thurs noon–2:30pm and 3:30–6pm; Fri noon–2:30pm, 3:30–6pm, and 7–10pm; Sat–Sun 11am–1pm, 2–4pm, and 5–7pm (8pm on Sat). Tube: Liverpool St.

This is London's only open-air rink, tiny but modern and surrounded by city wine bars. The state-of-the-art sound system will knock your skates off.

Queen's Ice Skating Club. 17 Queensway, W2. ☎ **020/7229-0172.** Admission £5–£6.50 ($8–$10.40) adults and children, plus £1 ($1.60) skate hire. Mon 10am–noon is the cheapest at £5 ($8); Fri–Sat night £6.50 ($10.40) inclusive of skate rental. Daily 10am–11pm; call for session times. Tube: Bayswater, Queensway.

Weekend disco nights are especially crowded at this large indoor rink right in the heart of Bayswater. It can handle about 1,000 skaters, and often does. There are also 10-pin bowling lanes.

SWIMMING & FITNESS

London Central YMCA. 112 Great Russell St., WC1. ☎ **020/7637-8131.** Admission £15 ($24) per day, £37.50 ($60) per week. Mon–Fri 7am–10:30pm, Sat–Sun 10am–9pm. Tube: Tottenham Court Rd.

Super-snazzy for a Y, this West End health and fitness center has a pool, weight room, squash and badminton, short tennis, cardiovascular equipment, sauna, and solarium. It's membership only, so you pay a flat fee to do as much or as little as you want. There are also beauticians, massage therapists, and a holistic therapy clinic.

Oasis Sports Centre. 32 Endell St., WC2. ☎ **020/7831-1804.** Pool £2.90 ($4.65) adults, £1.10 ($1.75) under-16s. Gym £5.40 ($8.65). Sauna £6.80 ($10.90) peak times, £3.70 ($5.90) before noon and 2–4pm. Exercise classes £4.50 ($7.20) for 45min., £5 ($8) for 1hr. Indoor pool Mon–Fri 6:30am–6:45pm, Sat–Sun 9:30am–5pm. Outdoor pool Mon–Fri 7:30am–9pm, Sat–Sun 9:30am–5:30pm. Tube: Covent Garden, Holborn.

This place has got pretty much everything and at very reasonable prices for London. But the irresistible draw is the roof-top open-air pool. Come and tune out after a hard day's sightseeing.

13 Spectator Sports

CRICKET

Lord's and the Oval are London's two cricket venues. Tickets to county games are the budget-friendliest at around £10 ($16), and you can just turn up on the day of the match. Book ahead for international Test matches and 1-day games. Tickets are dear at £25 to £50 ($40 to $80). The cricket season runs from April through September.

Foster's Oval. The Oval Kennington, SE11. ☎ **020/7582-6660.** www.surreyccc.co.uk. Tube: Oval.

Less stodgy and prettier than Lord's, except for the gasometer looming up behind it, the Oval is home to Surrey County Cricket Club. It also traditionally hosts the final game in the summer international Test series. The box office is open Monday to Friday 9:30am to 4pm.

Lord's. St. John's Wood Rd., NW8. ☎ **020/7432-1066,** or 020/7432-1033 for tours of the ground. www.lords.org/mcc. Tours & museum £6 ($9.60) adults, £4.40 ($7.05) concessions. Tube: St. John's Wood.

Lord's is home to both the Marylebone Cricket Club (which governs the game) and the Middlesex County Cricket Club, which plays league matches on this hallowed ground. The international Tests have the aura of high society, or at least corporate hospitality, events. The box office is open Monday to Friday 9:30am to 5:30pm.

You don't have to endure a cricket match to make a pilgrimage to Lord's. There are **guided tours** year-round at noon and 2pm. These include a visit to the **museum,** which has exhibits on legendary cricketers such as W. G. Grace and houses the Ashes trophy, for which the English and Australians compete furiously. The first-ever Test against the now-old enemy took place here in 1884, a century after Thomas Lord founded the Marylebone Cricket Club, originally in Dorset Square. It moved to St. John's Wood in 1811 and to its current location in 1816. The next big change was the building of the space-pod-style media center, a considerable shock to the establishment. On the tour, you'll also see the pavilion, where the dressing rooms are, and the "real tennis" court—Henry VIII enjoyed this early game so much he copied the idea at Hampton Court. Then watch bowling machines fire practice balls at 100 m.p.h. in the indoor school, before popping into Lord's Tavern.

FOOTBALL (SOCCER)

Footballers really have attained god-like status. A gilded relief of David Beckham, the Manchester United star and Posh Spice's hubbie, has taken the spot usually reserved for angels at the foot of the main Buddha statue in a Bangkok temple. This sport attracts quasi-religious devotion here, too. Yet, whatever you may have read about English fans in the past, the violent hooliganism that marred the national game has declined with the abolition of stands in favor of all-seat stadiums. The football season runs from August to April, with matches usually kicking off at 3pm on Saturdays or 7:45pm on Wednesdays. The capital has more than a dozen clubs in different leagues. All the newspapers carry listings, but for advanced info, you should surf **www.sportal.com**. Seats cost from £8 to £30 ($12.80 to $48), and more for gold-dust premiership tickets. London's glamour clubs are: **Arsenal,** Arsenal Stadium, Avenell Rd., N5 (☎ **020/7704-4000,** or 020/7704-4040 for the box office; www.arsenal.co.uk; Tube: Arsenal); **Tottenham Hotspur ("Spurs"),** White Hart Lane, 748 High Rd., N17 (☎ **020/8365-5000,** or 020/8365-5050 for the box office; www.spurs.co.uk; Tube: Seven Sisters); and **Chelsea,** Stamford Bridge, Fulham Rd., SW6 (☎ **020/7385-5545,** or 0891/121011 for the box office; www.chelseafc.co.uk; Tube: Fulham Broadway).

GREYHOUND RACING

Wimbledon Stadium. Plough Lane, SW19. ☎ **020/8946-8000.** www.wimbledondogs.co.uk. Admission: Main Grandstand £5 ($8), Popular Enclosure £3.50 ($5.60). Races Tues, Fri–Sat 7:30–10:30pm (stadium open 6:30pm). Tube: Wimbledon Park.

This people's sport has enjoyed a big renaissance over recent years, repositioning itself as *the* alternative night out. The greyhounds race around the track after a fuzzy mechanical hare. The minimum bet is £1 ($1.60), but the results are even less predictable than horse races. You can eat, drink, and make very merry at restaurants, bars, and fast food stalls. A good laugh and good value.

HORSE RACING

Royal Windsor Racecourse. Maidenhead Rd., Windsor, Berkshire, SL4 5JJ. ☎ **01753/865234.** www.windsorracing.co.uk. Admission £4–£11 ($6.40–$17.60). Race meetings:

Mar, Oct–Nov afternoons; May–Aug Mon evenings; start times vary. Train: Windsor Riverside, then Riverbus (☎ **01753/851-9000;** www.boat-trips.co.uk) from nearby Barry Ave. Promenade, £4 ($6.40) return.

Windsor does hold sporadic afternoon race meetings during the chillier months, but the festive summer Monday evenings are by far the best fun. The relaxed crowd is a mix of champagne Charlies and regular Joes, sampling the restaurants and bars, or diving into a DIY picnic. Even the journey is a delight. Turn right out of the train station, and follow the crowd to the Riverbus for the 35-minute trip up the Thames to the racecourse. It leaves on the hour, and at 20 and 40 minutes past, from an hour or so before the first race, to a ½ hour after the last one. Buy your ticket on board.

RUGBY UNION

The capital's three top clubs are **London Wasps,** Loftus Rd. Stadium, South Africa Rd., W12 7PZ (☎ **020/8743-0262;** www.wasps.co.uk), **London Irish** (☎ **01932/783034;** www.london-irish-rugby.com), and **Harlequins** (☎ **020/8410-6000;** www.quins.co.uk). Both the latter play at Stoop Memorial Ground, Langhorn Dr., Twickenham, Middlesex, TW2 7SX. This chest-thumpingly macho game can be very exciting. The season runs from August to May, with games on Saturday and Sunday afternoons. Tickets are relatively easy to get hold of (though it is wise to book ahead) and cost £10 to £25 ($40 to $16). For full fixtures listings, surf **www.rfu.com**.

Twickenham Stadium. Rugby Rd., Twickenham, Middlesex, TW1 1DZ. ☎ **020/8892-8877.** www.rfu.com. Museum and/or tour £5 and £3 ($8 and $4.80) adults, £3 and £2 ($4.80 and $3.20) concessions, £15 ($24) family ticket. Stadium tours Tues–Sat 10:30am, noon, 1:30, and 3pm; Sun 3pm. Museum of Rugby Tues–Sat 10am–5pm, Sun 2–5pm, match and post-match days from stadium opening to 1hr. after final whistle. Train: From Waterloo to Twickenham, then bus no. 281.

Twickenham is the headquarters of the Rugby Football Union and hosts international games (very hard to get tickets) and cup finals (a little bit easier). The annual Six Nations battle between Scotland, Ireland, Wales, England, France, and Italy takes place from January to March, whipping up a fever of patriotism.

Take the **Stadium Tour,** and you can walk through the players' tunnel to see what they see on the big day, visit the dressing room, and hear lots of sporting stories. There's a scrum machine (similar to a blocking sled in American football) in the **Museum of Rugby,** where you can test your own strength. It's crammed with memorabilia, of course, including the oldest jersey still in existence, and watch the best rugby moments of all time on film.

TENNIS

Ever since players in flannels and bonnets took to the courts in 1877, the **Wimbledon Lawn Tennis Championships** have drawn a socially prominent crowd. Now it's the people's game, too, and even anti-sport fanatics get drawn into the national tennis fever. Save up and savor the extortionately priced strawberries and cream that are part of the experience. It takes place this year from June 25 to July 8. Show court seats are mostly sold by ticket ballot. The allocation is random, so you can't request a specific court or date. To be included, write between August 1 and December 31 of the preceding year for an application form, enclosing a self-addressed envelope with an International Reply Coupon, to **All England Lawn Tennis Club,** P.O. Box 98, Church Rd., Wimbledon, SW19 5AE (☎ **020/8944-1066** or 020/8946-2244; www.wimbledon.org). A handful of show-court seats are sold on match day during the first 9 days of the tournament. People camp out in line the night before to get them; prices range from £25 to £63 ($40 to $100.80) for Centre Court, £16 to £34 ($25.60 to $54.40) for No. 1 Court, and £15 to £24 ($24 to $38.40) for No. 2.

During the earlier rounds, you can see lots of the stars playing on the outside courts if you just buy Ground Admission. Prices start at £12 ($19.20), winding down to £4 ($6.40) at the end of the 2 weeks when there's much less to see; or £5 ($8) falling to £1 ($1.60), if you come after 5pm to catch the tail-end of the day's play. There are two more great deals, too: People leaving the show courts are encouraged to turn in their tickets, which then go on sale at £5 ($8) before 5pm, £3 ($4.80) after, with the proceeds going to charity; and all prices are discounted on the middle Saturday of the tournament. The gates open at 10:30am. Come early because queues are long and stop moving all together when the crowd inside reaches capacity.

The **Wimbledon Lawn Tennis Museum** (☎ **020/8946-6131**) is open daily 10:30am to 5pm. Tickets cost £5 or £4 ($8 or $6.40) for under-16s, students, and seniors. It has all sorts of memorabilia tracing the social history of the game, from period room sets to costumes and tennis kit, as well as TV footage of famous matches, and some staggering statistics—did you know that Greg Rusedski's serve reaches 140 m.p.h.? A visit includes a tour of Centre Court. The museum is closed Friday to Sunday before the championships, the middle Sunday, and the Monday after it finishes. During the 2 weeks, it is only open to tournament visitors. It is also closed December 24 to 26 and January 1.

Take the Tube to Southfields, then a 39, 93, or 200 bus.

7

Shopping

The Brits tend to think of the United States as the home of the crazy consumer, but research done last year showed they're a little bit odd themselves. Wouldn't you know it, embarrassment is the main reason they buy online: Men rush at the chance to avoid having to guesstimate their partner's size in a sexy lingerie store, while women gratefully sidestep the technobabble from car and electronic salesmen. Otherwise, Brits still like to see, touch, scratch, and sniff what they're buying. Shopping is a buzz, and nowhere is buzzier than London.

Stores are usually open from 10am to 6pm, and most add on an extra hour, at least 1 night a week. There's late-night shopping, as it's called, on Wednesday in Knightsbridge, Kensington, and Chelsea, and Thursday in the West End. Around touristy Covent Garden, many doors don't close until 7 or 8pm every night. Shops can open for 6 hours on a Sunday, and many do, usually from 11am or noon. If you're planning to visit a particular store, always call ahead to check.

TAXES & SHIPPING

Most goods and services, with the exception of books, newspapers, groceries, and children's clothing, carry 17.5% value-added tax (VAT) in Britain. This is included in all prices. Visitors from non-EC countries can reclaim the tax on any shopping they take home. Before you buy, check whether or not the store participates in the refund scheme, as unfortunately not all do. And although there is no official minimum purchase requirement, some stores set their own, usually around £50 ($80).

To make a claim, you must show identification at the store and fill out a VAT reclaim form then and there. Keep the receipt, form, and goods handy to show to the British Customs office at the airport (allowing a ½ hour to stand in line). If you leave the country with your form unstamped, you've blown it. There are two ways to get the money: Either mail the form back to the store, choosing a credit card refund, or go to the airport Cash VAT Refund desk, where you will lose money on the conversion rate if you take other than sterling.

VAT is not charged on goods shipped directly out of the country by the supplier—some stores will do that for you, at a price. But you will have to pay import duty at home. To ship stuff yourself, call **London Baggage,** London Air Terminal, Victoria Station, 115 Buckingham Palace Rd., SW1 (☎ **0800/378-254;** www.londonbaggage.com), or **Excess Baggage,** which has branches in every Heathrow and Gatwick Terminal, and main London railway stations (☎ **0800/783-1085;** www.excess-baggage.com).

1 Top Tips for Bargain Hounds

Sadly for visitors, the muscular pound means London no longer offers the bargains it used to. But never fear. This super-shopper has pounded the capital's pavements to find the budget-friendliest stores and ideas for affordable but quintessentially English souvenirs (see the "London's Best Buys" box, below). With these cunning strategies, a couple of bucks will do the work of 10.

- **London for Less.** This $19.95 discount card and guidebook gets you 20% off at around 50 posh shops, including Burberry and Pringle, as well as cheap sightseeing, accommodations, dining, tours, and so on (see "Fifty Money-Saving Tips" in chapter 2).
- **Traditional Sales.** January sales are as English as plum pudding—and that's one thing always reduced by 30% after the holiday. London goes into a total frenzy, with people now giving I.O.U.s (gift certificates) as Christmas gifts and honoring them at a discount a day or two later. Harrods even has bargain-hunters camped out for days so they can be first through the door. At the sale's loony peak, the store takes over £1 million an hour. London's summer sell-offs are exciting, too, and start earlier every year—certainly by the end of June. For a year-round guide to sales and promotions, surf the fab **www.inshop.co.uk**.

  Buyer beware: By law, goods have to be available at the regular price for a certain amount of time before they can be marked down. However, many stores ship stuff in especially for sales, and it may be of lower quality.
- **Designer Warehouse Sales.** This company does just what its name suggests—stage 3-day jamborees, flogging off designer mens- and womenswear at 40% to 80% discount (see p. 258). Be prepared to do battle with seasoned local bargain-hunters.
- **High Fashion at High Street Prices.** The transfer of fashion from the catwalk to the streets of London is incredibly fast. And with knock-offs on every shelf and rail, it's tough for stores to stand out from the crowd. So many of them now commission top designers to create an exclusive collection just for them. Quality is usually high as famous names have reputations to protect. Travelers with designer desires but tight budgets should take the Tube to Marble Arch and head east along Oxford Street to **Marks & Spencer** and **Debenhams** (see "Department Stores," below), then to **Dorothy Perkins** and **Top Shop** (see "Contemporary" under "Fashion," below).
- **Factory Shopping.** London's handful of factory shops tends to be off-city center, which may mean taking a local train. But discounts from 25% to 80% on samples and discontinued lines more than repay the effort. Check out **Nicole Farhi** and **Burberry** (see "Discount" under "Fashion," below), and **Villeroy & Boch** (see "China & Glass," below).
- **Markets.** Knowledgeable locals and bargain-hunting visitors love to cruise London's outdoor markets (see "Markets," below) for food, clothing, furniture, books, antiques, crafts, and lovely junk. There are dozens catering to different communities. Stalls rarely open before sunrise, officially at least, but that doesn't stop the flashlight-wielding professionals who'll snap up gems even before they reach the display table.
- **Artful Dodges.** The vast sums paid by serious collectors make the art world seem a scary place. Not to mention the snobbery. But anyone can be an art lover, and buying is easy, too. It's largely a matter of timing. The **Art School degree shows** in May and June are great for hot talent at debut prices. If you're in London in October, visit the **Affordable Art Fair** (see "Will's Art Warehouse," below).

London's Best Buys

The smart shopper will stock up on oddities and specialties you can only find in Britain, or that are made better here than anywhere else. Here are just a few ideas.

- Unusual **pickles** and **preserves.** For cheese-friendly relishes, try **Jeroboams,** 51 Elizabeth St., W1, (☎ **020/7823-5623;** Tube: Victoria). **The Spice Shop,** 115–117 Drummond St., NW1 (☎ **020/7916-1831;** Tube: Euston, Warren St., or Great Portland St.) is a hotspot for authentic Indian chutneys. **Mr Christian's,** 11 Elgin Crescent, W11 (☎ **020/7229-0501;** Tube: Ladbroke Grove), has sweet preserves, such as quince and rose-petal jelly. London is in the middle of an organic food boom so browse the city's **markets,** too (see, "Markets," later in this chapter).
- **A budget afternoon tea.** First stock up on **PG Tips** or **Typhoo** for a much heartier cuppa than you'll get with brands at home. Then add **traditional British biscuits** to the shopping list: chocolate digestives and shortbread. Supermarkets sell all these and are great places to browse for gifts. Call to find out the nearest branch of **Marks & Spencer** (☎ **020/7268-1234;** www.marksandspencer.co.uk), **Sainsbury's** (☎ **0800/636262;** www.sainsburys.co.uk), or **Tesco** (☎ **0800/505555;** www.tesco.co.uk).
- **Stationery** is another best buy. Try **John Lewis** (see "Department Stores," below) for leather-bound address books, and **Paperchase,** 213 Tottenham Court Rd., W1 (☎ **020/7580-8496;** www.paperchase.co.uk; Tube: Charing Cross) for gorgeous papers and notebooks.
- And then there are the **splurges.** Unique, hand-made scents from **Penhaligon's** (see "Bath & Body," below); a classy umbrella from **James Smith & Sons** (see "Traditional British Goods," below); or the classic English trench coat from **Burberry,** at a conscience-salving discount from the factory shop (see "Discount" under "Fashion," below).

There are two big dates for fans of decorative arts and crafts. **New Designers 2001** is a super-degree show in July for students from all over Britain. **Hidden Art,** on the last weekend of November and first in December, is a fair and open-studio, where you can buy direct from working designers. See "Crafts," below.

2 The Shopping Scene

The **West End** is the heart of London shopping; its main artery is **Oxford Street,** a mile of mass-market chains and department stores like John Lewis, Selfridges, and Marks & Spencer. At the eastern end, St. Giles High Street is the gateway into **Covent Garden,** a warren of narrow streets lined with stores selling quirky specialties and the hottest fashion trends. The old market is home to boutiques and craft stalls, while the piazza is a nonstop street festival of mime artists, singers, and entertainers.

Oxford Circus is the first big intersection walking west along Oxford Street, where it crosses the patchily elegant **Regent Street:** Turn south for Liberty, Aquascutum, Austin Reed, Burberry, and Hamleys. The next landmark westwards is New Bond Street, which changes to Old Bond Street as it heads south through **Mayfair.** It's wonderful for designer window-shopping and for fine art and antiques.

Both Regent Street and Old Bond Street run into Piccadilly, to the south of which is **St James's** and some seriously upper-crust shopping. Here you'll find Hatchard's for books; Swaine, Adeney Brigg & Sons for fine leather goods and riding equipment; and the fabulous food halls of Fortnum & Mason. Jermyn Street is famous for shirt-makers; other fine shops include Paxton & Whitfield, a specialist cheesemonger, and Floris, which has been blending perfume since 1730. It's *the* place to see how the other half lives.

Continue west from Piccadilly and Hyde Park Corner, to posh **Knightsbridge** and the world-famous Harrods department store on Brompton Road. Off Knightsbridge (it's a street as well as a neighborhood), is Sloane Street, a millionaires row lined with the most rarified names in haute couture. This runs down to Sloane Square and **Chelsea's** King's Road. The latter was the center of Swinging London in the 1960s and of the punk revolution a decade or so later. Mainstream boutiques have invaded now, but there's still a healthy dose of the avant-garde.

Young fashion flourishes on **Kensington High Street.** Nearby **Notting Hill** is crammed with funky boutiques of every kind, especially around Portobello Market, though budget-busters are pushing out the neighborhood bargains. You have to travel east to find a hip shopping scene still on the way up: creative **Clerkenwell,** or **Brick Lane** in the city. As well as the market, the latter now has Dray Walk, a small private enclave of quirky studio-shops and galleries.

3 Shopping A to Z

ANTIQUES

There are thousands of antiques stores in London—hardly surprising since the place is ancient and the Brits never throw anything away. Like husbands at a barbecue, gangs of dealers naturally gravitate together and there are several arcades on the must-visit list. Otherwise, check out "Markets," and "Auction Houses," below.

Alfie's Antique Market. 13–25 Church St., NW8. ☎ **020/7723-6066.** www.ealfies.com. Tube: Edgware Rd., Marylebone.

With its 370-plus dealers, Alfie's would fox the most expert maze-builder. You name it, you'll find it here, from art-deco lighting to 20th-century ceramics, and at prices below the West End.

Antiquarius. 131–141 King's Rd., SW3. ☎ **020/7351-5353.** Tube: Sloane Sq.

Antiquarius houses more than 120 dealers in its Arts and Crafts–style building. They sell everything from classic luggage to art-nouveau sculpture and jewelry. Head for the lower-priced basement hall.

✪ **Camden Passage.** Off Upper St., N1. ☎ **020/7359-9969.** www.antiquescamdenpassage.co.uk. Tube: Angel.

Bargains are hard to find and certainly hard fought over by the luvvies who flock to Camden Passage, but it's wonderful browsing the arcades and malls, plus the specialty stores lining this little shop. Wednesday and Saturday, when the outdoor stalls are open, are the best days to look for bargain jewelry, silverware, and trinkets.

Grays Antiques Market & Grays in the Mews. 58 and 1–7 Davies St., W1. ☎ **020/7629-7034.** www.graysantiques.com. Tube: Bond St.

The main antiques market is red hot on jewelry, but the Mews is a better bet for bargain hunters, especially if they're looking for something pocket-size, like a model car or music box. There is also an enormous hall especially for books, antiquarian and merely secondhand. Grays is closed on the weekends. Call for details on regular exhibitions.

London Silver Vaults. 53–64 Chancery Lane, Chancery House, WC2. ☎ **020/7242-3844.** Tube: Chancery Lane.

This is a marvelous place to buy a wedding or christening present. Over 40 dealers trade in modern and antique silver, with prices starting at around £20 ($32).

ART & DESIGN

FINE ART

The herd instinct of London's art elite is extraordinarily powerful: **Cork Street,** Mayfair, is nose to tail with posh commercial galleries—strictly for browsing only.

Galleria Charlick. 138 Gray's Inn Rd., WC1. ☎ **020/7713-6206.** Tube: Chancery Lane.

This vaulted gallery is an extension of the deli next door, and you can have lunch there from 12:30 to 2pm, surrounded by the work of young artists. Exhibitions range from Italian sculptors, such as Viccardi and Elio Garis, to Robert Cooper ceramics or photography by Frank Herholdt.

October Gallery. 24 Old Gloucester St., WC1. ☎ **020/7242-7367.** www.theoctobergallery.com. Tube: Russell Sq., Holborn.

This gallery is dedicated to promoting avant-garde art from different cultures: *transvangarde,* they call it. It has shown everyone from Kenji Yoshida to Aubrey Williams and Sokari Douglas Camp, as well as hosting group exhibitions from Tibet, South Africa, Haiti, and Oceania. In the diary for November is Art from the Congo. There's a cafe here, too.

Will's Art Warehouse. Unit 3, Heathmans Rd., SW6. ☎ **020/7371-8787.** www.wills-art.com. Tube: Parson's Green.

Will Ramsay set up his warehouse in 1996 to debunk art-market snobbishness and offshore-bank-account prices. The 200 pictures on display change every 6 weeks. Customers can peruse the entire collection on a computer screen and choose which piece(s) they would like to see. Prices start at £50 ($80), and works can be purchased on Will's Web site as well. The venture has spun off into the annual **Affordable Art Fair** in Battersea Park where over 100 stands display work priced at under £2,000 ($3,200). It takes place from October 25 to 28: Entry is free for under-16s, £6.60 ($10.60) in advance or £7.50 ($12) at the door for adults, and £5.50 ($8.80) for concessions. Tube: Sloane Sq., then no. 137 bus.

AUCTION HOUSES

A Monet sold for millions to a mystery bidder always grabs the headlines, but it's a tiny part of what passes through London's salerooms: from toys to fine wine, Roman coins to rock stars' underpants. Emotions and prices run high, so it's a great spectator sport, and the lots go on view to the public for a few days beforehand. London's four biggest auction houses first banged their gavels in the 18th century. To find out what's on (little in August), contact their main salesrooms: **Bonhams,** Montpelier St., SW7 (☎ **020/7393-3900;** www.bonhams.com; Tube: Knightsbridge); **Christie's,** 8 King St., SW1 (☎ **020/7839-9060;** www.christies.com; Tube: Green Park); **Phillips,** 101 New Bond St., W1 (☎ **020/7629-6602;** www.phillips-auctions.com; Tube: Bond St.); and **Sotheby's,** 34–35 New Bond St., W1 (☎ **020/7293-5000;** www.sothebys.com; Tube: Bond St.).

✪ **Chiswick Auctions.** 1 Colville Rd., W3. ☎ **020/8992-4442.** Tube: Acton Lane.

This friendly local salesroom is a place where travelers on a budget can dare to raise their hands as prices start as low as £10 ($16). Loony lots often add to the party atmosphere:

fake marble columns from a props company or 5-foot-high bronze parrots. But there's good stuff, too. Chiswick Auctions handles a lot of private libraries. Viewing runs from Sunday afternoon until the auction starts on Tuesday—small goods at 5pm, furniture from 7pm, every week.

BATH & BODY

The Body Shop. 374 Oxford St., W1. ☎ **020/7409-7868.** www.the-body-shop.com. Tube: Bond St.

The internationally famous British chain sells organically based lotions, shampoos, and beauty aids all over London. It has lots of rivals now but has spruced up its act and is still worth a visit. Prices on some popular products are lower here than in the United States.

Crabtree & Evelyn. 6 Kensington Church St., W8. ☎ **020/7937-9335.** www.crabtree-evelyn.com. Tube: High St. Kensington.

This purveyor of very English toiletries caters to nostalgia queens with pastel-colored soaps, powders, and potpourri in pretty cottage-style packaging. There are also branches on James Street (Covent Garden), Regent Street, and Chelsea's King's Road.

Lush. Units 7 and 11, The Piazza, Covent Garden, WC2. ☎ **020/7240-4570.** www.lush.co.uk. Tube: Covent Garden.

You've probably never seen anything quite like Lush—it's a beauty shop that takes "organic" to a whole new level. Huge slabs of soap burst with pineapple slices (good for the skin) or poppy seeds (a great exfoliator). The store whips up fresh facial masks and keeps them over ice. Just scoop some into a take-home container and keep refrigerated. Lush is a fabulous source for gifts, especially for visitors from the U.S. or New Zealand, where the store has yet to open. The best-seller is the Tisty Tosty—a heart-shaped "bath bomb," which fizzes and scents the water. There are branches on King's Road, Chelsea, and Carnaby Street in Soho.

✪ **Neal's Yard Remedies.** 15 Neal's Yard, WC2. ☎ **020/7379-7222.** www.nealsyardremedies.com. Tube: Covent Garden.

Founded in 1981, this is still the best shop in London for herbal toiletries and medications, aromatherapy oils, homeopathic hair remedies, and other alternative medicines. Most of the products come in intensely blue glass bottles, and they make attractive and reasonably priced gifts. Try Remedies-to-Roll, roll-on essential oils to fit in your handbag, including one for sleep. The store is at the end of a short cul-de-sac off Short's Gardens.

✪ **Penhaligon's.** 41 Wellington St., WC2. ☎ **020/7836-2150.** www.penhaligons.co.uk. Tube: Covent Garden.

Barber William Penhaligon opened for business in 1841, and the scents are still made by hand according to his formulas. This lavish store sells soaps, eau de cologne, and shaving kits. It also has a fine selection of antique scent bottles and silver accessories, such as boxes, mirrors, and manicure sets. The most famous women's scents are Violetta and Bluebell. Love Potion No. 9 is irresistible.

BOOKS & MAGAZINES

London is one of the best places in the world for avid readers and bibliophiles. The city has 1,000 or so booksellers, dealing in new, not-so-new, and antiquarian volumes. Look for entire shops devoted to art, science fiction, religion, medicine, crime, politics, sport, and travel. Browsers should start from Leicester Square Tube station and walk north along **Charing Cross Road,** the heart of London's bookselling community.

And don't ignore side streets like St. Martin's Court and Cecil Court. Bloomsbury (**Museum Street** in particular) also has a number of bookshops, especially scholarly antiquarian dealers.

Blackwells. 100 Charing Cross Rd., WC2. ☎ **020/7292-5100.** www.bookshop.blackwells.co.uk. Tube: Tottenham Court Rd.

This is a London offshoot of the venerable bookseller that has served generations of Oxford students. As well as academic texts, it has a huge stock of "normal" books.

Books Etc. 421 Oxford St., W1. ☎ **020/7495-5850.** Tube: Bond St.

Books Etc. is part of the mammoth Borders and is one of the most user-friendly and well-stocked of the chains. It is very good on modern fiction and holds some backlist titles. This and several of its 16 other central London stores have posh coffee bars. For branch addresses and a diary of author signings, call ☎ **020/7379-7313.**

✪ **Books for Cooks.** 4 Blenheim Crescent, W11. ☎ **020/7221-1992.** www.booksforcooks.com. Tube: Ladbroke Grove, Notting Hill Gate.

This store stocks over 8,000 different cookery books: the classics, hot manifestos from celebrity chefs and recipes from virtually every ethnic cuisine. There's a test kitchen and a mini-dining area at the back, and different chefs come in to try out published recipes. It costs £12 ($19.20) for three courses. BFC also puts little books together of tested recipes—a great bargain buy.

Borders Books, Music & Café. 203–207 Oxford St., W1. ☎ **020/7292-1600.** www.bordersstores.com. Tube: Oxford Circus, Tottenham Court Rd.

London has really taken to this stateside book, music, and video giant. It stocks almost 250,000 titles and what is claimed to be the biggest choice of newspapers and magazines in the country. You'll find the busy Café Express on the second floor, where Borders holds readings and events. There's a second branch in Charing Cross Road.

Children's Book Centre. 237 Kensington High St., W8. ☎ **020/7937-7497.** www.childrensbookcentre.co.uk. Tube: Kensington High St.

A brilliant place for baby bookworms and parents who want to pass on a love of reading to their kids. There's something for every age group, from fiction to fun factual stuff. The shop is crammed with toys, CD-ROMs, videos, and audio tapes, too. Some Saturdays, it arranges "personal appearances" by popular cartoon characters.

Compendium Bookshop. 234 Camden High St., NW1. ☎ **020/7485-8944.** www.compendium-books.com. Tube: Camden Town.

This terrific shop is a paradise for the well-rounded reader. It has sections on cult and beat fiction, politics, psychology, women's issues, and new age. All the alternative and anarchist magazines can be found here. This is the place to come for what was once termed "underground" lit.

Foyles. 113–119 Charing Cross Rd., WC2. ☎ **020/7437-5660.** Tube: Leicester Sq., Tottenham Court Rd.

The famous, and famously old-fashioned, Foyles has books on virtually every topic under the sun. Fiction is still stacked under publishers' names, not alphabetically, and it has certainly been surpassed in efficiency by the big chains. Still, this is the place to find titles other shops have stopped stocking, or never did in the first place.

Garden Books. 11 Blenheim Crescent, W11. ☎ **020/7792-0777.** Tube: Ladbroke Grove, Notting Hill Gate.

Gardening has never been funkier in Britain, with endless backyard makeovers on TV and magazines launching for yuppies who'd rather have been seen dead than in the garden center a few years ago. This store opened in 1996 and now carries around 7,000 titles, including a section on interior design. If Garden's hasn't got the book, it's probably out of print.

Gay's the Word. 66 Marchmont St., WC1. ☎ **020/7278-7654.** www.gaystheword.co.uk. Tube: Russell Sq.

The fantastically comprehensive stock makes this Britain's biggest gay and lesbian bookshop. It has everything from literary fiction to detective novels and erotica, as well as issues-based titles, philosophy, and politics.

✪ **Hatchards.** 187 Piccadilly, W1. ☎ **020/7439-9921.** www.hatchards.co.uk. Tube: Green Park, Piccadilly Circus.

A holder of Royal Warrants from the Duke of Edinburgh and the Prince of Wales, Hatchards has been trading since 1797. It carries popular fiction and nonfiction titles, and all the latest releases. It's a pleasure to climb the creaking stairs and browse the venerable wooden stacks with its upper-crust clientele.

Jarndyce. 46 Great Russell St., WC1. ☎ **020/7631-4220.** www.jarndyce.co.uk. Tube: Tottenham Court Rd., Holborn.

This antiquarian bookseller recently turned itself from a simple office into a more browser-friendly shop, open on weekdays only. It specializes in 19th-century English literature.

Offstage Theatre and Film Bookshop. 37 Chalk Farm Rd., NW1. ☎ **020/7485-4996.** Tube: Camden Town or Chalk Farm.

Offstage is packed with drama students and the occasional famous actor thumbing through play and movie scripts. There is every kind of specialty book including sections on circus, stagecraft, cinematography, and commedia dell'arte. There's a big secondhand department, too.

✪ **Stanfords Map & Travel Bookshop.** 12–14 Long Acre, WC2. ☎ **020/7836-1321.** www.stanfords.co.uk. Tube: Covent Garden.

Stanford's is world-renowned for its exhaustive collection of travel literature, guidebooks, atlases, and maps of every kind, from maritime to historical, for biking or hiking, and covering every region of the world. It has a good selection of globes, too. Oddly enough, though, there are few guides to London—not exotic enough, obviously.

The Travel Bookshop. 13–15 Blenheim Crescent, W11. ☎ **020/7229-5260.** www.thetravelbookshop.co.uk. Tube: Ladbroke Grove.

This little gem carries a huge variety of travel literature and guidebooks, both old and new, mainstream and more adventurous.

✪ **Waterstone's.** 203–206 Piccadilly, W1. ☎ **020/7851-2400.** www.waterstones.co.uk. Tube: Green Park, Piccadilly Circus.

It feels a bit insulting to call this a mere bookshop. Spread over 7 floors in the building where posh store Simpson used to be, the new Waterstone's flagship is the very model of a modern emporium. There are over 265,000 titles here, as well as Internet access, a juice bar, cafe, lounge bar, and the Red Room restaurant. It holds regular events and is a great place for a free wee if you get caught short sightseeing and need the bathroom.

CHARITY SHOPS

Don't turn your nose up at charity shops (that is, thrift shops), especially those in the West End and well-heeled neighborhoods like Knightsbridge, Kensington, and Chelsea. The stock can be very good quality. **Oxfam** is Britain's fifth biggest retailer, selling Fair Trade products, gifts, furnishings, books, and secondhand clothes. **Oxfam Originals** stores concentrate solely on funky, retro fashions. There are three in Central London, at 123a King's Rd., Shawfield St., SW3 (☎ **020/7351-7979;** Tube: Sloane Sq.); 22 Earlham St., WC2 (☎ **020/7836-9666;** Tube: Covent Garden); and 26 Ganton St., W1 (☎ **020/7437-7338;** Tube: Oxford Circus). The British Red Cross has a shop in Chelsea, at 67–71 Old Church St., SW3 (☎ **020/7351-3206;** Tube: South Kensington). Imperial Cancer Research Fund also has one West End shop, at 24 Marylebone High St., W1 (☎ **020/7487-4986;** Tube: Baker St., Bond St.). Or try the Notting Hill Housing Trust in Knightsbridge, at 211 Brompton Rd., SW3 (☎ **020/7581-7987;** Tube: South Kensington), or Kensington, at 57 Kensington Church St., W8 (☎ **020/7937-5274;** Tube: Kensington High St.). Finally, one of the best charity shops around is the Salvation Army's at 9 Princes St., W1 (☎ **020/7495-3958;** Tube: Oxford Circus). It often has out-of-date, new stock in the main room, as well as secondhand children's clothes, and a selection of funky gear in a section called "Cloud 9" upstairs.

CHINA & GLASS

For that ultimate present from England—though you can buy it almost anywhere now—it has to be Waterford Wedgwood or Royal Doulton (see "Traditional British Goods," below).

Reject China Shop. 183 Brompton Rd., SW3. ☎ **020/7581-0739.** www.chinacraft.co.uk. Tube: Knightsbridge.

These stores carry a wide range of English china. As the name suggests, most of the stock is seconds or discontinued lines. Shoppers who know the going prices in the United States may pick up a bargain here. There are also branches in Regent Street and Covent Garden Piazza.

Villeroy & Boch Factory Shop. 267 Merton Rd., SW18. ☎ **020/8875-6006.** www.villeroy.com. Tube: Southfields.

This German company has been making high-class tableware since 1748. You can find it in all the top London stores, from Harrods to Selfridges and Liberty. However, take the Tube to the wealthy suburb of Wimbledon, near the end of the District line, and you'll save a whopping 30% to 70% on seconds and ends of lines.

CRAFTS

For years, popular prejudice lauded the noble artist and ignored his peasant cousin the craftsman. Not any more. Britain is in the grip of a passion for great design. Ceramicists, jewelry and textile-makers, glassworkers, and others command huge respect and all-too respectable prices. However, dozens of designers take part in a fair and open their studios to sell direct to the public, without the middleman's mark-up, during the **Hidden Art** festival (☎ **020/7729-3301;** www.hidenart.co.uk). It takes place in ever-so creative East London on the last weekend in November and the first weekend in December. For details of open-studio days year-round, contact the **Crafts Council** (☎ **020/7278-7700;** www.craftscouncil.org.uk).

The Crafts Council has two shops, one at the Victoria & Albert Museum (see chapter 6) and the other at its gallery, 44a Pentonville Rd., N1 (☎ **020/7806-2559;** Tube: Angel). Big pieces are look-but-don't-touch, but small ceramics, jewelry, or scarves shouldn't bust the budget. **Contemporary Applied Arts,** 2 Percy St., W1 (☎ **020/7436-2344;** www.caa.org.uk; Tube: Tottenham Court Rd.) is another browser's paradise.

The above are great for rising and risen talents. To catch designers and makers at the embryo—and hopefully cheaper—stage, make sure to visit the **art school degree shows.**

DEPARTMENT STORES

Debenhams. 334–348 Oxford St., W1. ☎ **020/7580-3000.** www.debenhams.co.uk. Tube: Bond St., Oxford Circus.

Dowdy Debenhams shocked the fashion pack when it became one of the first chain stores to persuade big name designers to descend to high street level. You'll find ranges by **Pearce Fionda, Jasper Conran** (for adults and toddlers), **Maria Grachvogel,** and recent additions **Edina Ronay** and **Betty Jackson,** as well as **Natalie Hambro** bags and jewelry by It-Girl favorite **Lulu Guinness.** Covetable womenswear designer **Elspeth Gibson** has created the Sweet Pea range for girls aged 3 to 8.

✪ **Harrods.** Knightsbridge, SW1. ☎ **020/7730-1234.** www.harrods.com. Tube: Knightsbridge.

Opened in 1849, Harrods claims to be the most famous department store in the world and that anything in the world can be bought (or ordered) here. The incredible ground-floor food halls are a feast for all the senses. And, for sheer theme-park excess, nothing beats the Egyptian escalator and the children's department with its theater, cartoon cafe, and specialty hairdresser. On the minus side, the store layout is very frustrating. With around 35,000 visitors a day, it can become a nightmare experience, like Disney World on the 4th of July. Harrods also has a snooty dress code: no dirty or unkempt clothing, ripped jeans, high-cut shorts, athletic singlets, cycling shorts, and bare tummies or feet.

Harvey Nichols. 109–125 Knightsbridge, SW1. ☎ **020/7235-5000.** Tube: Knightsbridge.

Harvey Nicks, as this elegant store is affectionately called by the It-Girl and fashion-pack clientele, could hardly be more different from its brash Knightsbridge neighbor, Harrods. Whereas the latter is crammed to opulent bursting point with everything under the sun, and much of it in dubious taste, Harvey Nichols is a cool haven of chic. It pioneered the showcasing of designer collections from London, Paris, and Milan—from Anne Demeulemeester to Gaultier, Tocca to Joseph—and has a decent menswear department, too. As well as the food hall and fifth-floor bar, cafe, and restaurant, Harvey Nicks also has a YO! Sushi concession (see chapter 5).

John Lewis. 278–306 Oxford St., W1. ☎ **020/7629-7711.** www.johnlewis.co.uk. Tube: Oxford Circus.

This is one of the few remaining traditional department stores that really does stock everything, from fashions and fashion fabrics, to curtain fabrics and furniture, clothing, washing machines, and lovely leather-bound diaries. John Lewis makes a big promise—"Never Knowingly Undersold." If customers find the same goods locally at a better price, the store will refund the difference. (And it employs an army of under-cover shoppers to check out the competition.) Sister store **Peter Jones,** Sloane Sq., SW1 (☎ **020/7730-3434;** www.peterjones.co.uk; Tube: Sloane Sq.), is the Sloane Ranger's spiritual home. It is having an £80-million refurb, due to be complete in 2004.

✪ **Liberty.** 210–214 Regent St., W1. ☎ **020/7734-1234.** www.liberty-of-london.com. Tube: Oxford Circus.

This is London's prettiest department store. It may be old-world on the outside (neo-Tudor, in fact), but everything here is beautiful and stylish. As well as colorful clothing with the famous Liberty imprint, it has a fantastic array of women's fashions by well-known and up-and-coming designers. And don't miss the world-famous furnishing and dress fabrics. Liberty is far from cheap, but if you're after a small gift to take home, you'll usually find something on the bazaar-like first floor.

Marks & Spencer. 458 Oxford St., W1. ☎ **020/7935-7954.** www.marks-and-spencer.com. Tube: Marble Arch.

In 1995, Vivienne Westwood's son Joe Corre launched his vampy undies shop Agent Provocateur with the slogan, "More S&M, less M&S." It has been a roaring success. Which may be why puritan, and ailing, Marks & Spencer forgave Corre's cheek and asked him to create the temperature-raising Salon Rose collection. The lacy bras, basques, and suspender belts are all machine-washable and at nonluxury prices. M&S has followed up with the Autograph label, designed by Katherine Hamnett, Betty Jackson, and others. There are new men's sportswear and baby kit (prams, car seats, and so on) sections. And M&S at last accepts credit cards. Even the ever-popular food hall, with its deli-style delights and ready meals, looks more inviting.

Selfridges. 400 Oxford St., W1. ☎ **020/7629-1234.** www.selfridges.co.uk. Tube: Bond St., Marble Arch.

Chicago salesman Harry Selfridge opened this store in 1909, stunning Londoners with his marble halls and sheer variety of goods. A 3-year revamp, just completed, has restored its slightly slipping fortunes. The ground-floor perfumery and cosmetics department is the biggest in Europe. Upstairs is a crammed with covetable designer fashions, while Miss Selfridge is several shops within a shop within a shop. It hosts high street names, including Oasis and Warehouse (see "Contemporary" under "Fashion," below), and some funky young designers. Selfridges also boasts one of the finest food halls in London (see "Food & Drink," below).

FASHION

CHILDREN

Feted womenswear designer Elspeth Gibson has turned to a younger clientele—girls aged 3 to 6—and created the delicious Sweet Pea collection for **Debenhams** (see "Department Stores," above). The store also has a 0 to 3 range by **Jaspar Conran,** Junior J, and its own label.

CONTEMPORARY

For **Miss Selfridge,** check out Selfridges in "Department Stores," above.

Dorothy Perkins. West One Shopping Centre, 379 Oxford St., W1. ☎ **020/7495-6181.** www.dorothyperkins.co.uk. Tube: Bond St.

London fashion doyenne Lucille Lewin has created a high street version of her Whistles collection for this otherwise unexciting store. The delectable Whistles Express includes knits, urban sportswear, tailoring, and evening wear. The bold body-flattering swimwear is by Liza Bruce.

Oasis. 292 Regent St., W1. ☎ **020/7323-5978.** www.oasis-stores.com. Tube: Oxford Circus.

Oasis has been staggeringly successful over the past few years. This fashion chain's brand of well-priced women's wear has a real laid-back chic. There's stuff to work and play in, in a mix of natural fibers and hi-tech new ones.

Pink Soda. 22 Eastcastle St., W1. ☎ **020/7636-9001.** Tube: Oxford Circus.

This is one of those supposedly well-kept fashion industry secrets that has now been thoroughly outed. In the wholesale garment district north of Oxford Street, it sells young and funky womenswear and accessories at fabulously low prices. Pink Soda is closed at the weekends.

Top Shop. 214 Oxford St., W1. ☎ **020/7636-7700.** www.tops.co.uk. Tube: Oxford Circus.

The huge, multifloored, multi-everything Top Shop is right on Oxford Circus. Long regarded as selling cheap tat for teenyboppers, its funky styles have now become top wannabuys for stylists and their pop star clients. The TS Design label boasts an army of A-list names: **Clements Ribeiro, Hussein Chalayan, Tracey Boyd,** plus rock chick faves **Sherald Lamden** and **Markus Lupfer.** And it's still amazingly cheap.

Warehouse. 19–21 Argyll St., W1. ☎ **020/7437-7101.** www.arcadia.co.uk. Tube: Covent Garden.

This high-street chain aims to set trends and isn't half bad at it. While it clearly aims at women in their 20s, it doesn't exclude nontiny people or anyone who doesn't want to display their belly button. Clothing ranges from seasonal staples to full-on party gear.

Discount

For 40% to 80% discounts on just-*passé* styles from 88 top fashion names, check out the monthly Designer Warehouse Sales at **The Worx,** 45 Balfe St., N1 (☎ **020/7704-1064** for info; www.dwslondon.co.uk; Tube: King's Cross). They run for 3 days, starting on a Thursday, which is when you should go for the best pickings. Entry is £3 ($4.80).

Amazon. 1–3, 7a, 7b, 19–22 Kensington Church St. No phone. Tube: High St. Kensington.

At one point, you couldn't bend down to tie your shoelace without another Amazon shop opening here at the bottom of Kensington Church Street. The same stock often appears in several of them, but there's a great mix of designer and high-end high street fashion for both sexes, at up to 70% off. It often has Nicole Farhi and French Connection.

Browns Labels for Less. 50 S. Molton St., W1. ☎ **020/7514-0052.** Tube: Bond St.

Browns is the sort of name that wins star treatment from a designer when the buyer visits a collection. The main boutique showcases only the best names and can make a hot young newcomer. Browns Labels for Less is inevitably less impressive. Still, it's well worth a visit for discounts of 30% to 70% on designers like Jill Sander and Sonia Rykiel, or Alan Scott for menswear.

Burberry's Factory Outlet. 29–53 Chatham Place, E9. ☎ **020/8328-4320.** Train: Hackney Central BR station.

Burberry is one of Britain's best-known luxury marques. It puts its distinctive tartan on everything—macs, wallets, umbrellas, even bikinis—and you'll find everything here, including samples and ends of lines. You have to take a local train, but savings of up to a third on the normal price will more than cover the cost of your ticket.

French Connection/Nicole Farhi Factory Outlet. 3 Hancock Rd., E3. ☎ **020/7399-7125.** Closed Sun–Mon. Tube: Bromley-by-Bow.

Here you can pick up old stock, seconds, and samples of these two labels. But you do need to be a serious fan to make it worth the trek. Try Amazon in Kensington Church Street first, as it's bound to be more convenient.

Paul Smith. 23 Avery Row, W1. ☎ **020/7493-1287.** www.paulsmith.co.uk. Tube: Bond St.

There are 3 floors stocking this hot British menswear designer. Most of the suits and other clothes are from last season. You'll also find accessories from hats to belts and socks. Discounts range from 30% to 70%.

Shoes

London's shoe stores almost outnumber pubs and churches. The best places to go are: Oxford Street for mid-priced popular footwear; Bond Street and Sloane Street for high-price designers; South Molton Street (just by Bond Street Tube), Covent Garden, and King's Road for trendy styles. Below are the biggest branches of the best of the chain stores.

British kids have been growing up in sensible **Clarks** shoes for 175 years. Now this staid brand has blossomed, selling a small collection of great-value high fashion shoes that won't give you bunions: Go to 260 Oxford St., W1 (☎ **020/7499-0305;** Tube: Oxford Circus). Pricier, but great for classy chic, are **Bertie,** 25 Long Acre, WC2 (☎ **020/7836-7223;** Tube: Covent Garden), and **Jones Bootmaker,** 57 King's Rd., SW3 (☎ **020/7730-5818;** www.jonesbootmaker.com; Tube: Sloane Sq.). Urban warriors and dolly birds will love mid-price **Office,** 57 Neal St., WC2 (☎ **020/7379-1896;** www.officelondon.co.uk; Tube: Covent Garden).

As well as the chains, London has two more must-visits. Action people looking for eco-friendly shoes should try the **Natural Shoe Store,** 21 Neal St., WC2 (☎ **020/7836-5254;** Tube: Covent Garden). It has full lines of Dexter, Ecco, Birkenstock, Arche, and Timberland, as well as shoes with specialized contours, arches, and soles. Last on the list is a footwear institution. At **Dr. Marten's Department Store,** 1–4 King St., WC2 (☎ **020/7497-1460;** Tube: Covent Garden), you can pick up a pair of the basic shoes for £40 to £50 ($64–$80). Camden Market has them at a discount.

Vintage & Secondhand

Don't forget to browse London's thrift shops, particularly **Oxfam Originals** (see "Charity Houses," above).

Blackout II. 51 Endell St., WC2. ☎ **020/7240-5006.** www.blackout2.com. Tube: Covent Garden.

Pick up your club costume at this fun emporium, where you'll find everything from feather boas to PVC coats. Whether you're looking for glam or kitsch, you'll find it here. Bell bottoms and other retro stuff, all at decent prices.

Cornucopia. 12 Upper Tachbrook St., SW1. ☎ **020/7828-5752.** Tube: Victoria.

The stock is so huge that there are definitely bargains to be found here, it just takes a bit of rummaging to find them. But that's so much fun with this treasure trove of costumes from the 1920s on, all arranged by era. Women off to the hottest parties in town come here for entrance-making evening wear and the costume jewelry to go with it.

Pandora. 16–22 Cheval Place, SW7. ☎ **020/7589-5289.** Tube: Knightsbridge.

Ladies who lunch don't throw last season's clothes away: They sell them through this Knightsbridge dress agency. Pandora is the grande dame of the secondhand scene, claiming to hold every famous designer from Armani to Zilkha (Ronit, that is). The stock is seasonally correct, and there are even sales: from July to August, and December to January.

Fun Feet Fact

Doc Martens—those funky, clunky boots with the air-cushioned soles that are requisite street wear for cool kids the world over—were invented by Dr. Klaus Maertens in post-war Germany as a comfort shoe for old ladies.

✪ **Steinberg & Tolkien.** 193 King's Rd., SW3. ☎ **020/7376-3660.** www.bestselections.com. Tube: Sloane Sq.

The vast array of stock spreads over 2 floors, organized by era and designer. The pieces are in prime condition and run from the mid–19th century to contemporary, with a host of legendary names from Chanel to Balenciaga to Vivienne Westwood. This is a fab place if you want a bit of celeb-spotting thrown in with the retail therapy.

Stitch Up. 45 Parkway, NW1. ☎ **020/7482-4404.** Tube: Camden Town.

If you're crazy about cashmere, you must visit this little boutique specializing in reconditioned knitwear. Most pieces are nearly as good as new, restored, cleaned, and dyed on occasion, and prices start at £15 ($24). The stock is a mix of vintage and patchwork house-designs made from recycled sweaters.

WOOLENS

The Scotch House. 2 Brompton Rd., SW1. ☎ **020/7581-2151.** Tube: Knightsbridge.

Lambswool sweaters begin at about £45 ($72), and prices rise with the quality and complexity of design. The emphasis here is on hand-knits, Shetland and cashmere, too, as well as machine-made woolens. Kilts, hats, socks, and scarves can be bought off the rack or made to order.

Westaway & Westaway. 64–65 Great Russell St., WC1. ☎ **020/7405-4479.** www.westaway.co.uk. Tube: Holborn.

The window mannequins at this fantastically old-fashioned store look like Hitchcock heroines frozen in time. The stock runs from Shetland wool sweaters and cardigans to tartans. Prices are old-fashioned, too, and the store is worth a visit if that's your style.

FOOD & DRINK

EDIBLE TREATS

Also check out London's markets, below.

The Chocolate Society. 36 Elizabeth St., SW1. ☎ **020/7259-9222.** www.chocolate.co.uk. Tube: Victoria, Sloane Sq.

The Chocolate Society uses the venerated Valrhona in all its chocolates. When you come into this little shop, stand and inhale the mouthwatering smell. Shelves groan with truffles, chocolate-dipped fruit, cakes, and much, much more.

Neal's Yard Dairy. 17 Shorts Gardens, WC2. ☎ **020/7379-7646.** Tube: Covent Garden.

This is *the* place for British and Irish cheeses—none of that foreign muck—from the very best old favorites to delicious new ones developed by little farmhouse cheesemakers. The names are wonderful—Lincolnshire Poacher, for instance—and staff are delighted for you to try before you buy. Then pop 'round the corner to **Neal's Yard Bakery,** 6 Neal's Yard, WC2 (☎ **020/7836-5199**), for still-warm bread to go with your selection. There is a second dairy at Borough Market, SE1 (see "Markets," below).

Paxton & Whitefield. 93 Jermyn St., W1. ☎ **020/7930-0259.** www.cheesmongers.co.uk. Tube: Green Park.

This is London's most venerable cheese shop, established in 1797. It concentrates on English and French farmhouse cheeses—about 200 in all—and matures each one itself. Prices are refreshingly reasonable despite the upper-crust location, and shelves groan with a big selection of wine and port to go with whichever cheese you choose.

Food Halls

London's department-store food halls are a Bacchanalian feast of vibrant colors and exotic smells. Pick your treats wisely, though. You could break the bank, and that will be all you have to eat or drink for the remainder of your holiday. Harrods is the king of food halls. There are close to 20 departments, of which the meat, fish, and poultry room—with its mosaics of peacocks and wheat sheaves, ceramic fish, scallop shells, boars, and more—is the most amazing. The best handbag-size buys are jams made with fruits rarely found at home, like gooseberries. Rows of food counters sell every kind of portable lunch, perfect for a picnic in Hyde Park across the road. Or try neighboring **Harvey Nichols,** lauded for its brand of stylish goods. The Selfridges food hall is much more compact than Harrods, but it packs an awful lot in, and the wine and choccy departments are separate. And so to **Marks & Spencer,** which holds a place in the hearts of most Brits. Best described as a very posh supermarket, with wine, packaged deli foods and ready meals, polished fruit, cut-up fresh vegetables, biscuits, and great sandwiches and salads. For more on all of these, see "Department Stores," above.

✪ **Fortnum & Mason.** 181 Piccadilly, W1. ☎ **020/7734-8040.** www.fortnumandmason.com. Tube: Green Park, Piccadilly Circus.

Fortnum & Mason is a department store but few shoppers penetrate beyond the food hall—unless it's to have English tea (see chapter 5). This is *the* place for aristocratic foods and empire-building delicacies you've only ever seen in period movies. Fortnum knows everything there is to know about tea: The house brand is pricey but outstanding quality. It's said that if you take along a sample of your tap water, they'll know which tea to pair it with.

Scotch

Cadenhead's Covent Garden Whisky Shop. 3 Russell St., WC2. ☎ **020/7379-4640.** www.coventgardenwhiskyshop.co.uk. Tube: Covent Garden, Holborn.

This shop specializes in single cask, single malts, and has an astonishing stock of old and rare whiskies. But if you prefer Irish whiskey to Scotch, you won't be disappointed.

Milroy's of Soho. 3 Greek St., W1. ☎ **020/7437-9311.** www.milroys.co.uk. Tube: Leicester Sq.

Milroy's has perhaps the longest whiskey list in London. There are hundreds to try from Ireland and Scotland, as well as American bourbons if you're feeling homesick. The store has moved into the cellar to make room for a bar at street level, open Monday to Saturday, 11am to 11pm.

The Vintage House. 42 Old Compton St., W1. ☎ **020/7437-2592.** www.sohowhisky.com. Tube: Leicester Sq.

This little store opened just after World War II and stocks over 700 whiskies, as well as rare old bottles of other spirits, champagne, fine wines, and Cuban cigars.

MARKETS

Farmers' markets may be old hat in the United States, but they're a new idea in London. The produce is all English, whatever's in season, and much of it chemical-free. Farmers sell only their own produce and also make the sausages, cheese, jams, and so on—even buffalo pastrami. You'll find the biggest range at **Islington Farmers' Market,** Essex Rd. opposite Islington Green, N1 (Tube: Angel), open Sundays 10am to 2pm. Others are: **Camden Farmers' Market,** West Yard, Camden Lock, NW1 (Tube: Camden Town), Wednesday and Friday, 11am to 3pm; **Notting Hill Farmers'**

Market, behind Waterstones on Notting Hill Gate, W11 (Tube: Notting Hill Gate), Saturday 9am to 2pm; **Swiss Cottage Farmers' Market,** Winchester Market, Avenue Rd., NW3 (Tube: Swiss Cottage), Wednesday 10am to 4pm. New markets are due to open at the rate of one a month (☎ **020/7704-9659;** www.londonfarmersmarkets.com).

Bermondsey Market. Bermondsey Sq., SE1. Fri only 5am–2pm Tube: London Bridge.

Forget Portobello Road, charming though it is. This is where serious antiques collectors and dealers come—burglary victims, too, tracking down their stolen possessions. It's a dawn start with stalls starting to close at noon. And the market is a bit of a trek from London Bridge. But that's all part of the adventure.

Borough Market. Borough Sq., SE1. www.londonslarder.org.uk. Fri noon–6pm, Sat 9am–4pm. Tube: London Bridge.

Celebrity chefs are said to fill their shopping baskets at this covered food market next to Southwark Cathedral. Stalls laden with meats (including bacon and venison), fish, olives, chocolates, bread, pies, and much more are wickedly tempting. The third weekend of every month, twice as many producers turn out for "The Big One."

Brick Lane Market. Brick Lane, E1. General Market Sun 8am–1pm; Laden Market Mon–Sat 11am–6pm, Sun 10am–4:30pm. Tube: Shoreditch, Liverpool St.

One of the last places you can try that oh-so English delicacy, jellied eels, yet one of the hippest markets in London. As well as fruit and veggies, cheap tat, and lots of leather, there's the new **Laden Market** at 103 Brick Lane—a covered space abuzz with young fashion and accessory designers, great for cheap unique gifts. Combine Brick Lane with a visit to neighboring Spitalfields Market (see below).

Brixton Market. Electric Ave., SW9. Mon–Tues, Thurs–Sat 8am–6pm, Wed 8am–3pm. Tube: Brixton.

Brixton is the heart of African-Caribbean London, and Brixton Market is its soul. Electric Avenue (immortalized by Jamaican singer Eddie Grant) is lined with exotic fruit and vegetable stalls. Turn right at the end for a terrific selection of the cheapest secondhand clothes in London. Granville Arcade, off the avenue, is crammed with foods, African fabrics, reggae records, and community newspapers.

Camden Market. Camden High St. and Chalk Farm Rd., NW1. Camden Market Thurs–Sun 9am–5:30pm; Camden Lock indoor stalls Tues–Sun 10am–6pm, outdoor Sat–Sun only; Stables Market Sat–Sun 8am–6pm; Camden Canal Market Sat–Sun 10am–6pm; Electric Market Sun 9am–5:30pm. Tube: Camden Town, Chalk Farm.

This vast market fills the streets, arcades, and courtyards, taking more money than the whole of the West End. Hundreds of stalls flog crafts, bric-a-brac, clothes and furniture, with a big hippy-trippy contingent. The Stables concentrates on clothing, almost-junk, and 20th-century collectibles. The best vintage clothing can be found on Buck Street, Camden High Street, and in Electric Market (good for cheap Doc

Fun Junk Fact

Traders who collected unwanted junk off the streets and by knocking on doors were known as rag-and-bone men. They drove horses and carts, and are a dying breed. But Mick the Trolley still trawls wealthy Chelsea. You can usually find him, as well as some impressive bargains, at the thrice-weekly car boot sale at Christchurch C of E School, Caversham St., SW3 (☎ **020/7351-5597;** Tube: Sloane Sq.). Call for dates. Entry is 50p (80¢).

Martens). By the canal, Camden Lock hosts a Farmers' Market on Wednesday and Friday. Come early, particularly on Sundays, as this is one of London's biggest tourist attractions.

Greenwich Market. From Greenwich High Rd. (opposite St. Alfege's Church), SE10. Antiques Market Sat–Sun 9am–5pm; Central Market indoor Fri–Sat 10am–5pm, Sun 10am–6pm, outdoor Sat 7am–6pm, Sun 7am–5pm; Crafts Market Thurs 7:30am–5pm, Fri–Sun 9:30am–5:30pm; Food Market Sat 10am–4pm. Docklands Light Railway: Cutty Sark, Greenwich.

The market is an essential part of a visit to this bustling and historic maritime borough. Greenwich is pretty chi-chi, which is reflected in the quality of stuff on sale: from upscale antiques to collectors' oddities, old and new. The Central and Food Markets are in Stockwell Street, just off the high road. The Craft Market is in College Approach.

Petticoat Lane. Middlesex St., E1. Sun 9am–2pm. Tube: Liverpool St. or Aldgate.

This ancient market is not what it used to be. Now stores open on Sunday, and other events draw the crowds. But it almost feels like discovering the real London, if you can ignore the hordes of tourists. Shoes and clothes are dirt cheap, and you'll find leather fashions at the Aldgate end.

✪ **Portobello Market.** Along Portobello Rd., W10, W11. Antiques Market Sat 4am–6pm; General Market Mon–Wed 8am–6pm, Thurs 9am–1pm, Fri–Sat 7am–7pm; Organic Market Thurs 11am–6pm. Clothes & Bric-a-brac Market Fri 7am–4pm, Sat 8am–5pm, Sun 9am–4pm. Tube: Notting Hill Gate, Ladbroke Grove.

Portobello Market is fantastic, despite the seething masses. Saturday is the full-on armoires-to-lava-lamps day. More than 2,000 antiques dealers set out their stalls at the southern, uphill, end: Head for Notting Hill Gate Tube station. For retro and street-chic clothing, secondhand music, and junkabilia, go to Ladbroke Grove instead. Cross the road out of the station to the passage left of the bridge. Weekdays, Portobello is an old-fashioned fruit and veggie market with organic food on Thursdays.

Spitalfields Market. From Lamb St. to Brushfield St., E1. Organic Market Fri–Sun 10am–5pm; General Market Mon–Fri 11am–3pm, Sun 10am–5pm. Tube: Liverpool St.

Like Brick Lane, this market is burgeoning under the wave of trendoids moving into the city fringes. It's mostly antiques and crafts during the week, with clothing stalls setting up at the weekend. That's also when the market turns into a cornucopia of edible delights. Come for one of "London's Best Buys" (see box earlier in the chapter), organic pickles and relishes.

MUSIC

Denmark Street is *the* musicians' hangout. This scruffy cut-through off Charing Cross Road is lined with shops selling everything you need to get a band on the road.

NEW RECORDS, CDS & TAPES

Check out the stores below, and especially Tower Records, for flyers offering cheap entry into some of London's hippest night clubs (see "Dance Clubs & Discos," in chapter 8).

HMV. 150 Oxford St., W1. ☎ **020/7631-3424.** www.hmv.co.uk. Tube: Oxford Circus.

This HMV is a mega-megastore, so whatever you want it's probably got it. Dance music is a real strength, and the ground floor has all the new releases, rock, soul, reggae, and pop. The range of world music and spoken-word recordings is huge. Last year, HMV closed its most famous store—where Brian Epstein cut the first demo discs of the Beatles—and opened a super hi-tech one twice the size across the road: 360 Oxford St., W1 (☎ **020/7514-3600;** Tube: Bond St.). It's the first music store in the country where customers can create their own CDs with digital downloads.

Tower Records. 1 Piccadilly Circus, W1. ☎ **020/7439-2500.** www.towerrecords.co.uk. Tube: Piccadilly Circus.

A warehouse of sound, Tower has 4 floors of records, tapes, and compact discs—pop, rock, classical, jazz, bluegrass, folk, country, soundtracks, and more, all in separate departments. Downstairs you'll find a fantastic selection of international music magazines. It's open until midnight every day except Sunday.

Virgin Megastore. 14–16 Oxford St., W1. ☎ **020/7631-1234.** www.virginmega.com. Tube: Tottenham Court Rd.

The Virgin Megastore is a microcosm of Richard Branson's ever-expanding empire. You can buy a mobile phone, an airline ticket, or an hour on the Internet, as well as hardware and software for computer games, videos, MP3 players . . . oh, and the usual albums and singles. And it holds regular live performances and signings.

VINTAGE & SECONDHAND

Hanway Street, close to Tottenham Court Road, has seven secondhand stores—it's a mecca for vinyl buffs.

Harold Moores Records & Video. 2 Great Marlborough St., W1. ☎ **020/7437-1576.** www.hmrecords.co.uk. Tube: Oxford Circus.

Classical heaven, this store is full of stock ranging from 78s to LPs and CDs, some rare and precious to the tune of thousands of pounds. But it also has great sales.

Mole Jazz. 311 Gray's Inn Rd., WC1. ☎ **020/7278-8623.** www.molejazz.co.uk. Tube: King's Cross.

Jazz fans come here for historic recordings, whether it be New Orleans traditional, swing, or modern. You can ring up or e-mail (jazz@molejazz.co.uk); ask for an auction list, too, if you're on the hunt for something really rare.

Music & Video Exchange. 36–42 Notting Hill Gate, W11. ☎ **020/7243-8573.** www.buy-sell-trade.co.uk. Tube: Notting Hill Gate.

This is four stores in a row, each specializing in something different. Together they offer bargain buys and collectible rarities; CDs, tapes, and vinyl; the classics, jazz, folk, dance music, and more. Surf the Web site for other branches because this company is a real gremlin. It even has shops selling retro housewares, movie memorabilia, and clothing.

TOYS

✪ **Hamleys.** 188–196 Regent St., W1. ☎ **020/7494-2000.** www.hamleys.com. Tube: Oxford Circus, Piccadilly Circus.

William Hamley founded Noah's Ark, as it was called, in 1760, and it is one of the largest toy stores in the world. There are 7 floors stuffed with more than 40,000 toys, games, models, dolls, cuddly animals, and electronic cars. There are even executive toys at very adult prices.

London Dolls House Company. 29 Covent Garden Market, WC2. ☎ **020/7240-8681.** Tube: Covent Garden.

Girls big and little will love this store. Collectible dollhouses can fetch £3,300 ($5,280), but kits start at £65 ($104) and delicious miniature furnishings at 50p (80¢).

Repro Rarities from London's Museums

If you think of museums just as sightseeing attractions, then you're really missing out. They're sophisticated retailers, too. Once, all you could buy was a tea-towel or dusty postcard, but many museums now sell replicas of the treasures in their august halls. These are great places to look for quirky affordable gifts. I'd love a pair of earrings and a brooch, copied from an ancient Egyptian or Greek design, from the **British Museum,** Great Russell St., WC1 (☎ **020/7323-8000;** www.britishmuseum.co.uk; Tube: Tottenham Court Rd). There's a wonderful bookstore, too. The **London Transport Museum,** The Piazza, Covent Garden, WC2 (☎ **020/7379-6344;** www.ltmuseum.co.uk/shopping; Tube: Covent Garden) is unbeatable for treats for the kids. The Underground sign and the Tube map are design icons, and you'll find them on everything. And there are lots of toys and models. Check out the **Science Museum,** Exhibition Rd., SW7 (☎ **020/7942-4000;** www.sciencemuseum.org.uk/shop; Tube: South Kensington) for oddball clocks and telescopes, books, high-tech games, puzzles, and other gimmickry—glow-in-the-dark t-shirts or a baby hot-air balloon. The replicas at the **Victoria & Albert Museum,** Cromwell Rd., SW7 (☎ **020/7942-2000;** www.vam.ac.uk/shopping; Tube: South Kensington) are pricier but beautiful: pewter, glass, ceramics, jewelry, and silk designs. It has books, games, and edibles, too. For more on the museums, see chapter 6.

Specialties

For top-notch knick-knacks, check out the box "Repro Rarities from London's Museums," above.

Anything Left Handed. 57 Brewer St., W1. ☎ **020/7437-3910.** www.anythingleft-handed.co.uk. Tube: Piccadilly Circus.

"Righties" will be amazed at how much they take for granted when they visit this unusual shop. It has scissors, rulers, DIY tools, kitchenware, corkscrews, pens, and mugs, all made for the southpaw.

Architectural Components Ltd. 4–8 Exhibition Rd., SW7. ☎ **020/7581-2401.** www.doorhandles.co.uk. Tube: South Kensington.

Ever yearned for those very English hearth implements, period doorknobs and knockers, snuffers, fireplace implements, and shaving stands? Here's where to find them. Some are quite reasonably priced.

BBC World Service Shop. Bush House, Strand, WC2. ☎ **020/7557-2576.** Tube: Temple.

This is great for suitcase-friendly gifts for Anglophiles of every age. It stocks videos of BBC TV shows and cassettes of classic drama and book readings from Radio 4, as well as lots of stuff for kids. There is another great shop at the **BBC Experience,** Broadcasting House, Portland Place, W1 (☎ **020/7765-0029**): see chapter 6 for more information on the attraction.

Coincraft. 44–45 Great Russell St., WC1. ☎ **020/7636-1188.** www.coincraft.com. Tube: Tottenham Court Rd.

For an unusual gift, check out this esteemed purveyor of collectible coins, banknotes, and archaeological objects. For less than £10 ($16), you could pick up a set of British Military Notes, used on army bases after World War II, or a Roman coin from a recent find in Eastern Europe.

The Filofax Centre. 21 Conduit St., W1. ☎ **020/7499-0457.** Tube: Oxford Circus.

Nothing was more emblematic of the booming 1980s than the Filofax loose-leaf organizer under every Yuppie arm. They're not cheap, but they're handy. Here at the British HQ, you can pick up every insert ever made for every size of filer. There's another branch in Neal Street, Covent Garden.

TRADITIONAL BRITISH GOODS

James Smith & Sons. 53 New Oxford St., WC1. ☎ **020/7836-4731.** www.james-smith.co.uk. Tube: Tottenham Court Rd.

Few things are more British than the umbrella, and the august James Smith & Sons has been making them since 1830. Traditional "brollies" come in nylon or silk, stretched over wood or metal frames. Prices start from about £30 ($48). A fancy umbrella or cane can set you back £300 ($480) or more.

Royal Doulton. 154 Regent St., W1. ☎ **020/7734-3184.** www.royal-doulton.com. Tube: Piccadilly Circus.

Founded over 200 years ago, Royal Doulton is one of the most famous names from the heart of English china production in Staffordshire. The company also produces Minton, Royal Albert, and Royal Crown Derby, all stocked here.

The Tea House. 15 Neal St., WC2. ☎ **020/7240-7539.** Tube: Covent Garden.

Besides teapots and tea balls, this wonderful-smelling shop sells more than 70 varieties of tea from India, China, Japan, and the rest of the world. Available loose or in bags, traditional English blends make excellent, light, and inexpensive gifts.

Waterford Wedgwood. 158 Regent St., W1. ☎ **020/7734-7262.** www.waterfordwedgwood.co.uk. Tube: Piccadilly Circus.

Waterford crystal and Wedgwood china share the same table at this upscale shop. Fine cut-glass vases, platters, and objets d'art come in a wide range of prices. You can even splash out on complete sets of the famous powder-blue and white Jasper china, and lots of other styles and patterns, too. There's a smaller branch on Piccadilly.

Whittard of Chelsea. 38 Covent Garden Market, WC2. ☎ **020/7379-6599.** www.whittard.com. Tube: Covent Garden.

Whittard has everything you need to make tea, even pure origin teas you can blend yourself. It sells a full range of coffees, too, and colorful ceramics that make appealing inexpensive gifts.

London After Dark

8

I hate to talk dirty again, after the revelation in chapter 7 that British men use the Internet to buy sexy undies for their sweethearts. But guess what caused the biggest bang on the London arts scene last year—another American star getting her kit off on stage. From the reaction to Kathleen Turner's unzipping in *The Graduate* at the Gielgud Theatre to Nicole Kidman in 1999's *Blue Room* at the Donmar Warehouse ("pure theatrical Viagra," one critic said), you'd think the Brits had never seen even a movie featuring anyone in the buff before. Jerry Hall later took over the Mrs. Robinson role to inevitable press comparison between Ms. Turner's and the ex-Mrs. Jagger's physical attributes.

Both theaters were at the forefront of a much more serious, but equally British, furor in 2000. Union Jacks flew at full mast when American bidders (note the irony!) failed to get their hands on two companies that jointly owned half the West End stages. Andrew Lloyd Webber and some City pals paid the Australian Holmes à Court family £87.5 million for the 10 Stoll Moss theaters, including the Gielgud. The Donmar and six others went to a group of investors, including some famous theater angels, for £18 million. The latter was exciting news, and not just for the terminally jingoistic. The Ambassador Theatre Group plans to commission, produce, and present new plays—a first, in such force, for the West End.

That's the real story—money, not sex, and lots of it, sloshing through the whole entertainment scene. And it's a great one for budget travelers. Lottery funds have poured into new work, old venues, and into democratizing the performing arts by improving facilities and restructuring ticket prices. Yet more millions, private this time, have transformed three redundant architectural treasures into what the media has dubbed the superclubs: together, **Home, Fabric,** and **Scala** can pack in 6,000 sweaty bodies. And they're really shaking up the competition.

BUY BEFORE YOU FLY West End shows, opera, ballet, big festivals, rock concerts, and other spectaculars all sell out very fast. If getting in is more important to you than getting a great deal, hand over the cash, and please try to book as far ahead as possible. Ticket-agency fees vary according to the event and seat quality. There's usually a handling charge, too. **Globaltickets (☎ 800/223-6108;** www.globaltickets.com) adds up to 20% to box offices prices, plus a

U.S. handling charge of up to $8. The office is open from 9am to 8pm Monday to Saturday, and noon to 7pm on Sunday. In London, the agency (☎ **020/7734-4555**) operates out of the Britain Visitor Centre, 1 Regent St., SW1. **Ticketmaster** (☎ **020/7316-4709;** www.ticketmaster.co.uk) takes phone and e-bookings around the clock for a fee of £1 to £5.50 ($1.60 to $8.80), plus a variable handling charge. It has branches in Tower Records and HMV (see chapter 7). **Firstcall** (☎ **0870/906-3838;** www.firstcalltickets.com) charges £1 to £5.65 ($1.60 to $9.05), plus a £1.50 ($2.40) handling charge, and never sleeps. Pop concert specialist **Stargreen** (☎ **020/7734-8932;** www.stargreen.co.uk) just imposes a £2 to £5 ($3.20 to $8) fee, and takes calls Monday to Friday 10am to 7pm, and 10am to 6pm on the weekend.

WHERE TO GET YOUR CULTURE INFO Even if you have zero intention of actually buying a ticket from them, surf the ticket agencies' Web sites for far-advance notice of what's going on. You can buy tickets online, at least for some shows, at **www.sceneone.co.uk**. However, the really cool thing about this site is its compilation of newspaper and magazine reviews for every event—theater, gigs, cinema, comedy, and so on. It regularly refers to—as you should—its listings bible *Time Out* (www.timeout.com), which comes out on Wednesdays. The *Evening Standard* (www.thisislondon.com) produces a supplement, *Hot Tickets,* on Thursdays. You'll also find good guides in the weekend broadsheet newspapers.

1 Entertainment on a Shoestring

Having a blast is a lot more affordable here than in other swinging cities. If you put in the legwork, join a few queues, and time your foray just right, you can cruise around town on a wave of dynamite deals. Below are our favorite London freebies and cheapies (£5/$8 and under), as well as some money-saving strategies.

FREEBIES

- **Holland Park Theatre** (see p. 278) Don't buy a ticket; just sit on the grass outside and soak up the music for free.
- **Barbican Centre** (see p. 279) There are informal **FreeStage** concerts here in the early evening most weekends and during festivals.
- **Royal Festival Hall** (see p. 281) Come for hot **Commuter Jazz** in the foyer on Fridays from 5:15 to 6:45pm.
- **Lamb & Flag** (see p. 291) Fantastic free jazz at a fantastically traditional pub in Covent Garden every Sunday night.
- **Bar Rumba** (see p. 285) Monday to Thursday, 5 to 9pm, drinks are two for the price of one, *and* there's no cover charge. So come early and stay late for free clubbing.
- **The Clinic** (see p. 286) Cool and cozy, this Chinatown nightclub plays progressive music, and entry is free before 10pm.
- **Subterania** (see p. 287) Come before 11pm on Saturday for a free night of all-style groove at this stalwart of the pre-cool Notting Hill.
- **WKD** (see p. 293) Live gigs by new bands on Monday and the groovin' Love4Love dance night on Friday at this Camden club-bar. Come in during happy hour before 9pm, and stay all night for free.
- **Mezzo** (see 155) Live music every night of the week at this giant Conran restaurant, from cabaret singers to jazzfunk, jazzgroove, and jazzwhatever-else-is-on-the-scene. No cover Sunday to Tuesday, and free for diners before 10pm Wednesday to Saturday.

- **Borders Books, Music & Café** (see p. 253) No reservations so come early for live music, readings, and talks at this mammoth bookstore, usually at 6:30pm.
- **Waterstone's** (see p. 293) This bookstore is so big there are even function rooms. Events tend to start around 7pm and most are free (or £1 to £2/$1.60 to $3.20). Booking recommended.
- **BBC TV and Radio Recordings** The Beeb is always looking for audiences for its radio and TV shows, and tickets are free. If you're a fan of quirky British humor, try and catch my absolute favorites, *The News Quiz* and *I'm Sorry I Haven't a Clue,* both on Radio4. For more information, contact **BBC Audience Services** (☎ **020/8576-1227;** www.bbc.co.uk/tickets).
- **Street Entertainment** Fire-eaters, mime artists, musicians playing Andean nose flutes, all throng at the Piazza at Covent Garden.

CHEAPIES

- **Royal Court Theatre** (see p. 271) The cutting edge of contemporary theater for £5 ($8) a ticket every Monday night. Last-minute standbys at the Theatre Downstairs cost a token 10p (16¢).
- **Shakespeare's Globe Theatre** (see p. 272) Just as the Bard did it, both the stage and production style. Stand in the raucous central yard for only £5 ($8).
- **The Gate** (see p. 275) "Pay what you can" on Happy Mondays at this theater above a pub in Notting Hill.
- **Soho Theatre** (see p. 275) Monday nights, all tickets are £5 ($8) at this recently re-launched hotbed of new writing and community theater.
- **The English National Opera** (see p. 276) Get here early for £2.50 ($4) day-of-performance Balcony tickets to see one of Britain's finest opera companies.
- **The Royal Ballet** (see p. 276) Who wants a restricted view or to have to stand? You do if it's Britain's premier ballet company and only costs £2 ($3.20).
- **Comedy Café** (see p. 282) The cover is only £3 ($4.80) on Thursdays. You can go for free on Wednesday, but that's when new acts try out.
- **Downstairs at the Troubadour** (see p. 282) The cover is a comical £4 ($6.40) at this Tuesday comedy night.
- **Social Bar** (see p. 283) Two indie bands gig here every Wednesday, a bargain at only £3 ($4.80).
- **Headstart** (see p. 285) Saturday night techno clubbing with low-tech cover, £5 ($8) before 11pm.
- **Atelier** (see p. 288) Gay house grooves on Thursday nights, free with a flyer before 9pm, then £5 ($8).
- **G.A.Y. at the Astoria** (see p. 288) Pick up a flyer to have fabulous fun at this club for just £1 ($1.60).
- **Central Station** (see p. 289) Never more than £4 ($6.40) cover for cabaret and cruisy club nights at this great gay and lesbian hangout.
- **Late View at the Victoria & Albert Museum** (see p. 207) Just £3 ($4.80) for an after-hours party night of exhibitions, live music, and lectures (plus £5/$8) at this stunning museum, from 6:30 to 9:30pm every Wednesday.
- **After-Dark Walking Tours** (see p. 240) Discover Jack the Ripper's haunts or the city's most haunted streets on a £5 ($8) walking tour . . . whooo!
- **Windsor Racecourse** (see p. 244) Take a boat up the Thames from the train station to see Monday evening horse racing, summer only: Tickets start at £4 ($6.40).

- **Wimbledon Greyhound Stadium** (see p. 244) A lot less posh than horse racing but doggone fun (sorry!): £5 ($8) in the main grandstand, £3.50 ($5.60) in the enclosure. Starts at 7:30pm.

EIGHT MONEY-SAVING STRATEGIES

1. **Flock to a Festival.** Time your trip to coincide with any one of a host of festivals for a blitz of entertainment, often at giveaway prices. It would be impossible to list every hot diary date, but you'll find the hottest in our "London Calendar of Events" in chapter 2. There are 20 London festivals covered in the brochure and e-listing compiled by the **British Arts Festivals Association** (☎ **020/7247-4667;** www.artsfestivals.co.uk). It's missing some, so check with *Time Out* and the **London Tourist Board** (☎ **020/7932-2000** or 020/7971-0026; www.londontown.com).
2. **Interrogate the Box Office.** Most performing-arts venues follow a few basic charging rules: Tickets may be cheaper on certain nights of the week, Monday especially, and for matinees; it's cheaper to see a preview; same-day tickets and standbys, on sale any time from 10am to 30 minutes before showtime, cost a fraction of normal prices; so do bad views and standing up; and seniors, students, and children almost always pay less.
3. **Wise up to the Web.** Just before you fly, scan **www.lastminute.com** for fab short-notice discounts of up to 50% on theater, musicals, comedy, cinema, classical music, rock and pop, and even VIP entry to nightclubs. **Firstcall** (see above) usually has one or two special offers, too.
4. **Buy a London for Less Card and Guidebook.** It can't guarantee ticket availability but an investment of just $19.95 does get you 20% to 25% off at West End theaters, and up to 80% (rarely that high) on concerts, opera, and ballet. See "Fifty Money-Saving Tips" in chapter 2.
5. **Theater Bargains, Part I.** For West End shows, go to the **Half-Price Ticket Booth,** run by the Society of London Theatre (SOLT), on the south side of Leicester Square, W1. It charges a £2 ($3.20) booking fee for day-of-performance tickets, a maximum of four per person, and no returns allowed. The booth is open Monday through Saturday from noon on matinee days (which vary from theater to theater), and from 2:30 to 6:30pm for evening performances, and it only accepts cash. SOLT was planning some changes, so check the Web site (**www.officiallondontheatre.co.uk**). And come early.

   Note: Scalpers cluster around the official booth. Don't succumb, and report any that try to rip you off to **SOLT,** 32 Rose St., WC2 (☎ **020/7557-6700**).
6. **Theater Bargains, Part II. The Big Bus Company** (☎ **020/7233-9533;** www.bigbus.co.uk) often includes theater tickets with its whole-day tour packages, for a great all-in cost of around £35 ($56).
7. **Go out Early for Some Discount Dancin'.** Nightclubs are keen to catch punters early and keep them as late as they can, so the cover is often cheaper at either end of the evening. Check both inside the main door of Tower Records on Picadilly Circus (see chapter 7) for promotional flyers and the clubs' Web sites. *Time Out* also prints a weekly Privilege Pass, which will get you a couple of quid off at selected venues.
8. **Head for a Happy Hour.** Not always half price and not always on all drinks, but even Scrooge would buy a round at happy hour. Here are some watering holes to check out in the early evening: **Bar Rumba** (see p. 285), **Central Station** (see p. 289), **Ku Bar** (see p. 289), **La Perla** (see p. 293), **The Match Bar** (see p. 293),

and **WKD** (see p. 293). These restaurant-bars from chapter 5 get happy, too: **Browns** (see p. 159), **Cactus Blue** (see p. 142), **Soho Spice** (see p. 156), and **Speakeasy at St. Christophers** (see p. 132).

2 London's Theater Scene

Prices for London theater are well below those in New York. There are about 40 West End stages with ticket prices from £10 to £35 ($16 to $56). Musicals tend to be the most popular and, therefore, the most expensive. But you can see them on tour in your hometown anyway. Instead, grab the chance to see great British actors doing great drama.

MAJOR COMPANIES

✪ **Royal Court Theatre.** Sloane Sq., SW1. ☎ **020/7565-5000.** www.royalcourttheatre.com. Jerwood Theatre Downstairs tickets £8–£19.50 ($12.80–$31.20) matinee; £10–£22.50 ($16–$36) evening; £5 ($8) restricted view; concessions £9 ($14.40) pre-booked, £5 ($8) on day of performance; all tickets unsold 1hr. before performance 10p (16¢). Jerwood Theatre Upstairs tickets £8 ($12.80) matinee; £10 ($16) evening; concessions £5 ($8). Mon evening, all seats in both theaters are £5 ($8). Tube: Sloane Sq.

The English Stage Company finally moved back home last year after spending £26 million on the Royal Court. The results are fabulous, mingling the best of this listed building with exciting new interior architecture—work even included digging out a new restaurant under Sloane Square (see chapter 5). The bill almost ruined the company, until the Jerwood Foundation wrote a big check—which is why its name is on the two spaces. Since staging the plays of the angry young men of the 1950s (John Osborne, Arnold Wesker, and so on), the Royal Court has built a world-class reputation as a forum for challenging modern writing. Conor McPherson's play *The Weir* moved into the West End and onto Broadway, as many do once the ESC has taken the "risk."

✪ **Royal National Theatre.** South Bank, SE1. ☎ **020/7452-3000.** www.nt-online.org. Tickets £10–£32 ($16–$51.20); matinee £10–£22 ($16–$35.20); seats with restricted view in Cottlesloe are £12 ($19.20); all tickets unsold 2hr. before performance in the Olivier and Lyttleton theaters £16 ($25.60); student standby may also be available for £8 ($12.80) 45min. before curtain at all 3 theaters. Tube: Waterloo, Southwark, Embankment (cross over Hungerford Bridge). Central London Fast Ferry: South Bank.

The Royal National Theatre is spread over three auditoria in this concrete bunker on the South Bank. The large open-stage **Olivier,** the traditional proscenium of the **Lyttelton** Theater, and the smaller, studio-style **Cottesloe** put on dozens of productions a year: reworked classics, cutting-edge premieres, musicals, and shows for young people. Beyond the productions, there's so much else going on. Backstage tours take place three to five times a day, depending on matinees, every day except Sunday: £4.75 ($7.60) adults, £3.75 ($6) children and concessions. Tickets to the early-evening **talks and readings** by hot names in the performing arts are almost given away at £3.50 or £2.50 ($5.60 or $4). **Celebriteas** are similar, but with a cream tea thrown in. They take place at 2:30pm on Fridays in August, and tickets cost £7 ($11.20). In July and August, the Theatre Square and the National's terraces are abuzz with **Watch This Space,** a free (yes, free) festival of music, mime, street theater, acrobats, and magic from all over the world. There are two elements: Taking to the Streets is on Wednesdays, Thursdays, and Saturdays at 1:15 and 6:15pm; Waterloo Sunsets is on Saturdays at 10:15pm. To join the events mailing list, call ☎ **020/7452-3327.** Otherwise, make your own party night, any night, in one of the bars, restaurants, or cafes here. The box office is open Monday to Saturday 10am to 8pm.

Royal Shakespeare Company. Barbican Centre, Silk St., EC2. ☎ **020/7638-8891** for box office. www.rsc.org.uk. Barbican Theatre £6–£28 ($9.60–$44.80). The Pit, midweek matinee £14 ($22.40), or £12 ($19.20) day of show; evening/Sat matinee £18 ($28.80), or £14 ($22.40) day of show. Bookable concessions: seniors £8–£14 ($12.80–$22.40) Wed matinee/evening; 4 children go ½ price with 1 adult ticket. Day-of-performance concessions: under-25s half-price; under-19s/seniors standby £10 ($16); full-time students standby £7 ($11.20). Tube: Barbican, Moorgate.

The Royal Shakespeare Company spends 8 months of the year in London, from October to May, and then either tours or goes back to Stratford-upon-Avon. Big productions, both the Bard's work and the occasional lucrative musical, fill the Barbican's 1,200-seat main auditorium. On the smaller stage of the Pit, the RSC puts on classical and contemporary works with a connection to Shakespeare. The Barbican box office is open daily from 9am to 8pm and can supply a full program for the London season. To see how the RSC works, call ☎ **020/7628-3351** (extension 7680), about the twice-daily backstage tours, Monday through Saturday during the Barbican season. Tickets cost £4 ($6.40) adults, £3 ($4.80) everyone else. The RSC also spends some of its London time at the **Young Vic** (see "Off–West End & Fringe Theater," below), and often has productions in the West End.

For information on the company's base in Stratford-upon-Avon, see chapter 9, "Easy Excursions from London."

✪ **Shakespeare's Globe Theatre.** 21 New Globe Walk, Bankside, SE1. ☎ **020/7401-9919.** www.shakespeares-globe.org. Tickets £10–£26 ($16–$41.60) adults; £9–£23 ($14.40–$36.80) concessions; £5 ($8) yard standing tickets. Price ranges reflect 4 levels of restriction to view. Season runs May–Sept. Tube: Mansion House and St. Paul's (cross over Millennium Bridge), Southwark. Central London Fast Ferry: Bankside Pier.

Just across the river at Bankside, this replica stands on the site of Shakespeare's original amphitheater, which burned down in 1613. It's an astonishing place, correct in every detail and constructed from the same materials. Four tiers of banked benches encircle the stage where the company performs the Bard's great works just as their predecessors would have done in his day—artistic director Mark Rylance played Cleopatra in 1999. The Elizabethan set shuns lighting and scenery. There are no little luxuries like cushioned seats or protection from the elements (hence, the summer-only season). Hawkers selling food and drink roam through the standing audience in the central yard during the performance.

This is so much more than just a theater, though. The late Sam Wanamaker's vision encompassed a learning network to educate the world about Shakespeare and the original performance style. The **Shakespeare's Globe Exhibition** charts the history of Elizabethan drama—bear baiting and stews, inter-theater rivalries on Bankside, penny stinkards, bodgers, and early special effects—and its modern portrayal. There's even performance footage taken from cameras sown into the actors' costumes. You can test your star potential at an interactive exhibit that allows you to record scenes from a Shakespeare play between those pre-recorded by actors, or edit a script on a

Parent Alert!

ChildsPlay at Shakespeare's Globe is a parent's dream. A drama workshop and story-telling session keep the kids (8 to 11 years old) happy and elsewhere, while you enjoy the Saturday matinee in peace. Tickets cost £9 ($14.40).

Central London Theaters

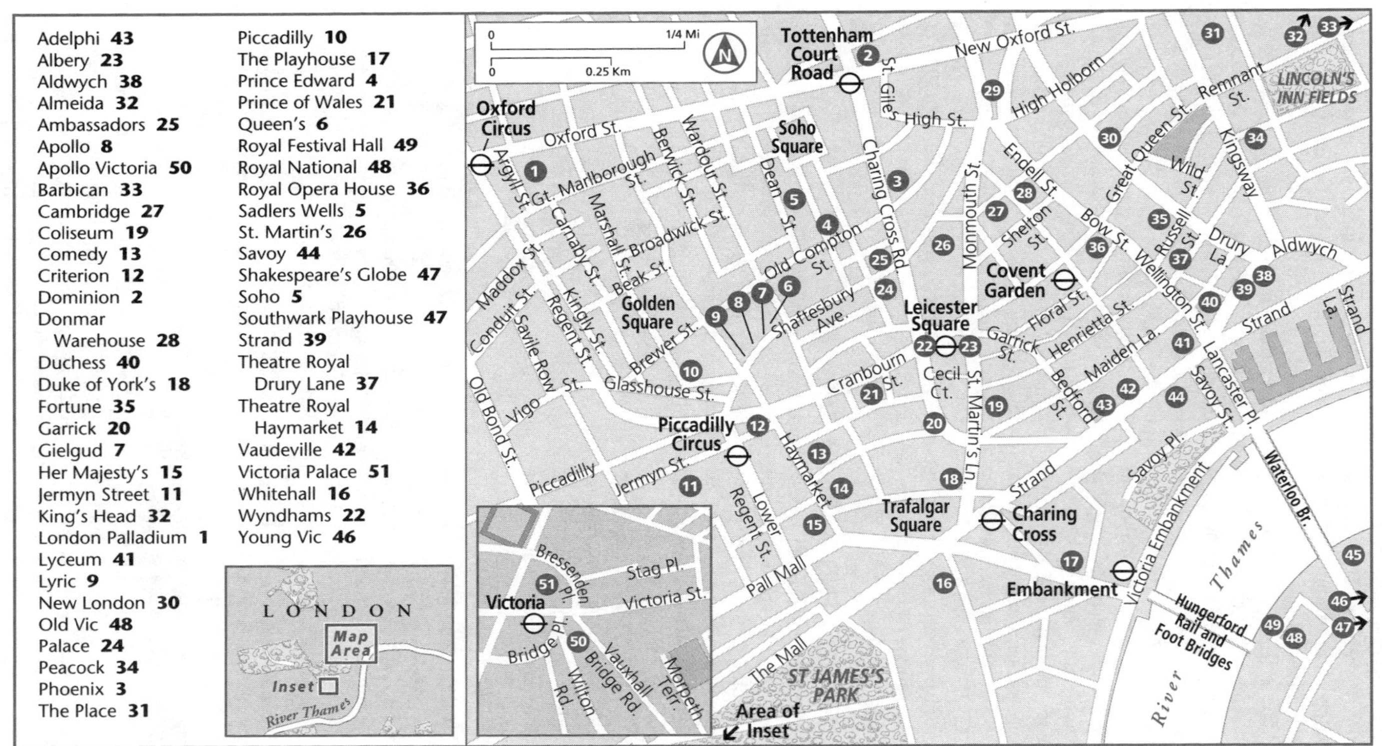

touch-screen exhibit. As of last year, all of this happens in the undercroft beneath the Globe. The exhibition's temporary home, the **Inigo Jones Theater,** is now used for rehearsals but will eventually stage winter performances. The exhibition is open daily, May to September 9am to noon and October to April 10am to 5pm, and tickets include a theater tour, unless matinees throw off the schedule (☎ **020/7902-1500**). Entry costs £5 or £7.50 ($8 or $12) with tour adults; £4 or £6 ($6.40 or $9.60) seniors and students; £3 or £5 ($4.80 or $8) children; £15 or £23 ($24 or $36.80) family ticket.

And call to find out about the huge range of **workshops** (stage fighting, voice work, and so on), **lectures, staged readings,** and **Walkshops**—guided tours of the historical sights of Southwark and a quick look round the Globe. Most take place on weekends, others on weekday evenings. Usually £5 to £9 ($8 to $14.40), tickets are free one weekend in the middle of June in celebration of Sam Wanamaker's birthday.

You can dine very well here, with superb river views: **Shakespeare's Globe Café** (☎ **020/7902-1576**) is open May to September from 10am to 11pm, October to April from 10am to 6pm; **Shakespeare's Globe Restaurant** (☎ **020/7928-9444;** reservations essential) has pre- and post-theater menus during the season and is open noon to 2:30pm, and 6 to 11pm throughout the year.

OFF–WEST END & FRINGE THEATER

Some of the most original theater in London is performed at the dozens of smaller theaters, many of them above pubs, devoted to "alternative" plays, revivals, in-your-face new drama, and so on, all across the city. Famous off–West End names carry huge cachet, but as long as you avoid the poshest seats, tickets are cheaper than at the glitzier theaters. Some of the best are listed below.

✪ **Almeida Theatre.** Almeida St., N1. ☎ **020/7359-4404.** www.almeida.co.uk. Tickets £11–£21.50 ($17.60–$34.40); £7 ($11.20) restricted view; £7–£11 ($11.20–$17.60) concessions. Mon–Thurs. Tube: Angel/Highbury.

This theater, in an old science lecture hall in Islington, has built such a white-hot reputation that million-dollar actors gladly play leading roles for under £300 a week. Ralph Fiennes transferred to Broadway with the Almeida's production of *Hamlet,* as did Dame Diana Rigg with *Medea.* Kevin Spacey, Liam Neeson, Cate Blanchett, and Juliette Binoche all treasure the accolade of having worked here. This year, after *The Tempest* closes on February 17, the theater finally begins its long-awaited refurbishment. But the show goes on, with a full program in 2001, including the annual Festival of Contemporary Music, a.k.a. Almeida Opera (June to July). The temporary home had yet to be announced at the time of writing, so call the box office, which is open Monday to Saturday 9:30am to 6pm.

Donmar Warehouse. 41 Earlham St., WC2. ☎ **020/7369-1732.** www.donmar-warehouse.com. Tickets usually £15–£25 ($24–$40), but vary for each show. Tube: Covent Garden.

Know Your Theater Lingo

When queuing up for tickets to a London show, be sure you know what types of seats you're buying. **Stalls** are the equivalent of orchestra seats in an American theater; the **Dress Circle** is actually the front balcony—except at Sadler's Wells (see section 4), which is waging a one-theatre war on elitist jargon: Here, it's the First and Second Circle. **Concessions** is a truly catchall term, though, usually covering students, seniors, and people with disabilities, who qualify for discounts.

Tableau Vivant

Actors re-create East London family life by candlelight at the Georgian and lovingly restored, **Dennis Severs' House,** 18 Folgate St., E1. (☎ **020/7247-4013;** Tube: Liverpool St.). Performances take place at 7:30pm on the first Monday of the month, and tickets cost £10 ($16).

Anyone shocked that a first-timer could have directed the smash hit *American Beauty* and won an Oscar for it should look at Sam Mendes's track record. He was only 24 when he took over the Donmar, now one of the hippest and most highly rated theaters in London. Under his artistic direction, the Donmar produces a huge range of old and new shows, including cabaret and performances by visiting companies. Nicole Kidman caused a rush of blood to every critic's head in 1999 during her less-than-fully-clad scenes in *The Blue Room.* Runs never last for more than 2 or 3 months. The box office is open from 10am to 6pm.

The Gate. The Prince Albert Pub, 11 Pembridge Rd., W11. ☎ **020/7229-0706.** Tickets £12 ($19.20), £6 ($9.60) concessions; Happy Mondays, pay what you can. Tube: Notting Hill Gate.

This tiny room above a pub in Notting Hill is one of the best alternative stages in London. Popular with local cognoscenti and young actors looking for a gold star on their resumes, the theater performs historic and contemporary international drama. The box office is open 10am to 6pm.

The King's Head. 115 Upper St., N1. ☎ **020/7226-1916.** Tickets £14 ($22.40); £10 ($16) concessions Sun–Thurs evenings, £15 ($24) Sat–Sun matinee; Fri–Sat evenings, no concessions. Tube: Angel, Highbury & Islington.

Arguably London's most famous fringe venue, the King's Head is also the city's oldest pub-theater and part of the arty Islington scene. Despite its tiny stage, it produces lively musicals and revues; some that originated here have gone on to become successful West End productions. Come for pub grub and a pint first. The box office is open Monday to Saturday 10am to 8pm, Sunday 10am to 4pm.

Soho Theatre. 21 Dean St., W1. ☎ **020/7478-0100.** www.sohotheatre.com. Tickets £9–£11 ($14.40–$17.60), £7.50 ($12) concessions; Mon all tickets £5 ($8). Tube: Tottenham Court Rd.

This theater had been closed so long people almost forgot it was there. But they cannot have missed last year's whizz-bang reopening of the amazing new Soho space: The highlight was four BBC radio plays recorded in front of invited audiences. The mission, and it is that evangelistic, is to foster new writing talent, which includes working with the local community and businesses like Marks & Spencer. There are writers' booths, seminar and rehearsal rooms, and a Café Lazeez downstairs (see chapter 5).

Young Vic. 66 The Cut, SE1. ☎ **020/7928-6363.** www.youngvic.org. Main House tickets £15–£18 ($24–$28.80), £12 ($19.20) concessions; preview performances £9 ($14.40), £7 ($11.20) concessions. Studio £8–£9 ($12.80–$14.40), £5 ($8) concessions. Tube: Waterloo, Southwark.

The Young Vic aims to introduce and hone new stage talent in its resident company. The studio space and main house stage an eclectic variety of productions, from last year's *'Tis Pity She's a Whore* starring yummy Jude Law, to Shakespeare's *Julius Caesar* on the schedule this year. The Young Vic also hosts and collaborates with the Royal Shakespeare Company and other touring companies. The faded decor and inadequate loos are somewhat redeemed by the delicious brasserie menu, available noon to 8pm, catered by wicked local deli, Konditor & Cook (☎ **020/7620-2200** for reservations). The box office is open Monday to Saturday 10am to 7pm.

3 The Performing Arts

OPERA & BALLET

Opera audiences have flocked to Covent Garden ever since the mid-18th century. All the world's great singers, from the legendary Adelina Patti and Maria Callas to the three tenors, have appeared at what is now the stunningly refurbished **Royal Opera House.** An Honours List of famous British composers has premiered works here: Sir Arthur Bliss, Sir Ralph Vaughan Williams, Sir Benjamin Britten, Sir Michael Tippett, and Sir William Walton. The **Royal Opera Company** moved here after music publishers Boosey & Hawkes bought the lease of the building after World War II. The other big opera venue is the beautiful **London Coliseum,** on nearby St. Martin's Lane, which is the home of the **English National Opera.** It sings in English, is much more cutting edge, and sets almost-affordable ticket prices.

After WWII, the Royal Opera House also invited Lilian Baylis and her ballet company to take up residence. But it was not until the big refurb that **The Royal Ballet,** as it is now known, got a custom-made performance space. Also newly renovated, **Sadler's Wells** no longer has its eponymous performers: Baylis's second company left there for Birmingham a few years ago. But the touring **Rambert Dance Company** usually has a Sadler's Wells season, as the **English National Ballet** does at the London Coliseum.

London is also a regular stop for international dance companies, both classical and contemporary. See "Dance," below for more on the sizzling modern scene.

MAJOR COMPANIES

The English National Opera. London Coliseum, St. Martin's Lane, WC2. ☎ **020/7632-8300.** www.eno.org. Tickets £5–£55 ($8–$88). Discounted day-of-performance tickets: £27 ($43.20) in Dress Circle Mon–Fri, Sat matinee; £2.50 ($4) in the Balcony, any day; on sale at the box office at 10am or by telephone from noon for matinees and 2:30pm for evening performances. Tickets unsold 3hr. before performance: £28 ($44.80) in Dress/Upper Circle, Sat evening; £18 ($28.80) seniors and students any day. Children under 18 are ½ price with an adult in the Stalls or Dress Circle. Tube: Charing Cross, Leicester Sq.

English National Opera (ENO) is a very innovative company. It thrills enthusiasts and rocks traditionalists with newly commissioned works and lively, theatrical, and often updated reinterpretations of the classics. The first half of 2001 will see four new productions, six revivals, and the world premiere of *From Morning to Midnight* by David Sawer from a play by Georg Kaiser (April 27). The ENO is also embarking on a mammoth production of Richard Wagner's four-opera Ring Cycle project, due to culminate in 2005: The first two are *The Rhinegold* in January and *The Valkyrie* in September. The ENO performs in the 2,350-seat London Coliseum, always in English, during a season lasting from September to July. Pre-performance talks are free (you must book) and start at 4:45pm. At Christmas and during the summer, the English National Ballet takes over the auditorium. If you're prepared to put in a bit of effort (hang around for standbys and so forth), tickets here are an incredible deal. The box office is open 10am to 8pm (9:30am to 8:30pm, by phone), Monday through Saturday.

✪ **The Royal Ballet.** Royal Opera House, Bow St., WC2. ☎ **020/7304-4000.** www.royalballet.org. Tickets evening £15–£60 ($24–$96), £6 ($9.60) restricted view or standing,

£12.50 ($20) standby available 4hr. ahead to concessions only; matinee £11–£35 ($17.60–$56), £2 ($3.20) restricted view or standing, children ½ price. Tube: Covent Garden.

Britain's leading ballet company is now firmly ensconced back at the Royal Opera House, but last year saw more than logistical upheavals. Long-time director Anthony Dowell has retired, to be succeeded by Ross Stretton, a former stalwart of the American Ballet Theater, then artistic director of The Australian Ballet. The company's repertoire is very varied but tilts toward the classics and works by its earlier choreographer-directors, Sir Frederick Ashton (*La Fille Mal Gardée,* this year) and Kenneth Macmillan (*Romeo and Juliet* and *Triad*).

✪ **The Royal Opera.** Royal Opera House, Bow St., WC2. ☎ **020/7304-4000.** www.royalopera.org. Tickets £15–£150 ($24–$240), £6 ($9.60) restricted view or standing, £15 ($24) standby may be available 4hr. before performance to concessions only. Tube: Covent Garden.

Despite promises to bring opera to "the people," the revamped Royal Opera House only sells 20% of its seats through the box office—the rest are filled by prosperous debenture holders and the corporate entertainment crowd. The good news is that prices have come way down. Restricted view and standing tickets cost about the same as a pizza, while bargain-rate seats for smaller operas cost even less on weekends, which is when most venues seem to inflate prices. The combined talents of the Orchestra of the Royal Opera House, the Chorus of the Royal Opera, and the dozens of guest artists and conductors are sublime, under the musical direction of Bernard Haitink. Operas are usually sung in the original language, and when they aren't, projected supertitles translate the libretto for the audience. This year's program includes Verdi's *La Traviata* and *Otello,* Puccini's *Turandot,* Mozart's *Die Entführung aus dem Serail,* and a new production of *The Queen of Spades* by Tchaikovsky (the schedules hop around the calendar). The International Concert Series boasts a performance by Kiri Te Kanewa on March 4.

CLASSICAL MUSIC

The city supports several major orchestras—the **London Symphony Orchestra** at the Barbican Centre, the **London Philharmonic** and **Philharmonia Orchestra** at the Royal Festival Hall, on the South Bank, and the wandering **Royal Philharmonic.** Then there's the host of choirs, chamber groups, and historic instrument ensembles, and the highly regarded but smaller venues (see below), where they often perform. Look out for the modernist **London Sinfonietta,** the **English Chamber Orchestra,** and the **Gabrieli Consort.** Lastly, London also draws top-name international musicians to its top-name venues, including the Royal Albert Hall (see "Major Arts Venues," below).

The **British Music Information Centre,** 10 Stratford Place, W1 (☎ **020/7499-8567;** www.bmic.co.uk), is *the* resource center for new British classical music. As well as running an online database of scores and recordings, the BMIC provides free telephone and walk-in information on current and upcoming events (open noon to 5pm, Monday to Friday). It also holds recitals (£6/$9.60 adults, £4/$6.40 seniors and students), usually on Tuesday and Thursday at 7:30pm. Call for exact times, then take the Tube to Bond Street.

London Symphony Orchestra. Barbican Centre, Silk St., EC2. ☎ **020/7638-8891.** www.lso.co.uk. Tickets £6.50–£35 ($10.40–$56); £3 ($4.80) per child accompanied by an adult at series concerts; £6.50 ($10.40) all tickets at family concerts; 20% discount for buying a ticket to every concert in a series. Tube: Barbican, Moorgate.

Performers in the Park

It might sound like utter lunacy in a place as rain-tossed, allegedly, as Britain, but there's a very strong tradition of open-air theater, music, and dance in London's parks. Stressed city folk love spreading rugs on the grass and tucking into their interval picnics. Alfresco dining gets comically competitive—silver cutlery and damask napkins, bottles of champagne, and strawberries. The **Open Air Theatre,** Regent's Park, NW1 (☎ **020/7486-2431;** www.open-air-theatre.org.uk; Tube: Baker St., Regent's Park), has been staging summer drama, from June to early September, since 1932. Tickets cost £8.50 to £22.50 ($13.60 to $36). **Holland Park Theatre,** Holland Park, W11 (☎ **020/7602-7856;** Tube: Holland Park), has opera, and a week of ballet, from June to August under a temporary canopy in the ruins of the Jacobean Holland House. Tickets cost £26 ($41.60), but savvy bargain hounds listen to the music for free while relaxing on the lawn outside. Perhaps the most famous open-air concerts are during July and August at the Robert Adam mansion, **Kenwood House,** Hampstead Lane, NW3 (☎ **020/7344-4444;** www.picnicconcerts.com). This is a magical scene, on Hampstead Heath, by a lake that reflects the spectacular firework finales—a favorite with unstuffy types enjoying popular classics. Tickets are £16 to £37 ($25.60 to $59.20) for a deckchair, or £14 to £20 ($22.40 to $32) to promenade. Take the Tube to East Finchley, and catch the courtesy bus. For more details on **Kenwood House & Iveagh Bequest,** see chapter 6. Also call **Somerset House** (see page 203) for about open-air concerts and theater in the stupendous courtyard.

London's top orchestra is a major international force under the direction of principal conductor Sir Colin Davis. You'll know its work already if you've seen *Star Wars, Episode 1: The Phantom Menace.* The LSO worked on the soundtrack with John Williams at the famous Abbey Road Studios. It stages 85 concerts a year at its main home in the Barbican. One of the highlights this year is the spring Bohemian Nights, a series of 10 concerts celebrating Czech composers. Reduced-price student standby tickets are sometimes on sale 90 minutes before a performance. The most taxing part of the evening will be finding your way around the labyrinthine arts complex, so allow plenty of time.

RECITAL VENUES

Don't forget to check out the magical candlelit concerts at **St. Martin-in-the-Fields** (see chapter 6).

St. John's Smith Square. Smith Square, SW1. ☎ **020/7222-1061.** www.sjss.org.uk. Tickets £6–£20 ($9.60–$32). Tube: Westminster, St. James's Park.

This baroque masterpiece, designed by Thomas Archer, provides a slightly bigger performance space than Wigmore Hall, but a lot less comfortable. It hosts chamber groups, choirs, and voice soloists. The Thursday lunchtime concerts at 1pm are a steal at £5 ($8). The box office is open Monday to Friday, from 10am to 5pm, for advance booking.

Wigmore Hall. 36 Wigmore St., W1. ☎ **020/7935-2141.** Tickets £7–£20 ($11.20–$32). Discounted standby tickets sometimes available for concessions. Tube: Bond St., Oxford Circus.

Wigmore Hall is considered by many cognoscenti to be the best auditorium in London for intimacy and acoustics. Buy the cheapest seats, as it really doesn't matter where you sit. All the tickets at The Sunday Morning Coffee Concerts, and those recorded for BBC Radio 3 on a Monday lunchtime, are £8 or £10 ($12.80 or $16)—an excellent deal. The box office is open Monday to Saturday from 10am to 8:30pm and 45 minutes before performance on Sunday.

DANCE

The **London Dance Network** is a publicly funded organization set up in 1998 to build both audiences and support for creating a National Dance House. Its Web site (**www.london-dance.net**) is a superb source of information on everything that's going on in the capital. Contemporary dance is certainly thriving here. Top international companies like Merce Cunningham, Twyla Tharp, and Trisha Brown appear at the Barbican Centre, Royal Festival Hall, and Sadler's Wells Theatre (see "Major Arts Venues," below). While smaller venues, like **The Place** (see below), focus on the even more avant-garde. Also worth checking out for the occasional dance events in their programs are: **ICA,** The Mall, SW1 (☎ **020/7930-3647;** www.ica.org.uk; Tube: Piccadilly Circus, Charing Cross); and **Riverside Studios,** Crisp Rd., W6 (☎ **020/8237-1111;** www.riversidestudios.co.uk; Tube: Hammersmith).

Many of these are among the host of venues for **Dance Umbrella** (☎ **020/8741-4040;** www.danceumbrella.co.uk), the internationally acclaimed fall showcase of contemporary dance. It runs for 6 weeks from the very end of September. Seats are usually available on the day of performance, except to see blockbuster companies, and cost as little as £8 ($12.80), depending on the venue.

The Place. 17 Duke's Rd., WC1. ☎ **020/7387-0031.** www.theplace.org.uk. Tickets £6–£10 ($9.60–$16). Tube: Euston.

This is *the* showplace for contemporary dance and has been since it was founded in the late 1960s by Robert Cohan of the Martha Graham Company. Now The Place is the permanent home of the Richard Alston Dance Company and the London Contemporary Dance School. Having finally got the funds for refurbishment, the theater is closed until April 2001, when it relaunches as a fully fledged commissioning venue with an all-new dance program. In the meantime, The Place is hot-staging around town and there will still be a "Resolution" season of up-and-coming British and European companies in January and February. The box office is open Monday to Friday (and Saturday performance days) from 10am to 6pm.

4 Major Arts Venues

✪ **Barbican Centre.** Silk St., EC2. ☎ **020/7638-8891.** www.barbican.org.uk. Tube: Barbican or Moorgate.

Reputedly the largest arts complex in Europe, the Barbican is so maze-like that yellow lines have been painted across its brick-paved walkways and piazzas to help visitors find their way around. If you see people walking ahead of you, don't automatically follow them thinking they know where they're headed. The sound of your footsteps will only reassure *them* they're not lost after all, probably wrongly.

The architecture may be the object of derision, but even detractors agree that the arts facilities inside the Barbican are superb. The complex contains two theaters, two art galleries, three cinemas, and several restaurants, bars, and cafes. The acoustically excellent concert hall is home to the London Symphony Orchestra (see "Classical Music," above), and hosts other festivals and large-scale events between LSO performances. The Royal Shakespeare Company (see "London's Theater Scene," above) takes up residence from October to May, with the other 6 months of the year taken up by the Barbican International Theatre Event (BITE). This festival of drama, music-theater, and dance comprises 19 productions and 180 performances, as well as foyer and outdoor events. Tickets range from free to £30 ($48).

The BITE talks and workshops are part of the regular **Barbican Plus** program: Some cost £5 to £8 ($8 to $12.80), but many are free. Call the box office, open daily from 9am to 8pm, for tickets. There are free concerts (**FreeStage**) at lunchtime and in the early evenings, most weekends, and as part of festivals, too. Call ahead to find out what's on.

London Coliseum. St. Martin's Lane, WC2. ☎ **020/7632-8300.** www.eno.org. Tube: Leicester Sq., Charing Cross.

The Coliseum was built in 1904 and is one of London's most architecturally spectacular houses. Prior to some modernization work last summer, the Coliseum was pure hell for the musicians: Temperatures in the orchestra pit used to reach 84°. The Coliseum is home to English National Opera and hosts touring companies when the ENO is resting or away. English National Ballet has a fleeting Christmas season and comes back again during the summer. The ENO Web site lists the full program. The box office is available by phone around the clock.

Royal Albert Hall. Kensington Gore, SW7. ☎ **020/7589-8212.** www.royalalberthall.com. Tube: South Kensington, Kensington High St.

In summer, a £3 ($4.80) standing ticket to one of the Sir Henry Wood Promenade Concerts at the Royal Albert Hall has to be one of the best buys of the cultural season. Known as "The Proms," this is the most famous classical music festival in the world. Every year, from mid-July to mid-September, the daily changing performances cover every conceivable spot on the classical music spectrum—and often two or three very different pieces a night. During the festival, the hall takes out all the central orchestra seats to leave an open unregulated space for the promenaders. They take over the show on the Last Night of the Proms, a national institution that's usually televised, with wild jingoistic flag waving and a swaying sing-along to the sounds of Elgar's most famous anthem, *Pomp and Circumstance.* The Victorian Royal Albert Hall, immortalized in a classic children's book as *The Great Jelly Mould of London,* has a massive 5,000 seats. The rest of the year, it puts on a spectacular range of entertainment. Joaquin Cortes, Robbie Williams, Sheryl Crow, Burt Bacharach, Tony Bennett, B.B. King, Cirque du Soleil, and the world's top stand-up comedians, tennis players, and sumo wrestlers—they've all appeared here. The Royal Albert Hall is another of London's major arts institutions going through a big refurbishment (until 2003), but this one is not closing. The box office is open daily from 9am to 9pm.

✪ **Royal Opera House.** Bow St., WC2. ☎ **020/7304-4000.** www.royaloperahouse.org. Tube: Covent Garden.

The Royal Opera House reopened at the end of 1999, on time amazingly, in its new guise as the "people's pleasure palace." The revamp is so stupendous that it has vanquished all controversy—a Herculean feat. The Royal Ballet has new performance and rehearsal spaces. The backstage area is crammed with high-tech equipment. The comfort factor is vastly improved in the main auditorium, where there's new seating and air-conditioning. The Vilar Floral Hall—a stunning, Victorian, glazed atrium—has been restored half a century after it was damaged in a fire. And a new "indoor street" called The Link runs through the ROH to the piazza colonnade, finally completed to Inigo Jones's design.

The ROH also seems to have picked up a few tips on open access from the Barbican and the South Bank Centre, which is why it now merits a separate listing as a major arts venue. The new Linbury Studio Theatre and Clore Studio Upstairs host a diverse range of talks, workshops, and student and visiting performers, both music and dance: Tickets cost only £5.50 to £20 ($8.80 to $32), or £3 to £6 ($4.80 to $9.60) standing. There are free (yes, free!) lunchtime concerts every Monday at 1pm during the season. Tickets are available from 10am on the day of performance at the information desk next to the box office. Pre-performance talks are also free. You can tour backstage, usually at 10:30am, 12:30, and 2:30pm, for £6 or £5 ($9.60 or $8) for concessions. Although eight tickets are held back to be sold on the day of performance, it is better to book as far ahead as possible—and I mean months.

The Link, its coffee bar, and the box office are open to the public Monday to Saturday from 10am to 8pm, the Vilar Floral Hall from 10am to 3pm. The Amphitheatre restaurant (☎ **020/7212-9254;** e-mail: searcys@roh.org.uk), with its terrace overlooking Covent Garden, serves modern European cuisine to the public as well as theater-goers at lunchtime. But it's a splurgy joint, with main courses costing £10.50 to £12.50 ($16.80 to $20), so have a starter and pudding instead.

Sadler's Wells Theatre. Rosebery Ave., EC1. ☎ **020/7863-8000.** www.sadlers-wells.com. Tube: Angel.

Recently rebuilt, this is one of the busiest stages in London and also one of the best, with superb sight lines. It hosts top visiting opera and dance companies from around the world, including the Rambert Dance Company. Each August, Sadler's Wells presents the Mosaics festival of new dance and physical theater, performed by over 30 young companies: Tickets are a steal at £6 to £8 ($9.60 to $12.80). Sadler's Wells is dedicated to making dance accessible, so there are always some seats within reach of the budget traveler (£7.50 to £45/$12 to $72). Prices are much the same at The Peacock Theatre in Holborn, initially a temporary home during the rebuild and now a permanent satellite venue staging longer runs of more populist musical theater and dance. Sadler's Wells shuns elitist jargon. So the "ticket office" is open Monday to Saturday 10:30am to 8pm, and seats are divided into the First and Second Circle.

South Bank Centre. Belvedere Rd., SE1. ☎ **020/7960-4242.** www.sbc.org.uk. Tube: Waterloo, Southwark, Embankment (cross over Hungerford Bridge). Central London Fast Ferry: South Bank Pier.

The constituent parts of this huge arts complex have all now ditched the umbrella name, in a bid to distance themselves in public perceptions from the concrete monstrosity they call home. The **Royal Festival Hall on the South Bank,** which celebrates its 50th birthday in May, comprises three music and dance venues: **RFH1** is the usual venue for big populist orchestral performances. The smaller **RFH2,** which used to be the Queen Elizabeth Hall, is known for chamber music, semi-staged opera, and special events. And the intimate **RFH3,** the old Purcell Room, usually hosts advanced students and young performers making their professional debut. All three stages are lit almost every night of the year, with ballet (including the Royal Ballet), jazz, pop, and folk concerts in the diary as well as classical music.

If you can, try to make it over for Meltdown (**www.meltdown.co.uk**) in the last 2 weeks of June. Each year, the RFH invites a different performer to devise their fantasy arts festival, so it's a uniquely diverse (or perverse, perhaps) event. Following in the footsteps of Elvis Costello and Nick Cave, the reclusive Scott Walker put together the 2000 Meltdown. The program included Blur, Smog, Jarvis Cocker, Radiohead, *Waiting for Godot* in French, and a piece by Mark Anthony Turnage, whose *Silver Tassie* had just premiered at the Royal Opera House.

Lastly, there's the foyer of the Royal Festival Hall, one of the city's hardest-working venues. Free informal recitals take place in front of the Festival Buffet cafe, daily from noon to 2pm. On Friday evenings, it's Commuter Jazz from 5:15 to 6:45pm. Blazing is a summer fest of mostly free events—music, mime, dance, poetry, workshops (paid-for), and more—on the Ballroom Floor. Booking is not usually required for any of these, but check with the box office, open daily from 10am to 10pm.

The **Royal National Theatre** (see "London's Theater Scene," above) and the **Hayward Gallery** (see chapter 6) are also part of the South Bank Centre. As is the **National Film Theatre,** the hub of November's London Film Festival (www.lff.org.uk). The **Museum of the Moving Image** is closed for refurbishment.

5 The Club & Music Scene

COMEDY & CABARET

Do be careful when you see laughably low-ticket prices in listings magazines: They may be for open-mike, talentless-spotting sessions. However, some deals really *are* too good to miss. At the **Comedy Café,** 66 Rivington St., EC2 (☎ **020/7739-5706;** Tube: Old St.), there's no admission charge on Wednesday, when new acts perform, and it's only £3 ($4.80) on Thursday.

Some pubs also have highly rated, regular comedy nights: **Bound & Gagged,** Tufnell Park Tavern, Tufnell Park Rd., N7 (☎ **020/7483-3456;** Tube: Tufnell Park), starts at 9:15pm on Saturdays, with a £6 to £8 ($9.60 to $12.80) cover, plus £1 ($1.60) membership; **Comedy at Soho Ho,** Crown & Two Chairmen, 31 Dean St., W1 (☎ **0956/996690;** Tube: Leicester Sq., Tottenham Court Rd.), is on Saturdays at 8:30pm, cover £5 to £6 ($8 to $9.60); **Downstairs at the Troubadour,** 265 Old Brompton Rd., SW5 (☎ **020/7370-1434;** Tube: Earls Court), is at 9pm on Tuesdays, cover £4 ($6.40). Typically, you need to get there half an hour or an hour before a show.

Canal Café Theatre. The Bridge House, Delamere Terrace, W2. ☎ **020/7289-6054.** Cover £7 ($11.20), or £5 ($8) concessions, plus £1 ($1.60) membership. Tube: Royal Oak, Warwick Ave.

For a really lovely evening out, come early and stroll along the canal in this very pretty part of Maida Vale. The Canal Café Theatre is a small but long-established fringe venue above a pub. Performances range from drama to cabaret, but the most famous is the topical sketch show *Newsrevue* (Thursday to Saturday at 9:30pm, Sunday at 9pm). You can buy tickets in person up to 45 minutes before the show, or book on the office line above, which is sometimes manned by an answering machine. Food is served until 10pm.

The Comedy Store. Haymarket House, 1A Oxendon St., SW1. ☎ **020/7344-0234.** www.thecomedystore.co.uk. Cover £12–£15 ($19.20–$24), or £8 ($12.80) concessions. Tube: Piccadilly, Leicester Sq.

Launched in 1979, The Comedy Store has nurtured such talents as Rik Mayall, Keith Allen, Dawn French, Ben Elton, Paul Merton, Jack Dee, and Eddie Izzard. It is still London's premier venue for current and up-and-coming stars. On Tuesday nights, the Cutting Edge performs a topical satirical revue. An improv group, The Comedy Store Players, takes the stage on Wednesday and Sunday. Shows start at 8pm, Tuesday to Sunday, with extra midnight performances on Friday and Saturday.

Madame JoJo's. 8 Brewer St., W1. ☎ **020/7734-3040.** www.madamejojos.com. Cover £10–£25 ($16–$40), £3–£5 ($4.80–$8) for plays Mon–Wed 7:30–9:30pm. Tube: Piccadilly Circus.

Paul Raymond, of Revue Bar fame, opened this drag cabaret club in 1986. Madame Jojo's changed hands recently. The revamp has stayed true to the tarted-up interior used in countless movies, including *Eyes Wide Shut,* but the entertainment is much more varied, and the clientele mainly straight. From Monday to Wednesday, the evening starts with an off-the-wall play. Silver Screen is a cult movie night, classics and "dirty ones," every second Monday. On Tuesdays, there's live music with Lady Carol and guests. On Wednesdays, DJs spin funk and 1980s grooves. There's more live music on Thursdays. Friday is Bizarre, funky house with a twist and the only night that still draws the gay crowd (trannies "dressed to impress" pay less to get in). As good as the cabaret can be, avoid Saturdays: Tickets are £25 ($40), and the club is swarming with raucous hen and stag parties. On Sunday, zone out to deep funk. Open Monday to Wednesday 7:30pm to 3am, Thursday to Saturday 10pm to 3am, and Sunday 9:30pm to 2:30am.

ROCK & POP

London has hundreds of live music venues—10,000-plus seaters, old theaters, radio halls, nightclubs, and intimate bars—hosting rock legends, pre-fab boy and girl bands, and the sharpest indie sounds. For big name gigs, you'll need to book well ahead—sometimes several months. The Web site **www.aloud.com** is an excellent source of advance info, as are the ticket agencies mentioned at the start of this chapter. But contact the box office directly to avoid the booking fee. These are London's premier venues: **Astoria,** 157 Charing Cross Rd., WC2 (☎ **020/7434-0403;** Tube: Tottenham Court Rd.); **Brixton Academy,** 211 Stockwell Rd., SW9 (☎ **020/7771-2000;** Tube: Brixton); **Forum,** 9–17 Highgate Rd., NW5 (☎ **020/7344-0044;** Tube: Kentish Town); **Shepherds Bush Empire,** Shepherds Bush Green, W12 (☎ **020/7771-2000;** Tube: Shepherds Bush); **Wembley Arena & Conference Centre,** Empire Way, Wembley, Middlesex (☎ **020/8802-0802;** Tube: Wembley Park).

For a laid-back session that you don't have to plan in advance, or spend a mint on, try one of the places below—and **WKD** in Camden for great Monday night gigs (see section 7 below). Otherwise, for the latest low-down on what's super-hot and where, consult the listings magazines.

The Bull & Gate. 389 Kentish Town Rd., NW5. ☎ **020/7485-5358.** Cover £4–£5 ($6.40–$8). No credit cards. Tube: Kentish Town.

Smaller, cheaper, and scruffier than its competitors, the Bull & Gate is the unofficial headquarters of London's pub music scene. Independent and unknown bands play back-to-back, sometimes three or four a night, starting at 8:30pm.

Social Bar. 5 Little Portland St., W1 ☎ **020/7636-4992.** Cover £3 ($4.80). Tube: Oxford Circus.

This great little bar hosts the Acoustically Heavenly night every Wednesday. There are always two bands in the line-up, and the gig starts at 7:30pm. Open Monday to Saturday noon to midnight, Sunday 5 to 10:30pm.

Spitz. Old Spitalfields Market, 109 Commercial Rd., E1 ☎ **020/7392-9032.** www.spitz.co.uk. Cover £4–£8 ($6.40–$12.80). Tube: Liverpool St.

This vibrant arts center puts on live music every night except Monday, at 7 or 8pm. Offerings range from drum and bass to electronica and funky fusions of everything in between. Spitz also has a bar, restaurant, club, and gallery. Open Monday 5:30 to 11pm, Tuesday to Sunday 11am to midnight.

FOLK

Cecil Sharp House. 2 Regent's Park Rd., NW1. ☎ **020/7485-2206.** www.efdss.org/events. Cover £3–£8 ($4.80–$12.80). Tube: Camden Town.

CSH was the focal point of the folk revival in the 1960s. The English Folk Dance and Song Society is based here, and it continues to document this music and nurture it. You'll find a whole range of traditional English music, Cajun, Irish, and anything else that's danceable.

JAZZ

There is a superb gig guide at **www.jazzservices.org.uk**; otherwise trawl the listings magazines. Freebie favorites include the **FreeStage** sessions at the Barbican (☎ **020/7638-4141**), at lunchtimes and in the early evening, on weekends and during festivals, and **Commuter Jazz** from 5:15 to 6:45pm on Fridays at the Royal Festival Hall (☎ **020/7960-4242**). For more information on both, see "Freebies," in section 1 above. The **Lamb & Flag** in Covent Garden (see "Pubs," below) also puts on free jazz on Sunday night from 7:30pm. So does **The 100 Club** noon to 4pm on a Friday (see below).

Jazz Café. 5 Parkway, NW1. ☎ **020/7916-6060.** www.jazzcafe.co.uk. Cover £6–£20 ($9.60–$32). Tube: Camden Town.

The sounds are very contemporary here, anything and everything from rap to Latin jazz. You must book your table ahead of time, but try to avoid going upstairs; the restaurant is pretty pricey. Music starts at 7pm. Open Monday through Thursday until 1am, until 2am on Friday and Saturday, and midnight on Sunday.

The 100 Club. 100 Oxford St., W1. ☎ **020/7636-0933.** Cover £6–£10 ($9.60–$16). Tube: Tottenham Court Rd.

The 100 Club really has got that thing. The smoky basement stage hosts jazz sets, swing, jive, rhythm and blues, as well as funk and soul. Every night is different, so give them a ring-a-ling to find out what's on. Don't miss the fab Friday Lunchtime Jazz—admission is free. Open Monday to Thursday 7:30pm to midnight, Friday noon to 3pm and 8:30pm to 2am, Saturday 7:30pm to "late," Sunday 7:30 to 11:30pm.

PizzaExpress Jazz Club. 10 Dean St., W1. ☎ **020/7437-9595.** www.pizzaexpress.co.uk. Cover £10–£20 ($16–$32), plus food. Tube: Tottenham Court Rd.

Unlikely though it sounds, the basement of this chain restaurant is one of the city's most popular jazz venues. The house band, the PizzaExpress All-Stars, shares the stage with leading traditional and contemporary names. Open Sunday to Thursday 9 to 11:30pm, Friday to Saturday 9pm to 12:30am.

✪ **Ronnie Scott's.** 47 Frith St., W1. ☎ **020/7439-0747.** www.ronniescotts.co.uk. Cover £15–£20 ($24–$32). Tube: Leicester Sq., Tottenham Court Rd.

Ronnie Scott's is the capital's best-known jazz room. It opened in 1959 and has featured all the greats, from Ella Fitzgerald and Dizzy Gillespie to Hugh Masekela, Roy Ayers, Charlie Watts, and Elvin Jones. For a Saturday show, you'll need to reserve a week in advance. On Sunday, an independent promoter puts on contemporary and world music. There's dancing "Upstairs" (£7/$11.20 cover): 1970s and 1980s jazz, funk, and soul on Wednesday and Thursday (Starsky & Hutch; no sneakers); on Friday and Saturday, it's salsa. It's open Monday to Saturday 8:30pm to 3am, Sunday 7:30 to 11pm.

DANCE CLUBS & DISCOS

Okay, so urban clubbers don't have quite the same mass urge to mate that characterizes party animals on islands like Ibiza and Cyprus, but in every other respect the London scene is the best in the world. Three new venues opened in 1999, unleashing the much-hyped battle of the superclubs. **Home, Fabric,** and **Scala** all boast of spending millions of pounds on transforming vast old buildings into iconic modern spaces with state-of-the-art sound systems. The high-octane competition has worked its magic on London's other clubs, too, lengthening hours, lowering admission charges, and forcing owners and promoters to work even harder to attract attention. Things are still pretty quiet at the beginning of the week, but from Thursday to Saturday even hardcore hedonists will find their heads spinning at the choice. The hot spots change from week to week, so it's impossible to make really reliable recommendations. Consult *Time Out* for the latest roster, and for the magazine's Privilege Pass, printed weekly, which will buy you cheap entry at a number of venues. For more money-saving tips, see section 1, above. *Note:* Always check the dress code because many clubs ban trainers (sneakers).

GROOVY SATURDAY CLUB NIGHTS

- **Big Fish** Dress "wet and wild" for a night of house and garage at the mermaid-themed club with a swimming pool, **The Aquarium,** 256 Old St., EC1, (☎ **020/7251-6136**). Cover £15 ($24). Open 10pm to 5am. Tube: Old St.
- **Blow Up** 1960s R&B, funk, and soulful jazz for a stylish post-pubescent crowd, at The Wag Club, 35 Wardour St. (☎ **020/7437-5534;** www.blowup.co.uk). Cover £8 ($12.80) before 11pm, £10 ($16) until 2:30am, then £3 ($4.80). Open 10pm to 5am. Tube: Piccadilly Circus.
- **Carwash** Glitzy 1970s night, and you'd better ABBA up, too, at Sound, 10 Wardour St., W1 (☎ **020/7394-9447;** www.carwashclub.com). Cover £12 ($19.20) before 2am, then £5 ($8). Open 10pm to 4am. Tube: Leicester Sq.
- **Freedom** Funky disco, U.S. house beats, garage, trance, and long queues, at Bagleys Studios, King's Cross Freight Depot, off York Way, N1 (☎ **020/7278-2777** or 08705/314444; www.freedom-nightclub.co.uk). Cover £14 ($22.40). Open 11pm to 7am. Tube: King's Cross.
- **Garage City** Underground garage, disco house, and dressy gear, at Bar Rumba, 36 Shaftesbury Ave., W1 (☎ **020/7287-2715**). Cover £6 ($9.60) before 11pm, £10 ($16) before midnight, then £12 ($19.20). Open 9pm to 6am. Tube: Piccadilly Circus.
- **Headstart** Techno club with open-doors attitude to guest DJs—big names and newcomers—and live acts, at Turnmills, 63b Clerkenwell Rd., EC1 (☎ **020/7250-3409;** www.headstartclub.co.uk). Cover £5 ($8) before 11pm, then £8 ($12.80). Open 10pm to 5am. Tube: Farringdon.
- **Rulin** U.S. garage, deep house, and designer streetwear, at the monster brand Ministry of Sound, 103 Gaunt St., SE1 (☎ **020/7378-6528**). Cover £15 ($24). Open midnight to 9am. Tube: Elephant & Castle.

GREAT VENUES

Also check out **Ronnie Scott's** (see p. 284), **Spitz** (see p. 283) and **WKD** (see p. 293).

✪ **Bar Rumba.** 36 Shaftesbury Ave., W1. ☎ **020/7287-2715.** www.barrumba.co.uk. Happy hour Mon–Thurs 5–9pm. Cover £3–£12 ($4.80–$19.20). Tube: Piccadilly Circus.

This club travels through the whole musical spectrum every week—from Latin sounds to cosmic disco house and garage (see "Groovy Saturday Club Nights," above). And get this: Drinks are two-for-one during weeknight happy hour, *and* there's no cover charge, so come early and you can club it up later for free. Open Monday to Thursday 5pm to 3:30am, Friday 5pm to 4am, and Saturday 7pm to 6am.

Camden Palace. 1a Camden High St., NW1. ☎ **020/7387-0428.** www.camdenpalace.com. Cover £5–£20 ($8–$32). Tube: Mornington Crescent, Camden Town.

This ex-theater and Britpop legend is a bit past its sell-by date but still a blast if you're in the mood. Depending on the night, you'll hear indie rock, house, trance, garage, or 1970s and 1980s revival. Open Tuesday 10pm to 3:30am, Friday 10pm to 6am, and Saturday 10pm to 7am.

The Clinic. 13 Gerrard St., W1. ☎ **020/7734-9836.** Cover free before 10pm, then £3–£8 ($4.80–$12.80). Tube: Leicester Sq.

This cool, cozy club promotes progressive music, from electronica to house, with reggae and soul thrown into the mix. It opens as a bar in the early evening: That's a seriously cool deal, too, because if you go before 10pm when the music starts, entry is free. Open Monday 5 to 11pm, Tuesday to Wednesday 5pm to 2am, Thursday 5pm to 3am, and Friday to Saturday 5pm to 4am.

The End. 16a West Central St., WC1. ☎ **020/7419-9199.** www.the-end.co.uk. Cover £5–£15 ($8–$24). Tube: Holborn, Tottenham Court Rd.

At this beautifully designed, cutting-edge club, the main sounds are techno, house, garage, and drum 'n' bass—a great West End gig. Be prepared for long lines, particularly for Saturday night's Subterrain, and check the dress code, which varies from night to night. Open Thursday 7pm to 1am, Friday 10pm to 5am, Saturday 10pm to 6am, and Sunday 8pm to 3am.

✪ **Fabric.** 77a Charterhouse St., EC1. ☎ **020/7490-0444.** www.fabric-london.com. Cover £7–£15 ($11.20–$24). Tube: Barbican, Farringdon.

Fabric is as hot as its origins were sub-zero. The 15 Victorian brick arches of this beautiful minimalist superclub (capacity 2,500) used to be the old cold-store for Smithfield meat market. There are three rooms, various bars, a roof terrace, and chill-out rooms. A hi-tech sound system pumps the beat from some of the city's best house, garage, techno, and drum 'n' bass up through the main dance floor—feel those vibrations. One grumble: Fabric is notorious for its mile-long lines, both to get in and for the *Ally McBeal*–style unisex bathrooms. Sunday is the gay Addiction to DPTM night (see below). Open Friday 10pm to 5am and Saturday 10pm to 7am.

Hanover Grand. 6 Hanover St., W1. ☎ **020/7499-7977.** www.hanovergrand.com. Cover £3–£15 ($4.80–$24). Tube: Oxford Circus.

Here's the scene: A dress-conscious crowd cavorts around a renovated theater to a maelstrom of musical styles. It's the home of youth, glitter, and glam—the kind of place to pack your high heels and sequins for, next to the comfy slacks and sightseeing shoes. Saturday night is the big one. Open Wednesday 10:30pm to 3:30am, Thursday 10:30pm to 4am, Friday 10pm to 4am, and Saturday 10:30pm to 6am.

Home. 1 Leicester Sq., WC2. ☎ **020/2710-0107.** www.homecorp.co.uk. Cover £4–£15 ($6.40–$24). Tube: Leicester Sq.

This is the daddy of the capital's trio of new superclubs. Home can pack in 2,700 people, stacked up over 7 floors (part members only), in tacky Leicester Square. In fact, it feels scarily like the department store where you used to lose your mom, so keep a tight grip on your friends. It's got the same promoters as the Home club night in Ibiza, and a roster of big name DJs rev up the atmosphere. Budget travelers should check out Thursday's Highrise: only £4 ($6.40) with a flyer, otherwise £7 ($11.20). There's a restaurant here, too—but it's pricey except for early birds—and a cybercafe that closes at 8pm—not a lot of use. Open Thursday to Friday 10pm to 3am, and Saturday 9pm to3am.

Legends. 29 Old Burlington St., W1. ☎ **020/7437-9933.** www.legends.co.uk. Cover £8–£15 ($12.80–$24). Tube: Green Park/Oxford Circus.

One of the city's more lavish but intimate spots, Legends is *the* place to show off your assets, world-weariness, and perma-tan, to the sounds of funky garage and house. Open Thursday 10:30pm to 3am, Friday 10pm to 4am, and Saturday 10:30pm to 4am.

Ministry of Sound. 103 Gaunt St., SE1, WC2. ☎ **020/7378-6528.** www.ministryofsound.co.uk. Cover £10–£15 ($16–$24). Tube: Elephant & Castle.

The first of the clubland power brands is awesome as it spins off into radio, e-publishing, merchandising, and so on. Not as super-hip as it once was, this is still a hot stop on the club circuit. There's a big bar and an even bigger sound system, blasting garage and house at the label-conscious crowd. It's not cheap and can afford to be selective. Not a place you'd go to for friendly conversation. Open Friday 10pm to 7am, Saturday midnight to 9am.

Scala. 278 Pentonville Rd., N1. ☎ **020/7833-2022.** www.scala-london.co.uk. Cover £5–£12 ($8–$19.20). Tube: King's Cross.

The third of London's superclubs is the smallest (capacity 800) and certainly the quirkiest. The shabby old independent cinema reopened in March 1999 as a live music venue, gallery, sometime film-house and nightclub. Surf the Web site because the schedule of DJs, promoters, and special events is astonishingly eclectic and changes from one week to the next, as does the cost to get in. Monday is a regular student night of R&B, drum 'n' bass, Asian breakbeats, swing, hip hop, and more—not to mention admission is only £6 ($9.60). It's the gay Popstarz on Fridays. Open Monday and Thursday 9pm to 3am, Friday to Saturday 9pm to 5am.

Subterania. 12 Acklam Rd., W10. ☎ **020/8960-4590.** Cover £5–£12 ($8–$12.80). Tube: Ladbroke Grove.

This frill-free stalwart of the Notting Hill night scene is under an elevated section of the A40 main road, close to Ladbroke Grove Tube. Friday is Rotation night, which pulls in the locals for phat, jazz, reggae, and hip hop. On Saturday, it's all-style groove and free entry before 11pm. Open Monday to Thursday 8pm to 2am, Friday to Saturday 10pm to 3am, and Sunday 7pm to midnight.

333 Club. 333 Old St., EC1. ☎ **020/7739-5949.** Cover £5–£10 ($8–$16). Tube: Angel.

This Hoxton Square club occupies 3 floors in a scruffy converted pub. The laid-back atmosphere draws a hip crowd in a neighborhood that's taking over—from now-too-wealthy Notting Hill—as the cutting edge of street chic. Club nights sometimes verge on performance art. Open Friday and Saturday 10pm to 5am.

6 Gay & Lesbian London

Old Compton Street in Soho is the epicenter of gay London life—the equivalent of Christopher Street in New York City. But there are plenty of bars and clubs elsewhere. To find out what's going on and where, pick up one of the free newspapers you'll find at most of the places listed below: the *Pink Paper* (www.sonow.net) and *Boyz* (www.boyznow.com), for instance. *QX* magazine (www.qxmag.co.uk) is another top guide, and there are gay listings in *Time Out.* Lastly, for purely online help, check out the very comprehensive www.gaytoz.com or www.rainbownetwork.com. Otherwise, the **Lesbian & Gay Switchboard** (☎ **020/7837-7324;** www.llgs.org.uk) is a round-the-clock information source on absolutely everything.

Note: Clubbers should check out the gay bars (see below) for discount flyers and jump-the-queue tickets. Trannies "dressed to impress" get cheap entry to **Madame Jojo's** on Friday nights (see above).

GROOVY CLUB NIGHTS

- **Atelier** Groovy laid-back house and food 'til 10pm for loungers from the media, music, fashion and film industries at The End, 16a West Central St., WC1 (☎ **020/7419-9199;** www.the-end.co.uk). Cover free with a flyer before 9pm, then £5 ($8). Open Thursday 7pm to 1am. Tube: Holborn, Tottenham Court Rd.
- **Addiction to DPTM** Latino house, funky grooves, and a few Sunday celebs, now at new superclub Fabric, 77a Charterhouse St., EC1 (☎ **020/7251-8778;** www.adptm.net). Cover £7 ($11.20) before 10pm, then £12 ($19.20). Open Sunday 9pm until late. Tube: Barbican, Farringdon.
- **Coco Latté** Get queue-jump tickets at The Box (see below) and join the mixed Mayfair crowd for a hot, hot night of garage, techno and 1970s sounds, at The Chocolate Bar, 59 Berkeley Sq., W1 (☎ **020/8806-2220;** www.cocolatte.net). Cover £7 ($11.20) before midnight, then £10 ($16). Open Friday 10pm to 3am. Tube: Green Park.
- **The Gay Tea Dance** Pop from the 1970s, 1980s, and 1990s in a converted gothic church, at Limelight, 136 Shaftesbury Ave., W1 (☎ **020/7437-4303;** www.ku-bar.co.uk). Cover £3 ($4.80) before 7pm with a flyer, then £6 ($9.60). Open Sunday 6 to 11pm. Tube: Leicester Sq.
- **Popstarz** Kitsch 1970s and 1980s in the Rubbish Room, plus indie and alternative sounds, at the Scala, 278 Pentonville Rd., N1 (☎**020/7738-2336**). Cover £8 ($12.80); or £5 ($8) before 11pm, then £6 ($9.60), with a flyer. Open Friday 10pm to 5am. Tube: King's Cross.
- **Spunk** Steamy bare-muscle cruising to NY garage and funk, at Substation Soundshaft, Hungerford Lane, off Villiers St., WC2 (☎ **020/7278-0995**). Cover £6 ($9.60). Open Friday 10:30pm to 5am. Tube: Charing Cross, Embankment.
- **Trade** Late-night techno, lasers, and the seriously body beautiful, at Turnmills, 63b Clerkenwell Rd., EC1 (☎ **020/7250-3409;** www.tradeuk.net). Cover £10 to £15 ($16 to $24). Open from 4am Saturday to 1pm Sunday. Tube: Farringdon.

GREAT VENUES

G.A.Y. The Astoria (LA1 and LA2), 157–165 Charing Cross Rd., WC2. ☎ **020/7734-6963.** www.g-a-y.co.uk. Cover £3 ($4.80) or £1 ($1.60) with a flyer, Sat £10 ($16) or £8 ($12.80) with a flyer. Tube: Tottenham Court Rd.

There are so many fab deals to be had at G.A.Y. that you've just got to call and get the low-down. This colossal club is less about posing and more about a young unpretentious crowd having fun. G.A.Y. Pink Pounder is on Mondays (plus cheap drinks) and Thursdays in the basement LA2. Camp Attack is a themed binge of 1970s and 1980s sounds in LA1 on Friday. But the biggest night is Saturday, when G.A.Y. pulls some special surprises—big-name personal appearances, for instance. Open Monday 10:30pm to 3am, Thursday 10:30pm to 4am, Friday 11pm to 4am, and Saturday 10:30pm to 5am.

Heaven. The Arches, Craven St., WC2. ☎ **020/7930-2020.** www.heaven-london.com. Cover £6–£10 ($9.60–$16), free with a flyer before midnight on Friday and £1–£4 ($1.60–$6.40) other nights. Tube: Embankment, Charing Cross.

The 2,000-capacity Heaven is London's most famous gay club, though its popularity has drawn a lot of heteros, too. It's like a self-supporting space colony, with 3 floors of separate bars and dance floors, including the smaller interlinked venue, Substation Soundshaft (see "Groovy Club Nights," above). Big name DJs and PAs power up the volume across the full musical spectrum. On a Monday, you'll get cheap drinks, with happy pop, disco trash, and dance downstairs, and indie upstairs. Wednesday is soul and heavy funk, Friday techno and hard house. Saturday is the one strictly gay-only night. Surf the Web site, and you can print off "flyers" to save a few pounds getting in. Open Monday and Wednesday 10:30pm to 3am, Friday 10:30pm to 5am, and Saturday 10pm to 5am.

PUBS, BARS & CAFES

These places keep regular pub hours—Monday through Saturday 11am to 11pm, Sunday noon to 10:30pm—unless otherwise stated.

The Bar. Chariots House, Fairchild St., EC2. ☎ **020/7247-5222.** www.gaysauna.co.uk. Tube: Old St., Shoreditch, Liverpool St.

This friendly cafe has a beer garden, music, and great-value global pub grub—nachos, baked potatoes, and Thai dim sum. Best of all, it's next to **Chariots Roman Baths** (☎ **020/7247-5333**), London's biggest gay sauna.

The Box Bar. Seven Dials, 32–34 Monmouth St., WC2. ☎ **020/7240-5828.** Tube: Leicester Sq.

A friendly, comfortable, and recently redesigned cafe-bar where people hang out and graze during the day, and gather for drinks in the evenings. It's astonishingly busy, especially for the Coco Latté Pre-Party (see "Groovy Club Nights," above) starting at 7pm on a Friday.

Candy Bar. 23–24 Bateman St., W1. ☎ **020/7494-4041.** Cover Fri–Sat £5 ($8) after 10pm, Sun (downstairs) £1–£3 ($1.60–$4.80). Tube: Tottenham Court Rd.

Britain's first-ever 7-night lesbian bar opened its doors 3 years ago and has been such a hit that it has just moved to bigger and better premises around the corner. There's more outdoor lounging, as well as earlier and later opening hours, but otherwise the same principles apply: great beer, great cocktails, and great club nights. Gay men are welcome as guests. Open Monday to Thursday 5pm to 1pm, Fri and Sat noon to 3am, and Sunday noon to 11pm.

Central Station. 37 Wharfedale Rd., N1. ☎ **020/7278-3294.** www.centralstation.co.uk. Happy hour Mon–Fri 5–9pm. Cover free–£4 ($6.40). Tube: King's Cross.

A pub with a difference—later hours and a laid-back crowd here for the cabaret, sports bar, roof terrace, and cruising at the basement's club nights (Monday and Thursday, men-only). Open Monday 4am to 3pm, Monday to Wednesday 5pm to 2am, Thursday 5pm to 3am, Friday 5pm to 4am, Saturday noon to 4am, and Sunday 11am to midnight.

Ku Bar. 75 Charing Cross Rd., WC2. ☎ **020/7437-4303.** www.ku-bar.co.uk. Happy hour daily noon–7pm. Tube: Leicester Sq.

Great place to start a night on the town as you'll find lots of discount flyers for clubs at this hip West End bar. All the beer is bottled, so no cheap pints. On Sundays, Ku Bar doesn't open until 1pm.

West Central. 29–30 Lisle St., WC2. ☎ **020/7479-7981.** Cover (bar only) £3 ($4.80). Tube: Leicester Sq.

Is it a pub? Is it a club? Yes, to both of those. There's a decibel and energy level to suit any mood at the 3-storied West Central. There's some kind of entertainment every

Trannie Heaven

Saturday nights at the chic basement bar of the **Philbeach Hotel** (see chapter 4) are a clubby megaton blast. So call the transvestite dressing service (☎ **020/7373-4848**) and get the full works—wigs, clothes, shoes, and make-up.

night for eyes, ears, and dancin' feet. The basement bar stays open latest, Wednesday and Thursday 10:30pm to 2am, Friday and Saturday 10:30pm to 3am.

The Yard. 57 Rupert St., W1. ☎ **020/7437-2652.** Tube: Piccadilly Circus.

This is a friendly spot, attracting a laid-back mixed clientele and a big after-work crowd. There's a blissfully secluded courtyard and two bars inside. The bar is closed on Sundays.

7 The Drinking Game: Pubs & Bars

The government is at last planning to drag the ridiculously outdated licensing laws in England and Wales into the 21st century. But even as the Home Office published the proposals last May, it warned that new legislation was unlikely before the next election, and that could take place any time during the year to spring 2002. Odds are that if you come to London this year, you'll find the same old rules apply. Normal pub opening hours are 11am to 11pm Monday through Saturday, and from noon to 10:30pm on Sunday, though some close in the afternoon. Under-14s can go into some pubs, if they have a family room, restaurant, or garden, but it is illegal for under-18s to buy alcohol, with one exception—16- and 17-year-olds may purchase "beer, porter, or cider," with a table meal.

For bars that do hold late licenses, see "After-Hours Drinking," below.

PUBS

There is nothing more British than a luvverly local boozer. People have tried copying the idea overseas, including the British Army, which travels with pop-up pubs. But it takes more than a formula of polished wooden bar, beer on tap, big ashtrays, and a few pictures of Queen Victoria. The atmosphere of the real thing is unique. Though we've listed public houses as evening entertainment, the locals go almost any time—to meet their mates, swap stories, tell jokes, and put away quite a lot of booze. Pubs serve every sort of alcoholic beverage, except fancy cocktails, but beer is the national drink. Expect to pay £1.70 to £2.70 ($2.70 to $4.30) for a pint, depending on what and where you're drinking. It would be hopeless to try and list all the great pubs in London, or even the merely good.

Note: In pubs, you order food as well as drinks at the bar; there's no table service and there's no tipping, either—though you'll make friends fast if you offer to buy the bartender a drink . . . and one for yourself.

Cittie of Yorke. 22–23 High Holborn, WC1. ☎ **020/7242-7670.** Tube: Chancery Lane, Holborn.

This pub's soaring high-gabled room must have the longest bar in England. You can still see the huge vats originally used to dispense wine and liquors. All along one wall are private wood-carved cubicles, supposedly designed for lawyers from the dozens of chambers in the neighborhood to meet discreetly with clients. The pub dates from 1430.

✪ **The Dove.** 19 Upper Mall, W6. ☎ **020/8748-5405.** Tube: Ravenscourt Park.

A perfect riverside pub at Hammersmith, with a terrace perfect for watching the rowers from the many local boathouses. Along with what must be one of the smallest bars in the world, it has a series of comfortable oak-paneled rooms with copper tables and settle seating. Get here early on sunny weekends.

The French House. 49 Dean St., W1. ☎ **020/7437-2799.** Tube: Tottenham Court Rd.

Actually opened by a Belgian, this Soho institution became the center of French life in London during World War II when de Gaulle and his circle gathered here. It still attracts a lot of French-speaking visitors. Beer is only sold in half pints—myths abound but no one really knows why.

✪ **The George.** 77 Borough High St., SE1. ☎ **020/7407-2056.** Tube: London Bridge.

There's been a coaching inn on this site since at least 1542—and possibly earlier—but the current building dates from 1676. Shakespeare's plays are thought to have been performed in the galleried courtyard—they certainly are today, if only during the summer. Dickens is also associated with the place.

The Grenadier. 18 Wilton Row, SW1. ☎ **020/7235-3074.** Tube: Hyde Park Corner.

This mews pub is always crowded. It was an officers' mess in the Duke of Wellington's time. Come to see the military memorabilia and the resident ghost of a soldier flogged to death for cheating at cards.

The Jamaica Wine House. St. Michael's Alley, off Cornhill, EC3. ☎ **020/7626-9496.** Tube: Bank (Exit 5).

This is one of the oldest bars in the City, where Caribbean merchants met to make deals over coffee and rum. Today, young bankers gather at the first-floor bar or downstairs in the cozier cellar to sip good wines, port, or beer.

The Jerusalem Tavern. 55 Britton St., EC1. ☎ **020/7490-4281.** Tube: Farringdon.

This pub pulls a mean pint, supplied by the St. Peter's Brewery in Suffolk. So it's no surprise that the tiny Georgian-style bar, with its open fire, is always packed and getting more so as Clerkenwell zooms up the list of London's coolest neighborhoods.

The Lamb. 94 Lamb's Conduit St., WC1. ☎ **020/7405-0713.** Tube: Oxford Circus.

The etched and hinged glass screens stretching round the bar here are called snob screens; they were put in so that customers didn't have to see the bartender. Apparently, they were the cat's pajamas at the turn of the last century when such Victorian niceties really mattered.

Lamb & Flag. 33 Rose St., WC2. ☎ **020/7497-9504.** Tube: Leicester Sq.

The Lamb & Flag is an old timber-framed pub in a short cul-de-sac off Garrick Street, Covent Garden. The poet Dryden dubbed it the "Bucket of Blood" after he was almost beaten to death here (no doubt for being too witty at someone else's expense). The Lamb & Flag can be hard to find, but the friendly atmosphere and list of 30 whiskies are ample reward for the effort. The food is good traditional pub grub, and there's free live jazz from 7:30pm on Sunday evenings.

Museum Tavern. 49 Great Russell St., WC1. ☎ **020/7242-8987.** Tube: Holborn.

As you'd expect of a pub in Bloomsbury, the Museum Tavern is the haunt of writers, publishers, and academics. Etched glass and oak provide Victorian atmosphere, but the pub actually dates back to the early 18th century.

After-Hours Drinking

If going home at 11pm makes you feel like Cinderella, try one of these places for later-night drinking: **Bar Rumba, Central Station, The Clinic, La Perla, Match, Social Bar, Spitz, West Central,** and **WKD.** Don't forget the restaurant-bars in chapter 5: **Blues Bistro and Bar, Boisdale, Corney & Barrow, Livebait!, Mezzo, Soho Spice, Yo! Below,** and **Belgo.**

Phene Arms. 9 Phene St., SW3. ☎ **020/7352-3294.** Tube: Sloane Sq., then no. 11 or 211 bus.

In the summer, the capital's privileged youth comes out to play in the Phene's delightful courtyard garden. Local eccentrics jostle with them for elbowroom.

Prospect of Whitby. 57 Wapping Wall, E1. ☎ **020/7481-1095.** Tube: Wapping.

Named after a coal barge that operated between Yorkshire and London, this is an atmospheric pub with a fine view of the river. Once frequented by smugglers and thieves, it dates back to 1520. Take a cab from the Tube station, or turn right and walk along the river.

The Punch Tavern. 99 Fleet St., EC4. ☎ **020/7353-6658.** Tube: Blackfriars.

Charles Dickens and a bunch of his friends founded the satirical magazine *Punch* here. It is one of the oldest pubs in London, though it's known now for its Victorian gin-palace interior. Next door to St. Bride's Church and, a little farther on, St. Paul's Cathedral.

Salisbury. 90 St. Martin's Lane, WC2. ☎ **020/7836-5863.** Tube: Leicester Sq.

This popular pub has lost none of its charm despite a recent revamp. The decor is quite over the top, from the Victorian etched glass and statuette lamps to plush velvet banquettes.

Spaniard's Inn. Spaniard's Rd., NW3, Hampstead. ☎ **020/731-6571.** Tube: Hampstead, then no. 210 bus.

This romantic pub has a lovely garden in summer and hearthside drinking in winter. Part of it dates back to 1585, and many a famous drinker has dallied here—from Keats and Shelley to Dickens and the highwayman Dick Turpin.

Windsor Castle. 114 Campden Hill Rd., W8. ☎ **020/7243-9551.** Tube: Notting Hill Gate.

It's a risky business meeting a friend at the Windsor Castle—the maze of small wood-paneled rooms are always crowded, and you can circle round hopelessly for hours. Come in the summer and enjoy a drink in the walled garden.

Ye Olde Mitre. 1 Ely Court, Ely Place, off Hatton Garden, EC1. ☎ **020/7405-4751.** Tube: Chancery Lane.

Ye Old Mitre is often called London's "best-kept secret." The pub is tucked away down a dingy passage, and first-time visitors often turn back, thinking they've come the wrong way. It has a delightful, snug Elizabethan interior.

COCKTAILS

Last seen several decades ago sporting a kitschy paper umbrella or a glacé cherry, the cocktail is making a huge comeback in London, but this time, it's very, very classy. Even Noël Coward would approve, though he'd no doubt have something opinionated to say about the groupie-gathering mixologists (bartenders, to you and me).

At £5 to £10 ($8 to $16) a pop, cocktails are very budget-unfriendly. So our listing includes two fab happy hours, as well as a chic hangout and a classy hotel bar. Also check out one of the quirkiest watering holes, the stylish Studio Lounge at the giant bookshop, **Waterstone's,** 203–206 Piccadilly, W1 (☎ **020/7851-2400;** www.waterstones.co.uk; Tube: Green Park, Piccadilly Circus), where the list runs to 19 cocktails and prices start at £4.95 ($7.90).

Dukes Hotel Bar. 35 St. James' Place, SW1. ☎ **020/7491-4840.** www.dukeshotel.co.uk. Tube: Green Park.

Gilberto claims his martini cocktails are the best in the world—nothing but the most expensive gin and vodka. You'll have to spend at least £9 ($14.40), and one member of the bar team will do that mixologist thing at your table. This is a very cozy, friendly, and English drinking den, in a very smart part of town. Open 11am to 11pm to nonresidents.

La Perla. 28 Maiden Lane, WC2. ☎ **020/7240-7400.** Happy hour 5–7pm daily, all night Tues from 5pm for Margaritas. Tube: Covent Garden, Charing Cross.

This is a Tex-Mex joint, so it's no surprise that tequila is the house speciality—there are over 60 kinds, plus mescals. Delicious Margaritas start at around £4.50 ($7.20); come on a Tuesday, and they're £3 ($4.80) all night. Don't despair if tequila turns your stomach. There are bourbons, whiskies, and lots of other cocktails. La Perla attracts a noisy young crowd, and the odd famous name. Open Monday to Saturday noon to midnight, Sunday 4 to 10:30pm.

The Match Bar. 37–38 Margaret St., W1. ☎ **020/7499-3444.** Tube: Oxford Circus.

Dick Bradsell has done much to fuel the city's cocktail frenzy. He's the Match mixologist and has a consultancy selling his expertise, and crowd-pulling name, to other bar owners. Look out for the Bramble, gin-based with crème de mûre, and other quirky berry concoctions. Cocktails start at around £5 ($8), and the service is charming. Open Monday to Saturday 11:30am to 11pm. **Match EC1,** 45–47 Clerkenwell Rd., EC1 (☎ **020/7250-4002;** Tube: Farringdon), is open Monday to Friday 11am to midnight, Saturday 6pm to midnight.

WKD. 18 Kentish Town Rd., NW1. ☎ **020/7267-1869.** www.wkd.bizhosting.com. Cover £1–£7 ($1.60–$11.20). Happy hour Mon–Fri 4–8pm, Sat–Sun 1–8pm. Tube: Camden Town.

Get your lips round the WKD Experience: This devil's mix of Kahlua, Amaretto, Baileys, and milk costs £4.95 ($7.90) a pop, or £7.50 ($12) a jug during happy hour, instead of £12.50 ($20). But WKD is much more than a shakin' cocktail spot: There's something going on every night at this great club-bar. Monday is The Studio, where you catch live gigs by bands just starting out. Love4Love is Friday's groovin' dance night. Come in for free before 9pm, and stay all night. Open Monday to Thursday noon to 2am, Friday and Saturday noon to 3am, Sunday noon to midnight.

WINE BARS

Wine lovers will thank their lucky stars for an alternative to the pub, where plonk predominates over fine bouquet. A bottle of house red or white generally costs £10 to £15 ($16 to $24), a great deal to share between two or three people, and most wine bars sell a selection by the glass. You can almost always eat there, which is why the full reviews are in chapter 5. For great wine lists at more than manageable prices, try: **Bleeding Heart,** Bleeding Heart Yard, off Greville St., EC1 (☎ **020/7242-8238;** Tube: Chancery Lane, Farringdon); **Cork & Bottle,** 44–46 Cranbourn St., WC2 (☎ **020/7734-7807;** Tube: Leicester Sq.); **Corney & Barrow,** 116 St. Martin's Lane, WC2 (☎ **020/7655-9800;** www.corney-barrow.co.uk; Tube: Leicester Sq.); and **Shampers,** 4 Kingly St., W1 (☎ **020/7439-9910;** Tube: Oxford Circus).

9

Easy Excursions from London

Spur-of-the-moment escapes may be great fun, but you won't be laughing when you realize how much you could have saved by making plans at the same time as you book the whole holiday—especially if you're traveling to a hot spot at a hot time in the summer when discount deals are snapped up very quickly. You can arrange tours, trains, and coaches, as well as get helpful advice, at the **Britain Visitor Centre,** 1 Regent St., SW1 (no phone; www.visitbritain.com), open Monday to Friday 9am to 6:30pm, and Saturday to Sunday 10am to 5pm (or 4pm in winter).

1 How to Save on Day-Trippin'

- **Play the Train Fare Game** Avoid traveling on Fridays when prices soar to profit from the mass exodus of city dwellers. There are dozens of different fares with varying restrictions, depending on where you're going and with which train company (see "The Train Ticket Dictionary," box in this chapter). So always ask for the cheapest, and then decide if it suits your travel plans.
- **Book Online** As long as you spend over £10 ($16), **www.thetrainline.com** will give you a £1 ($1.60) discount.
- **Train Passes** If you expect to make several trips out of London, call **BritRail** (☎ **888/BRITRAIL;** www.raileurope.com) about the **SouthEast Pass**—before you leave home as it is only available outside Britain. This flexipass gets you to all of the places we suggest for excursions except for Bath and Stratford-upon-Avon: $74 for 3 days and $105 for 4 days travel within an 8-day period, or $142 for 7 days travel within a 15-day period. Child passes are $21.
- **Bus Deals** The leading long-haul bus line is **National Express** (☎ **08705/808080;** www.gobycoach.com). If you're planning several trips, check out the **Tourist Trail Pass,** which allows unlimited travel on a set number of days, not necessarily consecutive but falling within a fixed time period: either 2 days to be used within a 3-day period, for £49 ($78.40); 5 days travel, valid for 10, for £85 ($136); 7 days, valid for 21, for £120 ($192); or 14 days, valid for 30, for £187 ($299.20). Under-25s and over-50s can buy a discount card for £9 ($14.40), which cuts pass and individual ticket prices by 20% to 30%.

How Long Should I Spend in Each Destination?

Of the excursions mentioned in this chapter, if you have **1 day or less** to spare, you can easily see **Cambridge** (see page 297) or **Windsor & Eton** (see page 301). On the other hand, while you can do **Bath** (see page 304), **Oxford** (see page 308), or **Stratford-upon-Avon** (see page 313) in a day, I think you'll want to **stay overnight** once you read about the lip-smacking delights they have to offer. To help you choose between them, we've put together a calendar of the must-see annual events ("Calendar of Events for London Excursions," below). The local tourist offices can fill in any gaps.

- **Car Deals** I beg people on bended knee not to drive in London, but the deals at **easyRentacar** are so good that it does make sense for a puttering-about kind of excursion into the English countryside (not for city visits, though). Bear in mind that there is only one depot, south of the river at London Bridge, which means crossing *a lot* of traffic-laden city if you're heading north. Daily rates fluctuate according to demand, so book early and you might only have to pay £14 ($22.40) to have a Mercedes A-Class for a day. Booking is online only (www.easyrentacar.com).
- **Discount Sightseeing** The **Great British Heritage Pass** gets you free entry into almost 600 historic properties around the country, including Anne Hathaway's Cottage and Shakespeare's birthplace in Stratford-upon-Avon; the Roman Baths and Pump Room at Bath, and Stonehenge nearby; Windsor Castle; Blenheim Palace, near Oxford; and in London, Hampton Court Palace, Kensington Palace State Apartments, and Royal Ceremonial Dress Collection. Passes are valid for 7 days ($54), 15 days ($75), or a month ($102), no discounts for children. Call **BritRail** (☎ **888/BRITRAIL;** www.raileurope.com) before you travel, or visit the British Travel Shop next to the BTA office in New York. (See "Visitor Information" in chapter 2.)
- **Follow My Leader The Original London Walks** (☎ **020/7624-3978;** www.walks.com) can get you a discount on a cheap day-return train ticket. It offers **Explorer Days** every Saturday to places like York, Oxford, Bath, Salisbury, and Stonehenge. You get guided walks in the morning and afternoon for £10 ($16) adults, £8.50 ($13.60) seniors and students, plus tickets to attractions (and rail fare). A great way to get the most from a stolen day out of the capital.
- **Take an Escorted Tour** The **London for Less** discount card gets you 20% off **Frames Rickards** (☎ **020/7837-3111**) 1-day coach tours, 10% on longer trips. For example, the £50 ($60) daily excursion to Oxford, Warwick Castle, and Stratford-upon-Avon would cost £40 ($64) per person with the discount. **Trafalgar Tours** (☎ **020/7976-5363;** www.trafalgartours.com) coach trips cost £44 ($70.40) per person to Bath and Stonehenge, or to Stratford, and £27 ($43.20) to Windsor. Both companies include entry to attractions in their prices.
- **Stopover Packages** British Short Breaks from **National Express** (☎ **08705/808080;** www.gobycoach.com) include return coach travel, hotel, and breakfast. It would cost two people £112 ($179.20) for a night in a nice hotel in Bath—cheaper than going independently and staying at two of our guest houses. Hotel chains such as **Forte** (☎ **0845/740-4040;** www.moments.com) and **Thistle** (☎ **0800/181716;** www.thistlehotels.com), also have hotspot special offers. Many are for a minimum 2- or 3-night stay, though. Thistle does do a **Stratford**

The Train Ticket Dictionary

These are the fares most likely to suit budget-travelers on an excursion from London.

- **Cheap day returns** For journeys under 50 miles, leaving London after 9:30am. No need to book specific train times. An ordinary **day-return** ticket allows travel during peak times.
- **Network Away Break** No need to book specific trains, but not available on some peak services. Return journey must be within 5 days.
- **Super APEX** Selected services only, off-peak. Must be bought 14 days before departure with fixed dates and times for both halves of the journey.
- **APEX** Selected services only, mostly off-peak. Must be purchased a week in advance with fixed dates and times for departure and return.
- **Super Advance** Must be bought by 6pm the day before departure with fixed times and dates, mostly off-peak.
- **Supersaver return** Walk on, but only outside the morning (after 9:30am) and evening rush hours. Not available on a Friday.
- **Standard return** A no-restriction splurge.

Theatre Flyer (☎ **01789/294949**): four-course early-bird dinner, tickets to the Royal Shakespeare Theatre, bed and full English breakfast, and bus tour of Stratford-upon-Avon, for £198 ($316.80) for two people sharing.

Calendar of Events for London Excursions

February

- **Cambridge University Rag Week.** Students dress up and play the fool to raise money for charity. February 27 to March 6.

March

- **Bath Literary Festival.** High-profile writers give readings at this bookish knees-up. Call ☎ **01275/463362** (www.bathfestivals.org.uk). March 3 to 11.

April

- **Shakespeare's Birthday.** Foreign dignitaries flock to Stratford-upon-Avon for celebrations and unfurling of flags along Bridge Street. Great fun, but it mucks up sightseeing. Call ☎ **01789/204016** (www.shakespeare.org.uk). April 28.

May

- **Cambridge University May Week.** Graduation celebrations. May 14 to 21.
- **Bath International Music Festival.** Classical and early music at beautiful venues. Call ☎ **01275/463362** (www.bathfestivals.org.uk). May 18 to June 3.
- **Bath Fringe Festival.** "Anything people want to do, as long as they can do it in public," plus a traditional Bedlam fair on middle Saturday. Call ☎ **01225/463362** (www.bathfringe.co.uk). May 27 to June 10.
- **Oxford Eights Week.** Inter-collegiate rowing championship. May 23 to 26.

June

- **Cambridge Strawberry Fair.** Free fest of music, arts, and crafts on Midsummer Common. Call ☎ **01223/560160** (www.strawberry-fair.org.uk). 1st or 2nd Saturday of June.
- **Encaenia.** Begowned university bigwigs and lucky dignitaries process at noon through **Oxford** to the Sheldonian Theatre for the bestowing of honorary degrees. June 20.

July

- **Cambridge Shakespeare Festival.** Open-air performances of uncut texts at beautiful old colleges. Call ☎ **01223/357851.** Early July to late August.

September

- **St. Giles' Fair.** Street mayhem in Oxford, usually the first weekend in September.
- **Windsor Festival.** Concerts and events in Windsor Castle, Eton College, and the Wren-designed Guildhall. Call ☎ **020/7286-8811.** Last 2 weeks in September.

2 Cambridge

55 miles N of London

Cambridge and Oxford compete fiercely in everything. Oxford is grander and older. A thriving town before the first college opened its doors, it has a busy industrial area, now centered around the Science Park. Cambridge has a much more somnolent air and an immediately captivating beauty. But behind the lazy romance of this town on the banks of the Cam is a dot.com business boom. Ever since Microsoft set up its European research center here, Cambridge has become known as "Silicon Fen."

Settled by the Romans, the city did not begin to flourish until the 13th century when the first college was founded. Cambridge University now has 31, the grounds of which are open to the public year-round. Some are worth visiting, others less so, and admission fees can quickly add up. We recommend a trip to the Fitzwilliam Museum, Kettle's Yard, and then one or two of the colleges, before taking a stroll along the backs or a punt on the river. During the summer holidays, the colleges are crowded with visitors.

Note: Cambridge University **term dates** for 2001 are: January 16 to March 16; April 24 to June 15; and October 2 to November 30.

A WEEK AT A GLANCE

Monday: no choral service at King's College Chapel; Fitzwilliam Museum and Kettle's Yard closed. **Sunday:** farmers' market in Market Square.

ESSENTIALS

GETTING THERE Trains depart from King's Cross station and take 55 minutes. The day-return fare is £16.10 ($25.75); cheap day return £13.50 ($21.60). From Cambridge station, take the Cityrail bus to Market Square, in the middle of Oxford. Call **National Rail Enquiries** (☎ **08457/484950**). **National Express buses** (☎ **08705/808080**) leave from London's Victoria Coach Station, take 1 hour and 55 minutes, and cost £11.40 ($18.25) return, £8.50 ($13.60) same-day return. If you're driving from London, take the M11 motorway to Exit 11.

ORIENTATION Cambridge (pop. 111,000) has two main streets. **Trumpington Road**—which becomes Trumpington Street, King's Parade, Trinity Street, and finally St. John's Street—runs parallel to the River Cam. It's close to several of the city's colleges. **Bridge Street,** the city's main shopping zone, starts at Magdalene Bridge; it becomes Sidney Street, St. Andrew's Street, and finally Regent Street.

VISITOR INFORMATION The **Tourist Information Centre** (TIC), Wheeler St. (☎ **01223/322640;** www.cambridge.gov.uk/leisure/tourism.htm), is behind Guildhall. It'll tell you everything you need to know on transportation and sightseeing, and has useful maps as well. The office is open all year Monday to Friday 10am to 5:30pm, Saturday 10am to 5pm, Sunday 11am to 4pm. To find out more about Cambridge University, surf its rather dry Web site (**www.camb.ac.uk**).

The TIC **Accommodation Booking Service** (☎ **01223/457581**) charges a £3 ($4.80) fee and 10% deposit, and operates from 9:30pm to 4pm Monday to Friday. Otherwise, for a super-cheap sleep, the **Cambridge Youth Hostel,** 97 Tenison Road (☎ **01223/354601;** e-mail: cambridge@yha.org.uk), charges £15.10 ($24.15) a night for adults, £11.40 ($18.25) for under-18s.

WALKS & TOURS

Walking tours leave from the Tourist Information Centre at least twice a day, at 11:30am and 1:30pm, from April to October—more often at the height of the summer, less in the fall and winter. Tickets are £6.50 ($10.40) and include entrance to King's College Chapel. For more info on guided tours, call ☎ **01233/457574.**

VISITING THE COLLEGES

You won't have time to see all the colleges. And some are frankly not worth the admission charges of between £1.50 and £3.50 ($2.40 and $5.60) , so below are a few recommendations. A great way to see a lot more of them, from the outside, is to take a stroll along the backs—the meadows between the colleges and the Cam. This swath of green takes you up to **St. John's Bridge,** a replica of the Bridge of Sighs in Venice.

The undoubted must-visit is ✪ **King's College** (☎ **01223/331100,** or 01223/331447 for the chapel), founded by Henry VI in 1441. The chapel is internationally famous for its choir and the traditional Festival of Nine Lessons and Carols, which is broadcast every Christmas Eve. It has incredible fan vaulting, stained-glass windows, and a screen given by Henry VIII that bears his initials and those of his queen at the time, Anne Boleyn. Behind the altar is Rubens's *Adoration of the Magi,* painted in 1634. A small exhibition hall holds a display about the chapel's history.

Go for a choral service (Tuesday to Saturday at 5:30pm, Sunday at 10:30am and 3:30pm, call to check) for the full experience, but only during university terms. Then, the chapel is open Monday through Saturday 9:30am to 3:30pm, Sunday 1:15 to 2:15pm. During vacation, it's open Monday through Saturday 9:30am to 4:30pm, Sunday 10am to 4:30pm. The chapel is closed December 26 through January 1, and occasionally without notice for recording sessions and rehearsals. Admission to the chapel is £3.50 ($5.60) for adults, or £2.50 ($4) for students and children.

From King's, walk around the front court past the neo-Gothic gatehouse and screen. Then follow the passageway between the Gibbs's and Wilkins's buildings to the back lawn and the bridge that crosses the River Cam, before you leave via the North Gate.

Founded by Henry VIII in 1546, **Trinity College** (☎ **01223/338400**) is the largest and wealthiest of Cambridge's colleges. It has produced 29 Nobel Laureates. Famous alumni include the scientist Sir Isaac Newton; poets and writers Francis Bacon, Lord Tennyson, Lord Byron, Andrew Marvell, and John Dryden; and philosopher Bertrand Russell. The courtyard covers 2 acres. Traditionally, students try to run around it in the time it takes the clock to strike 12, a scene you may remember from

Cambridge

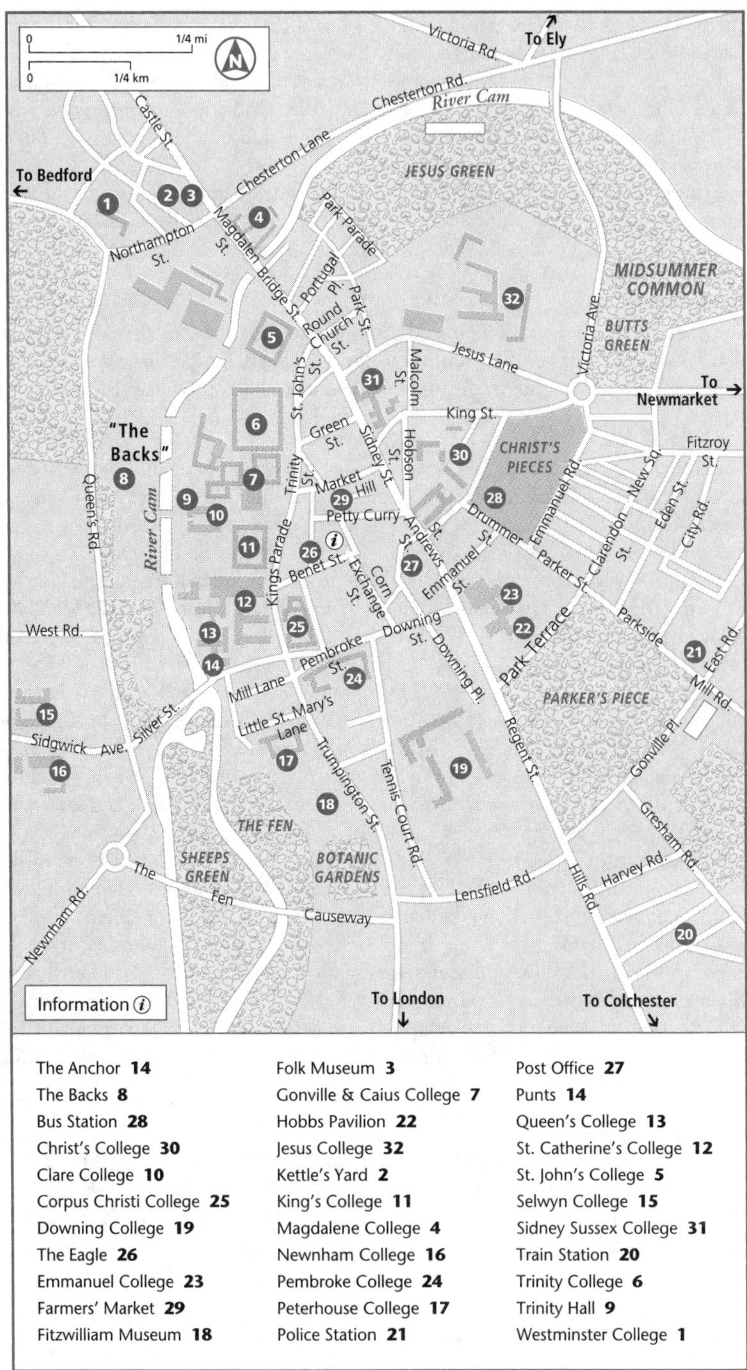

The Anchor **14**	Folk Museum **3**	Post Office **27**
The Backs **8**	Gonville & Caius College **7**	Punts **14**
Bus Station **28**	Hobbs Pavilion **22**	Queen's College **13**
Christ's College **30**	Jesus College **32**	St. Catherine's College **12**
Clare College **10**	Kettle's Yard **2**	St. John's College **5**
Corpus Christi College **25**	King's College **11**	Selwyn College **15**
Downing College **19**	Magdalene College **4**	Sidney Sussex College **31**
The Eagle **26**	Newnham College **16**	Train Station **20**
Emmanuel College **23**	Pembroke College **24**	Trinity College **6**
Farmers' Market **29**	Peterhouse College **17**	Trinity Hall **9**
Fitzwilliam Museum **18**	Police Station **21**	Westminster College **1**

the movie *Chariots of Fire.* More rakishly, it's said that the poet Byron used to bathe naked in the large central fountain. Note the statue of Henry VIII on the Great Gate clutching a chair leg instead of a sword—the result of a student prank. The impressive **Wren Library** was designed by Sir Christopher himself and holds many original works by famous former students. Admission is £1.75 ($2.80)for adults, or £1 ($1.60) for concessions.

Queens' College (☎ **01223/335511**) is arguably the prettiest of them all. Founded in 1448, it is named for Margaret of Anjou, the wife of Henry VI, and Elizabeth, wife of Edward IV. The most spectacular parts are the 16th-century half-timbered **President's Lodge** and the Tower, where the great scholar, Erasmus, lived from 1510 to 1514.

Other places to stop in at include **Magdalene,** to view the Pepys Library, the diarist's collection of 3,000 volumes; and **Jesus College,** for the chapel's stained-glass windows designed by Edward Burne-Jones and its ceiling by William Morris.

. . . AND BEYOND

"Punting," or pole-boating, is a Cambridge tradition. **Scudamore's Boatyards,** Granta Place (☎ **01223/359750**), by the Anchor pub, has been renting punts and rowboats since 1910. It costs £10 ($16) to hire one for 1 hour, and you have to leave a £50 ($80) refundable deposit. Summer only, daily from 9am to 10pm.

If you enjoy museums and galleries, there are two exceptional **freebies** to visit here in Cambridge. The **Fitzwilliam Museum,** Trumpington Street (☎ **01223/332900;** www.fitzmuseum.cam.ac.uk), is an eclectic treasure house of Chinese jades and bronzes, pages from beautiful Books of Hours, and the first draft of Keats's "Ode to a Nightingale," as well as china, glass, majolica, silver, clocks, and a superb Egyptian collection. The paintings range from medieval and Renaissance works to contemporary canvases. Feast your eyes on Titian's *Tarquin and Lucretia,* Rubens's *The Death of Hippolytus,* brilliant etchings by van Dyck, rare Hogarths, 25 Turners, works by William Blake, the impressionists, and more recent artists Paul Nash and Sir Stanley Spencer. Open Tuesday to Saturday 10am to 5pm, and Sunday 2:15 to 5pm.

Kettle's Yard, Castle Street (☎ **01223/352124**), is a very different kettle of fish. Jim Ede was the curator at the Tate during the 1920s and 1930s. He and his wife Helen acquired this collection of artworks, furniture, and decorative objects, displayed as he arranged them in his home. You'll find work by Ben Nicholson, Christopher Wood, and Alfred Wallis, and sculptures by Henry Moore, Henri Gaudier-Brzeska, Brancusi, and Barbara Hepworth. The gallery, meanwhile, holds exhibitions of 20th-century art. Open April to August, Tuesday to Saturday 1:30 to 4pm, and 1:30 to 3:30pm on Sunday and in winter. The gallery is open Tuesday to Saturday 11:30–5pm, Sunday 2–5pm.

WHERE TO EAT

The Anchor. Silver St. ☎ **01223/353554.** £1.95–£5.95 ($3.10–$9.50). MC, V. Food served Mon–Thurs noon–7:45pm, Fri–Sat noon–3:45pm, Sun noon–2:30pm. PUB.

The Anchor looks out on a raft of punts and the willow-fringed river. It's loaded with atmosphere—beams, sloping ceilings, and filled with odds and ends like cider pots, jugs, and prints. It serves traditional homemade English pub fare like battered cod and plaice, lamb-and-vegetable or leek-and-potato pies, and sausage, egg, and chips. Come here for real ale, as well as the usual selection of lagers and bitters.

The Eagle. Benet St. ☎ **01223/505020.** Lunch £3.25–£4.95 ($5.20–$7.90), evening main courses £4–£9.95 ($6.40–$15.90). Food served daily noon–2:30pm; Mon–Thurs 5:30–8:45pm, Fri 5:30–8pm. PUB.

The Eagle is an ivy-covered pub with a lovely galleried courtyard that serves as a beer garden. Inside are two bars and three sitting areas with scrubbed wood tables. Burned into the ceiling of the Air Force bar are the names and numbers of wartime officers. The pub offers good traditional pub fare—the top price is for a hefty T-bone steak.

Hobbs Pavilion. Park Terrace. ☎ **01223/367480.** Reservations recommended. PDQ lunch £5 ($8), fixed-price lunch £6.75 ($10.80), main courses £5.25–£11.50 ($8.40–$18.40), 3-course meal anytime £8.75–£12.95 ($14–$20.70). No credit cards. Tues–Sat noon–2:15pm and 6–9:45pm. Closed mid-Aug to 1st wk. Sept. CREPES AND GRILLS.

Hobbs lists 30 different crepes stuffed with everything from hot-chilied lamb to Dijon chicken and black pudding; from banana, ginger, and cream to lemon, sugar, and butter. Soups, salads, and char-grilled meat and fish—even a char-grilled Mars bar—are also on the menu, as are quirky ice cream flavors such as lavender and honey. The three-course all-in menu is an excellent deal at £12.95 ($20.70): It includes a side salad, a ¼ liter of wine, and coffee. Hobbs Pavillion is child-friendly and nonsmoking.

3 Windsor & Eton

21 miles W of London

Surrounded by gentle hills and lush valleys, this pretty riverside town—which the ancient Britons called Windlesore—is famous for two things: an enormous luxe fortress and a very posh private boys school. You'll need at least 1½ hours to look around Windsor Castle, and that's at a bit of a trot. Take it easy, and make sure to see St. George's Chapel and Queen Mary's Dolls House, too, at a pace that lets you really enjoy them. Then take a well-earned lunch break to refuel before one of these three great afternoon options: Visit Eton College for free; take a boat trip that goes past the school for a smallish fee; or splurge and head for the amazing Legoland theme park.

A WEEK AT A GLANCE

Monday: Summer evening meetings at **Royal Windsor Racecourse** (☎ **01753/865234;** www.windsorracing.co.uk). Admission £4 to £11 ($6.40 to $17.60). Take the Riverbus to the racecourse from just west of Windsor Bridge, paying your £4 ($6.40) return fare on board. **Saturday:** morning farmers' market at Windsor Central Station; in the afternoon, Eton boys in "mufti," not tailcoats and wing collars. **Sunday:** no Changing of the Guard, but cheaper entry to Windsor Castle as St. George's Chapel open for services only; Eton boys in "mufti" after church.

ESSENTIALS

GETTING THERE Trains depart from Waterloo for Windsor & Eton Riverside and take about 50 minutes. A standard return costs £11.40 ($18.25); a cheap day return is £5.90 ($9.45). If you have a London Transport travelcard that covers zone 4, you can hop on the same train, a few minutes into its journey, at Richmond—the District Line Tube and proper trains use the same station. Standard return is £8.50 ($13.60); cheap day return is £4.80 ($7.70). Trains to Windsor Central, very near Riverside station, start from Paddington and, inconveniently, you have to change at Slough. Call **National Rail Enquiries** (☎ **08457/484950**). **Green Line buses** (☎ **08706/087261**) leave from Bulleid Way, near Eccleston Bridge behind Victoria Station, and take around 1 hour. Day-return tickets cost £7 ($11.20). If you're driving, take the M4 west out of London to exit 6.

ORIENTATION Windsor is one place where there's little chance of getting lost. The castle is so enormous that you can always take your bearings from it. Eton is just on the other side of the river.

VISITOR INFORMATION Turn right out of the station, and follow Datchet Road round the walls of Windsor Castle. It turns briefly into Thames Street and then High Street. The **Royal Windsor Information Centre** is at no. 24 (☎ **01753/743900;** e-mail: windsor.tic@rbwm.gov.uk). It's open Monday to Saturday 10am to 5pm, Sunday 10am to 4pm. Windsor is a perfect day-trip, but if you fancy staying overnight, call the center's **Accommodation Hotline** (☎ **01753/743907**).

CASTLE HILL

✪ **Windsor Castle.** ☎ **01753/868286.** www.royal.gov.uk/palaces/windsor.htm. Admission £10.50 ($16.80) adults, £8 ($12.80) seniors, £5 ($8) under-17s; if any part of the castle is closed (e.g. chapel on Sun), admission discounted to £8.50 ($13.60), £6.50 ($10.40), and £4 ($6.40). Castle Mar–Oct daily 9:45am–5:15pm (last entry 4pm); Nov–Feb daily 9:45am–4:15pm (last entry 3pm); closed when Queen in residence (call to check). State Apartments same hrs., opening at 10am. St. George's Chapel Mon–Sat 10:45am–4:15pm (last entry 4pm); closed June 12–23, Oct 30–Nov 10.

It took 1.5 million gallons of water and 15 hours to put out the fire at Windsor Castle in 1992. The repair bill was so huge that it prompted the Queen to open Buckingham Palace to the public for the first time as a way of raising the necessary funds. The work is finished now, and the castle looks as spectacular as it ever did.

It lies on a bend in the Thames, surrounded by 4,800 acres of lawn, woodlands, and lakes. It has over 1,000 rooms and claims to be the largest inhabited castle in the world. Built more than 900 years ago, it is certainly one of the oldest. The **State Apartments** are open to the public as long as the Queen isn't in residence—if you see the Royal Standard flying, then you're out of luck. Room after room is filled with fabulous furnishings, tapestries, and paintings by Rembrandt, Canaletto, van Dyck, Rubens, and Holbein. **St. George's Hall** was one of the most laborious parts of the restoration. It is decorated with the heraldic arms of more than 800 Knights of the Garter going back to the founder, the Black Prince. The painter of the extraordinary pagan feast on the **King's Dining Room** ceiling got ideas above his station and put himself into the picture. See if you can find his face, or ask one of the guards to point it out.

But my favorite of all the treasures at Windsor Castle is the spectacular **Queen Mary's Doll House.** Designed by Sir Edwin Lutyens, it took 1,000 craftsmen more than 3 years to create. Everything in it actually works, from the plumbing to a tiny electric iron. Even the bottles in the cellar contain a drop of by-now vintage wine.

The **Changing of the Guard,** when soldiers march to a military band through the town to the castle's Lower Ward, takes place at 11am, from Monday to Saturday between April and June, and on alternate days the rest of the year. To find out if it's happening on the day of your visit, call the castle number and ask for extension 2347.

Edward IV founded ✪ **St. George's Chapel** (☎ **01753/865538**) in 1475. Within the castle precincts, it's one of the finest examples of late Gothic architecture in Britain. This is where Prince Edward and Sophie got married. Ten sovereigns have left their bones here, including Henry VIII, who completed the chapel, and his third wife Jane Seymour. St. George is patron saint of the Most Noble Order of the Garter, Britain's highest chivalric order. You can see the banners, swords, helms, and crests of each current member, as well as more than 700 metal stall plates, the oldest of which dates back to about 1390. Sadly, many have been lost, including those of the original founders in 1348. Visitors are welcome at Sunday services and also at daily Evensong.

. . . AND BEYOND

Have a wander through the cobbled streets, known as Guildhall Island, opposite the castle gates. Then turn down the High Street towards the river, which is where all the afternoon options start. Eton is across the bridge. You can catch the shuttlebus for

A Royal Retreat

Henry VIII bought the Little and Great Frogmore estates in the 16th century, but the present house is rather nouveau, only finished in 1684. Ever since then, the royals have used it as a retreat from Windsor—not retreating very far, as **Frogmore House** is in the park a mile south of the castle! The Queen spent part of her honeymoon here and still comes to stay. So the few days it opens each year, usually in May and August, depend entirely on her schedule (☎ **01753/869898;** www.royal.gov.uk/palaces/frogmore.htm). Also try to see the opulent Mausoleum built for Prince Albert. Queen Victoria, who lies at his side there, ordered the walls and ceilings to be painted in the style of Raphael, her consort's favorite artist.

Legoland from either Windsor Central Station on the left, or back at Windsor & Eton Riverside. And boat tours start just upriver from the bridge on the Windsor bank.

It's about a 10-minute walk from the bridge, past browsable antiques stores, to the most prestigious "public school" in England, **Eton College** (☎ **01753/671-0000;** www.etoncollege.com). Prince William graduated last year, but you might still see Harry wandering through the streets between lessons, in wing collar and tailcoat. Eton has educated many members of the British establishment, including 19 prime ministers. The **Lower School** has one of the oldest classrooms in the world (1443). Eton is open to visitors: March 29 to April 25 and July 3 to September 5, from 10:30am to 4:30pm; April 26 to July 2 and September 6 to October 1, from 2 to 4:30pm.

For a more leisurely peak at Eton, as well as several river islands, posh houses, and Royal Windsor Racecourse, take a **French Brothers boat trip** up the Thames from Barry Promenade. The bumper 2-hour cruise starts at 1:30 and 2:30pm, every day from Easter to the end of October. Tickets cost £5.80 ($9.30) for adults and £2.90 ($4.65) for children. Cheaper quickie tours, lasting 35 minutes, leave every ½ hour from 11am to 5pm, and cost £3.60 ($5.75) for adults and £1.90 ($3.05) for children. Call ☎ **01753/851-9000** (www.boat-trips.co.uk) for info.

Few theme parks are as extraordinary or impressive as **Legoland,** Windsor Park (☎ **08705/040404;** www.legoland.co.uk). It took 20 million of the famous Danish Toy company's little plastic building bricks to create Miniland. The park has 21 rides in all, including a roller coaster and a mad water ride, as well as shows, an imagination center, and freestyle workshops where the kids can build whatever comes into their heads. The shuttlebus from either station is free if you show a pre-booked Legoland ticket, or £2 ($3.20) without one. And it is essential to plan ahead, as queues can be terminally long in school holidays: **Buy online, and you'll get a 10% discount.**

One-day admission is £17.50 ($28) adults, £14.50 ($23.20) under-16s, and £11.50 ($18.40) seniors; 2-day is £23 ($36.80) adults, £20 ($32) under-16s, and £17 ($27.20) seniors. Legoland is open daily from 10am to 6pm—to 8pm during summer holidays.

WHERE TO EAT

Gilbey's Bar & Restaurant. 82–83 High St., Eton. ☎ **01753/854921.** Bar menu £2.95–£8.95 ($4.70–$14). AE, DC, MC, V. Mon–Fri noon–2:30pm, Sat–Sun noon–3pm; daily 6–11pm. WINE BAR.

Gilbey's is a specialist importer of French wine, which it sells at shop prices alongside bottles from its own English vineyard. The bar menu is delicious and reasonable, from fortifying soup with crusty bread at the cheapest end, to a double-size portion of smoked haddock fishcakes at the other. In the summer, you can eat out in the garden.

Sally Lunn's. 11 Peascod St., Windsor. ☎ **01753/862627.** Main courses £4.70–£7.70 ($7.50–$12.30), all-day "afternoon tea" £4.30–£4.80 ($6.90–$7.70), "high tea" £8.90 ($14.25). MC, V. Mon–Sat 10am–6pm, Sun 11am–6pm. TRADITIONAL BRITISH.

This deliberately "olde worlde teashoppe" is an offshoot of Sally Lunn's in Bath, where the good lady was a celebrated baker in the 17th century. Though you can gorge yourself on creamcakes and a cuppa, it has so much more. Whatever you think of as traditionally British, you'll find it here, from Cornish pasties to rhubarb crumble. And at more than reasonable prices.

4 Bath

110 miles W of London

Beautiful Bath is a UNESCO World Heritage city. Legend has it that King Lear's father, Bladud, founded the town when he was miraculously cured of leprosy after immersing himself in the hot springs. In fact, Bath had been a spa resort since Roman times. It became really popular at the beginning of the 18th century, when the gouty Queen Anne came to take the waters and brought the fashionable *beau monde* with her. Society flocked to the Pump Rooms, arriving early in the morning to bathe and drink up to a gallon of the foul-tasting but supposedly curative waters.

At the time, the Assembly Rooms and the grottoes and pavilions of Sydney Gardens played host to balls, concerts, firework displays, and other entertainment. Bath became a magnet for artists, musicians, and social climbers. Fashions and trends launched here, from Bath buns to Bath chairs, under the watchful eye of dandy Beau Nash, high society's unofficial Master of Ceremonies. Jane Austen came regularly, and Gainsborough made his name here as a portrait painter. Not everyone subscribed to the town's delights, though. Daniel Defoe lamented that "people go to Bath to commit the worst of all murders—to kill time." The fun lasted until the end of the 18th century, when the newly discovered benefits of sea bathing dented the spa's popularity.

The 18th-century town planning and architecture were the vision of John Wood and his son. They laid out elegant interconnected squares and crescents stretching from Queen Square to the beautiful Circus—30 3-story town houses, divided by 114 carved ionic columns, around a circular central green—and the Royal Crescent.

A WEEK AT A GLANCE

Monday: Royal Crescent House closed. **Saturday:** no afternoon, only evening tour of Bath led by one of the Mayor's Corps of Guides; first and third Saturday of the month, farmers' market at Green Park Station. **Sunday:** admission to Bath Abbey restricted to 1:30 to 2:30pm, and 4:30 to 5:30pm, except for those attending services.

ESSENTIALS

GETTING THERE Trains depart from Paddington, making the trip in about 1½ hours. A Supersaver return costs £31 ($49.60), the APEX fare is £17.50 ($28), and a Super Advance is £25.50 ($40.80). Call **National Rail Enquiries** (☎ **08457/484950**). **National Express buses** (☎ **08705/808080**) leave daily from London's Victoria Coach Station and make the trip in about 3¼ hours. Special day return is £12 ($19.20), while a standard return is £20 ($32). If you're driving from London, take the M4 motorway to Exit 18.

ORIENTATION Bath (pop. 83,000) lies in a steep valley along the River Avon. Most of the city's main sights, including the abbey and baths, are clustered near the two bridges that span the river. The bus and train stations are both at the end of Manvers Street, which turns into Pierrepoint Street, then North Parade, as you take the short walk into the city center. Turn left off the parade into York Street for the Roman Baths.

VISITOR INFORMATION The **Tourist Information Centre** is in Abbey Chambers, Abbey Church Yard (☎ **01225/477101;** www.visitbath.co.uk). It has a great free local guide and will help you find a room at a local B&B. The center is open May through October, Monday, Tuesday, Friday, and Saturday from 9:30am to 6pm, Wednesday and Thursday 9:45am to 6pm, Sunday from 10am to 4pm; November through April, Monday to Saturday from 9:30am to 5pm, Sunday from 10am to 4pm. The *Bath Chronicle* has an excellent what's-on Web site at **www.thisisbath.com**.

WALKS & TOURS

The Mayor's Corps of Honorary Guides (☎ **01225/477786**) leads a **free walking tour,** which lasts about 2 hours, at 10:30am, every afternoon except Saturday at 2pm, and at 7pm on Tuesday, Friday, and Saturday evenings. Meet in Abbey Churchyard.

The **Jane Austen Centre** (☎ **01225/443000**) leads a walk following in the famous author's footsteps—she lived at no. 4 Sydney Place from 1801 to 1805. This starts every day at 11am from the Tourist Information Centre. Tickets cost £3.50 ($5.60) for adults and £2.50 ($4) for children, except under-12s who go free. Otherwise, visitors with the inner strength to withstand a lot of teasing will enjoy the **Bizarre Bath** comedy tour (☎ **01225/335124**). Meet at the North Parade Passage at 8pm nightly: £4.50 ($7.20) adults, £4 ($6.40) students, no need to book.

Further afield, well-informed guides on the very friendly **Mad Max Tours** (☎ **01225/465674,** at Bath Youth Hostel) take small groups to **Stonehenge,** and several other stops in the beautiful countryside around Bath. The minibus picks up by the statue at the end of Cheap Street at 8:50am, returning at around 4:30pm. It costs £14 ($22.40), plus £4 ($6.40) if you want to get close up to the ancient stone circle.

ANCIENT BATH

Of all England's historic treasures, there are few more beautiful, better preserved, or so excellently explained as the ✪ **Roman Baths & Pump Room** (☎ **01225/4727785;** www.romanbaths.co.uk). Built between A.D. 65 and 75, they were originally dedicated to Sulis, a local Celtic goddess closely identified with the Roman Minerva. The spring pumps out 240,000 gallons of hot mineral water a day into the pools and the main bath, lit from underneath as part of the presentation. Tour with a personal headset, and you'll see the sauna and steam rooms, as well as the dry heat rooms where the Romans had their massages and escaped from the alien climate.

In the museum, computer-animated reconstructions and wooden models show the site as it probably looked in Roman times. It also holds striking excavation finds, including a gilt-bronze head of Minerva, 13,000 coins, the soles from sandals, a magnificent Gorgon's head, and several mosaics and stone carvings. Archaeologists excavating the spring even found several pewter and lead objects inscribed with such curses as, "whoever stole my gloves, may he lose his mind and his eyes in the temple."

A Money-Saving Ticket

Save a few pounds to spend on Bath buns by buying a combined ticket to the **Roman Baths** and the **Museum of Costume:** £8.90 ($14.25) for adults, £8 ($12.80) for seniors, £5.30 ($8.50) for children, and £23.50 ($37.60) for a family ticket.

The baths are open April to September daily 9am to 6pm; August daily 9am to 9:30pm; October to March daily 9:30am to 5pm. Admission is £6.90 ($11.05) adults, £6 ($9.60) seniors, £4 ($6.40) children, and £17.50 ($28) for a family ticket.

The 18th-century **Pump Room** (☎ **01225/444477**), with its Georgian interior, overlooks the baths. People come for lunch or tea and to sample the therapeutic water, with its 43 minerals, for 45p (72¢) a cup. My brother claims it tastes like his bath water! The Pump Room is open daily from 9:30am to 5:30pm, and admission is free.

Just across from the Pump Room, **Bath Abbey** (☎ **01225/422462**) dates from the late 15th century. The west front is the most striking; the troop of angels climbing a ladder to heaven is said to depict a dream Bishop Oliver King had, exhorting him to restore the church. He did so in 1499. Inside, you'll see stunning fan vaulting and stained glass—the East window depicts 56 scenes from the life of Christ. The abbey has some interesting memorials, too, including one to Isaac Pitman, inventor of Pitman Shorthand, as well as to Richard Beau Nash. The Abbey is open Monday to Saturday 9am to 6pm (November to Easter 9am to 4:30pm); Sunday 1:30 to 2:30pm and 4:30 to 5:30pm, although you can also attend any one of six services.

. . . AND BEYOND

Take a peek at **Pulteney Bridge,** which is off the northwest corner of Grand Parade, a 5-minute walk from the abbey. Designed by Robert Adam and finished in 1774, it is lined with small shops, which you rarely see today. The first two attractions below are on the same side of the river as the Roman Baths and the abbey. But the Holburne Museum & Crafts Study Centre is over Pulteney Bridge.

The **Museum of Costume & The Assembly Rooms,** Bennett St. (☎ **01225/447789;** www.museumofcostume.co.uk) traces the history of fashion and accessories, from silver tissue dresses made in the 1600s through 1920s beaded chiffon to the current dress of the year. Ever since 1963, the museum has asked a fashion expert to choose a dress or outfit to represent the most important new design idea. Karl Lagerfeld, Hussein Chalayan, and Philip Treacey have all given pieces to the collection. It is open daily 10am to 5pm. Admission is £4 ($6.40) adults, £3.60 ($5.75) seniors, £2.90 ($4.65) children, and £11 ($17.60) for a family ticket.

See "A Money-Saving Ticket," above for information on combined entry to the museum and the Roman Baths.

Five minutes' walk away is perhaps Bath's most famous architectural treasure, **Royal Crescent,** built by John Wood the Younger. To see a recreation of the 18th-century lifestyle, visit **Royal Crescent House** (☎ **01225/428126**). Lady guides, who are obvious enthusiasts, can tell you everything about the furniture and fabrics, kitchen equipment, and paintings that all give the house an air of lived-in authenticity. It's open mid-February through October, Tuesday to Sunday from 10:30am to 5pm; and in November, same days, from 10:30am to 4:30pm. Tickets are £4 ($6.40) for adults, £3.50 ($5.60) for seniors, students, and children, and £10 ($16) for families.

The **Holburne Museum & Crafts Study Centre** (☎ **01225/466669;** www.bath.ac.uk/Holburne), is in a lovely 18th-century building at the end of the once very fashionable, 100-foot-wide Great Pulteney Street. It holds a unique collection of decorative and fine arts—jewelry, silver, majolica, porcelain, and furniture—with new pieces set next to old to show how each craft developed. The museum also has paintings by all the English greats, as well as some stunning miniatures, and exhibits by contemporary artists and craftsmen. It's open mid-February to mid-December, Monday to Saturday 11am to 5pm and Sunday 2:30 to 5:30pm. Tickets are £3.50 ($5.60) adults, £1.50 ($2.40) children, and £7 ($11.20) for a family ticket.

WHERE TO STAY

The **Tourist Information Centre** (☎ **01225/477101**) accommodation service will find and reserve you a room for a 10% deposit and a £5 ($8) fee. The largest cluster of budget-priced B&Bs is along Newbridge Road, but those on streets, like Wells Road, in the south of the city are much nicer. Except during festival time (last 2 weeks of May, first week of June), you can usually get a room without prior reservations.

For a super-cheap sleep, go straight to **Bath Youth Hostel,** Bathwick Hill, Bath, BA2 6GZ (☎ **01225/465674;** e-mail: bath@yha.org.uk), which charges £10.85 ($17.35) per night for adults, and £7.40 ($11.85) for under-18s.

Leighton House. 139 Wells Rd., Bath, BA2 3AL. ☎ **01225/314769.** Fax 01225/443079. www.leighton-house.co.uk. E-mail: welcome@leighton-house.co.uk. 8 units, all with bathroom. TV TEL. £40–£80 ($64–$128) single; £55–£95 ($88–$152) double. Rates include full English breakfast. Lower rates apply midweek and winter. JCB, MC, V. No under-7s.

Proprietors Marilyn and Colin Humphrey offer terrific value in their spacious 1870s Victorian house, overlooking Bath. All the rooms are comfortable and nicely decorated—Leighton House is rated 5 Diamonds—some with period pieces, and all with hair dryers, tea-/coffeemaking facilities, radios, and complimentary toiletries. There's a large lounge, with sofas and armchairs around the fireplace, and a lovely garden. The breakfast is à la carte. Choose from traditional eggs cooked any style, kippers, or smoked haddock, then help yourself to cereals, fruits, and yogurt. The house is only a 10-minute walk from the town center, on a bus route. And there's a car park. Leighton House is also nonsmoking.

Oldfields. 102 Wells Rd., Bath, BA2 3AL. ☎ **01225/317984.** Fax 01225/444471. www.oldfields.co.uk. E-mail: info@oldfields.co.uk. 14 units, all with bathroom (some with shower only). TV TEL. £48 ($76.80) single; £42–£68 ($67.20–$108.80) double/twin; £57–£78 ($91.20–$124.80) four-poster room. Rates include full English breakfast. Discount available for 3-night stays. AE, JCB, MC, V.

This friendly and well-run hotel occupies a large, and very elegant, Victorian house, built out of honey-colored Bath stone. It has marvelous views over the city. The rooms are high-ceilinged and attractively modern, with hair dryers and tea-/coffeemaking facilities. An excellent breakfast is included, which is cooked to order from the full selection from a menu. Fruit, breads, cereals, and yogurt are out on a large sideboard. There's a large sitting room for guests and off-street parking. It's only a 10-minute walk from the city center. Oldfields is nonsmoking throughout.

✪ **The Old Red House.** 37 Newbridge Rd., Bath, BA1 3HE. ☎ **01225/330464.** Fax 01225/331661. 4 units, 3 with bathroom (most with shower only). TV. £26–£45 ($41.60–$72) single; £42–£68 ($67.20–$108.80) double. Discount for 3-night stays. AE, DC, MC, V.

This is my favorite B&B in Bath—a gingerbread house that really is red! The owner has such charm and the rooms have been decorated in a fetching personal style, often with canopies over the bed, eye-catching antiques, and treasures brought from as far afield as India. The largest one boasts stained-glass windows and a marble fireplace, but my favorite is in a separate little lodge at the back.. All the rooms are nonsmoking and have hair dryers, radio/alarms, and tea-/coffeemaking facilities.

WHERE TO EAT

As well as those listed below, the **Riverside Café** (☎ **01225/480532**) is a charming little hole-in-the-wall tucked away off Pulteney Bridge, looking out on the river. It's good for a spot of tea or light meals like toasted sandwiches, quiche, salads, and jacket potatoes—nothing is priced higher than £4 ($6.40).

Coeur de Lion. Northumberland Place, ☎ **01225/463568.** No credit cards. Mon–Sat 11am–11pm, Sun noon–8pm. PUB.

This has to be the smallest pub in Bath and one of the most charming. The first-floor bar, with its fireplace, is behind a storefront window. The food runs from sandwiches to cheese and pâté plates, as well as pasta and *moules marinières.*

Hullabaloos. 36 Broad St. ☎ **01225/443323.** www.hullabaloos.co.uk. Express lunch £5.25–£7.50 ($8.40–$12), fixed-price lunch £6.99–£8.50 ($11.20–$13.60); pre-theater menu £8.50–£10.25 ($13.60–$16.40), dinner £14.75–£17.75 ($23.60–$28.40). AE, DC, MC, V. Daily noon–2pm and 6–10pm. MODERN BRITISH.

You might see a large, soon-to-be naked, man in a policeman's uniform strutting through Hullabaloos if you come here in the evening. The basement room is where hen (bachelorette) parties and their strip-a-grams are kept separate from "regular" diners. This place is good-deal city. There's no corkage when you bring your own wine, and all the fixed-price menus give ample choice from the light modern British menu and daily chef's specials. You must book ahead because it is understandably very popular.

Sally Lunn's Refreshment House & Museum. North Parade Passage. ☎ **01225/461634.** Lunch £4–£8 ($6.40–$12.80); dinner main courses £7–£9 ($11.20–$14.40). Mon–Sat 10am–10pm, Sun 11am–10pm. No smoking. BAKERY/TRADITIONAL BRITISH.

Sally Lunn buns are famous far beyond Bath, named after the woman who set up as a baker in the 1680s in this house, which is said to be the oldest in town. A bit like extra large brioche, the buns can be filled with meats, cheeses, and salads, and served cold or toasted. Pick one topped with lemon curd, for a sweet treat, or hazelnut and coffee. This is the place to come for morning coffee, a quick snack, afternoon tea, or candlelit dining on traditional English dishes. You can see the original kitchen in the downstairs museum (admission 30p/48¢, free for seniors, kids, and diners).

5 Oxford

57 miles NW of London

Oxford contrasts dramatically with Cambridge. It's a modern, crowded, and busy place where town seriously competes with gown. After all, people were living here 2 centuries before the founding of the first college. Although scholars and students began to congregate as early as the 12th century, Oxford University didn't receive its charter from the Papal Legate until 1214. From 1249, colleges began popping up like mushrooms, starting with University, then Balliol in 1263, and Merton in 1264. Originally they were men only. The first one for women, Lady Margaret Hall, was established in 1878. In 1975, some of the men's colleges began admitting women, and the rest reluctantly followed. The university hit the headlines last year, accused of academic snobbery when it turned down a would-be medical student from a comprehensive school in the North of England, who then won a scholarship to Harvard.

Wedged between the Thames and Cherwell rivers, Oxford has more than 600 buildings listed for historical or architectural interest. If you really want to uncover the nooks and crannies, the history and personalities, then read *Oxford* by Jan Morris.

Note: Oxford University **term dates** for 2001 are: January 14 to March 10; April 4 to June 16; and October 7 to December 1.

A WEEK AT A GLANCE

Monday: Ashmolean Museum and Museum of Modern Art closed. **Wednesday:** general market at Gloucester Green. **Thursday:** flea market, same place; also farmers'

Oxford

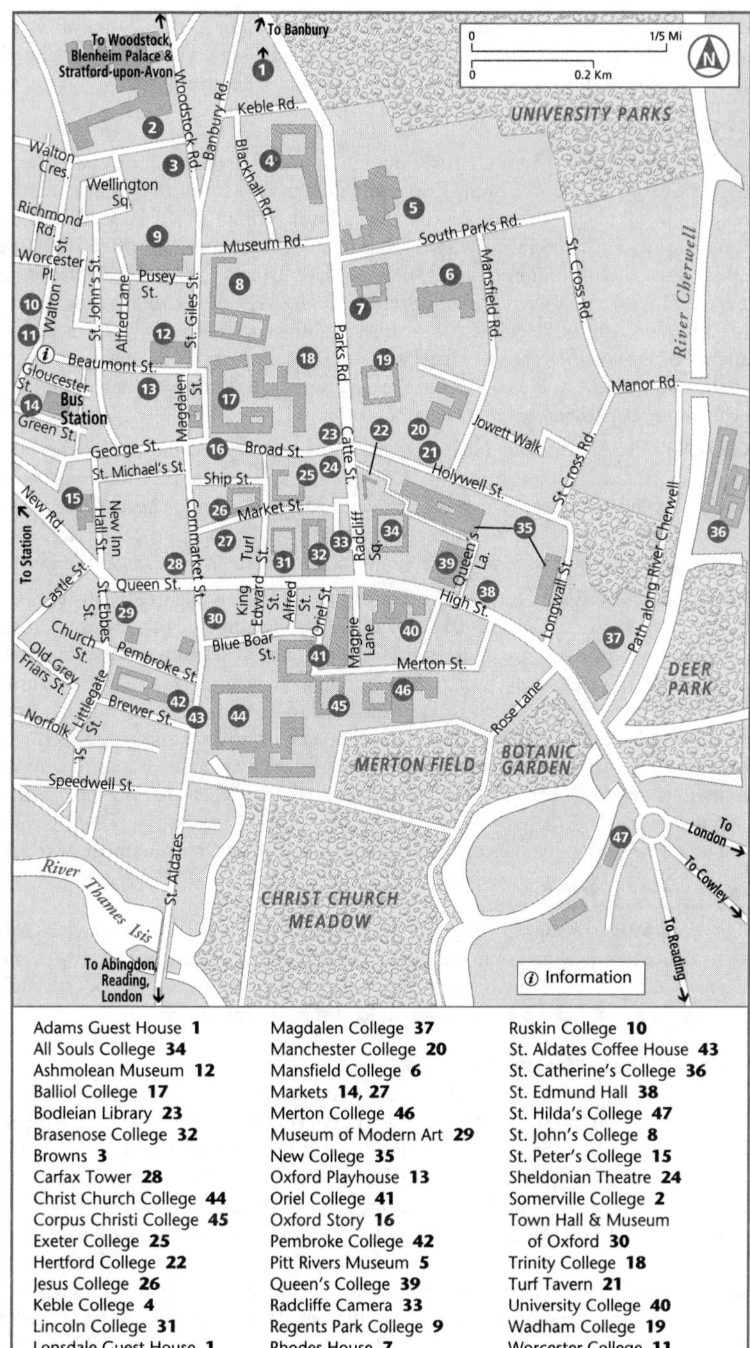

0
1/5 Mi
0
0.2 Km
N
To Woodstock, Blenheim Palace & Stratford-upon-Avon
To Banbury
UNIVERSITY PARKS
Keble Rd.
Woodstock Rd.
Banbury Rd.
Blackhall Rd.
Walton Cres.
Wellington Sq.
Richmond Rd.
Worcester Pl.
Walton St.
St. John's St.
Alfred Lane
Pusey St.
St. Giles St.
Museum Rd.
South Parks Rd.
Mansfield Rd.
St. Cross Rd.
River Cherwell
Parks Rd.
Beaumont St.
Gloucester St.
Bus Station
Green St.
Magdalen St.
Manor Rd.
Jowett Walk
George St.
Broad St.
Catte St.
Holywell St.
St. Michael's St.
Ship St.
Market St.
New Rd.
To Station
New Inn Hall St.
Cornmarket St.
Turl St.
Radcliff Sq.
Queen's La.
Longwall St.
Path along River Cherwell
Castle St.
Queen St.
King Edward St.
Alfred St.
Oriel St.
High St.
St. Ebbes St.
Church St.
Pembroke St.
Blue Boar St.
Magpie Lane
Merton St.
Old Grey Friars St.
Littlegate St.
Brewer St.
Norfolk St.
Rose Lane
DEER PARK
MERTON FIELD
BOTANIC GARDEN
Speedwell St.
To London
To Cowley
River Thames Isis
St. Aldates
CHRIST CHURCH MEADOW
To Reading
To Abingdon, Reading, London
Information
Adams Guest House 1
All Souls College 34
Ashmolean Museum 12
Balliol College 17
Bodleian Library 23
Brasenose College 32
Browns 3
Carfax Tower 28
Christ Church College 44
Corpus Christi College 45
Exeter College 25
Hertford College 22
Jesus College 26
Keble College 4
Lincoln College 31
Lonsdale Guest House 1
Magdalen College 37
Manchester College 20
Mansfield College 6
Markets 14, 27
Merton College 46
Museum of Modern Art 29
New College 35
Oxford Playhouse 13
Oriel College 41
Oxford Story 16
Pembroke College 42
Pitt Rivers Museum 5
Queen's College 39
Radcliffe Camera 33
Regents Park College 9
Rhodes House 7
Ruskin College 10
St. Aldates Coffee House 43
St. Catherine's College 36
St. Edmund Hall 38
St. Hilda's College 47
St. John's College 8
St. Peter's College 15
Sheldonian Theatre 24
Somerville College 2
Town Hall & Museum of Oxford 30
Trinity College 18
Turf Tavern 21
University College 40
Wadham College 19
Worcester College 11

market the first Thursday of the month. **Saturday:** additional official tour of Oxford at 1:45pm, starting at Carfax Tower and usually including a visit to Christ Church. **Sunday:** same additional tour as Saturday; Sheldonian Theatre closed.

ESSENTIALS

GETTING THERE Trains depart from London's Paddington Station and make the trip to Oxford in about 1 hour. Day-return tickets are £28.90 ($47.85); cheap day return £14.80 ($23.70); and Network Away Break £18.90 ($30.25). Call **National Rail Enquiries** (☎ **08457/484950**). **National Express buses** (☎ **08705/808080**) take 1 hour and 40 minutes, and round-trip fares from Victoria Coach Station are £9.50 ($15.20), with day returns for under £7.50 ($12). If you're in a car, take the M40 to the A40, to the A420. Don't drive into the city center, however, as parking and traffic are horrific. There are free **Park and Ride** car parks on the main approaches to the north, south, and west sides of the city. Buses run regularly from there into the heart of the city (there's a small charge).

ORIENTATION Known as **Carfax,** the city center ripples out around the crossroads where Cornmarket Street, St. Aldate's Street, Queen Street, and High Street meet. Most of the colleges are to the east, with **Magdalen Bridge** beyond the eastern end of High Street. The bus station and the tourist information center are in the northwest corner of Carfax, while the train station is further west, across the canal.

VISITOR INFORMATION The **Oxford Information Centre** is in The Old School, Gloucester Green (☎ **01865/726871;** www.oxford.gov.uk/tourism). It can provide you with maps, brochures for local sights and attractions, and accommodation booking. The office is open May through September, Monday to Saturday 9:30am to 5pm, Sunday 10am to 1pm and 1:30 to 3:30pm; October through April, Monday to Saturday 9:30am to 5pm, closed Sundays and Christmas week (as is most of Oxford). Otherwise, **Oxford University's** Web site (www.ox.ac.uk/visitors.htm) is refreshingly visitor-friendly, with information on all its colleges and museums, what to see and when.

For a what's-on guide, especially useful for stopovers, surf **www.oxfordcity.co.uk**.

WALKS & TOURS

Two-hour tours costing £4 ($6.40) for adults, and £2.50 ($4) for under-12s, leave from the center daily at 11am and 2pm. The 1:45pm tour, from Carfax Tower, only happens on Saturday and Sunday and usually includes free admission to Christ Church. You can pick up more walkin' info at the information center.

THE DREAMING SPIRES

It's an option, not a duty, but the animatronic presentation at **The Oxford Story,** 6 Broad St. (☎ **01865/728822**), will help put in context what you see during the rest of your visit. It tells the history of Oxford and student life, and is open daily: April through June and September through October from 9:30am to 5pm; July through August 9:30am to 5:30pm; November through March, daily 10am to 4:30pm (5pm at weekends). Admission is £5.70 ($9.10) adults, £4.70 ($7.50) concessions.

A cheaper way to plot out Oxford's dreaming spires is to scale the 97 steps to the top of **Carfax Tower** (☎ **01865/792653**). The attendant will give you a map identifying the individual rooftops. It's open daily from 10am to 6pm but closes at 3:30pm in winter. Admission is £1.20 ($1.90) adults, 60p (95¢) children, or half price with the official walking tour.

Today there are 41 colleges scattered throughout the city. Most open their quads and chapels in the afternoon only, except for Christ Church, Hertford, New College,

St. Hugh's, and Trinity College, which are open in the morning, too. Obviously you can't and probably wouldn't want to visit all of them, so we've picked the best of the bunch.

Founded in 1458, **Magdalen** (☎ **01865/276000;** pronounced "*Maud*-len") is one of the largest and most beautiful of the colleges—the hall has some particularly lovely carved wood paneling. Its tower (1492–1509) is a city landmark from which, on May mornings, you can hear the glorious pealing of bells. Magdelen alumni include Thomas Wolsey, Edward Gibbon, Oscar Wilde, and Edward, Prince of Wales. The college is open daily from 2 to 5 or 6pm, and admission is £2 ($3.20), or £1 ($1.60) for concessions. The Botanic Gardens, meadows, and Grove (where deer have roamed since the 1700s), which surround the college, make it a very peaceful retreat.

Built on the site of St. Frideswide's Monastery, **Christ Church** (☎ **01865/276150**) dates from 1546 and is both college and cathedral. The latter contains some beautiful medieval stained glass, including a depiction of the martyrdom of Thomas à Becket, and the St. Frideswide and St. Catherine windows by Edward Burne-Jones. Charles I took up residence in the Deanery during the civil war, when Oxford was his military headquarters. Sir Christopher Wren designed **Tom Tower** (1682), at the college gate.

The hall at Christ Church has a fine collection of portraits, including those of notable graduates William Penn, W. E. Gladstone, John Wesley, Anthony Eden, and Lewis Carroll. The cathedral is open in summer, Monday through Saturday 9:30am to 4:30pm, Sunday 1 to 4:30pm. There are four services on Sunday. Evensong is at 6pm weekdays.

All Souls (1438) is an unusual institution in that does not admit undergraduates. The chapel has a striking hammerbeam ceiling and finely carved reredos and misericords. The Great Quad was designed by Nicholas Hawksmoor, a pupil of one of the college's most famous graduates, Sir Christopher Wren.

The chapel at **New College** (1379) is one for culture buffs: It has some very famous artworks, including Epstein's *Lazarus* and El Greco's *St. James,* as well as fine stained-glass windows and woodwork, particularly the carving of the choir stalls. The paneled hall is the oldest in Oxford, while the gardens are some of the most beautiful.

Corpus Christi (1517) is a small college. Somehow it managed to retain most of its silver and other plate. It also has a charming sundial topped by a pelican in the middle of the Front quad and an altarpiece in the chapel, *The Adoration of the Shepherds,* attributed to Rubens. **Hertford** (1874) has its own Bridge of Sighs. Capability Brown laid out the gardens at **St. John's** (1555). And if you want to tread in Bill Clinton's footsteps, visit **University College** where he was a Rhodes Scholar in 1968.

. . . AND BEYOND

The attractions below are ranked subjectively by entertainment value. It is up to you how to mix and match them. Bear in mind that the Pitt Rivers Museum is only open for a few hours in the afternoon. The bustling **Covered Market,** which links Market Street and High Street, has fed the burghers of Oxford since 1774. It's a great place to take a breather from earnest sightseeing, as well as to grab food on the hoof for lunch.

Back on the history trail, let's start with a fabulous **freebie.** Founded in 1683, the **Ashmolean Museum,** Beaumont Street (☎ **01865/278000;** www.ashmol.ox.ac.uk), is

Fun Fact

At 9:05pm every day, the 7-ton "Great Tom" bell at Christ Church tolls 101 times. The tradition dates from the time when each chime represented a scholar and the tolling marked the closing of college.

England's oldest public museum. It's the sort of place where you don't quite believe what you're seeing is for real—things like Guy Fawkes's lantern, Henry VIII's stirrups and hawking gear, the mantle said to have belonged to Powhattan, father of Pocohontas and King of Virginia. It has a terrific archaeology collection, too, with Egyptian mummies, casts of Greek sculptures, silver, ceramics, and bronzes. The paintings are pretty impressive, including works by da Vinci, Raphael, and Rembrandt. The Ashmolean is open Tuesday through Saturday 10am to 5pm, Sunday 2 to 5pm.

Sticking to the haunts of academe, just off Broad Street you'll find the famous 1602 **Bodleian Library** (☎ **01865/277165**), which contains more than 5 million books. The **Radcliffe Camera** (1748) is England's earliest round reading room, designed by James Gibbs. The library is open for tours (£3.50/$5.60): Call for exact times.

To see where the university bestows honorary degrees during the Encaenia ceremony (June 26), visit the **Sheldonian Theatre** (☎ **01865/277299**). This concert hall was Sir Christopher Wren's first commission, completed in 1669. The interior is made entirely of wood except for the ceiling, which consists of 36 panels painted by Robert Streeter, court painter to Charles II. It's open Monday to Saturday 10am to 12:30pm and 2 to 4:30pm (to 3:30pm mid-November to March), but call ahead to check. Admission is £1.50 ($2.40) adults, £1 ($1.60) children.

The **Pitt Rivers Museum** on Park Street (☎ **01865/270949;** www.units.ox.ac.uk/departments/prm/) is free, and it's like a 3-D tour through the pages of *National Geographic.* General Pitt Rivers gave his collection of ethnic artifacts to the university in 1884 and there are now more than half a million objects. The spookiest section is on magic, which has a 17th-century silver phial, said to have a witch trapped inside. Most redolent of adventure are the 150 pieces collected during Captain Cook's second voyage, from 1773 to 1774, including a Tahitian mourner's costume. Arranged by type, rather than geography or date, the exhibits demonstrate how different peoples tackled the same tasks. The Pitt Rivers is open Monday to Saturday 1 to 4:30pm, and from 2pm on Sunday. To get to it, walk through the courtyard of University Museum.

The **Museum of Modern Art** on Pembroke Street (☎ **01865/722733**) could hardly be more of a contrast. This leading center for contemporary visual arts holds ever-changing exhibitions of sculpture, architecture, photography, video, and other media. It's open Tuesday through Sunday 11am to 6pm (until 9pm Thursday). Admission is £2.50 ($4) adults, £1.50 ($2.40) seniors, free for under-16s.

WHERE TO STAY

Accommodations in Oxford are limited, especially during the school term. The main roads out of town are lined with affordable bed-and-breakfasts; these are fine if you don't mind a healthy walk. The **Oxford Information Centre** (☎ **01865/726871;** www.oxford.gov.uk/tourism), will book rooms for a £2.50 ($4) fee and 10% deposit.

The **Oxford Youth Hostel,** 32 Jack Straw's Lane, Oxford, OX3 ODW (☎ **01865/762997;** e-mail: oxford@yha.org.uk) is a super-cheap sleep, charging £10.85 ($17.35) a night for adults, and £7.40 ($11.85) for under-18s.

Adams Guest House. 302 Banbury Rd., Summertown, Oxford, OX2 7ED. ☎ **01865/556118.** Fax 01865/514066. 6 units, all with bathroom (shower only). £30 ($48) single; £45 ($72) twin. Rates include full English breakfast. No credit cards. Bus: 2 from train station to South Parade; 2, 7, from coach station and city center.

One and a quarter miles from the middle of Oxford, in Summertown, Adams Guest House is one of the best B&Bs around. Rooms are comfortable and cozy. And the breakfast includes a vegetarian option. From this quiet neighborhood with a number of restaurants, shops, and a laundry, a bus runs every few minutes to the city center. It's opposite the Midland Bank.

Lonsdale Guest House. 312 Banbury Rd., Summertown, Oxford, OX2 7ED. ☎ **01865/554872.** Fax 01865/554872. 8 units, 6 with bathroom (some with shower only). TV. £32 ($51.20) single without bathroom; £50–£60 ($80–$96) double/twin with bathroom. Rates include English breakfast. No credit cards. Bus: 7, 7A, 2A, or 2B.

About 10 minutes by bus from the city center, the Lonsdale is a really cozy B&B in a 3-story Victorian terrace house. If you catch a local bus here, ask for the stop outside the BBC Radio Oxford building. Most rooms have a private shower and all have tea-/coffeemakers. And Christine and Roland Adams have won a "Heartbeat" healthy eating award from Oxford City Council for their breakfast. The B&B is totally nonsmoking.

WHERE TO EAT

Browns. 5–11 Woodstock Rd. ☎ **01865/511995.** Main courses £6–£15 ($9.60–$24). AE, MC, V. Mon–Sat 11am–11:30pm, Sun noon–11:30pm. ENGLISH.

This large, casual, upbeat brasserie is one of the best places to eat in Oxford. It serves hearty food, including a good traditional cream tea, and has a large convivial bar and a very pleasant outdoor terrace. Mummies and daddies come here with their high-achieving offspring when they come to visit them at the university. There is also a Browns in London (see "Mayfair," in chapter 5).

St. Aldates Coffee House. 94 St. Aldates. ☎ **01865/245952.** Main courses £2.60–£5 ($4.15–$8). No credit cards. Daily 10:30am–8pm. BRITISH.

Right opposite Christ Church, this pleasant diner has a long menu of delicious good-value grub, from soups and baked potatoes, to homemade pies like lamb and rosemary or steak and red wine. The cakes are wickedly irresistible. A great place to stop and refuel, right up to the early evening.

The Turf Tavern. 4 Bath Place. ☎ **01865/243235.** Main courses £4–£5.75 ($6.40–$9.20). Daily noon–8pm. PUB.

This delightful pub, tucked away down a cobblestone alley, gets very crowded. It has several bars in a series of long, low-ceilinged rooms decorated with rowing crew portraits and other Oxford memorabilia. The food is traditional pub grub, ranging from steak-in-ale pie, and fish and chips, to sandwiches and salads. It also has a good selection of cask ales and a pleasant beer garden.

6 Stratford-upon-Avon

92 miles NW of London

William Shakespeare was born in Stratford-upon-Avon in 1564 and died here, too, after setting the London stage alight, in 1616. So it is inevitable that this has become a mecca for tourists, which can often make it seem more like a theme park than a real place. If you can stand the competition, it is still well worth a visit. Stratford was a market town way before Will put in an appearance—ever since 1169, in fact—and the streets still follow the medieval grid pattern. In spring and summer, roses and honeysuckle seem to bloom everywhere, filling the air with a sweet fragrance. Statuesque chestnut and poplar trees shade picture-perfect, half-timbered houses, while lazy willows skim the surface of the River Avon. The Stratford Canal balloons into a narrowboat marina here. Take a Bard-break and wander along the banks of one of these waterways.

A WEEK AT A GLANCE

Friday: general market in Rother Street. **Saturday:** first weekend of the month, there's a farmers' market, same place. **Sunday:** no backstage tours of Royal Shakespeare Theatre.

ESSENTIALS

GETTING THERE Depending on the route, the train trip can take anything from 1½ to 2½ hours from London's Paddington Station. Direct trains leave every 2 hours. A saver return costs £22.50 ($36), cheap day return £19.50 ($31.20). Call **National Rail Enquiries** (☎ **08457/484950**). **National Express buses** (☎ **08705/808080**) leave from London's Victoria Coach Station, and make the trip in about 3½ hours. Tickets cost £12 ($19.20) for a same-day return and £15 ($24) for an open return. Driving from London, take the M40 motorway, then head north on A34.

ORIENTATION Stratford's simple layout is an important component of its charm. Just three streets run parallel to the river and three streets at right angles to it. Buses stop at the corner of Guild Street and Warwick Road.

VISITOR INFORMATION The **Tourist Information Centre,** Bridgefoot (☎ **01789/293127;** www.stratford-upon-avon.co.uk), offers helpful advice, maps, and an accommodations booking service. It's open April through October, Monday to Saturday 9am to 6pm, Sunday 11am to 5pm; November through March, Monday to Saturday from 9am to 5pm and Christmas Sunday (closed other Sundays).

BARD-WATCHING

There are five hotspots, known as the "Shakespeare Properties." Why not start with the three in town? Will was born in a three-gabled house on Henley Street on St. George's Day (April 23) in 1564. **Shakespeare's Birthplace** has some period furniture and a fine exhibition about his "life and times." Get here before 11am, when the masses of day-trippers arrive. It's open late March to mid-October, Monday to Saturday 9am to 5pm, Sunday 9:30am to 5pm; mid-October to mid-March, Monday to Saturday 9:30am to 4pm, Sunday 10am to 4pm. Admission is £5.50 ($8.80) adults, £5 ($8) seniors and students, £2.50 ($4) children, and £14 ($22.40) for a family ticket.

The next stop is **Nash House,** a 16th-century house on Chapel Street once owned by Thomas Nash, first husband of Shakespeare's granddaughter Elizabeth. **New Place,** next door, was the Shakespeare's retirement home. This was one of Stratford's poshest houses when he bought it in 1597—sadly, only the foundations and garden remain. Between the two lie the Elizabethan **Knott Garden** and the Great Garden, which has a mulberry tree said to have grown from a cutting planted by the Bard himself. It's open late March to mid-October, Monday to Saturday 9:30am to 5pm, Sunday 10am to 5pm; mid-October to mid-March, Monday to Saturday 10am to 4pm, Sunday 10:30am to 4pm. Admission is £3.50 ($5.60) adults, £1.70 ($2.70) children.

The last of the three in-town properties is **Hall's Croft,** Old Town (☎ **01789/204016**), where Shakespeare's daughter Susanna lived with her well-to-do husband, Dr. John Hall. The Tudor house, with its traditional oak furniture, has an exhibit on Elizabethan medical practices and a lovely walled garden at the back. It's open late March to mid-October, Monday to Saturday 9:30am to 5pm, Sunday 10am to 5pm; mid-October to mid-March, Monday to Saturday 10am to 4pm, Sunday 10:30am to 4pm. Admission is £3.50 ($5.60) adults, £3 ($4.80) concessions, £1.70 ($2.70) children, and £8.50 ($13.60) for a family ticket. Hall's Croft Club serves morning coffee, lunch, and afternoon tea.

Before you head off to the out-of-town Shakespeare properties, pop into the nearby **Holy Trinity Church,** Southern Lane (☎ **01789/266316**), where the Bard's grave is marked with a small plaque bearing the words, " . . . and cursed be he who moves my bones." Anne Hathaway is buried here, too. Open Monday to Saturday, 8:30am to 6pm from April to October, to 4pm from November to March; Sunday 2 to 5pm year-round.

Stratford-upon-Avon

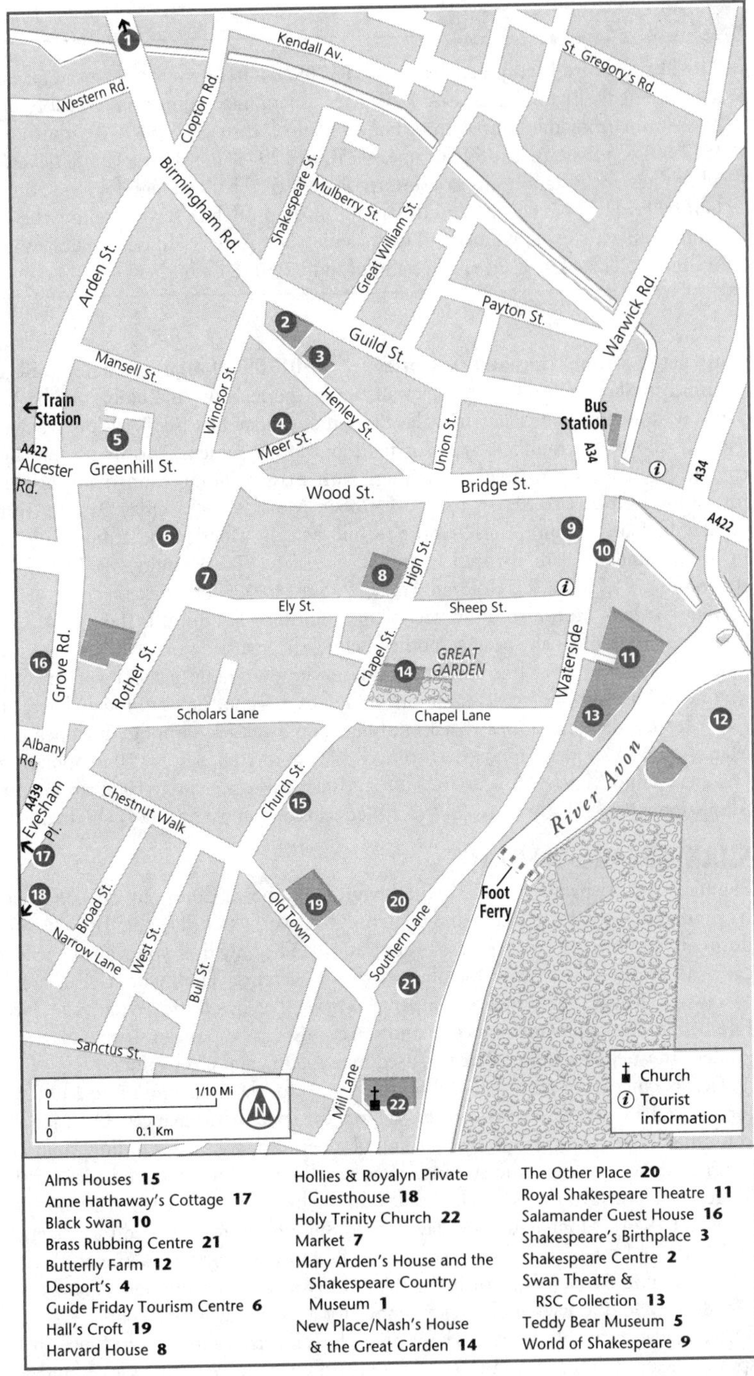

A Money-Saving Ticket

The **Shakespeare Birthplace Trust** (☎ **01789/204016;** www.shakespeare.org.uk) administers the five "Shakespeare Properties." Combined admission, available at all of them or from the Tourist Information Centre, costs £12 ($19.20) adults, £11 ($17.60) concessions, £6 ($9.60) under-15s, or £29 ($46.40) for a family ticket. At adult rates, for instance, this saves nearly £10 ($16). That's enough for a ride on the **Guide Friday** (☎ **017892/94466**) hop-on, hop-off bus service round the five properties, which you will need to use to visit Mary Arden's House, 5 miles away in Wilmcote. Tickets are £8 ($12.80) adults and £2.50 ($4) children.

To get to **Anne Hathaway's Cottage** (☎ **01789/204016**), 2 miles west of Stratford in Shottery, you can either walk across the meadow and along the marked pathway from Evesham Place, or take the Guide Friday bus (see "A Money-Saving Ticket," above). Surrounded by an orchard and lovely gardens, this pretty thatched cottage has a big open fireplace, ceilings with massive beams, and many original furnishings. Open late March to mid-October, Monday to Saturday 9am to 5pm, Sunday 9:30am to 5pm; mid-October to mid-March, Monday to Saturday 9:30am to 4pm, Sunday 10am to 4pm. Admission £4.50 ($7.20) adults, £3.70 ($5.90) concessions, £1.70 ($2.70) children, and £10 ($16) for a family ticket.

Mary Arden's House at Wilmcote, 5 miles north of Stratford, is thought to have been the home of Shakespeare's mother before she married John Shakespeare and moved to Stratford. It's a fine Tudor farmhouse with outbuildings and a working farm next door. Displays bring rural traditions to life, from Tudor times to today. There are also falconry demonstrations, blacksmithing, and livestock farming. It's open late March to mid-October, Monday to Saturday 9:30am to 5pm, Sunday 10 to 5pm; mid-October to mid-March, Monday to Saturday 10am to 4pm, Sunday 10:30am to 4pm. Admission is £5 ($8) adults, £4.50 ($7.20) concessions, and £2.50 ($4) children.

SHAKESPEARE ON STAGE

Founded in 1961 by Sir Peter Hall, the **Royal Shakespeare Company** puts on five or six productions—other classical and contemporary works as well as the Bard's plays—during its summer and winter seasons at Stratford. The only time you won't be able to catch a performance is early October to mid-November. The main stage is at the 1,500-seat **Royal Shakespeare Theatre,** on the banks of the Avon. The Neo-Elizabethan **Swan Theatre** seats 430 and stages post-Shakespearean works. The small modern theater, **The Other Place,** is used for experimental productions.

Tickets range from £6 to £26 ($9.60 to $41.60) for the Swan and up to £40 ($64) for the main stage, with discounts for seniors for some performances. Occasionally, you can get matinee seats on the morning of a performance, and standing room and returned tickets for the same evening. However, holding out for a good deal is risky. To get good seats, you must book ahead. Call the box office (☎ **01789/403403;** fax 01789/261974), Monday to Saturday 9am to 8pm; or write with credit-card details, an S.A.E., and international reply coupon to Box Office, Royal Shakespeare Theatre, Stratford-upon-Avon, CV37 6BB. In the U.S., you can buy through Globaltickets (☎ **800/2236108;** www.globaltickets.com), for a fee and handling charge.

Again, you're strongly advised to book ahead for a **backstage tour** of the Royal Shakespeare Theatre (☎ **01789/412602**). These usually take place Monday to Saturday at 1:30 and 5:30pm, and Sunday at noon, 1, 2, and 3pm, as well as after some evening performances. Tickets cost £4 ($6.40) adults, £3 ($4.80) for students and seniors.

WHERE TO STAY

There are lots of bed-and-breakfasts, but during the summer it's wise to book ahead. The **Tourist Information Centre,** Bridgefoot, Stratford-upon-Avon, Warwickshire, CV37 6GW (☎ **01789/293127**) can help you find somewhere to stay on short notice.

For a super-cheap sleep, try the **IYHF Youth Hostel,** Hemmingford House, Wellesbourne Rd., Alveston, Stratford-upon-Avon, CV37 7RG (☎ **01789/297093;** e-mail: stratford@yha.org.uk). It charges £14.90 ($23.85) a night for adults, £11.20 ($17.90) under-18s.

The Hollies & Royalyn Private Guesthouse. 16 & 17 Evesham Place, Stratford-upon-Avon, Warwickshire, CV37 6HT. ☎ **01789/266857.** www.royalynhouse.co.uk. E-mail: anyone@mighty.demon.co.uk. 11 units, 8 with bathroom (some with shower only). TV. £37 ($59.20) double without bathroom, £45 ($72) with bathroom. Rates include full English breakfast. No credit cards.

The lady who owns the Hollies guest house, in the old 3-story schoolhouse, has bought the equally comfortable Royalyn next door—that's where you need to be to get a tub-shower. All the rooms are comfortably English, and spotless. Tea-/coffeemakers and hair dryers are available on request—as is vegetarian breakfast. E-mail reservations to the manager, Annette Rigg, at the above address rather than through the Web site.

Salamander Guest House. 40 Grove Rd., Stratford-upon-Avon, Warwickshire, CV37 6PB. ☎ **01789/205728** (also fax). E-mail: SEJGET@nova88.freeserve.co.uk. 7 units, all with bathroom (most shower only). TV. £22 ($35.20) single; £44–£48 ($70.40–$76.80) double. Rates include full English breakfast. No credit cards.

Salamander is in a 1904 house facing a wooded park, 5 minutes' walk from the town center. Mr. and Mrs. Hind took over as managers in 1999, and they've repainted and carpeted throughout, and bought new matching bed linen and curtains. The rooms all have tea-/coffeemaking facilities, and you can borrow an iron and hairdryer at the reception desk. Salamander is nonsmoking.

WHERE TO EAT

Black Swan. Southern Lane, Waterside. ☎ **01789/297312.** £8–£16 ($12.80–$25.60). AE, MC, V. Bar food Mon–Fri noon–10pm, Sat–Sun noon–2pm and 5:30–10pm; restaurant Mon–Sun noon–2pm, Mon–Sat 7–10pm (from 5:30pm for booked pre-theater meal). PUB.

Affectionately known as the Dirty Duck, this popular pub has been a regular hangout for local actors since the 18th century. Autographed photos of patrons, including Lord Olivier, hang on the walls. The menu is mouthwatering, from venison medallions to smoked salmon with quail's egg salad. During cold weather, an open fire blazes in the hearth. When it's fine, you can take your drinks onto the terrace overlooking the river.

Desport's. 13–14 Meer St. ☎ **01789/269304.** E-mail: bookings@desports.co.uk. Main courses £11.95–£16.95 ($19.20–$27.10). MC, V. Tues–Sat noon–2pm and 6–11pm. MODERN EUROPEAN.

Don't worry if the main course prices make you gasp because you can choose a starter-size version of most dishes for £5.50 to £6.95 ($8.80 to $11.10). And before you say that isn't going to fuel a serious sightseer, have a listen to what you could be eating: seared monkfish with dill creamed potato, sweet pea puree, and orange vinaigrette; or mushroom fettuccini with black truffle oil and parmesan. It's no wonder this innovative restaurant has won such high praise. And the building, which is Tudor black and white inside and out, is enchanting and all part of the dining experience.

Appendix: London in Depth

London is the place to see history in the making. Two thousand years of continuous habitation have left their mark on the city's architecture, cuisine, politics, and just about any aspect of culture you care to mention. The city is like an ever-expanding time capsule, to which each generation adds its own contribution—from modern streets that still follow the arrow-straight Roman highways, to chic new-wave Indian cuisine that is the legacy of the Empire, and the ebb and flow of social mores. This appendix will help you to see beyond the superficial and immerse yourself in a truly 3D London experience.

1 London Today

British governments have an expiration date, rather than a set date, for re-election. The Prime Minister and party pundits read the runes, sniff the air, and poll thousands of voters to find the most propitious moment within their allotted 5-year term to "go to the country." Tony Blair's time runs out in May 2002, and the bookies have been taking bets for months on his calling a national election either 1 year or 6 months early. While few experts would risk a wager on William Hague, the long knives are out for Labour. It swept to power (as the cliché goes) with the healthiest credit rating of any new government for years, but debits have since piled up on its popularity balance sheet.

The inevitable winter flu crisis shoved the government's record on health under an unhealthy spotlight. The debacle over Rover and BMW highlighted internal strife over Europe every bit as heated as that within the Tory party. And pity poor Whinnie the Pig, tethered for months in Parliament Square by protesting farmers. Then there was the London mayoral election. In their farcical head-to-head, Tony looked like the back half of a pantomime horse, while erstwhile loony-lefty Ken Livingstone stole the show as heroic principal boy. The PM wants to privatize the Underground. Mayor Ken says oh, no, you don't. He has little real power, but his off-message beats any government spin.

It even turned a sure-fire public relations coup, the first baby born to a Downing Street Dad for hundreds of years, into a damp squib. There were celebrations, certainly, but it also cranked up the debate on European moves to improve employee rights. Would Tony take paternity leave? His missus was certainly all for it: Blair's wife Cherie Booth,

Impressions

"The only infallible rule we know is, that the man who is always talking about being a gentleman never is one."

—RS Surtees (1803–64), *Ask Mamma*

a leading barrister, was attacking government policy in the courts just a week before the birth.. And the newspapers all wanted to know whether midnight feeds might prompt the PM to reform the antiquated working practices at the House of Commons. One of "Blair's Babes"—the influx of young women MPs he was proud to be photographed with after the election—announced she wouldn't stand again because of the silly macho atmosphere and family-unfriendly all-night sittings.

Many of Labour's problems are undoubtedly its own fault for making such big promises. Yet, the maelstrom of change in Britain would sweep anybody off their feet. The fox-hunting crowd, a national icon in their red coats, get death threats these days. The Garrick Club, one of the last bastions of ungentlemanly chauvinism, is allowing women to dine at the men-only long table—though only on Fridays. Dotcom mania is creating new millionaires overnight, at least on paper, while blue-chip reliables like Marks & Spencer suffer.

The Queen officially met Camilla Parker-Bowles for the first time last year, though not at the shindig to celebrate the Queen Mum's 100th birthday, Princess Margaret's 70th, Princess Anne's 50th, and Prince Andrew's 40th. Prince William asked not to be called HRH yet, and revealed a royal talent for cooking, as he voluntarily broke the media black-out on his 18th birthday, just before leaving Eton. The public affection for William may yet convert the half of the population that considers the monarchy irrelevant in a democracy.

Democritization is the buzzword among the once elitist cultural institutions that have scooped up lottery millions. Children and seniors now get into most national museums for free, and the Culture Secretary has proposed a government-supported £1 charge, which may come into effect in September 2001. If it does, it will be a rare example of successful political meddling in the arts. Witness the contrasting fortunes of the Dome and Tate Modern: The latter was a roaring success from the moment it opened (like the new building at Tate Britain, the National Portrait Gallery, National Gallery, Science Museum); the former made a fat mark in red on New Labour's popularity balance sheet. Even a night at the lambasted Royal Opera House can cost less than a movie (if you're lucky), and its Monday lunchtime concerts are free!

The commercial entertainment scene is just as hot, hot, hot. Restaurant pioneers turn into empire-builders, leaving space at the bottom of the heap for yet more new ideas. The club scene is like Ibiza, without quite as much sex, as promoters bring their experience home and open huge venues in London. Or the young British artists—not called that any more, of course—who seem to have moved en masse to pump up the excitement in East London. You know the East is where it's at when arch-art marketer, the entrepreneur Jay Jopling, chooses that neighborhood for his second gallery, White Cube^2. The city's streets have become the center of the shopping universe—tough luck, Paris—particularly for anything to do with another national obsession, home decoration. Channel-hop any night of the week and you'll find wall-to-wall TV makeovers: One comic failure last year turned a mess deck on a new navy frigate into a 1950s American diner—instead of the traditional English pub (wouldn't you know it!) the sailors had specifically asked for.

This DIY obsession is tangled up with soaring property prices. It's said you have to be earning at least £49,000 a year ($78,400) even to buy a shoebox, while rumor has it Madonna paid over £10 million for her townhouse. The government has had to propose cheap loans for "key workers"—nurses and teachers, particularly—to stop a mass migration out of town.

That is just part of a wider, and unfortunate, problem—the polarization of society. Like any big multicultural city, London suffers from homelessness, poverty, drugs, crime, and violence. Even in Southwark—which Tate Modern has turned into one of the most visited boroughs and developers have yuppiefied by turning warehouses into apartments—the deprivation is still evident.

These are a few of the issues that will confront the campaigning Tony Blair.

2 A Look at the Past

Dateline

- **A.D. 43** Londinium settled by Roman invaders.
- **50** London Bridge built across the Thames.
- **61** Boudicca sacks London.
- **190–220** City walls built.
- **350** Saxons invade.
- **410** Romans retreat.
- **457** Londoners take refuge behind city walls.
- **604** First St. Paul's built. Mellitus appointed Bishop of London.
- **886** Alfred the Great takes London from the Danes.
- **1066** William of Normandy (the Conqueror) crowned king.
- **1078** Construction of White Tower begun.
- **1097** William Rufus builds Westminster Hall.
- **1123** St. Bartholomew's Hospital founded.
- **1176–1209** London Bridge built of stone.
- **1192** Henry FitzAilwin elected first mayor of London.
- **1214** King John grants city a charter.
- **1215** Magna Carta signed.
- **1348–49** Black Death sweeps London.
- **1381** Peasants' Revolt.
- **1397** Richard Whittington, a wealthy merchant, elected lord mayor.
- **1401** Water piped in from Tyburn.

continues

EARLY ROMAN, SAXON & DARK AGE LONDON London is very old by any measure. Archaeological excavations have unearthed evidence of settlements from as far back as 2500 B.C. Scholars hotly debate the origin of the city's name, but most believe it comes from the Celtic words *Llyn Din,* meaning "lakeside fortress." It's a fairly easy step from there to the Roman *Londinium.*

The British Isles began to feel the heat of Roman attention in A.D. 43. Julius Caesar visited twice and camped where Heathrow is today. The invaders were great engineers and put in impressive infrastructure throughout the empire. Some of London's modern streets still follow their original roads—Oxford Street, Bayswater Road, and Edgeware Road, for example. The London stone, set into the wall at 111 Cannon St., was probably the starting point for every distance measured in the country. As the Romans settled Britain, they transformed what began as a military base into an important trading center, putting up buildings with tiled roofs and mosaic floors. To see what it looked like then, visit the Museum of London, which has a very effective reconstruction. It also holds fragments of the massive Roman wall, built between A.D. 190 and 220 to protect the city against the "barbarians."

Two hundred years later, though, the Empire began to crumble and the Romans pulled out of Britain. The vacuum created by the sudden loss of a national governing force led to inevitable turmoil. The local tribes had to fend for themselves against Anglo-Saxon invasions.

From the 7th to the early 9th centuries, the tribal kingdoms of Kent, Mercia, Northumbria, and the West Saxons fought each other for control of Britain. Meanwhile, the Viking hordes descended, occupying the Saxon suburb that had grown up around Charing Cross, outside the walls (871–872). The Saxon king Alfred the Great fought back, then in 886 made peace with the Danes. Londoners abandoned the settlement and moved back inside the Roman walls. The population had grown by then to around 12,000 and the town was large enough to be divided into 20 wards. Few traces of this early period remain.

The rapacious Vikings began raiding again in the late 10th century. London resisted at first, but finally had to accept Sweni as king in 1013, and later his son Canute. After the latter's death, Edward, the son of Ethelred the Unready, came to the throne. It was he who moved the court out of the city, to a new purpose-built palace on the site of today's Westminster Hall. He also spent a tenth of his income rebuilding the nearby abbey of St. Peter. Not for nothing, was the king known as Edward the Confessor. When his beloved wife Eleanor of Castile died in Nottinghamshire in 1290, her funeral cortege traveled slowly back to London and Edward had a cross erected at every overnight stop. Only one survives in London—at Charing Cross, the last stop on the sad journey. You can visit his tomb in Westminster Abbey.

Edward's death on January 6, 1066, sparked a raging battle for the throne between the Saxons and the Normans—his mother's people. The city's merchants and barons sold their support to the Saxon Harold for the promise of certain rights and privileges. But he fell at the Battle of Hastings and William the Conqueror marched on London, burned Southwark, and forced a surrender.

MEDIEVAL LONDON William had himself crowned in Westminster. He was smart enough to understand the power the bigwigs wielded, and he fulfilled Harold's promises—though that didn't stop them fighting for more independence. William granted favored Norman barons tracts of land on which they built huge, fortified, stone houses, known as *burhs.* None survive, but street names such as Bucklersbury and Lothbury tell us where they once stood.

Throughout the 11th century, the old Saxon London of wood and thatch slowly transformed into Norman stone. William began the massive, impregnable White Tower (of the Tower of

- **1455** Wars of the Roses begin.
- **1461** Edward of York crowned king.
- **1483** Richard, Duke of Gloucester, imprisons (and possibly murders) Crown Prince Edward V and his brother; crowns himself Richard III.
- **1485** Henry Tudor defeats Richard at Bosworth. Henry VII launches Tudor dynasty.
- **1509** Henry VIII succeeds to the throne. Marries first of six wives.
- **1513** Henry VIII builds Navy and opens dockyards at Deptford and Woolwich.
- **1536–40** Dissolution of the monasteries. Church of England established, with king at head.
- **1553** Mary Tudor made queen. Lady Jane Grey, the "Nine Days' Queen," is executed.
- **1558** Elizabeth I (1558–1603) succeeds to throne.
- **1588** Spanish armada defeated.
- **1599** Globe Theatre built.
- **1600** London expands south of the Thames.
- **1605** Guy Fawkes and his Gunpowder Plot to blow up King James I and Parliament are foiled.
- **1631** Inigo Jones builds Covent Garden.
- **1637** Hyde Park opens to the public.
- **1642–58** Oliver Cromwell leads Parliamentary forces during Civil War and later Protectorate.
- **1649** King Charles I beheaded before the Banqueting House in Whitehall.
- **1660** Monarchy restored under Charles II.
- **1665** Great Plague strikes 110,000 Londoners.
- **1666** Great Fire destroys 80% of the medieval city.

continues

- **1675–1710** Wren rebuilds 51 churches, including St. Paul's.
- **1688** Bloodless Revolution: James II banished; William and Mary invited to throne.
- **1694** Bank of England established.
- **1725** Mayfair developed.
- **1739–53** Mansion House built.
- **1759** British Museum founded.
- **1780** In Gordon Riots, mobs protest against Papists.
- **1801** First census. Population: 959,000.
- **1802** West Indian Dock opens.
- **1826** University College established.
- **1829** Metro Police established.
- **1832** First Reform Bill enfranchises some property owners.
- **1837** Victoria, 18, succeeds her uncle, William IV.
- **1840s** Influx of Irish immigrants, fleeing famine and political repression.
- **1847** British Museum opens.
- **1851** Hyde Park hosts the Great Exhibition, which finances development of South Kensington.
- **1858** The Great Stink. Royal Opera House opens.
- **1861** Prince Albert dies, sending Victoria into deep mourning and 10 years out of the public eye.
- **1863** The first Underground connects Paddington to the City.
- **1877** First Wimbledon Tennis Championship.
- **1882** Law Courts built in the Strand.
- **1888** London County Council established.
- **1889** Great Dock Strike.
- **1894** Tower Bridge opens.
- **1900** Coca-Cola arrives in Britain.
- **1901** Queen Victoria dies. Edward VII ascends throne.

continues

London) in 1078, not only as a fortification against invaders, but also to intimidate his new London subjects.

But the City fathers went on wielding influence in later battles for the throne. King Stephen (1135–54) only held onto his because Londoners attacked Matilda, daughter of Henry I, and prevented her coronation at Westminster. Later, they kept the rebel William Longchamp in the Tower, and King John (1199–1216) in power. That earned them formal right, later enshrined in the Magna Carta and still in place today, to elect their own leader, the Lord Mayor of London. Which is why the monarch has to ask permission to enter the City.

Wars dominated the whole of the 12th, 13th, and 14th centuries: abroad, in the Crusades and the Hundred Years' War with France; at home, with the Wars of the Roses, between the House of Lancaster and the House of York for the English throne. Despite all this strife, London continued to grow and thrive, through trade largely, even though London Bridge was the only way across the Thames. The original wooden bridge was replaced several times, then work started on a stone version in 1176: It was to take 33 years to complete and cost 200 lives. It was 940 feet long, with 20 arches, and had a chapel on top of it, dedicated to Thomas à Becket. Timbered houses lined the 12-foot-wide cobbled roadway. It was across the new London Bridge that the medieval kings of England set out to Crécy, Potiers, and Agincourt. And they impaled the heads of traitors on the gate at the southern end (one foreign visitor in the 16th century counted 30 on display).

The River Thames was the city's main highway. It cost only two pence to travel from London to Westminster in 1372. Wharves lined the banks, each one assigned a particular type of cargo. There were a few roads wide enough for 16 knights to ride abreast (dubbed royal roads), but most were narrow, unpaved, and badly maintained. In the late 14th century, it took 4½ days to ride from London to York, traveling about 44 miles a day. Wagons took even longer.

London's wealth grew out of the wool trade, in particular: Sheep outnumbered people 300 to 1. A handful of merchants controlled the market, which was exporting a million yards of cloth to Europe by the 1480s. Other industries flourished, too. In 1422, the clerk of the Brewers Company recorded 111 city trades—drapers, soapmakers, cordwainers, goldsmiths, haberdashers, vintners, and many more. The guilds set standards, trademarks, and prices, and arranged pensions for their members. As prosperity grew, they built impressive halls. Many survive today, though often in 19th-century incarnations: Drapers' Hall, Fishmongers' Hall, and Goldsmiths' Hall, for instance. You can see the banners of the principal companies flying in the Guildhall.

Daily life was hard for most. The Great Plague killed 30% to 40% of the population between 1348 and 1349. At the height of the epidemic, one London cemetery buried 200 dead each day. Drink and religion were the common escape from the grind and the terrors. In 1309, there were 1,334 taverns, each brewing its own individual ale. London had 106 churches in 1371 and several monasteries. Holy Days, royal celebrations, and fairs, like the famous St. Bartholomew fair, provided blessed relief. When Henry VI visited in 1432, young women representing Mercy, Grace, and Pity dispensed the wine of joy and pleasure at the Great Conduit water pump in Cheapside. The conduits flowed with wine at every coronation, and celebrations lasted for days.

The Court had its own pleasures. Jousting tournaments took place in Smithfield and Cheapside and the king went hunting for deer, boar, and hare in what are now our favorite London parks. Among the wealthy classes, chess was so popular that *The Rules of Chess* was the second book Caxton chose to print.

Westminster was the center of government, linked to London by Whitehall and the Strand (but primarily via the Thames). From the early 14th century on, the king summoned his nobles to council there. The courts and the treasury were in Westminster Hall, where the exchequer kept the accounts with tally sticks. Notches marked out the money owed along the stick, which was then split in half, one part kept by the exchequer and the other by the debtor. It was the burning of these old sticks in 1854 that destroyed the original buildings at Westminster.

By the early 14th century, the population had reached 50,000 and living conditions were abysmal. Pigs, chickens, packhorses, and dogs roamed the city and the streets were open sewers. Under the Plantagenets, there's a record of one being piled so high with garbage it was nearly impossible to get down. Many people

- **1907** Central Criminal Court (the Old Bailey) constructed.
- **1910** King Edward VII dies and is succeeded by George V.
- **1914–18** World War I. London bombed from planes and airships.
- **1922** BBC begins broadcasting.
- **1936** King George V dies. Prince of Wales succeeds to throne as Edward VIII, but abdicates to marry Wallis Simpson.
- **1937** Edward's younger brother crowned King George VI.
- **1939–45** World War II. Air raids and rocket attacks destroy much of the city: 30,000 killed; 50,000 injured.
- **1947–48** New influx of Commonwealth immigrants.
- **1948** London hosts Summer Olympics.
- **1951** Royal Festival Hall opens.
- **1952** King George VI dies.
- **1953** Queen Elizabeth II crowned in first nationally televised coronation ceremony.
- **1955** Heathrow Airport opens.
- **1956** Clean Air Act passed to cut through famous pea-soup smog.
- **1960s** Swinging London—Mary Quant, the Beatles, et al. The controversial Centre Point Tower built. England beats Germany in the Football World Cup in 1966, and dines out on it ever after.
- **1965** Churchill (b. 1874) dies. Greater London Council formed.
- **1973** Britain joins the European Common Market, despite opposition from the old foe France.
- **1974** Covent Garden Market moves out to Nine Elms.

continues

- 1976 Royal National Theatre opens.
- 1979 Margaret Thatcher becomes Britain's first woman prime minister, heading a Conservative government.
- 1981 Charles, Prince of Wales, marries Lady Diana Spencer in St. Paul's Cathedral. Docklands Development Corporation established.
- 1982 The Thames Flood Barrier is completed downstream at Woolwich. Barbican Arts Centre opens.
- 1986 Margaret Thatcher abolishes the Greater London Council after battling for years with its bolshy left-wing leader, Ken Livingstone.
- 1990 Tories oust Margaret Thatcher and vote for John Major to replace her. Paparazzi shots of a possibly-tearful Maggie leaving Downing Street shoot round the world.
- 1992 Royal family rocked by scandals, and Windsor Castle fire. Queen agrees to pay income tax. And open Buckingham Palace to the public.
- 1994 Channel Tunnel officially opens.
- 1996 IRA bombs Docklands in first attack for 17 months. Two die. Prince Andrew and Sarah Ferguson's divorce becomes final. Charles and Diana divorce, too.
- 1997 Tony Blair wins election for New Labour. Princess Diana killed in Paris car crash; nation mourns with huge outpouring of grief.
- 1999 Scotland and Wales win partial self-government. Monica Lewinsky chooses Harrods to launch her book, *Monica's Story,* written by Diana biographer Andrew Morton. Prince Edward and Sophie Rhys-Jones marry at

continues

scraped a living as rakers and gong farmers—digging through the garbage and excrement. There was no clean water supply: It came straight out of the Thames at the Great Conduit in Cheapside. And fires were frequent.

TUDOR & ELIZABETHAN LONDON The modern history of London begins with the Tudors, who ascended the throne at the end of the 15th century. The first was Henry VII, who laid the solid administrative foundations on which his successors built a great nation and a strong monarchy.

Between 1500 and 1600, the population of London rocketed from 50,000 to 200,000. The city got wealthier and wealthier, due largely to the English Company of Merchant Adventurers. They traded wool to the Dutch in Antwerp and shipped back to England all kinds of things, from tennis balls, licorice, and Bruges silks, to warming pans, thimbles, and dye for cloth. These 800 or so wholesale traders were the richest men in England. It was they who, in 1571, founded the first financial institution in the city, the Royal Exchange, which went on operating until 1939.

Under the Tudors, England grew in economic and political power. Henry VIII was a powerful Renaissance prince who competed fiercely with archrival Francis I of France. It was he who laid down the foundations of the British Army and the Navy—incorporating the Fraternity of Artillery in 1537, establishing dockyards at Deptford and Woolwich, and commissioning ships like the *Great Harry.*

But Henry's most significant legacy was separating the English church from Rome in furious response to the pope's refusal to grant him a divorce. It was a huge step, and a very lucrative one, since the king went on to dissolve the monasteries and confiscate church wealth and lands, including Cardinal Wolsey's Whitehall Palace (he'd already taken over Hampton Court, Wolsey's country place, in 1529). Frustrated in his desire for a male heir, Henry married six times, executing two of his wives and divorcing another two. One died of her own accord and one outlived him. Anne Boleyn passed through Traitor's Gate at the Tower in 1536 on the way to her beheading. The executioner from Calais used a sword instead of an ax, which is said to have cut so cleanly and swiftly that that her lips were still moving in prayer as her head hit the ground. Catherine Howard was beheaded too, but she tested the block first and died proclaiming her love for Culpepper, who'd already got the chop for dallying with her.

Patronage of the arts and architecture was an important way to display power, and Henry VIII invited great painters like Holbein to his court. He built Nonsuch Palace (long gone), and embellished St. James's and Whitehall. Henry's greed was prodigious and his reputation for extravagance well earned. The kitchen at Hampton Court Palace, which you can visit, was 100 feet long and 38 feet wide, and had ceilings 40 feet high. He spent £300,000 a year on food and £50,000 on drink. At each of the two main meals of the day, the Great Master of the Household was permitted 10 gallons (80 pints) of ale and 6 quarts (12 pints) of wine. The Lord Chamberlain, however, was only entitled to 4 gallons of ale and 1½ quarts of wine. And female members of the court received 3 gallons of ale daily and a pitcher of wine, as well as what they could drink at the table. Little wonder people died of apoplexy (as that other over-eater, Queen Anne, did too). What is surprising is that, despite his ever-expanding waistline, the king had boundless energy for manly pursuits: He enclosed Hyde, St. James's, and Green Parks for his own hunting and other pleasures.

Windsor. New Labour makes hereditary lords pitch for parliamentary privileges, and ousts 600 of them.

- **2000** First Universal Day of new millennium starts at Greenwich. Dome's fortunes go downhill from there. Ken Livingstone elected as first London mayor. First official meeting between the Queen and Camilla Parker-Bowles. Prince William leaves Eton.
- **2001** Mayor Ken submits first budget for London. Tony Blair weighs up the most advantageous date for National Election, as his term runs out in May 2002.

Henry VIII may have plundered Catholic coffers and estates, but it was his fanatical protestant son, Edward VI (1547–53), who wreaked the greatest physical destruction on London's parish churches. He presided over the wholesale stripping of sculptures and decoration: One church lost 100 tombs and monuments. The Lord Protector Somerset demolished the cloister of St. Paul's in 1549 and used the materials to build Somerset House in the Strand. In 1550, Edward dissolved the bishopric of Westminster. The church returned to the Dean, but part of its revenues were transferred to St. Paul's; hence the English saying, "robbing Peter to pay Paul," still used today. Henry VIII's elder daughter Mary reestablished Catholicism in 1553. She was as hard-line as her brother had been, though of the totally opposing view, and many public executions took place at Smithfield.

Her sister Elizabeth ascended the throne in 1558, ushering in not only Protestantism again, but a period of unprecedented colonial expansion and economic growth. A popular queen and master politician, she held England at peace for 30 years while she advanced the nation's interests against those of Catholic France and Spain. In 1588, her Navy defeated a large Spanish armada that had set out to invade. Elizabeth gave thanks for this victory at St. Paul's.

Literature and the arts also flourished. Edmund Spenser dedicated his epic poem, *The Faerie Queene,* to Elizabeth. And the statesman and philosopher Francis Bacon; the soldier, explorer, and poet Sir Walter Raleigh; and others of equal versatility wrote pivotal books on history, science, and philosophy. At the same time, the English theater came into its own. James Burbage built the first playhouse, called simply "The Theatre," in Shoreditch in 1576, then the Rose on Bankside in 1587, the Swan in 1595, and the Hope in 1614. Play-going became a central part of London life, with as many as 40 productions a year presented at the Rose, including works by Christopher Marlowe,

John Webster, Ben Jonson, Thomas Middleton, and William Shakespeare, of course, who joined Burbage's company in 1599. Today, Bankside is experiencing a similar cultural flowering, with the rebuilding of the Globe Theatre and new Tate Modern.

STUART LONDON Elizabeth's death destroyed the longstanding political stability as an increasingly assertive, and largely Puritan, Parliament sought to build its power and limit that of the monarch. Known as the Virgin Queen, she had no direct successor and the throne passed to James VI of Scotland, who then became James I of England. James believed absolutely in the divine right of absolute monarchy, so couldn't help but fight with Parliament. He persecuted the Puritans, despite an avowed intention to begin a new era of religious tolerance after Elizabeth's harrying of the Catholics. And, though it was Catholic-led, he won no friends during the Gunpowder Plot when Guy Fawkes tried to blow him up at the state opening of Parliament.

If the conflict had simmered under James I, it exploded under his son Charles I, who was forced to dissolve several parliaments. In response, Parliament put the king's ministers on trial. It charged Thomas Wentworth, Earl of Strafford, with 28 crimes and he fought for 18 days in Westminster Hall to defend himself. Charles fled to York. In 1642, he raised his standard at Nottingham and London prepared for a Royalist attack. Parliament called out trained bands of men. Armed boats patrolled the Thames. And 100,000 men were pressed into digging 18 miles of trenches to link up the 24 bastions. The attack never came. The Royalist and Parliamentary troops waged their battles all over the country instead—at Edgehill, Oxford, Marston Moor, Naseby, and Preston.

Finally defeated, Charles I stood trial in Westminster Hall in 1649 and was condemned to death. He took his last walk through St. James's Park on January 30, flanked by guards with a troop of soldiers in front and behind, colors flying and drums pounding. The procession crossed a gallery at what is now Horse Guards Parade and entered the Banqueting House of Whitehall Palace. Four hours later, the king stepped out of the window onto the wooden scaffold. After saying his prayers, he pulled off his doublet, laid down his head, and the executioner wielded his ax. His last words were: "To your power I must submit, but your authority I deny." Today, a statue of a horseman stands looking down to the spot where he died. At the other end of Whitehall, outside Westminster Hall, there's a statue of Oliver Cromwell, the Puritan general who ruled England, as Lord Protector, after Charles's execution from 1649 to 1658.

Charles I had been a great patron of the arts and invited Van Dyck and Rubens to his court. In 1621, the latter painted the ceilings of the Banqueting House in Whitehall for £3,000 and a gold chain. Under Cromwell, the arts died. He closed the theaters and the city fell under a pall of fear and Puritan gloom. Diarist John Evelyn described Cromwell's funeral in 1658 as the "joyfullest . . . that ever I saw." The crowds impaled his head and those of his generals Ireton and Bradshaw and stuck them up on the roof of Westminster Hall. It's said Cromwell's remained there for 25 years until the wind blew it down and a sentry stole it.

The Restoration brought the Merry Monarch, Charles II, to the throne and brought the city back to life. The theaters reopened and the king kept a lavish court at Whitehall Palace. Political and social climbers flocked there to curry favor, either directly or with one of the many royal mistresses. Courtiers chatted with Charles while his wig was being combed and his cravat tied. One might win himself a frigate, another a company or a favorable judgment.

Two major catastrophes interrupted the merrymaking—another Great Plague (1665) and the Great Fire of London (1666). The first victim of black death died on April 12, 1665; by December, 110,000 had died. The king and his court left for Hampton Court, and most of the nobility dismissed their servants and fled. The unemployed roamed the city looting and pillaging. Men worked day and night digging mass graves, but couldn't keep up with the corpses, which piled up in mounds. The stench of death was horrific. When someone succumbed to the swellings in the groin and armpit (buboes), officials locked up their whole household for 40 days, and marked a red cross on the door. This merely multiplied the death rate. The innocent-sounding nursery rhyme "ring a ring o' roses" refers to the first marks to appear on the victim's skin.

Eventually, the rat-born plague ran its course and, in February 1666, the king deemed it safe enough to return to London. He'd been back only a few months when the Great Fire broke out, in the early morning of September 2, 1666, at the bakery of Robert Farriner in Pudding Lane (a monument marks the spot today). It spread like lightning through the city, fanned by strong easterly winds. Samuel Pepys describes the flames leaping 300 feet into the air, warehouses blazing, and people jamming the river and roads in a vain attempt to flee. The lord mayor, Sir Thomas Bludworth, was woken with the news but went back to bed with a dismissive, "a woman might piss it out." By mid-morning, when the fire had already consumed 300 houses, Pepys describes him running hither and thither wailing, "Lord, what can I do? I am spent. People will not obey me. I have been pulling down houses but the fire overtakes us faster than we can do it."

The Duke of York (later James II) was put in charge of fire-fighting, and the king himself helped too. The flames raged for 4 days, over 400 acres within the city walls and 60 more outside. It wiped out medieval London, destroying 87 churches, 44 livery halls, and 13,000 half-timbered houses. Ten thousand people were left homeless. From then on, it was decreed that all buildings must be constructed of stone and brick.

Although Charles II realized this was an opportunity to create an elegantly planned city, and even invited architects—Sir Christopher Wren among them—to submit plans, London needed rebuilding immediately. The medieval layout had to stay: To this day, London's streets follow the same routes as in the Middle Ages, hence the traffic jams. The streets were widened, though, and pavements laid for the first time. The king appointed six commissioners to mastermind the city's reconstruction. Wren was one of them: He rebuilt 51 churches (23 survive today, along with the towers of 6 others) and designed the 202-foot monument commemorating the fire. St. Paul's was his greatest achievement.

In 1688, England went through a "Bloodless Revolution." James II had succeeded his brother Charles and, after converting himself, tried to bring the whole nation back to Catholicism. It was too bitter a pill for the people to swallow. So they asked his Protestant daughter Mary and her husband, the Dutch Prince William of Orange, to take the throne. The couple did so, first signing a new bill of rights, fixing limits to a sovereign's power. England had taken its first step on the path to constitutional monarchy.

London went through a property boom between 1660 and 1690, especially in Piccadilly, the Strand, and Soho. In 1656, Covent Garden Market opened as a temporary arrangement in the Earl (later the Duke) of Bedford's garden. In their headlong flight from fire and plague, many of the aristocracy had suddenly woken up to the advantages of living outside London, in the villages north and west of the city—Bloomsbury, Kensington, Hackney, Islington, and Hampstead. As they developed their new suburban estates, London began to take on its current form. They built houses for rent and laid out formal squares, like Bloomsbury (1666) and St. James (1665)—the earliest dating from the late 17th and early 18th centuries.

18TH-CENTURY LONDON During the 18th century, London's population continued to multiply explosively, from 490,000 in 1700 to 950,000 in 1800. The city transformed in the process, as Mayfair and the West End began to develop. Private and corporate landowners laid out squares as the focal points of their estates. Each one had associations with a particular political faction: Hanover Square was the hub of the Whig aristocracy and the Earl of Scarborough; Cavendish Square was linked to the Tories under the Earl of Oxford; and lawyers ruled over Lincoln's Inn, New Square, and Bedford Square. Walk down Bedford Row even today, and you'll find shingles marking the chambers of many a lawyer-peer.

Wealth flowed back from overseas colonies in America and from those established in the 17th century by the East India Company, the Royal Africa Company, and the Hudson's Bay Company. The Port of London boomed, trade tripling between 1720 and 1780. Eighteen hundred vessels jammed into the Upper Pool of the Thames in a space designed for 500. Bigger ships lay downriver at Woolwich, offloading their cargoes onto 3,500 lighters, or barges. Because of the congestion, it sometimes took three or four weeks to unload one vessel. As the century progressed, though, the pivotal role of the Thames as a main trade and general highway began to decline. Other forms of transport, from the stage and hackney coach to the sedan chair, took over and more and more bridges began to span the river, like the one built at Westminster in 1749.

Other social developments helped change the face of the city, too. Greater wealth brought philanthropy and a growing concern for the poor. This led to the establishment of major public institutions like the Foundling Hospital (1742), Chelsea Hospital (1692), and Greenwich Hospital (1705); the British Museum (1755); and the Royal Academy of Arts (1768), all of which survive to this day (except the Foundling Hospital). The authorities set up a rudimentary fire department. And, by 1710, there were already 3,000 pupils at various charity schools, including such august institutions as St. Paul's, Westminster, and Christ's Hospital, which still survive today.

The major social institution, other than the church, was the coffeehouse, where literary and powerful men gathered to debate and gossip about politics and society. Addison, Steele, and Swift all met at Burtons in Russell Street; Samuel Johnson was a regular at the Turks Head at no. 142 the Strand; East India Company merchants thronged the Jerusalem Coffeehouse in Cornhill; and the first ever stock exchange started informally at Jonathan's Coffeehouse in 1722. In 1702, London got its first newspaper, the *Daily Courant,* which was reaching 800 readers by 1704. Later in the century the *Guardian, Spectator,* and *Rambler* all published regular editions. Grub Street hacks would anonymously fire off any kind of libel or satire for a fee—a tradition some might say the tabloids uphold to this day.

One word sums up the politics of the age—corruption. Hogarth captured the scene most acidly in his series titled *The Election.* Votes were bought and sold. Politicians stole from the public purse. For instance, Walpole was reckoned to have remodeled his house from skimming while he was prime minister. Riots were common; during the worst, the Gordon Riots in 1780, the mob torched several prisons and attacked the Bank of England and Downing Street.

Life was grim in the 18th century for the poverty stricken. Silk weavers in Spitalfields, the hub of that trade, hired out looms, employing female and child labor. Workhouses and prison workshops were common, too. To see the seamier side of London life, just take a look at Hogarth's *Gin Lane* or *The Rake's Progress.*

Those who could afford it took their leisure at Vauxhall Gardens (1660) or at Ranelagh Pleasure Gardens (1742). Their favorite fun was horse racing, archery, cricket, bowling, and skittles, as well as less salubrious pastimes like bullbaiting and prizefighting. Freak shows were very popular, too, at Don Saltero's Coffee House in Chelsea. And people flocked to Mrs. Salmon's waxworks in Fleet.

Though the prudish Victorians later hushed it up, London's sex industry has never been bigger than it was behind the elegant Georgian facades. Indeed, it funded much of the building. One in eight women (25,000) in the city was a prostitute in 1796, each one making more in a night than the average male worker earned in a fortnight. It was no big deal for celebs and wealthy Londoners to go to brothels, half-heartedly disguised as Turkish baths. As well as the wealthy courtesans of Marylebone, streetwalkers did brisk trade in Covent Garden, adding to the louche atmosphere of this theatrical neighborhood.

David Garrick and Richard Brinsley Sheridan were the best-known and very successful actor-managers, both at Drury Lane. Musicians and composers were feted at the courts of the Hanoverian kings (Georges I, II, and III): Johann Christian Bach, Franz Joseph Haydn, and Mozart all performed there. Handel is the composer most closely identified with the London of this period: It was during the reign of George III that the annual performance of that composer's *Messiah* began. Beyond court and the church, Thomas Britton fired a new musical tradition in the city, arranging weekly concerts from 1678 to 1714 in a loft above his Clerkenwell coal house.

Under the Georges, a great many artists rose to prominence, among them Sir Joshua Reynolds (who became head of the Royal Academy of Arts, founded by George III in 1768), Thomas Gainsborough, William Turner, and William Hogarth. Literature burgeoned too: The celebrity cast list includes the great lexicographer and wit Samuel Johnson, his biographer James Boswell, poet Alexander Pope, and the novelists Samuel Richardson and Henry Fielding. Edward Gibbon's multivolume *History of the Decline and Fall of the Roman Empire,* one of the great achievements of English literature, caused George III to remark, "Always scribble, scribble, scribble. Eh, Mr. Gibbon?"

19TH-CENTURY LONDON In the 19th century, London became the wonder of the world—a wonder based on imperial wealth and power. In 1811, at the age of 58, the Prince of Wales became regent for his father, mad George III. He set up an alternate court at Carlton House and at his extravagant palace in Brighton. At both, the prince entertained his mistresses openly and lavishly, including the famous Mrs. Fitzherbert (whom he'd married illegally). He treated his wife Caroline abominably, even banning her from his coronation, which took place in 1820 at the massive cost of £238,238. (As the French say, *Plus ça change, plus c'est la même chose,* or the more things change, the more they stay the same.) Though widely condemned for his extravagance and dissolute behavior, George IV did contribute to the city's architectural growth and harmony. He worked with architect John Nash to introduce urban planning to the city. Together they laid out Regents Street, a grand highway leading from Carlton House to Piccadilly.

Plump as a partridge, Victoria ascended the throne in 1837. As the century progressed, the city's transformation into a modern industrial society proceeded apace, shaped by the growing power of the bourgeoisie and the queen's strict moral stance. The raciness of the preceding three centuries seemed to disappear, but it actually just went underground.

Extremes of wealth and poverty marked life in Victorian London. Children worked long hours in factories and sweatshops, or as chimney sweeps. Immigrants—Irish and European—poured into the foul, overcrowded slums. Thirty percent of the population lived below the poverty line, in the appalling conditions graphically described in many of Charles Dickens' novels. The consumption of gin was huge in the 1820s. In an effort to reduce it, the government abolished tax on beer, and scores of ale houses opened as a result—probably why there are so many pubs in London today. The Thames was the city's main sewer, as well as the source of its drinking water, to which the Great Stink drew sensational attention in the hot summer of 1858.

Parliament passed the first Reform Bill in 1832 and social campaigners pressed for better conditions: Lord Shaftesbury strove for improvements in labor and education, Elizabeth Fry in prisons, and Florence Nightingale in hospitals. In 1870, the Education Act made elementary education compulsory.

The Victorians revolutionized public transport, too. In 1829, Shillibeer launched his horse-drawn omnibus. Underground trains started running from Paddington to Farringdon in 1863, carrying 12,000 passengers that year. And the first electric Tube ran on the Northern Line in 1890. Vast railway networks spread out across the country, all terminating at impressive Central London stations—Victoria, Charing Cross, St. Pancras, and Euston—several of which are virtually unchanged today.

In 1851, Prince Albert put his weight behind a celebratory Great Exhibition, housed in an astonishing iron-and-glass construction, Crystal Palace, built in Hyde Park. More than 6 million people flocked to see this showcase of the industrial and technological wonders of the age. Albert was a great promoter of new advances, like the revolutionary electric lighting that began to replace traditional gas lamps in London houses in 1880.

The middle class enjoyed a fantastic nightlife. By 1850, London had more than 50 stages, producing everything from popular blood-and-thunder melodramas to pageants at Christmas and Easter. The repertoire began to get more upmarket toward the end of the century, with works by Oscar Wilde, Arthur Wing Pinero, James Barrie, and George Bernard Shaw. Actor-manager Henry Irving and actress Ellen Terry lit up the Lyceum in the Strand. But music halls were even more popular. By 1870, the city had more than 400. People flocked to the Hackney Empire and the London Coliseum to hear Marie Lloyd, Dan Leno, and other stars belt out Cockney tunes and ribald variety shows.

Eating out became an upper-middle-class pastime, too. Once an exclusively male domain, mores slowly relaxed to let women in on the fun. They were already allowed to dine in a separate room at Simpsons, which opened in 1848. New hotel restaurants like the Savoy (1889), the Ritz (1906), and the Cafe Royal (1870) imposed no such segregation. From the 1890s to the 1920s, the last of these was a fashionable mecca for the famous artists and writers of the day, like Augustus John, Aubrey Beardsley, Oscar Wilde, Max Beerbohm, and James McNeill Whistler. Edward VIII and George VI also dined at the Cafe Royal, and later patrons included Sir Compton McKenzie, T. S. Eliot, and

J. B. Priestley. The opening of the first Joe Lyons in 1894 made eating out something the masses could enjoy, too. These friendly corner houses—there were 98 in London by 1910—served anything from a snack to a five-course meal.

Spectator sports took off in a big way in the 19th century—football, rugby, and especially cricket. The All England Croquet Club put in tennis courts in 1874 to revive its sinking fortunes. The ploy was so successful that the club held its first Wimbledon Championship in 1877. The manufacture of the safety bicycle in 1885 launched a craze, which gave women a taste of liberation: The "New Woman" of the 1890s took to the road on two wheels without a chaperone. Shopping, too, was becoming a national pastime. Department stores opened up to satisfy the urge to splurge—Whiteleys (1863, now converted into one of London's best shopping malls), Harrods (1860s), Liberty (1875), and Selfridges (1909), all famous names that still survive to this day.

Victoria celebrated her golden jubilee in this energetic capital, before ushering in the 20th century.

THE EARLY 20TH CENTURY The early 1900s, during the reign of Edward VII (1901–10), were filled with confidence. Britain was at the height of its power and Londoners looked forward to a radiant future. Looking back, though, some historians pinpoint this as the start of the economic decline, arguing that Britain was already losing markets and trade to the United States.

At home, the trade union movement gained recruits and women campaigned vigorously for the vote. They chained themselves to railings and protested at the Houses of Parliament. In November 1911, 223 women were arrested after going on a window-smashing spree, enraged by the government's failure to introduce a suffrage bill. The courts sent 1,000 suffragettes to Holloway Prison between 1905 and 1914, and it took World War I, with its social ramifications, to help women gain the franchise.

Rivalry with Germany had been festering for years, and war eventually broke out in 1914. British men marched off to do their duty, expecting certain and rapid victory. Instead, the war bogged down in the trenches and the slaughter wiped out a whole generation. Back home, 900 bombs fell on London, killing 670 people and injuring almost 2,000. The Great War shattered the liberal middle class's illusion that peace, prosperity, and social progress would continue indefinitely in a strong and beneficent British Empire.

The peace imposed on the Germans at Versailles led inexorably to economic dislocation, and ultimately to both the Crash of 1929 and the Great Depression of the 1930s. An unprecedented constitutional crisis further threatened Britain's stability in 1936, when the new and hugely popular king, Edward VIII, abdicated after refusing to renounce his love for the American divorcee, Wallis Simpson. His brother succeeded him as George VI.

Meanwhile, fascism was rising in Germany and threatening the peace with its expansionist ambitions. British and French attempts at appeasement failed. Hitler marched into Poland. And, in 1939, World War II began. The Blitz of 1940–41 and again in 1944–45 killed over 20,000 people in London and destroyed vast areas of the city. Bombs even hit the House of Commons. But Londoners' spirit proved indomitable. They dug trenches in public parks to resist the expected invasion. Night after night, they ran for their shelters as waves of German planes flew over with their deadly cargo. One hundred and fifty thousand slept in the Underground, others stayed home, and the defiant continued partying. The royal family remained in London despite the dangers.

Recordings of Winston Churchill's speeches still evoke pride, even among people who weren't born at the time. But for many who were there, the

What'd Ya Say?

Many Americans are shocked to discover that there's such a thing as British English. Believe it or not, the gulf between the two languages is wide enough to cause, if not a total communications breakdown, then at least some embarrassing and entertaining exchanges. The English use words and phrases you may think you understand, but their meaning is often quite different from the U.S. equivalent.

Troublesome Slang When the British call someone "mean," they mean "stingy." And "homely," isn't "ugly" or "plain," but "cozy and comfortable." Other slang can get you into much worse trouble. In England "pissed" isn't "angry," it's "drunk;" a "rubber" refers to an "eraser," not what you think it refers to; while "fag" means a "cigarette" as well as being a homophobe's term of abuse. "Fanny" in English is definitely not what you think it means. *Fanny Hill* might give you a clue—let's leave it at that.

Problematic Pronunciation The letter Z is pronounced "zed." Zero can be "zero," but is more often "nought," or interchanged with the letter "O," especially when people are telling you their phone number. French words can cause hiccups (or "hiccoughs," sometimes), too. The Brits put the emphasis on the first half of "*croi*-ssant" and "*ba*-llet," which is actually closer to the original.

Local Customs If you don't line up in London, you're a pariah. Except that the Brits "queue" instead.

Public Transport Whereas a "subway" is an underground pedestrian walkway, the actual subway system is "the Underground" or "the Tube."

Automobiles This is a tough topic. Very little is the same, except for the word "car": A truck is called a "lorry;" a station wagon is an "estate

memories are bittersweet: Britain won the war but lost the peace. Unlike Germany and Japan, which received American aid under the Marshall Plan, Britain was impoverished, and her industrial plants antiquated. Dissolution of the empire and a plummeting of national morale followed swiftly.

POSTWAR & CONTEMPORARY LONDON Postwar London was a glum place. Rationing continued until 1953. Only the coronation of Queen Elizabeth II in June 1953, watched by 20 million on their TV screens, seemed to lift the city's spirits. Heathrow formally opened in 1955, the same year Mary Quant launched her boutique on the King's Road. The coffee bar, rock 'n' roll, and antinuclear protests all arrived in the 1950s, setting the stage for the Swinging London of the following decade. It was then that young people all over the world went bananas over the Beatles, the Kinks, the Rolling Stones, The Who, Eric Clapton's Yardbirds, and the Animals. Sixties London was suddenly the fashion and arts capital of the world.

The swinging slacked off a bit in the 1970s when the Beatles disbanded. But the trendy movement continued as Terence Conran launched Habitat, Anita Roddick created the Body Shop, and the Saatchi & Saatchi advertising empire were born. In 1976, London finally got its Royal National Theatre, first conceived of in 1848. The Barbican Arts Centre opened in 1982.

Other less-heartwarming developments also took place during the postwar years. The number of West Indians heading for Britain each year rose from car." Even the bits are different: The hood is the "bonnet," the windshield the "windscreen," and the trunk is the "boot." Drivers "hoot" the horn and "indicate" before they turn. Oh, and gas is "petrol."

Groceries In a supermarket, canned goods become "tins," potato chips "crisps," rutabagas "swedes," eggplants "aubergines," green squash "courgettes," while endive is "chicory" (and, conversely, chicory is "endive"). Both cookies and crackers become "biscuits," unless they've got a specific name—digestives or crackers, for instance. A Popsicle is called an "iced lolly," candy is "sweets," and a soda is a "fizzy drink." If you want diapers, ask for "nappies."

Clothes Shopping This is a real red-face territory. Repeat after me: Undershirts are called "vests" and undershorts are "pants" to the English. Long pants are "trousers," their cuffs are called "turnups," and, unless you're looking for lacy things that hold up ladies' stockings, ask for "braces," not suspenders. Panties are "knickers" and pantyhose are "tights." Pullovers can also be called "jumpers," "jerseys," or "sweaters."

Nightlife The term "theater" refers only to the live stage; movie theaters are "cinemas." Some people still refer to "the pictures" or "the flicks," but plain old "film" is most common these days.

At Home Most of us know that an English apartment is a "flat," unless it's over two floors, which much-reviled estate agents (realtors) describe as a "maisonette," rather than a duplex. An elevator is a "lift." And the first floor is always the ground floor, the second floor the first, and so on. Once you set up housekeeping, don't vacuum—"hoover."

1,000 to 20,000 after 1952 when the United States closed its doors to them. They settled in particular areas—the Jamaicans in Brixton and Stockwell, Trinidadians and Barbadians in Notting Hill. Ultra-conservative politicians like Enoch Powell called for a slow down in immigration. And London experienced its first-ever race riots in Notting Hill in the summer of 1958. Parliament responded by restricting entry to Britain, but prohibiting discrimination in housing and employment. More riots followed in 1981 and 1985, and the race issue continues to fester as the second and third generations still find themselves treated as second-class citizens. In 1999, a public inquiry accused the Metropolitan Police of institutional racism after its failure properly to investigate the murder of 17-year-old Stephen Lawrence.

In the 1950s and 1960s, immigrants also began arriving from India and Pakistan; the Punjabi Sikhs gathered in Southall and the Bengali Muslims around Brick Lane. Their communities have also been under attack, but successful Asian entrepreneurs and businesspeople are fighting back and demanding justice. In contrast to other European countries, though, the shocking violence of the 1980s does seem to have helped mold a more honest cross-cultural society than most, despite what the tabloid references to "frogs" and "krauts" might suggest to the contrary.

The post-war economic decline was initially masked by Britain's continuing reliance on preferential trade with former colonies. Most Commonwealth exports flowed through London, making the port one of the busiest in the world. But many of these countries gained full independence in the 1960s and began to build their own industries and diversify. Germany, Japan, and the United States were tough competitors, too. The deathblow came for the dockyards when workers fought against containerization. The East India dock closed in 1967, followed by St. Katharine's in 1968, and the Royal Docks in 1981. Only Tilbury, which did containerize, survived. At the same time, manufacturing jobs went as big companies like Thorne-EMI and Hoover relocated to other areas. Unemployment in the poorer boroughs of London, like Tower Hamlets and Southwark, soared from 10,000 in the 1960s to 80,000 in the 1980s.

The Conservatives rose to power in 1979, with Britain's first woman prime minister at the helm, on the promise of revitalizing the economy. Margaret Thatcher's reforms were ground-shaking: privatization of major industries, from insurance companies to British Airways and British Rail These had all been taken into state ownership by the Labour government after World War II. Maggie also squashed the trade unions and dismantled parts of the welfare state. At the height of her power in the early 1980s, she mobilized British forces to rescue the Falkland Islanders from the Argentine invasion. The return to gunship diplomacy reignited English pride and won the Tories the next election.

Later, fiercely protective of British sovereignty, Maggie refused to agree to a German-backed monetary union within the European Community and opposed moves toward the creation of a federal entity. She angered many backbenchers in her own party in doing so. And, in 1990, the party rebelled and ended the longest tenure of any modern British prime minister, voting to replace her with the Chancellor of the Exchequer, John Major. His tired government limped along, but the Furies were on their tail.

The Tories couldn't seem to keep their hands off dodgy money and dodgy women. They fought amongst themselves, very publicly, about Britain's role in Europe. In 1994, the Channel Tunnel opened. An astonishing feat of engineering and a success now, but then it was a money-pit that had to seek repeated refinancing. And the monarchy, of which the political right has always been a loyal supporter, was in such disarray that it prompted louder calls for a republic than at almost any time since the Protectorate.

In 1992, Windsor Castle lit up the night sky as workers struggled for 15 hours to put out the blazing fire. Angry political debate about freeloading royals prompted the Queen to agree to pay income tax for the first time. And both her elder sons' marriages crumbled in the full lip-smacking glare of media attention. No wonder the Queen described it as her *annus horribilis*. The next year brought her yet more grief in the shape of published transcripts of taped almost-telephone sex between Charles and Camilla Parker-Bowles. The Royal marital farce reached its climax in 1996 with the divorces of Prince Charles and Diana, and Prince Andrew and Sarah Ferguson.

The British people were more than ready for change. Tony Blair moved the Labour Party way up the sexiness scale and to the political center, reassuring Middle England that it was no longer the party of high taxation. It worked, and the blessed Tony led his gang to a massive victory in 1997.

After 18 years of Tory rule, it felt like throwing off a particularly smelly and oppressive old dog blanket. The government promised so much to so many, in a new inclusive society: help for the disadvantaged, powerful support to British business, a revitalized education system and health service, backing for the arts, and so on. Blair's golden glow lit up their efforts, even surviving the misjudged sucking up to arts and media luvvies, and naff proclamations about how cool the country was, and especially its capital.

A year later, Britain had its dreadful Kennedy moment. Ask any local and they'll be able to tell you where they were when they heard about the death of Princess Diana: I'd fallen asleep with my radio on and awoke before dawn to hear a shocked journalist reading an unconfirmed bulletin. The nation plunged into mourning and turned on the royal family for their hidebound reaction. With the PM volunteering advice, they have been trying to "get real" ever since.

Tony may be good in a crisis, but day-to-day governing has proved tougher than he may have expected. Labour's moves to control welfare costs looked suspiciously Tory. Blair also had to try to persuade the Brits that, yes, they should send troops to Kosovo, staging a virtually unprecedented state-of-the-nation address on prime-time TV. Scotland and Wales have been a little wayward since getting their first taste of partial self-government. Dissenting politicians and terrorists forced the dissolution of the Northern Ireland Assembly. Labour also forced the hereditary peers to pitch for their parliamentary privileges, before ousting 600 of them from the House of Lords. You have only to look at the state of Blair's once-bouffant locks, now deflated and graying, to see what hard work it's been.

Even the monarchy was showing signs of backsliding into the past. Prince Charles and Camilla Parker-Bowles invited the paparazzi to the first formal photo-call. Prince Edward and Sophie had an evening, and therefore hatless, wedding (shock, horror!). But the proposal to allow unwed partners, even same-sex ones, at palace functions never made it onto the embossed invitations.

Londoners did chuckle when Prince Philip decided not to renew his Royal Warrant for Harrods, shortly after Mohammed Al-Fayed repeated his suspicions in court about the Diana and Dodi's car crash. I'm sure the Queen's husband has just found a corner shop nearer home, and it's all a coincidence.

3 Recommended Books & Films

BOOKS

GENERAL HISTORY There are gazillions of books on London, as you'll see below, but you might want to start with a broader British overview. Anthony Sampson's *Anatomy of Britain* and his later *Changing Anatomy of Britain* are a little dry but can't be beat for insights into the social institutions. Balance that with Bill Bryson's *Notes from a Small Island,* about his final walking tour around the country he had lived in for 20 years before he moving home to the U.S. *The English* is a mirror read about British quirks, without the humor, by arch-tiger BBC journalist Jeremy Paxman.

To mug up on the city, turn to the very personal portrait in John Russell's *London,* which is filled with anecdotes, observations, color photographs, and illustrations. *The London Encyclopedia* (Macmillan, 1983), edited by Ben Weinreb and Christopher Hibbert, is great for the sort of minutiae that wins

Impressions

"Every city has a sex and age which have nothing to do with demography. London is a teen-ager and urchin, and, in this, hasn't changed since the time of Dickens."

—John Berger, *Guardian,* March 27, 1987

Trivial Pursuit. Hibbert's *London: The Biography of a City* (Penguin, 1969) is another treasure from this very unheavy historian. Cultural bigwig Roy Porter brings the city to life in *London: A Social History* (Hamish Hamilton, 1994). *The Wonderful Story of London* (Odhams, 1956) will capture kids' imagination: You may have to hunt it down in secondhand bookstores. Other favorites include novelist and literary critic V. S. Pritchett's *London Perceived* (Hogarth, 1986) and Virginia Woolf's *London Scene: Five Essays* (Random House, 1986), which paints a picture of the city in the 1930s.

For history reviewed from a distance, read *London Life in the Eighteenth Century* by M. Dorothy George, an enlightened and readable study; *The Making of Modern London,* by Gavin Weightman and Steve Humphries, on the Victorian development of London; and *The Long Weekend,* by Robert Graves and Alan Hodge, a fascinating and straightforward account of Britain between the wars. And match that with gossip and tales from those who were actually there: Pepys and Evelyn on the 17th century; Daniel Defoe's *Tour Through London About the Year 1725;* and for an outsider's insight from the 19th century, Taine's *Journey Through England.* Coming right up to date with a sharp modern eye on recent events, particularly Thatcherism, read novelist Julian Barnes' *Letters from London.*

Then there are the specialty books. *Americans in London* (William Morrow, 1986) by Brian N. Morton is a great street-by-street guide to the clubs, homes, and favorite pubs of more than 250 famous Americans. Among the many literary guides, *The Writer's Britain,* by Margaret Drabble, is an illustrated favorite, although not strictly about London.

FICTION Of all the arts, England is probably richest in literature. Chronologically, start with Chaucer's wonderful portrait of medieval London in his *Canterbury Tales.* Follow with Shakespeare and Ben Jonson. Then the essayists Addison and Steele, whose *De Coverley Papers* portray 17th-century society and its concerns in graphic detail. Pepys and Evelyn, of course, are wonderful friends with whom to explore the London of this period. For the 18th century, take Fielding, Swift, and Defoe. Boswell's *London Journal* and his other books also make great reading. Anything by Dickens or Thackeray will unlock Victorian London for you. The period from the turn of the century to the 1920s and 1930s is best captured in the works of Virginia Woolf, Henry Green, Evelyn Waugh, P. G. Wodehouse, and Elizabeth Bowen. Contemporary authors who provide insight into London society are Muriel Spark, Iris Murdoch, Angus Wilson, V. S. Naipaul, Martin Amis, Angela Carter, Ian McEwan, Jeanette Winterson, Graham Swift, Anita Brookner, Kazuo Ishiguro, Hanif Kureishi, Allan Hollinghurst, Nick Hornby, and a legion of others.

Right now, London literati are reveling in the cult of the almost-child prodigy, and one of the hottest of these is Zadie Smith. She wrote the hugely successful *White Teeth,* about tangled immigrant lives in North London from World War II to now, while still at university.

Impressions

"I think the British have an almost adolescent take on their bodies and what they are for. But, compared to the other books, we had more Londoners coming forward specifically as a result of health issues or near death experiences. Having been through tough times, they felt they could do anything."

—American photographer Greg Friedler to *Time Out* on the publication of his clothed and unclothed study, *Naked London* (2000)

BIOGRAPHY The biography is definitely back in fashion too. Amanda Foreman's *Georgiana, Duchess of Devonshire,* the story of an 18th-century political and social siren, fashion icon, and chronic gambler, propelled the thirty-something blonde to media stardom. The latest hit is *Bosie, A Life of Lord Alfred Douglas* by another just-ex student, Douglas Murray—a companion read to Richard Ellman's *Oscar Wilde* (Knopf, 1988).

And there are so many others to choose from. Among the greats are Jackson Bate's study of Samuel Johnson, the many royal portraits written by Antonia Fraser, as well as her book on Oliver Cromwell, and Blake's *Disraeli.* For a portrait of Disraeli's opponent Gladstone, see those written by Richard Shannon or H. C. Matthews. When it comes to Winston Churchill, you can read his autobiography, or turn to Martin Gilbert's *Churchill: A Life* (St. Martin's, 1991). These days, politicians step down not to spend more time with their families, but to churn out the inevitably turgid tome. Also rated as a good read are the stories of Tory infighting and the substantial ghost of Maggie in John Major's *The Autobiography* (surprisingly), and the roaring indiscretions in the *Diaries* of Alan Clark, a minister for two terms under the Iron Lady.

As for the tabloid-harried royals, two books dredge up all the lurid details—Anthony Holden's *The Tarnished Crown* (Random House, 1993) and A. N. Wilson's *The Rise and Fall of the House of Windsor* (W. W. Norton & Company, 1993). For Diana's perspective on the whole family and her role in it, read *Diana: Her True Story* (Simon & Schuster) by Andrew Morton.

FILMS

Get out the popcorn, take the phone off the hook, and settle down for a big preview night of London at the movies.

Pierce Brosnan takes a rather speedy river cruise past some of the city's major landmarks to Docklands and on to Greenwich as James Bond in *The World is Not Enough.* You'll even get to see the Millennium Dome, which Tony Blair may have wished the special effects guys really had blown up. Brosnan is certainly more impressive than the real MI5, which tends to leave laptops in tapas bars, and get hoodwinked by baddies like 87-year-old "Red Granny" Melita Norwood. And the film goes perfectly back-to-back with the classic gangster movie that foreshadowed so much of the change in 1980s London, including the development of Docklands, *The Long Good Friday* with Bob Hoskins.

Blockbusters pay £10,000 or so, and low-budget movies £1,000, to film in the old city buildings. Merchant Ivory chose Mansion House for the new adaptation of Henry James's *The Golden Bowl,* starring Nick Nolte and Uma Thurman. For *Entrapment,* starring Sean Connery and Catherine Zeta Jones, the Lloyd's of London building became the inside of a New York insurance company, the goods entrance of a building in Kuala Lumpur, and an oil tanker's boiler room! The CIA headquarters in *Mission Impossible* wasn't in the United States at all, but the grand foyer of County Hall opposite the Houses of Parliament. *Patriot Games* showcased the Royal Naval College at Greenwich.

To tread in Gwyneth Paltrow's footsteps, head for the Church of St. Bartholemew's the Great in Spitalfields, where much of *Shakespeare in Love* was made. *Sliding Doors* sent the lovely Gwyneth and John Hannah all over London, but the rainy shot in the boat took place just by Hammersmith Bridge; and most of the cafe scenes were shot at Mas Café in All Saints Road, at the bottom of Portobello. *Notting Hill* really put this neighborhood on the map.

Fun Fact

Can you believe it? Movie director Neil Jordan had to wheel out the smoke machines to create just the right grimly gloomy London day for *The End of The Affair.* Relentless sunshine was holding back shooting on his £15-million adaptation of Graham Greene's classic wartime tale of uptight Brits doing it with people they shouldn't, starring Britain's sexiest thesp Ralph Fiennes.

Spotty-dog fans will recognize Burlington Arcade, in Piccadilly, as the location of several scenes in *101 Dalmatians.* The spotty taxis and buses lined up along Park Lane for the sequel caused a huge jam of rubberneckers.

Don't just restrict your preview pleasures to London-specific movies. Think of the following as British Culture 101. Start with the 1997 hit *The Full Monty,* if you haven't seen it already. Then add *Secrets and Lies, Naked, Trainspotting, Four Weddings and a Funeral, The Crying Game, Mona Lisa, My Beautiful Laundrette, Educating Rita,* and *A Clockwork Orange.* Oh, and the full Merchant Ivory backlist!

Index

See also Accommodations, Restaurant, and Afternoon Tea indexes, below.

General Index

General Index

D

General Index

ACCOMMODATIONS

RESTAURANTS

Afternoon Tea

Notes

Notes

Notes

Notes

Frommer's® Complete Travel Guides

Alaska
Amsterdam
Arizona
Atlanta
Australia
Austria
Bahamas
Barcelona, Madrid & Seville
Beijing
Belgium, Holland & Luxembourg
Bermuda
Boston
British Columbia & the Canadian Rockies
Budapest & the Best of Hungary
California
Canada
Cancún, Cozumel & the Yucatán
Cape Cod, Nantucket & Martha's Vineyard
Caribbean
Caribbean Cruises & Ports of Call
Caribbean Ports of Call
Carolinas & Georgia
Chicago
China
Colorado
Costa Rica
Denmark
Denver, Boulder & Colorado Springs
England
Europe
European Cruises & Ports of Call
Florida
France
Germany
Greece
Greek Islands
Hawaii
Hong Kong
Honolulu, Waikiki & Oahu
Ireland
Israel
Italy
Jamaica
Japan
Las Vegas
London
Los Angeles
Maryland & Delaware
Maui
Mexico
Montana & Wyoming
Montréal & Québec City
Munich & the Bavarian Alps
Nashville & Memphis
Nepal
New England
New Mexico
New Orleans
New York City
New Zealand
Nova Scotia, New Brunswick & Prince Edward Island
Oregon
Paris
Philadelphia & the Amish Country
Portugal
Prague & the Best of the Czech Republic
Provence & the Riviera
Puerto Rico
Rome
San Antonio & Austin
San Diego
San Francisco
Santa Fe, Taos & Albuquerque
Scandinavia
Scotland
Seattle & Portland
Shanghai
Singapore & Malaysia
South Africa
Southeast Asia
South Florida
South Pacific
Spain
Sweden
Switzerland
Thailand
Tokyo
Toronto
Tuscany & Umbria
USA
Utah
Vancouver & Victoria
Vermont, New Hampshire & Maine
Vienna & the Danube Valley
Virgin Islands
Virginia
Walt Disney World & Orlando
Washington, D.C.
Washington State

Frommer's® Dollar-a-Day Guides

Australia from $50 a Day
California from $60 a Day
Caribbean from $70 a Day
England from $70 a Day
Europe from $70 a Day
Florida from $70 a Day
Hawaii from $70 a Day
Ireland from $60 a Day
Italy from $70 a Day
London from $85 a Day
New York from $80 a Day
Paris from $80 a Day
San Francisco from $60 a Day
Washington, D.C., from $70 a Day

Frommer's® Portable Guides

Acapulco, Ixtapa & Zihuatanejo
Alaska Cruises & Ports of Call
Bahamas
Baja & Los Cabos
Berlin
California Wine Country
Charleston & Savannah
Chicago
Dublin
Hawaii: The Big Island
Las Vegas
London
Los Angeles
Maine Coast
Maui
Miami
New Orleans
New York City
Paris
Puerto Vallarta, Manzanillo & Guadalajara
San Diego
San Francisco
Sydney
Tampa & St. Petersburg
Venice
Washington, D.C.

Frommer's® National Park Guides

Family Vacations in the National Parks
Grand Canyon
National Parks of the American West
Rocky Mountain
Yellowstone & Grand Teton
Yosemite & Sequoia/ Kings Canyon
Zion & Bryce Canyon

Frommer's® Memorable Walks

Chicago
London
New York
Paris
San Francisco
Washington, D.C.

Frommer's® Great Outdoor Guides

New England
Northern California
Southern California & Baja
Southern New England
Washington & Oregon

Frommer's® Born to Shop Guides

Born to Shop: France
Born to Shop: Italy
Born to Shop: London
Born to Shop: New York
Born to Shop: Paris

Frommer's® Irreverent Guides

Amsterdam
Boston
Chicago
Las Vegas
London
Los Angeles
Manhattan
New Orleans
Paris
San Francisco
Seattle & Portland
Vancouver
Walt Disney World
Washington, D.C.

Frommer's® Best-Loved Driving Tours

America
Britain
California
Florida
France
Germany
Ireland
Italy
New England
Scotland
Spain
Western Europe

The Unofficial Guides®

Bed & Breakfasts in California
Bed & Breakfasts in New England
Bed & Breakfasts in the Northwest
Bed & Breakfasts in Southeast
Beyond Disney
Branson, Missouri
California with Kids
Chicago
Cruises
Disneyland
Florida with Kids
Golf Vacations in the Eastern U.S.
The Great Smoky & Blue Ridge Mountains
Inside Disney
Hawaii
Las Vegas
London
Miami & the Keys
Mini Las Vegas
Mini-Mickey
New Orleans
New York City
Paris
San Francisco
Skiing in the West
Southeast with Kids
Walt Disney World
Walt Disney World for Grown-ups
Walt Disney World for Kids
Washington, D.C.

Special-Interest Titles

Frommer's Britain's Best Bed & Breakfasts and Country Inns
Frommer's Britain's Best Bike Rides
The Civil War Trust's Official Guide to the Civil War Discovery Trail
Frommer's Caribbean Hideaways
Frommer's Adventure Guide to Central America
Frommer's Adventure Guide to South America
Frommer's Adventure Guide to Southeast Asia
Frommer's Food Lover's Companion to France
Frommer's Gay & Lesbian Europe
Frommer's Exploring America by RV
Hanging Out in Europe
Israel Past & Present
Mad Monks' Guide to California
Mad Monks' Guide to New York City
Frommer's The Moon
Frommer's New York City with Kids
The New York Times' Unforgettable Weekends
Places Rated Almanac
Retirement Places Rated
Frommer's Road Atlas Britain
Frommer's Road Atlas Europe
Frommer's Washington, D.C., with Kids
Frommer's What the Airlines Never Tell You